ASTROLOGY

OF THE

WORLD

VOLUME I:

The Ptolemaic Inheritance

TRANSLATED & EDITED BY
BENJAMIN N. DYKES, PHD

The Cazimi Press
Minneapolis, Minnesota
2013

Published and printed in the United States of America

by The Cazimi Press
621 5th Avenue SE #25, Minneapolis, MN 55414

© 2013 by Benjamin N. Dykes, Ph.D.

ISBN-13: 978-1-934586-39-6

ACKNOWLEDGEMENTS

Dedicated to Robert Zoller and Charles Burnett

I would like to thank the following friends and colleagues, in alphabetical order: Bernadette Brady, Charles Burnett, Hisham Khalek, and Vibeke Koehler. Special thanks goes to the Urania Trust, for their generous grant to study Arabic intensively at the University of Minnesota.

Also available at www.bendykes.com:

Designed for curious modern astrology students, *Traditional Astrology for Today* explains basic ideas in history, philosophy and counseling, dignities, chart interpretation, and predictive techniques. Non-technical and friendly for modern beginners.

Two classic introductions to astrology, by Abū Ma'shar and al-Qabīsī, are translated with commentary in this volume. *Introductions to Traditional Astrology* is an essential reference work for traditional students.

The classic medieval text by Guido Bonatti, the *Book of Astronomy* is now available in paperback reprints. This famous work is a complete guide to basic principles, horary, elections, mundane, and natal astrology.

The largest compilation of traditional electional material, *Choices & Inceptions: Traditional Electional Astrology* contains works by Sahl, al-Rijāl, al-'Imrānī, and others, beginning with an extensive discussion of elections and questions by Benjamin Dykes.

The famous medieval horary compilation *The Book of the Nine Judges* is now available in translation for the first time! It is the largest traditional horary work available, and the third in the horary series.

The Search of the Heart is the first in the horary series, and focuses on the use of victors (special significators or *almutens*) and the practice of thought-interpretation: divining thoughts and predicting outcomes before the client speaks.

The Forty Chapters is a famous and influential horary work by al-Kindī, and is the second volume of the horary series. Beginning with a general introduction to astrology, al-Kindī covers topics such as war, wealth, travel, pregnancy, marriage, and more.

The first volume of the *Persian Nativities* series on natal astrology contains *The Book of Aristotle*, an advanced work on nativities and prediction by Māshā'allāh, and a beginner-level work by his student Abū 'Alī al-Khayyāt, *On the Judgments of Nativities*.

The second volume of *Persian Nativities* features a shorter, beginner-level work on nativities and prediction by 'Umar al-Tabarī, and a much longer book on nativities by his younger follower, Abū Bakr.

The third volume of *Persian Nativities* is a translation of Abū Ma'shar's work on solar revolutions, devoted solely to the Persian annual predictive system. Learn about profections, distributions, *firdārīyyāt*, transits, and more!

This compilation of sixteen works by Sahl ibn Bishr and Māshā'allāh covers all areas of traditional astrology, from basic concepts to horary, elections, natal interpretation, and mundane astrology. It is also available in paperback.

Expand your knowledge of traditional astrology, philosophy, and esoteric thought with the *Logos & Light* audio series: downloadable, college-level lectures on CD at a fraction of the university cost!

Enjoy these new additions in our magic/esoteric series:

Astrological Magic: Basic Rituals & Meditations is the first book in our new esoteric series. It thoroughly introduces a magical cosmology and shows how to perform ritual correctly, integrating Tarot and visualizations with rituals for all Elements, Planets, and Signs.

Available as an MP3 download or physical CD, *Music of the Elements* was composed especially for *Astrological Magic* by MjDawn, an experienced electronic artist and ritualists. Hear free clips at bendykes.com/music.php!

Nights is a special, 2-disc remastering by MjDawn of the album GAMMA, and is a deep and powerful set of 2 full-disc soundtracks suitable for meditation or ritual work, especially those in *Astrological Magic*. Hear free clips at bendykes.com/music.php!

TABLE OF CONTENTS

TABLE OF FIGURES

INTRODUCTION

I am pleased to present *Astrology of the World I: The Ptolemaic Inheritance* (*AW1*), the first in a three-volume series on traditional mundane astrology. It will be followed *AW2*, on ingress charts, conjunctional theory, and astrological theories of history, and *AW3*, a translation of Abū Ma'shar's *Book of Religions and Dynasties* from the Latin edition by Burnett and Yamamoto—also known as *On the Great Conjunctions*. In this Introduction I will give a general overview of the book and Ptolemy's methods. Detailed introductions will precede each of the book's four Parts, with shorter introductions in each of the Sections which contain the translated texts. With these three volumes, my *Essential Medieval Astrology* series (see Appendix A) will come to a close, followed by a Greek and Latin Hellenistic series, an Arabic series, and later Medieval, Renaissance, and early Modern series.

The present works on mundane astrology are primarily *horoscopic*: that is, based on charts cast for a specific time and with an Ascendant. Thus, we will deal hardly at all with older omen-based astrology, apart from some lore on comets and, in *AW2*, time-lord theories of history that are not at all (or hardly) based on specific charts. I have given this volume the subtitle *The Ptolemaic Inheritance*, because most of our texts—most of which were written in Arabic even if later translated and redacted into Latin[1]—draw directly or indirectly on Book II of Ptolemy's *Tetrabiblos*, which itself is on mundane techniques. Some of the authors in the series speak about relating individuals' nativities to mundane charts, but for the most part they deal only with astrological phenomena which are present for the whole world: especially New/Full Moons and eclipses. Indeed, one challenge for mundane astrology is to make its judgments specific to a particular region or topic, and this is especially true for weather prediction. Let us first look briefly at the four Parts of the book, and then turn to Ptolemy and other topics.

---

[1] I have translated many of the texts from Latin, but others I have translated directly from Arabic (or from the Latin, with corrections based on separate Arabic manuscripts). I am grateful to the Urania Trust for a generous grant which allowed me to study Arabic more deeply at the University of Minnesota in 2012.

Structure of the book

Part I: Weather. In this Part, we will address traditional methods of weather prediction. Of our authors, al-Kindī is the most Ptolemaic: that is, he uses Ptolemy's naturalistic approach to astrology, in which the planets at certain New and Full Moons causally predict weather, with their ongoing transits being monitored to judge weather throughout the seasons. In fact, where Ptolemy is only very general or skimpy on details, al-Kindī is at pains to describe his understanding of this approach in great detail. But al-Kindī and the other authors describe many other methods as well: certain Lots of rains and winds, the lunar mansions, various versions of the "opening of the doors," the "centers" or "posts" or "foundations" of the Moon (which Ptolemy mentions only briefly), and so on. Some authors draw on Persian and Indian accounts. There is also disagreement on whether malefics cause rain or prevent it. All of this provides a wealth of resources for future research. And throughout these texts, we must remember that a chief job of the astrologer is to figure out how to *localize* the effects: if an application of the Moon to Saturn means rain, it cannot mean rain everywhere in the world at the same time, so how can we tell where the rain will fall? I will summarize a variety of answers in in Section I.1.

Part II: Prices & Commodities. Although Ptolemy does not deal directly with prices and commodities, later astrologers took many of his remarks and used their own ingenuity to decide how to use New and Full Moon (or even ingress) charts to predict prices—both of the market as a whole, and of individual commodities. Notable in this respect is al-Qabīsī, who provides a list of Lots for individual commodities. This topic is related to weather, since periods of little rain lead to a scarcity in crops, which directly affects prices. Some authors describe how to distinguish supply and demand in a chart.

Part III: Eclipses & Comets. Ptolemy himself had made eclipses (and to a tiny degree, comets) a central aspect of his mundane approach. Our authors follow Ptolemy to a great extent, but they emphasize the meaning of the eclipse chart in its own right as a statement about political events. For example, Ptolemy hardly spoke of the importance of the Ascendant and its lord at an eclipse, but our Arabic-speaking astrologers give it a prime place. From the eclipse chart, they reach in two directions: to effects on weather, crops, and animals (as did Ptolemy), and to political events they otherwise analyze from ingress charts. This "middle position" of eclipses was already inherent in Ptolemy's approach. Indeed, one of the frustrating things about Ptolemy's mundane astrology to my mind is that it does not proceed in an orderly manner like the other parts of the *Tetrabiblos* do. That is, while Ptolemy uses both lunation charts and eclipses, *Tet.* II can hardly be read sequentially: the text seems to constantly make references backwards and forwards, and at the end one is not always quite sure how to bring the techniques together. Later astrologers pretty much solved this problem by embedding lunations and eclipses within the broader framework of conjunctional and ingress theory.

Part IV: Chorography & Climes. One of the more unusual and less-known aspects of traditional mundane techniques is the application of chorography and climes. Chorography is the method of associating cities, countries, and territories, with the signs and planets. Climes are either discrete lines of latitude or bands of latitude on the earth, each of which comes under the management of either the signs or planets (or both). Of course in the ancient and medieval periods, these regions were more restricted: not much was known about southern latitudes (although they do appear here), nor about longitudes east of modern Pakistan and western India—to say nothing of the Americas. Ptolemy also developed a way of applying the triplicities mundanely (including special mundane triplicity lords which are mostly unknown now), as well as describing how individual cities may be associated with signs and planets based on their founding date or the nativities of their political rulers. For Ptolemy this was particularly useful in judging eclipses, since the sign in which an eclipse took place, determined both the regions and the types of beings (animals or humans) effected by it: for example, that an eclipse taking place in Libra would affect regions and beings ruled by Libra. In our texts, we will see some Ptolemaic-type attributions (such as in ibn Labban) as well as associations which have no explanatory context, simply asserting that such-and-such a region is ruled by (say) Mercury and Capricorn. A Greek text will purport to give the founding charts for certain cities, although more work will have to be done in order to understand what the charts are really based on. We will have to investigate further to understand how these types of rules may be applied to regions unknown to Ptolemy and the medieval Arabic-speaking astrologers.

Finally, in this volume I have decided not to provide an Index to methods or authors, since the extensive Sectioning and cross-referencing found throughout the book made it seem redundant.

Ptolemy's Mundane Astrology

To understand traditional, horoscopic mundane astrology, we really must begin with Ptolemy. His *Tetrabiblos* Book II provides foundational material for later works on weather prediction, eclipses, lunation charts that precede solar ingresses, chorography, and more. But here and throughout *AW1*, for the most part I will provide only summaries of Ptolemy's astrology, rather than direct translations. The summaries are based on the Robbins translation, in cooperation with Hübner's critical edition where necessary, as well as Schmidt's translation of parallel material in Hephaistio (who frequently copied Ptolemy's material, albeit with some changes). I hope this will help ease the reader into Ptolemy's approach, which he enjoys expressing in a way that is both very compressed and wordy. Throughout, I will provide chapter references and sentence numbers (in boldface) for the Robbins/Hübner editions, for those who wish to check the sources.

Let us begin with Ptolemy's opening statements about mundane astrology, before moving on to his theory of weather prediction. In his introductory chapter (*Tet.* II.1), Ptolemy recognizes two main branches of astrology (**2**): mundane (the "universal" part) and natal (the "individual" part), of which the mundane obviously has broader effects which sometimes override the normal expected outcomes of individuals' nativities (**3**). Here we are obviously interested in the universal, mundane part.

But within mundane astrology, there are also several divisions (**4**): one part considers broad changes and effects pertaining to regions, another to cities, another to various events like wars and natural disasters (pestilence, earthquakes, famine), and another to local weather trends. Ptolemy prefers to stick to regions, as he thinks it is very difficult to get down to localized particulars in mundane astrology (**1, 5**). (Of course this is one of the chief problems in traditional weather prediction, which I address a bit in Section I.1.)

In order to make these predictions, we need two types of information or tools. The first is some way of associating heavenly phenomena with the world (**5**), and for Ptolemy the chief ways involve associating geographic regions with the zodiacal triplicities, and the individual planets with the climes and ethnic groups in them.[2] The second is to identify which heavenly phe-

---

[2] See Section IV.2. Ptolemy's justification for this is based on his association of planets and signs with winds and physical processes.

nomena actually matter in mundane astrology (**5-6**): for Ptolemy, these include the visible eclipses of the Sun and Moon, lunar phases (especially those immediately preceding solar ingresses), and planetary phases and stations, particularly those of the superior planets. Later on, he will also include comets and other omens (II.9, II.13).[3]

So while Ptolemy does want to track ongoing transits and phases of various kinds, his mundane techniques rest on two types of charts: New/Full Moons (and the stages of the lunar month called the "centers" of the Moon, see Section I.1), and visible eclipses of the Sun and Moon. In each case he notes the signs involved, the rulers of those signs (see especially Section III.2), and the types of beings and areas of the earth affected (Sections I.2, III.2). In Sections I.2, III.2, and IV.2, I will go through Ptolemy's interpretive steps. But the reader should keep in mind that later astrologers went beyond Ptolemy in their interpretations: as an example, Ptolemy pays little attention to the Ascendant and its lord, but these take center stage in later authors.

Editorial conventions in this book

In putting together this set of translations, I have divided the book up in certain ways, and have also added details to the texts themselves. At the purely editorial level, I have divided it into four *Parts*, each of which is devoted to a different area of mundane astrology: weather, prices, eclipses and comets, and chorography. But within each Part is a variety of *Sections*: the first Section contains my own introduction, the second Ptolemy's approach (except for Part II, since Ptolemy has no doctrine of prices), with the rest of the Sections being devoted to other authors.

In addition, since 2012 I have decided to start adding sentence numbers to my translations. This is especially useful for translators comparing texts in different languages, but I think it will also be helpful for readers who are looking for precise references. In the text itself I indicate the sentence with a boldface number, such as: **5** And if Mars were in the seventh…. When citing a certain sentence in a footnote or in one of my introductions, I follow the usual reference with the boldface number. For instance, if something is found in the fifth sentence of Chapter II.3 of the *Tetrabiblos*, I will write: *Tet.* II.3, **5**. In a few cases it was important to indicate which language a sentence came from, such as when a text in multiple languages has a paragraph that

---

[3] See Section III.2.

only occurs in the Latin version: in this case, I normally prefix a letter to indicate the language: **A5** for Arabic, or **L5** for Latin. My short introductions to each Section usually indicate anything special I have done in this regard. Finally, chapter and heading titles in Latin and Arabic have also been assigned sentence numbers, but I do not include them in the text for aesthetic purposes: thus the reader will find sentences apparently skip a number between the end of one chapter or Section, and the next.

A note on traditional astronomy: apogees

Many readers of traditional texts will have noticed frequent mentions of different kinds of "increase" and "decrease": in computation, number, course, and so on. Unfortunately, not every author means the same thing by these terms. But even more importantly, they are mostly based on Ptolemaic astronomy, with concepts and procedures no longer in use. I have tried to define some of these terms in the Glossary, and in the future I plan to produce a book which will explain all of these concepts for the contemporary astrologer. Indeed, I will need to introduce much more of this in *AW2*, since Persian conjunctional theory deals with what are called "mean" conjunctions of planets like Saturn and Jupiter, *not* the visible conjunctions of their bodies. These mean conjunctions are directly related to the concept of apogees, which features prominently in our texts here in *AW1*. Let us turn to that now.

A planet's relation to its apogees is one instance of what it means to increase or decrease, or rise and sink. An apogee is a point on a deferent circle or epicycle which is furthest away from earth, while the perigee is the point opposite, where it is closest to the earth. When a planet is near its apogee it appears both smaller and slower, just as a person walking in the distance appears small and slow. When it is near its perigee, it appears both bigger and faster. A pair of apogee and perigee points are called "apsides," and the line between them the "apsidal line" (although this was usually only used to describe the apogee of the deferent). Below is a basic image of the deferent or eccentric circle of the Sun, the center of which is displaced from the center of the earth (which is what "eccentric" means).

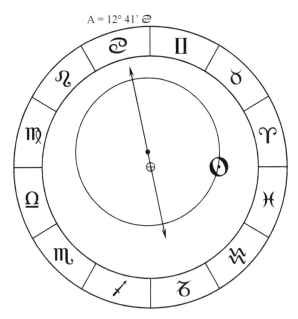

A = 12° 41' ♋

Figure 1: Apogee of Sun (1990)

In this diagram, the earth (⊕) is at the center of the universe. The center of the Sun's deferent circle is offset from the center, towards Cancer. From the earth's perspective, the Sun in the diagram is currently at 0° Aries. His modern apogee is at 12° 41' Cancer, which means that when he reaches it he will be moving apparently slower and be a tiny bit smaller. Since he is in that position in the summer (in the northern hemisphere), summer is slightly longer than the other seasons. Likewise, his apogee must be at 12° 41' Capricorn, whence he seems to move a little faster then and winter is a little shorter. The apogee moves extremely slowly forward in the order of signs. I began with the Sun because in Ptolemy's astronomy the Sun does not have an epicycle.[4] But other planets do, and we'll turn to them now.

In Ptolemaic astronomy, apogees were crucial for determining planetary positions. If we know where the apogee is on a given date (known as the "epoch date"), and we know exactly how fast the deferent circle moves, then we can know the position of a planet's epicycle on the deferent for any other

---

[4] Hipparchus and Ptolemy both knew that the Sun's motion could be described either using a single eccentric deferent and no epicycle, or else a circle centered on the earth but with an epicycle. Ptolemy decided the former was more natural, and Hipparchus chose the latter (Evans, pp. 216-17).

date we like. Likewise, once we know how fast a planet moves on its epicy-cle, we can know where a planet falls on it.

The angular distance between the planet's epicycle and the apogee, is called the "mean eccentric anomaly." That is, it is the difference (anomaly) between the apogee and the epicycle along the deferent (eccentric) circle, as measured in uniform (mean) motion. The point is that if the center of the epicycle is exactly on the apsidal line, then the mean eccentric anomaly is 0°. If the deferent has rotated so that the center is 60° away, then the mean ec-centric anomaly is 60°.

The following diagram reproduces what would have been Ptolemy's own calculations for the position of Mars in 'Umar al-Tabari's New Moon chart of May 785 AD (see Section II.4 below).[5]

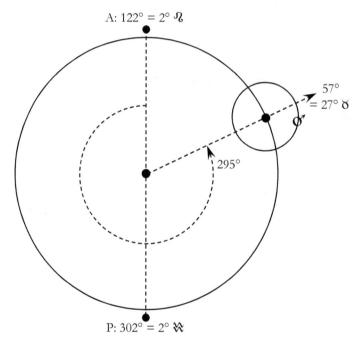

Figure 2: Mars and his apogees, May 13, 785 AD

---

[5] I have used the *Almagest Ephemeris Calculator* to generate these values (www.staff.science.uu.nl/~gent0113/astro/almagestephemeris.htm). But please note that this is not the accurate version which we can get using modern Ptolemaic tables.

In this example, in May 785 the apogee of the deferent of Mars was at 122° longitude, which is the same as 2° Leo; by definition, the perigee is opposite it, at 2° Aquarius. On the day of the Full Moon, the deferent of Mars had rotated by 295°: past the apogee, down towards the perigee, and up again. If we add 295° of rotation to the apogee (122°), we get 417° or 57° in longitude, or 27° Taurus. Therefore, the mean motion of Mars should have brought his position to 27° Taurus from the perspective of the equant circle (the large circle depicted here). This is not the same as his position as seen from earth: we need to apply some corrections to get that. But Mars is also rotating counter-clockwise on his epicycle (the smaller circle) at the same time, and on the day of the Full Moon he had rotated so as to almost come to the apogee of the epicycle again. Thus he is rising both towards the apogee of the deferent and to the apogee of his epicycle.

Astrologically this is of interest, because when a planet is near its apogee (small, apparently moving slowly), it indicates matters that are high or increase—such as prices. As it moves toward the perigee (and is larger, apparently moving faster), these things decrease. Then as it passes the perigee and moves "upwards" towards its apogee, things increase again. Thus, we want to know the zodiacal position of the apogee, and also roughly where the planet has average speed and size (somewhere around 90° from the apogee).[6] In the case of Mars above, his position of average speed and size will be somewhere around 2° Taurus and 2° Scorpio.

Following are the approximate apogees of five of the planets in their deferent circle using modern methods, which are good enough for general use in the 20th and 21st Centuries:[7]

---

[6] This position differs based on the planet involved. For our purposes, we can say it is roughly 90° on either side of the apogee.

[7] See Evans 1998, p. 368. For the Sun, I have used a separate table on p. 228. Unfortunately, I cannot currently find the correct apogees for Mercury and the Moon (both of whose theories are rather complicated in the *Almagest*). According to the values given by al-Bīrūnī in his *Book of Instruction* (§195), the apogee of Mercury should now be about 9° Scorpio—but according to the *Almagest Ephemeris Calculator*, it should be at about 28° Libra. Again, using the website calculator the Moon's apogee should be around 1° Scorpio, but I am very uncertain about these two values.

♄	00° ♑
♃	9° ♎
♂	28° ♌
☉	12° ♋
♀	8° ♋

Figure 3: Five recent apogees of the deferent circle

Now, in some texts in this book, the author seems to talk about the apogee, and then speaks of a planet being so many signs away from it. This seems to mean that the 360° distance around the apsidal line was conveniently converted into sign values: so, if the epicycle's center had moved 30° from the apogee, then it had moved "one" sign from it. Using this logic, a planet will move down and reach about average speed and size after three signs, and also at nine signs on the other side; likewise, a planet will sink down to the perigee after six signs, and begin to rise in the seventh sign. For our purposes, it is enough to know where the apogee is, and use our eyes to tell whether it is moving away from it or towards it. When a planet is very close to the apogee or perigee, we need to add certain corrections for greater accuracy.

One problem in our texts, though, is that while a planet may be advancing towards one of its apogees, it is also said to be "decreasing" in one way or another, and not every author seems to use the same terminology. For example, a planet may be increasing in number or computation or course: according to ibn Ezra, increasing or decreasing in "course" refers to going faster or slower than average speed—but since average speed is calculated from the equant circle (a concept I am not addressing here), we need to have more Ptolemaic astronomy under our belt to understand what that means for a given planet. Likewise, according to Robbins in his translation of the *Tetrabiblos* (p. 115, n. 4), adding in "motion" refers to a planet that is in the outer half of its epicycle near the epicyclic apogee, because then it will not only be advancing on the deferent, but also advancing on its epicycle—making it move more quickly. Other forms of increase and decrease have to do with the corrections that must be added to a planet's mean position, so as to determine its correct longitude from the terrestrial perspective.

PART I: WEATHER

Section I.1: Introduction

In this Section I will provide a general introduction to methods of weather prediction. This is especially necessary because not only do our authors endorse a variety of methods (which may not all be compatible), but they even have some differing accounts of which planets and signs indicate rain the most. For the most part, all of the methods describe three types of information: (1) When to cast a chart, and the time frame it covers. This is usually the New (but often the Full) Moon, and especially the one which most nearly precedes a solar ingress into a sign. But some authors also include ingresses themselves. Sometimes the lunation prior to the annual Aries or quarterly ingresses sets the tone for the season, with further lunations throughout the season giving indications for changes over weeks and days. (2) What planets should we take as the significator? For lunation charts, this is usually the Moon and the planet to which she applies next, but throughout the month we are supposed to watch similar things when the Moon is in one of her "centers" or "posts" or "foundations" (see below). But other approaches recommend the trio of Moon-Mercury-Venus, and the method of "opening the doors" looks at connections between planets whose domiciles are opposite each other (such as Mercury-Jupiter). (3) What planetary conditions should we take into account when predicting weather, and especially rain? These points must be examined individually for every method.

When thinking about these methods, there are certain challenges for any theory of astrometeorology. For one thing, which are the signs and planets that indicate rain? Authors differ on this point, though not with really absolute agreement. Second, what is the true role and nature of the lunar mansions, since they play such an important role in so many texts? The main thing here is that some authors consider the mansions mathematically, dividing the zodiac equally from 0° tropical Aries. But the older approach seemed to be sidereal, taking the mansions according to the chief fixed stars which define them (see below). This might not have been so important in antiquity, when the sidereal and tropical zodiacs did not differ so much; but in this century it is very important to figure out, and indeed it is surprising to me that even medieval authors like al-Bīrūnī and al-Rijāl recommended the tropical approach, since precession would have affected the mansions greatly by then.

Finally, what is probably the most important challenge is particularizing the methods for a certain location. Suppose we cast a chart for the New Moon, and the Moon is applying next to some planet indicating rain. But the Moon is in that situation at that moment for everyone in the world—and yet it will not rain everywhere in the world. There must be some way of making planetary conditions relevant to different locations. Fortunately, although none of the texts explicitly recognizes the problem, they do contain a number of ways of making weather localized. The most basic way is by noting the standard expected weather in a given region, which then only becomes *modified* by the indications in a chart: one would need a lot of special indicators to predict rain in the desert Southwest of the United States, but not many to predict it in the rather wet Northwest (such as in Seattle). Here are a few of the more interesting ones, apart from chorography itself:

- The Ascendant and its lord. Since the Ascendant is particular to a location (or rather, to broad stripes across a geographical region, this can be relevant.
- Angularity. Likewise, angularity is relevant to a region.
- Planetary hours. These are sensitive to latitude and seasons.
- Ascensions. In al-Kindī's *DMT* Ch. 4, he seems to say that the centers of the Moon should be measured in ascensions rather than ecliptical degrees. Ascensions, like the Ascendant itself, are sensitive to latitude.
- Lots. Our texts describe four distinct Lots of wind and rain, which are sensitive to location because they are cast from the Ascendant.

Since I do not have much experience working with these methods, I cannot vouch for any one of these in particular, but they should be helpful for further research.

In what follows, I will introduce the following seven methods or procedural templates for predicting weather (and especially rain). Most of these apply especially at the charts of New/Full Moons, but many texts also recommend watching ongoing transits:

(1) Centers/posts/foundations of the Moon.

(2) Lunar mansions.

(3) Opening of the doors.

(4) The Sun's ingress to 20° Scorpio.

(5) Moon-Mercury-Venus.

(6) Planetary hours at lunar ingresses.

(7) Lots of rain and wind.

First however, I will say a few words about the signs and planets which are said to indicate rain.

Rainy signs & planets

I place here a small table with representative lists of signs that indicate rain; please keep in mind that some authors add others:

Hermann Ch. 3, **15**	♋	♌	♏	♐	♑	♒	♓
Hermann Ch. 6, **16**	♋?	♌	♏			♒	♓?
Masha'allah *Chap.*, **49**	♋		♏			♒	♓
Ibn Labban Ch. 7	♋	♌	♏			♒	♓

Figure 4: Some rainy signs

Hermann (Ch. 4, **2-5**) also specifically mentions signs which indicate little rain: Taurus, Gemini. Virgo and Libra have only a modicum of rains, and Capricorn (which is described above as being a sign of rain) is here stated to show more cold than rain *unless* the Moon is in it and aspects another planet which is in a place of rain (at least, that is how I read it). As for rainy mansions of the Moon, see Method 2 below.

Likewise, many texts identify the planets with indicating or causing typical weather patterns:

	♄	♃	♂	♀	☿
Ptolemy *Tet.* II.8	Cold, Dry	Warm, Moist	Hot, Dry	Warm, Moist	Varies
Al-Kindī *DMT* 7, **7:L2-3**	Cold	Mild	Windy	Rainy	Varies
Al-Kindī *40 Chaps.* §674	Clouds Hail	Wind	Windy, Hot	Wet	Windy
Opening of Doors **4**	Clouds Cold	Wind	Windy, Hot	Moist	Windy
John *Epitome* I.6, **30-35**	Rain Cold	Mild	Windy, Hot	Moist	Windy

Figure 5: Planets and weather

This table provides the opportunity to note some differences between our authors. Although all authors agree that Venus indicates some kind of moisture, they are generally divided as to how the benefics and malefics indicate weather. For Ptolemy, the malefics do not standardly indicate moisture or storms, but the benefics do (although many authors associate Mars with lightning and violent weather). In Māshā'allāh's *Chapter on Rains*, **12-19** and **25-26**, Mars in particular *inhibits* rain. Ptolemy's attributions may be based on some experience, but are certainly embedded in his naturalistic theory of astrology: the extreme dryness represented by the malefics are not productive of rain. When Jupiter indicates rain, it is usually gentle or "safe" or "healthy" rain.

But on the other hand, Jafar's *Book of Heavy Rains* **27-31** takes the opposite view, with an explanation: malefics *cause* rain and storms precisely because they are immoderate and extreme in their activities and indications, whereas benefics are normally too temperate to create rain. But he does allow that Venus with the malefics can produce rain.

Yet a third view is found in places such as al-Kindī's *DMT* Ch. 6 and Māshā'allāh's *Chapter* and *Letter*. In these texts (among others), the trio of planets associated with rain are Moon-Mercury-Venus, and their configurations in particular are used in lunation and ingress charts. This trio seems to come from a separate tradition, and has many rules associated with it.

Method 1: Centers of the Moon

The "centers" or "posts" or "foundations" (hereafter, "centers") refer to specific degree-relations between the Sun and Moon throughout the lunar month. In traditional weather lore, they act as something like critical days in decumbiture charts: times in which, if certain conditions are met, there should be rain.

The first version of the centers in our texts comes from Ptolemy (*Tet.* II.12), who includes the lunar quarters and semi-quarters, as well as the trines and sextiles. When the Moon is in these positions, we must see what planets she is configured with, as well as what planets are making phases to the Sun (II.12, **6-7**).

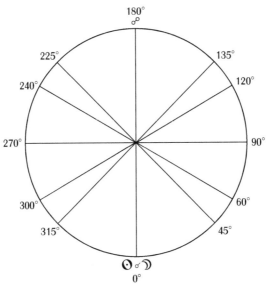

Figure 6: Ptolemy's centers of the Moon

Later authors adopted versions of this scheme, with some adding extra centers to account for the Moon's visibility at the beginning and end of the lunar month (and their opposites): that is, 12° on either side of the Sun, and the opposites of those. Remember that although the diagram shows the phases or aspects evenly spaced out, in reality the degrees will not be evenly spaced from the degree of the New Moon. For instance, let the New Moon be at 0° Aries. The first quarter of the Moon will not be 90° away at 0° Cancer, because the Sun is also moving: by the time she gets to the first quarter, he will have moved to about 7° Aries, which will put her first quarter at about 7° Cancer.

Some astrologers also seemed to want to combine the centers with the opening of the doors (see below), seeing if there was an opening of the doors at the same time as the Moon was in one of the centers. Likewise, some combined the centers with an appraisal of the lunar mansions.

Following is a list of most of the versions of the centers in our texts:

- Ptolemy, *Tet.* II.12, **5** (Section I.2).
- Al-Kindī, *DMT* Ch. 5 (Section I.3).
- Al-Kindī, *DMT* Ch. 7, Latin only (Section I.3).
- Al-Kindī, *Forty Chapters* Ch. 38.3 (Section I.4). This is the same as:
- 'Umar al-Tabarī, Ch. 84 (Section I.5).
- Jafar, **39-42**, two versions (Section I.10); cf. *Sages* **40-42** (Section I.11).

Method 2: Mansions of the Moon

The mansions of the Moon are divisions of the ecliptic or zodiac into equal parts. In the case of the Indians, there are 27 mansions of 13° 20' apiece; in the case of the Arabs, there are 28 with 12° 51' 26" apiece. In my *Choices & Inceptions: Traditional Electional Astrology*, I discussed the mansions at some length, so I will only offer a summary statement here. Our authors have a great interest in using the mansions to predict rain, focusing on whether the Moon or some other planet, or even a Lot, is in a rainy mansion at a certain time. But it makes a great difference as to whether one measures the mansions using a tropical zodiac, or with a sidereal zodiac that respects the fixed stars which traditionally defined them. For example, in a sidereal zodiac the two stars Sheratan and Mesarthim (in a horn of Aries) mark the first lunar mansion. But due to precession, in a tropical zodiac stars near the beginning of the constellation Pisces would mark the first mansion. Despite lists which specifically showed what stars marked what mansion, even some astrologers in the Middle Ages (both Arabic and Latin) insisted that one measure the mansions tropically. Others recognized the importance of the stars and gave their best values for precession so as to use the mansions side-really. My own sense is that using the mansions requires a sidereal approach, but I am not experienced with them enough to say for certain.

The table below is based on the lists and attributions of the mansions in al-Kindī's *DMT* (Section I.3) and John of Spain's descriptions (Section I.16). The names were drawn from Bos and Burnett 2000, and the identification of the fixed stars marking each one comes primarily from Kunitzsch. Since the Indian and Arab systems had different numbers of mansions, I have numbered each mansion according to the different systems: the Indian column (27#) and the Arab column (28#). The Arabs distinguished between *al-Zubānā* and *al-Iklīl*, which yields 28 mansions instead of the Indian 27. In the *Hebrew Letter II* version of al-Kindī's letter on rains (Section I.3), *al-Zubānā* is indeed marked as very moist, but since it is not distinguished from *al-Iklīl*, a sixth very moist mansion was identified instead: *al-Dhirāᶜ*. On the other hand, in the Latin manuscripts, which recognize 28, *al-Dhirāᶜ* is not very moist: instead, both *al-Zubānā* and *al-Iklīl* are. Both systems yield six very moist mansions.

In the column for "Rain," I show the properties as to moisture: VM = "Very Moist," M = "Moist," T = "Temperate" or neutral, and D = "Dry."

Finally, in the column titled "Luck," I have listed al-Bīrūnī's attributions from his *Chronology* (p. 351) in case they correlate with cheapness of prices, especially in Jafar's methods for prices (Section I.10): L = "Lucky," M = "Middling," U = "Unlucky."

27#	28#	Name	Stars	Rain	Luck
1	1	*al-Sharaṭān* "The butting"	Sheratan (β Aries), Mesarthim (γ)	T	M
2	2	*al-Buṭayn* "The little belly"	Botein (δ), ε, ρ Aries	D	L
3	3	*al-Thurayyā* "The Pleiades"	Pleiades	T	L
4	4	*al-Dabarān* "The two buttocks"	Aldebaran (α Taurus), or Hyades	VM	U
5	5	*al-Haqᶜah* "White circle of hair"	λ and φ Orion?	D	U
6	6	*al-Hanᶜa* "The camel's brand"	Alhena (γ Gemini), ξ?	T-M	L
7	7	*al-Dhirāᶜ* "The forearm"	Castor (α Gemini), Pollux (β)	M or VM	L
8	8	*al-Nathra* "The tip of the nose"	Praesepe (nebula near ε Cancer)	T	M

9	9	*al-Tarf* "The look, the eye"	ϰ Cancer, Alterf (λ Leo)	D	U
10	10	*al-Jabha* "The forehead"	Around ζ, γ, η, α Leo; ε Gemini	M	L
11	11	*al-Zubra* (or *al-Kharātān*) "The mane"	Zosma (δ), θ Leo	T	L
12	12	*al-Ṣarfah* "The diversion" or "The change"	Denebola (β Leo)	VM	U
13	13	*al-ʿAwwāʾ* The constellation Bootes	Zavijava (β Virgo), Zania (η), Porrima (γ), δ, Vindemiatrix (ε)	T	L
14	14	*al-Simāk* "Fish"	Spica/Azimech (α Virgo)	T-M	M
15	15	*al-Ghafr* "The coat of mail"	Maybe ι and ϰ Virgo	M	U
16	16	*al-Zubānā* "The claws"	Zuben Elgenubi (α Libra) & Zuben Eschemali (β)	VM	U
16	17	*al-Iklīl* "The crown"	Maybe Acrab/Graffias (β Scorpio), Dschubba (δ)	VM	U
17	18	*al-Qalb* "The heart"	Antares (α Scorpio)	D	L
18	19	*al-ʾIbrah* "The sting, tail"	Shaula (λ Scorpio), Lesath (υ); Acumen & Aculeus (in sting of Scorpio)	M	U
19	20	*al-Naʿāʾim* "The ostriches"	Near Ascella (ζ Sagittarius)	M	U
20	21	*al-Balda* "The place"	Maybe π Sagittarius	T	M
21	22	*Saʿd al-dhābih* "Luck of the slayer"	Algedi (α Capricorn), Dabih (β)	VM	L
22	23	*Saʿd al-bulaʿ* "Luck of the swallower"	Albali (ε Aquar.), μ, ν	T	M
23	24	*Saʿd al-suʿūd* "Luck of the lucks"	Sadalsuud (β Aquarius), ξ; *46 Capricorn?*	T-M	U
24	25	*Saʿd al-ʾakhbiyah* "Luck of the tents"	Sadachbia (γ Aquarius), π, ζ, η	D	M
25	26	*al-Fargh al-muqaddam* "The preceding spout"	Maybe Markab (α Pegasus) & Scheat (β)	D	L

26	27	*al-Fargh al-muʾakhkhar* "The following spout"	Maybe Algenib (γ Pegasus), Alpheratz (α Andromeda or β Pegasus)[1]	VM	M
27	28	*Baṭn al-ḥūt*[2] "Belly of the fish"	β Andromeda[3]	T	L

Figure 7: Table of lunar mansions

Method 3: Opening of the doors

The "opening of the doors" (or "portals" or "gates") is a technique unknown to most people today. Most of the authors are in broad agreement about its basics, but they differ in certain respects about when to use it, and what its different types are. The basis of the technique is simply this: aspects between two planets whose domiciles are opposite each other. Thus an aspect between Mercury and Jupiter, or Venus and Mars, or the Sun/Moon-Saturn, can be called an opening of the doors. But what is the meaning of this term? The Latin ʿUmar says:[4]

18 You should know that every one of the higher planets has one state, and the lower planets have another;[5] wherefore the higher ones are like spirits, and the lower ones are bodies, and no generating comes to be in the world except through the application and commixture of them, one with another, and of the superiors with the inferiors.

Likewise, Māshā'allāh says in the Latin *Letter* (Section I.7):

32 For the superior planets do not have power in themselves and by themselves, nor likewise do the inferiors, except from the superiors.

Traditional authors sometimes made this sort of statement about the Sun and Moon forming such a pair, but here the idea is extended further. Planets whose domiciles are opposed form a pair such that, when they make aspects

---

[1] According to Kunitzsch and Smart (pp. 15, 47), there was some confusion between the names and stars for α-γ Pegasus and α Andromeda.
[2] Also called *Baṭn al-rishāʾ*, "belly of the rope" (esp. the rope for a well).
[3] According to Kunitzsch and Smart (p. 50), this mansion originally involved a faint curve of stars meant to be like a rope, connecting to the Square of Pegasus.
[4] See his Ch. 82, **18** (Section I.5).
[5] The Ar. speaks as though each superior planet has a "bond" with a lower one.

at certain times, it is as though a door or channel of influence opens up, allowing higher influences to be received and manifested in our lower world. (Hermann explicitly speaks in this manner in his Ch. 5, **9**.) In the present case this idea is used to predict rain, but it seems to be a more general statement about the production of life itself—note 'Umar's spirit-body reference.

Following are the chief references to the opening of the doors in this book, with their variations on the method:

- Al-Kindī, *DMT* Ch. 5, **83ff.**, esp. **107** (Section I.3). Al-Kindī *seems* to prefer that the pair of planets not only be in any degree-based aspect with each other, but also with the Sun, while *in addition* the Moon is at one of her centers. Perhaps the Moon should also be aspecting the pair or even be transferring the light between them (**107**). Al-Kindī also hints that the centers (or even any of the aspects?) should be measured by ascensions and not just the ecliptic, which would help localize the effects.

- Al-Kindī, *Forty Chaps.* Ch. 38.3 (Section I.4). Here, al-Kindī wants the pair to apply to each other *by opposition* while the Moon is in one of her centers. He prefers that the Moon also be transferring the light from one to the other and also suggests that the luminaries be aspecting the Ascendant of the city or region (i.e., its founding chart):[6] this would also help localize the weather.

- 'Umar al-Tabarī Ch. 83 (Section I.5). 'Umar has two versions, each of which seems to involve the Moon being at one of her centers (**6**, and Ch. 84). First, that the Moon be transferring the light between the pair; second, that she is applying to Saturn (i.e., that she and Saturn himself are the pair).

- Māshā'allāh, *Letter* **6-10ff.** (Section I.7). Māshā'allāh's rules are varied, but he seems to want the pair of planets to be joined by opposition, especially in signs which belong to them: such as the Moon in Capricorn applying to Saturn in Cancer (**7**). But Māshā'allāh gives so many variations on the signs that it is difficult to make a summary statement. Nor does he seem to require that these configurations be while the Moon is in one of her centers, even though he does recommend looking at these at the Aries ingress and the Sun's entrance to 19° or 20° Scorpio (**17**).

---

[6] But perhaps the Ascendant of the Aries (or other quarterly) ingress would work?

- Hermann, Ch. 5, **31-32** and 6, **2-6** (Section I.12). In Ch. 5, Hermann suggests that the opening of the doors can only happen through a conjunction of a planetary pair. He also seems to allow that "they" (the luminaries? the pair?) apply to some other inferior planet after their separation. In Ch. 6, he wants the Moon to transfer light between the pair, but then seems to suggest that the pair ought to be in an opposition.
- *Doors* **1-11**, **36**, **38** (Section I.13). This text contains three types of opening. In the first (**1-3**), the pair are simply conjoined—although I am not sure whether this is a bodily conjunction or any aspectual connection. In the second (**36**), the Moon is transferring light between planets whose domiciles are opposite each other: this is the "double doors." In the third (**38**), we look for an aspect between the lord of the Ascendant of the lunation chart, with the lord of the seventh of the chart: by definition this will be a pair just like in the other versions, except that it identifies these two in particular. *Doors* does not seem to require that any of this happen while the Moon is at one of her centers.

To these variations, we may add statements by al-Kindī in a *Letter on the Phenomena of the Atmosphere*, **8-14**.[7] In this *Letter*, al-Kindī distinguishes a "greater" from a "lesser" opening. The greater opening is the application of the Sun to Saturn, especially (or only?) from a rainy mansion. The "lesser" involves the other pairs of planets (including Moon-Saturn). It is best if one or both of the planets involved aspects its own sign (**13**). However, al-Kindī then recommends that the Moon be transferring the light from one to the other (**14**).

Method 4: Moon-Mercury-Venus

I hesitate to call the material dealing with the triad of Moon-Mercury-Venus a "method," but the fact is that it seems to constitute a distinct body of lore, often set apart from other methods. When combined with other methods it is usually with the 20° Scorpio or Libra ingress approach (see below). The reason for choosing Moon-Mercury-Venus is probably because the

---

[7] Bos and Burnett, p. 417.

Moon and Venus are most closely associated with rain, and Mercury is associated with winds and changeability.

Unfortunately, this material is so varied (except perhaps for the easternness and westernness of Venus, see below), that it is hardly possible to summarize it. I can only direct the reader to the largest collections of this lore, which seem to be Māshā'allāh's *Chapter on the Rains in the Year* (Section I.6) and Hermann's *Book of Heavy Rains* (Section I.12).

Method 5: Sun at 20° Scorpio

Although most of the methods in this book are meant to be applied to lunar phases and centers (and occasionally an Aries ingress), the fifth approach looks at the Sun's transit into 20° Scorpio—with a variation using the Libra ingress. Why 20° Scorpio? *Sages* (**66**, Section I.11) says that it is because water is increased in wells around that date, but this cannot really be an explanation. Perhaps it is because in some climates the weather after November 10 (when the Sun is at about 20° Scorpio) turns more stormy on the seas, and snow and winter rains begin to fall.

In our texts, some of the passages deal only with the Libra ingress (but one implicitly refers to 20° Scorpio), others with 20° Scorpio; some include lore about Mercury or the Moon or others, some do not.[8] But all methods speak of the easternness or westernness of Venus: that is, whether she is in an earlier degree than the Sun and so rises before him (eastern), or is in a later degree than him and so sets after him (western).[9] So, we could consider this 20° method a special case of the very varied lore on the Moon-Mercury-Venus approach.

I have divided the passages into two primary groups: the 20° Scorpio group, and the Libra ingress group. Within the 20° Scorpio group, three texts also pair Venus and Mercury together in terms of easternness and westernness (marked with *):

---

[8] One passage (Hermann Ch. 5, **10-16**, in Section I.12) does not mention these ingresses at all, but still follows the general rule we see below: easternness means rain at the end of a period, westernness at the beginning.

[9] Hermann Ch. 5, **10-16** (Section I.12) is rather ambiguous as to when Venus's easternness and westernness should be examined.

20° Scorpio:

1. *Al-Kindī, *DMT* Ch. 6, **118-24** (Section I.3).
2. *'Umar Ch. 82, **2-5** (Section I.5).
3. Māshā'allāh, *Chapter on Rains*, **2-5** (Section I.6).
4. Māshā'allāh, *Letter*, **59-64** (Section I.7).
5. *Hermann, Ch. 5, **33-35** (Section I.12).
6. *Hermann, Ch. 6, **17-20** (Section I.12).

Only Māshā'allāh deals with Venus alone, and he is clear that if she is eastern at the 20° Scorpio ingress, rains happen at the *end* of the season; if western, at the *beginning*. In these cases, he is suggesting that she is actually visible and not under the rays. But if she is with the Sun in the same sign, the rain will come when they are joined: for "Venus under the rays is just like a woman under a man: it makes waters descend."[10] But of those passages which pair Venus with Mercury (i.e., al-Kindī and Hermann),[11] these situations are reversed: if Venus and Mercury are eastern, rain is at the *beginning*, while if western it shows rain at the *end*.

Then our texts have variations which deal only with the Libra ingress, or only implicitly with the 20° Scorpio ingress. Some also include applications of the Moon, and they also explicitly put Venus under the rays. They are:

Libra ingress:

1. Al-Kindī, *DMT* Ch. 8, **148-50** (Section I.3).
2. Jafar, **145-48** (Section I.10).
3. Hermann Ch. 5, **22-26** (Section I.12).
4. *Opening of the Doors* **30-32** (Section I.13).
5. John, *Epitome* I.6, **27** (Section I.15).

Here, the general rule is that if Venus is western and under the light of the Sun, rains happen near the *beginning* of the period; but if eastern and under the rays, near the *end*. Likewise, the Moon applying to a western planet indicates the beginning, but to an eastern one, the end.[12] *DMT* adds extra information which connects the Libra ingress to the 20° Scorpio method:

---

[10] *Letter* **62**; see also his *Chapter on the Rains in the Year*, **5**.

[11] Although 'Umar does deal with the easternness and westernness of Mercury and Venus, he relates it to the overall amount of rain, not to the time of the season.

[12] *Doors* **32** suggests ambiguously that if she were eastern and visible, the rain would be near the middle and end.

namely, if Venus were western in this way about 6 weeks into the season (when the Sun would actually be near 20° Scorpio), the middle of the season would have rain: this would be precisely because westernness means rain sooner, and it also suggests that easternness and westernness should be monitored throughout the season. No text in this group clearly states what it means for Venus to be *out* of the rays, but this may be intentional: since Māshā'allāh says that the Moon under the Sun's rays is what especially brings water, we would not expect as much from her when out of them.

So the majority of our texts agree that a western Venus (especially under the rays) shows early rains, while an eastern Venus (especially under the rays) shows late rains. Only al-Kindī's *DMT* and Hermann (who was probably taking information from al-Kindī) disagree. What accounts for this difference?

I suggest that the difference lies precisely in the fact that al-Kindī tends to follow Ptolemaic principles. And according to Ptolemy, eastern planets on the whole show things which happen sooner:[13] thus it makes sense that an eastern Venus would show rains early, a western one late. But Māshā'allāh and the others seem to follow a different principle, one in which a western planet is in a more nocturnal position—namely, one pertaining more to moisture and cooling. Thus a rainy planet such as Venus, being in a more feminine, moist, nocturnal relation to the Sun, would more likely indicate rains early.

Obviously, these methods cannot both be right (if they are correct at all), and I hope that future research will shed light on these phases of the planets in weather prediction.

Method 6: Planetary hours at lunar ingresses

Another approach mentioned in several texts deals with the planetary hours at lunar ingresses—one of the few worked-out examples of using planetary hours I have seen in traditional literature. We may see it in al-Kindī's *DMT* Ch. 6, **137** (Section I.3), which is incomplete in the Latin but apparently complete in the Hebrew version. I say "apparently" complete, because although the Hebrew version continues with another statement concerning the hour of Saturn, no other Latin text with the parallel sentence refers to Saturn: instead, they refer to other planets. Indeed an older Arabic

---

[13] See for instance the end of *Tet.* III.4 (Hübner, Schmidt) or *Tet.* III.3 (Robbins).

text (Māshā'allāh's *Chapter on the Rains in the Year*, see below) has close similarities to these other Latin ones. Moreover, a clue in Munich Clm. 11067 (96v) suggests that the reference to Saturn belongs in the planetary hour list, not in the concluding remark. Let us first look at the planetary hour list in the various texts, putting the variations in italics:

[al-Kindī, *DMT* Ch. 6, **137**] Another method. When the Moon will enter Cancer at the hour of the Sun, or Virgo at the hour of Venus, or Sagittarius at the hour of the Moon, or Gemini at the hour of Mercury, or Taurus at the hour of Mars, *or Leo (or even* Libra) at the hour of Jupiter, it signifies rain and wind[14] according to the nature of the sign; and what there is *with respect to her essence and the essence of these signs, will be likewise.*

[*Opening of the Doors*, **34**] Moreover, when the Moon enters Cancer at the hour of the Sun, and Virgo at the hour of Venus, or Sagittarius at the hour of the Moon, or Gemini at the hour of Mercury, or Taurus at the hour of Mars, or Libra at the hour of Jupiter, it signifies rain or winds, in the manner of the nature of the sign *in which the lord of the hour is.*

[John of Spain, *Epitome* I.6, **37**] And when the Moon enters Cancer at the hour of the Sun, or Virgo at the hour of Venus, or Sagittarius at the hour of the Moon, or Gemini at the hour of Mercury, or Taurus at the hour of Mars, or Libra at the hour of Jupiter, it signifies rain or winds according to the nature of the sign in which *the lord of that hour is.*

[Munich Clm. 11067, 96v] When the Moon enters Cancer at the hour of the Sun, or Virgo at the hour of Venus, or Sagittarius at the hour of *Saturn*, or Gemini at the hour of Mercury, or Taurus at the hour of Mars, or Libra at the hour of Jupiter, it signifies rain or winds in the manner of the sign in which *the lord of the hour is.*

In terms of the matching of signs with planets, the differences seem to be trivial and accidental: al-Kindī includes Leo along with Libra, and Munich

---

[14] Omitting "rain in hotness, and." The Hebrew reads, "rain in its proper times, and wind…".

pairs Sagittarius with Saturn instead of the Moon. But the use of Saturn does not seem trivial once we ask the question, "why these signs and hours?" Evidently there must be a relationship between the domicile the Moon is in, and the domiciles ruled by the planetary lord.

For the first two signs, the Moon is in a sign which is the twelfth from a sign ruled by the hourly lord: Cancer is the twelfth from Leo (ruled by the Sun), and Virgo the twelfth from Libra (Venus). If we follow Munich, we also get Sagittarius, which is the twelfth from Capricorn (Saturn).

On the other hand, if we look at the other members of the lists, some planets could be seen as offset from their proper place by one spot. For instance, the texts pair Libra with Jupiter: but Libra is the twelfth from Scorpio, ruled by Mars, the previous planet in the list. And although Taurus is paired with Mars, Taurus is the twelfth from Gemini, ruled by Mercury, the previous planet in the list. Finally, while Gemini is paired with Mercury, Gemini is the twelfth from Cancer, ruled by the Moon, who is the previous planet in all lists but Munich's. To me, this suggests that the original Arabic source was worded in such a way that it caused confusion, so that in each case the Moon is supposed to be in the twelfth from a sign whose planetary lord is currently in power. The only difficult part is deciding what sign should be paired with Jupiter, since he rules two domiciles. Since I cannot see any rationale for picking the other domiciles in the first place, for the moment we are left with conjecturing that it must be either Scorpio or Aquarius, since each is in the twelfth from a domicile of Jupiter (Sagittarius and Pisces, respectively).

Another important difference is that all of the other texts besides al-Kindī's say the effect will be according to the sign in which *the lord of the hour* is, not the Moon. To me this makes good astrological sense. Suppose that the Moon were in Virgo during the hour of Venus: since Virgo is in aversion to Libra (ruled by Venus), and no aspects of Venus to the Moon or Virgo or Libra are mentioned, the only obvious relevance which Venus has, must be something like her own nature or the sign she is in. The Hebrew itself only says "the sign," without saying whose sign, so at least it does not contradict this idea. The rest of al-Kindī's sentence is a kind of throwaway remark reminding us that the Moon and her sign are important too, which is not very informative when we are specifically talking about planetary lords.

And so, with the proviso that we do not know which domicile the Moon should be in for Jupiter's hour, I suggest that this planetary lord list should read as follows:

[Dykes's suggestion] Another method. When the Moon will enter Cancer at the hour of the Sun, or Virgo at the hour of Venus, or Sagittarius at the hour of Saturn, or Gemini at the hour of the Moon, or Taurus at the hour of Mercury, or Libra at the hour of Mars, or Scorpio/Aquarius at the hour of Jupiter, it signifies rain and wind according to the nature of the sign in which the lord of the hour is.

The last portion of the sentence, which exists only in Hebrew but has parallels in the other texts, runs as follows:

[al-Kindī, *DMT* Ch. 6, **137** (Hebrew)] For example: the Moon in Aquarius or Scorpio or Capricorn, in the hour of Saturn, indicates a change of weather.

[*The Opening of the Doors*, **35**] When Venus is in Scorpio or in Capricorn or in Aquarius, or when Jupiter [is conjoined to][15] the Moon or aspects her, it signifies much rain.

[Munich Clm. 11067, 96v] If Venus is in Capricorn or Scorpio or Aquarius, and *she* is being conjoined to the Moon or aspects her, it signifies much rain.

[John of Spain, *Epitome* I.7, **14**] Venus in Scorpio or Capricorn or Aquarius, denotes rain [if she is] in a proportion to the Moon,[16] and thus the three planets[17] joined in Aquarius.

[Jafar, *Book of Heavy Rains*, **149**] In fact, a multitude of rains especially pours forth while Venus and Mercury hasten to enter Scorpio and Capricorn, Aquarius, and Pisces; but even an application of them with

---

[15] Adding with Bos and Burnett, but see the parallel excerpt in Munich Clm. 11067.
[16] *Proportionalis Lunae*. I take this to mean an aspect.
[17] This must refer to the Moon, Mercury, and Venus: see Jafar immediately below.

the Moon from moist places (not without a regard):[18] which if they would bear themselves thusly, they show general rains, nor unuseful ones.

[Māshā'allāh, *Chapter on the Rains in the Year*, **11**][19] When you have established this firmly, look at the position of Venus and the Moon and Mercury, and if you have found these planets in signs of water, and you have found the Moon to be connecting with them, and she is not connecting with one of the infortunes: the rain was abundant in that year.

In al-Kindī, *The Opening of the Doors*, and Munich, this sentence immediately follows the statements about planetary hours. Note first that *only* al-Kindī connects its content to planetary hours, although it is hard to see the relevance of Saturn's hour to Scorpio. But in the *Doors* text and Munich, we are not even speaking of the Moon here to begin with, but rather Venus—so that the Moon-Mercury-Venus lore is being introduced. The version of *Doors* translated here, inexplicably has Jupiter being connected to the Moon, while Munich has the Moon being joined to that same Venus. The last three passages appear to mirror this interest in Venus being in these signs and connected to the Moon, specifically calling these rainy signs (with Jafar adding Pisces). The only extra element is the inclusion of Mercury, which is part of the general treatment found throughout our oldest reliable text, Māshā'allāh's Arabic *Chapter on the Rains in the Year*, and is also in a version of the 20° Scorpio approach in al-Kindī's *DMT*, Ch. 8, **142-43**. Finally, I note that in *DMT* Ch. 6, **131-35**, al-Kindī had already begun to address the Moon-Mercury-Venus material, and immediately begins to do so again in **138-41**[20]— just as the other texts immediately turn to it after the discussion of planetary hours.

So while al-Kindī may be reporting some teaching about the hour of Saturn, the more likely explanation is that Saturn belongs in the planetary hour list (per my suggested correction above), and that the end of **137**, like the other parallel texts, deals with some version of the Moon-Mercury-Venus lore, with some or all of them being in one of the rainy signs.

---

[18] Hugo/Jafar seems to mean that both a *conjunction* ("application") and an aspect will indicate these things.

[19] See also sentences **47**, **51**, and **57**.

[20] Because of the structure of the Latin text, these sentences do not appear until Ch. 8.

Method 7: Lots of rain and wind

Finally, throughout Part I our authors describe four different Lots of rain and/or wind, some of which are supposed to track the possibility of rain on a daily basis. I have not tested any of these Lots, but thought it would be good to put them together here for those who would like to research them further.

1. Sun-Saturn, Moon. The first Lot is described in al-Kindī's Latin *DMT*, Ch. 7 (Section I.3 above). According to Bos and Burnett (p. 382), it is the second of those listed in Abū Ma'shar's *Kitāb al-Sirr* ("The Book of the Secret"), which is found as an interpolation in 'Umar's Ch. 81 (Section I.5). It is substantially the same as *The Opening of the Doors* **17-18**, ibn Ezra's *Book of the World* §40 (Version 2), ibn Ezra's *The Beginning of Wisdom* Ch. 9, p. 153 (where it is attributed to Enoch or Hermes), and John's *Epitome* Ch. 1.7, **12-13** (Section I.15). Some versions clarify that it should be cast at dawn every day, and projected from the "degree" or "place" of the Moon, not simply her sign:

> **7:L2** If you wished to know what there is on any day in terms of rains, winds, thunders, and hail, take from the Sun to Saturn and project from the sign of the Moon: where the number will be ended, see what planet will be the lord in that house. **L3** If it were a house of Saturn, that day will be cold; if Jupiter, calm and mild; if Mars, a strong wind; if the Sun, a hot day; if Venus, rainy; if Mercury, variable; if the Moon, rainy.

A few sentences later, al-Kindī gives the same calculation (at dawn, using the degree of the Moon), and gives extra information on Mercury and Venus:

> **L7** If Mercury aspected this Lot, or it happened to fall with Mercury, there will be wind on that day. **L8** And a stronger sign is if the Moon would be with him, especially if Venus participated.

John adds: "And one must even see whether that same computation would be ended in a moist or dry mansion, according to what will judge."

2. New Moon-Moon, Ascendant. The second Lot comes from ibn Ezra's *The Beginning of Wisdom* Ch. 9, pp. 152-53. The calculation is performed daily (ei-

ther at dawn or dusk) and is supposed to be valid for countries ruled by the
sign the Moon is in. First, find the position of the most recent New Moon,
and the current position of the Moon herself. If done at dawn, measure from
the New Moon to the current Moon, and project that distance from the Ascendant; if at dusk, measure from the Moon to the New Moon, and project
from the Ascendant. If there is a planet "with this Lot in one of the angles,"
then it will rain when the transiting Moon reaches that planet.

This description has ambiguities in it. First, what is the reason for deciding to calculate it at sunset rather than sunrise? Also, in which angles is this
other planet supposed to be: in the whole-sign angles of the Lot itself, or in
the angles of the chart? Finally, what are the differences between the planets
in those angles: will it rain more heavily if it is Mars rather than (say) Jupiter?

3. *Moon-Venus, Sun.* This Lot is only found in Hermann's *Book of Heavy
Rains* (Section I.12, Ch. 5, **2-3**). At the Sun's Aries ingress (but perhaps also
the quarterly ingresses or even monthly ones?), measure from the Moon to
Venus by day, but from Venus to the Moon by night, and project from the
Sun. According to Hermann, "it being found in a place of waters, indicates a
rainy year."

4. *Mercury-dispositor of Mercury, Ascendant.* Finally, 'Umar describes a Mercu-
ry-based Lot in his Ch. 81, **19-24** (Section I.5). I am uncertain as to whether
this is also a daily Lot, or one to be calculated only at ingresses or even at
New Moons. It is worth quoting in full:

> **19** And help yourself in this with the Lot of air and winds, and make it
> be a partner with the significator. **20** And if you found Saturn or Mars
> with the Lot or its lord,[21] judge from them just as we said before about
> their appearance in the stakes[22] and in the aspects of the significator. **21**
> For you will take this Lot from the degree of Mercury (if he were not
> in his own house) up to the degree of the lord of the house in which he
> is, and add on top of this the degrees of the Ascendant, and project
> from the Ascendant:[23] and where the number is ended, there is the Lot.
> **22** And if Mercury were in his own house, take his own degrees, adding

---

[21] Reading with Burnett's 'Umar and the Tehran al-Kindī for al-Rijāl's "their lords."
[22] That is, "angles." See the Glossary.
[23] Burnett's 'Umar reads, "subtract."

the degrees of the Ascendant to them, and projecting from the Ascendant: and where [the counting] applied to, there is the Lot. **23** And you will do the same at the entrances of the Sun in the quarters (which are Aries, Libra, Cancer, and Capricorn). **24** You will do likewise at the entrance of the Sun into each of the twelve signs.

SECTION I.2: PTOLEMY ON WEATHER

In my Introduction to this book, I made some summary statements about Ptolemy's approach to mundane astrology. Here I will introduce Ptolemy's method of weather prediction in the following way. First, I will give Ptolemy's indications for the planets and their phases, and some comments about how to use them. Second, I will describe the indications for some fixed stars and the zodiacal signs, which for Ptolemy probably means the constellations themselves. Third, I will detail Ptolemy's own method. Fourth, Ptolemy makes a few comments about omens. Fifth, I will offer two chart examples and make some suggestions, some of which are adopted by later astrologers.

Indications of the planets [Tet. I.8, II.8]

General overview. In several chapters of *Tet.* II, Ptolemy develops a naturalistic theory of weather prediction, and in Section I.3 we will see how al-Kindī takes Ptolemy a bit further. First, in II.8 Ptolemy offers a lengthy description of the basic indications of the seven planets, not just for weather but other things as well: for example, we must keep these lists in mind when looking at the material on eclipses. Although he does want us to take the planets' signs and aspects into account, he first looks at what each planet means by itself, when it has sole rulership over the key places indicating the mundane effects.[1] I will give an abbreviated list of these indications from II.8 first, and then explain how Ptolemy wants us to use them.

Saturn (5-8)	Extreme cold, dryness.[2] Destruction by cold.
Humans	Chronic illness, fluid buildup, rheumatism, quartan fevers, exile, poverty, fear, death.
Animals	Scarcity and disease in animals used by people, and the people who use them.
Weather	Strong coldness, mist, pestilence, clouds, darkness, bad snowstorms, weather producing harmful animals.
Water/seas	Storms, shipwreck, scarcity/death of fish, flooding and polluted waters.
Crops	Scarcity of necessities, pestilence and infestations, destruction by hail, famine.

---

[1] As we will see below, this especially includes the sign in which an eclipse takes place.
[2] These elemental qualities are from *Tet.* I.4-5.

Jupiter (9-10)	Temperate heat, moisture. Increase generally.
Humans	Fame, prosperity, peace, health of body and mind, increases necessities of life, good rulers.
Animals	Increase of useful animals, decrease of unuseful ones.
Weather	Temperate, windy, moist, good for growing.
Water/seas	Good sailing, moderate rise in waters.
Crops	Abundant crops.

Mars (11-13)	Extreme dryness, heat. Destruction through dryness.
Humans	Wars, imprisonment, angry leaders causing deaths, fevers, tertian fevers, much death, violence, robbery.
Animals	Loss of [useful] animals.
Weather	Hot, pestilence, hot winds, lightning and hurricanes, drought.
Water/seas	Shipwreck, bad winds and lightning, water drying up.
Crops	Scarcity of crops, locusts, burning of supplies.

Venus (14-15)	Warmth, moisture. Like Jupiter but more pleasant.
Humans	Abundance, happiness, marriage, children, good relationships, neatness, health, good rulers.
Animals	Abundance of useful animals.
Weather	Temperateness, fertilizing rain, good wind and clear weather.
Water/seas	Successful and profitable trips and rising waters.
Crops	Abundance, high yields, profits.

Mercury (16-18)	Like the planets associated with him.[3]
Humans	Ingenuity but often by immoral means; dryness, coughs, consumption (with malefics); events regarding the priestly code, worship, government revenues, changes in customs and laws.
Animals	Destruction of [useful] animals (prob. with malefics).
Weather	Drying, but stimulates sudden strong winds, thunder and lightning, hurricanes, openings in the earth, earthquakes.
Water/seas	Unsuccessful trips if with malefics; if sinking,[4] diminishes waters, but arising,[5] raises them.
Crops	Destruction of crops (probably with malefics)

Figure 8: Ptolemy's mundane significations of planets

---

[3] Ptolemy seems to assume the worst things about Mercury here, perhaps because he says Mercury is very stimulating (16), which probably leads to sudden and unexpected events and weather patterns.

[4] This probably means sinking under the Sun's rays (or already being fully under them).

[5] This probably means arising out of the Sun's rays (or already being fully outside them).

You should have noticed that the Sun and Moon are absent from the list. This is actually Ptolemy's usual approach: treating the Sun and Moon as general indicators, with the other five planets giving specifics.[6] But here in particular he explains why (**2**): that the luminaries are arrangers[7] and leaders of the others, and are responsible over the rulership of the other five, not to mention their strength and weakness. Robbins (p. 179 n.1) helpfully points out a note by the anonymous commentator to Ptolemy, that this refers to the role of the Sun and the Moon in eclipses—we might also add their role in the charts for the lunation preceding solar ingresses, too. This makes sense to me, given how Ptolemy uses the eclipses and lunations to identify key signs and mundane regions in the first place. That is to say, he uses the luminaries as clocks and placeholders, to identify which sign rulers and so on to examine.

So, how should we use these planets? First, we must identify what places matter, and this would seem to be first of all the places of eclipses, but perhaps also the signs in which the annual, quarterly, and monthly lunations fall. When we find the appropriate sign, Ptolemy seems first to want to know what geographic regions of the earth the sign itself rules—because the weather would especially be relevant for that region. After identifying the region and classes of beings affected, Ptolemy wants us to discover the planet or planets ruling the zodiacal place (**21**), to notice whether or not it has a natural affinity or "familiarity" with the regions and beings affected (**21-22**),[8] and then to notice the following things about these ruling planets:

- The planets ruling the key places (**1, 19, 21**).
- Their combination with each other (**1, 19**).
- Their solar phases (and probably stations) (**19**).[9]
- Their combination with their sign-location (**1**).[10]
- Their combination with fixed stars (**4**).

---

[6] See for instance *Tet.* III-IV, on body types, character, profession, and so on.
[7] *Diataktai.*
[8] See Section III.2 for a discussion of this in connection with eclipses.
[9] In *Tet.* I.8, Ptolemy describes the elemental qualities of the planets in relation to the Sun.
[10] For the indications of the signs, see below.

To make a couple of these items clearer, in *Tet.* I.8 Ptolemy describes the planets' elemental qualities in relation to the Sun. Following is a diagram of the Moon's phases:

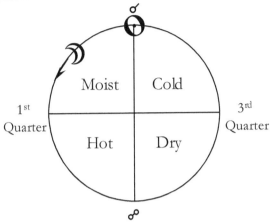

Figure 9: Lunar phases and elemental qualities (*Tet.* I.8)

For the superior planets (Mars, Jupiter, Saturn):[11]

- As morning planets, from arising out of the rays to their first station: moisture.
- As morning, planets, from the first station to being achronical or opposite the Sun: heat.
- From the opposition of the Sun to the second station, dryness.
- From the second station to sinking under the rays: coldness.

---

[11] Strictly speaking, this can only refer to the superior planets, since Mercury and Venus are never opposite the Sun. If we follow al-Kindī's understanding of this, the phases of Mercury and Venus should be the opposite, so that when they are closest to the earth they are more heating and drying: arising out of the rays direct (moistening), retrograding until they are under the rays (heating), emerging out of the rays retrograde (drying), and moving direct towards the Sun's rays (cold).

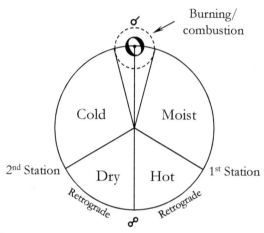

Figure 10: Superior planets' weather effects by solar phase (*Tet.* I.8)

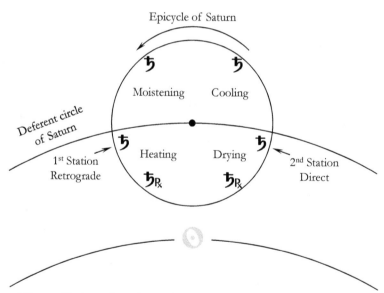

Figure 11: Superior planets' weather effects, in epicyclic form

Ptolemy does not offer an equivalent scheme for Mercury and Venus. But in his natal treatment of bodily form (*Tet.* III.11),[12] he says that when Mercury has arisen out of the rays (*anatolikos*) he indicates warmth, but when setting under them (*dutikos*) he indicates dryness. When Venus is arising, she is like

---

[12] This is III.12 in Hübner's edition.

Jupiter in being warming and moistening, and when setting under the rays she indicates greater moisture. It could be that because Mercury and Venus are always so close to the Sun, they cannot not exhibit the thorough variation which the superiors do. In *Tet.* I.8, Ptolemy conspicuously mentions that the Moon and the *superiors* go through all these stages, and so by omission implies that the inferiors do not.

In al-Kindī's account, the cycle of the inferiors has the following structure:

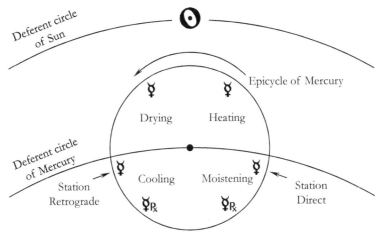

Figure 12: Al-Kindī's weather effects for inferior planets
(*DMT* Ch. 5, 68-69)

It is easy to see that al-Kindī has made the effects for superiors and inferiors mirror each other. In each case, a planet's nearness to the Sun indicates heating and drying: for the superiors this happens during retrogradation, for the inferiors during direct motion. A greater distance from the Sun leads to cooling and moistening, and again for the superiors this happens in direct motion, but the for the inferiors in retrograde motion.

Indications of the fixed stars (Tet. I.9)

As for the fixed stars, in *Tet.* I.9 Ptolemy famously listed numerous fixed stars and their associated planetary natures. For instance, the stars in the head of Aries (Hamal, Mesarthim, Sheratan) are like a combination of Mars and Saturn. Thus, it seems to me that if Mars were of importance in a particular weather prediction, and he were conjoined with those stars, they would enhance the weather indications listed under Mars above. One may consult any of the better astrology computer programs to find these stars' positions. I should point out here, though, that I cannot see a relationship between the weather indications for fixed stars listed in Ptolemy, and those of the lunar mansion stars (see Section I.1). That is, the stars to which Ptolemy assigns planetary qualities in *Tet.* I.9, are often the very stars which define the lunar mansions—but whereas Ptolemy's Martial stars in *Tet.* I.9 ought to indicate rain, the lunar mansions in which they appear do not necessarily do so. This suggests that the lunar mansions and Ptolemy's stellar qualities come from totally separate sources.[13]

Indications of the zodiacal signs (Tet. II.11)

In *Tet.* II.11, Ptolemy explains the general character of each zodiacal sign, and then divides each into thirds and into areas of northern and southern ecliptical latitudes. If one groups the signs by seasons, one may see that the general characteristics of the signs tend to follow the weather when the Sun is in them: thus the spring and summer signs (Aries through Virgo) tend to be hotter than the rest. But this is only a very general observation.

The table below summarizes the main points of *Tet.* II.11. In it, each sign has a general characteristic under its name; then each third is described (where "1st" means from 0° or the beginning of each sign or constellation, up to one third of it, and so on), then its indications in its northern ("N") and southern ("S") ecliptical parts. Following is also a key for common, abbreviated weather descriptors:

C = Cold	**Pest.** = Pestilential
D = Dry	**T** = Temperate
Destr. = Destructive	**Th.** = Thunder
EQ = Earthquakes	**Var.** = Variable, unstable
H = Hot	**W** = Windy
M = Moist or Rainy	

---

[13] Of course, one hole in Ptolemy's use of the fixed stars is that he sometimes assigns them qualities of the Sun and Moon, but he does not want to assign specific weather and other indications to them, as I mentioned above.

	1st	2nd	3rd	N	S
Aries Th., Hail	M, W	T	H, Pest.	H, Destr.	C
Taurus Warm	EQ, W, Misty	M, C	H, Th., Lightn.	T	Var.
Gemini Even	M, Destr.	T	Var.	W, EQ	D
Cancer T, Warm	H, EQ, Misty	T	W	H, D	H, D
Leo H	H, Pest.	T	M, Destr.	H, Var.	M
Virgo M, Stormy	Warm, Destr.	T	M	W	T
Libra Var.	T	T	M	W	M, Pest.
Scorpio Th., Fire	Snowy	T	EQ	H	M
Sagittarius W	M	T	Fiery	W	M, Var.
Capricorn M	H, Destr.	T	Stormy	M, Destr.	M, Destr.
Aquarius C, M	M	T	W	H	Cloudy
Pisces C, W	T	M	H	W	M

Figure 13: Weather indications of the signs (*Tet.* II.11)

Ptolemy mentions fixed stars in some of his descriptions, which suggests the use of either a sidereal or constellational zodiac. It is well known that the tropical and sidereal zodiacs roughly coincided around Ptolemy's lifetime, so if it is sidereal, then each sign is technically 30°, but certain stars in the constellation might fall inside or outside the neat thirds he mentions. But if Ptolemy is using the constellations themselves, then because the constellations are of uneven lengths, each third of the signs will not be equal to 10°.

Ptolemy's method (*Tet.* II.10, II.12)[14]

At this point we may now turn to summary statements of Ptolemy's method of weather prediction. One should notice that Ptolemy's method

---

[14] In Hübner's edition, these are *Tet.* II.11 and II.13 respectively, because Hübner split an earlier chapter up into two parts. Thus Robbins has 13 chapters in Book II, and Hübner 14.

forms a foundation for practices in later authors: for one thing, he uses the charts of New/Full Moons prior to Solar ingresses, except that here he is only concerned with weather, while later authors use them for social and agricultural matters, too. For another, Ptolemy introduces what are later called the "foundations" or "posts" or "centers" of the Moon: positions between the New and Full Moon, at which her condition and aspects ought to be examined for shorter-term influences.[15]

Ptolemy's method is in several parts:

1. Charts of New/Full Moons prior to the Sun's ingresses into the movable signs (II.10, II.12).
2. Charts of New/Full Moons prior to the Sun's other monthly ingresses (II.10, II.12).
3. The Sun's and Moon's relations to planets at her quarters, and other aspects (II.12).
4. Daily indications, as fixed stars make morning or evening appearances, risings and settings (II.12).[16]
5. Hourly indications, as the luminaries pass through the angles throughout the day (II.12).

Charts of New/Full Moons prior to ingresses. In *Tet.* II.10, Ptolemy argues that the New Moon prior to the beginning of the year is an appropriate time to judge the course of the year (**1**). He does not provide a real argument, but we might imagine that it is for a reason rather like choosing the date of Easter. Easter (at least in the West) is defined as the first Sunday after the first Full Moon after the spring equinox; but why such an odd definition? It has to do with light: Sunday is assigned to the Sun, the spring equinox defines when the length of daylight triumphs over night, and the Full Moon is when the Moon receives the most light from the Sun. This is a fitting time to celebrate a God whose story is thematized by resurrection out of darkness, revelation, life, and light. So we might expect that around the time of the beginning of

---

[15] For more on the foundations or posts or centers, see my Introduction in Section I.1.

[16] In this case, Ptolemy means something different than the planets' relations to the Sun's rays. In his *Phases of the Fixed Stars*, "morning" and "evening" refer to the time of day: that is, when the *Sun* is actually on the Ascendant or Descendant; "rising" and "setting" refer to where the *fixed star* is. Thus, the "morning rising" of a fixed star means that it is (a) actually daybreak, and (b) the star is rising in the east, in virtually the same place the Sun is; but the "evening rising" means that it is (a) actually sunset, and (b) the star is again actually appearing on the eastern horizon. See Denningmann 2007.

the year (marked by a solar ingress) and the new Moon, is a good time to evaluate the beginning and further development of the year.

So far, so good. But while Ptolemy agrees that the beginning of the year ought to happen at the Sun's ingress in one of the movable signs, he says it is hard to know which to prefer (**2**). For, other cultures have variously considered the movable signs as beginnings (**3-4**): the spring equinox because of the increase of daylight over nighttime, the summer solstice because the Nile floods and brings new life then, the sowing of future seed at the fall equinox once the harvest is over, and the lengthening of day from its shortest period just after the winter solstice. Which to use? Well, Ptolemy prefers to use all of them, and specifically the pre-ingress New Moon or Full Moon, whichever most recently preceded the ingress (**5**); and he is especially interested if any of these are also times of eclipses, since the eclipse method is so central to his conception of mundane prediction.

Thus, by casting the chart for the New or Full Moon most nearly preceding the Sun's ingress into Aries, Cancer, Libra, and Capricorn, we may see what types of weather the upcoming season has in store (**5**). Ptolemy does not explain why a time *before* the ingress should be more powerful than one *after* the ingress, but I suspect it is because we want a preview of the season, not an account after the season has begun (although this does not seem like a powerful argument to me).

For monthly charts (*Tet.* II.12), we do the same procedure, but with a twist: if the lunation most nearly preceding the seasonal ingress had been a New Moon, use only New Moons up until the next season; but if it had been a Full Moon, use only the ongoing Full Moons (**3**).

In evaluating the seasonal and monthly ingress charts, Ptolemy wants to note the following things (*Tet.* II.10.6-7, II.12.4):[17]

- The standardly expected weather for that season and location.
- The weather-inducing qualities of the signs involved. This probably means first of all the sign in which the lunation happens, but possibly (it seems to me) the Ascendant; but Ptolemy definitely includes the signs in which the rulers of the signs are.

---

[17] My list is somewhat tentative as to what to include, in part because Ptolemy states the method differently in each chapter, leaves out some items we might expect to see (like stations), and seems more interested in his own compressed writing style than spelling it all out for us.

- The qualities of the rulers of the lunation themselves,[18] and those of the angle *following* it, as with his eclipse method.[19]
- Planets in or aspecting the place of the lunation (and probably the signs in which they are).
- Weather indications of the planets' applications, separations, and phases with respect to the Sun's rays, and probably stations—probably primarily that of the rulers, but perhaps any other planet doing something like this at the time. Probably ongoing transits in or to the place of the lunation should be examined, as well, up until the time of the next chart.
- The "wind" to which the latitude of the Moon is inclined, "through the obliquity of the ecliptic."[20]

Unfortunately, Ptolemy leaves some questions unanswered, of which one is: should the Ascendant and its lord (and its sign) be examined, as with later authors? To me it would seem so.

Daily predictions (II.12) One ought to examine the luminaries' aspects to the planets whenever the Moon is in some configuration with the Sun (New or Full Moon, quarters, sextiles, trines), including at the semi-quarters (**5**): the planets and signs involved will show day-by-day modifications to the general weather patterns (**6**). This is Ptolemy's version of the lunar "centers." At these times, note especially when bright fixed stars are making their morning or evening appearances from out of the Sun's rays (**7**). Ptolemy also mentions the times when the luminaries pass over the angles (**7**), which I take to mean their transits over the angles of the *monthly lunation chart*, not when they pass across the axes by diurnal rotation throughout the day.

Hourly predictions (II.12) Ptolemy is rather vague on this, except to mention two things: when the luminaries appear on the angles (in this case, the local angles throughout the day), and the direction of the winds to which the latitude of the Moon inclines.

---

[18] Undoubtedly, the lords of the signs, but consider also the victor-type approach for eclipses (Section III.2).

[19] Unfortunately, Ptolemy does not explain what exactly he means by the angle "following" it: is this the fourth sign from the eclipse? Or the sign on the axial degree which is most immediately following it in the zodiac? And why should we do this?

[20] This probably refers to her declination (which is how al-Kindī understands it): in signs of northern declination, northern winds; in southern declination, southern winds.

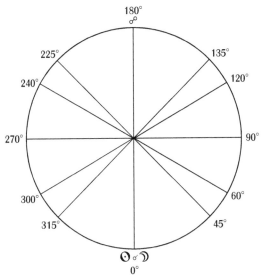

Figure 14: Ptolemy's version of the "centers" of the Moon

Omens and sights contributing to weather prediction (*Tet.* II.13)

In *Tet.* II.13, Ptolemy adds some details on using atmospheric effects to foretell weather. I will abbreviate these, because in many cases they are not strictly astrological but more commonsensical (for example, that if there are few clouds around the Moon, the weather will be clear for a while).

The Sun's appearances at sunrise and sunset, and also his aspects to the Moon, indicate weather from that point up until sunset/sunrise/the next aspect, respectively (**1**).

As for the Sun (**2-3**), if he appears clear and unobscured at sunrise or sunset, the weather will be fair; but if reddish and with reddish rays or surrounding clouds with long rays, there will be strong winds from the direction shown by the rays; and if he is dark and cloudy or with halos, it indicates storms.

For the Moon (**4-7**),[21] we ought to look three days before and after each of her four major quarters: in effect, this is nothing more than a version of the foundations or posts of the Moon (see my Introduction and the rest of the authors below), except that here Ptolemy looks for atmospheric effects

---

[21] See also *Tet.* II.12.5.

around the Moon's body instead of astrological configurations.[22] If the air around her appears thin and clear, it means clear weather; if thin and red but one may see the rest of the unilluminated portion, it means winds; if "dark, or pale, or thick" (I am not sure to what Ptolemy refers here), it means storms (**4-5**). But if she has halos around her, fewer halos means more clear weather, and more halos means more stormy weather (**6**), while yellow ones indicate winds, thick and misty ones, snow, and a combination means a combination (**6**). Ptolemy also says that halos around the planets and the brighter fixed stars indicate weather according to the color of the halos (or perhaps the colors of the stars?) and "the natures of the luminaries which they surround."

I omit Ptolemy's discussion of certain clusters (**8-9**), rushing and shooting stars (**10**), and rainbows (**11**), but I will mention his brief statements about comets (**10**) in Part III below.

Examples:

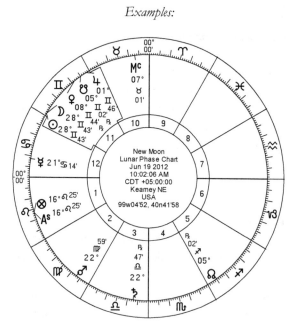

Figure 15: Summer lunation for Kearney, Nebraska, 2012

---

[22] But in an earlier chapter (II.12, see his general method below), Ptolemy *does* include aspects to planets in addition to other aspects like the trine.

Let's take an example of the method, assuming a normal tropical zodiac, and that the "angle following" the lunation means the axial degree following it: in this example, the Ascendant.

The chart is cast for the New Moon prior to the summer ingress into Cancer, in Kearney, Nebraska, USA, which suffered a terrible drought in 2012 (and was among the worst-hit in the country). As it is summer, the standard expected weather will be inclining to hot and dry (as it is summer).

The lunation is in Gemini, the last third: according to Ptolemy this suggests a kind of evenness with general variability: in other words, nothing distinctive one way or another. Two planets are in the sign of the lunation, Venus and Gemini. By sign they also indicate a kind of indifference, and in themselves they indicate pleasantness and fair weather: which was the case, the drought aside. Venus has just made a morning appearance from out of the rays, which suggests heating (which was the case) but also moistening (not the case). The planets most closely aspecting the degree of the lunation are Mars and Saturn, two drying planets which indicate scarcity and drought and burning, but strong storms when they do arrive. Saturn is also stationing, making his drying influence even more important.

Mercury rules the place of the lunation. He is often considered to be cold and drying by default, but he also has a sextile with Mars and Saturn. He does not aspect any moistening planet. He is in the last third of Cancer, which is temperate as a whole, but he is in the windy portion, and by being in northern ecliptical latitude it adds heat and dryness. He is moving direct and out of the rays, which for Ptolemy indicates warming (which was the case).

So far then, we see overall indications of clear, hot, and dry weather, with little to no rain. Of course, one problem may be Jupiter, which normally does produce profitable rains and is in the sign of the lunation, in a moistening phase: why does he not produce rain? One possibility is that the degree of his body is as close to the degree to the lunation as the malefics' aspects are, so he is more marginalized; another is that the overall thrust of the chart is for dryness and heat, so his moistening indication cannot overcome it. Then again, maybe something is wrong with Ptolemy's theory.

Two factors can help localize this chart. First, the Ascendant (which is also the angle following the lunation) is Leo, which is hot as a whole; its lord the Sun is likewise a heating and drying planet, again closely aspecting Mars and Saturn. Second, a few minutes before the lunation Hamal was on the Midheaven, and within seconds of the lunation Arcturus was on the IC. According to *Tet.* I.9, stars in the head of Aries (Hamal) are like Mars-Saturn, and Arcturus (in Bootes) is like Jupiter-Mars. Thus again we have strong drying influences.

On the other hand, look at the following chart for London, which has been experiencing the wettest summer in a century:

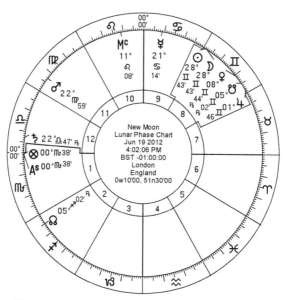

Figure 16: Summer lunation for London, 2012

Most of the features of the chart are the same as those for Nebraska. The angle following the lunation is still Leo. But now the local Ascendant is Scorpio, sign indicating thunder and snow: while it obviously did not snow, perhaps because snow is a type of precipitation it indicates rain and storms? Perhaps also this wetness brings out the storminess in its lord, Mars. About 10 minutes before the lunation, Deneb Adige (in Cygnus) was on the IC, but in a crooked sign that is faster moving, bringing it farther away from the IC. No significant stars were on the Ascendant or Midheaven within about 10 minutes of the lunation. Again, Mercury indicates warming; Venus indicates moistening.

Thus, without going into monthly ingresses or daily predictions, Ptolemy's method does not seem to distinguish very strongly between extreme drought and extreme rain, except in the case of the Ascendants of these charts. But as we will see, al-Kindī takes Ptolemy's method further, while Māshā'allāh and his followers have alternative ways of looking at weather, including the use of lunar mansions.

On the other hand, I do have a couple of suggestions for future research—even apart from adding the other methods endorsed by the rest of the astrologers in Part I:

- The drying conditions indicated in the charts might show that *worldwide* there are moisture problems, even if not in the region where a *particular* chart is cast. Again, we need to find reliable ways to particularize the charts (of which the Ascendant is one).

- London normally does not need help to get rain, nor is Nebraska known for being very wet. So, perhaps each needs only a small indication to make its typical weather more extreme: a watery sign rising to show extreme moisture in London, and a fiery sign rising to show extreme heat and dryness in Nebraska.

- Perhaps the New Moons preceding the ingresses are not the most important charts, and we ought to favor the seasonal and monthly ingresses themselves.

SECTION I.3: AL-KINDĪ, *LETTER ON AIR & RAINS*, OR *ON THE CHANGE OF SEASONS* (*DMT*)

This Section presents a translation of a scientific astrological *Letter* or *Letters* by al-Kindī, the most famous early Arab philosopher and scientific thinker (ca. 801-870 AD).[1] I say "*Letter* or *Letters*," because the only surviving copies of it are in two Hebrew *Letters*, and a single Latin one.[2] Of these Hebrew *Letters*, the first is equivalent to Chs. 1-6 of the Latin, and the second is roughly equivalent to Chs. 6-8. Some material appears only in the Hebrew, some only in Latin, and in the Latin work particularly, some material from Ch. 6 is repeated. Since we do not have the Arabic, and I have translated from the Latin (albeit with paraphrases and crosschecking against the Hebrew), I will abbreviate this work as *DMT* (*De Mutatione Temporum, On the Change of Seasons*). The Latin version was translated from an Arabic original (probably a different one than the source of the Hebrew), by a man calling himself "Master Azogont,"[3] and in his introduction to the work he proudly proclaims the "perfect wording" of his translation. In the Hebrew preface, the letter is addressed to a student called Habīb (which in Arabic means "dear, beloved"), and an earlier scholar named Steinschneider[4] says this was a Habīb ibn Bahriz, a known translator of Greek works who was part of al-Kindī's circle.

Readers of works like his *Forty Chapters* know that al-Kindī was no stranger to conventional astrological practice. But here he largely adopts a naturalistic attitude, using material from Ptolemy and Aristotle to develop his theory of weather prediction.[5] In this theory, al-Kindī consistently mentions

---

[1] For more on al-Kindī, see my translation of his *Forty Chapters* (2011). In this introductory section, I draw on Bos and Burnett's discussion (2000). Bos and Burnett published their critical edition of the Hebrew and Latin, with an English translation of the Hebrew and extensive commentary.

[2] Actually the situation is slightly more complicated. Bos and Burnett (p. 325) say that the Arabic title of the work itself is lost, but the second sentence of the introduction exactly corresponds to a *Letter* which Sezgin (p. 259) says was the topic of a lost work by al-Kindī. Bos and Burnett do not forcefully push for this *Letter* being that lost work, but it seems right to me and I suggest they are correct.

[3] Evidently a Latin rendering of something like al-Zu.....

[4] See Bos and Burnett, p. 325 n.2.

[5] The theory is not simply invented here, but also appears in his *Letter on the Proximate Efficient Cause of Generation and Corruption* (see for example Bos and Burnett, p. 331). See also Travaglia 1999 for his use of "degrees" in medicinal preparations, which is adapted here for levels of heating, cooling, drying, and moistening.

three planetary conditions which contribute to changes in temperature and precipitation: (1) a planet's place in its epicycle, (2) its declination, and (3) its relation to its apogee. (When a planet is under the rays of the Sun, the Sun tends to nullify its effects.) In fact, I am not convinced that al-Kindī's statements are always consistent with themselves, but generally speaking the closer the planet is to the earth, or the closer to the zenith of one's location (such as being in signs of northern declination, in the northern atmosphere),[6] the more intense its effects. In particular, al-Kindī draws on Ptolemy *Tet.* II.8 to say that when the planets are moving direct and therefore farther away from earth, they produce more cooling and moistening; but when retrograde and closer to the earth, they have heating and drying effects. Actually this is a bit more complicated with Mercury and Venus, because while al-Kindī makes this general statement often enough, in Ch. 5, **68-69** he says it is different for the inferiors: when the inferiors are direct (further from the earth, but closer to the Sun) they are heating and drying, but when retrograde (closer to the earth, further from the Sun), they are cooling and moistening. In Section I.2 above, we saw that Ptolemy also had some different and ambiguous rules for the inferiors, and I provided a diagram of al-Kindī's theory of the inferiors there.

Of course al-Kindī also feels obliged to draw on other sources, and in Chs. 6-8 we can see his versions of material also found in ʿUmar (see Section I.5), Māshāʾallāh (I.6-7), Jafar (I.10) and the *Sages of India* (I.11), and the *Opening of the Doors* (I.13), not to mention Hermann's later compilation (I.12) or material from John of Spain (I.15-16). These include the lunar mansions, the so-called "centers" or "posts" or "foundations" of the Moon, planetary hours, a Lot of rain, New and Full Moons, and the ingresses of the Sun into 20° Scorpio. (But remember that some of this material is only in the Latin version, not in the Hebrew.) References to weather omens, drawn from Ptolemy, are very few.

As a summary of the Chapter contents, most of al-Kindī's naturalistic theory is contained in Ch. 1, and applies generally to the study of temperature and humidity in Chs. 1-3. Chapter 4 puts the Moon into the general seasonal context, and introduces the theory of lunar "centers" and phases. Chapter 5 describes the "degree" theory of temperature, rehearses special qualities of the planets, and introduces al-Kindī's version of the "opening of

---

[6] For people in the southern hemisphere, it would be worth trying to treat the signs of southern declination as the heating signs, and the northern ones as the cooling withs.

the doors." Chapter 6 introduces special categories of the planets, mansions of the Moon, and extra lore on rain. Finally, Chs. 7-8 draw on ʿUmar, Māshāʾallāh, and are more astrological in content: for example, they include a Lot of rain.

One potential problem in a naturalistic approach like Ptolemy's, is that planetary motions are the same for everyone. That is to say, if Saturn is retrograde in Leo, he is retrograde there for everyone—and yet it does not rain everywhere or dry out everywhere at the same time. But sprinkled throughout the text are a number of methods and details that help to localize weather prediction, so that general planetary configurations may be made more particular to a specific region. Following are a few of the ways that al-Kindī allows the astrologer to localize the weather effects, and one should keep this in mind for other authors, as well:

- Ch. 4, **15**: In two places, al-Kindī says we must measure the distance between the Sun and the Moon's "centers" in ascensions, which are latitude-dependent.
- Ch. 4, **61-64**: Significators in the quarters of the circle (between the Ascendant and Midheaven, *etc.*) will mean different things, which is again dependent upon latitude and longitude.
- Ch. 5, **34-43**: One's distance from the Tropic of Cancer, and the time of day, affects what the significators mean.
- Ch. 5, **107-10**: The "centers" being measured by ascensions, as well as the peoples signified by the local Ascendant and IC, help to localize the effects.
- Ch. 5, **119-22**: Again, the local horizon matters, as does the geographical elevation of the place.
- Ch. 6, **137**: The local planetary hour at the times of lunar ingresses helps localize the indications, since the length of planetary hours are location-dependent.

Finally, let me say a few words about the sentence numbering in my translation. The sentence numbers in Bos and Burnett's Latin, as well as my translation of that, tend to follow the Hebrew, except in parts where only the Latin survives. Latin-only sentences begin with an **L**, usually with the chapter number as a prefix (such as **7:L10**). When multiple Latin-only sentences appear in a paragraph, I only add the prefix to the first one: for instance,

7:L10…**L11**…**L12**. Numbered sentences which appear in brackets are my own paraphrases of Hebrew-only sentences. Also, in all cases the chapter titles were designated as being the first sentence, but I omit it here: thus in all chapters the actual text begins with **2**.

Introduction

Comment by Dykes. This introduction is wholly contained in the Latin, although it replaces al-Kindī's own dedication to his "beloved" student with Azogont's advertisement for his own skill. Since Hebrew *Letter* I only covers Chs. 1-5, the Hebrew lacks sentences **16-18** below (which describe Chs. 6-8).

ဢ   ဢ   ဢ

1 In the name of Holy and Merciful God, and with His praise, the letter of al-Kindī on airs and rains begins, with the assembled, useful, and perfect wording translated by Master Azogont, from the Arabic.

2 I was asked to clarify those counsels of the philosophers in which they agreed on the superior impressions and the accidents of the air and what is cloudy, and the causes of moisture, dryness, hotness, coldness: **3** because the differences of those judging, and the distortion of their compilations, has removed them—due to which [differences and distortion] they have posited knowledge without its [proper] organization, **4** and they have withdrawn from the path [of knowledge] with words of credulity, without syllogism and proof, and they have imputed [this knowledge] to Hermes, and Ptolemy, [Dorotheus],[7] and other philosophers. **5** However, credulity is not a custom of philosophers in their positions, but rather clear proof and evident syllogistic are. **6** And[8] the sages knew that a man is not instructed in philosophy, nor does he know it, [unless] up to the point where he can enumerate the superior impressions with knowledge: **7** nor does he ascend to that knowledge unless it is after the quadruvial sciences, which are an introduction to philosophy (and they are the four mathematical ones); and after [that,] the one which they called the science of natures and their qualities); **8** [and] afterwards they knew the superior impressions, namely spiritual knowledge—

---

[7] Adding from the Hebrew. This could be a criticism of the Māshā'allāh lineage of astrologers, since the authorship of their material (particularly as it appears in *Judges*) is sometimes confused with Dorotheus. Nevertheless, many of their methods are identical to al-Kindī's. His complaint, however, is that they were not naturalistic and orderly in their explanations, but simply reported the techniques.

[8] The following few enumerated sentences are one long sentence in the Latin, and I have read it as such. I have eliminated the "if" which was the next word, because Azogont bit off somewhat more than he could chew. He begins the passage as an if-then statement, but by the time he finishes all of his parenthetical remarks, he has lost track of what he was doing. By removing the "if" we simply get a recitation of the types of knowledge one should acquire in order to attain wisdom.

which one who does not connect those things which I have named, does not acquire. **9** I congratulate one who is searching for the truth of things, and one wanting to contemplate the statements of the philosophers. **10** And I divide this letter into eight chapters:

11 The first chapter, on all of the accidents of the planets and their causes, and their impressions, in the upper atmosphere.

12 The second, on the diversity of motions in the quarters of the circle and the sections of the year.

13 The third, on the moist and dry quarters of the year, and how it is applied to those with respect to the area[9] of their retrogradation and direct motion.

14 The fourth, on dews and rains in every clime and city.

15 The fifth, on the way[10] of finding the hours of dews and rain, and the knowledge of the hour of its time in every place of the earth.

16 The sixth, on airs and rains according to the sayings of the sages.

17 The seventh, on the natures of the days.

18 The eighth, on the four seasons and the changing of the air from hotness to coldness, and conversely.

---

[9] *Parte.*
[10] *Qualitate.*

The first chapter of the book of al-Kindī: On clouds & rains & thunders & heat-lightning,[11] & winds, & their accidents

Comment by Dykes. Most of this chapter is contained in the Latin, except for **9-23** and a couple of others. In this chapter, al-Kindī reviews some ideas of Aristotle's (**2-28**), and then breaks down planetary motions into two categories: (1) how the Sun's motion through the zodiac (including by declination) produces effects of heating, chilling, moistening, and drying (**29-48**); (2) how the same things are shown by the planets besides the luminaries, in terms of both their epicycles and their deferents (**49-74**). But al-Kindī's comments about the planets seem to be really directed at the superiors only, and not the inferiors. For while he says that the planets will indicate heating and drying when closer to the *earth*, and mentions Venus in particular (Ch. 5, **89**), he later (Ch. 5, **68-69**) says that Venus and Mercury induce the opposite effects: they indicate heating and drying when they are in the portion of their epicycle that is closer to the *Sun*. Thus there is an important tension in the text as to how the inferiors operate.

ಬು   ಬು   ಲ

[Aristotelian reflections on the fifth element and the planets]

2 The philosophers agreed in this, that the nature of the heaven is one;[12] **3** nor did they say, "such a planet in its essence is hot or cold, moist or dry," nor [that] such a part of the circle of the signs in its own substance is hot or cold, moist or dry,[13] **4** nor does [any planet] undergo generation or corruption or diminution, neither according to itself [as a whole] nor according to any part, except through its own motion upon the epicycle, by direct motion, retrogradation, stationing, depression, elevation,[14] elongation [from the earth; and this is so for all] of the climes, in every season.

5-6 Rather, they saw their bodies be made greater and lesser because of their approach and elongation from us: for when something is elongated

---

[11] *Fulgetris.* Normal lightning flashes would be *fulguribus*, but Azogont might not have observed the difference.

[12] That is, it is composed of a single element, not many as are on the earth (Hebrew).

[13] This part about the signs is not in the Hebrew.

[14] Depression and elevation here mean being in the perigee or apogee of the deferent circle.

from view, it appears lesser; when it comes near, greater. [**7** Some also thought wrongly that the Moon is subject to generation and corruption, because of her waxing and waning; **8** but that is really because of how the Sun's light falls on her, depending on her position.]

[**9-12** Again, some thought the stars were fiery,[15] since fire is the highest of the four elements. But the stars are made of the fifth element. **13** The light of the stars themselves comes from the friction of the air through which they move, like when wood or certain metals glow from friction or striking. Since the region of air is very close to fire and the fifth element, it is able to be heated up by their movements.]

[**16-19** In *De Caelo* II.7,[16] Aristotle said that lead balls on the ends of arrows are melted when they are shot, although al-Kindī has not been able to prove it under testing; so maybe, he thinks the manuscripts are flawed. Nevertheless, arrows move from hotter air to colder air.]

[**20-23** So[17] the planets heat the air. But the fixed stars do not, because they are in the furthest orb, away from the realm of air and the heated air already produced by the Sun. The Sun himself heats, based on how close he is to the zenith in the sky.]

24 They[18] even say that a planet is not fiery, nor is its light fiery, **25** and that the greater and hotter planet is the Sun, because he is 166 (and a little more) times greater than the earth.[19] [**26** Jupiter is next, whose body is 81 ½ times greater than the earth. **27** Venus is also hotter than Saturn, because although his body is great, he is much farther away from the earth. **28** Now we will return to the topic at hand.]

---

[15] See Aristotle's *De Caelo* II.7 for this paragraph and the next.

[16] In *De Caelo* II.7, Aristotle reaffirms that the planets are composed of a fifth element: unlike the normal four elements, this one moves in a circular fashion rather than away from or towards the earth. He also tries to explain the stars' brightness as being caused by friction, using just the examples al-Kindī cites here (i.e., producing fire and heat from rubbing or striking wood, some stones, and metal). The part about arrows is a bit unfortunate, since it's hard to see how anyone could think that a flying arrow could melt lead on its tip through friction with the air. Aristotle's point seems to be that as an arrow flies through the air, it creates friction and heat in the air around it, though it itself is not fire; just so, the planets create light and heat through the friction they create, even though they themselves are not made of fire.

[17] Again, see *De Caelo* II.7 and *Meteorol.* I.3 for the essence of these ideas.

[18] For these statements about the volumes of the planetary bodies as compared with the earth, see Goldstein 1967. There, Ptolemy's values (in the Arabic version) are: Sun 166 1/3, Moon 1/40, Mercury 1/19,683, Venus 1/44, Mars 1 ½, Jupiter 82 ½ + ¼ + 1/20, and Saturn 79 ½.

[19] The Hebrew has 166 3/8.

[The Sun's motions and their physical effects]

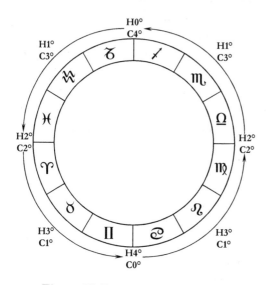

Figure 17: Increase and decrease of heat (H) and cold (C)

29 However, I say that the Sun has four seasons of equal greatness but of a diverse nature, because of his eccentric [circle]:[20] wherefore if he did not have an eccentric, each season would be of one [and the same] nature. 30 And so, I say that these planets are weakened and strengthened according to the elongation of the climes from the equinoctial line. [31 The intensity of heat and cold may be measured in four "degrees" or stages. At the extreme of northern declinations (i.e., Cancer), hot is at four degrees, and cold in its first degree. As the Sun moves towards the equinox and then to the extremes of southern declination (i.e., Capricorn), heat decreases and cold increases, to become cold to the fourth degree and hot to the first; likewise as he moves back up towards the northern signs. At the equinoctial points, heat and cold are evenly balanced at two degrees.][21]

32 And I say that if the circuit of the Sun was in the degrees of circles equidistant to the equator of the day, there would be a season of [only] one nature, hot or cold. 33 And the Sun, from the beginning of Libra to the be-

---

[20] What al-Kindī is really referring to is the *obliquity* of the ecliptic from the celestial equator, which makes him move through signs of northern declination (Aries through Virgo) and signs of southern declination (Libra through Pisces). If there were no obliquity, then the Sun would always mark the same arc across the sky, each sign would have a 0° declination, and the seasons would not change. So while it is true that his deferent circle (which defines where the ecliptic is) is eccentric with respect to the earth, it is not its *eccentricity* from the earth that makes seasons, but its obliquity from the equator.

[21] The Hebrew only spells this out in part, so I have expanded it. Al-Kindī is borrowing this language of degrees of heat and cold from his treatment of medicinal preparations, in which different chemical ingredients were taken to produce effects of hot and cold. See also Bos and Burnett (pp. 331-33) and Travaglia 1999 (pp. 77-84). See also Ch. 5, **13-36** below.

ginning of Capricorn, is elongated from the northern portion,[22] and that portion is made cold, and what is in it of moisture, flows, and it is coldness to the greatest extent while he comes to the beginning of Capricorn.

[**34** As[23] the Sun moves northwards in declination from Capricorn, there is an increase of heat, leading to melting and moisture in the air, **35** so the weather will be generally cold and moist. **36** At the beginning of Aries, there is more heating, **37** and so the weather is more hot and moist, up until he reaches Cancer. **38** Melting is at is maximum then, and the weather is generally hot and dry. **39** At Libra, the air is getting colder and the season is generally cold and dry.]

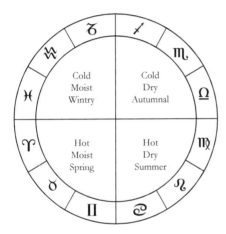

Figure 18: Elemental qualities by seasonal quarters

40 And so, there are four seasons, so that from the first of Aries, [it is] spring, and the air is hot, moist; from Cancer, summer, and the air is hot, dry; from Libra, autumn, and the air is cold, dry; from Capricorn, winter, and the air is cold, moist. **41** And the Sun and the wandering [stars] have a commonality in the four natures, due to the diversity of their own motions and the complexion of the air: which if the Sun's own proper action in this series[24] was without the planets, the air would always be the same [in a particular season]. **42** But it is not so: rather, the atmospheres of the year, month, [and] days vary, due to the diversity of the motions of the planets in themselves and in their distance from and nearness to the earth.

---

[22] That is, in declination.

[23] I am summarizing the Hebrew, because while the Latin covers many of the main ideas, it tries to cram sentences **34-39** into one, leading to some confusion.

[24] *Ordinibus*, which does not seem to correspond to any Hebrew word.

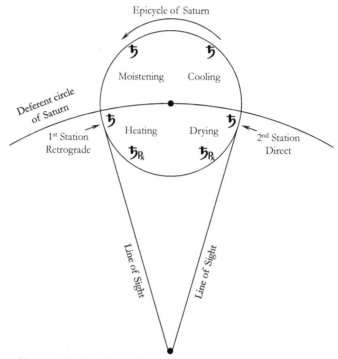

Figure 19: Weather effects in the epicycle of superiors

43 And I say that the hotness of the planets is stronger when they are ret-rograde, because they are closer to the air;[25] and their circuit around the earth[26] by one day and night is more than 360°, and is quicker, when they are direct. **44** Now, when a planet is retrograde in the second quarter of the circle,[27] and the Sun in the fourth quarter of the circle,[28] the complexion of that hour is cold, moist, [but] of weak virtue [due to the northern winds], **45** be-cause in that quarter the Sun loosens what he had congealed in the third quarter.[29] **46** Then, the nearness of the planets to the air[30] will heat up and

---

[25] That is, the region of air which surrounds the earth, just below the region of fire.

[26] Reading with the Hebrew for "upon the epicycle."

[27] That is, in the summer signs of Cancer through Virgo. See the figure with the Sun in Capricorn and Jupiter retrograde in Leo. Because it is wintertime (the Sun), the default weather is both cold and moistening; but because Jupiter is in a heating part of the zodiac, and his retrogradation brings him closer to the earth (adding more heat), al-Kindī would say that the season would become wetter and warmer than otherwise.

[28] In the winter quarter, from Capricorn through Pisces. Obviously this could only refer to Mars, Jupiter, and Saturn.

[29] As al-Kindī just stated earlier, in the winter quadrant there is a bit more heat, which leads to the melting of what was frozen during the autumn months. But al-Kindī takes all

loosen along with the loosening of the Sun, and moist vapor will be elevated, which the motion of the Moon will thicken, if she were in a good place from the Sun; and the southern wind from the side of the Sun will melt, **47** and the wind coming from the side of the planets which are loosening, along with the Sun, or from the side of the Moon which is thickening the clouds. **48** And when a wind will come from these quarters, the clouds will be made less and will be cut up; [but I will explain this below.]

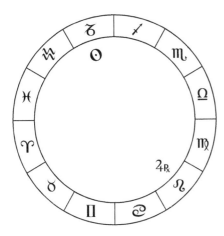

Figure 20: Melting weather in winter (Ch. 1.44-46)

[The motions of the planets in their epicycles and deferents, and their effects]

49 [So,] the cause of the four seasons is his eccentric circle. Nor is there missing a similarity to these seasons according to [the planets'] natures, since there is hotness according to the size of their bodies and the powers of their motions: **50** for they have eccentric [circles] and epicycles. [**51** For some tried to say that Jupiter is hot and moist when he is at the beginning of Cancer, but others said it was because of the planets' natures in the orb. **52** Others thought that the planets' effects are due to their periods, and not their orbs.] **53** [But] the planets have periods[31] of diverse natures, which I will affirm in the fifth chapter.[32]

54 And I say: when they will be [retrograde] from the beginning of Cancer to the beginning of Libra, they will be at the height of their hotness, and their complexion will be hot on account of [their] approach to the zenith of one's head in the north.[33] **55** And if they were then in the closer nearness of their

---

of this as being part of a process: he knows there will be more melting in the late winter close to spring, than there will be in the early winter.

[30] Remember, they are retrograde and in the summer signs, so they heat up the air by their closeness to it, and stir up the warm winds associated with those signs.

[31] *Tempora.*

[32] See Ch. 5 below, sentences **51**ff.

[33] For people near the equator, the Sun will be virtually at one's zenith around noon during this time of year (when he will be in signs of northern declination).

eccentric,[34] the hotness will be stronger. **56** For their hotness from there is in two ways: either with the hotness from the first station to the opposition, or from the opposition to the second station, with the conquering hotness which is at the limit of the stronger dryness.[35] **57** Because when a thing lasts, it is multiplied, and because of the duration of the hotness from station to station, it is multiplied in hotness, and because of that its operation is varied according to the proportion which there is between the two stations, in adding and diminution.

58 And if they were direct from that point, their hotness is weakened on account of the elongation from the earth, and they cool down according to their proportion to the hotness in that direction, and they proceed temperately by day and night through the advance of the epicycle in less than 360°. **59** At the second station [until] they are concealed under the rays of the Sun, their hotness is weaker, which is until it happens that the effect of hotness does not appear in them [at all]. [**60** At that point, cold will start to predominate. **61** Therefore many Greeks said that the planets are colder from the second station until concealment under the rays. Of course they are not colder in themselves, but their motions gradually produce no heat.] **62** When therefore a planet is concealed under the rays of the Sun, in no way does it have an effect in terms of hotness; but rather, it is weakened on account of its elongation from the earth, since the greatness of the Solar body, and the power of his heat, conquers [the planet's] light and heat. [**63** The planet's ability to heat, compared to the Sun's, is like comparing a point to a line. **64** Therefore, many Greeks said that this can produce rain, since cold is a factor in rain.]

65 Then, from the concealment to the first station, the planet begins to approach the earth, and it adds in hotness to the extent that many Greeks said "then there is a signification of moisture." **66** And they said this because they saw that when the Sun approaches the earth, it loosens what was frozen in the hour of its coldness at the greatest extent of its elongation from the zenith over one's head.[36] **67** And the planets stay upon that order [of effects], because they judged them as being chilled from the second station, up to hiddenness.

---

[34] That is, in their perigee, the part of the deferent that is closest to the earth.
[35] Al-Kindī is saying that by the time the planet goes from the lowest point of its epicycle to the second station, its heating effect will have produced a drying effect, as well.
[36] This is a reference to **54** above.

68 Then they ascribed hotness to it, after a planet is taken away from being burnt and it approaches the earth, [and it melts what had been frozen from the first station to the second concealment; **69** and one may conclude this through syllogistic reasoning.] **70** And this is a plausible thing[37] in which the philosophers agree in all of [the planets'] accidents, from the perspective of the epicycle. **71** But from the perspective of the eccentric, a need for those things does not emerge, because [strictly in terms of the deferent circle, a planet's][38] approach to and elongation from the earth, and from the north and from the south, is more powerful.

72 And if a planet were at the summit of its epicycle, and in addition at the summit of its eccentric, and it were in the fourth quarter of the circle,[39] this will be the limit of the weakness of its heat, so much so that the effect of its hotness would not appear on the earth, but rather that of [its] coldness, and the power of that would be increased. **73** But if it were in the second quarter of the circle,[40] and in addition it were at the lowest part of the epicycle and in the lowest part of the eccentric, then it will be the most extreme beginning of its hotness, until much dryness happens in the earth. [**74** So much for the planets in themselves.]

---

[37] *Speciosus.*
[38] Added for clarity.
[39] This must refer to the winter part of the zodiac (Capricorn through Pisces), reading "fourth" with the Hebrew for "first."
[40] The summer part of the zodiac (from Cancer through Virgo).

The second chapter: On the variation of the planets' accidents in the quarters of the circle

Comment by Dykes. Textually, only the first and last few sentences are missing in the Latin. In this chapter, al-Kindī explores different combinations of the planets (or rather, the superiors) being in signs of a certain season and declination, as compared to where the Sun is: for example, if the Sun were in summer signs, while the superiors were in wintry signs and in southern declinations.

ಬಿ   ಬಿ   ಆ

[2 In the previous chapter, we discussed planetary motions and changes in themselves. In this chapter, we will discuss how they relate to the seasonal quadrants of the zodiac,[41] thereby relating them to the Sun's own motion.]

[Summer, with the planets in summer signs]

3 And for knowing this, it is good to know [that] when they are retrograde from the beginning of Cancer to the beginning of Libra, and the Sun were with them in the same quarter, then it will be the height of heat in that portion (and it is the northern one),[42] and the southern one will be made cold, and northern winds will appear and complete the arrangement[43] of the fruits, and burn grasses up to the end, and a hot consuming wind will come to the northern portion. **4** If however they were harmonized so that they would be at the base of their eccentrics,[44] the hotness will be stronger. **5** And if [all] five were direct [and] eastern from there, the summer will be suitable, because then their heat will be weakened, and night will be cooled down.[45] **6** And their little wind[46] will be mitigated if the Sun were in the angle of the earth. **7** And if they were direct [and] western from there, that signification

---

[41] That is, the quadrants which define the seasons when the Sun is in them: Aries through Gemini are the spring quarter because in the northern hemisphere it is spring when the Sun is in them, and so on.

[42] These are signs of northern declination. Al-Kindī is associating the northern declination with northern winds and with spring and summer.

[43] *Digestionem.* The Hebrew reads, "ripening."

[44] In the perigees of their deferent circles, so that they are closer to the earth.

[45] Retrogradation brings the planets even closer to the earth, so being direct compensates somewhat for the fact that they are very close to the earth by being in their perigees.

[46] *Aurula.*

will be weaker [due to] their nearness to the earth; [but] since after the setting of the Sun they approach the zenith of the heat, and they will not come to the result of mild air.

[Autumn, with the planets in summer signs]

8 And if they were retrograde from the beginning of Cancer to the beginning of Libra, and the Sun was from Libra to Capricorn, then the Sun will have frozen up the northern half, [because] then his hotness will be weakened; **9** however,[47] these retrograde planets loosen what the Sun has frozen, by their motion and hotness; then that quarter will vary its complexion, inclining towards hotness, and [there will be] cold, northern winds. **10** If however they were direct, and in addition the Sun were from Libra to Capricorn, there will be frost to the greatest degree, for then the heat of the planets will be very weakened.

[Winter, with the planets in summer signs]

11 And if they were retrograde from there, and the Sun [was] from the start of Capricorn to Aries, [it will melt what was frozen in autumn, and the retrograde planets will heat and melt, and the temperature of the winter will be cold and very moist,][48] because then the Sun [and retrograde planets][49] dissolve the frost, unless the northern wind will be multiplied. **12** And when they will be direct, the signification of moisture in that season will be weakened, and especially if they were western of the Sun.

[Spring, with the planets in summer signs]

13 And if they were retrograde, and the Sun was from Aries to Cancer, that season will have a mild complexion, often with the wind of the north, because then the Sun loosens the frost with his dissolutions in [his] northern inclination, and the hot planets loosen it with him, and then moisture is made strong. **14** And if they were direct, the indication of moisture is weakened.

---

[47] Reading with the Hebrew, for "because."
[48] Filling in a lacuna based on the Hebrew.
[49] Adding with the Hebrew.

[Autumn, with the planets in autumnal signs]

15 But if they were retrograde from Libra to Capricorn, and the Sun will be with them, the northern wind will be multiplied with the power of the Sun's heat, along with the planets in that portion, and the air in that northern portion will soften the condensed frost. **16** And moisture will be multiplied there, on account of the elongation of the Sun from it, and southern winds will be impelled upon it, loosening what was congealed there. **17** And when they will be direct, and the Sun is with them, and they will be western, then there will be the height of frost from the direction of the north, and the winds from the south will calm down.

[Winter, with the planets in autumnal signs]

18 And when they will be retrograde from there, and the Sun [is] from Capricorn to Aries, it will be the height of moisture in that season, because the southern rains will be many, and in addition the Sun will loosen the frost in the north. **19** And when they will be direct from there, and the Sun is from Capricorn to Aries, and they will be western, that will signify a great diminution of the moisture in that season.

[Spring, with the planets in autumnal signs]

20 And if they will be retrograde from there, and the Sun is in the first quarter of the circle, that will be an indication of the moisture of the season. [**21** If they are direct from there, and the Sun is in the spring quadrant, it decreases the moisture.]

[Summer, with the planets in autumnal signs]

22 And if they will be retrograde there and the Sun is from Cancer to Libra, it is a sign of hotness in that hour, and of dryness, unless the southern winds will swell. [**23** If they are direct from there, the southern winds will be less, and there will be a diminution of heat.]

[Winter, with the planets in winter signs]

24 And if they were [retrograde] from Capricorn to Aries, and the Sun is with them, it is then a sign of moisture. **25** And when they will be direct [and eastern], it is a sign of dryness.

[Spring, with the planets in winter signs]

26 And if they were retrograde [there and the Sun is from Aries to Cancer], that will be a sign of the moisture of that season. [**27** If they were direct there, it indicates a decrease of moisture.]

[Summer, with the planets in winter signs]

[**28** If they are retrograde there, and the Sun is from Cancer to Libra, it indicates a southern wind, and the summer will become colder. **29a** If they are direct there, it indicates dryness.]

[Autumn, with the planets in winter signs]

[**29b** If they are retrograde there, and the Sun is from Libra to Capricorn, it indicates moisture. **30** If direct, it indicates dryness.]

[Spring, with the planets in spring signs]

[**31** If they are retrograde from Aries to Cancer, and the Sun is with them, it indicates much moisture. **32** If direct, it indicates dryness.]

[Summer, with the planets in spring signs]

33 And if they were retrograde, and the Sun from Cancer to Libra, it is a sign of the hotness of that hour, and its dryness. [**34** If direct, it is a sign of coldness, pleasantness, and balance.]

[Autumn, with the planets in spring signs]

[**35** If they are retrograde and the Sun from Libra to Capricorn, it indicates moisture unless the northern wind increases. **36** If direct, it indicates dryness.]

[Winter, with the planets in spring signs]

[**37** If they are retrograde and the Sun is from Capricorn to Aries, it indicates moisture. **38** If direct, it indicates dryness.]

[**38** The above statements are abbreviations, not a complete explanation of causes. But for those who have followed the instructions, this should be good enough.]

The third chapter: On the moist and dry quarters from the Sun, according to what can be acquired from the moist and dry things[50]

Comment by Dykes. This chapter consists of two parts: (1) Several sentences from *DMT* which are also in Hebrew *Letter* I (**1-14**); and (2) my summary of sentences **15-48**, which only appear in the Hebrew.

This chapter sets the stage for Chapter 4, by turning from general principles to indications for rain. Al-Kindī outlines typical indications for rain based on the retrogradations of the various planets along with the presence of the Sun in the signs. Of special interest for al-Kindī is the number of retrograde planets, which means different things depending on the season.

ଌ ଔ ଔ

2 In order that this may be discovered more easily, I will first put down the winter quarter[51] (then I will scrutinize the others, from quarter to quarter), **3** from the types of motion in the autumnal[52] quarter.

[The winter quarter: central example]

4 If the planets were all direct in [that quarter], I say that if the Sun were from the beginning of Capricorn to the beginning of Aries, and one of the planets [were] retrograde with him, the moisture will be little.[53] **5** If two, the moisture will be beautiful.[54] **6** If three, the moisture will be increasing. **7** If four, the moisture will be like a strong flood. [**8** And if five, there will be a flood.] **9** And [it will be] stronger in the spring quarter of the circle, or at the beginning of Cancer. **10** But if there were not one of the planets retrograde,

---

[50] Reading *rebus* for *horis* ("hours"), to match the sense of the Hebrew better.

[51] Al-Kindī means the winter portion of the zodiac: the signs marking the winter when the Sun is in them (Capricorn, Aquarius, Pisces), and so on with the other seasons.

[52] Following the Latin, but the Hebrew says "winter." Below, the Latin will likewise talk about the autumnal quarter, where the Hebrew says "winter." But since al-Kindī tends to judge planetary motions of a current seasons in comparison with those of the previous one, it is appropriate for him to mention autumn here and below, because the autumn will have an effect on winter.

[53] Since in al-Kindī's theory retrograde planets produce heat because they are closer to the earth than when direct, he means that they will cause melting and moisture in a normally cold and icy season like winter.

[54] *Formosa.* The Hebrew says "moderate." Perhaps Azogont or the Arabic al-Kindī thought that a moderate or smallish amount of rain was the most pleasant.

nor was there anything in their natures signifying moisture,[55] there will be dryness up until one of them goes retrograde. **11** And [what is] stronger in dryness is when this signification will be in the autumnal[56] quarter of the circle, with these significators appearing direct.

12-13 Wherefore,[57] if we found all the planets retrograde in that quarter[58] (or three or two or one), [and] afterwards they are made direct in the winter quarter, there will be [maximal] dryness. [And if the number of retrograde planets in winter is the same as the retrograde ones in the autumn, there will be moisture.] **14** And if [there were more in the winter, then there will be more moisture; but if less], the dryness will be strong according to the nature of the planets.

[**15-17** For winter, the retrogradation of Mars and Venus in winter is strongest, then that of Jupiter and Mercury, and then Saturn and the Moon's opposition to him.[59] By aspect, retrogradation from opposition is strongest, then trine, then the square.[60]]

[The spring quarter]

[**18-21** Compare the spring positions of the planets to their positions in winter (and this instruction is also applicable for other seasons). If they are direct in spring, especially if they were also direct in the winter, then they tend to show dryness; but the more that happen to be retrograde, the more they indicate rain.]

[**22-26** Again, dryness may be indicated by few planets retrograde in winter, or all of them direct in spring. Equal numbers of retrograde planets in

---

[55] Omitting *de parte temporum suorum*, as it does not appear in the Hebrew.

[56] Again, the Hebrew says "winter." But see my justification for keeping "autumn" in the footnote above.

[57] I have had to rewrite some of the sentences somewhat (following the Hebrew), as the Latin translator translated sentence **12** twice but differently, apparently mixing it up with elements of **13** and **14**.

[58] That is, the autumnal one—now the Hebrew agrees with the Latin.

[59] Note that these pairs of planets are precisely those involved in the opening of the doors (see Ch. 5 below).

[60] This probably refers to aspects of the planets to the Sun at the ingress. If so, then if, at the seasonal ingress, one of the superiors is retrograding in opposition to the Sun, that is strongest; then the trine and square. Since only Mars may be retrograde by around the square, he has more opportunities to indicate rain despite the fact that the square is less indicative. Venus and Mercury cannot aspect the Sun by any of these aspects. But al-Kindī might also be allowing planets to be retrograde in these aspects relative to the Moon at the ingress, too.

winter and spring continues the moisture; fewer in spring means less moisture, and more in spring means more. But one should not predict immediate
moisture or dryness based on the direct or retrograde motion of the moment—these things develop over time.]

[The summer quarter]

[**27-35** If all the planets were direct in both spring and summer, there will
be moisture but with pleasant weather. Retrograde in spring but direct in the
summer, there will still be moisture, but not enough to create pestilence (especially if the autumn had many direct planets). Being[61] retrograde in the
autumnal side of the zodiac as well as the winter one, will produce pleasant
weather, with a southern wind. Being direct on the winter side will also do
the same thing. If retrograde on the northern side, there will be pestilence
and plague, especially when retrograde in the summer quarter of the circle—
but if direct, it will be less and a hot northern wind will blow, and the southern wind less.]

[The autumn quarter]

[**36-43** Again, examine the planetary motions both in the summer and autumn. If all planets are retrograde, it indicates dryness; if only a few, there
will be some moisture but not much. If none are retrograde, it leads to cold,

---

[61] The next few sentences are confusing, and Bos and Burnett do not comment on them.
So far, al-Kindī has been monitoring retrograde and direct planets at the times of the
seasons themselves—that is, when the Sun is in the signs of spring, summer, and so on.
But he has not monitored *where* those direct and retrograde planets themselves have been:
he has only been counting their numbers from season to season. But now al-Kindī seems
to be doing something else: noting whether the planets are direct or retrograde *in the signs*
which are associated with the seasons—*not* if they are direct or retrograde when the Sun is
in them. The clue to this seems to be his use of the signs of southern and northern declination, and associating them with southern and northern winds. For the autumnal and
winter signs are precisely those of southern declination, and it is autumn and winter when
the Sun is in them; the same is true for the spring and summer signs being of northern
declination. So al-Kindī seems to be saying that when we are monitoring summer weather
(for example), we should see whether the direct and retrograde motions of the other planets are actually occurring on the autumnal/winter side of the zodiac (the southern signs)
or on the spring/summer side (the northern signs), because they will be productive of
southern and northern winds, respectively.

frost, and snow. If retrograde in the previous quadrant[62] but direct in the winter, there will be dryness (especially in a season that is already dry). But retrograde in the winter while direct in the previous one, indicates moisture. Planets[63] retrograde from Aries to Libra indicate dryness; but retrograde in signs of southern declination, moisture.]

[**44-48** Planetary motions in the middle and end of a season are more reliable and significant, because when they occur at the beginning of a season, it might indicate after-effects of the previous season. When planets are in signs of northern declination, maximum moisture and heat is indicated especially when they are retrograde, close to the zenith of a zone,[64] and in their perigees. The same is true for the southern declination. But if direct and maximally distant from a zone, and near their apogees, it signifies maximal frost and cold.]

---

[62] I am not sure if al-Kindī means "previous to the autumn," namely summer, or whether he has now switched to the autumn-winter pairing, so that the "previous" quarter is autumn.

[63] This sentence repeats the ambiguity from above. It probably means that planets which are retrograde in signs of northern declination are drier, while those retrograde in signs of southern declination are more moist—regardless of what the current solar season actually is.

[64] That is, close to the zenith at a particular latitude or clime or region, as the Sun is almost at the zenith of Mexico City at noon on the day of his Cancer ingress.

The fourth chapter: What can be acquired with respect to dews & rains, in the general variation of the nature of the season & winds, on the side of the north

Comment by Dykes. Textually, almost every sentence in the Hebrew *Letter I* is represented in the Latin. After the review of typical indications for rain in Chapter 3, al-Kindī now introduces the importance of the Moon (and especially charts of the New Moon) in the production of rain (**2-12**).

In **2-12**, al-Kindī introduces the importance of the Moon, particularly in the charts of New Moons, once it is known by other means that a period will produce rain (**7**). The text is not absolutely clear on all of the details, but al-Kindī's general view seems to be this: once we have decided that enough planets generally indicate rain during a certain month or season (Ch. 3 above), the Moon will indicate the time of the rain when she is both in certain ones of the "centers" or "posts" or "foundations," and also in a rainy mansion, and also in a close, degree-based "center" with respect to at least one of the other planets indicating rain (**8-11**). But we must also mention other conditions, such as the declination of the planets and their approach to the zenith, and the typical weather of the season itself, not to mention the time of day and the position of the planets in the quarters (**61-64**).

But there are three important ambiguities or unusual features of al-Kindī's approach, which cannot be resolved on the basis of the text itself. First, al-Kindī has two different versions of the "centers": the first, possibly composite version,[65] may be seen in this chapter (**13, 22-24**). The second, simpler version may be seen below, in Ch. 38 of his *Forty Chapters*. Which version should we use?

Second, al-Kindī is vague as to what ought to aspect what, in the case of the other planetary significators. That is, if the Moon is in one of the centers of the Sun, should the other (usually retrograde) planets be in a center from *her* (**11, 13**), or from the *Sun* (**22**)? For example, one of the centers is 12° from the Sun, while another is at 135°: when the Moon is 12° from the Sun, could this other planet be 135° from her, or should it be 135° from the Sun? I suspect that al-Kindī would prefer that all planets be in a center so as to aspect each other (for example, each one being nicely spaced at 90° or 120° from the others), but some of the centers do not allow this to be so. This problem

---

[65] For example, al-Kindī may be combining versions of the centers with versions of critical days (see Introduction).

returns in Chapter 5 (**83ff**), where other planets are supposed to aspect *each other* from the centers—but centers from which planet, we do not know.

Finally, al-Kindī makes the surprising claim that these centers must be measured according to ascensions, not zodiacal degrees (**15, 25**). There are two ways to take this statement. The first, more "astronomical" way would be to convert directly between degrees of right ascension and degrees of the zodiac: this is easy once the obliquity of the ecliptic is known. For example, if the Sun happens to be at 0° Aries (which has an RA of 0°) and the Moon were at the 60° center, we must convert 60° RA into zodiacal degrees: if the obliquity of the ecliptic were 23° 26', this center would actually be located at 27° 49' Taurus, just shy of Gemini.

One argument against this astronomical interpretation, is that al-Kindī says we must use the ascensions "of the climes," which is a typical way of referring to the second approach, ascensional times. If he does mean ascensional times, it would radically change the zodiacal positions of the centers. For example, if the Sun were at 0° Aries, we would have to add 60 ascensional times to that position in order to find the 60° center, and such ascensions vary by latitude. At the latitude of Minneapolis, Minnesota, USA (about 45° N), Aries has about 16.19 ascensional times, Taurus about 20.08, and Gemini about 28.01, for a total of 64.28. The 60° center in ascensional times would correspond to about 25° 24' Gemini, a difference of almost 30° as compared to the direct astronomical conversion![66] However, ascensional times were often used as a directive method in natal charts, and have the advantage of localizing the chart. The 60° center for Minneapolis would be in a rather different place than for Mogadishu, leading to very different types of lunar aspects (and therefore weather) for each region.

℞   ℞   ℞

2 True knowledge of their hours is very difficult, except for[67] where the planets cross over the zenith of one's head in the Midheaven. [**3** Astrologers have not used proper syllogisms or proof to discover it, so they have made many mistakes, and have only been correct by accident.] **4** And it is useful that I should set out ahead of time the ways of the Moon and her mansions,

---

[66] Of course we must also keep in mind that the centers are measured from the Sun, which is also moving: by the time the Moon moved into either of these positions, the Sun would have moved as well, and the actual degree would have to be adjusted a bit.

[67] Adding *nisi* to *ubi*, following the Hebrew and Bos and Burnett's suggestion.

in the regard of the Sun.[68] **5** For she signifies with respect to moisture, on account of the relation of her sphere to[69] the sphere of the earth. **6** It is even useful that I give priority to her approach to and elongation from the earth (and the zenith over one's head), in her own [mansions],[70] and [her] places in the regard of the planets[71] heating up the air, inasmuch as the generating of rains and the variation of the winds belongs to her in her conjunction with the wandering [stars][72] and the fixed ones.

7 I say that if a quarter signifies moisture due to the retrogradation of the planets and their periods, I would inspect the conjunction of the luminaries.[73] **8** For if it were a conjunction, where there is an application with a retrograde one, it is a sign of fair weather; **9** and likewise in [the luminaries'] opposition. **10** And in the wintry quarter, I would inspect the retrograde ones at the conjunction. **11** If the Moon were in the conjunction or in a center[74] from the Sun, and from retrograde planets, it will be the height of the matter. **12** And a stronger signification is that the five retrograde planets would be applied with the Sun.[75]

[The centers or posts or foundations of the Moon]

13 And this is a description of the centers of the Moon, from the Sun and from the planets. **14** For they are at 12°, 45°, 60°, 90°, and 120°.[76] **15** And if it happened that these degrees would be between them[77] and all the retrograde planets, with the ascensions of the climes,[78] there will be a great

---

[68] The Latin reads *respectu*, an aspecting word which suggests we should see if the Moon is in a rain-indicating mansion at the same time she is in one of the posts or centers or foundations.

[69] Reading more loosely and following the Hebrew, for the Latin "diversity of her proportion to the proportion."

[70] Adding with the Hebrew.

[71] That is, in their aspects.

[72] That is, the planets.

[73] Again, al-Kindī wants us to take everything in context.

[74] See below.

[75] Al-Kindī is probably only saying that if *any* of the retrograde planets applied to the Sun while the Moon is in one of the posts or foundations, that will be stronger than if the Moon applied to them.

[76] See below for more centers.

[77] That is, if some of the planets would be in these degrees of the centers or post or foundations *at the time of* the conjunction. Below, we will look for the planets to be in them when the Moon is passing through any of the others, as well.

[78] If al-Kindī really means these aspects to be reckoned ascensionally, it would help to confine the prediction to a particular geographical region.

amount of rain according to what the power of the quarter affirms, and the nature of the time of the signifying planets, and the Moon. **16** And if two were [in the centers], it decreases according to the limit of the quantity.[79] **17** And if it were one, it will decrease even [more]. **18** And if there will not be one in one of these centers, there will not be anything except a mild wind, moist air in the spring, cold in the winter.

19 Then, look to see when she will be [away] from the Sun after 12°. **20** If then some[80] of the planets will be in the centers, there will be great rain according to what the nature of the season affirms, with respect to its powers and weaknesses. **21** And if it were one of them, the moisture will be strong [but not as much]. [**22** And if none of them, there will be nothing.] **23** Then, [look] when she will be 45° from the Sun, and the aforesaid situations were in agreement; **24** and then, even when she will be 60° from the Sun, or 90° or 120° or 135° or 180° or 168° or 192° or 225° or 270° or 240° or 300° or 315° or 348°. **25** And these are all of the centers, with the ascensions of the climes. **26** And the stronger one of these significations is that the Moon would be in her closer distance [to the earth], increasing in her light.[81]

27 But the direction of the winds, [is] that when the Sun is in the southern declination,[82] he inclines the air toward the northern side, because the southern side becomes hot and the northern part is cooled

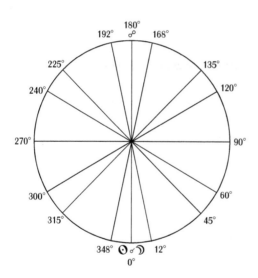

Figure 21: "Composite" diagram of al-Kindī's centers from the Sun (Ch. 5)

---

[79] That is, the fewer the planets, the more the amount will decrease from the maximum ("limit") quantity.
[80] Reading with the Hebrew, for "one."
[81] The Hebrew reads, "that the Moon, at its closest distance from the earth, is full, or at its furthest distance is diminishing in light." I do not really understand either the Latin or Hebrew versions.
[82] The Latin actually says "inclination," but I will follow the normal astronomical usage.

down. **28** And when a thing becomes hot, it flees towards a broader place.[83] **29** Then the air makes its way[84] to the condensed, [northern] side. **30** And if retrograde planets will be with the Sun in that quarter, the winds will be stronger on that side. **31** Still, the diversity of the winds on one day is from the touching[85] of the planets and the Moon, degree to degree, in their advancing from the east to the west, and from the conjunction of the Moon with the fixed [stars]. **32** And these winds are particular; however, the general ones [are] from the side of the Sun's motion.

33 And you should know that the "agreement" of the matter is if the Moon would be joined to one of the retrograde planets, and she is adding in her light, it is a sign of rain according to what the time of the planet affirms in terms of virtue and weakness, and how she may be in a center of the Sun and of a retrograde planet.[86] **34** When therefore she will be conjoined [to a retrograde planet] and will be subtracting [in light], it will decrease it. **35** And if then the retrograde planets will be in the first quarter of the circle, it will be a rainy signal, and more strongly so if the Moon were in the aforesaid centers from the Sun and the retrograde planets. **36** And if they will be retrograde in the second quarter of the circle [while it is] winter or spring or autumn, the signification will be stronger. **37** And if they will then be retrograde in the third quarter of the circle, it will be a more diminished signal, without very much,[87] because the southern wind will be multiplied from there.

38 But when they will be retrograde on the northern side, there will be rain with northern winds. **39** And if they were direct in the summer, and the Moon subtracting in her light,[88] and she will be connected with a direct planet, that will be a sign of hail and heat-lightning and [lightning]-rays and heat. **40** If they were direct on the northern side, or then retrograde on the southern side, that will be the height of hail and heat-lightning.

---

[83] This seems to be an *ad hoc* explanation, that heat will rise from the southern signs to the lower ones. But of course the signs are out in the heavens, not on earth.

[84] Reading *molit* for *mollit* ("softens").

[85] *Tactu.* The Hebrew reads, "retrogradation." Al-Kindī probably means, touching or "connecting" by aspect *with* a retrograde planet.

[86] Again, this means that the Moon is both in one of the posts or foundations (and in this case, also waxing), *and* in a degree-based aspect with a retrograde planet—thus both those situations come together at once or "agree."

[87] Bos and Burnett translate the Hebrew as saying that the *weakness* of the indication will not be very much.

[88] Omitting the Latin "and her body," in accordance with the Hebrew.

41 And if [the Sun] will be in the first quarter of the circle, and there will be a sign of moisture from the retrograde planets, we will look in that just as in the wintry quarter of the circle, and at the posited centers of the Moon. **42** I however say that if the Moon were adding in her light, [the signification is strongest].[89] **43** But if they were retrograde with the Sun in one [and the same] quarter, they will be stronger in the second quarter of the circle or at the beginning of Cancer, or even in the south, often because the moist southern wind is multiplied.

44 And if the Sun were in the second quarter of the circle, and there were a signification of moisture, inspect the centers which I have posited,[90] and [her aspects with][91] the retrograde planets; and when she is adding in her own light, [the indication for moisture] will be weakened because of this. **45** But when subtracting in her light, it will be strengthened. **46** Nevertheless, if the planets were with the Sun in one quarter, there will be very strong and burning heat. **47** And likewise if they were retrograde in the first quarter. **48** And if they were retrograde in the southern declination, the air will be mild. **49** And if the Moon will be applied from there to retrograde planets in the named centers, the air will be moved to a quality of clouds and hail and heat-lightning. **50** And if they will be direct from there, the signification will be weakened.

51 And if the Sun were in the third quarter of the circle, and the planets will be retrograde in that part, that is a sign of moisture, **52** and the hour of rain will be when the Moon is staying[92] in the stated centers from the Sun.

53 And it is an appropriate signification that the retrograde planets be closer, degree by degree, and one portion of them should be applied [to the other] from a trine, opposition, or square, or in the stated centers. **54** And if the retrograde planets were on the northern side, the signification will be stronger when the Moon will be conjoined to them, and the Moon[93] will be in the stated centers, and she will be adding in light. **55** Then, if the direct planets were on the southern side, and a planet will be retrograde on the

---

[89] Adding with the Hebrew.

[90] That is, look at them when the Moon is in them.

[91] The Latin suddenly acts as though the retrograde planets are increasing or decreasing in light, which does not really make sense; I have read it with the Hebrew, in which we (as usual) are talking about the Moon's light, waxing, and waning.

[92] *Manserit.*

[93] Again, the Latin reads as though the *Sun* is in the centers, and the *planets* are adding in light. But I have read it with the Hebrew, which makes more sense.

northern side, and the Moon[94] will be applied with it, and the Moon will be subtracting in light, it will be a sign of rain and snow then, because the direct planets then congeal the northern side. **56** And if the Moon were in a center from the retrograde planets [and the Sun, it indicates the melting of ice; but the retrograde planet is not enough to melt completely what the Moon had frozen],[95] while[96] the Moon is in the centers, then what was congealed will trickle down. **57** But if the Moon were adding in light, then it will dissolve it.

58 And you should know that when the planets are retrograde on the southern side, the southern winds come. **59** And when they are retrograde on the northern side, the northern winds come. **60** And it imparts it more strongly that[97] if the Sun were on the northern side, the northern winds come; likewise in the south.

61 You should even know that the days and nights are divided into four parts: from the first ascending of the Sun up to the middle of the day, is of the spring nature; and from midday to setting, of the summer nature; from setting to the middle of the night, of the autumnal nature; from the middle of the night to the ascending of the Sun, of the wintry nature. [**62** Significators are stronger in the first quadrant, a bit weaker in the next one, and so on through the last quarter. **63** One should avoid indications that are rather weak. **64** And if a signification is stronger, its opposite becomes weakened.][98]

65 And a planet in itself [transfers to the Moon when it is] with the Moon, and the [influence of the] Moon is distributed in the sphere of the world. **66** And the signification is concordant[99] until the Moon is being moved.

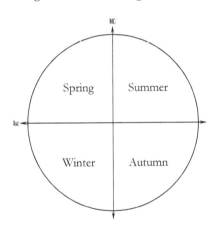

Figure 22: Seasonal analogies with the quadrants

---

[94] Reading with the Hebrew for "a planet."
[95] Adding with the Hebrew.
[96] Or, "until" (Lat. *donec*). I am not quite sure what role this word plays here.
[97] *Communicant potius*, reading as a singular. That is, no matter what, the Sun's influence will be more important.
[98] Adding based on the Hebrew. I am not sure what **64** means.
[99] The Hebrew reads, "stands still" or is inactive.

67 And while one of the light planets is being burned up in the autumnal quarter, and it was direct, it is a sign of coldness and frost. **68** And if it is being burned in the winter quarter, it signifies cloudy weather[100] and southern winds. **69** When however it is being burned up in the spring quarter, it signifies cloudy weather.[101] **70** But if in the summer one, it signifies hotness and heat-lightning and thunders. **71** And when heavy planets are burned up, the significations are of this kind except that they are weaker. **72** And the strongest of the Moon's centers is from the first [lunar] quarter (where she is at the beginning of 90°, and upon 180°, and upon 270°.

73 You should know that the Moon in the southern declination, when she is being applied with direct planets, is a signification of dryness; the air is moved to the extreme of coldness, if she were subtracting in light. **74** But if she were in the northern declination, and she [is] in the summer, and will be applied with retrograde planets, and she will be adding in light, a diversity of winds will be moved. **75** And if she were subtracting in light, it will be diminished.

76-77 These four chapters do not signify anything except after the knowledge of the fifth one. **78** For this reason, [namely that the last in order is the first in importance],[102] I have preferred that the Letter be according to this order. [**79** Let us begin, God willing.]

---

[100] Hebrew: "gales."
[101] Hebrew: "gales."
[102] Adding with the Hebrew.

The fifth chapter: On the manner of discovering dews & rains, & knowing the hours of their times in every place & land, & their causes

Comment by Dykes. Apart from a few sentences (particularly **31-41**), the Latin contains all of the relevant material found for this chapter in Hebrew *Letter* I. In this chapter, al-Kindī repeats that one's local latitude makes a difference, because the Sun's relation to one's zenith, combined with the degrees of heat and cold throughout the seasons, will affect the typical weather we can expect (**8-27, 37-43**). The time of day also matters, because when the Sun is in certain quadrants, he has other effects similar to those of the seasons (**28-33**), although al-Kindī describes these quadrants a bit differently than Ptolemy does (*Tet.* I.10). Al-Kindī relates the quadrants to seasons, while Ptolemy relates them to particular qualities:

	Al-Kindī *DMT* Ch. 5.28-33	**Ptolemy *Tet.* I.10**
ASC to MC/To East	Spring (hot and moist)	Drying
MC to Desc/To South	Summer (hot and dry)	Heating
Desc to IC/To West	Autumn (cold and dry)	Moistening
IC to ASC/To North	Winter (cold and moist)	Cooling

Figure 23: Quadrant effects for weather: al-Kindī versus Ptolemy

Then, al-Kindī reviews the typical weather indications for each planet based on its position in its epicycle and other conditions (**51-77**). He uses the zenith and the northern signs as a key situation in describing them, because when planets are near the local zenith, they will express their own natural effects most intensely and directly.

Fourth, al-Kindī introduces a new topic, the opening of the doors (**82-146**). I have already reviewed this a bit in my Introduction, but what is distinctive about the treatment here is that it is divided up by planetary pairs and blended with other considerations such as the centers, retrogradation, and the Moon.

Connected with the issue of the doors, is how the method indicates when the rain will actually come. This includes: when the planets or the Moon actually reach the exact position indicating rain, or when they reach the centers of the Sun or other planets using ascensions (see my Introduction to Ch. 4 above), or when the sign associated with a certain clime actually passes across the local horizon (**107**), or other indications, some of which I do not quite understand (**108-18**). Al-Kindī has a few other comments about the intensity of a signification, based on local topography and winds (**119-31**).

The last part of Chapter 5 is a review of weather omens and other data, largely derived from Ptolemy (**147-71**).

ℬ   ℬ   ℬ

2 I have already mentioned (before, in the fourth chapter) dews and rains according to the generality of every land. **3** Of course the path is more diffi- cult [when determining this] for a city, and in what place the [dews and rains] will be, in truth. **4** And Plato the philosopher has already written on this, [as has Empedocles];[103] **5** nor do they discover [it] nor advance by means of the progress whose description has preceded [this chapter], nor with its limita- tion;[104] and [my discussion] possesses part of what they have identified, except that I will state it by means of another path than the one which they did. **6** And I confess that it is nearer [to your level of comprehension] and easier for taking it just as I state it, because[105] in what preceded this we need what is simpler: what they have stated could not have been put into the form of only three Letters, **7** [while] *our* intent is [to write] an abbreviation and summary.

8 From there our knowledge has already preceded: that the cause of the four seasons is in the Sun, the motion of his eccentric; and that the natures of the seasons are not of the same power in every land, but rather they are added to and diminished according to the manner of the elongation of the place from the equinoctial [line] and its nearness to us.[106] **9** And seeing that it is so, I will posit an easy example for it, in the place where Cancer makes the zenith over one's head.[107] **10** Then, from this [we have] the knowledge of the power of the natures and their weakness in the northern part from the equa-

---

[103] Adding based on the Hebrew. The Hebrew attributes these views of Plato and Em- pedocles to a book called the "Activities," which Bos and Burnett (p. 349) say probably existed but surely was not by Plato or Empedocles.

[104] In the Hebrew, al-Kindī is speaking of his own treatment. What he means is that Chapter 5 contains only some material drawn from Plato and Empedocles, and overlaps previous chapters only in part.

[105] Reading the rest of the sentence somewhat loosely, following the sense of the Hebrew.

[106] That is, terrestrial latitude: weather indications will mean different things, the farther from the equator we are.

[107] Otherwise known as the Tropic of Cancer.

tor of the day. **11** (For what goes beyond that line from the southern part, does not pertain to us, because no one of our time has expressed to us [anything] about living there,[108] nor even in the books of the ancients before us.)

12 And so, I say that when the Sun makes the zenith over one's head, in terms of his latitude it is the greatest northern inclination, and as though the beginning of the height of heat among us [until the Sun reaches 15° Leo]:[109] because then [the heat] is very much multiplied. **13** Therefore let me posit in this example that it is then the fourth degree, of the portion which is the height of heat among them, and with the multiplication of heat and its greatest extent, dryness is multiplied, because it is made firm in power and it is a quality made from the multiplication of heat. **14** And let me posit that it is the end of the fourth degree in dryness.

15 Then, let me posit, from that greatest [amount] and [from] what is simple,[110] one degree [of quality intensity] for every 45° of the zodiac. **16** And I say that when the Sun is at the beginning of Libra, one degree of the four degrees is diminished, and it is the beginning[111] of the third degree of hotness, and likewise that of dryness. **17** And when one degree is taken away, one degree of the nature of its contrary succeeds it in its place, because when one of the contraries is taken away, what is left is increased [by the addition of the opposite]. **18** And then it will be the end of the first degree of cold and the end of the first degree of moisture.

19 And when the Sun will be in the fifteenth degree of Scorpio, it will be the beginning of the second degree of hotness, and the limit of the second degree of coldness. **20** And in this section their complexions are balanced, and these natures are equal in power and quantity among [those people]. Likewise, the [types of] air are varied among them.[112] [**21** When the Sun is at the beginning of Capricorn, it is the end of the first degree of heat and dryness, and the end of the third degree in cold and moisture.][113] **22** Now, when the Sun is in the fifteenth degree of Aquarius, it is the height of coldness and moisture among them, and the end[114] of hotness and dryness among them. [**23** When at the beginning of Aries, it is the end of the third degree of cold

---

108 That is, whether people are living south of the equator.

109 Adding with the Hebrew.

110 *Et simplici.* I am not sure of the function of this term here; it does not appear in the Hebrew.

111 The Hebrew reads "end," but I suppose it depends on which way one is looking at it.

112 This last statement about the air is not in the Hebrew.

113 Adding from the Hebrew.

114 The Hebrew reads, "the beginning of the first degree of heat and dryness."

and moisture, and the end of the first degree of heat and dryness. **24** At the fifteenth degree of Taurus, it is the end of the second degree of heat and moisture, and the end of the second degree of cold and dryness, so that their temperament is equalized. **25** At the beginning of Cancer, it is the end of the second degree of heat and dryness, and the end of the first degree of cold and moisture.] **26** And when the Sun is in the fifteenth degree of Leo it is the limit of coldness and moisture among them, and the height of hotness and dryness. **27** And these are the four qualities which are weakened and strengthened according to addition and diminution.

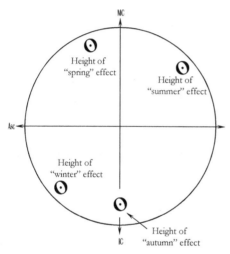

Figure 24: Position of Sun at daily "seasonal" effects

28 And from the rising of the Sun up to midday, is of the nature of spring; from midday up to setting, that of summer; from setting to the middle of the night, autumn; from the middle of the night to the ascending of the Sun, that of winter. [**29** The nature of autumn will be at its maximum when the degree rising from sunset will mark 90°,[115] namely at midnight.] **30** [But the nature of winter will be maximum when the degree rising from the arc will be a height of 225,° as the arc from sunrise to sunset will be] 180°, which is between rising and setting. [**31** The nature of spring is maximal between the height of 45°-90°. **32** The nature of summer is maximal at 135° of the arc. **33** In winter and at the fourth degree of cold and moisture, if the degree rising with sunset has an arc of height from 135°-280°, it will be the fifth[116] degree in cold and moisture.]

[**34-36** The season analogous to the time of day must be combined with the season in which the Sun is. So, although it will be the beginning of the fourth degree of coldness and moisture at midnight, if the Sun were also at the beginning of Aries (i.e., spring), it would not really indicate as much cold;

---

[115] That would be 90° in ascensions, namely where the IC is.
[116] This is perhaps a misprint in the Arabic, for "fourth."

likewise if it is daytime (which is hot) but the Sun is in a winter sign, or if it is night but the Sun is in a summer sign, or it is day but the Sun is in a spring sign.]

[37-41 People who live off the Tropic of Cancer will not have the same measure of heat as those who do. Determine the altitude of the Sun at noon for the location you want,[117] and subtract a proportion of the heat from the maximum expected at that time for the Tropic of Cancer; to the extent that you subtract heat, you must add cold (and likewise with dryness and moisture).][118]

42 Nevertheless, if you wanted to know the quantity of the nature of the time for the quarter you wanted, in what[ever] city you wanted, with respect to its nature, then for those for whom Cancer makes the zenith over one's head, take the measure of the elevation of that degree in that city, and the ascensions of the one in which Cancer makes the zenith over one's head, and you would know their proportional difference.[119] **43** Then, what[ever] it was, take that quantity of degrees which affirms the nature of the season for those for whom Cancer makes the zenith over one's head. What that will be, will be the quantity of the degrees of the nature of the season for you.[120] **44** Oh, how much we need this! You should know it and work by means of it.

45 However, we have already stated in the first Chapter that the essence of the heavens is one, and it is the fifth nature,[121] nor (they said) is there hotness, coldness, moisture, dryness, lightness, heaviness, nor change, in it, nor generation nor corruption. **46** Nor does the intellect comprehend its qualities except that the effect of the planets is varied in terms of the variation of the powers of their motion, and by means of their nearness and farness [from

---

[117] The altitude of a planet or star is the size of the angle it makes with the local horizon. So, if a planet were exactly at the zenith over one's head, its altitude would be 90°; if it were only halfway as high in the sky at one's location, its altitude would be 45°.

[118] The purpose of these paragraphs is to give more accurate "average" expectations for the kinds of heat, cold, dryness, and moisture, to expect in various places. Here, what al-Kindī broadly means is that locations on the Tropic of Cancer will represent the greatest quality of heat, when the Sun is at his noon position and in 0° Cancer: a summer sign, at the beginning of the summer quadrant in the heavens. So for other locations, see proportionally how much lower in the sky the Sun is at that time, and this will tell us how much less the expected amount of heat should be for that location. After all, we should not expect tropical heat in Iceland, in the same way we expect it in much lower latitudes. The same could go for other measurements of the Sun's position in various signs.

[119] *Proportionem.*

[120] That is, in the place you are investigating.

[121] That is, the fifth element or quintessence. See Ch. 1, sentences **2-4**.

the earth], and the co-helping place for receiving their effects.[122] [47-48 We have already described how the planets differ amongst themselves, but we will repeat some of it here.] 49 We have already said before that they heat up the air when they are retrograde, and chill it when direct, 50 and this is [according to] the generality of their significations. At the height of scrutiny,[123] the proper qualities of their natures are necessary for us.

[Specific indications for each planet]

51 I say that the proper quality of Saturn, [understood both] from the zenith over one's head, and if he were in his second station [going towards] concealment, is the height of coldness and dryness, according to the greatness of his body and his elongation and motion upon the epicycle. 52 And I posit for him a space for this as being from 15° of Taurus to 15° Leo.[124] 53 And if [in addition to being in][125] this portion, and were from his concealment to the first station, it signifies coldness and moisture according to what I said. 54 And if he were retrograde towards the opposition, it will be cold and moist, [but less so. 55 And from the opposition to the second station, it will be cold and moist,] except that his vapor[126] is weak, not having power, because of his approach to earth [and therefore] because he heats the airs, 56 with the height of his coldness [being] in this part: from midday to the rising

---

[122] Based on the Hebrew, what al-Kindī means is that the geographical place that receives their effects also contributes something to the season—just as he has argued that one's distance from the Tropic of Cancer will modify the expected effects.
[123] That is, to be really exact.
[124] In this section, al-Kindī is noting what a planet will mean if it is at the zenith of one's location, where its effects will be more intense and direct. In the northern hemisphere, this zenith relates to the region from 15° Taurus to 15° Leo, which also happen to be the most heating portion of the northern signs. So, by being close to the zenith, Saturn will automatically have more intense cooling and drying, because he is such a planet. But while in these signs, being in the moistening part of his epicycle will make him more moistening (53); in the heating portion, its cooling and moistening will be weakened (54), but presumably because he is on the zenith, his normal cooling qualities will still be evident; in the drying portion, there will have been enough heating that the cooling will be decreased noticeably (55), although I do not understand why al-Kindī is still speaking of moistening at all. Then al-Kindī seems to omit the fourth portion of the epicycle, which should lead to increased cooling and drying as he moves further from the earth. Of course, to actually be at the zenith he would have to be near the local Midheaven (56). But if he were going through these cycles while in the southern signs of the zodiac, which are further from the zenith (15° Scorpio to 15° Aquarius), he would still be a cooling and drying planet, but less intensely so (57).
[125] Reading with the Hebrew for "if he went beyond."
[126] *Nebula.* That is, his moisture in particular.

of the Sun when he is then in the Midheaven. **57** And if he were facing this portion,[127] in the fifteenth degree of Scorpio to the fifteenth degree of Aquarius, the decrease of coldness of multiplied,[128] as compared with what it was in the first portion.

58 Jupiter, however, is hot [and] moist, from the fifteenth degree of Taurus to the fifteenth degree of Leo. **59** And if he were in the first station to his opposition, he will be hot, [but] weakly moist. **60** And if he were in his concealment to the first station, [he is] hot, moist, of a good complexion, of balanced quantity in powers and all qualities. **61** And when he will be retrograde, he will add hotness to the active qualities. **62** (And you should know that Saturn is cold, dry; Jupiter hot, moist; Mars hot, dry; Venus cold, moist; Mercury a little bit dry.)

63 You should know that the effects of the hot planets [is stronger in the northern][129] declination and at the zenith over one's head, [while] their effect is weaker in the southern declination and facing[130] the zenith over one's head; likewise the cold planets, but their effects are stronger in the southern part (and that is an appropriate statement).[131] **64** You should even know that all of the heavy planets moisten from their concealment to the opposition, [and dry from opposition to concealment],[132] except that from the second station to combustion their complexion is [partly] cold, and from combustion to the first station their complexion is [partly] hot. **65** And the stronger hotness is at retrogradation, and the stronger dryness when they are in the northern inclination and near the zenith over one's head, and weaker in the opposition of that, and likewise the stronger moisture, **66** except that the coldness and moisture are more apparent in the southern inclination, and in the situation[133] of winter, because of their similarity to the nature of the season. **67** And you should know that the stronger heat of the planets[134] is when they are retrograde, and the stronger coldness when they are direct.

---

[127] That is, "opposite" it.
[128] That is, it will be warmer.
[129] Adding with the Hebrew.
[130] That is, "opposite."
[131] This may be an addition by Azogont or someone else.
[132] Adding with the Hebrew.
[133] *Facto.*
[134] That is, the *superior* planets.

68 But Venus and Mercury, at the hour of their arising,[135] if they are retrograde, until they go direct, are inclined towards moisture, **69** and from
direct motion and [until] burning with the Sun [they are] hot, and from the
conjunction and[136] their westernness [they are] dry, and from their retrogradation to the conjunction, cold.

70 Oh, how much we need the Moon! [And we must observe her][137] according to the truth of her natures with respect to the positions from the Sun
and the planets and the season; **71** and in the first quarter from the Sun, she
is hot, moist; if therefore she were ascending in the circle of her apogee, [she
is strong in heat and weak in moisture; but if she were descending in the circle of her apogee],[138] her nature will be very moist, and this is stronger in the
first quarter of the circle than the second quarter. **73** But in the second quarter of the month, her nature is hot, dry; and if she will be ascending in the
circle of her apogee and she is in this quarter, [she will be] dry according to
this nature; and if she will be descending, her nature will be a balanced hot.
74 But in the third quarter of the month her nature is cold, dry; and if she
were ascending [in the circle of her apogee], the coldness will be decreased; if
descending, its [cold] nature will be decreased [even more]. **75** But in the
fourth quarter, her nature is cold, moist; and in her ascension [in the circle of
the apogee], coldness will conquer; in the descent, moisture will conquer.

76 You should know that [a planet's] nature is stronger in the northern
half, and its influence[139] more apparent, if it were like the nature of the season. **77** And if one were in some city whose latitude is what is between 9° up
to 60°, they are cities in which there are rains; but in the others they only
have but hotness, dryness, or ice, due to the multiplication of hotness and
coldness [in those extreme latitudes].

78 If however you want to prophesy about rain according to its strength
and weakness, and it being little or much, first consider the nature of the
season and its power and weakness according to what I say about the degrees
of the nature of the season and cities. **79** If the nature of your season were at
the extreme of coldness and moisture, then a lesser signification of the plan-

---

[135] That is, out of the rays of the Sun. See the diagram in the introduction to Ptolemy
above.
[136] The Hebrew reads, "to" or "until."
[137] Reading more with the Hebrew for the Latin "sometimes" (*quandoque*).
[138] Adding based on the Hebrew.
[139] *Factum.*

ets will prophesy with a stronger signification of rains.[140] [**80** If the season normally indicates a lack of moisture, then many strong indications for rain will produce only a moderate amount.] **81** If however the nature of your season were at a balance of coldness and moisture, then a middling [amount of] significations will more signify [the rains'] powers, according to the signification of water.

[Predicting heavy or light rains by opening the doors I: Venus and Mars]

82 And if you knew this,[141] look to the nature of Venus and Mars. **83** If they were cold-moist or hot-moist, and between them there is an application from the opposition or one of the centers, and their latitude was one [and the same], and they (or one of them) will be connected with the Sun, consider the application of the Moon with the Sun, and the agreement of the previously-named centers in the preceding chapters.[142] **84** If the nature of the Moon were like their nature, it is a signal of water, but its power and weakness [depends on] if this figure agreed with these two and they [will or] will not be retrograde, and that season will be summery or spring-like. **85** For [if it were so], the [rain and] water will be very strong, and with this [there will be] thunder, lightning, wind, [and] much hail. **86** And there will be a multitude and scarcity [of rain] according to the nearness of the vapors of the earth; and the coldness of the wind, and hotness [will be] according to how the latitude of the Moon, and her mansion, and [her] portion from the Sun,[143] and the nature of the season, agreed [with that]. **87** And if this figure were in the winter or autumn, and they were not retrograde, the water will be weak, [merely] dripping during the season,[144] [and] a multitude of dryness.

88 And if they were retrograde, in the northern declination and in the time of spring and summer, in spring it will be at the height of what I am saying, **89a** less so in the summer due to the strength of their hotness in the

---

[140] That is to say, if the season already has a tendency to a certain kind of weather, only a few planetary indications will be enough to trigger that weather.

[141] That is, what the default expectations for weather were at the city in question (see above).

[142] Al-Kindī seems to mean we should prefer that all of these planets be connected from the centers—but again, it matters what centers these are, since some of them are at positions which do not match the centers from other planets.

[143] That is, what phase she is in.

[144] *Durante tempore*, which reads oddly here but was probably meant as an ablative absolute.

air, because of their approach to the earth; or [because] they will be at the foundation of their eccentrics.[145]

89b And if they were retrograde in the winter in the northern declination, it will be less than what I am saying.

[**90-91** When they are retrograde in the southern declination in the spring, it will be at its maximum; during summer, it will be slightly less.]

92 If in the southern declination, more so and hotter, [especially] if they will be retrograde and they will be at the foundation of the eccentrics. And if the application of the Moon with the Sun were then from the opposite, and likewise that of the two planets, in the spring [or summer],[146] it will be the limit[147] of the matter. **93** And in the winter and autumn, it will be decreased a little. And if it was at a conjunction of the planets [with the Moon], and the two planets connected one to the other from one of the centers, and the nature of the Moon were like them, and it will be in the winter and autumn, that is the height of rains. **94** If it were in the spring and summer, that is [the summit] of lightning[148] and many thunders, with water. **95** And if the two planets were conjoined with the Sun in a center, and[149] the Moon agreed with them in nature, that will be the height of rain, just as I am saying. **96** But the centers and the hours[150] [will be strengthened] when they are configured [and] the season and the Moon are helping through their nature, [and] if a planet other than Venus and Mars were in a likeness of their nature; **97** [and if there were six planets involved,][151] the matter itself will be increased so that it will be like a flood.

98 And if all seven planets were being configured in [a similar] nature, one to the other, and part of them were in the aforesaid centers, and it came to-

---

[145] In what follows there is a discrepancy between the Hebrew and Latin sentences. I have labeled the second half of this sentence **89b** and set it apart because it does not correspond to the Hebrew; then, I have summarized two sentences in the Hebrew (**90-91**) which do not appear in the Latin.

[146] Adding with the Hebrew.

[147] That is, an extreme.

[148] Reading Bos and Burnett's suggested *fulgetrorum*, for *frigiditatis* ("coldness").

[149] Reading with the Hebrew for "or."

[150] From here through "through their nature," I have loosely translated the Latin with the help of the Hebrew, as the Latin does not quite make grammatical sense to me.

[151] Adding with the Hebrew, since the next sentence goes further by mentioning all seven planets.

gether[152] that they are retrograde in the winter and summer, in the southern inclination, it will be, concerning dews and rains, such that they will kill people and cities and climes—except for a few. **99** And if they were retrograde in the southern inclination in the summer and in the spring, it will be similar except that the matter will not be shared in all places, **100** and in addition there will be thunders and lightnings and strong hail. **101** And if they were retrograde in the summer quarter of the circle,[153] and [in] the summer season, it will not be a signification for water; there will be the greatest dryness in the northern climes, and strong hotness, so that it will kill people, especially those who will be near the equator of the day.[154] **102** And if there were a rainy signification by two planets, or three or four, in the summer the air will have the greatest mildness, and little hotness,[155] nor will there be much water, unless there is a signification of five planets.

103 Now, in what places these are, or in what climes—O! how much error there is for those judging it, on account of the demanding difficulty of progressing [in this]! [**104** For one thing, Aristotle says[156] that the planets do not indicate absolute particulars; **105** for another, one must have detailed knowledge of many local regions and their weather tendencies. **106** But we will deal with all of this in a summary way.]

107 Identifying the hour of rain: it is when the planets will be at the most extreme point of signifying rain, and likewise the Moon, and in a place of signification and an application, degree to degree, from the centers of the Sun and the planets, with the ascensions of the climes, and the Ascendant of some people will be on the horizon—that is the sign of the hour of rain for those over whom it ascends.[157] **108** And if a wind blew in a direct line[158]

---

[152] *Concordaverit.* Or, "it so happened that…". The Latin is pointing out that multiple features and factors are coinciding.

[153] Reading more naturally for "in the quarter of the summer of the circle."

[154] Or rather, "the equator."

[155] The Hebrew reads that there will be a "tendency" for rain and moisture, expressing a similar idea.

[156] Aristotle does not say precisely this, but as Bos and Burnett point out (p. 359), the reference in the Hebrew to Aristotle's *On Generation and Corruption* may come from a later commentator on *Gen. et Corr.* II.10. In that chapter, Aristotle says that planetary motion along the ecliptic causes generation and corruption in the world, but points out that the details of how change works for every individual object depends on a lot of local details surrounding how each object is constituted (II.10 336b16-25).

[157] *Et erit ascendens supra orizontem aliquorum, illud est signum horae pluviae in illos supra quod* (sc. *quos*) *ascendit.* This seems to mean that it will rain when the sign associated with a certain region or clime or city, is actually coming across the horizon in that region.

[158] *Supra directum.*

from the direction in which it ascends, and wind did not happen to them, it is in the height of signification for one for whom the Moon is resting in that hour in his angle of the earth,[159] since it is with the peoples over whom it was ascending in a line equidistant to the equator of the day.[160] **109** And perhaps it was in the Ascendant [which was] ascending[161] over the horizon of other people: and this is if there was an intersection [of their horizon circles][162] upon the point which was ascending with the Moon in the circle of signs.[163] **110** And it was likewise a summit [of the indications, for those people] where the Moon was on their Midheaven; and if the Sun were then ascending, the matter is multiplied.

111 And if one of the signifying planets were in the angle of the earth (the angle of the earth of [that place], I say), or eastern to it or western, or in the Midheaven of it, the matter lasts until the significator-planets (with their being joined) are cadent from its four angles: [for when they are cadent], it is weakened. **112** Except that moistures will have lasted according to what lasts with respect to the degrees creating their application: [that is], the Moon and the Sun and the significator-planets being applied, one part of them to another;[164] **113** and the matter will be according to the planets' return to their angles of the earth,[165] then when the Sun and Moon and planets were cadent from the degrees of the application, part of them from the other. **114** Then, [since] the planets and the Sun and the Moon will be staying in their four angles, there will not be anything unless they [again] made an application; and that is just like the rainy nature.[166]

115 And the planets and the Sun and the Moon will be in a more worthy signification [if they are] in one of the four angles, degree to degree, **116** and

---

[159] The Hebrew reads as though the winds will blow for those who are "at" the pivot of the earth (which may mean that the sign on the IC is rising in their location).
[160] Hebrew: "as they are like those above whom it rises in a line parallel to the equator."
[161] Hebrew: "Perhaps it was rising...".
[162] Adding based on the Hebrew.
[163] In other words, for people whose Ascendant was on or near the same zodiacal degree which arises with the Moon.
[164] This may be a reference to different "orbs" of the planet's degree-based aspects, as Bos and Burnett suggest (p. 196). But in *Forty Chapters* §84, al-Kindī gives each planet a 6° orb (though he is unclear about this being 6° on either side of the planet, or 6° degrees total, leaving 3° on each side).
[165] The Hebrew has them simply returning to the four pivots themselves. But I confess this method is not wholly clear to me. Perhaps al-Kindī is referring to *how long* the rain will last.
[166] Hebrew: "the same holds good for the nature of rain." Since the whole method refers to rain, perhaps al-Kindī means to include winds as well.

what is like them.[167] **117** Test, therefore, what is from the application (degree by degree), and the amount [of distance][168] of the planets to their angles: nor will the matter be according to what it was at first in terms of their powers, but it will be much diminished unless the signification will be strengthened by another one, and even in itself. **118** And if the Sun were in the Midheaven of [that place] at the beginning of the significations, the matter will be weakened and diminished.

119 And if the places were elevated, the signification will be stronger; when sunk down, [weaker].[169] The matter with respect to moisture will be lasting until the natures are fulfilled[170] and the planets and the Moon are severed from the aforesaid centers. **120** And if the planets and the Moon were cadent from the angles of the horizons[171] of some people at the hour of the application[172] (degree by degree), the signification will be weakened among them and then there will be clouds. **121** And if the Sun were on the horizon of the east [in some location], and the Moon [in its Midheaven],[173] and the signifying planets on the horizon of its west, and [the Moon][174] in the angle of its earth, it is a sign of rains and their hours. **122** And if the Sun were on the horizon of its west, and the Moon on the horizon of the east, and one of the planets in the angle of its earth or its Midheaven at the hour of the application,[175] it is a sign of rain.

123 And you should know that weak significations do not signify for the shores of the sea, except for dews and clouds, on account of [their] great depressions;[176] but [weak ones] do signify for elevated places. **124** And if the Sun and the Moon and the planets were in the aforesaid rainy centers (one part [applying to the other] part) at the hour of the application,[177] degree by

---

[167] *Et simili illis.* The Hebrew reads, "In this way you shall draw analogies." Al-Kindī seems to mean that when we take all factors into account, we must note how one feature may enhance or mitigate another.

[168] Reading for *numerus*, in conjunction with the Hebrew ("…when the planets return to their pivots").

[169] Adding with the Hebrew. This seems to refer to the topography of the geographical regions (see **123** below).

[170] Hebrew: "changed."

[171] The Hebrew reads, "pivots."

[172] That is, of the *conjunction* of the luminaries.

[173] Adding with the Hebrew.

[174] Adding with the Hebrew, but notice that the Moon cannot be both on the Midheaven and the lower Midheaven.

[175] Again, the conjunction.

[176] That is, because sea level is a lower elevation than places farther from the coast.

[177] The conjunction.

degree, there will be rain. **125** And if one of the planets and[178] the Moon were making a signification for some peoples in one of the angles, if then the Sun were upon their zenith, the signification will be weakened.

126 And if there were a rainy signification in one of the places, nor will there be one for [people] in another place, [and] then a northern wind comes upon a people towards the south, they will know that it will be a signification in [their southern] part; **[127** But if it blows from the south towards the north, it will be in the][179] northern [part] from them. **128** If however it came from the west towards the east, they will know that [it will be] in the direction of the east.[180] **129** When from the east towards the west, they will know that [it is] in the direction opposite their east.[181] **130** For the air is dispersed towards the cold, moist, contracted direction, from the direction of hotness. **131** On account of those things, Aristotle said,[182] "When the method [for rains] goes astray, prophesy with winds according to the power of the method [for rains]."

[Predicting heavy or light rains by opening the doors II: Mercury and Jupiter]

132 And concerning dews and rains, prophesy with Jupiter and Mercury. **133** For if they were hot-moist,[183] [and] there will be an application between them from the centers, and from the Sun and the Moon, and the applications agreed, one with the other,[184] at the hour of the time of one, from the square and seventh[185] and trine and sextile and conjunction, that is the hour of rain. **134** Judge concerning them, and their powers and weaknesses, just as you have judged with Venus and Mars. **135** Likewise for their retrogradation and direct motion, and pausing,[186] and the hours of their signification in the places, **136** except that they signify less than Mars and Venus do.

---

[178] The Hebrew reads, "or."

[179] Adding from the Hebrew.

[180] Reading with the Hebrew for "west," and omitting *abstentatur a se.*

[181] *Orientis respectu sui.* That is, in their west.

[182] As Bos and Burnett point out (p. 356), this does not seem to be an authentic Aristotelian quote.

[183] The Latin also adds "cold-moist."

[184] This seems to mean that the applications between Mercury and Jupiter are in force at the same time as that between the luminaries.

[185] That is, the opposition.

[186] That is, their stationing. I have omitted *partis a parte* (which the Hebrew renders as "of one of them"), as it does not seem to make sense or contribute anything.

[Predicting heavy or light rains by opening the doors III: the luminaries and Saturn]

137 Likewise, look at Saturn and the Sun[187] and their natures. **138a** If they were cold-moist or hot-moist, judge with their applications and mansions[188] just as with Jupiter and Mercury, and Venus and Mars, except that what they signify is less than what Jupiter and Mercury do. **138b** Then, inspect any two [pairings] in a similar way, and the powers of the significations.

139 But the greater and stronger signification is when, to one signification, are added others, [or] so that there would be four significators, or five or six. **140** Likewise, the matter will be increasing up to seven, just as I said in what preceded. **141** And you should know that a signification of three is common in every place; and likewise [it is stronger of there were] four, five, six, [and] seven, nor does it ever fail from three up to seven. **142** And their powers are according to the manner of the elongation of the place from the equator of the day.

143 You should know that the stronger of the significations may perhaps deceive you in the summer, in [your] role as a prophet, as to the places in which there are waters; and in spring perhaps an average signification [will deceive you]; but in the winter a weaker one will always[189] fail. In autumn perhaps it will deceive with respect to the portion of dews, as to the hour. But in terms of the [fact of the] generation [of rain at all], nothing [we have told you] will lie. **144** And you should know that, according to a study of the places of the zodiac and their nearness and elongation from the earth, and [their] motion in adding and diminution, and latitude in the north and south, and escaping[190] from the rays, and from the quality of the four angles, or according to the latitude of the place at the beginning of the application, with the centers, degree to degree—that is a more sound and longer investigation. A certainty of those rainy hours, along with the revolution of significations and hours, [will be] according to the diminishment of that knowledge.[191]

---

[187] The Hebrew adds the Moon as well. Whether the Moon is included or not, the pairings al-Kindī has been using are meant to describe the opening of the doors.

[188] This does not seem to mean "lunar mansions," but simply their positions or where they are "staying" at the moment.

[189] Reading *semper* with the Hebrew, for the Latin *numquam* ("never").

[190] This should probably be read *emissione* ("emitting") with the Hebrew meaning, rather than *evasione*.

[191] That is, the less information you have, the less precise and accurate the prediction. I have omitted *et erit in summo in serenitate cum summo in significatione*, which is absent in the Hebrew, but seems to be mean roughly that one will be calm and confident, the more certain the indications are. One problem with that translation is that Azogont uses *serenitas*

145 And you should know that the height of signifying dews and rains is that there be a rainy signification at the hour of the conjunction of the luminaries (and that is more certain for every month), or at the hour of the position of the Sun in the centers which change the weather from one nature to [another] nature.[192] **146** For if there were a rainy signification, it will be stronger in every quarter up until there is a change to another season.

[Weather omens, derived from Tet. II.13]

147 It is even good that you prognosticate about the Sun according to his rising and setting. For when he arises clear, without darkness (or darkness is absent), it is likewise a sign of fair weather. **148** And if with his own body he is surrounded by[193] a circle, and its color will be varied towards redness, and there will be red rays spread out towards the outside of the circle,[194] and[195] there will be a thick darkness, or his roundness will be as though becoming red or it will be towards saffron, it is a sign of vehement winds. **149** But when he will arise [while] being changed with blackness and he will be in a cloud,[196] or his rays dark in winter, that signifies rains and snows.

150 Consider even the Moon three days before the New Moon, or likewise afterwards, and three days before the Full Moon or likewise afterwards. **151** For if you will see her clear in every case, not surrounded by anything, it signifies fair weather. **152** If however she were a little bit red, nor will there be a manifest light in her own body, and she will be as though moving,[197] it is a sign of winds happening from the direction of her shadow. **153** And if she will be black, tending towards the dark and pale,[198] and thickness in her, it signifies fearsome rains and winds. **154** Look even at the circles which are around her. **155** If there were one, and it is white, it signifies fair weather. If two or three, it signifies rain. **156** If there are many, and eastern, it signifies mists. **157** If western and elevated, winds. **158** And if there were a thickness

---

(correctly so) to mean "fair weather." So it is hard to know if he is talking about one's mind or the weather in this omitted clause.

[192] This seems to mean his ingresses into the movable signs, but might include all of his ingresses.

[193] Reading *circumdatur* to match the Hebrew meaning, for *comprehendet*.

[194] Omitting *aut intus* ("or inside it"), with the Hebrew.

[195] Reading with the Hebrew for "or."

[196] Hebrew: "with a black dust covering [him] totally or partly."

[197] Hebrew: "the light of [her] body is undefined and seems to move."

[198] Hebrew: "saffron."

of darkness, it signifies snows and rains in the winter, but in the summer, thunders [and] heat-lightning. **159** And if there were a swarthiness and blackness in it, it signifies long winters.

[Other weather omens]

160 Southern heat-lightning[199] even signifies [rains], and more strongly so if it was very brilliant. **161** Likewise, redness at [the Sun's] arising and setting, when it is with clouds on the horizon, is a sign of water. When the heat-lightning [is] northern, and [there is] redness, without a cloud, it is a sign of dryness.[200]

162 Likewise, when you will see the Moon having a strong arc, with [her] circumference clear, prophesy northern winds. But when [not with] a thick arc, nor a clear circumference, say southern winds.

163 Likewise[201] with the fixed stars:[202] if you saw them adding in light and greater than they were [before], it is a sign of winds. And it will be of the north or south, in that direction in which the fixed star will be. **164** And if you saw those which were illuminating before, and [in] a clear sky—[if], I say, you saw a thick darkness—it signifies water and cloud. [But if you saw them clear and illuminating, it indicates a strong wind.][203]

[Comets and shooting stars, from Aristotle and Ptolemy][204]

165 However, concerning the haired [stars],[205] Aristotle said that it signifies dryness.[206] I however say that if blackness and darkness circles them, it signifies a strong dryness and winds in the direction they appeared. **166** And its duration is according to the quantity of the light and darkness.[207] **167** And if they were from opposite directions,[208] it signifies [a confusion of][209] winds.

---

[199] The Hebrew reads "stars," but based on the Arabic text partly translated by Bos and Burnett (p. 358), the Latin seems to be correct.
[200] Reading with the Hebrew and the short Arabic text, for "darkness."
[201] See *Tet.* II.13.
[202] Reading with the Hebrew and Ptolemy, for "planets."
[203] Adding with the Hebrew.
[204] This section seems to be a mixture of Aristotle (*Meteorol.* I.7) and *Tet.* II.13.
[205] That is, comets.
[206] See Part III of this book for more on comets and Aristotle's view on them.
[207] The Hebrew mentions only darkness.
[208] This refers to shooting stars, which have been mixed up with comets in this paragraph. It would be very notable if comets appeared in opposite parts of the sky at the same time.

168 If from the four directions, it signifies rains and clouds with thunder and heat-lightning. **169** And if it were in the summer,[210] it signifies rains. **170** And likewise in the winter. [**171** When a multi-banded rainbow is seen in winter and it rains, it signifies clear skies; but if seen in a clear sky, it signifies rains.]

---

[209] Adding with Ptolemy.
[210] See Ptolemy II.13, who is describing the shapes of the clouds, not the season.

The sixth chapter: On airs & rains
according to the sayings of the ancient sages

Comment by Dykes. Textually, Chapter 6 consists of four parts:

- A passage which only appears in Latin (**6:L1-4**).
- A long passage which is only in the Hebrew, summarized here in brackets (**1-78**).
- A long passage almost completely shared between the Hebrew and Latin (**79-137**)
- A final short passage which only appears in Latin (**6:L5-6**).

In addition, much of the Latin was originally duplicated, in an alternate translation, in Ch. 8 below. I have omitted this duplicated material within Ch. 8, but used it where necessary to fill in blanks and clarify the Ch. 6 material here.

In terms of content, the chapter may be considered as having three main phases. In the first phase, al-Kindī rehearses his views on what the planets mean in both weather and politics, relying on a Ptolemaic approach to explain the reasons for these significations: that is, based on the planets' astronomical relation to the Sun.

In the second phase, al-Kindī formally introduces the names and classifications of the lunar mansions. Unfortunately, the lists are complicated by two facts: first, in the traditional material the Indians are reported as having 27 mansions, the Arabs 28. The reason for this is that the Indians apparently combined two mansions into one, which the Arabs treated separately: al-Zubānā and al-Iklīl, which are stars around Libra and Scorpio. So, the numbering of the mansions diverges mid-way through the list. Second, the Hebrew and Latin manuscripts do not always agree on which mansions belong in which classification (dry, very moist, etc.), with some manuscripts even giving the number of the mansion but not its name—or even including or omitting the "combined" mansion al-Iklīl. An example of this can be seen in the first category, the 10 or 11 moist mansions. The Hebrew list gives 10 by omitting al-Iklīl, while the Latin includes it, at least in some manuscripts. By consulting Bos and Burnett's book, and the other lists elsewhere, I believe I have accurate categorizations here. Moreover, I have sometimes used the lists from Ch. 8 rather than 6, but without alerting the reader at every point as to my choices.

Finally, the third phase of the chapter begins a set of miscellaneous methods which continue in Ch. 7: the 20° Scorpio method, the Moon's relationship to Venus and Mercury, planetary hours, and so on.

ℰℭ   ℱℭ   ℭℛ

[Latin Introduction][211]

6:L2 They said, if the Sun and Jupiter and Saturn were in one of the watery signs, and the Tail or Venus with them, one will have to fear many rains with torrents corrupting cities, in the direction of that sign,[212] and this is if they were adjoined in the winter; and likewise if in the summer, and there will be clouds, hail; or the keen eyesight of those riding:[213] and this will be according to the mansions of the Moon with them.

6:L3 And if the Sun were joined with Saturn and Jupiter and Mars in one watery sign, it will be a sign of rain and torrents and harmful rains. And [it will be] stronger if the Sun will be adjoined with Mars in a sign of water just as I showed you, and Saturn will aspect them from a square or be conjoined to them, if it[214] were in the tenth sign. **L4** Inspect Venus. When she will enter under the rays of the Sun, there will be much rain. For she is under the rays like a woman under a man.

---

[211] This Latin introduction seems to be a pastiche from other authors, because as Bos and Burnett point out (p. 381), this passage is the only one to mention the Tail, **L3** is very much like §674 in Ch. 38.2 of *Forty Chapters* (see I.4 below), and the statement about the woman under the man in **L4** evidently echoes Māshā'allāh's *Chapter on Rains*, sentence **4** (Section I.6) or his *Letter*, sentence **60** (Section I.7).

[212] *In illa parte signi.* If I'm reading this correctly, it either means the area designated by that particular sign (such as cities and peoples or even cardinal direction designated by that watery sign), or else perhaps the cardinal direction that sign occupies in the relevant chart.

[213] *Acies equitantium.* Bos and Burnett (p. 381) suggest that this could mean "battle-array of cavalry," an otherwise unknown term. Perhaps it refers to the visual judgment of travelers actually watching the Moon's position?

[214] I am not sure if this refers to Saturn, or the Sun-Mars combination.

[Introduction to Hebrew Letter II]

[1 Al-Kindī wishes that the reader be aided by God to find the truth.]

[2-6 Al-Kindī endorses the causal view that the celestial bodies have powers over the elements. But to understand the principles behind these powers, one must have studied many academic disciplines, such as mathematics, physics, and metaphysics. Moreover, one must understand how the different combinations of qualities work.²¹⁵]

[7-11 Al-Kindī mentions each of the mathematical sciences of the traditional *quadrivium*: arithmetic, geometry, and music, which are necessary for the fourth (astronomy). Music is relevant because it deals with principles of harmony: what fits with what, which is suggestive for understanding how planetary combinations will yield weather patterns.]

[12-15 One must also know physics and metaphysics, which study how the being of changeable, sensible things in the world are changed and affected by various powers—particularly by the celestial bodies.]

[16-18 Al-Kindī affirms that he has tried to make this easy for the reader to understand.]

[19-24, 26-27 There are nine spheres which encompass all of the sensible, moving bodies: earth and water together comprise the central sphere under the Moon, and they move downwards; air and fire are the second sphere, and they tend to move upwards, away from the center; then there are the spheres of the Moon, of Mercury and Venus together, then the Sun, Mars, Jupiter, Saturn, and the fixed stars.]

[The powers of the planets over weather]

[25, 28-32] The Moon, Venus, and Mercury are the main significators for rain, because they are the "essences"²¹⁶ of moisture and rain, water, and wind and air, respectively. The Moon's effect is more evident over earthy things and bodies of water (rather than fire and air), which is why she is connected with watery things especially. When Venus and Mercury are combined with the Moon, they will have very evident effects on generation and corruption.]

[33 The Sun pertains to the whole world, and is like a soul causing motion. He is also a source for sensible vision, which stands in parallel to the

---

²¹⁵ For example, how heat might be affected by moisture.
²¹⁶ Heb. *'Otzem*, which normally means "power" or "strength."

intelligibles, through which we mentally are able to "see" the truth more clearly.[217]]

[**34-37** The Sun is more akin to fire and air,[218] as the Moon is to earth and water. As the luminaries move, they create combinations and mixtures of the elemental qualities which lead to generation, corruption, and weather patterns.]

[**38-39** Mars, on the other side of the Sun, is not like water and earth (which are primary for the process of generation). He deals with heat and is harmful to the luminaries.]

[**40-46** Jupiter is indeed connected to water and earth; his sphere is not like sharp and fiery activities (like Mars), but is more calm, even, and lasting (so he is less like corruption, and more like generation and what lasts). He is compatible with the luminaries, and assists the Moon and Mercury. Jupiter can also undo malice caused by Saturn, but does not do so for Mars.[219] Venus is able to undo the malice of Mars.[220]]

[**46-49** Saturn is similar to water and earth, and affects coldness and cold things. When he is high, he is more drying like earth; while low, more moistening like water. He has no connection to heat. Like Mars, he is alien to the luminaries, and is generally harmful.]

[**50-52** The sphere of the stars acts upon seasons and the atmosphere, but not upon normal things subject to generation and corruption. When the luminaries are together by primary motion in some chart, especially in an angle (since that motion is caused by the rotation of that highest sphere), they cause appropriate effects at appropriate times.[221]]

[**53-55** But the Sun is more like the inferior planets and their effects on the earth. For one thing, the motions of their epicycles are coordinated with his. Also, the Sun is like a king who is in the middle of his country (between the three inferiors and the three superiors), and just as a good king bestows his largesse on the lower people, so he sheds his light on the inferior planets.

---

[217] This is a wholly Platonic doctrine, as befits al-Kindī's Neoplatonic understanding of Aristotle. The source of this Platonic doctrine can be found in places like the *Republic*. Note too, that Valens also relates the Sun to the soul (I.1).

[218] This is implied in al-Kindī's discussion.

[219] This is based on *Judgment 34* from Sahl's *Fifty Judgments* (probably ultimately taken from Māshā'allāh), most recently published in Appendix A of *The Book of the Nine Judges*.

[220] But not that of Saturn, according to the standard teaching.

[221] This seems to refer to charts of the conjunction of the luminaries at the New Moon. In timing procedures, the angles typically show things happening quickly or on time.

And so the Sun's motions determine the large-scale patterns of seasons and growth.]

[Other significations of the planets]

[**53, 56** The Sun is like the greater king, and the Moon like a lesser king. Both have great power over generation and sensible things.]

[**57** Mars is alien to the luminaries, so instead of their royal and noble qualities and virtues, he has more to do with war, injustice, crime, rebels, and so on.]

[**58-61** Jupiter agrees with the luminaries and institutional power, so he signifies good values and conditions like honesty and wealth, piety, supporting the law and religion. The Greek word for Jupiter, *Zeus*, comes from the verb *zaō*, referring to life.][222]

[**62** Venus is unlike Mars but is like Jupiter; but she focuses more on what is pleasant, like food, drink, sex, and pleasure.]

[**63-65** Although Saturn does not agree with the luminaries, he does agree with Jupiter and Venus. So he deals with socially constructive activities like construction and agriculture. He also indicates certain things like injustice, thought, and frivolity. But he does not indicate true perfection or completion of these positive things, because he cannot fully agree with the process of generation and such which is indicated by the luminaries—so whatever he indicates, will be somewhat lesser or lacking in that regard.]

[**66-78** Again, processes in the sublunar world take place due to motions in the celestial world. Rational beings like humans are able to take these general patterns and apply them to particular conditions and circumstances in the sensible world, in order to yield correct predictions. You must be able to properly value and rank the universal or general, and the particular.]

[The mansions of the Moon]

79 And al-Kindī said that the planets generating rain are Venus, Mercury, and the Moon; but the essence of Venus and the Moon is water, but that of Mercury winds. **80** However, the nearer and stronger impression of moisture and water in us is from the Moon, because her circle is closer to the earth.

---

[222] Based on sentence **61** and Bos and Burnett's footnote (p. 250).

81 The diversity of the seasons belong to the circle of the Sun and the complexion of the circle of the signs, and the position of the Sun with his advancement and retreat in it. **82** The circle [of the zodiac] is divided into 360°, [and] the Moon splits it by the month, which is called "lunar." **83** And the days of her [month] are 27 and 6/7 days,[223] [and she has a mansion in which she stays every night.] **84** But each of the 12 signs has 2 1/3 mansions. **85** And so, Aries has two, namely al-Naṭḥ (which is also called al-Sharaṭān), and al-Buṭayn, and one-third of al-Thurayyā. **86** And this is the consideration of the Indians, [who put al-Zubānā and al-Iklīl, of Scorpio, in the same mansion].[224] **87** [There are 27 mansions:] (1) al-Sharaṭān, (2) al-Buṭayn, (3) al-Thurayyā, (4) al-Dabarān, (5) al-Haqᶜah, (6) al-Hanᶜa, (7) al-Dhirāᶜ, (8) al-Naṭḥ, (9) al-Ṭarf, (10) al-Jabha, (11) al-Kharāṭān, (12) al-Ṣarfah, (13) al-ᶜAwwāʾ, (14) al-Simāk, (15) al-Ghafr, (16) al-Zubānā, (17/18) al-Qalb,[225] (18/19) al-Shawlah, (19/20) al-Naᶜāʾim, (20/21) al-Balda, (21/22) Saᶜd al-dhābiḥ, (22/23) Saᶜd bulaᶜ, (23/24) Saᶜd al-suᶜūd, (24/25) Saᶜd al-ʾakhbiyah, (25/26) al-Fargh al-muqaddam, (26/27) al-Fargh al-muʾakhkhar, (27/28) Baṭn al-ḥūt. **88** [By dividing the zodiac by 27 mansions, each mansion is 13 1/3°].

---

[223] This is probably calculated based on the Moon's appearance from under the rays, and/or her subsequent entry under them again. For her tropical cycle (in which she returns to the same degree she was in at the New Moon) is only 27.3 days, and her synodic cycle (when she returns to a conjunction with the Sun) is about 29.5 days.

[224] Adding with the Hebrew. This is significant, because the Arabic list has 28 mansions of 12° 51' 26" apiece, since the Arabic approach separated these two mansions. In what follows, I will retain the Indian numbering, but add a slash with the Arabic numbering so one may follow the two lists consistently.

[225] Again, the first number (17) is the Indian number, based on combining both al-Zubānā and al-Iklīl in the same mansion. But al-Qalb is 18 in the usual Arabic list, and so one with the rest.

89 And they posited that the [following 11 mansions] are moist:[226]

	Hebrew Letter II (n=10)	*DMT* Ch. 8 *MSS* BHP (n=11)
1.	4 [al-Dabarān]	4, al-Dabarān
2.	7 [al-Dhirāᶜ]	7, al-Dhirāᶜ
3.	10 [al-Jabha]	10, al-Jabha
4.	12 [al-Ṣarfah]	12, al-Ṣarfah
5.	15 [al-Ghafr]	15, al-Ghafr
6.	16 [al-Zubānā]	16, al-Zubānā
7.		17, al-Iklīl
8.	18 [al-Shawlah]	18, al-Shawlah
9.	19 [al-Naᶜāʾim]	19, al-Naᶜāʾim
10.	21 [Saᶜd al-dhābiḥ]	21, Saᶜd al-dhābiḥ
11.	26 [Al-fargh al-muʾakhkhar]	26, al-fargh al-muʾakhkhar

Figure 25: Ten moist mansions

90 And when she stays in six of them, rains are multiplied, as well as dew and water. And they are:[227]

---

[226] In the table below, I give two versions from the *mss*. The first is the list from Hebrew *Letter* II, which lists the numbers of the mansions but not their names. The other version is from *DMT* Ch. 8, but only from *mss* BHP. (Manuscript R does not seem reliable here, and has some odd transliterations that I cannot match with the Arabic.) The Hebrew list gives the numbers but not the names, while *DMT* gives both the numbers and the names. The Hebrew list gives only 10 moist mansions, because it reflects the aforesaid combining of *al-Iklīl* with *al-Zubānā* into the same mansion (16) and so does not list *al-Iklīl* separately. But the Latin list shows indications of being translated directly from an Arabic source (namely, their use of the *dhamma* or *u* at the ends of the words), and they have 11 mansions because they insist on listing al-Iklīl separately.

[227] In this list, we see that the Latin list continues to list *al-Zubānā* and *al-Iklīl* separately, but omits *al-Dhirāᶜ*. Actually, the Latin list gives *al-Iklīl* as the second one right after *al-Dabarān*, which looks suspicious to me. Probably the Hebrew list is correct.

Hebrew Letter II (n=6)	DMT Ch. 8 MSS BHP (n=6)
4 [al-Dabarān]	al-Dabarān
7 [al-Dhirāᶜ]	
12 [al-Ṣarfah]	al-Ṣarfah
16 [al-Zubānā]	al-Zubānā
	al-Iklīl
21 [Saᶜd al-dhābiḥ]	Saᶜd al-dhābiḥ
26 [Al-fargh al-muᵓakhkhar]	Al-fargh al-muᵓakhkhar

Figure 26: Six very moist mansions

91 And six are dry, nor do they signify rain, namely:

	Hebrew Letter II & DMT Ch. 8 MSS BHP
1.	2 [al-Buṭayn]
2.	5 [al-Haqᶜah]
3.	9 [al-Ṭarf]
4.	17 [al-Qalb]
5.	24 [Saᶜd al-ᵓakhbiyah]
6.	25 [Al-fargh al-muqaddam]

Figure 27: Six dry mansions

92 Another eleven are neutral, neither dry nor moist, namely:[228]

	DMT Ch. 8, MSS BHP	
1.	1 [al-Sharaṭān]	Neutral
2.	3 [al-Thurayyā]	Neutral
3.	6 [al-Hanᶜa]	Neutral / very moist
4.	8 [al-Nathra]	Neutral
5.	11 [al-Kharātān]	Neutral
6.	13 [al-ᶜAwwāᵓ]	Neutral
7.	14 [al-Simāk]	Neutral / very moist

---

[228] The Hebrew Letter does not list them. The fact that the Latin (which comes from an Arabic source) mentions a 28th mansion, indicates that it follows the Arabic numbering.

8.	21 [al-Balda]	Neutral
9.	23 [Saᶜd bulaᶜ]	Neutral
10.	24 [Saᶜd al-suᶜūd]	Neutral / very moist
11.	28 [Baṭn al-ḥūt]	Neutral

Figure 28: Eleven neutral (but sometimes moist) mansions

93 Among them are three which are perhaps more rainy than the six aforesaid moist ones **94** (the reason for which has been set out before), **95** namely: al-Simāk, al-Hanᶜa, Saᶜd al-suᶜūd. **96** And those [others which are] are neutral, [are] without moisture and dryness, because of their neutrality. You should know them.

97 [For knowing about rain generally in its season, see] when one luminary would be conjoined with the other one, in the same minute of one of the twelve signs.[229] **98** One should take from the first minute [of Aries] to the last one (that of the Sun and Moon), and see the quantity of the degrees which there are, and distribute 13 1/3° to each mansion, starting from Aries; but where the number will be ended, it will be moist or dry or in the middle. You should know this. **99** Operate likewise with the planets. Consider the hour of the conjunction of the Sun and Moon, and take from the first minute of Aries to the degree of each planet in its own place; then see how many degrees there are, and give 13 1/3° to each mansion of the Moon, starting from Aries; where the number will be ended, the planet will be in that mansion. **100** Therefore, you should know that I am considering the places of the planets from these moist and dry and neutral mansions.

101 And do it thusly four times in every month: at the conjunction, first quarter, prevention, second quarter. **102** And then distribute the Sun and Moon and the stars [around the chart]. **103** And you should know their aspects and complexions and applications, because, if the Moon will be in a moist sign, and a planet will aspect her or be conjoined to her, it signifies the generating of rain, especially if some infortune aspected her. For if an infortune will aspect, or she will apply to it, going towards it, when the Moon will reach it, it will be the hour of rain. **104** And if the Moon were with Saturn, or will aspect him in a mansion, the rain will be light, calm. **105** If with Mars, it signifies rain with lightning and thunder and hail. **106** With Mercury, a strong

---

[229] This sentence is a hybrid of those in Chs. 6 and 8, to approximate the Hebrew as well as possible.

wind, intermittently trickling down. **107** And if the luminaries were in the same mansion, they signify much rain with large drops.

108 The signification of Saturn over rain is black clouds; the clouds of Mars, saffron-red with a mixture of whiteness; the clouds of Mercury, pale[230] and smoky; **109** the clouds of the Moon (as an individual [planet]), white, of much water and hot air; the clouds of the Sun, saffron; but Venus does not signify a cloud, and she signifies moistures and dews and mists; Jupiter signifies the saffron color of the air, and mild wind.

110 If therefore Venus and Mercury and the Moon will be in one of these ten[231] moist mansions, it signifies much rain. **111** And if the Moon were in one of the moist mansions, nor does Venus nor Mercury aspect her, it will not signify rain. **112** And if Venus and Mercury and the Moon did agree [by aspecting or being] in one of these ten [as was just described], much rain is signified.

113 Moreover, you should know the places of the application of Mercury with the three superiors,[232] and with which one he is applied, and from which one he was separated. **114** If [he has an application] with Saturn, there will be strong wind with black darkness and dust. **115** If with Jupiter [and Venus],[233] it signifies a mild wind without rain. If with Mars, hot winds. **116** If with the Sun, a hot wind with corruption. **117** If Venus would be applied with Saturn, it signifies rain, and perhaps there will be hail with her, small, and rain as though like dust.[234]

[The 20° Scorpio method]

118 And if the Sun were in the twentieth degree of Scorpio, consider the application of the Moon with the planets. **119** For if she applied with Venus and Mercury, it signifies many rains in that year. **120** And[235] if Venus and Mercury in that hour were in [the east and][236] a sign of water, it is a sign that there would be rains at the beginning of the year. **121** And if Venus and Mer-

---

[230] Hebrew *Letter* II reads, "saffron."

[231] Or eleven, depending on how one counts (see above).

[232] Hebrew *Letter* II suggests that this is the three planets, the Moon, Mercury, and Venus. Nevertheless we are still supposed to note the following applications of Mercury.

[233] Adding with the Hebrew *Letter*.

[234] Reading more with the corrected Hebrew, and omitting *non residens in ea.*

[235] For these solar phase relations, see my Introduction.

[236] Adding with the Hebrew. But this really means "eastern," i.e., by solar phase.

cury were western[237] in any sign of water, it signifies many rains are going to be at the end of the year. **122** And if either of them were eastern, the other western, so that both would be in a sign of water, they both signify the generating of rain at the beginning of the year and at the end, but little.[238] **123** Even see whether the Moon would be applied with Venus or with Mercury, whether eastern or western. **124** If her application were with an eastern one,[239] it signifies that the rain at the beginning of the year will be more than at the end; if with a western one, more at the end than at the beginning.

[More on planetary applications]

125 And there is another method for you. If Mercury applied with Mars, there will be intermittent rain, and wind, and lightning. **126** And if Venus with Jupiter, there will be generous rain, and it will fall and be profitable. **127** If the Moon with Saturn, it will signify black, congealed[240] clouds. **128** If with Mars, clouds cut through with ice and lightning, and perhaps a rainbow will appear, nor will there be a general rain. **129** But if the Moon with Venus and Jupiter, there will be white clouds and dew of great usefulness. **130** If the Moon with Mercury, there will be pale[241] clouds of smoky color, and good wind with rain.

[More on the Moon's applications to Venus and Mercury, at her quarters]

131 Another method. Look at the Moon, at the hour of the conjunction and prevention, and the first quarter and second quarter, to see with whom she would apply at that hour. **132** If with Venus and Mercury, it signifies the generating of rain in that week, **133** and the hour of it will be according to the quantity of the degrees which are between the Moon and the two planets to whom she applies; and put down days and hours [for each degree]. **134** When the Moon gets to the degree of that planet to which she applies, and it

---

[237] Omitting "or eastern," following Bos and Burnett's suggestion. Again, this might be western by solar phase, and not by house placement.

[238] Omitting *sic*, which does not really play an informative role here. Bos and Burnett (p. 297) suggest it might stand for *siccitatem* ("dryness"), which they say agrees with Jafar (see his sentences **145-48**) but I do not quite see the parallel.

[239] That is, of Venus and Mercury, if the one to which she applies is eastern. Again, the Hebrew reads as though this is in the east or west of the chart itself.

[240] Reading *congelatas* for the humorous *conculcatas* ("trampled under one's foot"), and omitting *una pars conculcans aliam*.

[241] The Hebrew reads, "saffron."

is Venus in Scorpio or Capricorn or Aquarius, there will be many rains. **135** Likewise, when Mercury stands in one of these three, it signifies rain. **136** And if Venus and Mercury were in the aforesaid signs, and the Moon opposite to or conjoined to them, or in their square, it signifies rain.

[Planetary hours at lunar ingresses][242]

137 Another method. When the Moon will enter Cancer at the hour of the Sun, or Virgo at the hour of Venus, or Sagittarius at the hour of the Moon, or Gemini at the hour of Mercury, or Taurus at the hour of Mars, *or Leo (or even* Libra) at the hour of Jupiter, it signifies rain and wind[243] according to the nature of the sign; and what there is with respect to her essence and the essence of these signs, will be likewise. [For example: the Moon in Aquarius or Scorpio or Capricorn in the hour of Saturn, indicates a change of weather.][244]

[Latin addition to Ch. 6]

6:L5 Another brief method. Consider the conjunction of the month of the Arabs, and which of the planets is there. If it were a fortune, there will be trust with respect to rain. If an infortune, there will not be. Likewise with the other angles of the Ascendant. **L6** And look to see when the Moon will be in the opposite to the degree of the Ascendant of the conjunction, and one of the planets signifying rain will aspect her: there will be rain.

---

[242] See my Introduction for a discussion of this passage.
[243] Omitting "rain in hotness, and." The Hebrew reads, "rain in its proper times, and wind…".
[244] Adding based on the Hebrew. But see my Introduction for variants.

The seventh chapter: On the natures of the days

Comment by Dykes: This chapter concerns Lots and other methods which monitor weather over periods between one and seven days. It exists only in the Latin *DMT*, and is comprised of fifteen sentences, **7:L1-15.**

ℬ   ℬ   ℭ

[A Lot for daily weather][245]

7:L2 If you wished to know what there is on any day in terms of rains, winds, thunders, and hail, take from the Sun to Saturn and project from the sign of the Moon:[246] where the number will be ended, see what planet will be the lord in that house. **L3** If it were a house of Saturn, that day will be cold; if Jupiter, calm and mild; if Mars, a strong wind; if the Sun, a hot day; if Venus, rainy; if Mercury, variable; if the Moon, rainy.

[The Moon with different planets]

7:L4 And[247] you should know that the hot planets are Jupiter, Mars, the Sun, the Head of the Dragon; but the cold stars are Saturn, Venus. **L5** And if the Moon encountered a hot star,[248] the wind will speed up and the air will get hot; if with a cold one, the wind will come slowly and the air will be chilled down.

---

[245] According to Bos and Burnett (p. 382), this Lot is the second of those listed in Abū Ma'shar's *Kitāb al-Sirr* ("Book of the Secret"); it is also found in *The Opening of the Doors*, sentences **17-18**. See also ibn Ezra's *Beginning of Wisdom* Ch. 9 (p. 153), and the second version of his *Book of the World*, §40. See my list of weather Lots in Section I.1.

[246] This should probably be the "degree" of the Moon, as in **7:L6** below.

[247] Here Bos and Burnett note that their *mss* have two readings. I have preferred the minority reading here, but several others give the following: "And you should know that the hot planets are Mars, the Sun, the Head of the Dragon; but the cold ones Saturn, Jupiter, Venus."

[248] This should perhaps be read with **7:L9** below, where her application is determined at the moment she enters a sign.

[The same daily Lot, explained differently][249]

7:L6 Look even at the Lot of days: namely, take from the degree of the Sun to the degree of Saturn, and project from the degree of the Moon at[250] the rising of the Sun every day.[251] **L7** If Mercury aspected this Lot, or it happened to fall with Mercury, there will be wind on that day. **L8** And a stronger sign is if the Moon would be with him, especially if Venus participated.

[Lunar ingresses]

7:L9 And[252] it is even from the completion of the arranging of the Ascendant,[253] when the Moon is in the first minute of a sign: see which of the planets aspects her, and judge according to this. For it will signify with respect to an increase of the knowledge of the things of the air.[254]

[An alternate version of the posts or foundations][255]

7:L10 Another way. It will be signified from the degree[256] of the luminaries in the divergence of their ways, in what there is between the conjunction and the Full Moon, in the first and second quarter. **L11** And when it will be the middle of the body of the Moon, and her quarter and three quarters, and when she is in the trine and sextile from the Sun; and you should look[257] at

---

[249] This second version of the daily Lot is the same as described in the interpolation at the end of 'Umar Ch. 81 (Section I.5), where it is explicitly attributed to Abū Ma'shar.

[250] *Versus*, lit. "towards."

[251] *Totam diem*, suggesting "throughout" the day. But the meaning in 'Umar's Ch. 81 is clearer.

[252] This reports the same method as the interpolation at the end of 'Umar's Ch. 81.

[253] *De complemento directionis ascendentis*: that is, another method is to calculate the Ascendant at the time of her ingresses into signs; again, the meaning in the interpolation to 'Umar Ch. 81 is clearer. Speaking of calculating or determining using *dirigo* seems to be an idiosyncrasy of Azogont.

[254] In the 'Umar interpolation, this planet will generally signify the weather for as long as the Moon is in that sign—after which one must obviously look at her applications in the next ingress.

[255] In this Latin-only version of the centers, it is unclear to me whether the 12° distances from the New and Full Moons are included. For although the text speaks of the "divergence" of the luminaries, it seems ambiguous as to their divergence being from their exact conjunction and opposition, or based on her emergence from the Sun's rays at 12° (and the opposite region).

[256] *Parte.*

[257] Following Bos and Burnett's suggestion of *inspicias* for *inspiciet ipsa.*

the planets in that hour, and at their places from the degree[258] of the luminaries, and at the Ascendant and their angles,[259] and the aspect of the planets, and the application of their degree with a degree.[260] **L12** And you should know the more worthy one of them (and [this is] the significator), according to the greatness of their natures and the power of their complexion with the power of the planets and the signs: [thus] one will know what happens in the air, in terms of winds, thunders, and hail, motion or rest.

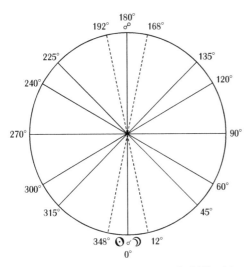

Figure 29: Another version of al-Kindī's centers of the Moon (Ch. 7)

[Heliacal risings and settings of fixed stars?][261]

L13 And it will even be signified with the fixed stars at their easternness and westernness,[262] and the airs will change just as the Moon does if she were in an angle.[263]

---

[258] *Parte.*

[259] Perhaps the angles from the luminaries, but this should probably be *eius*: the Ascendant and *its* angles.

[260] *Partis eorum cum parte.* That is, degree-based applications, and not just aspects by sign.

[261] This seems to refer to weather and seasonal predictions using the lunar mansion stars, as described by al-Bīrūnī (*Chronology*, pp. 335ff; see my discussion in my own *Choices & Inceptions*, Introduction §5). Calendar days and some weather prediction were determined by which fixed stars emerged from the Sun's rays.

[262] That is, the heliacal risings and settings.

[263] I belive the Latin author means that when certain mansion stars make their heliacal risings, it will indicate a seasonal change just as the Moon does when she is in the posts or foundations, above.

[More lore about the Moon][264]

L14 And the New Moon and her concealment have significance over the generating of rain and snow and wind, according to the greatness of [her?] inclination toward the north and south and east and west, and latitude toward some degree from the degree[265] of the quarters of the circle, in which there is moist [or] dry wind.

L15 Therefore, he who wished to know the accidents in the air, should inspect what I have said.

---

[264] I believe this section is saying that we should see in which direction of the chart the New Moon takes place, to see what kinds of winds will blow. For example, if it were directly to the east, there would be eastern, spring-like winds; but if more towards the south, there would be hotter and dryer, more summery winds. Probably we should look at her declination as well (e.g., northern declination suggests warmer winds, southern declination suggests colder ones.

[265] *Partem partis de parte*, lit. "a degree of the degree, from the degree." This seems to be a literal rendition of Arabic, which expresses phrases like "one of the men" as "one man of the men."

The eighth chapter: On the four seasons & the changing of the air in terms of hotness & coldness

Comment by Dykes. This chapter consists of four parts:

- A Latin addition (**8:L1-44**), which was taken verbatim from 'Umar's *Book of Questions* Chs. 81-82 (but attributed here to al-Kindī), and an unknown work by Māshā'allāh. It contains many different methods, such as New Moon charts, a Lot of rain, and so on. See I.5 of this book for all of 'Umar's material.
- An alternative translation of sentences **79-107** and **137** from Ch. 6, but omitted here as redundant.
- A summary of several sentences from the Hebrew *Letter* which were not in the Latin (**138-41**).
- The remainder of the Latin (**142-65**), which is shared with the Hebrew.

 හ   හ   ශ

[Latin addition: from 'Umar's Book of Questions Ch. 81][266]

8:L2 And this[267] will be known from [1] the conjunction and its degree, and [2] the Ascendant of the conjunction and opposition which is before the Sun's entrance into the first minute of Aries, and [3] the places of the luminaries in the signs.

8:L3 And so, if you found Saturn in the angles of the Ascendant, or arranged in [one] of the angles of the lord of the Ascendant, in a portion of his authority, especially in the angle of the Midheaven, it signifies the changing of the air, with corruption and its darkness. **4** And it will help in addition according to the tendency[268] of that season if it were a hot one, and according to the strength of the coldness if it were a cold season, **5** and he will add to that if it were in its own season.[269] And if he removed [himself] from the

---

[266] See the fuller form of this chapter below, in I.5.

[267] See the title sentence above.

[268] *Incurvationem.*

[269] Just as in my comments to 'Umar, I disagree with the statement in Arabic that Saturn will increase heat and increase cold. This is against astrological thinking as well as other statements to the contrary in these texts. It should be read as though Saturn makes heat

angles, the weather will be according to its own [normal] manner, nor will it be changed. **6** If Saturn [were] in [one] of the angles of the lord of the Ascendant (as I said), it will be less in his work, and weaker in deed [than if he were in an angle of the Ascendant].[270]

8:L7 And if it were Mars instead of Saturn (and it will be according to this that, I say, Saturn was [in an angle from the Ascendant or the lord of the Ascendant],[271] and [especially][272] in the Midheaven), the nature of heat will be increased if it were a hot season, and the nature of cold will be diminished if it were a cold season, and the essence of the season will be made balanced if it were a balanced season—[but] it will tend towards hotness.

8:L8 And if it were Jupiter or Venus or the Moon instead of both, the air will be made even and its complexion mellowed, and whatever was planted or sown in that season will grow.

8:L9 And inspect Mercury: if he were in the Midheaven from the sign of the Ascendant of the conjunction or opposition, or[273] he were in one of the signs of winds, or he were in any of the angles of an infortune, he signifies the disturbance of the air, and its corruption, and a multitude of impeding winds. **10** Say likewise if one of the infortunes fell in the angle [of Mercury, and Mercury was in an angle from][274] a fortune: it will do what an infortune does in the sign of the conjunction.[275]

8:L11 Concerning [any planet] which you have found in one of the angles of the Ascendant of the conjunction, or in what follows the angle of the Ascendant of the conjunction,[276] make it the significator. **12** Then inspect the complexion of Saturn and Mars [to the significator] from the square or opposite or conjunction. **13** And if Mars were in hot signs (which are Aries and its triplicity), he adds in the nature of heat if it were a hot season, and he

---

more moderate (because his coldness counteracts it), but he will increase any cold already indicated.

[270] Adding based on 'Umar.

[271] Inserting based on the statements above, for the Latin *cum eo* ("with him"). As Bos and Burnett point out, the Latin translator might have inserted *cum eo* so as to account for his misreading of Jupiter in the next phrase.

[272] Omitting *Iupiter*, and reading with the Arabic.

[273] The Arabic reads, "and."

[274] Correcting based on the Arabic; the Latin of *DMT* has the infortune in the angle of the *Ascendant*, and treats Mercury as though he *is* a fortune.

[275] I do not understand this last sentence: how could an infortune harming Mercury by square, but Mercury being related to other fortunes, be in any way related to an infortune being in sign of the conjunction itself?

[276] That is, being either angular or succeedent in the chart of the conjunction.

takes away from the nature of cold if it were a cold season. **14** And if the aspect were from the trine or sextile and he were in hot signs, it signifies as I say, however it diminishes. **15** If the aspect of Saturn and the complexion of the significator planet, and the application with it, were from the square or opposite or conjunction, and Saturn were in the cold[277] [and] dry signs or the cold, moist ones (like the watery ones), he will add cold to their natures if the season were cold, and will take away from the heat if the season were hot. **16** And if the complexion of the significator were from the trine or sextile ([he being], as I said, in these signs), it will be less. **17** And if Saturn were in the hot, moist signs (like Gemini and its triplicity), and the significator will be complected with him from the opposite or square or conjunction, it signifies mild air and what is of a good complexion, and the increase[278] of every vege-table thing because of the evenness of the air. **18** Likewise if the significator will be complected with him in the trine or sextile, so that [Saturn] is in those signs.[279] **19** Likewise, if the significator will be complected [with] Mars (or he will be complected with it), and in the cold, dry signs and the cold, moist ones, and it was from the square or opposite, it will even out the air and its complexion becomes good, and every vegetable thing and what sprouts, will grow.

8:L20 And he testifies with the Lot of winds, [and make it a partner with the significator].[280] **21** And it is that you take from the degree of Mercury (if he were not in his own house) to the degree of the lord of his house, and add on top of that the degrees of the Ascendant, and project from the Ascend-ant: and where it is finished, the Lot is in that. **22** And[281] if you found Saturn or Mars with the Lot or its lord, judge from them just as we said before about their appearance in the angles and in the aspects of the significator. **23** And so, if Mercury were in his own house, take from his degree, and add on top of that the degrees of the Ascendant: and where it will be ended, there will be the Lot. **24** Operate likewise according to the positions of the Sun in the quarters which are after Aries (and they are Cancer, Libra, Capricorn). And operate likewise at the Sun's entrance in every sign.

---

[277] Here and below, I follow the 'Umar text for Azogont's "hot."

[278] Reading *incrementum* for *crementum*.

[279] 'Umar adds that this situation will be even better.

[280] Reading with the Arabic for "and its motion with this evenness." Bos and Burnett suggest how the Latin translator misread the Arabic.

[281] Reading this sentence with 'Umar, for "If he were with the Lot of Saturn and Mars, say just as you said before when he was in his own house, even if he was not."

[Latin addition: from 'Umar's Book of Questions Ch. 82][282]

8:L25 But: the generating of rains and thunders and heat-lightning and winds and their multitude and scarcity. **26** Look in [a matter] of this kind from the entrance of the Sun into the twentieth degree of Scorpio.[283] Determine the Ascendant to that hour, and [also] its angles and the planets. Then, consider Venus and Jupiter and Mercury: **27** if they were western or of a slow pace, or retrograde, it signifies many dews and rains in that year. **28** And if they were eastern or direct, or of a quick pace, it signifies contrariwise.

8:L29 And consider Mars: if he were in any of the angles, especially in the Midheaven, in airy signs, and he would invest Mercury,[284] it signifies much with respect to thunders and heat-lightning and rains that are cut off quickly, and many locusts and the corruption of the air. **30** And if Mars were in the angle of the earth in earthy signs, and a fortune is cut off from him,[285] and he invests Mercury, it signifies a tremor of the earth and the appearance of fires from the earth, and fear, and there will be a corruption of minerals and the sulphurs of the earth. **31** And if Mars were, as I said, in hot signs in the angle of the earth, it signifies the burning of the land and the corruption of its substance, and its minerals, and the burning of seeds with paleness,[286] and corruption with mishaps. **32** If, however, according to what I said about the hot signs, he were in watery signs in the angle of the earth, it signifies the diminution of water and the corruption of it, even [the corruption] of anything which stays in the water, in terms of animals and other things. **33** And if a fortune invested him [or formed a conjunction with him],[287] the thunders and heat-lightning [will be less harmful; and if the fortunes had no commixture with him, thunder] and many lightning flashes will corrupt [and cause losses].

34 And if it were Saturn instead of Mars, especially if he were in the Midheaven and in airy signs, and Mercury invested him, and a fortune fell away from him, [it signifies harm in the atmosphere, and many damaging and lasting rains, and they will not be cut short. And if Saturn were in the angle of the earth just as we said before, and in earthy signs, and he had a commixture

---

[282] See also below, Section I.5.
[283] Or rather, 20° Scorpio.
[284] That is, if they would be mixed together.
[285] That is, the benefics are in aversion to him.
[286] *Pallore.* Perhaps the Latin translator is thinking of seeds being "blanched."
[287] Adding with 'Umar here and throughout the sentence, as there are several lacunas.

with Mercury, and the fortunes fell away from him],[288] tremors of the earth will happen, and shocks, and black waters and the like will appear from the earth. **35** And if he were in the watery signs and under the earth in the angle of the earth, and a fortune fell away from him and he invested Mercury, the waters of rivers and wells and springs will be diminished, and animals of the water and other things will be corrupted. **36** And if he were in the hot signs in the angle of the earth, and a fortune will fall away from him, and he invested Mercury, [it signifies harm on the land and what properly belongs to it, and in minerals. And if Mercury did not have a commixture with him, the aforesaid significations][289] will however be easier. **37** And if a fortune did not fall away from him, [mix the significations of the year, and][290] the signification of the aforesaid things will for the most part be eased.

8:L38 And you should know that every one of the superior planets is bound with some inferior one, [and] the superiors in themselves [are] in the soul, the inferiors in the body, nor is there generation nor corruption in the world, except with their application and complexion.

[Latin addition: a view of Māshā'allāh's][291]

8:L39 Another way: Māshā'allāh on airs. **40** Look,[292] in the revolution of the year, at the Ascendant and the angles, and the places of the planets, and their transits, and the blocking of their operations, and the projection of their rays according to what they signify in every clime in terms of the essences of animals and vegetation, and the separation of their ways, from the changing of the Sun in the signs, and their natures in the changing of the air in the four seasons (namely spring, summer, autumn, winter), and what the signs signify with their natures.

8:L41 If Mars stayed in hot ones, he will add to its hotness, but Saturn takes away. But when Saturn will be in an earthy one, he will add to its coldness, but Mars takes it away. Mars in an airy one will add to its hotness, but

---

[288] Adding from 'Umar. Because both this statement and the previous one have identical phrases about mixing with Mercury and the fortunes being in aversion, the Latin translator accidentally skipped this section.

[289] Reading with 'Umar, for "these will be earthquakes."

[290] Adding with 'Umar.

[291] Bos and Burnett (p. 384) say they have not been able to find the source for this attribution.

[292] Bos and Burnett point out that these two paragraphs are summaries of what appears in a longer form in 'Umar Ch. 81 (see above).

Saturn will take away from it. Saturn in a watery one will add to the coldness, Mars takes it away. **42** These are the positions of Saturn and Mars in the twelve signs: when they are in them, they change their atmospheres. **43** And every planet which will be under the rays in the revolution of the year, signifies according to[293] the weakness of its clarity, and the corruption of its ways.

8:L44 The letter of al-Kindī on airs and rains ends.[294]

[Another version of the 20° Scorpio method][295]

[138-41 Determine the Ascendant for the Sun's ingress into 20° Scorpio, as well as the angles and the planets. See if any of the rainy planets (the Moon, Mercury, Venus) are conjoined. If conjoined in the east, there will be rain at the beginning of the year; if in the west, at the end.[296] If they are increased in calculation, there will be more rain.]

[Signs and planets of rain][297]

142-43 When one member of the three planets of water (namely Venus, Mercury, the Moon) will be in one of the signs of water, [which are Scorpio, Cancer, and Aquarius],[298] and will be moving direct in it, rain will abound to the extent that it will harm the people.

[A victor in the revolution of the year]

144 Another method, as to when there will be much or little rain in the year. **145** Look,[299] in the revolution of the year, at its lord,[300] and at the

---

[293] Or rather, "because of."

[294] I have omitted the end of this sentence ("Another treatment of the same thing as above:"), because it introduces the repeated translation of the material on lunar mansions from Ch. 6. I continue the text below.

[295] Again, this is four sentences from Hebrew *Letter* II which were omitted in the Latin.

[296] Again, other versions of this technique suggest that they are eastern and western by solar phase, not in the eastern or western parts of the chart.

[297] Now we return to the Latin *DMT.*

[298] Adding from the Hebrew.

[299] The Hebrew reads differently: "Look at the sign of the end of the year, the lord of the return of the year, the Moon, the Lot of Fortune, the lord of the Lot of Fortune, the *fardār,* the ray; [and] which planet is rising above [sc. lord over] all of these." The "sign of the end of the year" evidently refers to a mundane profection (usually called a "terminal" place in Arabic), the *fardār* to a mundane *fardār* or *firdārīyyah,* and the "ray" to a mundane

Moon, and the Lot of Fortune and the lord of the Lot, and the *kardajas*,[301] and which one had rulership over all of them.[302] **146** If [the victor is] Saturn, Venus, Mercury, or the Moon,[303] there will be much rain in the year, especially if they were in rainy signs: Aquarius or the end of Capricorn, and Aries and Taurus and the beginning of Leo.[304] **147** And in addition to them,[305] Scorpio and Pisces and Aquarius.

[The Sun's ingress into Libra, and beyond]

148 And if you wanted to know whether it will abound in rain at the beginning of the year or in the middle or at the end, look to see when the Sun enters into Libra. If Venus were under him, western, it signifies much rain at the beginning ([but] if eastern, very little at the beginning), [and] much at the end. **149** If her westernness were after that hour by a month and a half,[306] it signifies much rain in the middle of the year; **150** and by how much more Venus will be under the rays, the air will be changed to rain all the more.

151 And[307] if you wanted to know the day of the rain, revolve your year for every conjunction and opposition from the Sun's entrance into the beginning of Libra up to his entrance at the beginning of Gemini, and take into testimony the lord of the degree of the conjunction and opposition, and Venus and Mercury and Saturn, **152** as you took it before at the beginning of

---

distribution or direction of a mundane Ascendant through the bounds. I will discuss these mundane methods in greater detail in *Astrology of the World III*.

[300] Probably the lord of the Ascendant at the revolution.

[301] This may have been a misread for the *fardār* or *firdārīyyah*. But Bos and Burnett refer this to the quick and slow *kardajas*, degree-based intervals in astronomical tables (see Glossary). Nevertheless, the use of this word here does not make much sense, and we should probably prefer the Hebrew's reference to the *fardār*.

[302] That is, the victor over all of them, the one with the most, or most powerful types, of rulerships over these places.

[303] Reading with the Hebrew. The Latin has "and" separating these planets, without really indicating what their role is supposed to be.

[304] The Hebrew has Leo and the beginning of Taurus, not the other way around.

[305] The Hebrew reads that these are the "strongest" ones.

[306] That is, if she were western of him about six weeks after the ingress into Libra. This would put him close to the position of 20° Scorpio, which is the centerpiece of another method discussed in several texts (including just previous to this paragraph). Since westernness makes it rain early, al-Kindī is saying that westernness around the middle of the season will make it rain then.

[307] For this paragraph, cf. *Doors*, sentences **13-15** and **20-21**. I confess that between the middle of sentences **154-55** I do not understand what al-Kindī or his source is talking about.

the year.[308] **153** And see the application of the Moon: if she is with the degree[309] of planets of water and in signs of water, rain will happen, [and also] at the place of equal distance.[310] **154** And if she were in changeable signs,[311] then [it will be] days according to[312] the number of degrees, and the bodies [are] to the maximum amount with a body. **155** And this is when the equal distance[313] would be closer than the number of degrees; but the number of degrees [is] closer than the maximum amount of the bodies. **156** The changeable signs signify quickness, and the double-bodied signs what is in the middle, the fixed ones a longer time.

[The posts or foundations of the Moon]

158 Even[314] look at the center of the Moon at the hour of the conjunction, [until] the next conjunction. **159** If the Moon were in one of the centers, [see] which planet she is applied with, and follows,[315] and each one of them will aspect the house of its partner, or both the house of one, or both the houses of both, or the luminaries will aspect them: rain will happen at the hour in which the Moon reaches the planet, and the hour of [the rain] being cut off[316] will be up to the point at which the applying one is at an equal distance or changing in what there is between it, in terms of changes.[317]

---

[308] The Hebrew adds that this will indicate "a minimum," which Bos and Burnett believe means a minimum "amount of days."

[309] *Parte.* That is, in the same degree by conjunction (Hebrew).

[310] That is, the opposition (per the Hebrew).

[311] That is, the movable ones (Aries, Cancer, Libra, Capricorn).

[312] *Post*, the Latin translator's synonym here for *secundum*.

[313] This should mean the opposition, as in **153**. But I do not understand what the author means. The Hebrew reads, "and the number of degrees is more than the maximum in the body."

[314] This version of the posts or foundations is very unclear to me in terms of the distances being discussed.

[315] *Sequitur.* But the Hebrew refers to the planet being in its own fall, which makes more sense.

[316] The Hebrew seems to read this as the Moon stopping somewhere, but Bos and Burnett are uncertain what it means.

[317] For the last part of this sentence, the Hebrew refers to the planet that is in conjunction, is "parallel" to the other planet, and one of them "moves to what is between them towards the other." Again, the meaning is unclear.

[The sound of the thunder][318]

160 If Mars aspected Mercury or the Moon, if it[319] was of the nature of Mars, thunder will happen.[320] **161** And if he was [retrograde][321] at the same time that he aspected the Sun and a planet signifying rain, a strong commotion will happen, and voices and gloom; **162** [this is doubled][322] when it was in changeable signs or signs[323] of voices. **163** And[324] if it were Saturn instead of Mars, or Mercury in his place and in the nature of Mars,[325] and both were according to what I am saying about Mars and Mercury, especially in signs lacking voices, the rain will be lasting and the air dark, nor will be there be movement nor voice in it. **164** Do likewise when there will be a question about rain, **165** and this will suffice for what you have asked.

165 The book of al-Kindī on the impressions of the air, ends.

---

[318] Bos and Burnett put this in the same paragraph as that on the posts or foundations, but I do not see the link; therefore I have separated the following paragraph.

[319] I am not sure what this refers to.

[320] Or rather, the sound of the thunder "will be bad." Only Hebrew *MS* C gives the same reading as the Latin, which I have retained here.

[321] Adding with the Hebrew.

[322] Adding with the Hebrew.

[323] Reading with the Hebrew, for "lords."

[324] I do not understand the conditions laid out in this sentence.

[325] The Hebrew does not specify Mars. This could be Saturn, so that the author is trying to say that Mars causes sound, while Saturn does not.

SECTION I.4: AL-KINDĪ, *THE FORTY CHAPTERS*

Comment by Dykes. Following are two complete chapters from al-Kindī's *The Forty Chapters*, which I recently translated from the Latin versions by Hugo of Santalla and Robert of Ketton (2011). The text is based on the Latin, but I have also consulted the Arabic edition in Bos and Burnett (pp. 395-402), and the Latin and Arabic al-Rijāl. Following are my sources:

Text	Arabic (Bos & Burnett)	Latin *Forty Chapters* (Dykes 2011)	Latin al-Rijāl (1485)	*Nine Judges* (Dykes 2011)
Ch. 38	Ch. 38	Ch. 38		§Z.8
Ch. 39		Ch. 39	Ch. VIII.31.1	§Z.9

The primary methods used in these chapters are: the charts of New/Full Moons, the opening of the doors, and the centers of the Moon. In Chapter 39, al-Kindī discusses how to judge the general quality of the year in terms of disease and health.

ะ๐   ๕๑   ๛

Chapter 38: On changes in weather

[Chapter 38.1: The year, quarters, & months]

§669. For a complete recognition of those things in the atmosphere which are renewed[1] through individual years, it is good that the Ascendant of the assembly or opposition[2] which came before the Sun's ingress into the beginning of Aries, be established. Therefore, whatever sign Saturn claimed in that hour, the year seems to imitate its nature: for a hot one means heat; cold, cold; dry, aridness; moist, moistening.

§670. Moreover, when the Sun enters the individual quarters or seasons of the year,[3] Jupiter comes to be noted: one will have to judge about him in that

---

[1] Hugo means the revolution or cycle of years: the Sun's return to Aries every spring.
[2] The Ar. has only the assembly/conjunction, not the opposition.
[3] That is, his ingresses into the other movable signs: Cancer, Libra, Capricorn.

same quarter of the year, in the way it was stated above [about Saturn]. But the consideration that is made of [both] the signification of a quarter and the signification of the year, will exhibit the truth in revealing the judgment.[4]

§671. Moreover you will note [1] with whom the application of the lord of the assembly or opposition[5] (preceding the beginning of the year or quarter) comes to be. For the sharing [of indications] that is made of that star (just as was stated above), lays bare what will be.

§672. Moreover, with no less attention should you care [2] with whom the application of the lord of the Ascendant of[6] the assembly, or [3] of the lord of the Ascendant of the year, comes to be. For once a discernment of all of them is had, they suggest what must be said. Moreover, [4] the lords of the assembly and opposition[7] in every month should be noted. In this way, let there be a report about those future things which are imminent.

§673. In addition, if the significator and giver of hail (or heavy rains or dryness) is regarding the [Sun or Moon at the][8] assembly or opposition of the month or year—the Sun for planets of the year, but the Moon for the planets of the year and the months[9]—it signifies that those things which follow its nature are imminent—especially [if] placed in a bound or house of its complexion.[10]

---

[4] That is, by combining the indications. Burnett's translation of the Ar. makes it seem that we should also look at Saturn at every quarterly ingress, but to me the sense is that Saturn is for the year as a whole, and Jupiter for the quarters. Certainly Robert and Hugo read it that way.

[5] Again, the Ar. has only the assembly/conjunction.

[6] Adding with Robert and the Ar.

[7] In this case, the Ar. does allow for the opposition.

[8] Adding with Robert and the Ar. That is, see if the planet which has been identified as the primary indicator, actually aspects the luminaries at the time of their conjunction or opposition.

[9] Adding with Robert and the Ar. The sense seems to be that planets examined at the beginning of the year (Saturn, planets at the annual conjunction just before the ingress) should aspect the Sun, but any of them may aspect the Moon when looking especially at monthly times. But this does not really make sense, since by definition any planet aspecting one luminary at the New or Full Moon will also be aspecting the other.

[10] Reading with Robert (Ar.: "according to its nature"). Hugo reads, "in agreement with the nature of the one to which it applies," but in this paragraph we are not considering applications.

[Chapter 38.2: Individual planets' indications]

§674. And so[11] it seems one must note that Venus principally signifies wetness, Mercury stirs up winds, Saturn multiplies clouds and the darkness of the air, and hail, Mars incites the southern winds [and heat] (but especially in Capricorn [and less so its pivots]);[12] moreover Jupiter in a house of some authority of his own (but especially in Cancer)[13] sends in the northern winds. The Sun introduces heat and dryness.

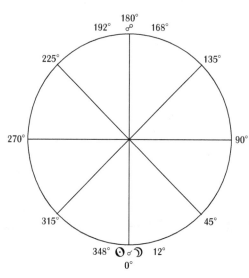

[Chapter 38.3: The posts[14] of the Moon, the opening of the doors]

§675. Moreover, let the [Ascendant of every assembly of the Sun and Moon][15] be principally established. But no less will you note, with the equal attention of your mind, [the following] twelve points, for they are these: the assembly, opposition, the two squares (namely the tetragons), and the cross-quarters of the tetragons, the 12° before the completion of the assembly and opposition, [and] the same amount after their completion.

Figure 30: Al-Kindī's twelve posts of the Moon (*Forty Chapters* Ch. 38)

§676. Therefore, when the Moon is found in any of these, if any of the inferiors would apply to a superior by opposition,[16] it testifies that what is in

---

[11] Cf. §677 below.

[12] Adding bracketed material with the Ar.

[13] The Ar. seems to allow other dignities as well, but especially his exaltation in Cancer.

[14] Ar. *marākiz*, which comes from a verb (*rakaza*) very similar to the Arabic (*watada*) and Greek (*kenteō*) verbs used to derive the words for the pivots or angles: "to ram into the ground, set up a pole, position or fix firmly." In this volume, we are usually calling these the "centers," "posts," "foundations."

[15] Adding based on the Arabic.

[16] The Ar. reads as though any inferior can apply to any superior, but al-Kindī is describing the "opening of the doors," in which an inferior must apply to the superior planet

agreement with its nature will happen, if a common regard of the Sun and Moon would be present, and if the Ascendant of the region or city does not lack their regard,[17] [and] even should they be supported by a regard of their own lords.

§677. In addition, if the Moon would advance and apply from some inferior to the superior opposite it,[18] both as mediator and key-bearer, it indubitably forces the natural [qualities] of its superior to come about. Which if this administration is ascribed to Mercury, in addition to heavy rains he begets winds; and if to Venus, it multiplies rain clouds [and cold];[19] and if to Saturn, it sends down hail, covers the atmosphere, and prolongs [destruction],[20] putting clouds over clouds. Moreover, the Moon brings about a multitude of rain clouds. Finally, in the same way the Sun taints the atmosphere alternately: now with fire, now with clouds.[21]

§678. The significators (or [especially][22] the Moon) being individually in the regard of Mars, stir up thunder and send down lightning strikes. Moreover, Saturn as the author of this administration, even [indicates cold and][23] overturns buildings; [and when Mars, there will be cold.][24] [The judgment must be made analogously for all qualities.][25]

[Chapter 38.4: Other indicators]

§679. Furthermore, the moistening places of the circle seem to be worthy of consideration, because they multiply waters.[26] Moreover, the retrogradation of significators furnishes an overflowing of waters.

---

which rules the domicile opposite its own: Mercury to Jupiter, Venus to Mars, and the luminaries to Saturn. Here, al-Kindī says the *aspect* must be an opposition.
[17] This probably means the Ascendant of the founding of a city or country. See Part IV for a list of some cities' alleged Ascendants and founding charts. Perhaps it could include the annual Ascendant of the year at the Aries ingress, or some other epochal Ascendant.
[18] The Ar. only says that the Moon is applying to an inferior planet.
[19] Adding with the Ar.
[20] Adding with the Ar.
[21] Ar.: "air, and darkness."
[22] Adding with the Ar.
[23] Adding based on Robert and the Ar.
[24] Adding from the Ar. But this does not make sense, and we should read this as "heat." But this is not the only time in which the Arabic sources seem to report the wrong qualities: see 'Umar's Ch. 81, sentence 3, in Section I.5 below.
[25] Adding with Robert, mirroring the Ar.
[26] Apparently, if significators are in them. It is unclear as to whether al-Kindī means the rainy signs (see my Introduction for a table of these) or the rainy mansions (see *DMT* Ch. 6, in Section I.3 above).

§680. And[27] this happens at the hour of the Moon's separation from an indicator of [rain], and likewise at the hour of the inferiors' departure from the superior significators. [By separating from an indicator, it means] the lunar departure from the four principal [posts],[28] which tends to alternate and vary any quality of the air [from one] to another. The Sun's [standing] there [does] likewise, but more powerfully so the Moon.

§681. Furthermore,[29] the rest of the stars imitate the Sun in this, but not so manifestly nor with such effectiveness. For example, they operate their own effects in their own orbits [of the apogee and perigee] and the rest of their own places, just as the Sun does in corresponding places, even though they do it more secretly and known to fewer.

§682. Finally, a studious reader should not neglect to scrutinize this attentively: any [star] traversing in north [latitude][30] seems to enlarge the effects of its own peculiar signification and indication; also, in the south [it is] weaker. Moreover, ascending into the north is more powerful than if it is descending in the [north]. But declining in the south [is] more slack than if its ascent in [the south] would be happening.

Chapter 39: On years of plague & good health

§683. First of all, with the Ascendant of the year being placed,[31] then too will follow an awareness of the Ascendant of the assembly or opposition which precedes the Sun's ingress into Aries. And so, let those Ascendants and the Moon be made clean of the infortunes, and no less should the lord of the assembly or opposition appear free [of them]. An application of [that lord] having been made with the fortunate ones, or that same [lord] being in the regard of the Sun and Moon (or at least the one which obtains the shift), introduces a healthful year and one without disease.

§684. Moreover, the lords of the [two] Ascendants, and the Moon, and also the lord of the assembly or opposition (or the majority of them), being

---

[27] This paragraph is a *pastiche* of Robert, Hugo, and the Arabic. The Arabic, however, does not speak of the inferior planets separating, but only that the Moon's departure from the four principal quarters indicates changes in weather.

[28] That is, at the lunar quarters.

[29] Reading this paragraph with Robert.

[30] This is a conjecture of mine, which Burnett also shares. But it might also refer to declination.

[31] That is, the Ascendant of the chart of the Sun's ingress into Aries.

unfortunate and unlucky, convey the pestilence of disease, and this is agreed[32] to happen according to the manner and harshness of the corrupting [planet], and the nature of the infortune, and the place in which the corruption comes to be.

§685. Which if there would be an application of those which rule the Ascendants, and of the Moon (the aforesaid misfortune having been observed), with the lord of their eighth,[33] a plague is designated which will kill many. But if it happened otherwise, [it will kill] very few. Which if a manifold disease[34] is present, still it will oppress few.

§686. Furthermore,[35] these significators (or one of them), retreating from scorching, and applying with the lord of its own eighth, introduces a sudden kind of ruin but without disease. But if any lord of them would apply with it, once a signification of disease would already be had, the slowness of its natural course multiplies the disease and renders it long-lasting; but the quickness[36] of [its] course removes the steadiness of its long-lastingness.

[Latin al-Rijāl VIII.31.1]: And if the planet which was more supported among all of these significators, applied to the lord of its own eighth, many sudden deaths will occur, without any long sickness. And if the lord of the sixth house of any of these significators would apply to the [main] significator, there will be diseases with long infirmities. But[37] if the significators applied to the lords of their own sixth [houses], the infirmities will not be long.

§687. Which if this corruption would proceed from Mars, it generates hot[38] diseases, particularly [assuming] the quickness of his course, [and] he even being strong and dwelling in a hot and dry sign. But Saturn arriving as

---

[32] Reading *constat* for *constans*.
[33] That is, of the lords with the eighth from that Ascendant, or of the Moon with the eighth from her own position. See a similar treatment in §692 of Ch. 40 of *Forty Chapters*, and §403 of Ch. 11.6.
[34] Robert: "much and difficult." Al-Kindī could mean a serious illness that kills few, or perhaps many diseases that kill few.
[35] I have added the version from the 1485 al-Rijāl below, because it departs so radically from Hugo's version.
[36] Reading *celeritas* for *caelestis*.
[37] This sentence does not seem to appear in the Arabic.
[38] Reading with al-Rijāl for "acute."

the corruptor, indicates the steadiness of the disease, particularly [with him being] slow, strong, and arranged in a cold and dry sign.

SECTION I.5: 'UMAR AL-ṬABARĪ, *BOOK OF QUESTIONS*

Comment by Dykes. Following are six chapters from 'Umar's *Book of Questions in the Judgments of the Stars*,[1] Chs. 81-85, and 138. Bos and Burnett (pp. 433-48) edited and translated the Arabic of Chs. 81-85, as well as a parallel text by al-Kindī, from Tehran (pp. 421-33). The Latin al-Rijāl and the *Book of the Nine Judges* also have translated the same 'Umar material, but Bos and Burnett say (p. 422) that differences between the version in the al-Kindī text and the others suggests that 'Umar might have been transmitted in an eastern form (Tehran) and a western one (the rest).

My own translation is from the Latin al-Rijāl, but in consultation with the Arabic. In the table below, "+" means the source has more than just 'Umar in it, while "-" means it has something less than the full 'Umar chapter. For the sentence numbers, I have departed from Bos and Burnett's practice. They employ different letters and numbers based on which sentences are shared between 'Umar's Arabic and *DMT* Ch. 8, or other texts. Since all of my translations come directly from al-Rijāl, I will instead follow his sentence numbering. As with al-Kindī, the first sentence tends to be the title itself, so the chapters will begin with 2.

Text	Arabic (Bos & Burnett)	Tehran: *On Rains & Winds*	Latin al-Rijāl (1485)	*Nine Judges* (Dykes 2011)
Ch. 81	Ch. 81	*On Winds*	VIII.26	§Z.2
Ch. 82	Ch. 82	*On Rains +*	VIII.27 +	§Z.3
Ch. 83	Ch. 83	*On Winds*	VIII.28	§Z.4
Ch. 84	Ch. 84	*On Winds -*	VIII.29	§Z.5
Ch. 85	Ch. 85	*On Winds*	VIII.30 +	§Z.6
Ch. 138			VIII.32 +	§Z.7

In these chapters, 'Umar has all of the primary techniques we saw in al-Kindī and in my Introduction: New/Full Moon charts, a Lot of air and winds, the 20° Scorpio method, the opening of the doors, centers of the Moon, *etc.* Chapter 138 has extra information on floods which I confess I do not completely understand.

---

[1] I am using Sezgin's title (Sezgin, pp. 112 #2). Bos and Burnett use an alternative title which does not appear in Sezgin, a *Shortened Book of Questions* (*Mukhtasar al-Masa'il*).

ೞ   ೞ   ೞ

'Umar al-Tabari: *Book of Questions* Ch. 81:
On the knowledge of the weather, the times & seasons,
and how they effect change in heat & cold
(from al-Rijāl: *Book of the Skilled* VIII.26)

2 This will be known from [1] the place of the meeting or opposition[2] of the Sun and Moon, and from [2] the Ascendant of the meeting or prevention, which was before the entrance of the Sun into Aries, and from [3] the place of the luminaries in the figure (and likewise from the places of the planets).[3]

3 Whence, if you found Saturn in one of the stakes from the Ascendant, or in any of the stakes from the lord of the Ascendant, [Saturn] being firm in that same place, in any of his own dignities (and especially in the stake of the Midheaven), it signifies diversity in the air, harm, and darkness, and in a time of heat it diminishes[4] the heat, and in a time of cold it makes great cold. **4** And if he were remote from the stakes, the seasons will be stable and even, just like they should be. **5** However, if Saturn were in the stakes from the lord of the Ascendant,[5] his signification will be less and weaker than when he will be in the stakes from the Ascendant.

6 And if Mars were in that very status which we stated with respect to Saturn, and especially in the stake of the Midheaven, heat will be increased in a time of heat, and cold will be diminished in a time of cold;[6] and spring and autumn will incline towards heat.

---

[2] Burnett's 'Umar and the Tehran al-Kindī only have the meeting or conjunction, but Hugo agrees with the Latin al-Rijāl.

[3] I have put this last part in parentheses, because they are not explicitly stated in 'Umar's Arabic but are obviously relevant in what follows.

[4] I am reading with al-Rijāl here, who agrees with the Tehran al-Kindī *On Rains* (*kasara*, "it breaks"). Burnett reads *kathrah*, "abundance." But this does not make astrological sense, and throws off the parallels with Mars below. Because Saturn naturally signifies cold, he should diminish heat and increase cold.

[5] Burnett's 'Umar makes this the angles of the Ascendant itself, not its lord; but the Tehran al-Kindī and Hugo affirm it is the lord of the Ascendant, which makes more astrological sense: for 'Umar has already said the angles of the Ascendant will be powerful in their signification.

[6] Reading with the Tehran al-Kindī and Hugo; Burnett's 'Umar has the cold increasing, not decreasing.

7 And if Jupiter or Venus or the Moon[7] were in the manner which we said, they make the air fit, and temper [it], and make it be of a good complexion, and [make] what is sown and planted, sprout and grow.

8 And look likewise at Mercury: because if you found him in the Midheaven from the Ascendant of the meeting,[8] and he were in any of the airy signs, and any of the infortunes were in any of the stakes of Mercury himself,[9] it signifies diversity in the air, and many damaging winds. **9** And you will judge in this way if you found any of the infortunes[10] in the angles from Mercury, and Mercury [were] in an angle from the fortune: because this is worth as much as if the infortunes[11] are in the sign of the meeting.[12]

[The significator with Mars or Saturn]

10 Whence, whatever planet you found in the stakes from the Ascendant of the meeting (or in [its] succeedents), make that one a significator.

11 Afterwards, inspect to see what kind of commixtures it has with Saturn and Mars: and if you found it to be mixed with Mars from the square or from the opposition or assembly, and Mars were in one of the fiery signs, heat will increase in a time of heat, and cold will be decreased in a time of cold. **12** And if the aspect were from the trine or sextile, and Mars [were] in the fiery signs, it signifies what we said, but not so much.

13 But if the significator-planet had a commixture with Saturn[13] from the square or from the opposition or assembly, and Saturn were in the cold and dry signs, or in the cold and moist signs, cold increases in a season of cold, and heat is diminished in a season of heat. **14** And if the aspect were from the trine or sextile, and Saturn [were] in the signs which we said before, it signifies what we said before, but not so much. **15** And if Saturn were in the hot and moist signs (which are Gemini and its triplicity), and he had a com-

---

7 The Ar. has all of them doing this, but 'Umar might mean "any one" of them being in such a condition.

8 That is, the conjunction or New Moon (but we should probably follow al-Rijāl in adding the New Moon).

9 Burnett's 'Umar and Hugo put the infortune in the same angular place as Mercury, not merely in any of the angles of Mercury.

10 Reading *infortunarum* with Burnett and Hugo, for the Latin al-Rijāl's *fortunatarum*.

11 Again, reading *infortunae* with Burnett and Hugo, for *fortunae*.

12 I do not understand this last sentence: how could an infortune harming Mercury by square, but Mercury being related to other fortunes, be in any way related to an infortune being in sign of the conjunction itself?

13 The Ar. specifically mentions a "connection," indicating a degree-based aspect.

mixture with the significator from the opposition or square or assembly, it signifies that the air will be tempered and of a good complexion. **16** And if this commixture were from the trine or sextile, with [Saturn] appearing in the signs we said before, the signification will be greater, and of greater [proper] mixture,[14] and a better complexion. **17** And likewise, if Mars had a commixture with the significator, and he were in the cold, dry signs, or the cold and moist signs, and the commixture were from the square or opposition or conjunction, it tempers the air and makes it be of a good complexion and manner. **18** And if the aspect were from the trine or sextile, with [Mars] appearing in the aforesaid signs, the tempering will be greater and every thing which sprouts and is generated will increase.

[The Lot of air and winds]

19 And help yourself in this with the Lot of air and winds, and make it be a partner with the significator.[15] **20** And if you found Saturn or Mars with the Lot or its lord,[16] judge from them just as we said before about their appearance in the stakes and in the aspects of the significator. **21** For you will take this Lot from the degree of Mercury (if he were not in his own house) up to the degree of the lord of the house in which he is, and add on top of this the degrees of the Ascendant, and project from the Ascendant:[17] and where the number is ended, there is the Lot. **22** And if Mercury were in his own house, take his own degrees, adding the degrees of the Ascendant to them, and projecting from the Ascendant: and where [the counting] applied to, there is the Lot. **23** And you will do the same at the entrances of the Sun in the quarters (which are Aries, Libra, Cancer, and Capricorn). **24** You will do likewise at the entrance of the Sun into each of the twelve signs.

---

[14] *Temperiei.*
[15] This sentence differs greatly among the authors. The Tehran al-Kindī says to consult the Lot "with these indications"; Hugo says that this Lot's testimonies "resemble the significators" mentioned above; Burnett's ʿUmar says to consult the Lot "and the partners of these indicators." To my mind, al-Rijāl's reading here is the clearest and most natural.
[16] Reading with Burnett's ʿUmar and the Tehran al Kindī for al-Rijāl's "their lords."
[17] Burnett's ʿUmar reads, "subtract."

[Interpolation: Abū Ma'shar's Lot of days][18]

7:L6 And Abū Ma'shar spoke of another Lot [although it does not belong in this book],[19] which is called the Lot of days: and it is taken on any day from the degree of the Sun up to the degree of Saturn, and is projected from the degree of the Moon when the Sun arises on any day. **7** Whence, if Mercury aspected this Lot or he were with it in one place, say that on that day there will be wind; **8** and the judgment will be nailed down more if the Moon were with him, and if Venus had any commixture there, it will be more.

7:L9 There is another way of judging by the days: determine the Ascendant at the hour in which the Moon enters the first minute of a sign, and look to see which [planet] aspects the Ascendant: you should take that as the significator, and judge by that one[20] as long as the Moon was in that sign, and you will find what you wanted, by God.

'Umar al-Tabarī: *Book of Questions* Ch. 82:
On the knowledge of rain, thunder, lightning, & winds
(from al-Rijāl: *Book of the Skilled* VIII.27 [part])

2 You[21] will know this from the entrance of the Sun into 20° and one minute[22] of Scorpio. **3** Whence, determine the Ascendant, the stakes, and the planets at that hour, and afterwards look at Venus, Jupiter, and Mercury. **4** And if you found all three to be western, [slow], or retrograde, judge that in that year there will be many rains and moistures. **5** And if you found them to be eastern or direct or of a great course,[23] it signifies that in that year there will be few rains and moistures.

---

[18] What follows is a later interpolation, which corresponds to *DMT* Ch. 7:L 6-9 (lines labeled as such here). 'Umar was dead by the time Abū Ma'shar's astrological career was getting underway, so 'Umar could not have written this himself.

[19] Adding based on the Arabic. According to Bos and Burnett, this Lot is the second of those listed in Abū Ma'shar's *Kitab al-Sirr* ("Book of the Secret"). See my list of Lots of rain and wind in Section I.1.

[20] That is, according to the typical weather patterns it suggests.

[21] Burnett continues the line numbering from the previous chapter, even though the Arabic clearly labels this as a new one.

[22] Or rather, once he enters 20° exactly (Ar., "to the minute"), because then he will be in the first minute of that degree.

[23] That is, moving quickly.

6 Afterwards, look at Mars: and if you found him in one of the stakes, and especially in the Midheaven, in any of the airy signs, and he had some commixture with Mercury, it signifies thunderings in that year, lightning flashes, damaging and strong rains which come at one hour and then afterwards withdraw; and it signifies locusts and harm in the atmosphere. **7** And if Mars were in any of the earthy signs, in the stake of the earth, and the fortunes were cadent from[24] [him] and he had a commixture with Mercury, it signifies earthquakes and the appearance of fires from the earth,[25] and terrifying things, and loss in minerals and earth which has sulphur in it. **8** And if Mars were in the stake of the earth in fiery signs, it signifies the burning of the earth,[26] and all things properly belonging to the earth are harmed,[27] and minerals, and the harvests will be harmed and burnt. **9** And if Mars were in the stake of the earth in a watery sign, it signifies diminishment for waters, and loss in all of that which is of animals and other things.[28] **10** And if the fortunes had a commingling with him,[29] they diminish and block the harm of thunder and lightning flashes in that year. **11** And if the fortunes had no commixture with him, thunder and lightning flashes will make losses in that year, and there will be many rays [of lightning].

12 And if Saturn were in the role of Mars in this, and he were in the Midheaven, and in one of the airy signs, and he had a commixture with Mercury, and the fortunes were remote from[30] him, it signifies harm in the atmosphere, and many damaging and lasting rains, and they will not be cut short. **13** And if Saturn were in the stake of the earth just as we said before, and in earthy signs, and he had a commixture with Mercury, and the fortunes were remote from him, earthquakes will happen, and black waters and the like will appear above the earth.[31] **14** And if he were in the watery signs and in the stake of the earth, and the fortunes were remote from him, and he had a commixture with Mercury, waters in wells will be diminished, and every thing which spends time in the water (in terms of animals and other things) is

---

[24] Reading with the Ar. and Hugo, for "supported/strengthened" (*appodeatae*).
[25] Reading with the Ar. and Hugo, for "in the air."
[26] Reading with the Ar. for a bit of garbling and confusion between air and earth in the Latin.
[27] The Ar. specifically mentions precious stones.
[28] That is, of those things which live on or near the water.
[29] The Ar. specifically mentions a connection, i.e. a degree-based aspect.
[30] That is, "in aversion."
[31] That is, such water will appear from out of the earth and be on the surface.

harmed. **15** And if he were in the fiery[32] signs under the earth, and the fortunes remote from him, and he had a commixture with Mercury, it signifies harm on the land and what properly belongs to it, and in minerals.[33] **16** And if Mercury did not have a commixture with him, the aforesaid significations will however be less and easier. **17** And if he did have the commixture of the fortunes, mix the significations of the year, and they will be more temperate, and the loss and evil which we said before will be diminished.

18 You[34] should know that every one of the higher planets has one state, and the lower planets have another;[35] wherefore the higher ones are like spirits, and the lower ones are bodies, and no generating comes to be in the world except through the application and commixture of them, one with another, and of the superiors with the inferiors. **19** And God has ordained it thus, and wills it through his authority.

'Umar al-Tabarī: *Book of Questions* Ch. 83:
On the knowledge of the opening of the door: the rain, winds,
heat & cold, every individual door in its own door
(from al-Rijāl: *Book of the Skilled* VIII.28)

2 When you wished to know the opening of the doors for rains or winds, or heat or cold—any of these in the season appropriate for it—and the season were fit for receiving that thing, look at the Moon. **3** And if you found her separating herself from Venus and applying to Mars, or separating from Mars and applying to Venus, that is the opening of the doors. **4** And if you found her separating herself from Jupiter and applying to Mercury, or separating from Mercury and applying to Jupiter, it is likewise an opening of the

---

[32] Reading with the Ar. for "earthy."
[33] This also includes precious stones, as above.
[34] Bos and Burnett (pp. 383-84) suggest that this passage may be originally from Māshā'allāh's *Letter on Rains & Winds*, **32** (Section I.7).
[35] The Ar. speaks as though each superior planet has a "bond" with a lower one. This is probably through the opposition of their domiciles as with the "opening of the doors" in the next chapter.

doors. **5** And if you found her applying to Saturn, and she[36] has a separation from the planets (or not), it is likewise an opening of the doors.[37]

6 To the extent that it happens with the aforesaid things,[38] look at the Moon to see if she were in any of the aforesaid openings, by taking in addition what there is of the foundations: the matter which is signified is made certain, whether it is rain, wind, heat, or cold.

7 And look to see if you found the Moon in a moist sign, applying to a moist planet, even if there is not an opening of the doors there: because then you could have trust in rain.

'Umar al-Tabarī: *Book of Questions* Ch. 84:
On the knowledge of the foundations[39]
(from al-Rijāl: *Book of the Skilled* VIII.29)

2 If the Moon were with the Sun in one minute, it is a foundation; and when she is in 12° from him, it is a foundation; and when she is in 45° from him, it is a foundation; and when she is in 90° from him, it is a foundation;[40] and when she is in 135° from him, it is a foundation; and when she is in 168°, it is a foundation; and when she is in 180°, it is a foundation; and when she is in 192°, it is a foundation; [and that point is the undoing of the knot.][41] and when she is in 225°, it is a foundation; and when she is in 270°, it is a foundation;[42] and if she were in 315°, it is a foundation; and if she were in 348°, it is a foundation. **3** And after that they are conjoined and are made fit for another turn. **4** Whence, look to see if something of a foundation is made certain with one of the openings of the doors, and judge according to its nature. **5** Afterwards, determine the Ascendant of the meeting or prevention,

---

[36] Reading with the Ar. for "Saturn." Since the Moon's domicile (Cancer) is opposite one of Saturn, she cannot separate from herself.

[37] Ibn Labban (see I.8 below) has a more natural reading, which he is evidently getting from 'Umar: that we look at "the Moon's separation from Saturn, since Capricorn is in opposition to Cancer."

[38] This phrase is very close to Hugo, suggesting that he and al-Rijāl were using a common manuscript transmission for 'Umar that differed from those used by Burnett.

[39] That is, the "centers" of the Moon.

[40] 'Umar's Ar. uses a word derived from Persian, meaning "half-full" (i.e., the first lunar quarter).

[41] Adding based on the Ar.

[42] 'Umar: it is the second phase of being half-full.

and look at the Ascendant of the meeting or prevention, and[43] look at the lord of the seventh sign (from whichever one of the two you determine it). **6** And if you found an application or aspect between them,[44] or a transfer[45] of light or a collection or reception, and[46] the Moon were in the openings or in a foundation which we said before, judge that there will be rains at that time (in a time of rains), or cold in a time of cold, heat in a time of heat, and wind in a time of wind.

7 However, what confirms the significations of the Moon is that Venus and Mercury would be western, or retrograde, or of a slow motion, or that some planet (or two) of the higher ones would be retrograde or of a slow motion: **8** because then there will be rain, without a doubt.

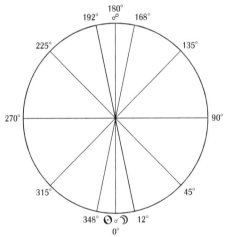

Figure 31: 'Umar's centers of the Moon (Ch. 84)

---

[43] The rest of this sentence is based on Burnett's emendation from al-Kindī. The Latin al-Rijāl is garbled and unclear.
[44] That is, between the lords of the Ascendant and the seventh of the chart cast for the time of the conjunction or prevention.
[45] Reading with the Tehran al-Kindī and al-Rijāl, for 'Umar's and Hugo's "returning."
[46] 'Umar's Ar. reads "or," but the Tehran al-Kindī also says "and."

'Umar al-Tabarī: *Book of Questions* Ch. 85:
On the knowledge of the time of rain
(from al-Rijāl: *Book of the Skilled* VIII.30 [part])

2 Look at the significator of rain:[47] and if you found it entering one of the stakes from the Ascendant at the hour which I told you that you should determine for knowing rains (and that is from the entrance of the Sun into 20° and one minute of Scorpio),[48] and it aspects the planets which signified rains in that year, and if they were received by it (and particularly by the Moon, when it was conjoined with her or was in the square or opposition),[49] there will be rain on that day. 3 And if it were without reception, there will be rain, but not so much. 4 And if the significator were in a stake just as we said before, and it were joined bodily with the Moon, it signifies thunder, lightning flashes, earthquakes, and the like.

'Umar al-Tabarī: *Book of Questions* Ch. 138:
On the knowledge of conflicts, wars, burnings, & submersions
(from al-Rijāl: *Book of the Skilled* VIII.32 [first part])[50]

2 Know that if the Moon was in the joining,[51] and it was in the twelfth, in a hot sign, and they both are being connected to an unlucky planet under the earth, then judge that on that day, in that country, a tribulation takes place.

3 And likewise, if they were falling [in this way] at the middle of the day, connecting with an infortune under the earth, [and] they were falling [in a watery sign],[52] judge and decree a submersion at that same time.

---

[47] 'Umar's Arabic specifically states that this is the lord of the Ascendant of the year (which is probably the lord of the Ascendant for the chart of the Sun's ingress), but the other texts do not mention it. Moreover, in 'Umar's Ch. 81, the significator was said to be any planet in an angle from the Ascendant in the chart of the conjunction or opposition of the luminaries.

[48] See 'Umar's Ch. 82 above.

[49] For the opposition here, 'Umar reads "or receives it." The Arabic words for opposition and reception are very close.

[50] I have translated sentences 2-5 directly from al-Rijāl's Arabic, as the Latin al-Rijāl is confused in several ways.

[51] Al-ḥāq, that is, the conjunction with the Sun at the New Moon.

[52] Adding based on a similar statement in Hugo, which accounts for the watery event (just as the fiery sign does for fire, below).

4 And likewise, if the Moon was in the joining and they both were connecting to an unlucky planet under the earth in a fiery sign, decree that places
in that country will be burned, and it will be in that time when the lights are
in the twelfth and the ninth;[53] except that if they both are located in the
twelfth, the misfortune will be at the beginning of the day; and if they are
located in the ninth, the misfortune is at the end of the day.

5 And if she was in the joining in the evening, decree that the tribulation
takes place at the passing of the day.

6 And if the Moon were in the conjunction [while] descending southern
[or] descending in the circle (I want to say that she is in Libra or Scorpio),[54]
diminished in light and number, and she had all of these misfortunes without
the aspect of any fortune, judge that burning or a quarrel or an earthquake
will happen in the city in that hour, and perhaps this evil will befall many
cities.

7 And you should know that if both infortunes will be joined with the Tail
in Aries, the mishaps will happen in small beasts and in the nobles;[55] and
judge in this manner through all of the other signs.

8 And if they will be joined in Virgo, the mishap will be in crops, and this
in those things which are of the form of men. **9** And you will recognize the
signs, because Aries is at the beginning of the eat, and Leo in the middle of
the east, and Sagittarius at the end of the east; and Taurus is after the east,[56]
and likewise its triplicity according to what we have said about Aries; and
Gemini is at the beginning of the west, with its triplicity likewise in this manner.[57]

10 And consider when the Sun enters Aries, [to see] which planet was
eastern, or which were more quickly eastern:[58] because that one will be the

---

[53] That is, if the time of the New Moon put them in the twelfth or ninth, as in the previous sentences.

[54] 'Umar means that she is decreasing in declination, since she would be moving from the
northern signs into the southern ones.

[55] Small beasts, because Aries signifies small quadrupeds; nobles, because the fiery signs
are known as the "royal" signs, and signify people of higher rant.

[56] That is, in the south. 'Umar is moving from the east, to the south, to the west—and
then omits the north.

[57] See Hugo's version in *Judges* §Z.7, and an alternate form based on finding fugitives in
Judges §7.123 and al-Bīrūnī §357. In general, fiery signs indicate the east, airy ones the west,
watery ones the north, and earthy ones the south.

[58] This seems to mean, "which one is outside of the rays and rises before the Sun, or the
one which *will* be out of the rays in such a position, sooner." But it is possible that he
would allow planets coming out of the rays on the setting side of the Sun (i.e., rising after
the Sun, being in later zodiacal degrees).

significator of the year. **11** Because if Jupiter were eastern, it signifies goodness, improvement, and the good of the year. **12** And if Venus, it signifies fertility and good things for sale. **13** And if Mercury were eastern, the year will be mediocre. **14** And if Saturn were eastern, provisions will be dear, and there will be great cold. **15** And if Mars were eastern, there will be quarrels, complications, and burnings.

16 Likewise, look to see when the Sun enters any of the quarters: because that planet which was eastern, will be the significator of that quarter, according to this way. **17** Look[59] also at the connection of the Moon to the Sun, and decree according to their relationship.[60]

---

[59] I have translated this sentence directly from Arabic.

[60] Reading as *al-walā'*, which seems to mean simply the New Moons (and perhaps the Full Moons, too). But it is possible that al-Rijāl means *al-walā*, the "manager" of them (i.e., the sect light).

SECTION I.6: MĀSHĀ'ALLĀH / JIRJIS: CHAPTER ON THE RAINS IN THE YEAR

Comment by Dykes. This is my own translation of the Arabic *Chapter on the Rains in the Year*, attributed to Māshā'allāh. Although many of the statements here differ from his *Letter* (Section I.7 below), many of the methods and themes are the same: the Scorpio ingress (or more likely, 20° Scorpio), the Aries and other quarterly ingresses, focusing on the lord of the Ascendant and the lord of the bound of the Ascendant, Moon-Mercury-Venus lore, and New (and perhaps Full) Moon charts.

This material is also paralleled in two other texts: the "Dorotheus" and Jirjis Sections on weather in Hugo of Santalla's *The Book of the Nine Judges*. The Jirjis passage below has some other related sentences not clearly identical with those here, and I have added sentence numbers to Jirjis to show how it relates to Māshā'allāh's *Chapter*. The following table shows the parallels:

Chapter On Rains	"Dorotheus"	Jirjis
§1	§Z.10	
§2	§Z.11	
§3	§Z.12	
§4	§Z.13	
§5	§Z.13	§Z.14

℘ ℘ ℘

A CHAPTER ON THE RAINS IN THE YEAR
from the sayings of Māshā'allāh

2 If you wanted to learn the abundance of the rain and its scarcity, or is the rain the most abundant at the beginning of the year or at the end, [then] see when the Sun entered Scorpio,[1] [and] look at Venus, [to see] whether she was rising eastern in the early mornings: the beginning of the year was scarce in rain, and the end is abundant in rain. **3** And if she was western, in front of

---

[1] Or rather, 20° Scorpio.

the Sun, the beginning of winter[2] was abundant in rain. **4** And know [that] if Venus was with the Sun in a sign, the rain in the year was most abundant in the month in which they meet in it. **5** And she is like the woman when she is under the man, bringing down his water.

6 Then look: if you wanted knowledge of the abundance of rain and its scarcity, look to see when the Sun has entered the first minute of Aries, [and] erect the Ascendant at the hour he arrives at the beginning of the sign. **7** Then see how many degrees of it are arising, [and] take the lord of [the] portion[3] of the degree of the Ascendant. **8** Then erect the four stakes, and know that[4] the lord of the portion of the Ascendant is the lord of the year for rain.

9 Then look at the lord of the year: does it connect with Venus or Mercury, and is it gathered with one of them in a sign? **10** Then look at the Ascendant: is it of the signs of water, or is it not? **11** When you have established this firmly, look at the position of Venus and the Moon and Mercury, and if you have found these planets in signs of water, and you have found the Moon to be connecting with them, and she is not connecting with one of the infortunes: the rain was abundant in that year.

12 And if you found Mercury made unfortunate by Mars, and[5] he is under the rays, and you found the Moon to be connecting with Mercury, know that the rains decrease at the beginning of the year, and increases at the middle of it. **13** And the rains are with thunder and lightning, and the corruption of the atmosphere, and an abundance of winds.

14 And if you found Venus to be connecting[6] with Mars or under the rays, then the rain decreased [that whole year].[7]

15 And if you found Mercury to be connecting with Saturn and the Moon to be connecting with Mercury or with Saturn, then it is a statement that the rains are increasing at the beginning of the year, and it increases the calamity[8] of the air, and [its] corruption.

---

[2] Bos and Burnett (p. 376) suggest that this should read "year." But Māshā'allāh's *Letter*, sentences **60** and **64** (Section I.6) also clearly say "winter."
[3] *Juz'*. Below, Māshā'allāh clarifies that this is the bound lord of the Ascendant.
[4] Reading *'inna* for *'in*.
[5] This should probably read, "or," just as with Venus below.
[6] This should probably be understood in terms of being made unfortunate by him, as with Mercury above.
[7] Tentatively reading for the Ar., which actually says, "in the knowledge of all of it."
[8] Tentatively reading *ṭāmmah* for *ṭalmah*. Hugo reads, "with a density of clouds being made, and the corruption of the air."

16 And if you found Jupiter in a sign of water, and Venus and the Moon connecting with him, judge with respect to the safety of the rain and its abundance. **17** And if you found [him] in a sign of fire,[9] and Mars is being connected with him, judge with respect to the scarcity of rain in that year.

18 Then, look at the lord of the bound of the Ascendant, which is the lord of the year, and [see] if it was in the stakes, [applying to the fortunate ones]:[10] truly[11] that year indicates rains at its beginning and end. **19** And if you found the lord of the year made unfortunate by Mars, or Mars was with it in the sign, indeed[12] it reduces the rains at its beginning and its end.

20 With all of your effort, if you found the lord of the year with Venus and the Moon, connected with Mars, then indeed the clouds and the winds increase and the rain decreases. **21** And if the sign in which the lord of the year gathers with Venus is of the signs of air, and the Moon is connected with Mars, say the air is corrupted by moisture [which is] not from rain. **22** And if you found Venus to be connected with Saturn, or the Moon was connected with Saturn, say indeed that the dew and the fog increases until it is similar to rain, and they burden the earth in that year from that moisture [which is] not from rain.

23 Then, look at the lord of the year, which is the lord of the bound of the Ascendant: and if it was Mercury, and he was made unfortunate, then truly the rains decrease and increase in that year, with corruption from the winds and clouds. **24** And if the lord of the year was Jupiter, and he was made unfortunate by one of the infortunes, then the rains decrease and there is no corruption in the atmosphere and the winds, as there was with the corruption of Mercury. **25** And if Venus was the lord of the year, and she was made unfortunate by Mars, or were under the rays, then the fog and moisture increase on the earth, from what is not rain. **26** And if the lord of the year was Mars, the dew and the rains and the clouds decrease. **27** And if it was Saturn, the rains decrease and fog increases.

28 And truly[13] it was these three planets (which are the Moon and Venus and Mercury) which were the planets which indicate the increase of rain and its scarcity. **29** And the connection of the fortunes and the infortunes, [is]

---

[9] Reading with *Judges*. Della Vida's Arabic reads, "of plants."
[10] Adding based on *Judges*; the Arabic has a lacuna indicated by Della Vida.
[11] Reading as *'inna*.
[12] Reading as the particle *fa-*, for Della Vida's *qa-* (i.e., *fa-qallala* for *qa-qallala*).
[13] Reading *'inna* instead of *'in*.

what blocks the rains (of the planets, [they are] the Sun and Mars and Saturn, unless if Saturn was in a sign of rains).

§2: A chapter on the knowledge of the rains in the quarters of the year

31 See when the Sun has entered the first minute of [Cancer or][14] Libra or Capricorn, and then erect the Ascendant and preserve [in your memory] the stakes which I have instructed you [to do] for that, and the Ascendant of that sign. **32** And see where Venus and Mercury and the Moon are, in that quarter, and with whom they have connected. **33** And see where the position of Mars is in every quarter, and the connection of these planets. **34** Then judge these planets, [and] then judge each one of these with respect to the topic of dew and rains and clouds and fog and winds; and when you judge what you want, if you discovered the first connection of some with the others, look in it as you looked at the beginning of the year, God willing. **35** And the Sun, when he enters Libra, judges as to what there is in this quarter up to when he begins in Capricorn (and that is the autumn). **36** And if he came to Capricorn, erect the Ascendant at the hour he enters Capricorn (or Aries), just as I demonstrated to you at the beginning of the year, God willing.

§3: A chapter on the knowledge of the year at the meeting and the opposition

38 If you wanted knowledge of the rains in every month, look at the hour of the meeting of the Sun and Moon in one degree, or the hour [when] the Sun opposes the degree of the Moon: and this is when the Moon moves in the seventh sign from the Sun, when [it is in] the degree of the Sun. **39** Erect the Ascendant of that hour just as you erect the Ascendant of every month, and indeed from it you will learn what there is. **40** Then, look at the Moon: and if you found her to be connecting with Venus or with Mercury, there is rain in that month. **41** And if you wanted a correction of that,[15] if the Moon reached the stakes and a connection with Venus or with Mercury, there is rain on that day—unless the Moon is being connected with Mars at the beginning of the [lunar] month: [because] if it

---

[14] Added by Dykes.
[15] That is, if you want a more exact prediction.

was like that, the thunder and flashing and winds increase, and the rain decreases until she reaches the opposition; and it is not rooted[16] in that half.

42 If you found the Moon to be connecting with the fortunes when she withdraws from the Sun, the rains are abundant after this half [of the lunar month]. **43** And the position of the meeting of the Sun and Moon, and their opposition, falls to you:[17] and it is that half of the month until the time when you erect the Ascendant at every half of a month.

44 And if you learn what there is in terms of rains in every half, then if you found the Moon to be connecting with Saturn when she withdraws from the meeting or opposition, and Venus was connecting with Saturn, in a rainy sign,[18] know that the rains increase at that meeting and opposition, unless Saturn is in a sign of fire.

45 And if you found Mars to be already [in] a connection with Saturn, then truly the clouds increase and the winds increase, and the rain decreases, and it corrupts the atmosphere from what is not dew, but [rather] what it does not receive with that,[19] and the rains decrease in that meeting and opposition.

§4: The rains in the days

47 If you wanted knowledge of rain, as to which day of that half of the month it is, then connect the Moon from a sign, and if she entered one of the stakes and is connected with Mercury or Venus or with the planet which was connected with her at the beginning of the month, and she entered one of the signs of water, and [there is] a connection with these planets which I mentioned to you, rain occurs[20] on that day, God willing.

---

[16] Treating *ʾaslan* as an adverb. As I have translated it, Māshāʾallāh seems to mean that the rain will decrease until it is not supported at all after the Full Moon. But Hugo understands this to mean that the opposition or Full Moon provides a new opportunity (and a new chart) for judging rain in the second half.

[17] Ar. *wa-ʾasqaṭa ʿanka.*

[18] It is unclear to me exactly which planets must be in signs of rain, although Hugo certainly reads it as being Saturn.

[19] Reading the Ar. as *ʾillā mā lā tanālu.* This last clause seems to be redundant, and Hugo omits it.

[20] Reading *jarī* for *jā.*

§5: A chapter on rain for every day at the entrance of the Moon [into] the rainy signs

49 Know that the rainy signs are Cancer and Scorpio, and Aquarius, and Pisces; and the most intense planets for rain are Venus and the Moon.

50 And if Venus was in one of these rainy signs, and Venus was at the beginning of the sign or the middle, then the Moon has passed [through] the rainy signs and has connected with Venus, it indicates rain on that day, and the rains gush forth[21] until the country is floating from the abundance of rains.

51 And if Venus and Mercury were in the watery signs, and the Moon passed through the watery signs, and was connected with one of those two, and she was at the end of the sign, it indicates an abundance of rain, but it is less than [at] the beginning.

52 And if you found the Moon and Venus in the rainy signs, and Mercury was not in the rainy signs, it indicates rains.

53 And if the Moon and Mercury approached the rainy signs, and Venus was in not-rainy signs, it indicates rain.

54 And if the Moon was at the beginning of the rainy signs, and she connected with Venus and Mercury, or it was[22] in the sign in which the Moon [herself] was, it indicates the duration of the rain until the Moon departs from it.

55 And Venus and Mercury and the Moon, if they did not connect with the infortunes, and the infortunes were not gathered[23] with them in the signs, it indicates rains on that day.

56 And if they were connected with the infortunes, or they were [present] with the [two infortunes], they indicate the holding back[24] of the rains.

57 And Venus and Mercury and the Moon, if they entered in the signs of rains, they indicate rains on that day.

58 And Venus, if she was with the Moon and Mercury in a sign, or gathered[25] with Mercury and the Moon, she indicates rains on that day.

---

[21] Reading *tanbuᶜu* for *tantabᶜu*.

[22] Ar. *kāna*. I take this to mean that "the situation" takes place in the Moon's sign, but this would obviously require that Venus or Mercury or both would be there, too.

[23] Ar. *mujmaᶜāni*. I take this to be equivalent to being "assembled" together in the same sign.

[24] Ar. ᵓ*iḥtirās*. The idea is literally that the rains are being guarded—that is, kept from us.

[25] In this case, I am not sure what distinction Māshā'allāh is trying to draw between being with them in the same sign, and being "gathered" there.

59 Mercury and Venus, if one of them was in Capricorn, and the Moon in Taurus or Scorpio or Pisces, it indicates rain on that day.

60 And if the Moon was in Taurus or Virgo or Capricorn, and she connected with Venus or with Mercury from an opposition, it indicates rain: and that is strongest if the Moon was with the Tail of the Dragon in one sign.

61 If the Moon was in Taurus with the Tail, and the Moon departing from Saturn, and Venus and Mars were in Aquarius, and Mercury in Pisces or Capricorn, it indicates rains, God willing.

೮ ೮ ೞ

Judges §Z.14: On rains—Jirjis

Therefore, whenever the Sun enters a turning sign,[26] Venus being in a watery sign, regarded by a Moon that is traversing outside a watery one, it suggests moderate rainstorms at that time. But [the Moon] regarding from a watery sign portends their excess.

Or otherwise: with the Sun wandering through the eighteenth[27] degree of Scorpio, Venus in watery [signs], generates rains to the level of flooding.[28] She appearing in a moist sign, middling [rains]; in a dry one, moderate ones. Moreover, the Moon dropping off from Mars means rains on that day, especially in a watery sign.

49 But through individual days, the determination will be through the signs which are devoted to rainstorms (but they are Cancer, Scorpio, Aquarius and Leo, especially Aquarius and Leo).

49/50 Moreover, the stars significative of rains are Venus, Mercury, and the Moon (especially Venus and Mercury. Venus occupying any of the aforesaid [signs],[29] while she lingers at the end or middle of the sign, moreover should the Moon apply to Venus while [the Moon is] crossing through watery signs, it means an excess of rains on that day.

---

[26] That is, his quarterly ingresses into the movable signs.
[27] This should probably be 20° Scorpio, as with the earlier accounts. But medieval texts are often unclear as to cardinal and ordinal numbers, so this might refer to the Sun's ingress into 19° Scorpio.
[28] *Submersionem.* Technically this should be "drowning," but that does not seem quite right here.
[29] The signs just mentioned.

51 Moreover, Venus and Mercury, while they walk through signs of that kind, and likewise the Moon applying to either one, and it[30] holding onto the end of a sign, conveys rains, but less than the prior ones [just described].

52 Moreover, the Moon and Venus in watery signs, with Mercury being removed from [the watery signs], has a judgment of rains.

53 Nor is it otherwise while Mercury and the Moon would reach signs of this kind, even though Venus is not walking through a rainy sign.

54 Moreover, the Moon being in those same signs, applying to Venus and Mercury (while they step in similar [signs] or traverse with her), renew rains until the Moon is separated from them.

---

[30] As in §Z.13, I am not sure whether this is the Moon or one of the others, but they would all have to be there for the application to perfect.

SECTION I.7: MĀSHĀ'ALLĀH, *LETTER ON RAINS & WINDS*

Comment by Dykes. This is an updated translation of a *Letter on Rains & Winds* attributed to Māshā'allāh, which originally appeared in my *Works of Sahl & Māshā'allāh* (2008). For my primary text I used the edition by Šangin in *CCAG* XII (pp. 210-16), but found it very valuable to have Paris BN lat. 7316a (69v-71v), which often gave better readings. In the introduction to Paris, the medieval Latin translator names himself as being an Amagro Drogone (or perhaps, Amagrus Drogo in the nominative). Šangin suggests (p. 210) that the Latin translator was John of Spain (Johannes Hispalensis), but this does not explain the attribution to Amagro/Amagrus.

The *Letter* is not very well organized, sometimes taking up a new topic and then returning to a previous one. Occasionally the details are incomprehensible, perhaps based on Arabic idioms or expressions that are garbled in translation. Much of the opening material is devoted to the opening of the doors, starting with a long passage focusing on the Moon and Saturn (**1-26**), and then describing the pairing of Mercury-Jupiter, with only a gesture at Venus-Mars. Other material includes the 20° Scorpio method, ingress charts, and much lore about Moon-Mercury-Venus combinations, as we also find in his *Chapter on Rains in the Year* (Section I.6 above). In a couple of places Māshā'allāh suggests that these rules may also apply to horary questions about weather, but he might simply mean that a client is asking a question about what an *ingress chart* is telling us. Finally, at the very end he mentions two fixed stars and appears to refer to lunar mansions (*casā*), but these amount to only two barely-developed sentences. This may be typical of Māshā'allāh, as we know from his *Chapter on Rains* that he is not very much interested in mansions or fixed stars.

ᛒᛜ   ᛤᛜ   ᛣᛉ

1 Māshā'allāh said: Inspect the inferior planets and the portions of their heavens; and you should know that the heaven of the Moon is extended up to the heaven of Saturn, and the Moon takes from him, and she allots much with respect to dews and hail, and the Moon receives the vapor of the earth.[1] **2** Therefore, when it is connected from the heaven of Saturn up to the heav-

---

[1] See *Tet.* I.4.

en of the Moon, and the Moon was descending and Saturn standing still,[2] it will be a sign of rains lasting a short amount of time, and it will happen when the clouds meet[3] in the air, degree-to-degree with each other. **3** If however Saturn were descending and the Moon ascending, and the portal of the heavens were open, one to the other, that is a signification of rains in that hour, especially if Saturn were in Cancer and the Moon in Capricorn, and they were in agreement with the Tail,[4] or the Tail was in Aquarius. **4** And if[5] one of them is descending, and the other is ascending, and the Moon added in [her] advancing, that year will be very rainy and watery.

5 If[6] however the Moon were on Venus (in addition to this description), and Venus western from the Sun and descending, it signifies a multitude of winds and dews, and their duration. **6** And if Saturn were retrograde and the Moon advancing less (she will be subtracted in her number), and the Tail in Aquarius, it signifies a multitude of obscurities [in the air], and a scarcity of rains, and the condensing of cold, and snows, and they will be multiplied until where the snows approach,[7] up to six days or more or more.

6 And you should know that the Moon is tied up in the heaven of Saturn. **7** If therefore Saturn were in Cancer, and the Moon in Capricorn or Pisces or Scorpio, it is a signification of waters; and in Libra, which is the exaltation of Saturn, and Aquarius (the house of Saturn), the lastingness of rain and the multitude of snow are signified. **8** And if Saturn were in Aquarius, but the

---

[2] *Stans.* But this should probably read, "ascending," to mirror the opposite situation in **3**. This vocabulary of descending and ascending must refer to (a) being angular or succedent, versus cadent; or (b) being on the ascending hemisphere of the chart (from the IC eastward up to the Midheaven) versus the descending side (from the Midheaven down to the IC); or (c) rising and falling in ecliptical latitude. For in **29** Māshā'allāh changes to saying "falling" or "cadent" (*cadens*), which suggests (a); but Māshā'allāh is also known for labeling one side of the zodiac "ascending" and the other "descending," which derives ultimately from *Carmen* V.27.26—that suggests (b). On the other hand, in **49** Māshā'allāh clearly refers to rising and falling in ecliptical latitude.

[3] *Nubes obviant sibi.* This should probably read "when *these two planets* meet each other," as Māshā'allāh is about to affirm that he is talking about the opening of the doors.

[4] This probably means that the Tail is in one of those signs, as well.

[5] Adding with Paris, rather than continuing the sentence with *CCAG*.

[6] Reading with Paris rather than *CCAG*, although neither is ideal. They read (with Paris and *CCAG* underlined, in that order): *Si autem fuerit Luna cum hac narratione in Venere et Venus occidentalis a Sole et descendens/ et occidentalis et descendenti, Venus* significat.... First of all, the *in Venere* is ambiguous: while it may suggest a transit, this is not how it is normally expressed in Latin or Arabic. Second, Paris at least says something grammatical and clear about Venus, but *CCAG* puts Venus at the end of the second clause, and reads *descendenti* rather than the expected *descendens*.

[7] Reading *accedant* with Paris for *accederat*.

Moon even in Leo (opposite it), and one of them ascending and the other descending, it signifies an abundance of waters; and to the extent that the Moon will proceed up to Leo, descending, the waters of the springs which are in Aquarius will descend to the river banks, and this signifies rains. **9** And if both were ascending, the winds will be strong and hot, with obscurity, and they will become rains while they descend, [and] afterwards there will be winds and the rains will be halted. **10** And if Saturn were in another place from this (namely that he would be in Aries or Taurus or Gemini), nor will he be in signs in which his nature is strengthened, there will not be rains.

11 And you should know that there are places in which rains are frozen,[8] just as in Armenia, in elevated places in the seventh clime, from the entrance of the Sun into 19° of Scorpio up to his entrance into 19° of Taurus: and this, because the heat of the Sun is not strengthened in the third clime, and that obscurity will become hot in the air or be calm,[9] and strengthened. **12** But if the Sun were in the nineteenth degree of Taurus up to the nineteenth degree of Scorpio, rain will be multiplied in southern estates, and those who are from the direction of the south, and estates which are near the line of the equator of the day: and they are those of the blacks and the Zanj,[10] and 'Aden,[11] and southern estates, and estates which are near the equator of the day in the first clime.

13 And they even look in it from the first minute of Aries and Libra in the root of the signification, and where the planets of rains are from the entrance of the Sun in 10° after they will be calculated. **14** And if Venus were with the Sun and the Moon will be conjoined, and if certain planets of the hours of the Moon,[12] it is a signification for rain. **15** And the stronger signification belongs especially to the Moon, because she has moisture. **16** And whatever planets [were] in the nineteenth degree of Taurus, it is a signification for rain, [but] not just like the signification of the Moon (because she is opposite the heaven of Saturn).

---

[8] Lit., "congealed."

[9] From here through the first clause in the next sentence, reading with Paris. *CCAG* has reversed the order of certain words.

[10] A largely black region of East Africa south of modern Somalia (Lat. *Zingi*).

[11] A port city in Yemen at about 12° 48' N (Lat. *Oaden*).

[12] There is an obvious error in the manuscripts. By reading *si quidam* as *siquidem* (as Paris does), we could have "and the Moon will be conjoined, and even supposing planets of the hours of the Moon." Paris itself reads, "and the Moon will be conjoined, *it is* of the hours of the Moon, *whatever planets [they are]*." No matter how we read it, it does not really make any sense.

17 If therefore you wished to know that, inspect the entrance of the Sun in the [first] minute of Aries or 19° Scorpio, and if the planets were lords of their own heavens[13] and they would look at them,[14] and the Moon would aid them, that signifies a multitude of rains. **18** But if the Moon did not inspect the lord of the heaven of her binding,[15] nor at a planet, and she was subtracting in her advance, then it signifies rains. **19** And the Moon signifies likewise, like Saturn if he[16] were under the rays of the Sun or in his opposite: for then it signifies rains, because[17] in these two hours [that location] receives it and it falls down in [that] place.

20 And then inspect the place of Saturn and the Moon. **21** If therefore they were as I have said, and you wanted to know the hour of rain in that year, look: if the Sun were in Aquarius and the Moon is turning with him,[18] it signifies a scarcity of rain; likewise if Venus would turn with the Sun in that sign, and likewise Mercury: and if they were conjoined, the rain will not cease in that year, until Venus and Mercury will be removed from the Sun. **22** If therefore the Sun were in Aquarius (namely, the house of Saturn), and the Moon in Leo (namely, the house of the Sun), it signifies many rains and in that hour. **23** And if Venus and Mercury were with the Sun, it signifies many rains. **24** And if the Sun were in Pisces or in Aries, and the Moon in Cancer or in Libra, or in Virgo, it signifies rain (or [in] Sagittarius toward its first part, namely because of the pure vapor that is in it). **25** And if Mars inspected the Sun or the Moon or Venus or Mercury, or one of the two luminaries,[19] it signifies many rains, especially if they aspected each other by the square or opposite aspect: because then it signifies great fearful things, such as heat-

---

[13] Or perhaps, "and there were planets [which are] lords of their own heavens." This probably means that some of them are in their own domiciles.

[14] Reading *ea* (indicating "heavens") with Paris for *CCAG*'s *eam* ("her"). This suggests that planets either are in, or aspect, their own domiciles. But if the *CCAG* is correct, the "her" refers to the Moon.

[15] Reading *non inspexerit Luna dominum caeli sui ligamenti*. This is a hybrid of Paris ("if she did not inspect the lord of the Midheaven of her binding") and *CCAG* ("if the Moon did not inspect the lord of the heaven of her liquid" [*liquamenti*, sic?]). The lord of the heaven of her binding must be Saturn, as she was already said to be tied up with him. The reference in Paris to the Midheaven is probably a mistake, albeit intriguing. Finally, the text puts the objects of the inspection or aspecting into dative, which is bad Latin but does express the preposition in Arabic which must follow the verb *naẓara*.

[16] It is impossible to say from the Latin, whether this is Saturn or the Moon, but I have read it as though it is Saturn.

[17] Reading *quia* with Paris, for *quod* ("that").

[18] This seems to mean that she is with him in the same sign.

[19] Reading with Paris for "or one or the other of the two" (*aut unum duorum vel varium*).

lightning, thunder, and what is of this kind. **26** And if Mars were retrograde, the rain will be fearful.[20] **27** And if the Moon were in Taurus [and] Mars in Scorpio, or the Moon in Scorpio and Mars in Taurus (which is the exaltation of the Moon), and the Sun in Aquarius or in Pisces, or in Aries, it signifies many rains and heat-lightning and flashes of lightning. **28** And if Mars were in Pisces and the Moon in Sagittarius, and the Sun in Pisces, it signifies rain and flashes of lightning. **29** And if the Sun were in Scorpio or in Sagittarius, and the Moon in Scorpio or Sagittarius or Pisces, and Mars in Gemini or in Virgo or in Taurus, it signifies the movement of heat-lightning, and not much rain, and a continuation of heat-lightning with the Sun in Aries, because it is the house of Mars. **30** If however it[21] aspected the Moon or were in Pisces (which sign is the exaltation of Venus), and the Sun in Scorpio (the house of Mars), or the Sun in Libra (the house of Venus), there will be cold winds, and with the Sun going out in Capricorn or Aquarius (the houses of Saturn).

31 Note even that the heaven of Jupiter and Mercury are bound together, likewise those of Venus and Mars. **32** For the superior planets do not have power in themselves and by themselves, nor likewise do the inferiors, except from the superiors.

33 If therefore Mercury aspected Jupiter in a revolution of the years (which I have reported), and one of them were falling and the other ascending, and the falling one aspected the ascending one, it signifies a multitude of winds in that year, because the heaven of Jupiter is a multiplier of winds, and Mercury signifies winds. **34** If even the Moon were in Taurus and Mercury aspected her from Aquarius or from Pisces, and Mercury was received by Jupiter in the root of the revolution, it signifies winds. **35** And if Mercury were in Aquarius, the Moon in Leo, or Mercury in Pisces and the Moon in Sagittarius or in Virgo, or the Moon with Jupiter (or with Mercury being in this sign),[22] it signifies winds. **36** If Jupiter will be in his own exaltation, and Mercury in Aries or in Pisces, and he aspected Jupiter and will be connected with him, then winds are signified. **37** And if Mercury [were] in Scorpio, Jupiter in Taurus or Leo, and the Moon will be connected with Mercury from Aquarius or from Pisces or Taurus or Leo, winds are signified. **38** And if Mercury were in Scorpio and Jupiter in Taurus or in Sagittarius, and the

---

[20] Paris reads *plura* for *pluvia*: "there will be *many* fearful things."
[21] I take this to be Mars.
[22] Reading the ablative absolute with Paris.

Moon will be connected to him from Gemini or from Virgo, winds are signified. **39** And if the Sun were in Scorpio or Sagittarius, or Aquarius or Libra or
Pisces, or Aries, and Mercury [were] under the rays of the Sun, many winds
are signified. **40** And if Venus aspected him, there will be rains. **41** And if
Mars aspected him, there will be heat-lightning and lightning flashes. **42** And
if the Moon crossed over through him,[23] there will be rain.

43 And inspect as I have said, with respect to Mercury. **44** However, the
heaven of Mars and of Venus are tied together.[24]

45 And look, in a revolution of the year, to the Moon and Venus, from
their opposition or in the hour of a [square] aspect[25] (which signify that it will
be), and it will not be fulfilled in that hour.[26] **46** But if it were from Scorpio,
the rain will not last. **47** If Venus will be in Taurus or in Aquarius, and the
Moon aspected her from Scorpio, and Mercury[27] [was] with the Moon, there
will be rains with heat-lightning and thunders, and there will be strong hail.

48 If Saturn aspected the Moon, there will be hail damaging the harvests
and killing winged things.

49 And if the Moon at the revolution were in Scorpio or in Sagittarius, or
in Aquarius, or in Pisces, if Mars were aspecting the Moon from the opposite
(unless it[28] is in Scorpio), it signifies a diminution of what was said before. **50**
And if it were from Scorpio, it will not make harm on account of the vapor
which is in Scorpio.

51 And if Venus were in Scorpio or in Sagittarius, or in Taurus, it signifies
rains. **47** The retrogradation of Venus in Scorpio or Capricorn, or Aquarius,
signifies many rains.

52 And when the Moon will have withdrawn from a superior planet in the
foundation of the question, and she will apply to an inferior planet (or equally [the other way around]), it will signify rains.

53 But if Mars were falling and the Moon ascending southern, it signifies
rain if the Moon aspected him from Leo or Virgo.

---

[23] This probably means a transit by body (*transierit per eum*).
[24] These two sentences were probably a single one in Arabic, so that Māshā'allāh is telling
us to treat combinations of Venus and Mars, just as we have Mercury and Jupiter.
[25] Tentatively adding *quarti*, since this is usually paired with the opposition.
[26] Māshā'allāh seems to be introducing conditions that lead to short rains or other things
besides rain.
[27] Paris reads, "Mars."
[28] I take this to refer to the Moon, since being in Scorpio was one of the signs just mentioned.

54 If Venus were under the rays of the Sun and the Moon aspected her from Pisces, with Venus going out into Taurus, or the Moon aspected her in Aries from[29] Libra, it signifies much rain in that season. **55** And if Mars cut off their light, it will take away from that rain.

55 If the Moon and Venus and Mercury were in Pisces in the revolution, rains are signified.

56 And if the Moon or Venus were in Aquarius, there will be rains. **54** If however they were in Aries or in Taurus, a diminution of rain is signified.

57 The Moon in the revolution even being opposite the Sun or Saturn or Venus, signifies the corruption of the air and rain by dew. **58** If the Moon and the lord of her house were adding, the corruption will be from much dew, if God wills.

59 When the Sun enters the first minute of 20° Scorpio,[30] take the Ascendant. **60** If it were a watery sign, and the Moon is even in a watery one, and likewise Venus, the beginning of winter will be rainy, and the end moistening. **61** If Venus were western, weak, and the Moon ascending in watery signs, the beginning and end will be likewise moist. **62** It must be noted[31] that Venus under the rays is just like a woman under a man: it makes waters descend. **63** If Venus were eastern of the Sun, the beginning will be dry. **64** But if she were not ascending from watery ones, nor were the Moon in a watery one, the beginning of the winter will be rainy and the last part dry.

65 And[32] if the Ascendant were an enflamed one,[33] and its lord in a watery one, then the weather will be tempered, with neither much nor little rain: and it will be inclined a little bit to moistures and heat-lightning. **66** And if the Ascendant were enflamed, and its lord in an enflamed sign, the diminution[34] of rains in that year will be signified. **67** And if the Ascendant were fiery and its lord in a windy sign, there will be few rains and many winds in that year. **68** And if the lord of the hour were moist and dewy, it will be a good year. **69**

---

[29] Reading with Paris for "and in."

[30] *CCAG* incorrectly puts the number of degrees in the next sentence.

[31] Reading *notandum* with Paris, for *hodie* ("today"). See a parallel statement in Māshā'allāh's *Chapter on Rains*, sentence **5** (Section I.6).

[32] In this paragraph, Māshā'allāh goes through other Ascendants. One would expect this to be connected to the previous paragraph (in which there was a watery sign on the Ascendant), but now he suddenly begins to speak of the lord of the Ascendant, which he had ignored before. See his *Chapter on Rains* (Section I.6), where he uses the lord of the bound of the Ascendant.

[33] That is, a fiery sign (*ignitus*).

[34] Reading *diminutiones* with Paris for *durationes* ("lastingness").

And if it were dry, it will corrupt the year. **70** And if the Ascendant were an earthy sign, and its lord in a watery sign, it will be a good year with many rains and dews. **71** And if the lord of the hour [were] in a fiery sign and the lord itself[35] in an angle, there will be great dryness in that year. **72** And if the Ascendant were watery, and its lord in a windy sign, there will be many dews and winds and mists in that year. **73** And if the Ascendant were fiery and its lord in a watery sign, that quarter of that year will be very moist, with little rain: or, fair weather will be multiplied and rain will be diminished. **74** And if the Ascendant were windy and its lord in an earthy sign, it signifies many winds, few dews.

75 Likewise, with the Sun will be conjoined in the Ascendant with any of the three superiors, and one of them is in the fourth house, rains are signified in the first quarter of the month or year; likewise if it were in the seventh, it will be in the middle quarter of the year; likewise if in the tenth, there will be dew in the third quarter[36] of the month or year; likewise if in the fourth, it will be at the end of the year. **76** Likewise in its opposite and in its square,[37] the signification hastens particularly in the winter or in the spring.[38] **77** Take its correct signification, and believe in[39] rains and the flowing of waters. **78** Likewise in the summer, it signifies strong hail: this is if there were a conjunction or opposition in the earthy or watery signs, for this signifies a multitude of flowing water. **79** If however they were in fiery signs, it will signify wars, battles, captivities, slaughter, burning, fires, and the destruction of vegetation. **80** If his conjunction were in a sign of winds, and one of them will square some earthy sign, it is a signification of winds and their roaring, and it signifies the corruption of fruits and a multitude of tempests. **81** If you want to know the hour, know when the Sun will apply to the place of the planet which is in [his] square,[40] and this signification will be prolonged if the Moon were in the Ascendant or the opposite.

---

[35] Reading *ipse dominus* with Paris for *prope dominum*.

[36] Reading *tertia quarta* for *tribus quartis* ("three quarters"), evidently an error. Paris reads, "in two quarters of the month or year."

[37] This may mean, "if the superiors are opposing or squaring the Sun, rather than one of them being conjoined to him in the Ascendant."

[38] Reading with Paris for "it hastens with Sagittarius or Venus" (i.e., reading *significatio aut vere* for *Sagittario aut Venere*).

[39] Reading *crede in* for *concede in*.

[40] Reading *planetae* with Paris for *pluviae*.

82 If someone said, "where will this be," inspect the conjunction of the planets.[41] **83** If it were in the Ascendant, from the direction of the east; if in the Midheaven, from the south; if in the seventh, in the west; if in the fourth, in the north: base it on this, and you will find it, God willing.

84 If there were a strong dryness, and if perhaps you wanted to know when it will rain upon the face of the earth, one will see where the Head of the Serpent is,[42] or the star which is called *Adhafera*.[43] **85** When one of these was in a cabin[44] which is said to be watery, calculate the Moon herself: when she will descend in a watery cabin, it will rain quickly.

---

[41] Omitting *amplius* ("also, in addition").
[42] That is, α Ophiuchus, or Ras Alhague.
[43] Lat. *Azaphora*. That is, either ζ Leo or the Coma Berenices cluster nearby (see Kunitzsch and Smart, p. 41).
[44] *Casa* here and below, which suggests perhaps Māshā'allāh is talking about the moist mansions. But what is supposed to be in them? Possibly a key planetary transit, such as the Moon's transit in them. At any rate, these two sentences to not fit well together. Compare with his *Chapter on Rains*, sentence **47** (Section I.6), which speaks of the *Moon* in the rainy *signs*.

SECTION I.8: THE LATIN AL-RIJĀL

Comment by Dykes. In addition to containing his own transcription of several chapters from ʿUmar al-Tabarī (see Section I.5 above), al-Rijāl's *Book of the Skilled* has several other passages on weather. Below I have listed all of the relevant chapters with the Latin titles from the 1485 edition, and have translated from it *only* those non-ʿUmar portions. In a couple of cases, all of al-Rijāl's chapter was from ʿUmar, so only the title appears here. In others, part of the chapter was from ʿUmar, part was from some other author. I list them all here so that the reader may see an exhaustive list of the chapters.

These passages were translated from the Latin 1485 edition, but for difficult or unclear phrases I have also consulted two Arabic manuscripts of al-Rijāl's work, Br. Lib. Ar. 23399 and Nuruosmaniye 2766.

ℬ ℬ ℭ

The Book of the Skilled VIII.26:
On knowing the accidents & diversities of the air in the seasons, heat, & cold[1]

The Book of the Skilled VIII.27:
On rains & thunders & lightning flashes & winds [part][2]

20 For rains, the root is that you should look at the Ascendant of the conjunction or prevention which was before the Sun's entrance into any one of the signs. **21** And look at the lord of the Ascendant, and the lord of the bound[3] of the conjunction or prevention. **22** And if these lords were in moist places, and moist and rainy signs, it signifies much[4] rain. **23** And if they applied to moist and rainy planets, it likewise signifies rain.

24 And on the other hand, if the significator were western or retrograde or of a slow motion, it likewise signifies rains. **25** And[5] if it were burned up it signifies rains, except if it were Mars: indeed, his being burned up reduces

---

[1] This chapter represents ʿUmar al-Tabarī's Book of Questions Ch. 81 (Section I.5).
[2] The first part of this chapter represents ʿUmar al-Tabarī's *Book of Questions* Ch. 82 (Section I.5). This second part of the chapter is from an unknown author.
[3] Reading *ḥadd* with the Ar., for "place."
[4] Adding with the Ar.
[5] Reading this sentence with the Ar., to clarify the Latin.

[the rains]. **26** And you should know that if the significator were descending in its latitude or in the circle of its apogee, it signifies rains (and the other way around).[6]

27 And you should know that if there were rains on account of the significations of the infortunes, it will be with harm: if they were through Saturn, there will be pillaging[7] and submersions; and if they were through Mars, it signifies rays [of lightning][8] and the burning of the air.

The Book of the Skilled VIII.28:
On opening the doors for rains, & other things[9]

The Book of the Skilled VIII.29:
On the foundations[10]

The Book of the Skilled VIII.30:
On knowing the times in which one may hope that it rains [part][11]

5 And[12] you will know how the rains will be in the year, in such a way: you will look at the Moon, Venus, and Mercury. **6** And if you found them to be joined in Pisces at the hour of the revolution of the year, it signifies rains and moistures and many clouds in that year. **7** And if they were in Aries or Taurus, it signifies that the year will have few rains, [and be] dry and in need.

8 And if the Moon were connecting with Venus[13] from one of the houses of Mercury, it signifies many lasting and soaking[14] rains in that year.

9 And if the Moon were in the opposite of the Sun, Venus, or Saturn, it likewise signifies many rains and dark clouds.

10 And if Mercury and Venus meet[15] in one bound, there will be great rains. **11** And if in addition they were in a sign of rains, and the Moon aspect-

---

[6] For example, ascending in the circle of its apogee would indicate few or no rains.
[7] *Diruptiones*, reading this noun as deriving from *diripio*.
[8] Adding with the Ar.
[9] This chapter represents ʿUmar al-Tabarī's *Book of Questions* Ch. 83 (Section I.5).
[10] This chapter represents ʿUmar al-Tabarī's *Book of Questions* Ch. 84 (Section I.5).
[11] The first part of this chapter represents ʿUmar al-Tabarī's *Book of Questions* Ch. 85 (Section I.5).
[12] Source material unknown at this time.
[13] Reading with the Ar. for "Venus applied to Mercury."
[14] Reading with the Ar. for "lasting and fixed."
[15] Reading with the Ar. for *integer*.

ed them from a trine, there will be strong and lasting rain, until one of those planets goes out from that bound.

12 And what would make the rains in the winter stronger and more lasting is if, in the revolution of the year, Mercury applied to Jupiter, the Moon to Saturn, and Venus to Mars: because each of these planets unfolds what it receives from the other planet which is opposite its own house.[16]

13 And if Venus were in front of the Sun, it signifies that that year will have many clouds and dews and moistures, but few rains.

14 And if Venus will be retrograde, with the Sun appearing in Aries or Taurus, there will be many rains in that year, and the spring of that year will be complete and most fertile, and have many and good rains. **15** And if her retrogradation were in Capricorn, Aquarius, or Pisces, the rains in the spring will be diminished, and there will be many in the middle of the winter, and that winter will be very moist.

16 And if Mercury were stationary and slow, in whatever sign he was, moistures will happen in the air in that season, and rains, and clouds, according to that season. **17** And what makes greater rains, and stronger ones, is if the planets of rains are being joined in signs of rains, and especially that Venus would be stationary: because Venus is more supported and a greater signification of rains and moistures.

18 And if Mercury were in a dry sign, and the Moon and Venus in rainy signs, the rains will be tempered; and if Saturn aspected them from a cold sign, the rains will be with strong cold, darkness, and iciness.

---

[16] Or rather, "from the planet whose *domicile* is opposite its own," just as Sagittarius (a house or domicile of Jupiter) is opposite Gemini (belonging to Mercury).

The Book of the Skilled VIII.31:
On epidemics, health, dryness, & abundance [part][17]

[Chapter VIII.31.2]: If you wanted to know the dryness or abundance of the year[18]

11 Look at the place of the conjunction or prevention preceding the revolution of the year of the world, and consider the lord of that place, [to see] to which of the fortunes or infortunes it applies. **12** And[19] if that which was connecting with it was Jupiter, and especially if he had a claim in the section of the conjunction or prevention,[20] or he was the lord of the Ascendant or the lord of the Ascendant was fortunate, along with the safety of the lord of the Ascendant from the two infortunes, and the terminal point of the year by the direction of the religion,[21] and the turning of the middle,[22] [came] to the place of Jupiter or Venus in the examination, or in the rays [of them], the fertility happens in that year, and especially if the lord of the second in the revolution of the year is making the lord of the Ascendant fortunate or is being connected with it from an aspect of friendship (whatever planet it

---

[17] The first part of this chapter represents al-Kindī's *The Forty Chapters* Ch. 39, and may be seen in Section I.4.

[18] Original source unknown at this time, but it is substantially the same as al-Rijāl VIII.2 (Section II.8), so they are either from the same source, or perhaps VIII.2 is al-Rijāl's own abbreviation of these ideas.

[19] I have translated this sentence from the Ar., as the Latin was problematic. The Latin reads: "And if it applied to Jupiter, and Jupiter had some dignity in the place of the conjunction or prevention, or he was the lord of the Ascendant of the revolution or the year or of the conjunction or prevention, or he made the lord of the Ascendant fortunate, and the lord of the fourth house were safe from the infortunes, and there were an application of the year (by the direction of that law or by a direction of the greater conjunction) to the place of Jupiter or Venus, or by aspect or rays, there will be fertility and abundance in that year—and more so if the lord of the second house of the revolution of the year made the Ascendant fortunate or it applied to it from an aspect of friendship (whatever planet it was); likewise especially if it made the lord of the Lot of Fortune fortunate, or the lord of the Ascendant."

[20] This suggests that rulership by bound (or triplicity or exaltation) would be relevant, and not just by domicile.

[21] This suggests the primary direction (or distribution, that is, directing through the bounds) of the Ascendant of the "conjunction of the change": the Saturn-Jupiter conjunction which shifted into a new triplicity and announced a new creed or religion. For the early Arabic writers, this would have been the 571 AD conjunction heralding the coming of Islam.

[22] *Al-dawr al-ʾawsaṭ*. "Turn" (*dawr*) refers to several different predictive methods, and normally I would expect the author to be referring to a mundane version such as found in Abū Maʿshar's *Book of Religions & Dynasties* I.1.25-31. But based on the parallel passage in al-Rijāl VIII.2 (Section II.8), this might simply mean a mundane profection.

was), especially if it was making the lord of the Lot of Fortune fortunate, or better yet the lord of the Ascendant. **13** These are the things which signify fertility and abundance.

14 And if all such things were testified to, there will be great fertility, the assets of the people will be multiplied, and they will profit in all ways and even in merchant dealings. **15** And if all such things were not [testified to], the fertility will be according to what [the testimonies] were, and the needs and dryness of the year will equally be contrary to these. **16** Because if Saturn had rulership in the conjunction or prevention, by application or by body, and likewise he had rulership in the Ascendant and made it unfortunate, and the lord of the fourth were harmed by the infortunes (especially by Saturn, and stronger than that if Saturn had a commixture with Mercury)—because whichever of the two infortunes made the year unfortunate and had a commixture with Mercury, that misfortune will be greater and more fixed. **17** And it will be likewise if the contrary constellations happened to the second house and the Lot of Fortune, and the Ascendant and the lord of the Lot of Fortune: of those things which we stated about fortunes, the indication for dryness, need, and diminution is strengthened.

18 And you should know that the constellations and fortunate things which we described through Jupiter, if they happened through Venus, such significations will be good, except that they will be weaker than those which are through Jupiter. **19** And likewise the misfortunes which we stated about Saturn, if they will be through Mars, they will have less evil and harm than through Saturn, except that the harms which were through the significations of Mars will be through dryness, burning, and strong rays, and what is likened to those; and the harms which were through Saturn will be through thirst or submersions in water. **20** And you will discern which of these two contrary [possibilities] it was, by the sign in which Saturn was: because if he were in a moist sign, it will be through submersion; and if in a dry sign, it will be through thirst.

The Book of the Skilled VIII.32:
On knowing when conflicts, wars, burnings,
& submersions will happen[23]

---

[23] The first half of this chapter represents 'Umar al-Tabarī's *Book of Questions* Ch. 138 (Section I.5). The second half is on comets (Section III.8).

SECTION I.9: IBN LABBAN ON WEATHER & DISASTERS

Comment by Dykes. In this Section I will summarize Kushyar ibn Labban's account of weather prediction, from Chs. 3 and 6-7 of Part II of his *Introduction to Astrology*. Kushyar is dependent upon other authors, but his succinctness makes his descriptions easier to grasp. Bolded numbers indicate the numbered paragraphs (not sentences) in the edition by Yano.

ℰ   ℰ   ℰ

Chapter 3. Here, ibn Labban is first of all concerned with planets in the angles of various charts, and draws on 'Umar al-Tabari's Chs. 81-82 (Section I.5). If Mars is in the tenth place in a quarterly ingress or a New/Full Moon chart, he indicates fires and meteors; this is especially so if the sign is airy, or if Mercury is conjoined or opposed to him, or if the Moon is made unfortunate by him (**1**). Similarly, if Saturn is in the fourth of any of these charts, it indicates earthquakes and a lunar eclipse;[1] likewise, this is especially so if the sign is earthy, or Mercury or the Moon are in the situations described for Mars (**2**). These situations for the malefics are even enhanced if they are rising in the circles of their apogees (**3**).

Ibn Labban then outlines further indications for earthquakes, which we have also seen in 'Umar: if Mars is in the pivot of the earth, with an earthy sign, and the benefics in aversion, and Mercury applying to him; it also indicates things like fires from the earth, earthquakes, and problems with minerals (**4**).

Finally (**5**), if the tenth of any of these charts is an airy sign, with the malefics or an unfortunate Moon in it, it again shows comets and meteors and storms in the heavens. But if the fourth were earthy and with the same situation, we again have earthquakes and a "lunar eclipse."

Chapter 6. Ibn Labban begins with a brief account of the opening of the doors, which is taken from 'Umar al-Tabari's Ch. 83 (**1**). But he later emphasizes (**10**) that the opening of the doors ought to take place when the Moon is in one of the "centers":[2] in that case, the pair of planets involved will determine the type of weather: Mars-Venus shows moisture, Saturn-Sun shows

---

[1] This does not make sense to me, as lunar eclipses are well defined independently of Saturn's position.

[2] Ibn Labban clarifies in his II.1.5 that he only means the places of the New and Full Moons, and the Moon's quarters.

cold in cold seasons and heat in hot ones, Moon-Saturn shows cooling and moisture, Jupiter-Mercury shows winds.[3]

He then lists indications for winds: the signs indicating winds are the airy signs, and the windy planets are the Sun, Mercury, and Jupiter (2); if two or three of the windy planets are gathered in the airy signs, it indicates winds (4).

Ibn Labban then turns to considerations that largely concern the malefics, much of which is again taken from 'Umar (Ch. 81). In a revolution of the year, each malefic will enhance the heat or cold of a sign which matches it, while counteracting the qualities of a sign which does not (3). Therefore Saturn in fiery and airy signs will counteract and decrease the heat, while Mars will enhance and increase it; Saturn in earthy and watery signs increases coldness, while Mars will counteract and decrease it.

In a similar way (5), Saturn in or aspecting the airy signs at a quarterly revolution or New/Full Moon, will indicate cold winds, while Mars in the same situation shows strong winds accompanied by heat. But if Jupiter, the winds will be good albeit stronger than Saturn's. If Venus, pleasant winds. Mercury, soft winds. The latitude of the planet indicates which direction the winds will come from.[4]

Continuing the theme of the airy signs (7), Saturn in them causes cold, mistiness and clouds, and ice; Mars, heat and drought; Jupiter, gentle moist winds; Venus, gentle and peaceful winds; Mercury, moderate and changing winds. (The fact that this is so similar to the paragraph above, suggests that ibn Labban is simply copying from two related sources.)

Finally, a few stray bits of lore. If the Sun reaches Gemini while the Moon reaches Sagittarius, the winds on those days will be good for the whole year, in terms of being beneficial or not (6). If Mars is eastern at the Sun's ingress into Cancer, it means excessive heat (8); but if Venus were eastern at the Sun's ingress into Capricorn, excessive cold (8). If the Moon separates from a bodily conjunction of Saturn in an earthy sign, it means cold and snow (if the season is appropriate for it); but if separating from an opposition with Mars, excessive heat in a season appropriate to it (9).

Chapter 7. In this chapter, ibn Labban is mostly concerned with rainfall, with lore reminiscent of Māshā'allāh's *Letter* or *Chapter on Rains* (Sections I.6-7). He begins by indicating the rainy signs and planets (1): the rainy signs are

---

[3] Ibn Labban then repeats this in his II.7.6.
[4] Remember that in Ptolemy, the *Moon's* latitude or declination was supposed to show this (*Tet.* II.12.1 in Robbins, *Tet.* II.13.1 in Hübner).

the watery signs, Leo, and Aquarius; the rainy planets are the Moon, Venus, and Mercury. The Moon especially shows floods and widespread rains, Venus fogs and darkness accompanying rains, and Mercury, while not showing very much rains (but rather winds), alternates between fairer weather and clouds (**2**). Mercury seems to be somewhat unusual, because he is mainly a stimulating planet (**3**): when changing signs and moving slowly, he stimulates fog and darkness, and violent changes in weather especially when the Moon and Venus happen to be in rainy signs at the same time; if it were in a season normally indicating rain, then the rain is long-lasting. If[5] the Moon applies to Venus from a sign of Mercury, it also agitates fog and rain, especially if Mercury is with Venus (**4**).

And in general, when rainy planets reach rainy signs, it shows much rain when the season is appropriate for that, but winds, darkness, and dust at other times (**5**). Again,[6] Venus being western at a time of rain, means much rain; if she were also in a rainy sign and being aspected by a rainy planet, it means rains—but the less these conditions are present, the less so (**8**). If the majority of the planets are in the watery triplicity, there will be so much rain it is harmful (**9**).

Ibn Labban then turns to some chart considerations. If the lord of the Ascendant at any of the quarterly ingresses or of a New/Full Moon happens to be one of the rainy planets, and is in a rainy sign, and is aspected by the other two rainy planets, then there will be much rain in the time appropriate to it, according to the kind of rainy planet it is (**2**). At a New/Full Moon, if the lord of the Ascendant and the lord of the seventh have an application or transfer of light or collection of light, and there is also an opening of the doors, it indicates that the normally-expected weather for that time will be present: rain if in a normal time for rain, winds at times of winds, and so on (**7**). Or, if the lord of the Aries ingress is Mars, and other planets are applying from watery signs, and he is in the Midheaven or between the Ascendant and the Midheaven, in a watery sign, it means excessive water—even worse if he were retrograde (**11**).

The Moon has several ways of indicating increased rain (**10**): moving faster, being near a New/Full Moon, rising in the circle of her apogee.[7] If one of

---

[5] For this sentence, see al-Rijāl's Ch. 30, sentence **8** (Section I.8).

[6] Cf. 'Umar's Ch. 82, sentences **2-5** (Section I.5).

[7] Ibn Labban defines this as being from her first quarter to Full, and from the second quarter to New, which does not make sense to me as a definition of rising in the circle of her apogee.

these is happening at a quarterly ingress or at a New/Full Moon, and the Moon is between the Ascendant and the Midheaven (or the opposite quadrant), then it shows rains for that period; if in the opposite conditions, the opposite (**10**).

Again, a few stray bits about planets' relations to their apogee:[8] Saturn, Venus, Jupiter, or the Moon descending in their apogees create excessive water, although Saturn is the more harmful (**11**).

---

[8] I would normally expect this to mean the apogee of the deferent circle. But ibn Labban puts this right after, and verbally connects it to, the statement about Mars being retrograde. Now, when Mars goes retrograde he does descend from the apogee of his *epicycle*, and while remaining retrograde he remains in its lower half; but I would have expected ibn Labban to mention the epicycle specifically. Besides, if he meant the epicycle, it would be virtually synonymous with the planets being retrograde, which the Moon never is.

SECTION I.10: JAFAR, *THE BOOK OF HEAVY RAINS*

Comment by Dykes. This work by "Jafar" or "Jafar Indus" (Jafar the Indian) was translated from Arabic into Latin by Hugo of Santalla (early 12ᵗʰ Century AD), and dedicated to his patron, Bishop Michael of Tarazona (in Spain). According to Hugo, it represents Indian teachings which were then put into a more concise form by Hermes, referred to here by one of his titles, the Cyllenian Mercury. According to Burnett (2004, p. 63), it is based on the same Arabic work represented by the less complete *The Sages of India* in Section I.11, and I have followed him in applying sentence numbers from Hugo to their parallel places in *Sages*. The two works should be read together.

After a typically tortured introduction, Hugo speaks without irony of the difficulty of translating such texts; he also praises the exalted nature of astrology, and suggests that real expertise in astrology is only possible for those with a suitable natal chart. After this, the text rehearses the usual methods we have seen so far: the opening of the doors, lunar mansions, the centers of the Moon, Moon-Mercury-Venus lore, and so on. As for the 20° Scorpio method, Jafar explicitly states that we must track planetary configurations from the Libra ingress *up through* the Sun's entrance into 20° Scorpio, and not just look at the latter alone (**67, 131, 145**). Jafar credits the Indians with this view.

The reader should keep in mind that Jafar's weather indications for each planet are not exactly the same as those we have seen so far. In previous Sections, Venus and Jupiter indicate productive and fertilizing rain, but here they do not. Or rather, Jupiter indicates fair weather, while Venus by herself is more productive of mists and dew. Only when supported by other rainy indications can Venus really produce rain. Even so, she does not really produce the strong (or even destructive) rains indicated by a planet such as Mars.

One should also keep in mind Hugo's difficult Latin style, which I have not tried to disguise here. It takes patience to get through his flourishes, circumlocutions, and double negatives, but he is generally an accurate translator of Arabic, so is worth studying. Some of his vocabulary may seem odd, particularly his use of the Latin *duco* and *ducatus* ("to lead/guide, leadership/guidance") when translating the Arabic verb for "to indicate/signify, indication/signification." He actually has valid reasons for choosing this vocabulary, but it will be unfamiliar to some.

ᛒᚩ   ᛥᚩ   ᚼ

The *Book of Heavy Rains,*
written by an ancient astrologer of the Indians
but then abbreviated by the Cyllenian Mercury, begins:

2 Just as the authority of the Indians warns, we ought to attend with all desire to the unshaken truth of the higher teaching, to guard what is attained with the greatest effort, and to beware lest the sacred mysteries of [one's] memory flee. **3** For, just as it is more worthy and more powerful than the other disciplines, so it ennobles those who profess it, by means of a certain privilege of worthiness and as it were the titillation of a certain gladness.[1] **4** But no impulse is able to aspire to it, unless naturally [so]—namely that which comes especially from his own [natal] constellation, and a certain inspiration[2] of a divine gift.[3] **5** Wherefore, once compensation of this kind is had, it is good that we have received it (namely we who have already recognized its causes and progress, and have tasted certain things of its effect), foresee [things] with the greatest diligence, [and] defend [this] both saintly and sublime science (and one conveyed from heaven), so that it may favor us with its necessary, matching truth, and lest it be dealt with by unworthy hands or be exhausted by the foolish scoffing of sophists. **6** Next, too, for any person wanting to approach an understanding of this in a worthy manner, we must disclose the secrets which are sufficient for it.[4]

7 Moreover, it comes to be noted that some extra things are contained in these volumes (which, following the treatments and examples of earlier things, are being translated into different languages), the effects of whose teaching have been diverted[5] from their proper place and signification by their use of terms, nor are they (through their foolishness) consistent with the intelligence of readers, at which time they veer off[6] from the proper path. **8** But we believe these come to be from two causes, namely the fault of

---

[1] Or, "elation, ecstasy" (*elationis*). This is a refreshing point one does not usually see in traditional texts. Normally, writers stick to issues of virtue and goodness, not that one may get a certain joy out of doing astrology.

[2] *Aspiratione*, but Hugo seems to be using it to mean inspiration.

[3] In other words, being a true astrologer requires inborn qualities from the nativity, and some divine gifts—it is not like other, everyday practices.

[4] *Huius quae sufficiant reseranda secreta.*

[5] Reading *pervertuntur* for *praevertit.* Throughout the text, Burnett has preferred *praeverto* to *perverto*, but I argue that *perverto* conveys Hugo's meaning better. Note the parallel between *perverto* here and *declino* ("veer off") later in the sentence.

[6] *Quorum occasiones...declinant.*

[both] scribes and those interpreting [the material].[7] **9** Often even, an interpreter (but then one in no way faithful), sighing amongst the pressures of [these] difficulties, translates some foreign word as he feels like it, lest he seem to miss something or, already doing something foolish, lest he fool around more—[since these foreign words], either through diverse marks above the letters or a lack of them,[8] [and] even more often the unmanageable differences between languages (through all of which the meaning of the etymology is varied), do not suffer to be converted correctly; so that although the nature [of the matter] denies it, still he really shakes it off through the arrogance of [his] elation.[9] **10** Secondarily though, [there is] the persistent and less perfect erudition of the writers—but all of these things cannot escape the industry of the reader.

11 Therefore, my lord high-priest Michael, since I have always understood that you wish for not only compendious [works] but even unerring[10] ones and those improved to a tee,[11] I, Hugo of Santalla, offer to Your Worthiness this little book on rains written by an ancient astrologer of the Indians named Jafar (and then corrected with an eye to conciseness[12] by the Cyllenian Mercury), especially so that your benignness may lavish on posterity what the modern astrologers of the French lament is lacking among them.[13]

The course of the book begins

13 The universal judgments of astronomy (just as the antiquity of the Indians asserts emphatically), are believed to emanate especially from the lunar guidance. **14** (But after that, they trace the source [of judgments] from an

---

[7] Or perhaps, "expounding" or "translating" (*interpretantium*). Hugo means that intermediaries between him and the original text have distorted the text itself as well as its meaning. To me it is quite outrageous that Hugo should complain about bad writing in the midst of one of his typical, groan-inducing introductions.

[8] This is especially true in the case of Arabic. For many letters, the only difference between them is the presence and number of little dots, which are sometimes misplaced or missing—which affects things such as the tense, person, number, and mood of verbs.

[9] Hugo seems to mean that some writers get so excited about what they are doing, that they ignore or "shake off" (*excutiat*) the problems they are creating through their shortcuts.

[10] *Certa*. Or, "certain, reliable."

[11] *Ad unguem correcta*. Or, "corrected to a fine point," etc.

[12] *Sub brevitatis ordine*.

[13] This interesting comment suggests that Michael may have had a little political rivalry and one-upmanship in mind with these translations, and not merely his own contribution to the history of thought and the sciences.

admixture of [her guidance] with the rest of the stars.)[14] **15** For she, as they say, assumes a completed property (and one more full than the rest) in the effecting the generation of worldly things. **16** But among all the rest, she affirms this singular and individual [role], insofar as she, as a mediator, assumes the guidance of all science and knowledge because of her total and intact perfection.[15] **17** This was declared among the sages of the ancients, with many arguments.

18 A general signification over things even proceeds from the efficacy of the stars, while they are blended with the nature of the Moon. **19** For in fact, the Moon really claims the universal figures of the stars. **20** Whence she is admixed with them necessarily, just as Mercury is blended with her: **21** For among the Indians, there is no difference between Mercury and the Moon as long as she is associated with him, and he traverses with her.[16] **22** But the Moon [is] more perfect than he is in the status of receiving [other influences], and [is] of more evident effectiveness: namely because she traverses more closely to the universal center (of the earth, I say), and the effecting of all things in this world is embraced under her. **23** For her operation (as was already stated) is discovered to be constantly present and tireless and more evident, at the *ijtimāᶜ* and *istiqbāl*[17] (the meeting, I say, and the opposition), and the tetragon—from which the situation of generation and corruption (while she increases and decreases in light and computation, even with her ascent and descent in the ether[18]) proceeds, one and then the other, without a doubt. **24** Nevertheless too, her deviation into the south and north, the rendering of counsel and her application,[19] and whatever configurations happen to her, suggest the same things. **25** The action of all of them, and of

---

[14] See *Sages*, which spells this out a bit more clearly. Hugo means that while they first credit the Moon with the significations, they must also agree that because of her role vis-à-vis the other planets, the other planets matter, too.

[15] *Ex sui summa et integra perfectione.* I am not quite sure what Hugo means here, but see sentences **22-23** below.

[16] This may mean that the Moon and Mercury each have a kind of neutrality, since they take on the qualities of whatever they are associated with.

[17] Lat. *alestima et izticbel.* That is, the conjunction and opposition of the luminaries at the New and Full Moons.

[18] This probably refers to her passage across the sky, which relates to tides; but Hugo or his source text might also be referring to ascending and descending in the circle of her apogee.

[19] But normally pushing management (or rendering counsel) is the same as an application, so what is Hugo distinguishing here? Note that the equivalent statement in *Sages* simply says, "conjunction or aspect."

her,[20] are discerned most easily through the effective power of the Moon in animals and germinating things of the earth.

On a fortune and an infortune

27 And so, Venus and Jupiter are fortunate stars (as the authority of the Indians [claims]), but they judge all the remaining ones to be unfortunate. But among some people, Saturn and Mars in particular claim misfortune, while the rest of the stars are arranged in a balanced mixture of evenness. **28** And so, in the way they reckon it, an application of the Moon with the malevolents, [and] with the lucky ones wholly in aversion, undoubtedly brings about rains; but if she would apply to the fortunate ones, [and] not be invested in any way with the malevolents, there will not be rains.[21] **29** For the fortunate ones clear the air, rarify [it], and make [it] fine, and whatever thick vapor had ascended above, they bear it away by squeezing it out.[22] **30** But the nature of the malevolents, and the affinity of their likeness to vapor,[23] once [that nature] is united, they introduce heaviness, showing an increase of virtue; finally they congeal [the moisture]. **31** Venus, however, since she is one of the benevolents, because she redounds in excessive liquid, if (I say) she would be clothed by the malevolents and respond to them with some kind of configuration, she portends rains.[24] And for this reason the superiors[25] tend to pour forth rainy vapors.

32 In addition, certain mansions of the Moon participate in moisture, some in dryness, but others in a balance of each; the occasion for which is believed to emanate not only from the nature of the star established in that mansion, but even from a precise place of the circle, all of which can be discovered from the origin of the root.[26] **33** Moreover, a division of these mansions was made not otherwise than that the rays of the planets touch places of the dignities—namely in whose order the natures take part, being

---

[20] *Ipsiusque,* but it is possible this word refers to something else.
[21] Note how this is directly opposite to the view of Māshā'allāh in his *Chapter on Rains.*
[22] *Exprimendo. Sages* has them "dissipating" the density of the vapors.
[23] *Earumque cum vapore similitudinis affinitas. Sages* has a clearer reading, but the mechanism being described here does not make sense to me.
[24] Compare with *Sages,* which has Venus with the Moon here.
[25] *Hac superiorum de causa.*
[26] *Ex ipsius radicis primordio.* Hugo is probably referring to the lunation and ingress charts which predict for various lengths of time and so act as "roots" for future events.

proportionate [to them].[27] **34** But they are drawn forth by a heart of lines in the circle, their arc being referred by a certain habit of thought to a tetragon, trigon, and hexagon;[28] **35** nevertheless, too, the places out of which a strong application of the stars comes to be, [are] configured to the place of each star, namely from wherever they apply (from a male place, I say, or a female one, namely of the nature of the places related to the four elements); in the same way even, if they would apply to each other from a particular longitude and latitude. **36** Therefore, once an application of the stars from places of this kind has been determined, the matching and firm reception which is had shows the most certain effects. **37** For this reason, learned antiquity wanted to attend to the mansions (which they call the "knots" or rather "bonds"), [and] to designate and distinguish and note them and their effects.

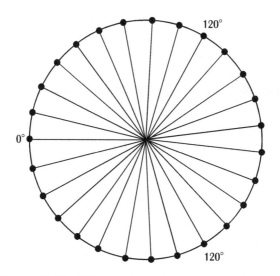

**Figure 32: The 27 mansions as measured by lines
or strings tied in knots[29]**

---

[27] What Hugo seems to mean (following *Sages*) is that we must look at the nature of the mansion along with the aspect (or type of aspect) which falls in it, in addition to the types of stars in them. See the next few sentences.

[28] See the diagram below.

[29] I have drawn this diagram to illustrate what I believe Hugo's source means when speaking of a "heart" of lines, their "knots," and the arc which is referred to various aspects by a "certain habit of thought." The source seems to imagine many different strings which are anchored at the center of the circle (its "heart"), which are then pulled or drawn out towards the circumference, and tied there. The angles between the strings determine the size of the aspects, and the knots show where planets and mansions would have to be, in

On having an understanding of heavy rains

39 For having an understanding of heavy rains, I believe it is appropriate[30] to attend most diligently to the hours of the assembly and the opposition,

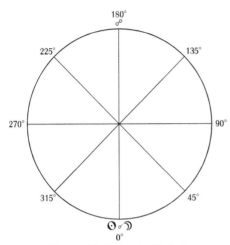

and even each tetragon and the middle of each tetragon, because from these eight configurations of the Moon, the most experienced of the ancients used to foresee the flowing of moisture.

40 But the majority of the Indians took care to attend to these four (namely the assembly and the opposition and each tetragon), with the rest being set aside[31]—while however certain others do not abandon the rest. **41** Moreover, these four figures which we said were the greatest, have eight other lesser ones put under them (and these are called the twelve "centers" of the Moon). **42** However, these are whenever the Moon is distant from the degree of the assembly by 12°, [and] not

Figure 33: Hugo's/Jafar's eight preferred centers

---

order to aspect each other. The reason that the lines are referred to squares and so on "by a certain habit of thought," is probably because the number of mansions—27 or 28—do not fit easily into the aspect scheme the way the signs do, certain mansions can only be said to square or trine each other by analogy with the signs. I have noted which mansions form a 120° angle, to emphasize that only a few actually aspect each other in the conventional way. Another possibility is that no single aspect by itself actually makes a square or triangle or other shape. For instance, an aspect between 15° Aries and 15° Cancer forms a 90° angle, but this is not really a "square," because a square has four sides. So the arcs that define the aspects, can only be called squares or triangles or hexagons by a convention or "habit" of thought adopted by astrologers and geometers. For these reasons too, the mansions are called "knots" or "bonds," because in order to find them, one must calculate angles and then draw lines to their relevant places on the circle, which are imagined as being tied onto the circumference.

[30] *Ob hoc congruum existimo.*

[31] *Postpositis.* This can also mean "put in second place," but since the next clause says that others do not "abandon" the semi-squares, I take Hugo's Jafar to mean that the majority of the Indians ignore them altogether.

otherwise for the opposition; but she does not abandon this arrangement for each tetragon.

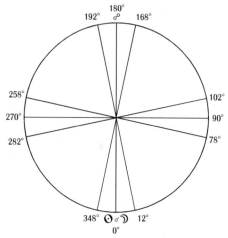

Figure 34: The centers according to "the majority" of the Indians

On the natures of the mansions of the Moon

44 However, concerning the mansions of the Moon, they left one un-touched. For since they numbered them as being 27, [then while] distributing the degrees of the whole circle equally among them, each one of them claimed 13 1/3 degrees. **45** But because of this, the aforesaid mansion is tak-en from the number of the whole, wherefore the Moon (as they claim), occupying each mansion with the Sun, **46** that mansion of the assembly without a doubt retains no signification of an effect.[32] **47** Whence even, and in an equal way, after the Moon withdraws from the Sun, while applying or

---

[32] This passage is somewhat complicated. First, Jafar seems to be arguing that there are in fact 28 mansions (as the Arabs have it), and that the Indians have only 27 because they don't count the one in which the New Moon takes place: in other words, at the New Moon, only 27 would be visible. This does not make sense, since the only way to get man-sions 13 1/3 degrees wide is to divide the whole zodiac by 27: it has nothing to do with a missing mansion. If there were in fact 28 (one of them being hidden), then each mansion would be only 12° 51' 26" wide, which is not what is attributed to the Indians here. Below (**48-50**), Jafar suggests a second reason for only 27 mansions: that the Indians did not recognize two mansions around the claws of Scorpio (or the pans of Libra), which the Arabs do: see al-Kindī's *DMT* Ch. 6 (in Section I.3) to see how the numbering of the mansions diverges, depending on whether one uses a 27- or 28-mansion system. Probably, the number of mansions is probably really related to the days of the Moon's visibility and her tropical cycle.

conjoined to another star, the whole signification (even the force and power of the effectiveness) is altogether left to the Sun once the Moon and the mansion have been left behind. **48** For this reason even, they wanted to note particularly and principally the one which is called *al-Zubānā*, because those two stars in every way complete the sign of Libra and its shape.[33] **49** For the Moon in the hands of Virgo is discovered not elsewhere, **50** in the same way, because the degrees of the one where these two [stars] exist, sit at the beginning of Scorpio, and there the Moon stays while she prowls around the scorched path; wherefore, they took its proper beginning from there.

51 And so, the Cyllenian Mercury disclosed all of these things [which were] hidden by[34] the ancients (in terms of explanation, not in terms of the effect of their operations). **52** But in what follows I will classify in what way an affair of this kind may be investigated with these particular (and as though woven-together)[35] mansions of the Moon themselves. I will even disclose the hours of dews and rain, even that of things for sale and illness, also journeys and the opinions about individual things which pertain to this little work, adjoining them in the required places for the greater evidence of the reader, in an appropriate order. **53** But the philosophers of the ancients appoint the places of the circle as [indicating] vapors or exhalations.

The mansions

55 Of the 27 lunar mansions therefore, which above are agreed to be called "knots," 10 in number are referred to moistures and rains because of the quality of their complexion. **56** The first of them among the Indians is *al-Dabarān*, the second *al-Dhirāᶜ*, the third *al-Jabha*, the fourth *al-Ṣarfah*, the fifth *al-Ghafr*, the sixth *al-Iklīl*, and after that *al-Naᶜāʾim*, *al-Balda*,[36] *al-Fargh al-muʾakhkhar*.[37] **57** Moreover, 6 of the number of the aforesaid particularly designate natural moisture, and they assume exact guidance for dews, because they claim the greater portion of moisture. But these are: *al-Dabarān*, *al-Dhirāᶜ*, *al-Ṣarfah*, *al-Iklīl*, *al-Balda*, *al-Fargh al-muʾakhkhar*. **58** For, the

---

[33] The pans of Libra are also the claws of Scorpio.

[34] *Occultata*. Or perhaps, "hidden *from* them"?

[35] Note Hugo's literary connection between the mansions as "knots" and their being "woven" together.

[36] Note that al-Kindī (*DMT* Ch. 6, **92**) treats al-Balda as neutral. If we follow al-Kindī, this should be *Saᶜd al-dhābiḥ*.

[37] Jafar's list is missing one of the mansions. Following al-Kindī (*DMT* Ch. 6, **89**), it should be *al-Shawlah*.

Moon being placed in mansions of this kind, or at least lit up [in them],[38] while she applies to stars signifying dews, or she would be staying in their assembly, really will agree with pouring forth heavy rains: in what way this happens, will be stated in what follows.

59 Moreover, they want 6 others of the mansions to be partners of dryness, of which the first is *al-Buṭayn, al-Haqᶜah, al-Ṭarf, al-Qalb, Saᶜd al-ᵓakhbiyah, al-Fargh al-muqaddam.*

60 But they ascribe the rest, as being moderate, to a state of balance: *al-Naṭh*[39] is of a temperate and equal complexion, then *al-Thurayyā, al-Hanᶜa, al-Nathra, al-Kharātān, al-ᶜAwwāᵓ, al-Simāk, Saᶜd al-ᵓakhbiyah,*[40] *Saᶜd bulaᶜ, Saᶜd al-suᶜūd.* **61** But 3 of these balanced mansions designate moisture because of the affinity and likeness of their nature: namely *al-Hanᶜa* and *al-Simāk* and *Saᶜd bulaᶜ*.[41] **62** Now, while the Moon, traversing in these, should be conjoined to stars designating dews, or she should approach them with a strong application, it portends there will be heavy rains in that same place.

63 Again, they connect these mansions ([which have been] described) with each other, by means of a likeness of property (as I reckon it). For they associate *al-Nathra,*[42] *Adatarf,*[43] *al-Jabha, al-Shawlah, al-Naᶜāᵓim,* and the Belly of the Fish,[44] and one will have to investigate with the rest which follow this, as it is had in a figure of rains.

On the changing of the atmosphere

65 Whenever, therefore, one will have to have knowledge about rains and their status, but even about the changing of the atmosphere, also about winds and dews, about rainy clouds and not-rainy ones, and no less at what hour or what time of year these things would happen, even about [their] increase and decrease, [one should look][45] just as the most experienced of the

---

[38] *Accensa.* But what is the difference between being placed in them, and being "lit up" in them? Perhaps Hugo meant *accessa*, which means "having approached" them. Normally we would expect an extra preposition to express that, but in sentence **102** he seems to use *accedo* without one to mean the same thing.
[39] An alternative name for *al-Sharaṭān*.
[40] But this was already listed as a dry one.
[41] In al-Kindī (*DMT* Ch. 6, **94-95**), this is *Saᶜd al-suᶜūd*.
[42] *Anathe.*
[43] This might be either *al-Ṣarfah* or *al-Ṭarf*.
[44] The last mansion, called *Baṭn al-ḥūt*.
[45] I have inserted this phrase because Hugo has gotten so carried away in his lengthy string of clauses, that he has forgotten to supply the essential verb.

Indians took care to describe in a figure according to the position of the circle. **66** Therefore, at the hour of the assembly or opposition (namely while[46] the Sun enters the first point of Aries or Libra), it is necessary for the Sun and Moon to be explicitly located or rather calculated. **67** However, the antiquity of the Indians instructed that this should happen at the ingress of Libra itself and when the Sun himself walks through the twentieth degree of Scorpio, because these signs really announce the hours of heavy rains in the middle climes.

68 Finally, once the Sun and Moon have been calculated for these two hours (namely those of the assembly or opposition) or for the aforesaid two signs, it will be good to pay attention, with the greatest effort, to what mansions of the circle they are holding onto, which could be discerned thusly. **69** Taking equal degrees from the first point of Aries up to the place of the assembly or opposition itself, remember to grant what pertains to the individual mansion (namely 13 1/3 degrees). **70** Once that is discovered, one must note [whether] it is moist or dry or bears itself in a balanced way. After that, too, attend to the places of the rest of the stars, and their mansions, just as was done for the Moon. **71** Finally, once they have been compared with certain understanding, one will have to search for the one to which the Moon would apply after the assembly.[47] **72** For if she, traversing in a moist mansion, [would apply to a] Saturn equally appearing in a moist one, and each being under the same bond,[48] nor does another star impede their application by any figure, it unwaveringly portends suitable, persistent, and gentle heavy rains, even black, obscure clouds wholly occupying the atmosphere. **73** But if the two inferiors, applying in the aforesaid regard, would supply their own testimonies, they wholly increase what was said before; which if they would be holding onto the same bond (or rather, knot) with them, they mean an overflowing of rains, the falling of houses, and submersions to be feared.

74 Moreover, the Moon: with guidance of this kind being assumed, the degrees of application undoubtedly lay bare at what hour these things ought to happen. **75** Therefore, once it has been discovered how many degrees there are of the application (whether the assembly or opposition or tetragon, or what is of this kind), it is necessary for there to be that many hours or days in between, until it begins to rain. **76** If therefore it was a regard from a

---

[46] Or rather, "before."
[47] Or after the opposition, whichever it is.
[48] This undoubtedly means being "in the same mansion."

convertible[49] or double-bodied [sign], it really suggests hours; but from a firm one,[50] days. **77** The quick course of the Moon really decrees a quicker or slow outcome, even an increase of light and computation, or her traversal in the quick *kardajas*,[51] or in opposite places of this kind. **78** While these things bear themselves thusly, the one to which the Moon applies likewise portends the number of hours. **79** Which if they bore themselves in the converse way, it signifies days and introduces slowness. **80** Now if a closer[52] regard of a benevolent to Saturn is had, and with rays thrown in between, and even their own traversal in their own dignities, these things seem to alternate: and it is a sign of delay and slowness. **81** The best is with the Moon pursuing the body or tetragon or opposition of Saturn: for thus there will be no delay. **82** For in fact it makes a judgment of delay whenever neither Saturn nor the other star[53] would possess a moist knot or mansion, nor would they be supported by the testimony of the inferiors.[54] **83** But with these things bearing themselves as was stated above, the signification of the Moon will not be able to be turned aside,[55] and with her speaking the truth,[56] praise and glory will in no way flee away.

[The Moon applying to different planets]

84 Moreover, a lunar application having been made to a Saturn who is lingering in a dry mansion, while they do not traverse in the same sign, nor do they acquire the testimony of inferiors, it shows persistent clouds but without heavy rains.

85 But if the Moon would apply to Jupiter from out of similar places, and they would be lingering in the same knot and equally a moist mansion, they being blessed by whatever testimony of Venus and Mercury, clouds or a kind of clouds will really occur. **86** With the testimony of these being denied, rains

---

[49] That is, a movable sign.

[50] That is, a fixed sign.

[51] See Glossary.

[52] Reading *propriori* for *proprio*. Remember that benevolents were generally not productive of rain.

[53] That is, Mars (see sentences **111** and **118** below for similar phrases). Note that Jafar connects this with the opening of the doors later in the sentence, by speaking of the support of the inferiors.

[54] This may be a reference to the opening of the doors.

[55] Reading *perverti* with some of Burnett's sources, for *praeverti* ("be anticipated").

[56] Reading *veradicente* with one of Burnett's sources, for *veradicentem*.

and dews with clouds are denied unless (I say) Jupiter, applying then at last to Saturn, will introduce part of those things which were said.

87 The Moon applying in just the same way to Mars, and with the testimony of feminine [planets], and she being placed in a knot and mansion of the Moon which portends moistures, it shows complicated and mixed clouds, likewise thunders and flashing, even lightning and often those without heavy rains, unless (I say) an application of Mars himself with Saturn and Jupiter is discovered: for because of such an application, there will be rains present. **88** Here it even comes to be noticed that Mars, from any regard, greatly increases the signification of heavy rains; in every way it also helps the Moon and the star to which she applies, in generating rains, for with her applying particularly and principally to it,[57] there is a delay. **89** But if it happened otherwise, it does not signify it; and it does corrupt, but the clouds which the Martial nature brings forth [will] be having the redness of saffron from above, not without brightness.

90 The Moon applying to the Sun. **91** Moreover, the lunar application with the Sun spoils and blocks heavy rains, while if the testimonies of the stars are present (certain ones of which being in a bond and moist mansion), [and] should the Sun apply to Saturn and Mars in places where he has neither dignity nor power, it portends the harshest falling of rains and inundations of waters; moreover, it generates saffron clouds and ones which are quickly dissolved, and afterwards it makes the atmosphere calm. **92** The Moon[58] should be applying to the Sun from a tetragon; but from the opposition and assembly, it will in no way be called an application. **93** Moreover, one must note that an application of the Moon with the malevolents in that week bestows rains. **94** However, the benevolents (by any aspect) dissolve and block the dews and efficacy of that unfortunate one, and they turn aside[59] the hour of the future signification. **95** The Moon being conjoined to that same malevolent, and being clothed by it, really restores[60] the certain and inviolable outcome of that hour.

96 The Moon applying to Venus. **97** In addition, the Moon applying to Venus and being in the same connection, and moist signs and mansions, announces future heavy rains, nor could this be frustrated if the superior stars (the infortunes, I say), would particularly be regarding [them], whether Mer-

---

[57] That is, if the Moon *only* applied to this other planet, *without* the help of Mars.
[58] This sentence seems to be clarifying the use of "application" in the previous sentence.
[59] Reading *pervertunt* for *praevertunt*.
[60] *Reducit.*

cury is testifying or not. **98** But if she would not be applying to these superiors, since she is then fortunate, the signification of heavy rains is made to totter. **99** Venus however, applying just then[61] to a superior star, while they were in the same knot, will convey the greatest heavy rains, and persistent ones. **100** Nor will there be falseness in Venus in anything while they bear themselves thusly. For while she appears fortunate, the lunar promise will not be certain while they linger neither in the same knot nor a moist sign nor a moist mansion. **101** Now, if the Moon would apply to her and they bear themselves thusly, it introduces clouds and dews but even mists, however without heavy rains. **102** Whenever, however, as we have said, they bore themselves thusly and the Moon would approach Saturn and Mars after [their] commixture, it brings back an excessive rushing of rains.

103 The Moon applying to Jupiter and the Sun. **104** Likewise, with her applying to Jupiter and the Sun, while there is some configuration between each (a regard, I say, or an application), heavy rains will not pour forth. **105** With the Moon then in an optimal place (namely, in one of the centers, the places devoted to this signification), since she is made fortunate, she shakes and even turns aside[62] her own proper guidance while she already responded to the fortunate ones by means of some configuration. **106** These general situations should wholly be noted. **107** Even the bright white clouds which are then generated portend many and inconstant dews.

108 The Moon applying to Mercury. **109** But if the Moon would apply to Mercury in the same knot, and being in a moist mansion, it prefigures quick and continuous heavy rains. **110** Also, the added testimony of Venus really introduces an overflowing of rains. **111** Mercury, however, applying with the superior stars (or to either of them),[63] warns of submersions and even collapses to be feared, because of the overflowing and persistence of the rains. **112** But however much there would not be a Mercurial application with the superiors, there will be rain. **113** Moreover, that same Mercury applying to the malevolents after he approached Venus, [indicates that] one must fear submersion and collapse and the persistence of heavy rains. **114** Moreover, Mercury regarding Venus from a watery sign and a moist mansion, or being placed in the same knot or bond, [means that] the rains will go beyond the

---

[61] *Tunc demum. Demum* could mean "only," but I take this to be part of Hugo's typical style: that the Moon is applying to Venus, and Venus also happens at the same time to be applying to a malefic.

[62] Reading *pervertit* with some of Burnett's sources, for *praevertit.*

[63] By the "superior" stars, Hugo or Jafar means the malefics, Mars or Saturn.

limit. **115** Which if a regard was present, while they bore themselves otherwise than was said above, a mediocrity of rains is denoted. **116** Even though Mercury indicates dews (as we have already said), if he would regard the benevolents in their own bounds or dignities, [and there is] an effect of that same kind and of their nature being admixed, it necessarily makes the Moon a liar, and perverts her leadership,[64] and will introduce other effects, of which kind is a manifold fury of winds, driving the clouds from the air, from every direction. **117** And the quantity of the winds will be according to the power of the star whose kind he assumes. **118** Nor do the twin stars[65] traveling the sky (namely, if the Moon would apply to them) pollute with lies, but rather they will rejoice in truth and wholly release what was promised—unless, I say, their status and condition would be especially be referred to Jupiter and Sun (as was stated above) through any kind of configuration: for thus it wholly changes the Moon's promises. **119** Their application with Saturn and Mars after the Moon approached them, is never made a liar, but it introduces the increase of [their] required and persistent indication, while it greatly increases rains, [and] introduces dews and mists. **120** But if they should presume to vary what was stated about rains, they will not be able to turn aside[66] the densest clouds and moisture of the air, but it will generate mists and raise up long-lasting moistures in the air.

121 All of these things are ascribed to their efficacy, particularly insofar as they bear themselves thusly. **122** Wherefore, those things which have now been explained about secrets of this kind [are] in no way fictional, and a happy and well-advised response by the one judging should be had.

A tested chapter on the changing of the weather

124 In addition, the Moon even traveling alone in a moist mansion, and being cadent from all stars, and being solitary from them in one of the centers,[67] and even being singular in her nature and action, introduces clouds and manifold dews, moistens the air, and in turn conveys many types of

---

[64] Reading *pervertit* for *praevertit*. What this phrase can also literally mean is that it turns her indication aside, in the sense of a finger pointing off in the wrong direction, or how a guide indicating a path may go astray.
[65] I take this to be the malefics again. In other words, if the Moon applies to them the effect will be certain and she will not give false information, *unless* they would be interfered with by Jupiter and the Sun.
[66] Reading *pervertere* for *praevertere*.
[67] All of this points to her being "wild": see *Introductions to Traditional Astrology (ITA)* III.10.

heavy rains; the clouds out of which the horizon is filled up will become hot; it stirs up diverse winds from which thunders, flashing, and lightning are created. **125** But if after that she would apply to a star which holds onto the category of the aforesaid star (if, I say, it were fortunate), it dissolves the aforesaid; for, it being a malevolent will exhibit a double efficacy [as compared with] the rest of the stars.[68] **126** Whence, I warn that one must note that while she traverses alone in the loosening up[69] of the aforesaid, she is found to be most strong. **127** From the aforesaid it is manifestly clear that the Moon being with the benevolents or in their lodging-place[70] or even with stars which apply to fortunate ones, in no way declares heavy rains; but to the contrary, traversing with the malevolents generates rains.

128 Laying bare the general significations of the Moon with the individual stars, as in the *ijtimā* (that is, the assembly), in those things which seemed necessary for having understanding of this kind, I have arrived at what was written above, in an appropriate order. **129** Therefore, the way in which it must be done at the opposition or tetragon, should now be explained next. **130** (And so, it is a tetragon whenever the Moon is withdrawing from the assembly by 90°, or from the opposition by the same number.)[71] And this must be performed four times in the individual months, as it was stated above:[72] for once these [observations] (which I added as roots) have been carried out fully, no variation or ambiguity in the renewal of the air will occur. **131** Therefore, the beginning of this matter is led from the first ingress of the Sun into Libra, up to where he walks through the twentieth degree of Scorpio. **132** But this same operation should be followed through up to the end of the year. **133** This same thing will even have to be pursued at the cycle of mundane years.

134 Moreover, one must note that the Moon has other guidance. **135** And so, once the assembly or opposition and each tetragon has been discovered just as was stated above (in order that knowledge of rains may be had), let the business of the aforesaid method carry out those things which we stated,

---

[68] That is, if she then applies to a benefic or neutral planet, the weather will clear; but if to a malefic, it will suddenly become more severe.
[69] *Solutione.* This seems to mean that she is "releasing" bad weather and making it happen, which is another meaning for *solutio.*
[70] This is a term occasionally used by Hugo to denote zodiacal signs.
[71] Reading for Hugo's awkward *ad conventum accedens gradus xc, ad oppositionem recedens pari numero distiterit.*
[72] But is Hugo/Jafar telling us to calculate a chart complete with the angles, at every quarter of the Moon, or simply to note the current transits at the time?

[but] before the assembly [and] after it, [and] in the same way even on this side of the opposition and beyond it, by 12°. **136** But these are the twelve centers of the Moon enumerated above, with which one will have to pursue the same affair, before and after.[73] **137** For they assume a certain power and efficacy in all of these things, while knowledge of them obtains the power of a root and a building.[74]

138 And so, the Moon traversing in mansions of balanced complexion, or dry ones, if she would then apply to inferior stars (which are places[75] of dew) or to superiors in watery signs, for the most part it makes a judgment of rains. **139** But the signs which introduce dews are watery and moist, like Cancer, Leo, Scorpio, and Aquarius. **140** But the stars which portend dews and moisture are the Moon, Mercury, and Venus. **141** If therefore they would regard the Moon from signs of this kind, or they would stay with her, [then] should the Moon even apply to them from moist places, it means heavy rains that should be feared. **142** She applying or regarding from dry or balanced places, wholly introduces mediocre rains. **143** Moreover, the Moon conveys, through her singular and own proper nature, sparse and bright white mists and clouds.

144 But however much the things which were said above may suffice in this place, the matter and [this] place recommends that [we] append certain no less useful things. **145** The condition of a rainy year depends especially on the ingress of the Sun into Libra up to the twentieth degree of Scorpio, [and] no less from the lunar application with the rest of the stars. **146** Therefore, should the star to which the Moon applies be eastern, it shows the end of the year or month or even week to be rainy. **147** Western, it decorates the beginnings of the aforesaid with the benefit of heavy rains. But this application being made especially with Venus and Mercury, means what was said before. **148** One being eastern, the other western, while the Moon would apply to them, denotes common rains and throughout the whole year, and the greatest [rains]. **149** In fact, a multitude of rains especially pours forth while Venus and Mercury hasten to enter Scorpio and Capricorn, Aquarius, and Pisces; but even an application of them with the Moon from moist places (not with-

---

[73] That is, just before and just after each quarter, when the Moon is 12° from angles of the Sun.

[74] Note that the other Arabic term for these in 'Umar and al-Kindī ("posts," "foundations") also recalls ideas of foundations.

[75] Or rather, "planets": see **140**. But perhaps Hugo means *in* places of dew, just as he has superiors in watery signs next.

out a regard):⁷⁶ which if they would bear themselves thusly, they show general rains, nor unuseful ones. **150** With the Moon applying to one while the other would regard the Moon, while that regard would be there until it is separated from her, a multitude of rains will not be absent.

151 The Moon applying with Saturn. **152** Moreover, the Moon applying to Saturn shows soft and sweet rains, but even quiet ones, and obscure and black mists. **153** But if to Mars, it brings heavy rains, thunders, and flashings, often stones and hail and saffron clouds having redness and bright whiteness from above. **154** With a signification of this kind being assumed, Mercury announces rains, a fury of winds, and their harshest traversal, even intermittent and dispersed clouds, [and] introduces saffron ones and those having the color of smoke. **155** If however the Sun assumes a signification of this kind, it portends great drops and saffron clouds. **156** But Venus, with the same [signification] being assumed, really generates soft and continuous rains, many dews, [and] clouds like mists. **157** Jupiter has fair weather and favorably-disposed winds.⁷⁷ **158** Not otherwise too, will a common gathering or admixture of the other stars being made with one another exhibit a general efficacy (as was stated above); but it will even be allowed to watch their significations and the successive colors of the clouds and the variations of the atmosphere throughout the whole year, with every difficulty being removed (once these things have first been compensated for).⁷⁸

[The stars of the mansions of the Moon]

159 Since therefore the more skillful people of any occupation⁷⁹ often impede those less experienced in knowledge, so that they do not recognize the place of the Moon and the mansion in which she traverses, in a full and certain calculation, I have taken care to append this matter in an abridged way, so that knowledge of the aforesaid may be had before one's eyes. **160** For I am writing down the mansions of the Moon according to the number of their stars in a table,⁸⁰ so that while one may recognize with which of [the

---

⁷⁶ Hugo/Jafar seems to mean that both a *conjunction* ("application") and an aspect will indicate these things.

⁷⁷ *Iupiter namque aera serenum et ventos habet propicios.*

⁷⁸ *Compensatis.* Hugo seems to mean, "once the indications have overcome the default assumption of fair weather."

⁷⁹ Reading *occupationis…impediunt* for *occupatio…impedit*, otherwise we could make no sense of the use of *prudentiores* here.

⁸⁰ According to Burnett, none of the sources contains a table.

stars] the Moon is staying, one may discover even in which mansion she was, most exactly. **161** For once the place of the Moon in the mansions has been noted, and also the places of the rest of the stars have been discovered (namely which of the mansions they are not fleeing),[81] no hesitation about the condition of the atmosphere and its change will be left. **162** For they are certain individual lunar mansions in the zodiac (which namely the Sun, with the Moon and the rest of the stars, walk though), in an apportioned and delimited division.[82]

Tested knowledge of heavy rains and winds

164 The knowledge of winds from the experience of rains, just like that of heavy rains, depends wholly on the assembly and opposition and the two tetragons. **165** Wherefore, the matter recommends that one attend to the three stars which designate winds: namely Mercury, Mars, and the Sun. **166** For while Mars greatly increases winds, Saturn blocks them, particularly [while] retrograde and traversing in an earthy sign; no less too, do the watery signs speak against them. **167** However, Mercury is a star of winds, and equally the airy signs. **168** In order therefore that you may foresee winds coming, it will be good to attend to Mercury. **169** For the Moon, withdrawing[83] after the assembly, applying to him, and traversing with him in the same bond, in a contrary mansion, announces the blowing[84] of winds.

170 Again, an application of Mercury with Saturn, or he traversing with him in the same knot and an airy mansion, nor is he[85] retrograde, brings about dark winds and varies the atmosphere; often, even, a terrible fury of winds emerges. **171** Whence it comes to be noted that the retrogradation of Saturn (even if Mercury should apply to him) wholly contradicts winds.

172 Moreover, with Mercury applying to Mars, or being in his assembly or the same knot, and a mansion which indicates winds, hot winds go forth and heat is generated in the air, and clouds will possess the horizon, often fires from the ether will be broken up or will appear in it, and the color of winds is altered—especially with Mars being retrograde. **173** With Mars lingering in

---

[81] *Quae videlicet mansionum has vel illas non fugiunt.* This last part is an unusual circumlocution, even for Hugo, and I have simplified it here.
[82] Reading *partitione* for *partitio.*
[83] Reading *recedens* for *recedit.*
[84] *Discursus.*
[85] I believe this is Saturn, based on what follows.

an earthy sign, there is a lesser signification of winds, but he grants many rains from that reduced[86] traversal of winds.

174 Now, that same Mercury applying to Jupiter or Venus, or in a mansion shaping rains, if he would be in the same knot, it brings back the beneficial winds. **175** However, Jupiter assumes a greater effectiveness for winds than Venus does; for he has the favorability[87] and mildness of all winds.

176 Moreover, Mercury being configured to the Sun, or holding onto the same knot and mansion which has winds, generates heating winds and the worst ones.

177 However, the common gathering or admixture of Mercury and the Moon with the rest of the stars is of the most subtle inquiry: which if it would happen, nothing will flee from [your] intention.[88]

[The Sun and the four winds in the seasons]

178 Here it even comes to be noted that the cycling of the Sun through the signs renews the changing of seasons. **179** Whence, that part of the four parts of the world which he holds onto (namely the east or west, south or north), comes to be noted with the utmost effort; no less, too, the lunar appearance from [the rays of] the Sun, and what her manner was at the opposition. **180** For the Sun's traversal in Aries really generates the eastern wind, which is called Eurus, up until he crosses the end of Gemini. **181** And where he is located [then], until he occupies the last part of Virgo and the first [part] of Libra, stirs up the southern wind (namely Aquilo). **182** There, even, and up to the beginning of Capricorn, Zephirus is generated. **183** Again, from thence up to the last parts of Pisces, it is necessary that Auster arise. **184** Taurus and Gemini are between Eurus and Aquilo, Leo and Virgo will possess the middle between Aquilo and Zephirus; likewise Scorpio and Sagittarius are placed between Zephirus and Auster, but Aquarius and Pisces between Auster and Eurus.[89]

---

[86] *Modico.*

[87] *Propiciacio.*

[88] *Proposito.* Recall above (**20-21**), when Jafar had stated that Mercury and the Moon are similar in their taking on the qualities of what is around them. This suggests that an application between them will be difficult to judge.

[89] After this sentence, the Jafar text largely turns to matters of elections and questions (which will appear in my future edition of *Judges*); but sentences **196-207** are on prices and commodities, and appear in Section II.12.

SECTION I.11: *THE SAGES OF INDIA*

Comment by Dykes. As I stated before, *Sages* is a Latin translation of the same Arabic source as Jafar's *Book of Heavy Rains* (though probably not the same manuscript). It is shorter than Jafar and incomplete, but reads more easily and directly than Hugo's Latin does. I have followed Burnett in adding boldface sentence numbers where the text stands in parallel to Jafar. The "Almersius" in the first paragraph is an unknown person, and according to Burnett (2004) only the oldest manuscript refers to him.

ꙮ   ꙮ   ꙮ

Almersius said: With respect to rains, the sages of India judge according to the Moon, considering her mansions and conjunctions, and the aspects of the planets to her. Other sages refer the majority of judgments about rains, to the Moon.

13-17 The Indians attribute the whole judgment to the Moon alone, claiming she is the significatrix of this world, and a mediator between earthly things and the planets, and [that] she receives power from the superior planets and the fixed stars, which she [then] gives to lands, **22** because she is nearest the point of the earth. We comprehend this with [our] sight, **23** because her manifold effects manifestly appear in the oppositions [and] conjunctions [and] squares,[1] and the manifold changes of corruption and generation appear according to the increase or diminution of her light and computation,[2] and according to her elevation or descent, both in the circle of the point of going out[3] and in the epicycle, **24** and her motion into the right or left, and her conjunction or aspect to any of the planets.

27 The Indians even claim that Jupiter and Venus are fortunate planets, [but] all the rest unfortunate. However, the most subtle of them claim only Saturn and Mars are unfortunate, [but] all the rest temperate, which seems to be more closely related to the truth. **28** But if the Moon has a conjunction or aspect with a planet [that is an] infortune, [it means that] rain will proceed from thence; but from a conjunction or aspect of a fortune, not at all—unless that same fortune would have a conjunction or aspect with an infor-

---

[1] Reading *quadratis* for *qua ratis*.
[2] Reading with Jafar for "knowledge" (*notitiae*).
[3] *Puncti egressi.* This is probably a misunderstanding in the Latin, and must refer to her relation to her apogee in the deferent circle.

tune: **29** because the fortunes dissolve the atmosphere and make it more fine, and they dissipate the density drawn together from the vapor[4] ascending from the earth, **30** and the infortunes increase the density according to the relation of their circles to the earth: because their operation is like vapor on the earth, and they attract moisture and vapor from the earth more abundantly, and they thicken the prior density and bind it, whence comes rain. **31** And even though Venus is a fortune, because she works moisture, her being conjoined to the Moon does bring about rains—but it does not bring [them] about unless they have the conjunction or aspect of an infortune.

32 However, certain ones of the mansions of the Moon are moist, certain ones dry, certain ones temperate: which happens due to the operation of the fixed stars which are in them, and according to the nature of the place from [its] part of the circle, **33** and according to the rays **34** of the aspect of the trine, sextile, square, [and] contrary[5] of the planets, which they perfect in the aforesaid mansions, and accordance with the planets being in the regard of the Ascendant (namely whether in the angles or after the angles or in the fallen[6] houses), **35** and according to the places in which the Moon and the planets are, namely the masculine or feminine signs, and according to the nature of the signs in which they are (fiery or watery or airy or earthy). Moreover, [judge] according to a completed or incomplete conjunction with the planets as considered from longitude and latitude, and likewise an aspect. For unless they are complete, it will not show a completed matter.

40 But the Indians consider the conjunction of the Sun and Moon, and the opposition, and the square. **41** Many others consider besides these the middles of the squares, and **42** the eight[7] doors, which are the 12° before the place of the conjunction, and that many after, and that many before and after the place of the opposition. **44** The Indians even claim exactly 27 mansions of the Moon, but others 28.[8] Whence, according to the Indians' division of the circle into 27, 13 1/3 degree fall to the individual mansions.

51 We do not know the reason for this division, but from certain ones of them which reach us we understood this, **48** namely [that] the mansion which others call al-Zubānā is not regarded by the Indians as being among the num-

---

[4] *Fumo*, literally "smoke," here and below.
[5] That is, the opposition.
[6] *Lapsis*, that is, "cadent."
[7] Reading for "seven." Eight are mentioned here, as they are in Jafar.
[8] The Latin text reads "29," obviously a misread for the 28 in the Arab theory of mansions.

ber of the mansions, because this is close to the hand of Virgo, **49** which is one of the mansions and is part of that mansion. **45** Others offer this reason, that even though there are 28,[9] the Indians do not count the one in which the Moon is conjoined to the Sun, **46** because the Moon then has no power in it when she is conjoined to the Sun, nor does she have power **47** until, in the next mansion, she appears separated from the Sun and has a conjunction or aspect with some planet. **55** And there are 10 mansions which administer much moisture, **53**, and they are called the "vapor of the circle," which are: **46**

al-Dabarān, which is the middle of Taurus
al-Dhirāᶜ
al-Jabha
al-Ṣarfah
al-Ghafr[10]
al-Iklīl / al-Zubānā[11]
al-Shawlah
al-Naᶜāʾim
Saᶜd al-dhābiḥ[12]
Al-fargh al-muʾakhkhar

Figure 35: Ten moist mansions, according to *Sages*

Whence, if the Moon were in al-Dabarān, al-Dhirāᶜ, al-Ṣarfah, al-Iklīl, al-Balda,[13] [or] al-Fargh al-muʾakhkhar, [it indicates even more rain, as these are very moist].[14] And[15] more if she were separated from the conjunction of the Sun **58** and has a conjunction or aspect with an infortune (namely Saturn or Mars or even Venus), it means rains. But al-Dhirāᶜ, which is the middle of Cancer, signifies much rain; and all of the remaining ones a scarcer amount.

---

[9] Again, the Latin text reads "29."
[10] Reading with mss. *CQ*; *PR* have *Alchard* but out of order; I take it to be this mansion.
[11] In mss. *CQ* and *PR*, respectively.
[12] Reading with mss. *PR*.
[13] *Aveldah*. But following al-Kindī, this should be *Saᶜd al-dhābiḥ*.
[14] Adding based on al-Kindī and Jafar.
[15] Reading the rest of this paragraph with mss. *PR*.

59 But six of these mansions are dry, which are:

al-Buṭayn
al-Haqᶜah
al-Ṭarf
al-Qalb
Saᶜd al-ʾakẖbiyah
al-Fargh al-muqaddam

Figure 36: Six dry mansions, according to *Sages*

60 The rest are temperate, **61** of which three have little moisture, which are:

al-Thurayyā[16]
al-Simāk
Saᶜd bulaᶜ[17]

Figure 37: Six mansions with little moisture, according to *Sages*

62 …in which, if the Moon were conjoined with a rainy planet, rain occasionally comes forth.

65 You will discover the causes of rains and the changing of the atmosphere, and the causes of winds and cloudy [days], even if[18] the rain is in the future, and also in what season of the year it is going to be, in this way: **66** you will seek, most diligently, the place and hour (with the degrees or minutes) in which the future conjunction (or opposition) of the Sun and Moon is, whether it is closer to the ingress of the Sun into Aries, and into Libra.[19] Besides this, the Indians even discovered the hour when the Sun enters the twentieth degree of Scorpio: and from that time they affirm that water is increased in wells.[20] **70** You will even discover, most diligently, by how many degrees and minutes the individual planets are distant from the beginning of Aries at the first hour of the conjunction or opposition, and in

---

[16] Reading with mss. *PR*, as *CQ*'s spelling (*Albechae, Albechabe*) cannot easily be identified (although Burnett believes it may be al-Hanᶜa.

[17] Reading with mss. *CQ*, as *PR* mention one that was already listed in another category (*Saᶜd al-dhābiḥ*).

[18] Reading *etsi* for *et si*.

[19] The author is assuming that we are casting the chart only for the nearest future ingress.

[20] That is, the water in wells allegedly increases around that date, which suggests a time of increased moisture.

what cabin[21] of the mansions the individual planets are, by counting 13 1/3 degrees for one mansion, starting from the beginning of Aries itself.

71 Thirdly, you will inquire as to which planet the receding Moon has a regard,[22] from the minute of the degree in which the conjunction or opposition comes to be. **72** Which if she aspected Saturn, and each was in a moist mansion, and if Saturn is not impeded by an aspect of Jupiter, there will be black clouds, and slow-moving and lasting rain. **73** If the inferior planets (namely, Venus and Mercury) aspected Saturn, the rain will be greater and more lasting. And this is a consideration for knowing the rains of the year.

75 Likewise, you will consider the conjunctions and oppositions and the squares in individual months, for discovering the rains of the months, and for finding the day on which it begins to rain. Search, therefore, for the distance in degrees in which the conjunction or opposition or square was, to the degree of a rainy planet: **76** and if the Moon were in a movable sign, give one hour to each degree[23] of distance; and in a firm one, a day to each degree; and if in a common one and in the first half, individual days to individual degrees, [but] if in the second [half], one hour to each degree. And where the distribution will be ended, the beginning of rain will be on that day or hour.

77 The most subtle of the Indians consider the slowness and quickness of the rain according to the quickness and slowness of the Moon's course, and according to the increase of her light and computation,[24] saying that the quickness and increase of rain follows [that].

78 If the planet to which the Moon gives [her] power[25] is like the Moon in the aforesaid accidents, after that many hours for the degrees lying in between the Moon and the planet, you will count that many days in quickness and slowness and in subtraction, so that the rain may come.[26] Which, in addition to the aforesaid Mars aspected Saturn, the delay is greater **81** until the Moon reaches the place of Saturn, or [his] opposition or square. **84** And if Saturn were in a dry mansion and the Moon would give him power, and neither of the inferior planets would aspect him, there will be cloudiness without rain. **85** And if the Moon would give power to Jupiter, with each

---

[21] *Casa.*
[22] That is, the planet to which the Moon first applies, after separating from the conjunction or opposition with the Sun.
[23] Reading *gradui* correctly with two of Burnett's sources, for *gradus.*
[24] Again, reading with Jafar for "knowledge" (*notitiae*).
[25] *Vim dat*, probably the Arabic "pushing power," here and below.
[26] Jafar seems to say that that if the Moon is applying to a planet which portends rain, then the degrees between them indicates hours; but if not, days.

appearing in a moist mansion, should either one of the inferiors aspect Jupiter, there will only be dew or cloudiness. **86** Which if (with the Moon and Jupiter being so placed) neither of the inferiors would aspect Jupiter, and he himself would aspect Saturn, there will be rain. **87** And if the Moon and Mars would be in moist mansions, and either of the inferiors would look at Mars, terrible cloudiness will follow, [and] thunders and meteors[27] and hail, and it will not rain unless Mars aspected Jupiter or Saturn—if God, the glorious and sublime manager of the seasons, wills.

The Book of Heavy Rains ends.

---

[27] *Lampadas.* This can also simply mean bright lights (suggesting lightning flashes high in the clouds).

SECTION I.12: HERMANN OF CARINTHIA, *THE BOOK OF HEAVY RAINS*

Comment by Dykes. This short work by Hermann of Carinthia seems not to be a direct translation of any single work, but a condensed summary of many different texts, as was his *The Search of the Heart* (Dykes, 2011). For example, a couple of sentences can be traced back to uncannily similar ones in Māshā'allāh's *Letter*, even though they do not match exactly.

This translation is based on Low-Beer, but I also found it useful to consult four other manuscripts, listed in the Bibliography.

ℭ   ℭ   ℭ

Chapter 1: Introduction

2 Since the authority of the Indians has handed down many and varied precepts for the understanding of heavy rains, I have taken care to run through them in a general way, and to bring the diverse opinions of different people under a certain abridgement, so that whatever the great number of their words has hidden, or the dissonant multitude of the philosophers has given variety to, even what the disconnected digressions of those writing has often drawn out—the brevity of a simple page will represent it, without any worry. **3** Whenever, therefore, a concerned inquirer would approach the falling of heavy rains, a most certain judgment pours forth[1] from what is written below.

Chapter 2: Universal rules

2 Now, the Sun in the southern hemisphere,[2] and Venus being under the rays, with the Moon applying to her, portend there are going to be heavy rains on that same day and very hour. **3** No less too, with Mercury being scorched, if the Moon would apply to him or his opposite, and he[3] would be lingering in Scorpio; the assembly of Mars and Venus in Scorpio will even

---

[1] *Mano.* This is a nice little pun on Hermann's part.
[2] That is, in signs of southern declination.
[3] Or perhaps, "she" (the Moon).

indicate this same thing. **4** With the Sun even in Aquarius, the Moon applying to him or placed in his opposition, and should Venus be lingering in that same place, rains will be present in that hour itself. **5** In the same way too, an application of Jupiter or Venus to the Sun, and the Moon traversing in their opposition or tetragon, while Venus was scorched, makes a certain indication of rains. **6** Which if they would assemble,[4] and Mercury equally would traverse with them, it reports continuous heavy rains and winds on that same day. **7** Even the lunar aspect to them [means that] heavy rains will not be absent. **8** However, the Sun in Libra, Venus in Sagittarius, with the Moon accompanying them, introduces rains on that very day. **9** With the Sun in Aquarius, the Moon in Leo (the house of the Sun, I say, or at least being in his sovereignty),[5] a course of excessive heavy rains will be present. **10** But[6] especially in Leo (the same thing in Sagittarius), on account of the clouds of Leo and its lightning; some of these even exist in the Pleiades and equally at the beginning of Taurus. **11** But Mars regarding the Sun and the Moon, while Venus and Mercury accompany[7] him or her, suggest present heavy rains and thick drops. **12** Likewise, too, in a house of Venus or Mars (Aries, namely, and Scorpio), large drops, thunders, and lightning flashes are generated. **13** Moreover, the Sun traversing in Pisces or Aries, with the Moon lingering in Virgo or Libra or Sagittarius (namely, in vaporous places),[8] conveys an abundance of heavy rains on that day.

---

[4] I take this to mean an assembly by body in the same sign. But this word (*conveniant*) can also mean to "agree," and suggests that more than one of the conditions just mentioned, would occur at the same time.

[5] That is, his exaltation (Aries).

[6] Reading with Cambridge. This sentence is somewhat vexed in the MSS. Low-Beer reads, "if in Leo especially, the same; in Sagittarius on account of its rivers, [and] even the clouds of Leo), and some of these exist [*consistit*, sic.] in the Pleiades and equally at the beginning of Taurus." Munich reads, "…but especially in Leo. The same thing in Sagittarius on account of its rivers, and the clouds of Leo; some of these even exist in the Pleiades and equally at the beginning of Taurus."

[7] Reading *comitantur* with Cambridge for *committuntur*.

[8] This may mean they tend to indicate only dews and mists, since in Ch. 4 below these signs have only a modicum of rains.

Chapter 3: On abundant rains

2 In addition, Venus or Mercury traversing in the same places with the Sun in a house of Venus (and even the Moon),[9] portends the most severe drops of heavy rains, meteors,[10] and thunders. **3** But in Leo, Pisces, [and] even Aries, Libra, and Scorpio, with the Moon in the Sun's opposition or traversing with Venus, it sends drops (not without meteors), thunders, and lightning. **4** In the same way, too, the Moon in Leo generates meteors, thunders, and lightning, and in an equal way in regions subject to the equinoctial line[11]—in the second clime, I say, [and] the third and fourth of these, there will be middling [amounts]; in the fifth and sixth, more slack. **5** Mars[12] being retrograde, if she[13] regarded him, heavenly lightning will fall. **6** The Moon being the lodging-place of Mars (namely Scorpio), however[14] Mars traversing in the opposite of his house, even the Sun being positioned in Aquarius or Pisces, they note the abundance of rains on that day. **7** With the Sun in Pisces, being regarded by the Moon and Mars, there will be lightnings and thunders, and a flowing of intermittent rains, and the falling of lightning. **8** The Sun in Aries or Scorpio, the Moon in Leo or Sagittarius or in the assembly of the Sun, prefigures the same thing. **9** However, the Sun in Capricorn, the Moon in Taurus or Virgo, Pisces, or Scorpio, generates the coldest winds. **10** No less, too, with him being in Capricorn, and especially appearing in Aquarius, while Saturn would traverse in their opposition and the Moon regarded one [of them].

11 In addition, Mars regarding Venus from Scorpio at the cycle of the year,[15] emanates with heavy rains. **12** Venus appearing in Scorpio, and being regarded by Mars, makes a judgment of rains on account of the seas which Scorpio has.[16] **13** But if she would lack the aspect of Mars, there will not be

---

[9] This is ambiguous, because by definition the Moon will be in the same sign as the Sun during the New Moon. Perhaps it refers to the ongoing transits of the Moon, along with those of Venus and Mercury.

[10] *Lampadas.* Hermann might also simply mean many flashes of light.

[11] That is, in the first clime, near the equator.

[12] For this sentence and the next, see Māshā'allāh's *Letter* **25-27**.

[13] But Munich says "if *the Sun* regarded him."

[14] Reading *autem* for *aut*, since Māshā'allāh's *Letter* explicitly has the Moon in Scorpio and him in Taurus.

[15] *Anni conversione.* That is, the annual ingress into Aries. But remember that most of these methods are also supposed to be used on a quarterly (seasonal) and monthly basis.

[16] Here and in the next sentence, Hermann and his source are speaking of the constellations themselves, a reminder of the constellational background to these techniques (such

much fertility of heavy rains from the remaining signification. **14** Moreover, should Venus, the Moon, and Mercury, traverse in places of rains at the cycle of the year, that cycle will convey an abundance of rains.

15 However, the places of rains are: each Saturnian house and their opposite (namely Leo and Cancer); in the same way Pisces will be of their number (on account of the streams it has, and rivers), just as even Sagittarius is (on account of the seas which are in its last part), and Scorpio (on account of its [seas]). **16** And so, the Moon applying to Venus in these very places, portends there will be rains.

Chapter 4: On poor rains

2 Moreover, there are signs of few rains: Taurus and Gemini. **3** True, the beginning of Taurus and the end of Aries do indicate rains, on account of the clouds which they have. **4** No less, too, Virgo and Libra (namely, they have a modicum of rains). **5** Capricorn, however, has more cold than rain. **6** Nor do heavy rains come to be in [Capricorn], unless the Moon regards[17] a star in places of water from it. **7** Venus[18] and Mercury being under the regard of the Moon and Mars, should Mars himself cut short and block the Moon's light from them, unless, I say, it is an assembly or opposition: for thus it also conveys rains.

---

as with the mansions of the Moon). According to Bernadette Brady, the area around Aquarius "governed a cosmic sea which contains the constellations" Pisces, Cetus, Capricorn, Delphinus, Eridanus, Piscis Australis, and Hydra. But Scorpio is not near this cosmic sea. Brady conjectures that Scorpio might be associated with late autumn storms—and thus, I suppose, the weather on the actual, not constellational, seas (private communication, 1/23/2013).

[17] Reading *respiciat* (sing.) with Munich, for *respiciant* (pl.). But perhaps Hermann meant to say "the Moon *and Mars*," has he does in the next sentence.

[18] For this sentence, cf. Māshā'allāh's *Letter* **54-55**. As written here it is unclear, and Hermann's style is to blame. My sense is that the first part (Venus and Mercury aspecting the Moon and Mars, with Mars cutting the light) means there will be no or little rain; but if it is from the opposition or conjunction, then there will be more rain.

Chapter 5: On rains, at the beginning of the year[19]

2 In addition, the Lot of rains[20] must be noted at the cycle of the year; now, it being taken up by day from the Moon to Venus (conversely by night), and with the beginning being taken from the Sun, it will really occur under the ending of the number.[21] **3** Therefore, it being found in a place of waters, indicates a rainy year.

4 Also,[22] when the Moon will reach Mars, heavy rains will really be present on that day, and there will not be another judgment with respect to Venus.

5 Moreover, for individual months, once the east has been established, the conjunction of the Sun and Moon, and the assembly and application of the stars, should be noted: for they generate winter rains. **6** One must even note this with the greatest effort: that Venus under the hands of the Sun[23] portends heavy rains and dews.

7 Moreover, an application of Venus with Mars, Mercury with Jupiter, [and] the Moon with Saturn, must be noted.[24] **8** But a greater judgment of the Sun pertains to dews.[25] **9** Since Venus is as though the door of Mars, Mercury of Jupiter, [and] the Moon of Saturn, whenever they assemble together or would enjoy a mutual aspect, they bring together dews with heat.

10 With[26] Venus being retrograde, the Sun in Aries or Taurus, it indicates a very rainy spring. **11** Moreover, she appearing retrograde while the Sun would be lingering in Capricorn or Aquarius, [indicates that] that winter will have few heavy rains. **12** However, all of these things come to be noted at the ingress of the year. **13** Now, while [Venus] will be retrograde (as has already been stated), and the Sun is walking through Capricorn or Aquarius or Pi-

---

[19] As we will see below, what follows is actually a collection of lore mainly to do with Venus, at the quarterly ingresses (not merely at the Aries ingress).

[20] See Section I.1 for the various Lots of rains.

[21] That is: by day, measure from the Moon to Venus, and project from the Sun; by night, from Venus to the Moon (still projecting from the Sun).

[22] This sentence does not seem to be connected with the Lot of rains, so I have made it its own paragraph.

[23] That is, under the rays.

[24] This is an example of the opening of the doors.

[25] Hermann means that Saturn with the Moon indicates rains, while the Sun with Saturn indicates only dews.

[26] This paragraph is very ambiguous to me, with respect to the easternness and westernness of Venus. Normally these considerations are examined at the Libra ingress and the Sun's entrance to 20° Scorpio, and they pertain only to winter rains. But Hermann seems to extend them to multiple ingresses and seasons.

sces, she being made eastern in the spring introduces a modicum of heavy rains. **14** But it moistens the beginning of winter with manifold rains. **15** Now, if she would appear eastern in the winter, the beginnings of it will redound in sparse, but at the end many, [rains]: **16** unless[27] any star would traverse more closely[28] to the Sun, and the above-written judgment about the arrival of rains would be wholly changed. **17** Moreover, the traversal of Venus in the east or any of the pivots, makes a certain and strong judgment of rains. **18** The leader,[29] even, regarding the Sun at the assembly or opposition, will boil with manifold heavy rain.

19 Then[30] should Venus, being under the rays or under any regard, walk through or be traversing the degrees of the pivots, it multiplies the most severe heavy rains. **20** But whenever the Moon would apply to her,[31] it brings about rains, and most firmly with respect to the Sun in this manner, and indeed in any degree of its[32] pivot or its east.

21 Also, the lord of the east being in a watery sign, in the assembly of the leader or applying to it, [indicates] the same.

[The Sun's ingress into Libra]

22 Now, in its[33] ingress to Libra, Venus traversing before the Sun by less than 30° and being direct, moistens the beginnings of winter with many rains. **23** But if she did not distance herself from him,[34] it permits the same thing around the end [of winter]. **24** But a distance of greater than 30° is present, the beginning of winter will redound in cold but few heavy rains, until

---

[27] Reading *nisi* with Cambridge and Bernkastel-Kues, for Low-Beer's *ubi* ("where").

[28] *Affinior.* This is an unfortunate word, because while it does mean "closer, more neighboring," like the more common *proprior, affinis* also suggest family relationships which in some contexts suggests rulerships—so that Hermann's word choice leads the mind in directions we perhaps should not go.

[29] *Dux*, in Arabic probably "indicator." This must be some chief planet or victor in the chart of the ingress. It is not (or not necessarily) the lord of the Ascendant as we see in **21** below. Sometimes Arabic texts refer to the Moon as a general significator or indicator, but since she is by definition with or opposed to the Sun at these times, it must not refer to her.

[30] Reading this sentence with Munich, because it supplies the verb and context that makes sense to me (*partes cardinum perambulet seu discurrens*). Low-Beer and other MSS have "being under the rays in the/any regard of a degree [*partis*] of the pivots."

[31] *Eidem.*

[32] Here and a few words later, I am not sure if this refers to the angular degrees of the chart, or of the Sun himself.

[33] *Eiusdem.* I take this to mean the Sun.

[34] *Si vero nec abinvicem destiterit.*

she makes the space between [them] be a lesser quantity. **25** Whenever, however, the distance of approach will be less than one sign under [her] direct course, that year will have manifold rains. **26** Also, the progressing of the Sun and Venus in the same sign generates a greater abundance of heavy rains.

27 Moreover, a star traversing in any house of its own nature, and being received while the receiver is holding onto a good place, [indicates that] the required[35] effect wholly follow. **28** The best thing, and the greater certainty of effectiveness, [is] if it would be in its own nature.

29 In addition, even, the Moon with Jupiter, Venus, or Mercury, applying from one degree, generates boiling heavy rains; in the south, [it generates something] more appropriate through the heavy rains, especially with Venus and Jupiter being received, and should the Moon have escaped the Solar degree at the assembly.[36] **30** Then Saturn, in a moist sign, in no way speaks against rains, and one will have to pursue it in this manner with the application of the Moon.[37] **31** But if they would be conjoined in the same degree, while the inferior would be staying below the superior (of which sort is Mercury and Jupiter, Venus and Mars, even the Moon and Saturn), [it indicates rains]. **32** Whenever therefore, both[38] would apply to some inferior, after the inferior had escaped from the superior, it is necessary to [predict][39] dews.

[The 20° Scorpio method]

33 One must even note whether the Sun himself would be walking through the twentieth degree of Scorpio; it will also be good to establish the east in individual years, to calculate the stars, and to attend most diligently to the place of the Moon, [and] even to whether the Moon would apply to Venus or Mercury. **34** Therefore, the easternness of Venus and Mercury greatly bestows rains at the beginning of the year, westernness at the end. **35** Then,

---

[35] *Debitus.*

[36] This may mean that *while* the Moon is in a bodily conjunction with Venus or Mercury (who are always somewhat close to the Sun), she is not under the rays.

[37] This may simply mean that if he is in a moist sign, her applications to him will work just as they do with the other planets just mentioned. Of course, her applications to him would also (under appropriate circumstances) be an opening of the doors. See the next sentence.

[38] Both luminaries?

[39] Reading for *aestuare*, which means to "boil" and which Hermann has used before to indicate heat; but in this case it seems misplaced since the sentence seems to be instructing the astrologer what to do.

the Moon, adding in light and computation, portends an abundance of heavy rains; but decreasing, more abated.

Chapter 6: The doors

2 On the other hand, the most experienced of the ancient astrologers took care to attend to the places which they said were of the "doors," of which this is a description: **3** namely, whenever the Moon, withdrawing from Venus, would apply to Mars, or she withdraws from Mars while she would apply to Venus, she thus really brings back a signification of rains. **4** Moreover, withdrawing from Mercury, and applying to Jupiter (or contrariwise), she presents no other judgment. **5** These however, belong to the individual stars as though [they are] certain places of pouring,[40] which are appropriately enough called the "openings of the doors." **6** And so, an opposition of these stars being discovered (with a trine and square being avoided, and towards the southern direction and higher land)[41] flows down with its own rains—**7** if (I say) they would be lingering between the nineteenth degree of Scorpio and the nineteenth of Taurus. **8** Moreover, a signification of heavy rains from out of the southern[42] direction will then occur whenever they would walk from the nineteenth of Taurus to the nineteenth of Scorpio.

9 In addition, one must note the cycle of the year and the seasons, at the initial ingress of the Sun into the four turning [signs]—Aries, I say, and Libra, Cancer, and Capricorn. **10** For from these quarters can be discovered what may be renewed in the general regions (in the east, namely, and the west, the north and the south). **11** Therefore, once the east has been established for these aforesaid beginnings, attend diligently to where the Moon is traversing, and whether she is walking through hot and moist signs, or hot and dry, cold and moist, or cold and dry. **12** If even the one to which the Moon applies would be co-rising,[43] it will be a greater indication of rains; if she would be

---

[40] *Manatoria.* I take this to be from *mano.*

[41] I am not at all certain about the meaning or correct translation of this parenthetical statement (*declinante tertio et quarto et ad partem australem et altiorem terram*). What I have translated as "trine" and "square" might even refer to the third and fourth climes.

[42] This should probably read, "northern."

[43] I am unsure of this reading, but it makes more sense than the alternatives. Low-Beer reads, "is not encouraged" (*non cohortatur*), while Munich and Cambridge and Oxford seem to read "reason/method" (*ratio*) but in the wrong grammatical case, and then Munich has "co-rises" (*coortatur*), while Cambridge and Oxford have "is made narrow" (*coartatur*).

applying to the lord of the circle,[44] who is arranged after the lunar one, more strongly so. **13** Moreover, the Moon descending southern,[45] applying to a southern and descending star, brings in heavy rains in many ways. **14** With her even applying to Mars, or if, withdrawing from him she would apply to Venus, it brings about rains or dews. **15** Also, her withdrawal from Jupiter and an application made with Mercury, or while she would leave Saturn behind she would be applying to the Sun, it will not give another judgment. **16** More powerful than what we have said, [is] an application made from the opposition and in signs which signify waters (of which kind are Aquarius, Leo, and Scorpio), in 8° of them.[46]

16 In the same way even, with an assembly or regard being discovered in Gemini and Sagittarius, and the Moon (being in her own house) applying to Saturn, or in Pisces to Venus, or in Aquarius with Venus and Mercury— introduces most useful[47] and manifold heavy rains more quickly.

17 One must even note when the Sun reaches the first[48] degree of Scorpio; but if Mercury and Venus happened to be eastern, there is no indecision [but that it indicates] there will be rains at the beginning of the year. **18** More powerfully is if the Moon, waxing in light, would descend into the south, regarding [both] Venus and Mercury—or at least, while she would be separated from one, she would apply to the other—and received on each side: for being thus at the beginning of the year,[49] it undoubtedly imports rains. **19** Moreover, the westernness of each,[50] and an application of the Moon with each (or at least either one), she even being western while namely she ascends at the beginning of the month to the seventh or eighth day,[51] and she goes after the Sun towards sinking, and she even descending, quick in course and waxing in light, portends future heavy rains at the end of the year. **20** But

---

[44] This sounds like the "lord of the orb," which is a natal technique in which planets are treated as time lords according to their zodiacal order (see *ITA* VIII.2.3), but I am not sure what it means in this context, nor what the next clause about coming after the "lunar one" means.

[45] I take this to mean descending in the southern ecliptical latitudes, but this might actually be descending into the signs of southern declination (Libra through Pisces).

[46] I am not sure of the significance of 8°.

[47] Reading *utilissimos* for *utillimos*.

[48] My sense is that this should be the "twentieth" (i.e., 20°), as what follows is part of the usual lore for the 20° Scorpio approach.

[49] Perhaps in some sense Scorpio is meant to indicate a new phase of the year.

[50] That is, Venus and Mercury.

[51] The "ascending" language might refer to movement through signs of northern declination. I confess I am unsure what exactly Hermann is describing.

if the Moon and stars of this kind happened to be received by the lords of their houses or sovereignties, the richness of produce and the means of subsistence is saved by the manifold (and not unuseful) abundance of heavy rains.

Chapter 7: On the virtues of the doors

1 But there is a virtue of these doors, and the best signification, such that the atmosphere begins to be varied on some day or hour by clouds or rains, through individual regions, cities, or even neighborhoods. **2** At the first precipitation of heavy rains or drops, one must examine carefully, with the greatest diligence, the east and the place of the Moon, but even the one to which the Moon is applying (to the superiors, namely, or the inferiors); no less too, whether that application of the Moon would come to be from the hexagon or tetragon or even the opposition, or the assembly, and even whether she is received. **3** In addition, in how many degrees the one to which the Moon applies, is standing, [and] even is it quick or slow, or in the middle, descending into the south, or is it climbing in the north. **4** Once all of these have been discovered in a certain order, the lunar application with a star (on the day it first begins to rain) will give a certain judgment about heavy rains through individual days—namely, up until that star crosses over to the next sign. **5** However, once it has entered the next sign, in no way should one make a presumption about a judgment of rains on this or that day, until you can really determine when the Moon applies to it again.

6 But if that application points out some heavy rains, one will have to report it with respect to its multitude and scarcity, according to that manner and number—but even according to the nature of that sign (namely, were it moist or dry, or in the middle). **7** In the same way too, [judge] the sign of the star with which the lunar application is happening. **8** For on that day on which you expect heavy rains, it seems that the quick course of the Moon (or its slowness), and her descent into the south or being raised up into the north,[52] must be noted, and in this manner also that of the star to which she is applying. **9** For the increase of heavy rain pours forth to no little degree from the status of a star of this kind. **10** Moreover, the latitude of the Moon

---

[52] This probably refers to being in signs of southern or northern declination, as Hermann mentions ecliptical latitude just below.

and of the star should equally be noted. **11** For, each one being southern and appearing closer to sight, and likewise the latitude, [means that] it greatly bestows a rushing of rains on that day. **11** But with the latitude [of each] being different, nor is there reception present, it portends sterile clouds or ones not fertile enough.

Chapter 8: In all the places the rain seems to fall

2 Those things which we have said will have to be discovered in this manner: in whatever region, city, estate, or district, with respect to an application and reception of the Moon (or the contrary), from her position in the aforesaid places (or not), even with respect to the nature of the signs and the star to which she applies. **3** Nor should another judgment be given unless,[53] I say, she would apply to another quicker star or she would be in its assembly.

4 Should she therefore merit this signification, one will have to return a judgment according to the forces of her power and weakness. **5** Even the degree of the assembly or opposition [of the luminaries] throughout individual months, [or] even the one to which the Moon applies until she returns to the assembly of the Sun (or at least she would be separated from the opposition), should in no way raise the trouble of forgetfulness. **6** Now, if she would apply to Mercury or Venus [by bodily conjunction] at that assembly or opposition, it pours out rains. **7** But if you saw the Moon applying from another sign (namely from the hexagon or tetragon, even the trigon or opposition), the star to which she applies (once the assembly or opposition has been left behind) holds the path of judgment, according to [its] quick course or slowness, descent or ascent, no less too according to the nature of that place, and according to the latitude of the Moon and that star, as was stated above. **8** For if she would be traversing in that same degree[54] from any of the pivots, and the star with which the lunar application is happening would be staying under the earth, it makes a judgment about what was said before; but if that star does not regard the east when she[55] regarded it by any figure, a renewal of heavy rains will follow. **9** In this manner too, with the aspect of the Moon to the east or to that star itself being denied, while how-

---

[53] Reading *nisi* and the rest of the sentence with Cambridge and Bernkastel-Kues
[54] *Parte*, but this might mean "direction."
[55] The Latin does not name the subject here, but I take it to mean that the Moon aspects the Ascendant while the one to which she applies, does not.

ever it[56] would designate rains without the obscuring quality of clouds, there will be a sudden coursing of rains.

Chapter 9: On the mansion of the Moon

2 Concerning the Moon's mansion, pay attention to the opinion of the Indians: namely, it is moist or dry. **3** As the Indians' faith has it, the Moon in a moist mansion, applying to a star appearing in a moist one, shows rains, most especially if she were abiding in that same knot[57] and moist one; which if they traversed in different moistening ones ([but] even if not), still there will be general rains. **4** With her being placed thusly,[58] applying to a star placed in a middling one and in one knot, it allots few heavy rains, whose beginnings will be stronger [but there will be less later].[59] **5** Now, with the Moon appearing in a middling one, while however her application would happen with a star appearing in a moist one and one knot, even though [there will be] less at the beginning, still at the end a manifold overflowing will be present. **5** On the other hand, if they would in no way be holding on-to that knot,[60] a middling amount of heavy rains (and sometimes even clouds) would occur, but sterile ones.

---

[56] *Ea.* This could refer to the Moon or the other star.
[57] See for example Jafar's *Book of Heavy Rains*, sentences **85** and **109**.
[58] That is, in a moist mansion.
[59] Reading for *sine ipso*, with the logic of the paragraph. Where the Moon is, indicates the beginning; the star to which she applies, indicates the end.
[60] Reading *nodum* with Cambridge and Bernkastel-Kues, for Low-Beer's *non, dum.*

SECTION I.13: *THE OPENING OF THE DOORS*

Comment by Dykes. This short Latin work is translated from the edition in Bos and Burnett 2000 (pp. 386-89), and at a couple of points I had occasion to compare it to Munich Clm. 11067, which has short excerpts on weather from many of our sources (see Section I.18). Neither this nor the Bos-Burnett version is a critical edition taken from all possible sources. Readers may consult the notes to the 2000 Latin version, which contains comments about many variant readings, and indeed the *Epitome* attributed to John of Seville (Section I.15) contains information which can be traced back to *Doors.*

In terms of the technique called the "opening of the doors," *Doors* describes three types, which can also be found in Māshā'allāh and 'Umar al-Tabarī:

- When the lords of opposite domiciles are connected (**1-3, 5-11**).
- The "double doors," when the Moon is assisting such planets by transferring light between them (**36**).
- When the lord of the Ascendant of the lunation joins with the lord of its seventh of it (**38**).

Indeed, *Doors* has information that can be found in a number of other sources. For example, it mixes bits from Māshā'allāh (**30-32**) with other material from 'Umar and al-Kindī. Like al-Kindī's *Forty Chapters* Ch. 38 (Section I.4), it provides a temporal hierarchy based on planetary rank: Saturn is an annual indicator, Jupiter a seasonal one, Mercury and Venus monthly and also semi-monthly. The Moon is highly tuned to daily rains when she is either part of an opening of the doors or at the centers or posts. There is also a daily Lot of rain.

℘ ℘ ℧

[Simple opening of the doors]

1 "Opening of the doors" is especially said when an inferior planet is being conjoined to a superior planet, and in addition their houses are opposite [each other].[1] **2** However, the openings of the doors are the conjunctions of

---

[1] That is, the domiciles they rule, not the houses they happen to be in at the moment.

the Sun and Moon with Saturn, or their aspect towards Saturn himself. **3** And in the same way Jupiter with Mercury, Venus with Mars.

4 But[2] Venus signifies moisture, Mercury winds, Saturn cloudiness[3] and cold, Mars winds but heat from the right, Jupiter a moderation of the air and winds from the left[4] (which he signifies more in Cancer, just as Mars does in Capricorn).

5 And so, if Mercury aspected the lords of the opening of the doors,[5] or he were with them, and conjoined at the conjunction of the Sun and Moon or in [their] opposition, there will be wind and rain. **6** Which if the opening of the doors were with Mars (as was said about Mercury), there will be meteors,[6] thunders, and lightnings. **7** Add to this or subtract [from it] according to the nature of Mars and the sign and the bound in which he is. **8** Which if Saturn is aspecting instead of Mars, and in a house of earth,[7] it signifies the destruction of houses. **9** If in a house of water, it signifies cold, heavy rains, and darkness. **10** Which if a retrograde planet were there, it signifies great rain. **11** But the Moon signifies rain. **12** However, if the Sun [were] in the lowest circle,[8] and together with the inferior planets, it signifies rain; and if the superiors, it signifies fair weather.

[Timing by application of the Moon]

13 And so, wanting to know the day of the rain, consider the day of the conjunction of the Sun and Moon, and likewise the time. **14** And see how many degrees are between the Moon and the next rainy planet, and for every degree take it according to the quickness of the signs.[9]

---

[2] For this sentence, see §674 of al-Kindī's *Forty Chapters* Ch. 38 (Section I.4).
[3] *Nubila.*
[4] Compare with Ptolemy's winds and mundane triplicity lords (Section IV.2), where Mars is associated with southwestern and western winds, and Jupiter with northern winds.
[5] This sentence is unclear to me. Does it mean that Mercury (and other planets, see the following sentences) is one of the planets forming the pair that opens the doors, or that he is aspecting them and so adding his indications to what *they already* show?
[6] *Lampadas.* But this can also indicate brightness and lights.
[7] That is, an earthy sign.
[8] This must refer to being in or near his perigee.
[9] This probably refers to quadruplicities: movable signs will show shorter units or spans of time, fixed ones longer, and common ones in the middle. If this is supposed to be done at every lunar month, then the units and spans of time could not exceed about four weeks.

[The posts or foundations of the Moon]

15 And see the doors of the Moon, and which planet will aspect the Moon, or which one is joined: **16** because then from that you will know the day of the beginning and end of rain.

[A Lot of daily rain]

17 And look at how many equal degrees are between the Sun and Saturn, and count that many degrees from the degree of the Moon; and where it came out, there is the Lot of rain.[10] **18** Which, if [the Lot] were in a house of the Moon or of Venus, it will signify rain; if in a house of Mercury or Jupiter, winds; if one of Mars or the Sun, fair weather; if Saturn, cloudiness.

[Timing by angularity and quadruplicity]

19 You even ought to know that sometimes there is rain at the conjunction or opposition itself, if there is an opening of the doors then, but sometimes it is delayed: you should not be ignorant of the reason for this. **20** And so, if at the opening of the doors the Moon is conjoined to the Sun or opposed to him, [and] the Moon herself were in the tenth angle and she was in a movable sign, then there will be rain at that conjunction or opposition itself. **21** If however she were in the other angles (either in one that has slipped by or one after the angles),[11] the rain will be delayed, according to it being a movable or fixed or common [sign]. **22** And then expect a great rain, namely when the Moon will have reached the opposition of the sign of the Ascendant at [the time of] the conjunction or opposition. **23** And the rain will last in accordance with whether she will already reach an aspect of the planets, and signs signifying rains.

---

[10] See Section I.1 on Lots of rain and winds.
[11] That is, a cadent or succeedent place, respectively.

[Rainfall determined annually and quarterly][12]

24 Wanting even to know the nature of the air in individual years, consider it at the conjunction of the Sun and Moon (or consider the opposition), which is before the Sun enters into a hot sign.[13] **25** And being in his own[14] bound, it takes away from the hotness; and if it were in a bound of Mars, the hotness of the year will be increased, and thus with respect to the others of the aforesaid significators,[15] according to their nature. **26** Also, you should mix with Saturn the natures of the planets which are associating with him[16] or which aspect him. **27** Judge thusly with respect to Jupiter, when the Moon is associating with the Sun and is in the opposition before the Sun enters[17] one of the other movable signs—the movable signs are the beginning of a quarter of the circle.[18] **28** Also, you will mix the nature with the nature of the sign in which Saturn is, and [with] the nature of whatever bound, as being the nature of its lord. **29** Thus too will be the judgment of Venus and Mercury in each month, and at the time of the conjunction or opposition of the Sun and Moon; thus even the judgment of the Moon in each of the aforesaid doors.

30 Moreover, wanting to know if there would be much rain at the beginning or middle or end of the year, see the place of Venus when the Sun enters Libra. **31** Which if she is with the light of the Sun and is western,[19] there will be much rain at the beginning of that year which begins from Libra, and at its end. **32** If eastern and visible, the rain will be to the contrary.

---

[12] In this little section, the author follows something like al-Kindī's approach in *Forty Chapters* Ch. 38 (Section I.4), treating Saturn as an indicator for the year, and Jupiter for the seasons.

[13] Normally this would be Aries, which is probably what the author means. Doing this for every hot sign, or rather fiery sign, would not be an annual determination.

[14] As Bos and Burnett point out, this is probably Saturn.

[15] Reading *ducum* for *ducis*.

[16] That is, are in the same sign (the closer, the more relevant).

[17] Reading *intret* for *interest*.

[18] Or rather, they define the beginning of a season.

[19] This seems to mean that she is under his rays and invisible, but in a later zodiacal degree (and so setting after him).

[Signs indicating rain]

33 The signs of much rain are the watery ones, Aquarius, and the end of [Capricorn, Aries, Taurus, and Leo. The stronger ones of these are Pisces],[20] Aquarius, and Scorpio.

[Lunar ingresses and lords of the hours][21]

34 Moreover, when the Moon enters Cancer at the hour of the Sun, and Virgo at the hour of Venus, or Sagittarius at the hour of the Moon, or Gemini at the hour of Mercury, or Taurus at the hour of Mars, or Libra at the hour of Jupiter, it signifies rain or winds, in the manner of the nature of the sign in which the lord of the hour is.

[Venus in the signs]

35 When Venus is in Scorpio or in Capricorn or in Aquarius, or when Jupiter [is conjoined to][22] the Moon or aspects her, it signifies much rain.

[Opening of the "double doors"]

36 And when the Moon is being separated from the conjunction or aspect of some planet, and is being conjoined to another planet by body or aspect, and the houses of those planets are contrary to each other—suppose if she would be separated from Venus and be joined to Mars—then this is called an opening of the "double doors,"[23] in which it is necessary for winds to come, or rain, according to the nature of those planets.

---

[20] Following Bos and Burnett, who have added the missing words from John of Seville's *Tractatus pluviarum et aeris mutationis*. But Munich Clm 11067 (96r), which also contains this section, reads "the stronger of these are Aries, Pisces, Scorpio."

[21] See the Introduction for a discussion of this method.

[22] Adding with Bos and Burnett, but the parallel excerpt in Munich Clm. 11067 (96va) says "and she," meaning *Venus*. See my Introduction.

[23] *Valvarum*.

[Feminine places and retrograde planets]

37 And again, if the Moon were in a feminine quarter and feminine sign, and a retrograde planet in a feminine sign[24] aspected her, by necessity it must rain, as we have always experienced.

[A third opening of the doors]

38 In addition, it is also called an opening of the doors when the lord of the Ascendant[25] aspects the lord of the seventh house (or is conjoined to it).

---

[24] The parallel passage in Munich Clm. 11067 (96rb) does not put the retrograde planet in a feminine sign.

[25] That is, the lord of the Ascendant of the chart cast for the New or Full Moon.

SECTION I.14: *SATURN IN ARIES*

Comment by Dykes. This translation is based on the Latin edition by Bos and Burnett (2000, pp. 457-66), but I have also consulted a manuscript version, Munich BSB Clm. 667 (17v-20r). As Bos and Burnett point out (p. 459), it is attributed to several people and the manuscripts have many variants.

Saturn in Aries focuses on what all of the non-luminaries mean in the signs, according to their solar phases. Since the luminaries are excluded here, it suggests that we should be examining these planets at the New/Full Moons. But should we look at every planet's position at the same time, or just that of the chief significator in the chart, or is this really about the planet to which the Moon applies at key times: such as directly after the New/Full Moon, or at the opening of the doors, or at her centers.

One unusual feature of this text is its use of "morning" and "evening" statuses: Arabic texts (like Latin ones) usually just speak of being eastern and western, or arising or sinking. The vocabulary of morning and evening suggests that a Greek text might be lurking in the background somewhere. Since these adjectives can also be used as substantives, I have added "planet" throughout in order to make the designations clear to modern English readers.

Note too the overlap between purely atmospheric and agricultural considerations, and occasional references to leaders of the country or other personages (such as soldiers for Mars in Sagittarius).

The mentions of "good health" (*sanitas*) refer generally to the notion that disease is caused by unclean or imbalanced air. The author might not have had a strictly scientific theory of this (such as the now discredited "miasma" theory of illness), but it certainly means that changes in seasons, and mixtures of dry and moist air (etc.) correspond to people getting ill.

The reader should note carefully how "complexion" is used here (and throughout medieval texts). In weather, it refers to the overall balance of temperature and moisture which is appropriate for the season and generally pleasant—that is, without harmful and painful extremes or sudden changes, clashes of warm and cold air, and so on. But when speaking about a *planet's* complexion, it refers to how it mixes with other planets by aspect or conjunction.

Note here that the weather indications here have little or nothing to do with planetary dignities. For instance, Jupiter in Capricorn is in his fall, but when it comes to weather his position there is not a bad thing.

Finally, there is often ambiguity in the texts as to whether the weather is foggy, misty, or cloudy—in Latin, all of these draw on words like *nubes* and *nebula*, and it is sometimes hard to know exactly what is meant. So, we should keep an open mind about these overlapping meanings.

℞   ℞   ℞

1 Saturn in Aries, under the rays, makes rains and brightness, and many mistinesses. But in men he makes infirmities from rheumatism.[1] If however he were an evening planet, he signifies the coldest winds; but if he were a morning one, eastern, he shows a good complexion. If he were stationary, he will bring to completion thunders and lightnings. **2** Jupiter in Aries, under the rays, makes rains. However, as an evening planet he sprinkles mists or dews. But as a morning one, eastern, fair. If however he were stationary, he signifies thunders and an abundance of fruits and hay. **3** If Mars were in Aries, under the rays, he signals fair weather. If however he were an evening planet, the contrary. As a morning one, eastern, a confusion of weather. Stationary, lightning and thunders. **4** With Venus appearing in Aries, under the rays, there will be no wind. As an evening planet, she signifies wind. As a morning one, eastern, thunders and rains. **5** Mercury in Aries, under the rays, stormy. As an evening planet, not well-complected enough. As a morning one, eastern, he signifies clean air.

6 Saturn in Taurus, under the rays, signifies a good complexion and good weather. But as an evening planet, dryness. However, as a morning one, eastern, a good complexion and good health. Stationary, heavy rain, stormy, and thundering. **7** Jupiter in Taurus, under the rays, signifies a middling quality of the air. As an evening planet, heavy rays. As a morning one, eastern, he makes an abundance of fruits and pasture. Stationary, an abundance of fruits and the good health of the pasture. **8** Mars in Taurus, under the rays, makes the weather be without wind. As an evening planet, fair weather. As a morning one, eastern, he moves winds. Stationary, he dries the air out. **9** Venus in Taurus, under the rays, signifies thunders. As an evening planet, fair weather. As a morning one, eastern, a good complexion, and it is useful. **10** Mercury in

---

[1] *Reumatismo.* This should be understood as any kind of inflammation of connective tissue.

Taurus, under the rays, is stormy and with heavy rains. As an evening planet, of a good complexion. As a morning one, eastern, dewy and clean.

11 Saturn in Gemini, under the rays, is dry and without moisture. As an evening planet, arid. As a morning one, eastern, of a good complexion. Stationary, he increases in infirmity. **12** Jupiter in Gemini, under the rays, signifies a good complexion. As an evening planet, good health. Likewise, being stationary repels infirmity and declares good health. **13** Mars in Gemini, under the rays, signifies infirmities in men. As an evening planet, most hot. As a morning one, eastern, he works contrarieties and contradictions[2] in men. Stationary, hot and dry. **14** Venus in Gemini, under the rays, dries out excessively. As an evening planet, she is windy. As a morning one, eastern, good weather. **15** Mercury in Gemini, under the rays, stirs up winds on the sea and on land. As an evening planet, he dries out. As a morning one, eastern, he signifies a good complexion.

16 Saturn in Cancer, under the rays, makes obscure days and powerful winds, and squalls on the sea. As an evening planet, he renders the sea fit for sailing. As a morning one, good and well complexioned. Stationary, he introduces long-lasting infirmities into human bodies. **17** Jupiter in Cancer, under the rays, signifies a tranquil sea and an abundance of fish. As an evening planet, a good complexion. As a morning one, eastern, a good complexion and good health. Stationary, ease in matters. **18** Mars in Cancer, under the rays, signifies burning. As an evening planet, infirmities. As a morning one, conflict among men. Stationary, hotness and dryness. **19** Venus in Cancer, under the rays, makes the weather be without wind. As an evening planet, a good complexion. As a morning one, fair weather. **20** Mercury in Cancer, under the rays, raises the seas. As an evening planet, he makes tranquility. As a morning one, eastern, a good complexion and good health.

21 Saturn in Leo, under the rays, makes rheumatism in the body, and disturbances from moisture, and dryness in the air. As an evening planet, he makes aridness. As a morning one, a good complexion and great good health. Stationary, aridness and dryness. **22** Jupiter in Leo, under the rays, introduces annual[3] winds. As an evening planet, a good complexion. As a morning one, eastern, he shows physical strength in the emperor and the

---

[2] Perhaps this means that the weather drives people to fight and argue.
[3] *Annuales.* But this could mean "seasonal."

success of Fortune.[4] Stationary, a remission and diminution of infirmities. **23** Mars in Leo, under the rays, [shows] an infirmity for the emperor. As an evening planet, he declares heat. As a morning one, eastern, destructions. Stationary, he is a significator of infirmities. **24** Venus in Leo, under the rays, makes heat. As an evening planet, the infirmity of beasts of burden. As a morning one, a good complexion. **25** Mercury in Leo, under the rays, brings forth wind from the west. As an evening planet, he makes suffocations. As a morning one, fair weather.

26 Saturn in Virgo, emerging under the rays,[5] is harmful, for it brings infirmity to men. As an evening planet, the difficulty of the air. As a morning one, dryness. Stationary, he makes infirmities in men. **27** Jupiter in Virgo, under the rays, signifies abundance. As an evening planet, a good complexion. As a morning one, the firmness of good health. Stationary, goodness, good health, and every joy. **28** Mars in Virgo, under the rays, makes the harmfulness of infirmity for men. As an evening planet, he is suffocating. But as a morning one, he makes conflicts and contentions. Stationary, he shows the dryness of the air. **29** Venus in Virgo, under the rays, dries out. As an evening planet, she gives a good complexion. As a morning one, she presents moisture. **30** Mercury in Virgo, under the rays, signifies powerful squalls on the sea. As an evening planet, dryness. As a morning one, he is somewhat moist, and well-complexioned.

31 Saturn in Libra, under the rays, introduces infirmities of the eyes. As an evening planet, an unevenness of the air. As a morning one, cold and dry winds. Stationary, he introduces quartan fevers. **32** Jupiter in Libra, under the rays, signifies air of a good complexion. As an evening planet, good health. As a morning one, he expels infirmities. Stationary, he makes the weather good and makes it firm. **33** Mars in Libra, under the rays, makes the air dry and arid. As an evening planet, he is rainy. As a morning one, he signifies disturbances and thunders. Stationary, arid and dry. **34** Venus in Libra, under the rays, is moist. As an evening planet, she is well complexioned. As a morning one, she is *famissica*[6] and moistening. **35** Mercury in Libra, under the

---

[4] Note the overlap between strictly material considerations of weather, mundane politics, and the person of the emperor. Many ancient peoples connected the well-being of the nation with the well-being of the emperor.

[5] *Sub radis nascens nocens est.* Based on the previous formulas, we would expect this to read "being under the rays, is harmful *to what sprouts*"; but that would require *nascenti*.

[6] Unknown at this time, but perhaps related to famine (*fames*) or being dry (*sicca*). Another manuscript simply reads "dry" (*sicca*, Munich BSB, Clm. 667, f. 19r). So perhaps it shows an alternation between moisture and dryness (which is not very informative).

rays, is a significator of the strongest contrary winds. As an evening planet, well complexioned. As a morning one, he is somewhat moist, and advantageous. **36** Saturn in Scorpio, under the rays, makes the air cold. As an evening planet, freezing. As a morning one, he is a significator of northern and cold winds. Stationary, he makes obscure days. **37** Jupiter in Scorpio, under the rays, makes cold rain. As an evening planet, a good complexion. As a morning one, good weather and an increase of fish. Stationary, tranquility and quiet. **38** Mars in Scorpio, under the rays, signifies tranquility. As an evening planet [and]⁷ a morning one, winds. Stationary, he brings about thunders and lightning. **39** Venus in Scorpio, under the rays, is without rain. As an evening planet, rainy. As a morning one, much rain. **40** Mercury in Scorpio, under the rays, is stormy. As an evening planet, without rain. As a morning one, rainy.

41 Saturn in Sagittarius, under the rays, signifies rain and mistiness. As an evening planet, dryness and aridness. As a morning one, coldness and freezing. Stationary, he makes infirmity for men. **42** Jupiter in Sagittarius, under the rays, [indicates] good preservation and a good complexion. As an evening planet, many rains. As a morning one, fair. Stationary, he signifies prosperity in all things. **43** Mars in Sagittarius, under the rays, is without moisture. As an evening planet, infirmity and pestilence. As a morning one, the movement of many soldiers.⁸ Stationary, imperfection and harm. **44** Venus in Sagittarius, under the rays, is rainy. As an evening planet, cold, windy. As a morning one, she signifies a good complexion. **45** Mercury in Sagittarius, under the rays, signifies much rain. As an evening planet, he is without moisture. As a morning one, he signifies a good complexion and good health.

46 Saturn in Capricorn, under the rays, makes northern winds with the obscurity of the air. As an evening planet, coldness, As a morning one, cold northern [air]. Stationary, he signifies obscure days. **47** Jupiter in Capricorn, under the rays, [indicates] moist air. As an evening planet, rain. As a morning one, he signifies tranquility on the sea and in rivers. Stationary, he is a significator of waters. **48** Mars in Capricorn, under the rays, nourishes. As an evening planet, a good complexion. As a morning one, he makes wintry days throughout places. Stationary, tranquility and perfection. **49** Venus in Capri-

---

⁷ Following Munich, f. 19r. Bos and Burnett believe there is a lacuna here, which seems reasonable given the pattern of indications in the other signs.
⁸ Bos and Burnett indicate one manuscript which reads "the movement of clouds."

corn, under the rays, is icy. As an evening planet, she is cold. As a morning one, rainy. **50** Mercury in Capricorn, under the rays, is always rainy.

51 Saturn in Aquarius, under the rays, makes a hard winter. As an evening planet, fear on the sea and in rivers. As a morning one, rain and winter. Stationary, snowy, likewise cloudy and frozen. **52** Jupiter in Aquarius, under the rays, a good complexion. As an evening planet, much rain. As a morning one, he repels much infirmity. Stationary, he conveys rain and nourishment. **53** Mars in Aquarius, under the rays, aridness. As an evening planet, an absence of winds. As a morning one, their movement. Stationary, he signifies harm on the sea. **54** Venus in Aquarius, under the rays, foggy. As an evening planet, hot and windy. As a morning one, rainy and foggy. **55** Mercury in Aquarius, under the rays, snowy. As an evening planet, icy and turbulent. As a morning one, rainy.

56 Saturn in Pisces, under the rays, is snowy. As an evening planet, rainy. As a morning one, a good complexion. Stationary, he signifies unevenness. **57** Jupiter in Pisces, under the rays, an increase of fish. As an evening planet, a good complexion. As a morning one, tranquility on the sea and in rivers. Stationary, he signifies a good and temperate rain. **58** Mars in Pisces, under the rays, a scarcity of fish. As an evening planet, aridness. As a morning one, lightning and thunders. Stationary, he signifies an unevenness in bodies. **59** Venus in Pisces, under the rays, icy weather. As an evening planet, watery and windy. As a morning one, a good complexion, and she nourishes the grass and a fetus. **60** Mercury in Pisces, under the rays, is stormy and rainy. As an evening planet, a good complexion. As a morning one, he is most tranquil and shows a good complexion.

SECTION I.15: JOHN OF SPAIN, FROM THE
EPITOME OF ALL ASTROLOGY

Comment by Dykes. Following are several chapters from the *Epitome of All Astrology* (*Epitome totius astrologiae*) attributed to John of Spain. According to Burnett (2004, p. 61 n. 19), this is a later and retitled edition of the earlier *Liber Quadripartitus*, which is excerpted in Section I.16. The reader will note that rather than being a true epitome (i.e., a condensed summary of essentials), this portion of the book is a pastiche of many sources, sometimes repeating the same material—note the headings which say "In an older copy, thus," and so on.

I have tried to indicate, when convenient, what some of the sources of the material is. For instance, much of Ch. I.6 is right out of al-Kindī's *Forty Chapters* Ch. 38 (albeit not in Hugo's nor Robert of Ketton's Latin), which I have labeled using its section numbers. Other passages are from *Doors* or are reminiscent of 'Umar al-Tabarī.

꙰   ꙮ   ꙮ

Chapter I.6: On the disposition of the air

2 Wanting to know generally whether the year is going to be rainy, consider, at the revolution of the year (namely at the hour of the conjunction or opposition) whether it is a sign of water, and of a watery mansion of the Moon, and is its lord watery or in a watery sign, or in a watery mansion, and what is the nature of the degree of the conjunction or opposition, and from there the nature of the planets appearing in the aforesaid places, or regarding them. **3** Which if there were more signs of rain than of fair weather, it will be a rainy year; if otherwise, it will be the contrary.

[§669] 4 Saturn is important in this judgment, for if he is in a dry, moist, hot, or cold sign, the year will even be such. **5** In this hour (in which the Sun enters into Aries), it even co-signifies in this hour according to the status of the Ascendant and its lord. **6** And as the status of Saturn signifies with respect to the Sun's entrance into Aries, and in the preceding conjunction or opposition, **[§670]** so Jupiter must signify at the conjunction or opposition before the Sun's entrance into any of the other quarters. **7** Thus even Venus and Mercury are considered at every conjunction or opposition of each month.

An addition from another copy:[1]

9 For the conjunction of the month, if the Ascendant is a firm sign, it will signify for the entire month.

10 On the other hand, [the following] are called the "openings of the doors" by the professionals [of astrology]: the conjunction of the Sun and Moon with Saturn (or their aspect to Saturn) at their conjunction or opposition; moreover in the same way, either the meeting or aspect of Jupiter with Mercury, or of Venus with Mars. **11** From these, the status of the Moon is considered, when she begins to enter into any of the aforesaid doors. **12** For the weather will be according to her status, until she enters into another door.

[§674] **13** Of the rest, Venus signifies moisture, Mercury winds, Saturn mist and cold, Mars winds from the right (or south), and heat from the north (the left), Jupiter the good mixture of the atmosphere and winds from the left: which he signifies more in Cancer, just like Mars does in Capricorn, and the Sun in Aries, [and] thus with the rest.

14 And so, if there were an opening of the doors with Mercury, there will be wind with rain. **15** If Mars would look at the conjunction or opposition of the Sun and Moon, or its lord, there will be meteors,[2] thunders, lightning. **16** However, increase or [subtract from this according to][3] the nature of Mars [and] the nature of the sign or bound in which he is. **17** Which if Saturn would be aspecting instead of Mars, and he is in a sign of earth, it signifies the destruction of houses; if in a sign of water, he threatens cold, mist, darkness. **18** Which if a planet were retrograde there, it signifies great rain.

19 The Moon has power with respect to rain. **20** The Sun signifies now rain, now fair weather; but in the lower place of his circle[4] he signifies rain, in the upper one fair weather. **21** It is the same judgment for the rest of the planets.

---

[1] *Exemplari.*
[2] *Lampadas*, which can indicate flashing light generally.
[3] Reading with *Doors* **7**, for the puzzling *deme*.
[4] That is, in the perigee of the deferent.

22 Moreover, the Moon accepts virtue from the planets just as their nature demands,[5] and as the planets are changed:[6] from the right to the left (and conversely), or from quickness to slowness (and conversely), or from [their] ascent from the lower part of the circle to the upper one (and conversely), or from their entrance or departure from the angles. **23** The conjunction or aspect of a planet does likewise. **24** The aspects of the fixed stars even signify thusly, according to their nature, especially if they would happen to be in the angles.

In an older copy, thus:

26 But the status of the Moon is considered when she begins to enter into any of the aforesaid doors: for the weather will be according to her status up until when she enters into another door.

27 It is even considered where Venus is, while the Sun is entering into Libra: which if she is in a rainy sign, and is under the light of the Sun, western, there will be much rain at the beginning of the year, but little at the end; if she were eastern, conversely.

28 The signs of many rains are the watery signs, namely Aquarius, the end of Capricorn, Aries, Taurus, Leo; stronger than all are Aquarius, Pisces, Scorpio.

29 And whenever Saturn is conjoined to the Sun and Moon, either by body or ray, or Jupiter to Mercury, or Venus to Mars, it signifies future rain.

30 And Saturn signifies rain with cold. **31** Jupiter, the balanced quality of the air. **32** Mars, winds from the right, and heat. **33** The Sun, hotness and dryness. **34** Venus, moisture. **35** Mercury, winds. **36** But the Moon takes the proper qualities of the planets, which she bestows upon the earth.

37 And[7] when the Moon enters Cancer at the hour of the Sun, or Virgo at the hour of Venus, or Sagittarius at the hour of the Moon, or Gemini at the hour of Mercury, or Taurus at the hour of Mars, or Libra at the hour of Jupiter, it signifies rain or winds according to the nature of the sign in which the lord of that hour is.

---

[5] Reading *exigit* for *existit*.
[6] Compare this list of planetary conditions with changes in times (see my discussion in the Introduction to *Choices & Inceptions*).
[7] See my Introduction for a discussion of this passage (Section I.1).

38 It[8] even denotes rain thus, if the Moon is separated from the light of another planet (by conjunction or aspect), and she enters the light of another (by conjunction or aspect), but so that their houses are opposites: for example, the Moon is being separated from Mars and conjoined to Venus (namely, whose houses, Aries and Libra, are opposites).[9]

39 Thus, with the Moon appearing in the fourth, and a feminine sign, if a retrograde [planet] appearing in a feminine sign would look upon her, there will be rain.

An addition from another codex:

41 Which if the Moon is in the sign of some city, or in any of its angles, it is said that what she signifies is going to be in that city; if however she is after the angles, but [still] in a sign aspecting the sign of the city, the signification will be less; and if in a sign not aspecting the sign of the city, the signification will be shaken.

Chapter I.7: On the same thing

2 However,[10] you will judge particularly with respect to the changing of the atmosphere, thus: at the conjunction of the Sun and Moon, consider what sign is ascending in it, and of what nature it is, whether it is a moist mansion or a dry one; and the lord of the sign: whether it is of a rainy nature or not; and the sign in which it is: of what nature it is; and what planets are in the ascending sign or with its lord, or likewise in their aspect; which ones are conjoined to the Moon or aspect her then, or in what house or what mansion the Moon herself is. **3** Which if more testimonies of the aforesaid planets and signs are for rain, that half of the lunation will be rainy (namely, up to the time of the opposition). **4** Which if more would agree in fair weather, it will be fair. **5** If equal, it will be indifferent.

5 Which if you found that [the atmosphere] is going to be rainy, then it will make rain when [the Moon] will be conjoined to some rainy planet, or if

---

[8] Cf. *Doors* **36**.

[9] A marginal note in the printed edition reads: "In another codex. And this is the opening of the great folding doors, in which it is necessary for winds or rains to come about, just as the nature of those planets is."

[10] For this paragraph, cf. the opening paragraph of Ch. I.6 above.

she looked upon it, or entered any rainy sign. **7** Which if it is not going to be rainy, the conjunctions or aspects of the planets with the Moon would barely be able to change the atmosphere.

8 The atmosphere is even altered if one of the planets would cross over from right to left (or the reverse), or from quickness to slowness (or the reverse), or from the apogee to the opposite [of that] (or the reverse), or from direct motion to retrogradation (or the reverse), or it would enter some sign or go out from it: for with these things coming upon [us], the air is frequently made to be stormy (or conversely).

9 And as we judge from the conjunction to the opposition through the Ascendant and its lord (and so on), as was stated before, we judge thusly through the opposition up to the conjunction. **10** Always, however, at the opposition we consider the degree of the luminary appearing above the earth.

11 Which if the Moon is under the light of a rainy planet, by conjunction or aspect, at the hour of the conjunction or opposition, by how many degrees she is then distant from the planet up to the perfection of the aspect or conjunction, it will begin to rain once that many days have been finished (after the hour in which the conjunction or opposition of the luminaries is).

12 Moreover, the greatest testimony of rain is that it be seen every morning how much there is from the Sun to Saturn, and that much be computed from the place of the Moon. Which if the computation would be ended in a house of the Moon or Venus, it denotes rain; if in a house of Mercury or Jupiter, winds; if in a house of Mars[11] or the Sun, calm weather; if in a house of Saturn, mist. **13** And one must even see whether that same computation would be ended in a moist or dry mansion, according to what will judge.

14 Venus in Scorpio or Capricorn or Aquarius, denotes rain [if she is] in a proportion to the Moon,[12] and thus the three planets[13] joined in Aquarius.

15 But one must note in a summary way, that two testimonies of rain in the season of summer, are worth less than one in the winter. **16** Thus [also], two of fair weather in the winter do less than one in the summer.

17 And that it rains in one land, but cannot be so in another, [is] either because at the hour of the cycle it has another Ascendant, or because the sign of one land at that hour has a rainy plant, and the sign of the other land has a fair planet. Therefore, let us look at the planets and sign on each side.

---

[11] See Section I.1 for a discussion of the Lots of rain.
[12] *Proportionalis Lunae.* I take this to mean an aspect.
[13] This must refer to the Moon, Mercury, and Venus: see Jafar's *Book of Heavy Rains* sentence **149** (Section I.10).

Chapter I.8: On the parts of the world distributed
to the planets and the signs (part)

*[I omit here a section on chorography in favor of the second half of the chapter,
on weather and the quality of the year.]*

Aphorisms found in another codex:

25 Always consider, if the Moon would be joined [to another planet] from
the conjunction or opposition of the Sun, which of the planets is closer to
the Sun at his entrance into the beginning of Aries, [and] with which planet
she is being joined or who aspects her by a complete aspect: and if it is a fortunate planet, the year will be good, it will rain in its own [proper] season,
and the [rain] of the month will be much, of much fruit, flock-animals and
the like. **26** And if that planet gives power[14] to an unfortunate planet, or if
the Moon gives power to one standing in an angle, and that planet gives
power to one standing in a fallen house, the end of the year will be bad.

27 And every planet harms, as its path [dictates]. **28** And the path of Saturn is a source of suffocation in water, when Saturn is in a house or in any of
the signs which are called the portions[15] of the Sun. **29** It signifies submersion in waters, if Saturn is in those which are called the portions of the
Moon. **30** If he were in a hot sign it signifies heat and dryness. **31** If he is in
signs of a human figure, it signifies wars, robbers, and there will be a powerful war at the entrance of Mars under the light of the Sun or into the house
of his disgrace;[16] and Jupiter having entered the light of the Sun [also] signifies thus. **32** Consider whether Mars is eastern or western, or from the right
or from the left: on the side in which Mars is, they will overcome.

33 And if Mercury were with Mars at the beginning of the year, or in one
of the four angles, it signifies mortality in the lands which the sign (in which
they are joined) denotes. **34** If Saturn will be with Mercury, and they were in
one sign, it signifies an earthquake.

---

[14] *Dat vim.* This might not be as technical as "pushing power," and may simply be an applying aspect.

[15] *Partes*, here and in the next sentence. This sounds like the solar half of the zodiac (from
Leo through the end of Capricorn) and the lunar half (from Aquarius through the end of
Cancer).

[16] That is, his fall or descension (Cancer).

SECTION I.16: JOHN OF SPAIN, *TREATISE ON RAINS* *& THE CHANGING OF THE ATMOSPHERE* (PART)

Comment by Dykes. This short description of the lunar mansions from John of Spain's *Liber Quadripartitus* was translated from Burnett's edition (2004, pp. 124-30). John uses the Arab, 28-mansion system (despite the attribution to the Indians), and explicitly links them to particular fixed stars: another reason to suppose that the mansions must be used sidereally and not tropically. In fact, one manuscript source (London, Brit. Lib. Sloane 702, see Burnett p. 125) specifically points out that about 10° of precession has taken place, which must be taken into account: thus the first mansion actually begins at about 10° of tropical Aries, not at 0°. Obviously that is a medieval value, and precession is even greater today. At the end of the translation, I append a table which summarizes the mansions and their likely stars, along with my own rendering of the little star images which appear in Paris lat. 7316a, fols. 46v-47a (in Burnett 2004, pp. 140-41).

℞ ℞ ℞

The Indians divided the circle into 28 parts,[1] which they called "mansions of the Moon." Each embraces 12 6/7 degrees.

1. And the beginning of them is from the two great stars which are called the Horns of Aries; this is their likeness. *Temperate*.
2. The second part is called the Belly, which is three stars, in this manner. *Dry*.
3. The third is called the Head of Taurus, which is six tiny stars, and it is what they call the Tail of Aries (but the Arabs [say it is] rainy). *Temperate*.
4. The fourth, a great and red star, and in front of it small stars. The great one is called the Left Eye of Taurus. *Moist*.
5. The fifth is the Head of the Strong Dog, and there are three small stars between two big ones, in this manner. Certain people call these the Three Fingers. *Dry*.

---

[1] Normally the Indians are said to have used a 27-mansion system, which John elsewhere attributes to "certain people" (Burnett 2004, p. 125). John is using the Arab, 28-mansion system.

6. The sixth is what the Indians call the Small Star, of great light. *Temperate.*

7. They call the seventh the Arm of Leo, and there are two bright stars. *Moist.*

8. They call the eighth Misty, and there are two stars with a cloud in the middle.[2] *Temperate.*

9. But they say the ninth is the Eye, there are even three stars. *Dry.*

10. The tenth is called the Brow; there are four stars. *Moist.*

11. The eleventh is called Fur,[3] there are two stars. *Temperate.*

12. The twelfth is called the Tail of Leo, it is the greatest star. *Moist.*

13. The thirteenth is called the Dog, there are four stars. *Temperate.*

14. The fourteenth is called the Ear of Grain;[4] it is the greatest star. *Temperate.*

15. The fifteenth is called the Covered;[5] there are three small stars. *Moist.*

16. The sixteenth is two great stars joined to each other, which are called the Horns[6] of Scorpio. *Moist.*

17. The seventeenth is called the Crown; there are three stars above the head of Scorpio, put in a straight line, of great light. Near them in that line are two others, in this manner. *Moist.*

18. The eighteenth, the Heart of Scorpio,[7] and it is a great, red star in between two small ones. *Dry.*

19. The nineteenth is the Tail of Scorpio; there are two shining stars, [and] nine other stars in the same line. *Moist.*

20. The twentieth is called a Beam;[8] there are eight bright stars, four in the belt[9] [but] the others outside it. *Moist.*

21. The twenty-first is called the Desert, and it is a place without stars. *Temperate.*

22. The twenty-second is called the Shepherd; there are two small stars, one set up on the left, the other descending on the right. The

---

[2] *Nube media.*
[3] *Capillus.* Or, hair on the head, perhaps a mane.
[4] *Spica,* which can also mean a "point": that is, the star Spica.
[5] Or perhaps, "Covering" (*Cohoperta,* a medieval misspelling for *Cooperta*). Other sources say "Drape" (*Velamen*).
[6] Or rather, "claws." These are also the pans of Libra.
[7] That is, Antares.
[8] *Trabs.*
[9] That is, actually in or near the zodiac.

Arabs however, call it the "killer of health," which is had in front
of another star said to be the Ram. *Moist.*

23. The twenty-third is called Gulping,[10] and there are two small stars.
    Temperate.

24. The twenty-fourth is called the Star of Fortune, and there are two
    stars, one shining more than the other. *Temperate.*

25. The twenty-fifth is called the Butterfly; there are two stars behind,
    four stars in front. *Dry.*

26. The twenty-sixth is called the First Drawer of Water, and there are
    two bright stars. *Dry.*

27. The twenty-seventh is called the Second Drawer of Water, and
    there are two bright stars. *Moist.*

28. The twenty eighth is called the Tooth of the Fish. *Temperate.*

The Indians say that the mansions which signify rain are 11, namely: the
Eye of Taurus, the Arm, the Brow, the Tail of Leo, the Covered, the Horn of
Scorpio, the Crown of its head, its Tail, the Beam, the Shepherd, and the
Second Drawer—namely the 4th, 7th, 10th, 12th, 15th, 16th, 17th, 19th, 20th, 22nd,
27th.

And six mansions are dry, namely the Belly of Aries, the Head of the
Strong Dog, the Eye, Heart, Butterfly, the First Drawer: the 2nd, 5th, 9th, 18th,
25th, 26th.

Eleven others are temperate, namely the 1st, 3rd, 6th, 8th, 11th, 13th, 14th,
21st, 23rd, 24th, 28th.

In a month,[11] you ought also to consider the hour of the conjunction of
the Sun and Moon, and their opposition and their square, from the right and
the left, and in which mansions of the Moon the five planets are (namely
moist or dry), and in what mansion the Moon herself is in, and what mansion
of the Moon is ascending from the east: and thus you could know on what
day of the month there is going to be rain. And you always ought to consider
the sign of that land and its angles, and its lord, and its every aspect.

---

[10] *Gluciens*, but reading as *Gluttiens*.
[11] This paragraph is very close to the anonymous passage following Hermann's *Book of
Heavy Rains* in Munich Clm. 11067 (Section I.18).

	Name	Star	Type	Image
1	Horns of Aries (*al-Sharaṭān*)[12]	Sheratan (β Aries), Mesarthim (γ)	T	
2	Belly (*al-Buṭayn*)[13]	Botein (δ), ε, ρ Aries	D	
3	Head of Taurus (*al-Thurayyā*)[14]	Pleiades	T	
4	Eye of Taurus (*al-Dabarān*)[15]	Aldebaran (α Taurus), or Hyades	M	
5	Head of Strong Dog (*al-Haqʿah*)[16]	λ *and* φ *Orion?*	D	
6	Small Star (*al-Hanʿa*)[17]	Alhena (γ Gemini), ξ?	T	
7	Arm of Leo (*al-Dhirāʿ*)[18]	Castor (α Gemini), Pollux (β)	M	
8	Misty (*al-Nathra*)[19]	Praesepe (nebula near ε Cancer)	T	
9	Eye (*al-Ṭarf*)[20]	ϰ Cancer, Alterf (λ Leo)	D	
10	Brow (*al-Jabha*)[21]	Around ζ, γ, η, α Leo; ε Gemini	M	
11	Fur (*al-Zubra*)[22]	Zosma (δ), θ Leo	T	
12	Tail of Leo (*al-Ṣarfah*)[23]	Denebola (β Leo)	M	
13	Dog (*al-ʿAwwāʾ*)[24]	Zavijava (β Virgo), Zania (η), Porrima (γ), δ, Vindemiatrix (ε)	T	

[12] "The butting" (Lat. *Alnath*).

[13] "The little belly" (Lat. *Albethain*).

[14] "The Pleiades" (Lat. *Althoraie*).

[15] "The two buttocks" (Burnett) or the star Aldebaran (Lat. *Addavenam*); but "the Follower" (Robson).

[16] "A (white) circle of hair on a horse" (Lat. *Alhathaya*).

[17] "The camel's brand" (Lat. *Alhana*).

[18] "The forearm" (Lat. *Addirach*).

[19] "The tip of the nose" (Lat. *Alnayra*).

[20] "The look, the eye" (Lat. *Attraaif*).

[21] "The forehead" (Lat. *Algebhe*).

[22] "The mane," according to Burnett (Lat. *Aҫobrach*). This mansion is also called *al-Kharātān*, meaning uncertain (but Weinstock p. 50 believes this might be "Two Hares," after the Greek of the *Codex Cromwellianus 12*.

[23] "The diversion" (Dykes) or "The change" (Burnett), Lat. *Aҫarfa*.

[24] The constellation Bootes (Lat. *Aloce*).

14	Ear of Grain (al-Simāk)[25]	Spica/Azimech (α Virgo)	T	○
15	Covered (al-Ghafr)[26]	Maybe ɩ and ϰ Virgo	M	○○ ○
16	Horns of Scorpio (al-Zubānā)[27]	Zuben Elgenubi (α Libra) & Zuben Eschemali (β)	M	○ ○
17	Crown (al-Iklīl)[28]	Maybe Acrab/Graffias (β Scorpio), Dschubba (δ)	M	○○○ ○○
18	Heart of Scorpio (al-Qalb)[29]	Antares (α Scorpio)	D	○◯○
19	Tail of Scorpio (al-ʾIbrah)[30]	Shaula (λ Scorpio), Lesath (υ); Acumen & Aculeus (in sting of Scorpio)	M	○○ ○○○○○○○○
20	Beam (al-Naʿāʾim)[31]	Near Ascella (ζ Sagittarius)	M	○ ○ ○ ○ ○ ○ ○ ○
21	Desert (al-Balda)[32]	Maybe π Sagittarius	T	
22	Shepherd (Saʿd al-dhābiḥ)[33]	Algedi (α Capricorn), Dabih (β)	M	○○ ○
23	Gulping (Saʿd bulaʿ)[34]	Albali (ε Aquarius), μ, ν	T	○ ○
24	Star of Fortune (Saʿd al-suʿūd)[35]	Sadalsuud (β Aquarius), ξ; 46 Capricorn?	T	○ ○
25	Butterfly (Saʿd al-ʾakhbiyah)[36]	Sadachbia (γ Aquarius), π, ζ, η	D	○○ ○○ ○○

---

[25] Meaning unclear, but this word does mean "fish" (Lat. *Açimech*).

[26] "The coat of mail," according to Burnett (*Algarf*).

[27] "The claws," according to Burnett (Lat. *Açebone*): namely, the claws of Scorpio or pans of Libra.

[28] "The crown" (Lat. *Alidil*).

[29] "The heart," or *Cor Scorpionis* (Lat. *Alcalb*).

[30] "The sting" (Lat. *Yenla*), also called "the tail" (*al-shawlah*), *Cauda Scorpionis*.

[31] "The ostriches" (Lat. *Alimain*).

[32] "The place" (Lat. *Albeda*).

[33] "Luck of the slayer" (Lat. *Sahaddadebe*).

[34] "Luck of the swallower" (Lat. *Zadebolal*).

[35] "Luck of the lucks" (Lat. *Zaadescod*).

[36] "Luck of the tents" (Lat. *Sadalabbia*).

26	1st Drawer of Water (*al-Fargh al-muqaddam*)[37]	Maybe Markab (α Pegasus) & Scheat (β)	D	○ ○
27	2nd Drawer of Water (*al-Fargh al-mu'akhkhar*)[38]	Maybe Algenib (γ Pegasus), Alpheratz (α Andromeda or β Pegasus)[39]	M	○ ○
28	Tooth of Fish (*Baṭn al-ḥūt*)[40]	β Andromeda[41]	T	○○○○○○○○○ ○○○○○○○○

Figure 38: Mansion stars according to John

---

[37] "The preceding spout" (Lat. *Fargalmocaden*), also called *al-Fargh al-awwal* ("the first spout").

[38] "The following spout" (Lat. *Alfargamahar*).

[39] According to Kunitzsch and Smart (pp. 15, 47), there was some confusion between the names and stars for α-γ Pegasus and α Andromeda.

[40] "Belly of the fish" (Lat. *Bathnealoth*), also called *Baṭn al-rishā'*, "belly of the rope" (esp. the rope for a well).

[41] According to Kunitzsch and Smart (p. 50), this mansion originally involved a faint curve of stars meant to be like a rope, connecting to the Square of Pegasus.

SECTION I.17: ROBERT GROSSETESTE, *ON THE IMPRESSIONS OF THE AIR,* OR *ON PROGNOSTICATION*

Comment by Dykes. This is a translation of part of a treatise on weather prediction by the famous medieval theologian, philosopher, and scientist, Robert Grosseteste (ca. 1175 – 1253 AD), who was also Bishop of Lincoln and teacher to the more famous Francis Bacon. It was written in 1249, shortly before his own death. We should take it more as an illustration of an approach to weather, rather than relying on his chart or skill as an astrologer.

The first part of the selection is a review of some basic principles in astrology, including a version of the "weighted victor" procedure, in which planets are assigned different sets of points according to which of their own dignities they happen to be in. Then, I omit a longish astronomical section which is not of much astrological import, and finally turn to his description of several example charts. As I point out below, Grosseteste's values for most of his planets are 10-11° off from a properly precessed tropical zodiac. Since John (Section I.16) says that precession has offset the constellations by 10°, Grosseteste may have had something like this in mind: he may have calculated all of the planets accurately according to tropical ephemerides (except for Mercury), and then thought he should subtract about 10°. Nevertheless the editor, Baur, says that a marginal note added to the manuscript claims his prediction about 1255 AD came true.

Grosseteste also does something very strange in his weighted victor calculation: he lets one planet with dignities in a place, take away from the points belonging to another. In his 1249 example, both Venus and Mercury are in Taurus. Venus has 5 points because she has dignity by domicile; but because Mercury is in his own bound (2 points), Grosseteste allows him to take those 2 away from Venus, leaving her with only 3 points total. This is totally against traditional practice (among those who used victors), and should be viewed as an error by an educated man but not an experienced astrologer.

ॐ   ॐ   ॐ

In order to know beforehand the diverse, future disposition of the air, on account of the diversity of the superior motions, it is necessary that the powers of the signs, the natures of the planets, also the qualities of the quarters of the circle described by the diurnal revolution,[1] be scrutinized.

Therefore, there are twelve houses, and they are distinguished by the nature of the elements: because Aries, Leo, [and] Sagittarius are of the fiery nature, hot and dry; Taurus, Virgo, and Capricorn of the earthy nature, cold and dry; Gemini, Libra, and Aquarius of the airy nature, hot and moist; Cancer, Scorpio, and Pisces, of the watery nature, cold and moist.

The natures of the planets are these: Saturn is extremely cold and correspondingly dry, and thus to that extent he is an enemy to all nature. But Jupiter is temperately hot and moist, and thus a friend to every nature. However, more heat abounds in him than does moisture. But Mars is hot and dry in an overflowing way, of a choleric nature, and thus in a certain way contrary to life; but more hot than dry. But the Sun [is] hot and dry in the most temperate way, or as I may say more truly, among all qualities supremely balanced. But Venus [is] temperately hot, moist in an overflowing way, whence she is reported to have rulership over venereal acts. However, Mercury is inclined through his nature towards that one of the planets and signs to which he is complected (however, in himself he is said to be cold and dry). But the Moon's nature is said to be temperately cold and extremely moist, whence she is said to be the source of moisture, just as the Sun is the source of heat (even though he is temperately hot).

However, in the aforesaid signs there are certain strengths which are attributed to the planets, which are called "powers" or "dignities" or "testimonies," as are the house, exaltation, triplicity, bound, face, aspect. And the house is said to have 5 strengths, the exaltation 4, the triplicity 3, the bound 2, the face 1.[2] Whence, the house has in itself five strengths, [which are equal to] five faces, and thus with the rest.

And[3] for this reason the house is compared to a man in his own house and own rulership. The exaltation is compared to a man in his own kingdom and glory. The triplicity is just like a man in his own honor and among allies. However, the bound is just like a man among relatives and [his] clan. How-

---

[1] For example, that the places from the Ascendant to the Midheaven are spring-like, hot and moist, etc.

[2] In the earlier Arabic period, the bound and triplicity values were switched. See *The Search of the Heart* for this and other victor methods.

[3] This paragraph shows that Grosseteste might be consulting al-Qabīsī: see the parallel text in *ITA* I.8. But al-Qabīsī does not include the statements about aspects below, nor does he consider Venus to be *hot* and moist. So Grosseteste might be relying on some intermediate, medieval Latin text which itself drew on al-Qabīsī.

ever, a planet in his own face is just like a man in his own profession. But a good aspect is just like a strong army escorting the king; but a bad aspect is just like a contrary army.

But the exaltations of the planets are these: the Sun is exalted in Aries, the Moon in Taurus, Saturn in Libra, Jupiter in Cancer, Mars in Capricorn, Venus in Pisces, Mercury in Virgo. And just as the Sun is exalted in Aries through his own virtue, thus in Libra is his descension, since it is the sign opposite Aries; and one must even understand it thusly for the rest.

However, the house of the planets is said to be the sign in which it was created at the origin of the world.[4] Therefore, Leo is the house of the Sun, Cancer of the Moon, Virgo of Mercury, Scorpio[5] of Mars, Sagittarius of Jupiter, Capricorn of Saturn. And one must note that the five planets have accidental powers in the five remaining signs, like Saturn in Aquarius, Jupiter in Pisces, Mars in Aries,[6] Venus in Taurus, Mercury in Gemini. Whence, they are called their accidental domiciles.

Figure 39: The *Thema Mundi*

It is called a triplicity of a planet, when it is in a sign of the same nature as the sign in which it was created, so that, if the Sun is in Sagittarius or Aries (which are hot and dry signs just like Leo, in which he was created); and the Moon, when she is in Scorpio or Pisces (which are cold and moist signs just like Cancer, in which she was created); and thus with the rest.[7]

---

[4] The so-called "birth chart of the world," or *Thema Mundi* (see below). For more information, see *ITA* III.6.2, and Firmicus Maternus's *Mathesis* III.1.1-2.
[5] In the *Thema Mundi*, the planets are arranged from Cancer through Capricorn. I have corrected Grosseteste's text, which had Aries here and Scorpio below.
[6] Again, correcting Grosseteste, who had Scorpio here.
[7] Of course, this is not true: Saturn was created in Capricorn, but he does not belong to the earthy triplicity. Robert may have known this but decided to ignore it, since going through all of the planets would have revealed that his explanation did not make sense. The way to attribute the planets properly to their triplicities is through the joys (which I

Triplicity	Diurnal	Nocturnal	Participating
Fire	☉	♃	♄
Air	♄	☿	♃
Water	♀	♂	☽
Earth	♀	☽	♂

Figure 40: "Dorothean" triplicity lords

However, different people feel different things about the bounds. The more famous ones are the bounds of the Egyptians, which are these: Jupiter has the first six degrees of Aries, Venus the six following, and thus with the rest, as is laid out in this table:[8]

♈	♃ 0°-5°59'	♀ 6°-11°59'	☿ 12°-19°59'	♂ 20°-24°59'	♄ 25°-29°59'
♉	♀ 0°-7°59'	☿ 8°-13°59'	♃ 14°-21°59'	♄ 22°-26°59'	♂ 27°-29°59'
♊	☿ 0°-5°59'	♃ 6°-11°59'	♀ 12°-16°59'	♂ 17°-23°59'	♄ 24°-29°59'
♋	♂ 0°-6°59'	♀ 7°-12°59'	☿ 13°-18°59'	♃ 19°-25°59'	♄ 26°-29°59'
♌	♃ 0°-5°59'	♀ 6°-10°59'	♄ 11°-17°59'	☿ 18°-23°59'	♂ 24°-29°59'
♍	☿ 0°-6°59'	♀ 7°-16°59'	♃ 17°-20°59'	♂ 21°-27°59'	♄ 28°-29°59'
♎	♄ 0°-5°59'	☿ 6°-13°59'	♃ 14°-20°59'	♀ 21°-27°59'	♂ 28°-29°59'
♏	♂ 0°-6°59'	♀ 7°-10°59'	☿ 11°-18°59'	♃ 19°-23°59'	♄ 24°-29°59'
♐	♃ 0°-11°59'	♀ 12°-16°59'	☿ 17°-20°59'	♄ 21°-25°59'	♂ 26°-29°59'
♑	☿ 0°-6°59'	♃ 7°-13°59'	♀ 14°-21°59'	♄ 22°-25°59'	♂ 26°-29°59'
♒	☿ 0°-6°59'	♀ 7°-12°59'	♃ 13°-19°59'	♂ 20°-24°59'	♄ 25°-29°59'
♓	♀ 0°-11°59'	♃ 12°-15°59'	☿ 16°-18°59'	♂ 19°-27°59'	♄ 28°-29°59'

Figure 41: Table of Egyptian bounds

However, the faces of the signs are distinguished thus: each sign is divided into three equal parts (and each one consists of 10°), which are called "faces," and by another name "decans." The beginning of the faces is from the first degree of Aries. Therefore, the first face is up to the tenth degree of Aries, and is said to belong to Mars. The second is up to the twentieth, and is said to be the face of the Sun (who succeeds Mars in the order of the circles,

---

will describe at a later date). Below is a table of traditional triplicity lords as found in Dorotheus and other ancient authors. See also Ptolemy's *mundane* triplicity lords (Section IV.2).

[8] Grosseteste's table apparently listed the amount of degrees for each bound, not the actual degrees included in them. I have supplied the latter, as it is easier to use.

that is, the spheres). The third face is from the twentieth up to the end of Aries, and is said to be the face of Venus. And thus with the rest according to rank, as is laid out in the following table:[9]

Sign	0° - 9°59'	10° - 19°59'	20° - 29°29'
♈	♂	☉	♀
♉	☿	☽	♄
♊	♃	♂	☉
♋	♀	☿	☽
♌	♄	♃	♂
♍	☉	♀	☿
♎	☽	♄	♃
♏	♂	☉	♀
♐	☿	☽	♄
♑	♃	♂	☉
♒	♀	☿	☽
♓	♄	♃	♂

Figure 42: Table of "Chaldean" faces or decans

These are the testimonies which the planets take from the signs. There are other strengths and weaknesses which the planets take mutually from each other, so that through a good aspect one planet takes strength from another, but weakness through a bad one.

But there are five aspects, namely: the opposite, square, trine, sextile, conjunction. The opposite aspect is if a planet were in some sign, and another in the sign directly opposite.[10] But such an aspect is said to be the worst, and especially if the planets were of contrary qualities, and also the signs: such as if Venus were in Aries, and Saturn in Libra (whence, just as sign contradicts sign, so planet [contradicts] planet). Whence, there is contrariety or contradiction there from every side, namely from the position [and] from the quality of the signs and planets. But the trine aspect is if two planets are in signs just like each other, and they contain between themselves one-third of the firmament. And it is said to be the best aspect, because there is not con-

---

[9] Again, Grosseteste's own table just gives the amount of degrees in each face, not the actual degrees themselves. I have supplied the latter.

[10] Note the use of whole-sign regards or aspects or configurations—not degree-based ones.

trariety there in the qualities of the signs. Whence, if the planets were concordant (like Jupiter and Venus), no contradiction will be found in such an
aspect. But the square aspect is if there were three whole signs between the
two planets, like if the Sun were in Aries, Saturn in Cancer. And it is called a
square, because the aforesaid planets contain one-fourth of the zodiac between them. And this aspect is said to be bad in a middling way, and it is
impeding just like one laying a trap. However, the sextile aspect is if there
were two whole signs between the two planets, namely one-sixth of the zodiac, and it is said to be good in a middling way, on account of the
concordance of the signs in one of the primary qualities. The conjunction, as
it is taken here, is if two planets were in the same sign. But the astrologers
say this aspect is the strongest; we however have found the opposite and the
trine to be stronger.

And there are other strengths and weaknesses which the planets take from
the diverse being in their short circle (namely, the epicycle): namely arising,
sinking, [forward] progress, stationing, retrogradation. It is called the "arising" of a planet when it goes out from under the solar rays and manifestly
appears to the world without the impeding brightness of the Sun. But "sinking" is such an entrance into [the rays]. It is called "[forward] progress" when
it is sensibly moved against the firmament. But retrogradation is when it is
moved more quickly from the east towards the west, than the firmament is.
However, "stationing" is when it remained for a long time in the same minute. And these differences are compared to the four seasons.[11]

However, there is another difference for each planet, from its different
condition in its deferent, which is admirable and worthy of memory more so
than the rest; and for that reason one must treat of it in a more expanded
description, since up to this point it has been overlooked by others...[12]

ꝏ   ꝏ   ꝏ

...And just as it appears with respect to the works of the Sun and Moon
in these lower things, likewise you should consider it with respect to the rest
of the planets. Whence it is clear that all planets, to the extent that they are

---

[11] Cf. Ptolemy's and al-Kindī's models of how planetary motion is like the elemental qualities, in Section I.2.
[12] At this point, Grosseteste goes into a longish description of the deferent circles and
some other geometrical considerations, as well as the Moon's effect on the tides. I have
omitted this, and continue with the more astrological material in the next paragraph.

more remote from the earth, they are that much stronger; by how much more near, they have operations that are much weaker in these lower things.

Their operations are even varied according to their approach to, and elongation from, the zenith over our head, because when they are near, then they operate more strongly; when however they are elongated, more weakly.[13]

Therefore, these are the essential and accidental testimonies of the planets, which are necessary for our suggested proposal. In order therefore to comprehend all of the aforesaid without labor and the wearying of [our] power, let me describe to you a figure of eight circles. Therefore, the first of these is the circle of the signs, the second the circle of Saturn, and thus with the rest, just as they are ranked in their orbs. And I will divide all of the circles into twelve equal parts according to the distinction of the twelve signs, and in every circle I will put the testimonies of the planet in the direct line of the sign in which they are found.[14] Therefore, for the house I put 5, for the exaltation 4, for the triplicity 3, for the bound 2, for the face 1. If therefore you wished to prognosticate the disposition of the air to some certain point in time,[15] it is good for you first to find that place of the planet through the tables. This being done, you will record their testimonies in the signs, and you will judge through the planet having more of their testimonies. For that planet which had more testimonies, will be the dispositor[16] of that weather.

For example, behold:[17] I seek the places of the planets in the completed year of the Arabs 646—that is, the year of Grace 1249—in the fourth month, the fifteenth day of the month (that is, 17 Kalends of May). And the Sun was found in the twenty-second degree of Aries, the Moon in the twenty-first

---

[13] See al-Kindī's *DMT* Ch. 5 (Section I.3).

[14] What Grosseteste means is that because the planets flow along their own circles below the fixed stars and the zodiac, the planets are never really "in" the zodiacal signs themselves: we only see them against the *background* of the signs. So in order to discover what place or degree a planet is "in," we are really drawing lines from the earth, through the planet, to the circle of the zodiacal signs, in line with our sight: where the lines fall, show where in the zodiac the planet "is."

[15] *Terminum.*

[16] *Dispositor*, lit. "arranger."

[17] Based on the positions of the Sun and Moon, it is clear that Grosseteste means for this to be a New Moon chart. But a comparison with the modern recalculation shows that most of his values are about 10-11° behind, suggesting an improperly precessed chart. (Note that John of Spain also recommends a precession value of 10° in his *Treatise* on the lunar mansions: see Section I.16.) Adding this amount gets us close to the actual positions of the luminaries, Saturn, Mars, and Venus. Grosseteste may simply have made a mistake with Jupiter, since subtracting 10° from his true position does get us the first degrees of *Capricorn* rather than Aquarius. Mercury is completely wrong.

degree of the same sign,[18] Saturn in the tenth degree of Scorpio, Jupiter in the first degree of Aquarius, Mars in the twenty-eighth degree of Aquarius, Venus in the seventeenth degree of Taurus, but Mercury in the fourteenth degree of Taurus.

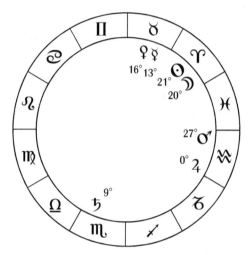

Figure 43: Grosseteste's New Moon chart for 1249 AD

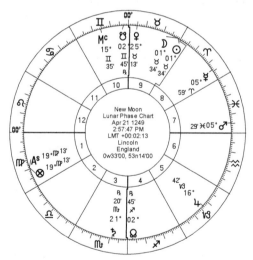

Figure 44: Grosseteste's chart recalculated

---

[18] Note that Grosseteste has virtually cast the chart for the New Moon, which is the usual traditional practice but he has not mentioned it before. Unfortunately, the New Moon did not occur with the planets in such signs in the spring of 1249 (see my notes above).

Therefore, proceed thusly. The Sun (extremely tempered in nature, or temperately hot and dry) is in the twenty-second degree of Aries, namely in his exaltation, where he has 4 testimonies; and in his own triplicity, where he has 3 testimonies; and thus in all he has 7. Nor is he impeded by any contrary planet. Therefore, if you remembered what was said before, he will arrange the air according to his own nature.

Moreover, Venus (hot and moist) is in the seventeenth degree of Taurus, which is her house, where she has 5 testimonies.

But Mercury, cold and dry in his nature, is in the fourteenth degree of Taurus, where he has 2 testimonies. Therefore, he takes away 2 testimonies from Venus, and thus only 3 testimonies remain to Venus.[19]

Likewise Saturn, cold and dry, is in the tenth degree of Scorpio, and thus in an opposite aspect with Venus. Lacking testimonies, he is retrograde, and thus he does not permit the witnesses of Venus to bear fruit. But because he is exalted in his own deferent and is near [his] apogee, and thus as though acquiring the favor of the judgment, he renders the testimonies of Venus suspect, and thus Venus is weakened in her own signification.

Moreover, Jupiter, hot and moist in nature, is in the first degree of Aquarius, lacking testimonies; but, however, he has proceeded forward in his own arising, and is thus as though a boy about whom one has hope; and thus he is in a certain way favorable to the Sun.

Likewise, Mars in his own nature is hot to an overflowing extent, and dry, in the twenty-eighth degree of Aquarius, lacking testimonies. And however, he has proceeded forward in his own arising and he aspects the Sun himself by a sextile aspect. Therefore, he prepares aid for the Sun in the hot and dry.

However, the Moon is cold and moist in her own nature, in the twenty-first degree of Aries, lacking testimonies. She is however near the apogee of her deferent, and thus proceeds very moist and cold.

Therefore, the Sun's testimonies remain wholly unshaken, wherefore he will be the indicator of that time, and the weather will be disposed in a temperate way according to the hot and dry—which was the case.[20]

---

[19] This is an unusual approach I have never seen before. Normally, planets only gain in their own dignities, but here Grosseteste has them taking them away from each other.

[20] Baur indicates the following, which he removed from the text: "And in that same time, there appeared two circles of great magnitude, containing the Sun." This must refer to a "Sun dog," when ice crystals in cold air create a halo and mirroring effect, producing the appearance of two extra Suns to the right and left of the actual Sun.

Therefore, this is the general form according to which you will proceed in judgments. If therefore you wished to prognosticate outstanding future heat, consider the many testimonies of the hot planets, concurrently with the trine aspect. For example, since the Sun in the year of Grace 1249 (in the month of July) will be in Leo and thus in his own house, [and] Mars at that same time will be in the first decan of Aries, and thus in his own house and face. Therefore, he will manage that time in what is hot and dry, in an overflowing way. However, Saturn will be in Scorpio, without testimonies, and in the square aspect with the Sun, and thus he will take away a little bit from the heat of the Sun.

If you wished to foresee outstanding cold, you will consider the many, concurrent testimonies of the cold planets. For example, in the year of the Lord 1255 Saturn will be in his own house (namely in Capricorn); for five continuous years he is going to stay in that same place and in Aquarius. Therefore, for five continuous winters he will manage according to his own nature, and he will impede heat and summers much on account of his opposite aspect with the Sun,[21] and thus he will impede the maturing of fruits. And so, the seasons of autumn will be pernicious in cold and the killing of flowers. One must therefore fear the annual grain revenues and especially that of vines and fruits, except that sometimes Mars or Jupiter will contradict [Saturn] in the aforesaid manner. However, his effect in all of the aforesaid will be diminished, because he will be very distant from the zenith over our heads.

But when you desired to know the abundance of rains, you will consider the moist planets abounding in testimonies, and more richly than you estimate, what you were seeking will happen, especially if in the first aspect[22] the moist planets aspected each other in watery signs.

The treatise on the impressions of the air according to the man of Lincoln, ends.

---

[21] Because in the summer the Sun is in Cancer and Leo, which are opposite Capricorn and Aquarius.

[22] *In primo aspectu.* I am not sure what Grosseteste means by this.

SECTION I.18: MISCELLANEOUS EXCERPTS, *MUNICH CLM.* 11067

Comment by Dykes. This Section is really a catalogue of several passages which suddenly appear after Chapter 6 of Hermann's *Book of Heavy Rains*, in Munich Clm. 11067, fols. 95rb-96rb. (Low-Beer notes that one of her manuscripts also contained this insertion.) I have mentioned several times that the same short texts describing various techniques are often found scattered across many different authors, and the snippets below testify to the fact that writers and scribes seemed to want to take their favorite rules from wherever they could. Below, I list the incipits and explicits, and identify their sources in this volume.

ဢ ဢ ဢ

1. (95rb-95va) Inc.: *Item Lunae cum malivolis applicatio.* Expl.: *Supradictum est se habeant pluviarum denotatur mediocritas.* Source: Jafar's *Book of Heavy Rains*, sentences **93-97** *passim*, and **110-15** *passim*.

2. (95va) Inc.: *Nota quod anni pluviosi status ab ingressu Solis ad Libram usque ad 20 gradum Scorpionis.* Expl.: *Et nubes croceas ruborem de vespere et candorem habentes.* Source: Jafar's *Book of Heavy Rains*, sentences **145-53** *passim*.

3. (95va-96ra) Inc.: *Temperies [sic.] causas pluviarum et aeris mutationem et causas ventorum et nubilorum.* Expl.: *Et non pluet nisi Mars aspexerit Iovem vel Saturnum.* Source: *Sages of India*, sentences **65-88**.

4. (96ra) Inc.: *In coniunctione Solis et Lunae considera signum ascendens et eius naturam et de qua mansione lunae.* Expl.: *Horam in qua est coniunctio solis et lunae vel oppositio incipiet pluere.* Source: John's *Epitome*, Ch. I.7.

5. (96ra-96rb) Inc.: *Volens etiam scire naturam aeris in singulis annis considera.* Expl.: *Piscis, Scorpius.* Source: *Opening of the Doors*, sentences **24-33**.

6. (96rb) Inc.: *Nota quod tempore aestatis duo testimonia.* Expl.: *Et alterius terrae signum habet planetam serenum.* Source: John's *Epitome*, Ch. I.7.

7. (96rb-96va) Inc.: *Ventorum cognitio ex pluviarum experiencia sicut.* Expl.: *Zephirum et Austrum nam inter Austrum et Eurum Aquarius et Pisces locantur.* Source: Jafar's *Book of Heavy Rains*, sentences **164-84**.

8. (96va-b) Inc.: *Cum intrat Luna Cancrum hora solis vel virginem hora veneris.* Expl.: *Dominus ascendentis aspiciat dominum septimae vel cum ei coniunctus.* Source: *Opening of the Doors* (sentences **34-38**), while the first sentence is itself an alternate reading of al-Kindī's *DMT* Ch. 6, **137**.

PART II: PRICES & COMMODITIES

SECTION II.1: INTRODUCTION

This Part is devoted to short works on predicting prices and market fluctuations, usually offering only general indications for prices, but also (though less often) identifying particular commodities. The similarity of doctrines across the selections, suggests that there were only a few common sources, probably Māshā'allāh and 'Umar.

Most of our authors rely on the charts of New and Full Moons, obviously borrowing from Ptolemy's approach to weather and other matters from *Tet.* II. But al-Qabīsī adds Lots, and all apply some standardized rules for prices which one might find relevant to many types of charts. For example, a planet that is exalted or in the tenth may indicate high prices, just as such a planet in a nativity might indicate an exalted person or something of great positive value for some area of life. They rarely refer to the charts of Solar ingresses (of which the Aries ingress would be the most important), but when they do so, their treatment suggests that annual and seasonal ingresses provide a baseline expectation and context for the year or season, while individual New and Full Moons between the ingresses point to short-term fluctuations and changes. In what follows, I will distinguish three approaches to prices, list some questions and problems, briefly summarize each author's method, and suggest some general principles.

Overall, I believe there are three ways of indicating prices in these texts, sometimes within the same author. First, there are (1) general indicators of markets, prices, and scarcity. This tends to include the Moon and the lord of the Ascendant in the lunation chart, but some authors also suggest that Saturn and Jupiter offer general guidance for understanding scarcity and abundance. In Māshā'allāh's foundational *Book of Prices*, he assigns the sign of the lunation and its lord to oil, and the Ascendant and its lord to prices. Unfortunately, he does not systematically connect them or explain their difference: is this a distinction between basic or necessary foodstuffs ("oil") and the prices of more specialized commodities? Or is it the condition of cooking oil versus its price? What is the difference between something's condition and its price?

Next, (2) there are commodities identified by planetary signification, such as cheese for the Moon or jewels for Venus. For example, one might take any planet in the tenth (at the lunation) to indicate a high price *only for that commodity*.

Finally, (3) one may identify commodities by mundane Lots, an approach found only in al-Qabīsī. His treatment is very brief, but one may see that his rules for the Lot and its lord are borrowed from (1), looking at angularity, benefic/malefic qualities, and transits.

After studying the methods in this Part, I have several questions about them:

- When the treatment is very general (e.g., lord of the Ascendant, Saturn/Jupiter), what exactly is being tracked? For, different commodities may experience different fluctuations. On the other hand, since in agriculture some things affect others, maybe it refers to an overall impression of the market. For instance, drought creates scarcity for feed, driving up the price of raising animals, leading to high prices for meat. Thus a general judgment of scarcity and expensiveness could be accurate for, or at least affect, a broad spectrum of commodities.

- Modern governments try to minimize wild swings in prices, so how dramatic should we expect the fluctuations indicated by the chart to be? Perhaps the charts show changes and fluctuations apart from these moderating forces, so that the real-life outcome for consumers is not as dramatic as the chart suggests.

- Where should the chart be cast for? Perhaps in a modern state we should use the location of the agricultural exchange (such as the Chicago Board of Trade); but maybe in more decentralized economies and areas, or even in places specializing in only a few crops, we should rely on local charts.

- For commodities identified by Lots, should we also take the Lot of Fortune into account?

As with other areas of this book, I do not have much experience in these techniques and cannot yet provide something like answers to these questions.

As for the actual methods, I discuss each author individually in my comment to each Section. But here I will provide a brief overview, so you may get a sense of how they approach prices.[1]

Dorotheus. The first selection comes from 'Umar al-Tabarī's Arabic translation of the Pahlavi version of Dorotheus's astrological poem. In Ch. V.43 of 'Umar's version, Dorotheus describes how the declination and phase of the Moon affects prices in transactions (as well as other conflicts, probably financial ones). We are fortunate to have two other versions: that of Māshā'allāh (from his *Book of Prices*), and the original versified Greek itself, quoted in Hephaistio's *Apotelesmatica* Ch. III.16. Later in 2013 I will publish a complete translation of Hephaistio III, but I have compared 'Umar's version with the Greek, and made a few comments. Dorotheus's treatment of this topic is electional, not mundane, but Māshā'allāh adopts the rules right into his own mundane material (just as he adopts some electional material into horary questions). From there, it was repeated by other authors, as can be seen in my *Choices & Inceptions.*

Māshā'allāh. Next is Māshā'allāh's *Book of Prices*, which I have translated directly from an Arabic manuscript. It was useful to compare it to the medieval Latin version, of which several manuscripts survive. The work covers a number of approaches related to prices, and seems to be a collection of smaller pieces, since one heading in the Arabic is entitled, "Another writing from him" (**A58**). First, Māshā'allāh gives general indications for looking at the New Moon chart, especially looking at the lord of the Ascendant of the lunation. Then, he uses a rare (but problematic) example which he says is from his own career, examining transits and planetary distances to determine the amount of change in prices, and when it will happen. He provides some general significations for different types of signs, and then appears to turn to question charts about prices, crediting an unknown Abū al-Hawl with rules for judging them: this is odd, since 'Umar seems to believe that these rules belong to Māshā'allāh himself. Following this, Māshā'allāh gives other rules on how to gain greater precision, rules about the apogee of the deferent or epicycle, and some more instructions on questions. Finally, he relates the

---

[1] Originally, I had translated the chapters on prices from Hermann of Carinthia's Latin summary of Sahl's *Book on the Revolutions of the Years of the World* (which Hermann called the *Fatidica*, translating roughly as *Prophetic Sayings*). But after comparing Hermann's brief account with Sahl's Arabic version, I decided I cannot justify using Hermann's text to represent Sahl's views. Instead, I will translate Sahl's work later for my projected Arabic series.

rules by Dorotheus and lists some more significations of the signs. The Latin manuscripts also contain extra information not found in the Arabic.

'Umar al-Tabarī. 'Umar's approach (as related by al-Rijāl) is to look at New Moons chiefly (although he includes rules about Full Moons). He follows a standard approach used for question charts by identifying a victor or chief significator, which will typically be the lord of the Ascendant or the Moon anyway. If planets are increasing in motion (or perhaps in other ways), prices rise; if decreasing, they go down. Likewise, angularity (especially with reception) helps prices rise, while cadency or applying to cadent and to decreasing planets makes them go down. 'Umar is also valuable for including two charts, which he interprets in some detail (though not everything is clear to me). Finally, if benefics are in the angles, then while they do indicate abundance (and thereby low prices for commodities), the value of coin will increase; if malefics, then coin depreciates but commodities appreciate.[2] (I do not understand this, and it probably relates to economies based on the gold standard. Nor do I understand his comment about houses other than the angles in sentences **18-19** of his Ch. 89.)

Al-Kindī. Al-Kindī's short discussion from *The Forty Chapters* is largely based on 'Umar's Ch. 89, and generic statements that could be based on Māshā'allāh or 'Umar's Ch. 86. First, he identifies the victor of the lunation preceding the Aries and other quarterly ingresses, but he does also examine the lord of the Ascendant and the lord of the place of the lunation. This seems to be an attempt to cover all his bases, which Māshā'allāh seems to do early in his *Book of Prices.* Again he follows 'Umar in numerous details, including a badly worded version of benefics and malefics in the angles. 'Umar's Ch. 89 had said that angular benefics indicate abundance and low prices, but *in commodities themselves,* while coin would appreciate (and the contrary for malefics): al-Kindī, or at least in Hugo's translation, does not make this distinction. Al-Kindī does specify that key places to watch for transits are the angles of the sign of the lunation. Finally, he seems to expand Dorotheus's rule about the Moon's declination (as reported by 'Umar) to all planets.

Abū Ma'shar. I have included a short section from Abū Ma'shar's *Flowers* (the Latin version), in which we are to include the charts of Jupiter-Saturn conjunctions (or perhaps the ingress charts for the years in which they happen). Abū Ma'shar examines ingress charts and the lord of their Ascendants,

---

[2] 'Umar also claims that the Moon indicates prices, and the Sun indicates coin and its value.

to determine their condition and the status of Jupiter and Saturn themselves: Jupiter indicates years of lower prices or at least more balance between buyers and sellers, while Saturn indicates burdensome years. The sign in which the lord of the year or quarter is (and perhaps even by ongoing transit) indicates the types of commodities affected; we should also examine the general significator of any given commodity, and watch its behavior.

Abraham ibn Ezra. Ibn Ezra primarily follows a few rules of Māshā'allāh's from early in the *Book on Prices.* But he also claims that fiery and airy signs indicate high prices, and earthy and watery ones low prices—especially whatever signs Saturn and Jupiter are in, and especially where their conjunction takes place. These statements about Saturn and Jupiter do recall Abū Ma'shar's *Flowers,* but also al-Rijāl's unattributed Ch. VIII.2 (below).

Al-Rijāl. Book VIII of al-Rijāl has three selections on prices in which the author is currently unknown. In the first (Ch. VIII.2), the item of interest is that Saturn tends to show high prices precisely because he indicates sterility (which leads to low agricultural yields and scarcity), while Jupiter shows abundance (and by implication, lower prices).

The second selection (Ch. VIII.33.1), also bears similarities to Abū Ma'shar, and claims to quote ibn Ezra. We are to examine the annual lord of the year (from the Aries ingress), but also the quarters and monthly New/Full Moons—this basically tells us to look at every kind of chart. But we are especially supposed to examine the signs in which Saturn and Jupiter are. Also, if the lord of the year is low in the circle of its apogee or epicycle, or is retrograde, it indicates low prices for whatever kind of commodities it naturally signifies. In fact, any planet which is exalted or increasing, shows expensiveness for such things. Likewise, the Moon being slow in speed or defective in light, or connecting with a decreasing or retrograde planet, shows cheapness. Finally, al-Rijāl quotes ibn Ezra (or a pseudo-ibn Ezra), stating that Saturn in the angles shows high prices, especially if in one of his own dignities.

The last selection (Ch. VIII.33.3), is attributed to a Filius the Roman (see my comment). Here, Filius says that any planet in the Midheaven of an Aries ingress, or the planet to which the lord of the Midheaven is connecting, will be the general significator of prices. As with other authors, being elevated and increasing show high prices, and the contrary the contrary. Finally, this Filius quotes a "Dorotheus" and says that eastern planets indicate high prices for the commodities they naturally signify (and contrariwise for western planets).

Ibn Labban is wholly derivative in his treatment, valuable mainly as a summary of some of the primary doctrines on prices. I will refer to it below.

Jirjis and "Aristotle." These selections from the *Book of the Nine Judges* have some interesting if derivative material—one passage is wholly lifted from Māshā'allāh's *Book of Prices.*

"Al-Qabīsī." In a few paragraphs from a mundane work attributed to al-Qabīsī, angular planets mean high prices in the commodities they naturally indicate—though the Ascendant and the Midheaven indicate the highest prices. Cadent planets show something in the middle, which does not make sense to me: surely succeedent houses should show middling prices, while cadent ones show cheapness.

Jafar or *Jafar the Indian* is the most unusual of our authors. His selection is in two parts: first, a Lot-like method involving Saturn and the fixed stars which define the mansions of the Moon; second, a general treatment of the lord of the year and angularity that is virtually identical to paragraph 6 of ibn Labban.

Al-Qabīsī is our only author who explicitly deals with Lots, providing some general rules for using them which stick closely to the principles we have seen before: angularity, exaltation, and increasing in motion or other ways, etc., show higher prices, and vice versa. Generally, if the Lot or its lord are with benefics, it indicates abundance; with malefics, scarcity.

Our authors do not agree on everything, but from them, and especially ibn Labban's summaries, we can find a few that they tend to agree on:

- Ingress charts for the seasons provide basic contexts for weather and abundance and prices, while New Moons (and to a lesser extent, Full ones) show more short-term fluctuations.
- When planets—especially the more important planets in the chart—are angular, or exalted, or moving faster than average, or eastern, or perhaps rising towards their apogees, or are applying to such planets, they indicate increases in price. Contrary conditions indicate the contrary.
- Benefics (and especially Jupiter) indicate cheapness, precisely because they suggest abundance; malefics (and especially Saturn) indicate expensiveness, precisely because they suggest scarcity.

- To these categories (high/low price, abundance/scarcity), ibn Labban adds another intriguing idea: that a planet in its own dignity, or received, indicates *demand*. That is, if Jupiter were in a poor condition, it would lead to even lower prices, because the bad condition suggests poor demand—adding low demand to an overabundance of goods. But if Saturn were in a good condition, then on top of his high prices (due to scarcity) he would add high demand and trade, leading to even higher prices.

Finally, I offer a table of typical commodities attributed to the planets, based on ibn Labban, Jirjis, "Aristotle," Māshā'allāh, and "al-Qabīsī" (attr.).

Saturn	Black things, drugs, lead, low-quality metal, wool, agricultural instruments, hides.
Jupiter	Common grains (wheat, barley, rice), sweet things, cotton, olive oil, silk, honey, raw silver, white fabrics, white wine.
Mars	Pungent herbs and vegetables, iron, weapons, red wine, red gold and copper, high-quality steel and iron, animals used in war, laxatives.
Sun	Gold, golden wine, saffron-colored textiles, saffron-colored copper, garnets, fine reddish textiles.
Venus	Jewels and ornaments, silver, perfume, slaves,[3] fats/ointments, sweet-smelling commodities and spices, pearls.
Mercury	Gold, painted and dyed things, coins, small grains and nuts, finely-woven fabrics.
Moon	Common animals used for labor, incense, milk, cheese.
Fiery	Precious stones and metals, meat, barley.
Airy	Human capital/labor,[4] animals, meat, barley.
Earthy	Foods derived from the earth.
Watery	Plants, water, fish and other aquatic animals.

Figure 45: Commodities of planets and signs

---

[3] According to ibn Labban. This might mean domestic help, maids, nannies, and so on.
[4] Specifically, slaves (ibn Labban); but I imagine that thinking of people in terms of labor and capital is suitable enough for modern times.

SECTION II.2: DOROTHEUS ON THE MOON & PRICES

Comment by Dykes. Below is my own translation of 'Umar al-Ṭabarī's Arabic version of Dorotheus, *Carmen* V.43.1-8, and I have also consulted the equivalent Greek passages in English translation, from Hephaistio's *Apotelesmatica* III.16 (publication forthcoming, 2013). Māshā'allāh's version of sentences **4-8** are found in his *On Prices* sentences **A94-98** (Section II.3).

In this passage, 'Umar's Dorotheus connects prices to a mixture of speed and latitude (**2-3**), as well as lunar phases (**4-8**). Prices are also connected to her declination (**1**), which was apparently not in the original Greek poem. In general prices increase in proportion to her northerly latitude, her increase in computation and declination (if we follow 'Umar), and light; the contrary conditions indicate a decrease. Although Dorotheus is writing in the context of personal elections, I thought it appropriate to include this material here as it illustrates general ideas found in other texts on prices. For more on elections like this, see my *Choices & Inceptions: Traditional Electional Astrology* (2012).

ℰ   ℰ   ℭ

[Prices according to declination and ecliptical latitude]

1 The Head is called "the rising," and its Tail "the falling"; and the signs which the scholars of the stars called "the obscured"[1] are indeed from Leo to Capricorn, and that is the side of downfall; and from Aquarius to Cancer is the side of ascent.[2]

2 Look, and if the Moon is on the side of ascent,[3] increased in calculation, then indeed he who bought with that, bought at high cost, and an increase over the price which is appropriate for it.[4] **3** And if the Moon was on the side of downfall, and she was defective in calculation, then indeed he who bought

---

[1] Or, "covered up" (*al-mughaṭṭāh*).
[2] 'Umar is being imprecise here. The signs which decrease in declination are from the beginning of Cancer to the end of Sagittarius (i.e., the *beginning* of Capricorn); those which increase in declination are from the beginning of *Capricorn* to the end of Gemini (i.e., the *beginning* of Cancer). At any rate, the Greek Dorotheus (Heph. III.16, **11**) is not interested in declination at all.
[3] In the context of the Arabic, this would seem to mean "declination," but perhaps also being on the North Node. In Hephaistio's report of this passage (III.16, **11**), Dorotheus includes being (1) full or increased in light, (2) moving quickly or "additive in longitude," (3) increasing in latitude, and (4) on the North Node.
[4] Lit., what is "equal" or "equivalent" to its true value (see the next sentence).

with this, bought with cheapness and at less than the price which is appropriate for it.

[Prices according to lunar phase]

4 And look with respect to the phase of the Moon. **5** And her phase when she went out from under the rays of the Sun, to where she reaches the left square of the Sun, indeed he profits in this whose intention in buying and selling is that of sincerity and faithfulness; and indeed he who bought the commodity at that hour[5] bought it at what was equivalent [to its value]: there is not cheapness in it, nor expensiveness. **6** If the Moon moves from the square of the Sun to where she reaches the opposition of the Sun, then indeed he profits in this sale and [in] the initiating of a lawsuit.[6] **7** And if she went from the opposition of the Sun to where she reaches the right square of the Sun, then indeed the buyer profits in this, and what is sought in the truth.[7] **8** And if the Moon went from the right square of the Sun until she comes to a stop at the position of the Sun, then indeed people profit in this [whose] intention is in the truth and justice.[8]

---

[5] Both 'Umar and Māshā'allāh seem to have the same ungrammatical phrase, which literally says, "at that commodity," but with a gender mismatch between "that" and "commodity." Since "hour" in Arabic is spelled almost identically to "commodity," I have inserted both words.

[6] Or simply, "quarrel" (*al-khuṣūmah*). That is, it is better for the seller or one who demands the payment.

[7] That is, what is sought or demanded with honest intentions (referring to quarrels and lawsuits). This word (*ḥaqq*) can also refer to what one is properly entitled to. 'Umar is a bit more generous than the Greek, which says that it not only good to buy but even to steal (Heph. III.16, **16**): perhaps this means that one gets much better deals than one should.

[8] And, the buyer (according to Māshā'allāh's translation). The Greek is worded strangely: "if you give little from much, better will this be for you" (Heph. III.16, **17**).

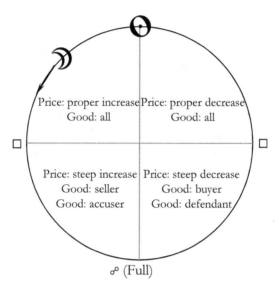

**Figure 46: The Moon and prices, by lunar phase
(based on *Carmen* V.43.4-8)**

SECTION II.3: MĀSHĀ'ALLĀH, *THE BOOK OF PRICES*

Comment by Dykes. The following is my translation of an Arabic version of Māshā'allāh's Arabic *Kitāb al-Asʿār* or *Book of Prices*, which was rendered into Latin as the *De mercibus* (*On Merchandise*) or *Liber super annona* (*The Book on the Price of Grain*).[1] According to Sezgin (p. 104), the Arabic seems only to exist in several excerpted versions, and indeed the Latin manuscripts sometimes have more, sometimes less, than what the Arabic contains.

For this provisional edition, I first translated a Latin version from five manuscripts: Berlin Lat. 246 (111vb-113ra), Munich Clm. 11067 (120ra-122ra), Oxford Hertford Coll. 4 (105r-107r), Erfurt Quarto 372 (56r-60r), and Cambridge Emm. MS 70 (1.3.8; 147v-149r). Of these, Cambridge shows clear signs of an Arabic original, because it often transliterates words and then translates them in the equivalent of parenthetical notes. Munich was the easiest to read, and so I used it as the basis of my translation. But Berlin was especially useful because it presented the prologue in the clearest way, explaining why Māshā'allāh had written the book. This translation was the basis of the Latin sentence numbers (**L##**) which parallel most of the Arabic, but supply a prologue (**L1-3**) as well as extra paragraphs I have placed at the end (**L91-111**), because they do not easily fit within the structure of the Arabic text.

For the Arabic, I used Bodleian Marsh. 618 (225a-229b), a manuscript in somewhat difficult handwriting (for example, often using single dot indifferently for *fāʾ* and *qāf*). It is undoubtedly not identical to every part of the other two manuscripts mentioned by Sezgin (p. 104, #3), but it parallels virtually every sentence in the Latin manuscripts, and so probably represents the majority of Māshā'allāh's material.

On the other hand, the text as we have it shows evidence that either (a) various scribes and commentators added their own opinions, or (b) the text itself is a compilation by a third party, with extra commentary. First of all, in several places the text reads, "Māshā'allāh said…". Likewise, in **A62** the text suddenly announces that the method just described is "weak," and that the reader should prefer a previous one. And again, **A58** is a section titled, "Another writing from him." So the *Book of Prices* should be considered primarily a pastiche of short works by Māshā'allāh gathered from other, unknown places.

---

[1] But Munich 11067 calls it *Judgments of Expensiveness* (*Iudicia caristiae*).

But why is it "primarily" by Māshā'allāh? In **A53** the writer suddenly introduces the views of an Abū al-Hawl on how to ask a horary question about a purchase. Unfortunately, I cannot find any reference to such a person in Sezgin: is this a predecessor of Māshā'allāh, or someone from a later century whose views the compiler has inserted himself? The name itself means "father of fear," suggesting perhaps a euphemistic title for someone. It is also the nickname for the Egyptian Sphinx, so it is even possible that Māshā'allāh is being labeled a sphinx.

At any rate, this collection of pieces by Māshā'allāh covers a lot of material. The compiler announces that it is in three parts, which seem to correspond to the long opening section, then the shorter sections headed by **A58** and **A72**. These include treatments of New Moon charts, ingresses, a confusing Lot-like procedure for specific commodities, Māshā'allāh's translation of Dorotheus on the phases of the Moon, horary questions, and more. The compiler seems most impressed with the opening material, which has to do with New Moons—although Māshā'allāh could be clearer in it. The sign of the New Moon (the "meeting" of the luminaries) and its lord indicate the matter and condition of "oil," while the Ascendant of the New Moon and its lord signify "prices."[2] But it is by no means clear to me what the difference between them really is, nor even why "oil" in particular is important: because it is a basic foodstuff? Does the Ascendant indicate prices of other things besides oil? In practice, most of the work is concerned with the Ascendant and its lord, and the principles seem clear on how to use it. The position of the lord of the Ascendant tends to show the default or baseline expected price, and its angularity and the angularity of other planets modify that price. Thus if the lord of the Ascendant is angular, and is applying to an angular planet, then prices will go sharply up; but if the lord is cadent while still being connected to an angular planet, then the prices will remain steady (the angularity of the other planet mitigating the lowered price of the cadent lord of the Ascendant). These rules appear in several places.

Māshā'allāh applies two techniques to an example chart, which he claims was part of his own practice when he was in a foreign city. Kennedy[3] has dated the chart based on his use of Escorial Ar. 938 (ff. 69v-70), and I have cast the chart for that date, in Baghdad.

---

[2] According to ibn Ezra in Section II.7, Māshā'allāh specifically meant olive oil *and its price* taken together. But we will see that the Ar. by no means is explicit about that.
[3] 1971, p. 185.

As a linguistic note, Māshāʾallāh frequently speaks of a planet "withdrawing or falling" (*zāylān aw sāqṭān*). Usually Māshāʾallāh seems to mean that they are either cadent from the angles, or else in aversion to the angles; but he also speaks of a planet withdrawing from an angle by zodiacal motion. So this phrase must be understood in context. Also, I have translated *watad* as "stake" instead of the Latinate "angle," following the Arabic emphasis on the angles forming four posts or foundational points in the chart.

ಐ ಏ ೪

L1 Māshāʾallāh wrote this book on account of one of his friends who was a merchant, and they both made a partnership for profit, and they earned a lot of money the very first time. **L2** Pay attention, therefore, to what I will say, and work according to this in whatever estate or place you were.

L3 Therefore, establish the Ascendant and its degree most exactly, and even establish the four angles for the hour of that same Ascendant, according to equal hours: for in this is a great instruction for those who are skilled, and many have gotten rich through it, with the aid of God.

A1 Māshāʾallāh's *Book of Prices*

A2 Know that I have composed this book in three sections, and this section is closer to what he follows, and a clearer indication.[4] **A3** So, attest to the Ascendant of the meeting [of the luminaries], and confirm the meeting and its sign. **A4** For from the side[5] of the sign of the meeting and its lord one knows the matter of oil and its condition, and from the side of the Ascendant of the meeting, and its lord, one knows the matter of the price and its condition in every month.

A5 If the indicator of oil or the indicator of the price were empty in course, then know its place: and if the lord of the sign of the meeting were in the Midheaven, then oil yields an extremely high price. **A6** And if it was in

---

[4] Reading tentatively for what seems to be *hadhā wa-awḍaḥā dalālah*. The Latin reads, "it is an easier and more certain method."
[5] Ar. *qubl*, here and in the next sentence. That is, its role and situation. But it might be *qibal*, its "power" or "ability."

the stake of the earth, it becomes cheap, and our ointments[6] will be terribly diminished. **A7** And if it was in the Ascendant, it is demanded in that month (all of it), and it is a little expensive in it. **A8** And if it were in the seventh, it is brought down in that month, and our ointment is diminished a little bit.

A9 And from that, if the lord of the Ascendant was in a stake, and if it is aspecting it, then look at [it just as through][7] the lord of the sign of the meeting: and if the lord of the Ascendant is being connected with a planet in a stake, and [the lord] is in a stake, then the price increases. **A10** And if the lord of the Ascendant was in a stake and is being connected with a withdrawing or falling planet, the price or oil is lowered a little bit until it separates from it; and if it was separated from it, the price is strengthened to its own [normal] condition. **A11** And likewise, if the lord of the Ascendant was withdrawing or falling, and was connecting with a planet in a stake, it indicates the persistence of the price until it separates from it; and if it separated from it, it lowers the price. **A12**[8] And also, if the lord of the Ascendant was withdrawing or falling, and was connecting with a planet in a stake, it indicates the increase in price as long as it is connected to it; and if it was separating from it, the price diminishes. **A13**[9] It is that indicator of increase for the whole time until it withdraws from the stake: and on the day on which it withdraws from it, the price diminishes, with the permission of God.

A14 *A section on decrease.*[10] Māshā'allāh said: And if the indicator of the price or oil was withdrawing from the stakes or falling away from the Ascendant, and it was connecting with another planet [that is] withdrawing or falling, it indicates the lowness of the price, and its diminishment. **A15** And if it was withdrawing or falling, and in addition it was retrograde, it also indicates the ruin of the price, and this is disastrous.

A16 *A section.* And if the lord of the Ascendant was in a stake, and was connecting with a falling or withdrawing planet, it lowers the price or oil a little bit until when it separated from it: it would be steady, and it does not

---

[6] Ar. *nift* or *naft*, nowadays often equated with petroleum, but a general term usually referring to various medical ointments. It is a transliteration of naphtha, and so is related to the use of flammable oils in warfare.

[7] Adding from **L15**, else this sentence would not really make sense.

[8] Note that this sentence is substantially the same as the previous one.

[9] Again, this seems to be redundant.

[10] This little section seems pretty redundant, except that it supplies the missing condition from the previous paragraph: that a cadent lord of the Ascendant is connecting with a cadent planet.

diminish until the time it withdrew from that stake; and when it withdrew from it, the price diminishes, by the permission of God.

A17 *The knowledge of how much the price increases or decreases.* If you wanted to know how much the price increases or decreases, or the oil too, [look at] that indicator over increase or the indicator of decrease, in every country. **A18** The work in that is if you subtract the lesser one in degrees from the greater one, what remained is the increase in the price or its diminishment in the condition which belongs to it, [a whole number][11] of dirhams; and as for the fractions, then indeed if you subtracted the lesser from the greater, see what is left. **A19** Know the name of it from thirty, and whatever it was,[12] a dry measure of food or oil increases [by that]: understand [and you will succeed],[13] God willing.

A20 And therefore I give you an example: work according to it, and I judged it in what was not [my] native country and place. **A21** I looked in the matter of oil at the hour of the meeting of the luminaries: and their meeting was in Cancer, in 10 degrees of it, and Mercury was in it, in 15 of it, and Mars in Virgo, in 8 of it, and Jupiter in Scorpio, in 9 of it, and the Moon in Cancer, in 10 of it, and the Sun in it, also in 10 of it; and Saturn in Virgo, in 4 of it; and also Venus in Capricorn, in 23 of it; and the Ascendant of the time of the meeting was Gemini, 8 degrees.[14]

A22 The indicator of oil was Cancer, and the Moon was the lord of the sign of the meeting, and the Moon is not connecting with a thing except Mercury, and they were each falling away from the Ascendant, so they indicated, in their fall from the Ascendant, a decrease.

---

[11] Reading for an uncertain word, which seems to be يتسال.
[12] Reading *f-mā kāna* for what seems to be *f-malikān* ("two kings").
[13] Tentatively reading for تصب, which has to do with overflowing; perhaps Māshā'allāh means one will be overflowing in wealth?
[14] According to Kennedy (1971, p. 185), the date of the chart is June 24, 773; I have cast it for the actual New Moon on the next day. Note that the text has put Venus in an impossible sign (opposing the Sun) and Mars in the sign opposite the correct one.

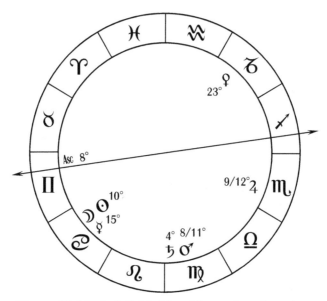

Figure 47: Māshā'allāh's New Moon chart for prices

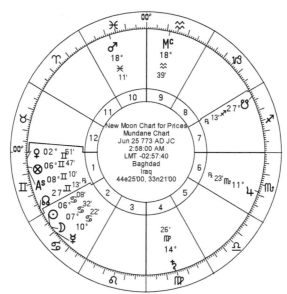

Figure 48: Likely chart for Māshā'allāh's example

A23 And oil was diminished according to what we have presented: for we subtracted the lesser from the greater, and that one (indeed the Moon) is in 10 degrees of Cancer, and Mercury in 15 degrees of it, so we subtracted 10 from it (I mean from 15): the remainder was five, so we said that the oil decreases by five dirhams in [that time].[15] **A24** And if a township does not bear[16] an increase of the dirham, divide five into thirty: it is one-sixth, and say it increases one-sixth from [that] five: and that [is] five-sixths of the dirhams;[17] [he worked][18] with it and tested [it]: [you will succeed],[19] God willing.

A25 Another example on the increase and decrease, and that is if you see what is between the indicators: you subtract the lesser from the greater, and you will know what remains. **A26** That remainder is how much it is from thirty: one-half or one-fourth or one-third or one-sixth, so that resembles the name [of units by which][20] it increases or decreases.

A27 *Another example.* Māshā'allāh said: And if the indicator was connecting with two planets, or three, or with more, the work in this is if you assemble the dirhams, then say in the increase and decrease [that] it is by that unit; then whenever the indicator separated from a planet, it subtracts from the total by that unit, just as if it was connecting with a planet [it is] increasing in its value, based on the unit of the degree of that planet. **A28** Māshā'allāh said: Therefore I am giving you an example with the Ascendant of the meeting mentioned above.[21] **A29** It was Gemini, 8 degrees, and Mercury[22] in Cancer, on 15, and Venus in 23 Capricorn, and the Moon in 10 Cancer, and Saturn in 4 Virgo, and Jupiter in 12 Scorpio, and Mars in 11 Virgo. **A30** The indicator in this arrangement was Gemini and Mercury, and he is the lord of the As-

---

[15] Reading tentatively for a rather illegible word which seems to be المنحرم.

[16] This seems to mean that the economy or scale of prices cannot increase by full units of the currency. If a gallon of oil normally costs $1, one would not expect it to rise by $5 overnight; but an increase of 1/5 is more likely.

[17] This is imprecise. What Māshā'allāh seems to mean is that the proportion of the sign represented by the degrees, shows the proportion of the *actual price*. Thus, five degrees is one-sixth of a sign, so the increase or decrease should be one-sixth of whatever the actual price happens to be in that area. This is shown in the following paragraph.

[18] Tentatively reading for an illegible word, which seems to be فقصص. This word can refer to telling a story, so perhaps the text means that Māshā'allāh is "relating" the method; but this does not make sense of the به immediately following.

[19] See above note for تصب.

[20] *Ism.* That is, the number in units. Thus, instead of increasing by (say) four units, it increases by one-fourth; or instead of by five, by one-fifth.

[21] In this example, Māshā'allāh is trying to show how the angularity of the planets makes prices rise as the significator of price connects with each in turn. But the details make no sense to me, since the numbers he assigns to the differences between them do not seem to bear a relation to their positions in either chart. Moreover, the method does not make a lot of sense if the significator happens to be Jupiter or Saturn: how can they show much fluctuation over a month, since they move so slowly?

[22] Lit. "the writer" (Ar. *al-kātib*).

cendant (I mean, of [that] meeting), which was the indicator of the price. **A31** And Mercury was connecting first with Saturn, and he is in a stake, and Mercury is falling and withdrawn from the Ascendant: so his connection indicates increase. **A32** And the price on the day of the phase[23] (I mean, the meeting) was 3 dirhams: so we subtracted the lesser of them in degrees, from the greater of them, [and] one remained. **A33** From that we knew that the price in dirhams increased by three upon his connection to Saturn, degree by degree. **A34** Then he separates from him and connects with Mars as well, and he is in a stake: it signifies an increase by his connection with him. **A35** So we subtracted the lesser of them from the greater of them, and the remainder was six, by which we knew that the price would also increase by six dirhams upon his connection to Mars—or, one-sixth the value— and that is until he connects to him degree by degree. **A36** And when he separates from him and connects with Jupiter, both of them are withdrawing from the stake, falling from the Ascendant: it signifies the lowness of the price and its diminishment. **A37** So, we subtracted the lesser of them from the greater of them, and the remainder was six, and [therefore] one-fifth of thirty remained: and we said the price decreased by one-fifth of its value, and that was when he was connecting to him, degree by degree. **A38** And when he separated from him, his course is free[24] until he connects with Venus, for then the price is lowered and becomes cheap; and God knows [best].

A39 And know that if it was the lord of the Ascendant and it was not going retrograde in a stake,[25] then say what the price increases or diminishes, and [*unclear*][26] remains based on its condition. **A40** And it was said that if an infortune is aspecting the indicator or it was with it, it indicated expensiveness, and likewise if it was aspecting the Ascendant from hostility, or it was in it (and the fortunes [are] contrary to that), unless that infortune or the lord of the Ascendant was retrograde. **A41** For if they (or one of the two) were

---

[23] Ar. *tasīs*. As Bos and Burnett explain (p. 447), this and its variants (such as *ta'sīs*) is a misread for the transliteration of the Gr. *phasis*, or solar phase.

[24] That is, empty or void; reading *sayyarah* for *sarah*.

[25] To me this sentence is unclear, because I am not sure what is being grouped together. Māshā'allāh could mean that it is the lord of the Ascendant, and it is not: going retrograde in a stake. But he might also mean that it is the lord of the Ascendant—provided it is not retrograde—and that it is *also* in a stake. See **A65** below, for the lord of the Ascendant being in a stake and retrograde, decreasing the price.

[26] The Ar. seems to read كانكة. This sentence is missing in the Latin mss., but see below where it seems that retrogradation causes a reversal of the usual condition.

like that, and the price or the oil was expensive, it becomes cheap; and if it was cheap, it becomes expensive. **A42** *A section.* And they said,[27] If the Ascendant was fixed by sign, the price in that month[28] would be stable. **A43** And if it was double-bodied or an infortune was in it, that commodity becomes expensive until it increases [so that] it is as though doubled.[29] **A44** And if a fortune was in it and[30] a fortune was aspecting it, that commodity becomes cheap until it decreases from it as though halved. **A45** And if it was convertible[31] by sign, it teaches that that thing is not desired if an infortune was aspecting it or an infortune was in it; and as for if a fortune was aspecting it or a fortune was in it, it teaches that it is not desired, [and] it cheapens it. **A46** And the infortunes are three: Saturn and Mars and the Sun; and the fortunes are three: Jupiter and Venus and the Moon. **A47** If a fortune did not aspect the indicator, nor an infortune, the commodity is not costly and it does not cheapen it, until a fortune or infortune aspects it. **A48** And if an infortune[32] aspected it, it indicates expensiveness, and if the fortunes aspected it, it indicates cheapness; and God is more knowledgeable.

A49 *A section.* And they said that the fiery and airy signs have meat and barley and oil, and the watery and earthy signs have safflower[33] and saffron and henna and red dye[34] (all of it) and figs and flax.[35] **A50** If Saturn and Mars[36] were in one of them, and Jupiter is in a square to it, those things become expensive; and God is more knowledgeable.

A51 *A section.* And if the lord of the Ascendant fell[37] from the Ascendant, and one of the planets was in the Ascendant or in another stake, then that planet does what the lord of the Ascendant did. **A52** And if it were in agreement with the Ascendant, it indicates compromise and increase; and if it

---

[27] It is unclear who this refers to.
[28] Reading the singular for *shuhur*, or else the demonstrative pronoun would have been *tilka*.
[29] The Ar. reads "as though halved," just as in the following sentence. But double-bodied signs double things, so I take this to be a scribal error.
[30] But this might simply mean "or."
[31] That is, a movable sign.
[32] Reading the singular to match the verb.
[33] Or especially the red dye prepared from its flower heads: see later in the sentence
[34] Or perhaps, anything dyed red.
[35] Or, "linen" (Ar. *al-kattān*).
[36] But perhaps one should understand, "or" Mars. The Latin understands this to mean that it will be "less" expensive: that is, it will be expensive because of the infortunes, but not too much because of Jupiter.
[37] Reading as *saqaṭa* for *āsqaṭa*.

were not in agreement with the Ascendant, then it indicates the corruption and decrease: the prices are not settled peacefully.

A53 Abū al-Hawl[38] said: If you asked[39] about a commodity or price, then look in that time from the lord of the Ascendant and the Moon: and if the stronger of them was connecting with a planet in the stake of the Ascendant or in the Midheaven, know that that commodity or price is expensive. **A54** And if it was connecting with a planet in the stake of the earth, the price is what is suitable, except that it is sought. **A55** And look in addition from the planet which you find in what is other than these stakes: for if it was received in its position, and it also is receiving the lord of the Ascendant or the Moon, it indicates a high price, and we are assisted[40] by the permission of God, be He exalted. **A56** And if the Moon or the lord of the Ascendant was connecting with a planet [which is] falling from the Ascendant, it is not received and it is also not receiving the Moon, then that indicates the lowness of the price, and its cheapness, and it lessens the demand for it. **A57** But if the stronger of them was connecting with a planet [which is] falling from the Ascendant, and that falling planet is received in its position, and it is also receiving the Moon or the lord of the Ascendant, then the price increases, [and] the seeking of it, however it is not expensive.

A58 *Another writing from him*

A59 Take[41] the sign of the meeting and its lord, and it is taken as the indicator of oil, according to what we are presenting. **A60** And take the Ascendant of the meeting and its lord, and it is taken as the indicator of the price (and indeed what he did in that was correct).[42] **A61** And some of them believed that he reckons the name of the hour in which the two luminaries meet, [and] the name of the thing whose money he wants to know, and the name of the city at the calculation of the birth [of the month], and he finds

---

[38] Unknown at this time (ابو الهول), but lit. "father of fear." This could either simply be a name, or a title (and indeed is the common title for the Egyptian sphinx). But note that when 'Umar discusses this topic (in his Ch. 89, in Section II.4 below), he cites Māshā'allāh, not an Abū Hawl. Perhaps Māshā'allāh is being called a sphinx?

[39] Reading *sā'alta* for *salta*. This now seems to be a horary or question chart, rather than a lunation or ingress chart.

[40] Reading *nuʿān* for *nuʿānahu.*

[41] Reading *khudh* for *khad*, as in sentence **A60.**

[42] This parenthetical comment must be some later commentator or compiler; see a second comment below at the end of **A62.**

28 28, all individually.[43] **A62** Then you assemble what remains from the name, all together after[44] the casting away,[45] and he finds 12 12, and what is left he casts away from Aries: where the number leaves off,[46] so it is the Ascendant of that commodity (and this example is weak: the first one is correct and more right).

A63 *A section.* Then, look from the lord of the Ascendant: for if it was in the stake of heaven, empty in course, and it is eastern, increased in calculation, rising in latitude[47] towards the north, then the price increases based on the units of increase of the planet in its latitude and its height, a carat[48] for every 90 minutes.[49] **A64** And if the lord of the Ascendant was in a stake, increasing, and connecting with an increasing planet, then the price increases based on the units of their increase. **A65** And if the lord of the Ascendant was in a stake, and it was retrograde, void in course, then it diminishes what is increasing in price, or it decreases.[50] **A66** And if the lord of the Ascendant was withdrawing from the stakes, decreasing in calculation, lowering in latitude towards the south, then it subtracts from the price, on every day, the number of its decrease in its height and its latitude, a carat for every 90 minutes from the height, and it subtracts from the latitude, carats for every 12 minutes. **A67** And if the lord of the Ascendant was increasing, and it was withdrawing from the stakes, and connecting with an increasing planet in a stake, then the price continues [as it is], [while] that planet remains in the stake—until when it withdraws from the stake, and then the price decreases on that same day. **A68** And if the lord of the Ascendant were decreasing, and connecting with a decreasing planet, it indicates the lowness of the price. **A69** And if the lord of the Ascendant was in the tenth and it was increasing, east-

---

43 كل على حدّته. I am not sure what is meant by this nor how Māshā'allāh is using this Lot-like method. Unfortunately, the Latin is missing for this method.

44 Reading as *ba'da*.

45 *Al-ṭarḥ*, here and later in the sentence. This can mean "subtraction," but I take it to mean something like a Lot calculation, where the amount is cast off or projected from some point.

46 Reading as *'athā*.

47 Reading *'arḍ* (lit. "breadth") as later in the sentence, for *'arḍ* ("earth"). In sentence **A61** below, there seems to be a distinction between degrees of latitude and degrees in the deferent circle; but since the mentions are so brisk and few, it is hard to tell.

48 Ar. *qīrāṭ*, exact value uncertain (but probably the source of our *carat*).

49 The Ar. uses *abjad* numerals, where a letter represents a number. The Arabic manuscript has ص (90), but the Latin text has 60, which makes more sense. In *abjad* numerals, 60 would be the other "s" letter, س: and perhaps that was originally the value.

50 This seems to mean that it either slows down a price which is also increasing, or it reduces something from its original price.

ern, empty in course, then the price becomes expensive and is sought until the lord of the Ascendant withdraws from the stake: and when it was withdrawn, the price decreases. **A70** And if the lord of the Ascendant was increasing in the Ascendant, and was connecting with an increasing planet in the stake of the tenth, it indicates the increase of the price until the lord of the Ascendant separates from it: then the price is stable with that based on its own condition, until the indicator decreases, and on the day it begins the decrease, the price decreases based on the units of its decrease. **A71** And if it was a little bit, a little bit; and if it was much, then much.

A72 *The knowledge of rising and descending, and increase and decrease*

A73 If you wanted this,[51] then subtract the apogee of the planet from its mean, and you see what remains. **A74** And if what remained was from a sign [to] three signs, then the planet is northern, upper,[52] decreasing in the course and computation, entirely rising from the middle of the belt[53] to its highest [point]. **A75** And if what remained was from 3 signs to 6 signs, then that planet is opposite the receiver,[54] southern, decreasing in computation, increasing in course, declining from the highest point of its ascent to the middle of the belt. **A76** If what remained was from 6 signs to 9 signs, then that planet is rising up, increasing in computation and course, entirely declining from the middle of the belt to its bottom. **A77** And if what remained was from 9 signs to 12 signs, then that planet is southern on the side of elevation, and increasing in computation and the course, rising from the bottom of the belt to its middle.

---

[51] This paragraph is based on geocentric astronomy. For the most part, Māshā'allāh is asking where the planet is relative to its apogee, counted by quarters: if it is between 0°-90° from it ("a sign to three signs"), then it appears to be moving more slowly than its mean motion, because it is farther away and so appears slow. But if it is closer to its perigee, it will be faster, etc. But Māshā'allāh also seems to be mixing in other considerations, such as if it is northern, and what its relation to the ecliptic is. His mixture of increasing and decreasing in number and course is a little puzzling to me. Generally, a planet closer to its apogee, or northern in latitude or in declination, shows increased prices; the opposite shows the opposite.

[52] Reading as *fawqiyy*.

[53] That is, the zodiac (*minṭaqah*).

[54] I am not sure what this means.

A78 And[55] likewise, the appraisal in category or its rank[56] in selling and buying: he advised that the Ascendant belongs to the seller, and the seventh to the buyer, and the tenth to the price,[57] and the fourth to what is offered for sale and [what] he buys. **A79** For where the fortunes were (of these [places]), or they bore witness to it by aspecting, that [signifies][58] the good, and good faith, and profit; and where the infortunes were, or they bore witness to it by aspecting, that [signifies] harm, and corruption and the ill-fated. **A80** And they also said that the Moon herself belongs to what he is selling or buying: and the planet which the Moon is separating from, belongs to the seller, and the planet which the Moon is connecting with, belongs to the buyer. **A81** The one to which the fortunes were bearing witness by aspecting or assembly, it is the good, and profit to its master, and also the one to which the infortunes were bearing witness, then truly it is the ill-fated, and harmful to the master.

A82 If you were asked about a seller of a thing (or the purchase of it), look from the lord of the Ascendant and the lord of the seventh. **A83** If one of them was connecting to the other, or it was a planet by a transfer of the light of one of them to the other, it indicates the completion of that matter by the hand of a man [who] enters in between them, [having] the characteristic of that planet transferring the light between them; and if you do not find that, [then] likewise what is left to you is the Moon. **A84** And if she had testimony in the Ascendant, see with whom she is connecting, and from whom she is separating: and her separation indicates the matter of the seller, and her connection indicates the matter of the buyer. **A85** Then, look at the planet from which the Moon was separating, and the one with which she is connecting: for if one of them is aspecting the other,[59] then the transaction is concluded between the two of them (the sale and the purchase); and if they are not facing each other, it is not concluded.

A86 And if you were asked about something for sale, without knowing the buyer,[60] then look at the lord of the Ascendant: for if it was in a stake, it

---

[55] For the next few sentences, see *Carmen* V.9. These sentences must represent Māshā'allāh's own translation of his Pahlavi copy of Dorotheus.

[56] *Al-ḥisāb fī bāb wa-jātihā.*

[57] Or, "value."

[58] Reading with the Latin here and later in the sentence, for an unclear word that looks like فغمي.

[59] Or literally, "if some of them aspect some."

[60] That is, if the question is a general one such as "Will I sell my car to someone this year?"

indicates he is not made known except later, also it is difficult; and it is also what that is, when the lord of the Ascendant was in the stake, slow in course, and when it was connecting to another planet also in a stake: for it indicates that that thing is not sold in that year, and it will not leave the hand of its owner. **A87** And if it was made unfortunate in a stake, and it did not have testimony in the place in which it was, it indicates that he is not made known. **A88** Also, if there were an infortune in the Ascendant, it indicates a delay, [and] it is on the part of the owner of the goods or the commodities for quitting the sale, and it indicates the misfortune of the lord of the Ascendant[61] in this matter. **A89** And if the infortune were in the seventh, that corruption is rather on the part of the buyer. **A90** And in whichever domain there was a fortune, say there is the evidence and indications [of success]. **A91** If there was withdrawing,[62] it indicates the promptness of the sale. **A92** And as for if the infortune were in the fourth, it indicates the promptness of the sale, and the departure [of the goods], and an increase in the value of it which is equivalent.[63] **A93** And if it was from the perspective of descent,[64] and it is defective in computation, then what he is purchasing in that, he is rather purchasing with cheapness, [down] from the value which is equivalent [to it].

A94 And[65] look with respect to the phases of the Moon: and if she was going out from under the rays up to where she reaches the first square of the Sun (and it is the left square), then he profits in this whose ambition was sincerity and completing [it]; and he who bought the commodity at that hour[66] or crossing,[67] bought it at what was equivalent [to its value]: there is not cheapness in it, nor expensiveness. **A95** And know that in six days[68] is the extent of the left square, and in nine days is the extent of the left trine, and on the fourteenth day she is in opposition, and on the twenty-first day is

---

[61] Or rather, the person indicated by it.

[62] This must mean at least being cadent, but perhaps also succeedent.

[63] This seems to mean that the price will be a bit higher than what is is actually worth ("equivalent" to its true value).

[64] See sentences **A67**ff above.

[65] This paragraph represents Māshā'allāh's translation of *Carmen* V.43.4-8. See Section II.2 above.

[66] Both 'Umar and Māshā'allāh seem to have the same ungrammatical phrase, which literally says, "at that commodity," but with a gender mismatch between "that" and "commodity." Since "hour" in Arabic is spelled almost identically to "commodity," I have inserted both words.

[67] That is, by transit.

[68] Normally this is seven, as the Latin has it.

the extent of the right square: and it is the first view[69] from the square [on the right]. **A96** If the Moon went out from the left square up to her attainment of the opposition, then the seller profits from that, and the initiator in a lawsuit. **A97** And if she went out from the opposition, up to her reaching the right square, then indeed the buyer profits in that, and what is sought in the truth.[70] **A98** And if she is going out from the right square up to her reaching the position of the Sun,[71] then the buyer profits in this, and people whose intention is in the truth.

A99 And[72] look during the birth of the year (and it is the entrance of the Sun [into] Aries). **A100** If the Ascendant was Aries, fish becomes cheap and meat becomes expensive. **A101** And if the Ascendant was Taurus, wheat becomes expensive, and barley, and meat becomes cheap. **A102** And if the Ascendant was Gemini, things become expensive (all of them), and wheat becomes cheap. **A103** And if the Ascendant was Cancer, it diminishes waters and dews, and multiplies fire. **A104** And if the Ascendant was Leo, produce[73] and grapes become cheap. **A105** And if the Ascendant was Virgo, fats become expensive. **A106** And if the Ascendant was Libra, dinars become expensive, and dirhams, and silver becomes expensive, and gold becomes cheap, and prices become expensive (all of them). **A107** And if the Ascendant were Scorpio, rains are diminished, and the prices too, and the trees bear [fruit], and produce thrives. **A108** And if the Ascendant were Sagittarius, it stirs up unrest and its agitation, and the prices become cheap. **A109** And if the Ascendant was Capricorn, meat becomes cheap and produce and fruits become expensive. **A110** And if the Ascendant was Aquarius, waters diminish and prices become expensive. **A111** And if the Ascendant was Pisces, things do not become expensive and they do not become cheap, and it indicates moderation.

A112 *And God has prayed over our master Muhammad and over his family.*

ɞ   ɞ   ᦏ

---

[69] Or, "aspect."
[70] This seems to mean, "honestly."
[71] Reading with 'Umar's translation of *Carmen* V.43.8, for "the square of the thing."
[72] The following sentences about the Ascendant of the year are also reflected in the work of "Jirjis," in *Nine Judges* §7.70, who evidently took this material from Māshā'allāh.
[73] Or, "the yield" (Ar. *thamar*), which can also refer to fruits themselves.

[More rules on questions about sales/purchases][74]

L91 And if the lord of the second is being joined to the lord of the Ascendant (and conversely), and the lord of the second was in a good place from the Ascendant (namely in its trine or sextile aspect), it signifies that that same object will be sought well enough, and there will be profit for the owner. **L92** And if the lord of the Ascendant is being joined to the lord of the second from a good aspect, it signifies that the lord is seeking one to whom he may sell his thing. **L93** And if it were in a bad place,[75] the thing will not be sold.

L94 And[76] consider the lord of the Ascendant: which if it were in any of the angles, it signifies that the thing for sale will not be out of the hands of the owner unless [it is] slowly. **L95** And if the lord of the Ascendant were outside the angles, and is being joined to a planet appearing in an angle, it signifies that the thing will be sold by the owner.

L96 Consider even where the Moon is: for if she is being joined to some planet in the Ascendant, it signifies profit for the owner of the thing. **L97** And if she is being joined to some planet in the angle of the earth, it signifies little profit. **L98** Which if she is being joined to an unfortunate planet and one cadent from an angle, it signifies that there will be loss and harm for him in that matter.

[More rules about ingresses and prices]

L99 Consider diligently the ingress of the Sun into the first minute of Aries, and see the lord of the bound of the Moon, and if it were a fortune or infortune; and see of what nature is the sign in which it is found. **L100** And prices which were of the nature of that sign, will be at a good market rate throughout the whole year [and] cheap, if the planet were a fortune; which if it were an infortune, there will be a bad market rate for them throughout the whole year, and expense.

---

[74] Now follow extra sentences from the Latin translation, which did not fit easily within the context of the Arabic.
[75] Or perhaps, "in a bad aspect"? Māshā'allāh means that if the lord of the second joins with the lord of the Ascendant, the buyer is seeking the seller (leading to an easy sale); but if the other way around, the seller is seeking a buyer, which makes things more difficult.
[76] This paragraph is close to **A86** and **A91** above.

L101 And[77] consider in what sign the Moon was, at the revolution of the year: which if she were in signs which are arising straight (which are from Gemini up to Sagittarius),[78] it signifies that all prices will be dear, while the Moon were in those same signs, up until she enters Capricorn. **L102** And they will be cheap while she was from Capricorn up to the end of Gemini— and it will be so throughout the whole year.

L103 Look even in the revolution of the year (namely at the entrance of the Sun into Aries), to see which planet is closer to the lord of the year or who is being joined to him.[79] **L104** And if it were the Sun, then wheat and barley and cooked bread will be at a good market value, and they will be cheap in the first parts of the year, but in the last ones they will be dear. **L105** And look at the lord of the year [to see] what sign it is in, and in what part of that same sign. **L106** Which if it is found in the first half, the aforesaid will be at a good market rate and cheap; and if it is found in the last half, they will be dear. **L107** If you found Jupiter to be closer to the lord of the year, wheat and olive oil will be at a good market rate in the last half of the year. **L108** And if Jupiter were in the first half of the sign, the aforesaid things will be dear; and if he were in the last half, they will be cheap. **L109** And just as it is said about Jupiter, so it is said in the same way about the Head of the Dragon and Venus, namely if they were in the first half of a sign or in the last one— and you will look at it, if you were wise.

L110 Even make a consideration at the revolution of the year or in its quarters, or in any conjunction of the Sun and Moon, and see where the Moon was: and[80] if she were increased in number, wheat, bread, and barley

---

[77] This paragraph represents Māshā'allāh's version of *Carmen* V.43.1-3 (Section II.2). But note that Māshā'allāh's takes the opposite view. For 'Umar, the crooked signs (Capricorn through Gemini), in which the Moon moves towards upwards into northern declinations, make things overly expensive; the straight signs (Cancer through Sagittarius), in which she moves downwards into southern declinations, makes things overly cheap. But the difference could lie in what the Moon really means: if she represents the growth of things, then perhaps being southern makes things scarce, leading to higher prices (and vice versa): that would support Māshā'allāh's interpretation. In any event, Dorotheus (as represented in Hephaistio) does not include declination.

[78] Or rather, the *end* of Gemini and the *beginning* of Sagittarius.

[79] I think the distinction here is between being near him by body, versus by aspect. In either case, we want the closer one.

[80] This represents Māshā'allāh's version of *Carmen* V.43.2-3. 'Umar's translation has the Moon's increase/decrease in computation (here, "number") happening concurrently with her being in signs of various declinations (see above). But in this paragraph, Māshā'allāh allows this to be a distinct consideration.

likewise increases in price. **L111** Which if she were diminished in number, the price of the aforesaid likewise is diminished.

SECTION II.4: 'UMAR AL-TABARĪ, *BOOK OF QUESTIONS*

Comment by Dykes. This Section contains translations from Latin versions of Chs. 86-89 of 'Umar's book on questions, from two sources: the Latin al-Rijāl and *Nine Judges*. Where the al-Rijāl text is available I have used that, and have also availed myself of the Arabic version in Brit. Lib. Ar. 23399. The Latin *Nine Judges* passages are only used where nothing in al-Rijāl was available.

Many of 'Umar's rules seem to depend on Māshā'allāh's *Book of Prices* or their common source. The following table provides an overview of the source material. As in other tables, a + symbol means more is contained in the Latin source than just 'Umar's material.

Arabic Umar	Latin al-Rijāl (1485)	*Judges*
Ch. 86	VIII.33.2+	§7.60
Ch. 87		§7.61
Ch. 87?[1]		§7.62
Ch. 88		§7.63
Ch. 89a	VIII.33.2+	§7.64
Ch. 89b	VIII.33.2	§7.65

In Chapter 86, 'Umar describes how to find the primary significator for prices in charts of New Moons. His rules about this planet's angularity, speed, and so on, are typical. Chapters 87-88 are valuable for providing actual examples from consecutive months (likely from 785 AD), even if his method for tracking fluctuations in price are not always crystal-clear. In Chapter 89, 'Umar claims to review the doctrines of Māshā'allāh (and indeed some of it does match Māshā'allāh's *Book of Prices*), but he also includes special rules for judging the value of coinage as opposed to commodities. Sentences **L65-67** and **L83** stand out as apparently contradicting the normal rules for benefics and malefics: if the Moon first connects with a benefic after the New/Full Moon, prices increase, while a malefic will make them decrease. Normally,

---

[1] In his Table of Contents for *Nine Judges* (privately provided), Burnett questions whether this was part of 'Umar's Arabic. It is very close to *Nine Judges* §7.69, attributed there to Dorotheus.

benefic planets lead to an abundance of commodities (and thus low prices), while malefics do the opposite.

ॐ   ॐ   ॐ

**'Umar al-Tabarī: *Book of Questions* Ch. 86:
On things for sale, and their status
(from al-Rijāl: *Book of the Skilled* VIII.33.2)**

L12 These are the statements of al-Tabarī on the price of things.

[Choosing the significators]

L13 He said that if you wanted to know the expensiveness or trade in the prices of things, and the condition of men in life and their affairs, you will know this from the situation of the luminaries. **L14** Therefore, look in any month at the conjunction of the luminaries, and calculate[2] the Ascendant at that hour. **L15** And you should know that the Ascendant and what was in it, are the significators of the condition of men and the atmosphere, and the lord of the house of the lord of the Ascendant aids them in the signification.

L16 And a peregrine planet in the Ascendant which was not suited to the Ascendant, signifies harm in that month if it were an infortune, or harm according to its nature and witnessing.[3] **L17** And if you found a planet in an angle, and it is the lord of the exaltation of the Ascendant, infer from that one, if you found the lord of the Ascendant separated;[4] any planet which was in an angle, having power there, will likewise be a significator. **L18** If the lord of the Ascendant were absent[5] from the angles, and the planet which was in an angle [were] peregrine, it[6] will be the significator while it was there, until it goes out from there. **L19** However, if the lord of the Ascendant were in the Ascendant or in any of the other angles, or in the eleventh, or in a good place, aspecting the Ascendant, it manifestly has more signification than any

---

[2] *Apta.*
[3] Reading with the Ar. for "power."
[4] Reading the first part of this sentence with the Ar., for: "And if you found a planet in an angle, having dignity in the Ascendant (especially the exaltation), take it as the significator."
[5] Reading with the Ar. for "remote." This probably means, "cadent."
[6] That is, the peregrine and angular planet.

[other], and especially if it were eastern, going out from under the rays and appearing in its own light, being light[7] in motion.

[Judging prices]

L20 Because if [the significator][8] were thus,[9] it signifies that men will get their means of subsistence and will profit, and will ascend in it in all ways in terms of what is scarce or plentiful,[10] according to the power of the planet, and especially on days in which the Moon was in the fourth from the Ascendant, or in the Ascendant, or aspecting the lord of the house of the Ascendant. **L21** However, if it[11] were in the opposite of it,[12] it will be the contrary of this. **L22** And[13] if it were increased in motion, the price of bread-grains will be increased; and if it were deficient, applying to the opposite of the Ascendant, and it aspected the lord of the Ascendant, it signifies [the price] is weak.

L23 And look to see if you found the lord of the Ascendant received, and the receiver was increased, in an angle: it signifies that for that whole month the price of bread-grains will be increased; and the lord of the house of the lord of the Ascendant is more supported at the opposite of the luminaries.[14] **L24** And if you found the lord of the Ascendant received, and it and the lord of the house of the lord of the Ascendant were increased,[15] the [expensiveness of supplies and their][16] expensiveness will be more established, and this according to their increase.

---

[7] *Levis*, that is, quick.

[8] 'Umar will generally continue to speak as though the significator is the lord of the Ascendant.

[9] 'Umar is referring to the conditions in the previous paragraph, which I have distinguished from this one because we are now transitioning to a new topic.

[10] *De pauco et multo.*

[11] This seems to be the Moon.

[12] This probably means that either the Moon or the significator is in the places/conditions opposite those just mentioned.

[13] The Arabic appears to read differently, but the sentence seems incomplete. For example, it says that if the significator (or the Moon?) were increased, and was in the Ascendant and aspecting the Ascendant, it shows deficiency; and if deficient, it shows increase.

[14] 'Umar seems to be suggesting that the lord of the Ascendant at the New Moon or conjunction, primarily indicates for the first half of the month, while its own domicile lord indicates for the second half. Thus, if both of them were received (as in the beginning of the sentence), then the entire month will be good.

[15] Reading with the Ar. here and at the end of the sentence, for "ascending."

[16] Adding from *Judges.*

L25 And if the lord of the Ascendant and a planet appearing in an angle applied to a cadent planet or a deficient one,[17] it depresses the price. **L26** And if the lord of the Ascendant were diminished, and the one which receives it is likewise diminished, the price is even depressed, and this will be according to their diminishment. **L27** And the cheapness of their prices will be more intense[18] if both were cadent from the angles, because this signifies that the cheapness will be fast. **L28** And if both applied to a planet cadent from an angle, or a diminished one, the cheapness of the price is likewise affirmed.

L29 And[19] if a planet were in the Ascendant, having any testimony there, there will be increase and cheapness according to the status of that planet in improvement and harm; and in addition the lord of the Ascendant will be a partner with it. **L30** And if the lord of the Ascendant were not received, you will not make it be a partner with it, because it alone will be the significator.

L31 And if the lord of the Ascendant and the luminaries were in such places at the figure of the conjunction [such as to be] in the Ascendant of the conjunction or in its angles, or in the angles from the place of the conjunction, it signifies that the price will remain what it is. **L32** And if the lord of the Ascendant or the luminaries were received and increased, and they were in the eleventh or fifth, it signifies that the price will increase.

L33 And[20] a connection of the lord of the Ascendant [to] an increasing planet, signifies an increase [in price] on the day it connects with it.

L34 And if the luminaries and likewise the lord of the Ascendant were deficient, and in the third or in the ninth or in the twelfth, it signifies the abasement of the price; however, the angles always signify steadiness[21] in what it is. **L35** And if a deficient planet applied to the lord of the Ascendant, it signifies a similar abasement, and more so if the lord applied to the planet. **L36** And if the lord of the Ascendant were deficient, and the lord of its house increased, it makes no increase of the lord of the house, because the root, power, and signification are in the lord of the Ascendant unless it was cadent and there were another planet in an angle; but if the Ascendant were

---

[17] This probably means decreasing in number, as above.

[18] Reading with the Ar. for *affixa* ("fixed, established").

[19] *Judges* includes an extra sentence here: that if there were a cadent or subtracting planet in the Ascendant, it indicates a decrease in price even more so.

[20] Reading with the Ar. for "And if a planet of the Ascendant applied to the lord of the Ascendant, it signifies an increase in price on the day of the application."

[21] *Fixionem*, which is more appropriately "fixity," but I have used Hugo's term for clarity.

one of the houses of the luminaries, look at their increases and their diminu-
tions in number, and at their places in the figure (how they are [arranged]
with respect to the Ascendant).

'Umar al-Tabarī: *Book of Questions* Ch. 87:
When prices are going to be more burdensome, or easier
(from *Judges* §§7.61-62)

Judges §7.61: When they are going to be more burdensome or easier

2 But whether one would surpass the other (namely increase or diminution), or when it would happen, could be discovered thusly. **3** And so, with it
decreasing from the apogee (or rather, the orbit),[22] that which is left over
from the sixth up to the seventh, is mediocre; but from the seventh to the
twelfth, and from one up to the third, the worst.[23] **4** Which if there is a question about addition, it will be good to attend to their computation: for when
first added,[24] it is necessary that the provisions be altered. **5** The lunar application to a quick course especially claims the same thing, and the power of
the lord of their domiciles and of their signification.

6 Therefore, once these things have been diligently observed, one should
choose the signification of the present affair from a joint observation of
them, with an alert memory. **7** However, in order that a firmer and absolute
method be applied to the opinion written above, with a question of this kind
being present, I have undertaken to append this example, and to note the
Ascendant and the places of the stars.[25]

8 Therefore, Cancer was the east, whose lord, the Moon, was staying outside a pivot. Then, the intention of the mind being drawn back to the east
and the rest of the pivots, one finds nothing of the stars there.

---

[22] *Abside*, which is a general term (Gr. *apsis*) referring to the apogee and perigee of the
deference circle. 'Umar is saying that when a planet is moving away from its apogee, prices lower; but when it moves towards it, they increase.
[23] See my Introduction to the book. 'Umar seems to be dividing up the zodiac according
to how far away a planet is from its apogee, but this does not quite match the description
below. For both Venus and Mars are indeed moving toward their apogees in 785 AD (9°
33' Gemini and 6° 52' Leo, respectively), but 'Umar says below that they are "decreasing."
An Arabic translation of 'Umar is needed to help clear up some of these difficulties.
[24] I believe this means that we must see when the planet actually begins to add in course,
for that will indicate the time.
[25] Omitting *consilium*.

9 [1] Once the eastern lord is taken account of, while I have drawn back its apogee. Furthermore, it is left to 5 signs.[26]

10 [3] From there, once recourse is had to the lord of [the Moon's] lodging-place, [Venus] is found to be decreasing,[27] and in the entrance to scorching.

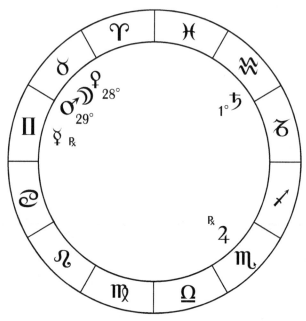

Figure 49: 'Umar's chart for *Judges* §7.61, based on the 1509 diagram

---

[26] Some texts say 6.

[27] At this point it seems that what 'Umar is referring to is not the proximity to the apogee of the deferent, but of the epicycle. Both Mars and Venus are direct and moving towards their apogees—both of their deferents *and* of their epicycles. But to correct their positions using Ptolemaic-style tables, a certain correction has to be *subtracted* from another value. This seems to mean that they appear further behind in the zodiac from our perspective, than from the perspective of the equant circle. In the future I hope to produce a book which will explain these points of geocentric astronomy.

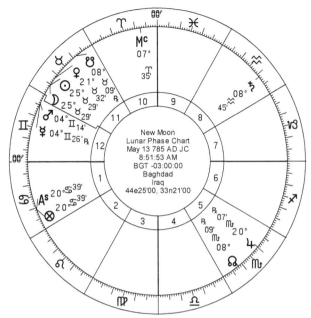

Figure 50: Likely chart for *Judges* §7.61 (in whole signs)

11 [2] Considering the status of the Moon, I found her applying to Mars without reception. **12** Therefore, the Moon being in [her] sovereignty or in [her own] house, was portending the steadiness of the burden of things for sale, until she herself crossed the east.[28] **13** Once that has happened, she [will have] conceded the signification to Mars, to which Venus was applying ([Venus] being the lord of [the Moon's] own lodging-place). **14** Thus therefore, both [Venus and Mars are] decreasing, [and] are entering scorching: and so they indicate the greatest increase and diminution,[29] in terms of points in the multitude of each *kardaja*.[30]

15 And so, their signification in the third part of the month (namely, once ten days have passed by), and in the last of them, testifies that things for sale that are of an easier price will become not-moderately so. **16** It is even agreed that the month is divided into three parts in this way. **17** Because [1] at its beginning, the Moon was enjoying the rulership of the east: whence she, add-

---

[28] I am not sure if this means the degree of the Ascendant, or the entire ascending sign.
[29] This seems to mean that the Moon signifies a good increase, while Venus and Mars signify decrease. See the next paragraph.
[30] For the basic definition of a *kardaja*, see the Glossary. Nevertheless I do not understand exactly how 'Umar (through Hugo's difficult Latin) is using this term.

ing in computation, indicates burdensome things for sale. **18** Then [2] Mars, to whom she was applying, takes away from the price, because he is decreasing, and because of [his entrance] into scorching.[31] **19** [3] Venus assumes the signification of the third part, [and is] indicating the same thing Mars does, because she is decreasing and is equally entering into scorching. **20** It will be permitted to observe all of these things through the appended description.

Judges §7.62: [More on the same topic][32]

2 Moreover,[33] just as was interpreted in this figure, it is agreeable to note the east and its lord at the beginning of the month, also to establish the pivots, and to consult the places of the stars, in order.

3 Therefore, once these have been interpreted in such an order, it seems that an observation of [1] the eastern lord is greatly necessary. **4** No less too, must [2] its application with adding stars (or those which are decreasing in computation) be noted, or their application with it. **5** In addition even, it seems that those stars which are holding onto the pivots must be observed, and their status up until they depart from them, but even the reception[34] of one to another.

6 [2] Again, in this place it comes to be noted that adding and decreasing stars (namely those which [happen to] apply to the lord of the east, or it to them), if they assume no testimonies with it, they undoubtedly portend an increase or diminution at the time of the application.

7 [2] Which if a star applying to [the lord of the east] would then possess a pivot (or [it did so in the preceding cycle of the month),[35] [and the lord of the east], I say, being drawn back, and applying to it in a pivot, it does not harm with an increase until it is separated from it. **8** Likewise, with it withdrawing, a diminution follows, namely in accordance with the withdrawal of

---

[31] Because the Sun moves faster than Mars, Mars is going under the rays and entering scorching.

[32] For this section, cf. "Dorotheus" in *Judges* §7.67, which has helped untangle some of Hugo's meaning. This material must derive from Māshā'allāh, since Dorotheus credits Māshā'allāh for this whole view, and 'Umar does so in a similar passage in §7.64.

[33] I have brought this sentence up from the bottom of the section, since it connects this section with the previous one, and links with the use of "order" in the next paragraph. I have omitted Hugo's *rationi consentanea omnimodo comprobantur* as not really having a clear role in the passage.

[34] This seems to mean how they apply to one another and receive each other's aspects, not classical reception proper.

[35] Reading for Hugo's "or a cycle of the month preceded."

the applying one which then possesses a pivot.[36] **9** And it signifies the alteration and constancy of the status.

10 Moreover, the eastern lord and equally [3] that of its lodging-place, if they would apply to a star in the Midheaven, they make things for sale costly, especially while they were adding. **11** For if they would be decreasing, they bring forth a moderate increase, but a steady one.

12 However, the increase of [the lord of] the east, and the one which is opposed to it,[37] do not convey much addition again, but decreasing they signify harm; still, they are examined and do not lack value. **13** If therefore [the planet to which it applied] would be holding onto the pivot of the earth as was stated, they introduce steadiness (if, I say, they do not recede from [their] average course).

'Umar al-Tabarī: *Book of Questions* Ch. 88: [Another example of prices, from the following month] (from *Judges* §7.63)

2 The east[38] was Sagittarius, and its lord [Jupiter] decreasing in computation;[39] the five stars were staying in the opposite [of the Ascendant]. **3** Of them, Mercury was cadent, while [4] the rest occupied a pivot.[40] **4** However, the Sun [is] wholly arranged rightly,[41] the Moon increasing, applying to a decreasing[42] and corrupted Mars. **5** Venus too was likewise adding, with no aspect being conveyed to the lord of the east, until she first gives up the sign

---

[36] But according to 'Umar's method, angular planets show increases; so why would it only show an increase *after* it departed the angle?

[37] This phrase should really read something like: "and of a planet in the house opposed to the east, namely the seventh." In Ch. 89 below, 'Umar clarifies that if the lord of the Ascendant or the Moon would apply to planets in the Ascendant or Midheaven, the increases will be more dramatic; but if to planets in the seventh or fourth, it is less dramatic. See the rest of this paragraph.

[38] This example should be easy to follow, with the exception of Mars allegedly decreasing in speed. 'Umar's point is that, at the beginning of the lunar month and up to and including the Full Moon, many planets will be angular and moving fast. And, the planets which will perfect aspects to the lord of the Ascendant, will also be moving quickly. So, this suggests a stable increase in prices.

[39] Jupiter is retrograde, so he is moving slowly.

[40] Again, suggesting that 'Umar uses quadrant divisions to determine angularity.

[41] *Recte.* This word is sometimes used to speak of the angles, and what Hugo means is that the Sun is exactly (or almost exactly) on the degree of the Descendant.

[42] Actually, Mars is increasing in speed.

which she is holding onto. **6** That portends the same thing which we related above about the eastern lord, the Sun, and the Moon.[43]

7 The signification of Mars pertains to diminution, until Venus herself gave up that place, once she has applied to the eastern lord (namely after ten days),[44] then finally even the Moon will undergo his assembly.[45] **8** Therefore, the aforewritten places of the stars, and their positions, designates that things for sale are confined to a suitable status, nor completely changed in anything, until 13 days of the month are reached. **9** But after that, up until her departure, their adding is noted, but nevertheless it seems an increase of this kind proceeds from the staying of the stars in the pivots.[46]

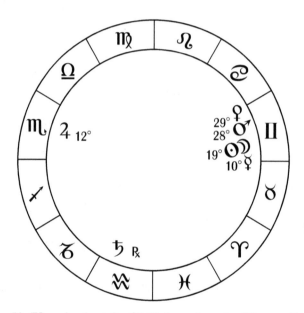

Figure 51: 'Umar's chart for §7.63, based on the Vienna diagram

---

[43] This might refer to §7.62 above, where it was said that an adding planet will increase prices when it aspects the lord of the Ascendant.

[44] Since 'Umar believes Venus is at 29° Gemini, and Jupiter is retrograde at 12° Scorpio, it should only take her about 10 days to make an exact trine to him.

[45] That is, the Moon will then conjoin with the lord of the Ascendant (Jupiter) while she is still waxing. She will do this a few days after Venus trines Jupiter, and just before the Full Moon—which is why 'Umar says that this will be the situation for 13 days. On about the fourteenth day, the Moon will be full and will then wane.

[46] 'Umar probably means that just before and during the Full Moon, the Sun and Mercury, and the Moon will all still be in the angles (showing a stable increase).

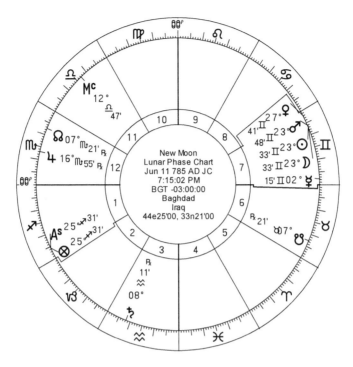

Figure 52: Likely chart for 'Umar's §7.63 (in whole signs)

'Umar al-Tabarī: *Book of Questions* Ch. 89:
[Māshā'allāh and others on the increase and decrease of prices]
(from al-Rijāl: *Book of the Skilled* VIII.33.4)

L43 These are the statements of Māshā'allāh on the increase and decrease
of prices.[47] **L44** He said, if you wanted to judge the increase or decrease of
things, look at the lord of the Ascendant and the Moon: and if the one of
them which was stronger applied to a planet appearing in the Ascendant or
in the Midheaven, judge that the price of provisions will be increased. **L45**
And if the planet were in the angle of the west or the earth, the provisions
will be of a middling price, but they will be sought.

L46 And likewise,[48] look in that time at the planet which was in the square
of these two bad ones:[49] because if it were received, or it received the lord of

---

[47] See generally Māshā'allāh's *Book of Prices*, sentences **A53-54**, where this material is attributed to an Abū Hawl.
[48] Cf. Māshā'allāh's *Book of Prices*, sentences **A55-57**.

the Ascendant or the lord of its house or its bound, it signifies expensive-ness. **L47** And[50] if there is a connection with a cadent [planet], and it does not receive it, then indeed commodities become cheap, and it reduces their demand. **L48** The worse status in sales is when the Moon and the lord of the Ascendant applied [from the stakes][51] to a cadent planet and it does not re-ceive them. **L49** And[52] if they were connecting with a planet,[53] and it was received, and the Moon or the lord of the Ascendant were receiving, then indeed it guarantees demand for them, however [the price] will rise.[54]

L50 And he said (in his book which he made for his student),[55] that Ptol-emy[56] and a portion of the sages with whom he came in contact in Egypt, are in agreement that the work of this matter has to do with the luminaries: and they used to begin to know this from the Sun's entrance into Aries, and from the conjunction preceding each quarter [of the year], and from the conjunc-tions and oppositions which were in every month. **L51** Because Ptolemy says that the revolution of the year of the world is the conjunction or opposition which was before the Sun's entrance into the beginning of Aries, and he says that the things and accidents of this world come to be through the conjunc-tions and oppositions, so that all generations of things, and accidents, come to be and happen through the conjunctions, and the removals of things come to be through the oppositions: because the Moon is a lesser world, and she is closer to the world than all [the rest of the] seven [planets]; and she in partic-ular[57] walks through the world of generation and corruption. **L52** And the things of generation and corruption are found in the months, through her increase.

L53 And after this speech, he found her to be placed and affirmed [in this role], because she is the first of the seven planets, and because likewise every thing, after it is completed, is diminished: they first gave the power of trees, animals, and everything which is generated in this world of generation and

---

[49] Reading with the Ar., which would suggest any planet in the Ascendant or Midheaven.
[50] Reading this sentence with the Ar.
[51] Adding with the Ar.
[52] Reading this sentence with the Ar.
[53] Probably the cadent planet just mentioned, as explicitly stated in Māshā'allāh's sentence **A57.**
[54] But Māshā'allāh's *On Prices* **A57** says that while it will rise, at least it will not be expen-sive.
[55] Probably al-Khayyat. Hugo writes that this opinion is now coming from Thābit bin Qurra.
[56] See my introduction to Ptolemy in Section I.2.
[57] Reading *proprie* for *primo* ("first").

corruption, to the Moon. **L54** And they made the Sun a partner with her, because these changes happen through the conjunction of the Moon with him (and his opposition); and likewise they gave Venus and Mercury to her as partners, because their heavens are near to the heaven of the Moon, and because they become eastern and western many times, and move lightly; and they made the Moon and the Ascendant be contrary (namely, one to the other).

L55 And likewise, they made the assets of coins and other things which are sold, to likewise be contraries (namely, one to the other). **L56** And when one is increased, the other is depressed, just like gold and silver, and bread-grain and cloth: because for little coin they will give much of a thing, and for little of a thing they will give much coin.

L57 And he said that the more noble places of heaven are the angles. **L58** And if fortunes were in the angles, coin will increase and appreciate, and other things will decrease and be depreciated. **L59** And if the infortunes were in the angles, coin decreases and is depreciated, and other things appreciate. **L60** And if the fortunes were in the other houses which are not angles, things appreciate and coin depreciates. **L61** And if the infortunes were there, it will be the contrary. **L62** And if some of the infortunes were in the angles and others in the other houses, judge through the more supported of them. **L63** However, the depreciation which comes through a fortune could not be great. **L64** And every planet [which is a] fortune, if it were retrograde or in a weak place, its virtue will then be weak; and the same thing for an infortune, if it were in its own exaltation.[58]

L65 And if you wanted to judge the quarter or middle of the year, or the whole of the year, look to see when the Moon is being separated from that conjunction or prevention, to see with which of the planets she is first joined. **L66** And if it were a fortune, the price of things which are sold will be increased, and will become dear; and if she will be joined with an infortune, they will be depreciated and cheap. **L67** And in this, the aspect is like what the conjunction is. **L68** And if the Moon were in an angle, the expensiveness increases, and she does likewise if she were in her own exaltation, safe from the infortunes.

---

[58] What Māshāʾallāh means is that its power to be a *malefic* is weakened, or rather that it is better than a problematic benefic: see Judgment 18 in his *Fifty Judgments* (in my *Works of Sahl & Māshāʾallāh*, or the Appendix to *Nine Judges*).

L69 And if the Sun reached[59] a fortune, or a fortune reached the Sun, just as if he reached Jupiter or Venus, coin increases and things become depreciated and cheap, especially if the Sun were in an angle or his own exaltation. **L70** And if the Sun reached an infortune, coin would be depreciated, especially if he were remote from the angles.

L71 Mercury has a signification in the two coins (which are gold and silver), and Venus has a role in them. **L72** The role of Venus in them is the beauty of [their] appearance and the clarity of [their] color. **L73** And the role of Mercury in them is the pictures and writing. **L74** Nevertheless, Mercury has greater authority especially in gold, because he is of the division[60] of the Sun. **L75** Whence, if they were eastern, coin ascends (that is, things are cheap), especially if they were in their own exaltations. **L76** And if they were western, coin is depreciated, especially if they were weak. **L77** And if Mercury were with the Sun, gold is honored and appreciated and the other things go down and become cheaper. **L78** If Venus were with the Sun, silver is honored and men love it. **L79** And if they were not with the Sun, and they were elevated in the circles of their apogees, coin is honored (that is, things become cheap), and especially if they went towards easternness or they were in their own exaltations or houses or dignities. **L80** And if they declined in their heavens, going toward westernness, or they were in places of their weaknesses and in which they do not have dignities, coin is depreciated (that is, things become dear).

L81 And if you made the Ascendant of the year or quarter, or month, or middle of the month, and you calculated[61] the angles and you knew the degree of the house of assets,[62] if you found the lord of the house of assets in any of the angles, and especially in a place where it has some dignity, and it is a fortune, coin is honored. **L82** And if there were an infortune in an angle just as we said before, coin is valued but not honored, because low-class men will have it.

L83 But you will judge the honor and cheapness of other things through the appearance of the fortunes and the infortunes in the signs, because if there were a fortune in the signs, the things which were of the division of that sign will be dear; and if an infortune were there, it is depreciated: be-

---

[59] *Attigerit,* here and below. I take this to include aspects, and not just reaching it by body.
[60] This could mean that Māshā'allāh understands him to be more like the diurnal sect.
[61] *Aptaveris.*
[62] An indication that 'Umar uses quadrant-based houses.

cause whatever sign has a role in this (just as small beasts are given to Aries, and the other signs according to their roles)—judge according to that.

L84 And you should know that the Ascendant always signifies the head of an animal, and the fourth house the belly, and the seventh the tail and rear part of the body, and the tenth the spinal [area]. **L85** Whence, that one of them in which there was an infortune, or in which there was [a planet] made unfortunate, there will be harm in that. **L86** However, the Ascendant of a man signifies the head, the second the neck, the third the shoulders and hands, and thus in order through all twelve houses, just as we have declared at the beginning of this book. **L87** However, in vegetable things, only front and back parts can be had, whence the Ascendant is the front part, and the seventh the rear part.[63]

L88 And if you were asked about some vegetable thing, if it will sprout well or grow, or what there will be concerning it, give the Ascendant and its lord, and the Moon and her lord, to it. **L89** And if all of these were fortunate, judge that it will last and go towards the good. **L90** And if they were unfortunate, judge that it will be harmed. **L91** And if two were fortunate and the other two unfortunate, say that it will be mediocre and you will be made certain according to this, by God.

---

[63] But see an alternative in *The Search of the Heart* II.3.1.

SECTION II.5: AL-KINDĪ, *THE FORTY CHAPTERS*

Comment by Dykes. This short chapter from my translation of the Latin al-Kindī's *Forty Chapters*[1] is useful as a statement of principles. Most of it bears a close resemblance to other material by ʿUmar and Māshāʾallāh, with a quick, unattributed reference to Dorotheus at the end.

In these passages we can see that al-Kindī is primarily resting on two sources: Māshāʾallāh's *Book of Prices* (in §662, which is also close to ʿUmar's Ch. 86), and ʿUmar's Ch. 89, which is at least partly a report of Māshāʾallāh.

ᙏ   ᙎ   ᙗ

Chapter 37: On prices & commodities

§662. If someone, worried, would inquire into the price of things for sale, let him note studiously the victor of the degree[2] of the assembly or opposition (which preceded the Sun's ingress into the first point of Aries), and let it take possession as the significator. If therefore the significator itself would be adding, or there would come to be an application of it with a star [that is] adding,[3] it seems to signify that the price of things will be more burdensome, and according to the nature of the sign which it is holding onto. No less should the understanding of the lord of the Ascendant of the year and of the Ascendant of the conjunction [or opposition] be judged as necessary.

§663. Moreover, the pivots being blessed with the light of the lucky ones makes the price of things for sale more burdensome; but that of the unlucky ones, the contrary. Moreover, the Sun and the Moon in a pivot declare coin to be costly. And so the Sun designates gold, the Moon silver.

§664. Venus [and] Mercury even testify in this manner: for Venus resembles the Moon in signification, Mercury the Sun. Which if these significators would be cadent from the pivots, they mean the cheapness of gold and silver, but they commend what is bought with these at a greater price.

---

[1] This may also be seen in *Nine Judges* §7.66.
[2] Reading with Robert. Hugo reads, "the victor, namely the lord of the degree…". But the victor assumes a decision procedure: it is not merely the lord of a place of a degree. Note however that *Forty Chapters* Ch. 3, which lists several victors, does not explain the victor of a particular degree. Perhaps al-Kindī is thinking along the lines of *Forty Chapters* §§699-700, which suggests the most important ruler of the degree which also regards it.
[3] This probably refers to increasing in speed, as ʿUmar has it in his Ch. 86 (see Section II.4).

§665. Therefore, one should note with an ever-watchful mind, what kind of assent the fortunes show.[4] But the fortunes make things more expensive, the infortunes the contrary.

§666. This same thing must be considered in the individual quarters [of the year] for the price of things at that time, and in the individual conjunctions and oppositions (just as done here at the beginning of the year), and a moderating judgment [made] from all of these.[5]

§667. If[6] therefore the significators of things for sale were cadent, they convey low[7] [prices] or a manifold abundance of them. Then the ingress of [the lord] of the Ascendant [of the year][8] or of the opposition or the assembly, into the Ascendant itself or into one of the pivots, determines the hour at which these things should happen. The lords of the annual quarters do not even deny what the lords of the Ascendant [of the year] and of the assembly [or opposition] testify to.

[Robert]: The ingress of the aforesaid significators into the places designated above will bring about the time of the foreseen alleviation or burdensomeness [of the cost]: namely, [1] the [ingress of the] victor of the degree of the conjunction or opposition into [that place itself], or [2] the entrance of the ruler of the east of the year, or the lord of the conjunction or opposition, into the east itself.

§668. Moreover,[9] the ascent of the stars into the north, increases the price of things; but into the south, the contrary.

---

[4] This probably means that we must keep watching the transits throughout the year, and not only at the ingresses. See below.

[5] Using Robert's more succinct version of this paragraph.

[6] I add Robert's version below, because he gives a slightly different version of the ingresses. Hugo has the lord of the Ascendant or of the assembly/opposition entering the Ascendant of the year or any of the pivots. Robert allows these significators to enter the Ascendant, but also lets the lord of the assembly/opposition enter the place of the assembly/opposition itself.

[7] *Graves.* I am a bit unsure about this, because in other places *gravis* and *gravescor* refer to higher and more burdensome prices. But one would expect the price and value of things to go down in the cadent places.

[8] Adding based on Robert.

[9] This is ultimately based on Dorotheus (Section II.2). 'Umar's translation of Dorotheus has the Moon in northern and southern *declinations*, while the Greek text has her in northern and southern *ecliptical latitudes*. Here, al-Kindī (or Hugo) is speaking of the planets generally.

SECTION II.6: ABŪ MA'SHAR, *FLOWERS*

Comment by Dykes. In this Section I simply reproduce without comment a short passage by Abū Ma'shar on prices, taken from the Latin *Flowers of Abū Ma'shar*.[1] For the full version with footnotes and comments, see *AW2*.

ಔ   ಜಿ   ಞ

Chapter III.1: On high and low prices

2 However, you will know these things from each of the superior planets, since every burden is of the work of Saturn, and all ease is of the work of Jupiter. **3** Therefore, however often you saw Saturn (in the revolution of the quarters of years) in a sign in which there was a conjunction which signified a sect, and Jupiter (or Venus with the Head), did not aspect him, without a doubt this will be of the signals of severity. **4** Therefore, commingle your account of him [using these factors], and do not have fear. **5** And if it were so that the Tail were with [Saturn] in one [and the same] sign, judge the burden of the yield and the terror of men, unless Jupiter aspects this place at the hour in which the Tail is being separated from him. **6** Moreover, the years that signify famine, are themselves those over which Saturn is in charge, in the conjunction or opposition in which the revolution was, and more severely so if he were in the conjunction or opposition of Mercury—this is [in the revolutions] of years. **7** For the months, if you saw him in the ninth place or the third at the conjunction or opposition, this will be a signal of ease.

8 Therefore, know the Ascendant of the prevention or the conjunction. **9** After this, look at its lord: which if [the lord] were increased in light or course, then the yield will be increased in price in that same month; and likewise, if it were increased in the Midheaven, the price of the yield will be increased in the same way. **10** And if it were decreased in course, the price of the yield will be decreased. **11** And if it were going to its own descension, likewise the price of the yield will go down. **12** But if it were in the subterranean angle, or in the seventh [angle], the price will be stable in its own condition.

---

[1] This was a Latin translation of a distinct Arabic work on mundane techniques by Abū Ma'shar (Sezgin pp. 142-43 #3), whose title in some manuscripts can be abbreviated as *The Report.*

13 However, in other matters besides wheat and barley, you should look at the manager of the year, to see if it were made fortunate; look even to see in what kind of sign it is, and what the essence of that same sign is. **14** Which if it were of the essence of fire, this will be in silver and gold, and in everything which is worked through fire. **15** Which if it were in the earthy ones, this will be in earthy things. **16** If however it were in a sign of air, then this will be in animate things: look at the place of that same sign from the Ascendant, and speak about that. **17** Look to see if it were in watery signs: this will be in animals of the water, and in everything which comes from out of it. **18** However, all of these [are] places in which there will be every burden of the yield. **19** If however [the lord of the year] were in Aries or its triplicity, it will be in the direction of the east; if in Taurus or its triplicity, in the direction of the south; if however in Gemini or its triplicity, it will be in the west; but if in Cancer or its triplicity, it will be in the north.

20 Consider the market value of the yield when the Sun has entered the first minute of Aries or the signs in which the exaltations of the planets are (which are the movable ones). **21** Now, the dismounting of the Sun onto the first minute of Aries is stronger and more lofty than all of his [other] dismountings in the beginnings of the movable signs, and more lofty than his dismountings at the beginnings of each sign. **22** Know this secret in market value, and do not pass over it, and do not look at [anything] else. **23** And if you wanted to have the knowledge of some thing by name, look at the planetary significator of that thing, and of the market value of that thing, [and] in what kind of sign it is; and look at what [*illegible/incoherent*] to that sign and to that planet. **24** And I have already made [*illegible*] to you in this book on the natures of the signs. **25** Therefore, know and work through that, and you will discover [it], if God wills.

SECTION II.7: IBN EZRA ON PRICES

Comment by Dykes. The following passages are translations or summaries taken from two different editions of the mundane works of Abraham ibn Ezra (ca. 1089-1168 AD), who wrote two similar but distinct Hebrew works on mundane astrology, both called *The Book of the World* (here designated *BW1* and *BW2*), published in an admirable critical edition with English translation by Shlomo Sela (2010).

Below, I have either summarized Sela's edition (with his section numbers), or translated from the Latin 1507 Venice edition (with its folio numbers). In the latter case, I have consulted Sela's edition for accuracy, and inserted bold-face sentence numbers that correspond with his.

Like ibn Labban, ibn Ezra is valuable for his summary of principles, almost all of which he gets from careful citations of Māshā'allāh's *On Prices*: see Section II.3.

ℬ ℬ ℬ

(*BW1* §40 / *BW2* §27) Generally, fiery and airy signs indicate high prices and famine, and earthy and watery signs low prices and plenty. Note especially which ones of these Saturn and Jupiter happen to be in, particularly at their conjunction (and perhaps in any revolution). Likewise Saturn and/or Jupiter in cold signs indicates high prices, and low prices in the hot signs.[1]

The lord/victor of the Ascendant, for commodities prices

(*BW1* §42 / Venice fol. 82v) **1** Moreover, Māshā'allāh says we ought to consider, in any conjunction (whether a great one or middle one or lesser one),[2] [and] in addition even in the revolution of any year, the ascending sign at the hour of the conjunction or opposition of the luminaries, which was in any place before the Sun enters the sign of Aries. **2** And you ought to look at the lord of the sign of the Ascendant at the hour of the conjunction or op-

---

[1] This last sentence does not seem right, since the fiery and airy signs are hot, but signified high prices. Perhaps ibn Ezra or his source means that the signs can be ranked on a spectrum, where fiery and earthy signs represent opposite extremes that are the most inimical to agriculture, while airy and watery signs are in the middle.

[2] These are the cycles of Saturn-Jupiter conjunctions, to be discussed further in *AW2* and *AW3*.

position: and the victor is the one which has dignity in that place,[3] provided that it aspects it. **3** Which if we found the victor or lord to be in the first angle[4] or in the tenth, this signifies the great expense of grain or grass in that land, and more burdensome if it were increased in its own course (that is, that it would go more than its own average motion); for if it would be moved less than its own average motion, or it was retrograde, the expenses will be diminished, day by day. **4** It is the same judgment if it gave its own power or strength[5] to a planet which was in one of the said angles. **5** Which if it were in one of the remaining angles, the [price][6] will be mediocre, and it is [lowered] like that in the succeedents of the angles; but in the cadents, it will be cheap. **6** But if the victor were burned up by the Sun, detriment or impediment will happen to the grasses:[7] and if it were [burned up] in one of the angles, then the detriment will be greater; [but in the cadents, it will be less].[8] **8** You should do it this way in every year, and also every month.

(*BW2* §25, **5-7**) If the lord of the Ascendant is in its exaltation, prices will rise; if in its fall, they will fall. If it moves faster than its average motion, then look at the luminaries as well: all three of them moving faster than average will raise prices; slower than average will lower them.

The lord of the place of the New/Full Moon, for oil

(*BW1* §43 / Venice fol. 82v) **1** Māshā'allāh claims that the place of the conjunction signifies the oil of olives—for he was experienced [in this]. **2** And you ought to look at the victor over the place of the conjunction, and judge according to what you saw in the same way that you judged according to the victor over grass.[9] **3** And know that if the victor were in the house of its exaltation, it will become more dear, but less so if it were in its own house. **4** Which if this one were in the house of its fall, there will be the greatest

---

[3] That is, the Ascendant.
[4] The Ascendant.
[5] That is, "pushing power" (see *ITA* III.16), but authors like Māshā'allāh seem to want simply an application ("pushing management").
[6] Reading with the Hebrew, for "thing, matter" (*res*).
[7] That is, to the commodities: ibn Ezra is assuming an agricultural economy.
[8] Adding with the Hebrew.
[9] That is, the lord or victor over the Ascendant signifies the *expense* or *price* of grasses, grains, and other commodities.

cheapening. **5** If however in the house of its detriment, there will be cheapening, but not so much as before.[10]

(*BW2* §29, **2**) The lord or victor over the place of the New/Full Moon signifies the *price* of olive oil, increasing or decreasing insofar as it moves faster or slower than its own average speed.

---

[10] That is, not as much as in its fall.

SECTION II.8: THE ARABIC AL-RIJĀL ON PRICES

Comment by Dykes. The following selections from al-Rijāl represent various points of view on prices, and include attributions to ibn Ezra, Dorotheus, and "Filius the Roman."[1] Except for parts of sentence **2** in both VIII.2 and VIII.33.1, all of the following has been translated from Arabic.

ᛒᛟ   ᛊᛟ   ᛊᚱ

Chapter VIII.2: On years which signify fertility or sterility[2]

2 If you wanted to identify the years in which the earth gives the fertility of things, or in which it is sterile, look at the Ascendants [and planets][3] of the meeting or fullness preceding the revolution, and their portions.[4]

3 And if the portion of the conjunction or fullness was connecting with Jupiter, and [especially] if Jupiter had rulership in it, and the lord of the Ascendant was made fortunate, with the safety of the lord of the fourth house, and the terminal point[5] from the Ascendant of the religion or the transfer of the triplicity has arrived at the place of Jupiter or Venus by body or ray, it determines fertility in that year, and especially if the lord of the second was in the good fortune of the lord of the Ascendant or was being connected with it, or aspecting it from a fortunate place, and especially if its witnessing was of the Lot of Fortune: indeed, this indicates the increase in fertility.

4 And as for years of sterility[6] and those things which are in them, Saturn being the governor over the meeting or the fullness by rulership or connec-

---

[1] Since *filius* in Latin means "son," just as *ibn/bin* does in Arabic, the Arabic would seem to be translated from a Latin author, mistakenly taking a description of his lineage as being his first name. And yet it seems unlikely that an Arabic author would have borrowed from a Latin text.

[2] Note the similarity between this chapter and Ch. VIII.31.2 in Section I.8. The source of this chapter is interesting because it uses vocabulary I have not seen before, justly calling planets "nomads" (Gr. "wanderers"), the prevention or opposition of the luminaries the "fullness," and even speaks of their conjunction as a kind of "knot." This suggests that the Arabic source was translating directly from a Greek one.

[3] Adding with the Ar. which literally calls these "nomads" (just as *planeta* means "wanderer"). Al-Rijāl's source might be speaking specifically of the Sun and Moon, which are the wanderers defining the place of the New/Full Moon.

[4] Reading with the Ar., for "places." The Arabic may be suggesting their bounds, here and in the next sentence.

[5] Ar. *intihāʾ*, which normally refers to profection: in this case, a mundane profection.

[6] Or, "drought" (Ar. *al-jadb*).

tion, and especially if he was the lord of the Ascendant or the victor over it, or he was hostile to it, or Saturn was in the stakes,[7] and the corruption of the lord of the fourth by the infortunes (and especially Saturn); and the worst is this, if he was parallel to[8] Mercury.

5 If Saturn was in the stakes of the nomads which I presented (he mentioned them),[9] or in the centers,[10] indeed that is significative of high prices. **6** And likewise, if the Moon was falling towards him[11] at the time of revealing herself from the knotting,[12] and if Saturn was rising,[13] it signifies severe expensiveness, whichever of the two infortunes was causing the misfortune; more difficult than that is if there was a mixing of Mercury with both of them.

7 And if misfortune happened to the second [house] and the Lot of Fortune and the Ascendant from the lord of the lord of the Lot of Fortune,[14] there would be an increase in sterility. **8** And what there was in it from the unluckiness of Saturn on this topic, is more difficult than the unluckiness of Mars. **9** And likewise, the good fortune of Jupiter in the topic of fertility is more powerful than the good fortune of Venus.

10 And as for rains, if Mars (in a revolution of the year in which one carried out the elevation [of a king] in it) was in the houses of Saturn, it signifies a scarcity of rains. **11** And if he was in his own houses, it signifies an abundance of them. **12** And if he was in the remaining houses, it signifies a middling amount.

---

[7] I have followed the Latin in abbreviating the Arabic, which says, "or Saturn was in the centers of the *al-marīsah* (and they are the stakes)." Currently I unsure of the meaning of *al-marīsah.*

[8] Ar. *muwāziyān* (adverb). The Castilian translator took this to mean "opposed to," which is a closely related verb, and it might indeed mean being in opposition. But in Tr. 5 of the *Book of Religions and Dynasties,* Abū Ma'shar uses this to mean that a planet is "in" a sign, that is, tracing a circle parallel with the zodiac. So al-Rijāl's source might mean that Saturn and Mercury are conjoined or that their epicycles are moving together.

[9] Ar. *fī awtād al-bawādī illatī qaddamtu dhakarhā.* This seems to be a parenthetical remark by al-Rijāl himself, referring to sentence **2** above. Again, the nomads or wandering planets mentioned here are probably the luminaries.

[10] Again, these were identified as the angles or stakes.

[11] The Latin has "applied," but again this source seems to use different vocabulary.

[12] That is, once she separates from the conjunction and begins to move out of the rays.

[13] This may mean rising in the circle of his apogee.

[14] Compare this with the conditions in the parallel passage, al-Rijāl's VIII.31.2, **12** and **17** (Section I.8).

Chapter VIII.33.1: On prices

2 If the lord of the year were at the end of its stake,[15] wanting to go retrograde, or if it were descending in the circle of the apogee, or if it were at the foundation of the circle of its epicycle,[16] it signifies the cheapness of the essence [of what] belongs to the house in which it is, if it was of jewels or fiery or southern or vegetable.

3 And the Moon too, if she were deficient in light and computation at the birth of the year or month, or she was connecting with a deficient planet [which was] turning back, indeed that indicates a cheapness of price, and the humbleness of food.

4 Know[17] the increase of price from the variation of the condition of the significator at the beginning of the year, and from the arising of the four seasons (which are the signs of the turning points),[18] and from the meeting of the Sun and Moon [in] one degree in every month, and from the entrance of Saturn or Jupiter into the signs of the regions of the countries, the eastern and western ones.

5 And the misfortune of the planets in these places indicates decline and cheapness, and humbleness. **6** And their good fortune indicates increase. **7** And every planet with elevation or increasing[19] at the birth of the year, or honor,[20] [whether] it had testimony or not, it indicates an expensiveness of price, and an increase of it in the assets of that planet, [and][21] the essence of the sign in which it is: such as if the Sun is in Aries, he has precious red stones, and gold, and precious jewels. **8** Or, [if] it is Venus, she has pearls[22] and precious stones and pearls and coral and pearls, and what is like that. **9** And every planet falling down and declining,[23] that indicates lowness and

---

[15] *Watadahi*, although we would then expect to read *"or* wanting…". The Latin reads as though it is at the end of its direct motion, which makes more sense.

[16] I have translated these terms from the Latin, as the Arabic seems more vague.

[17] Note the similarity to Abū Ma'shar, in Section II.6.

[18] That is, the four movable signs (Aries, Cancer, Libra, Capricorn).

[19] This probably means rising in the circle of its apogee, which is how the Latin understands it.

[20] This probably refers to exaltation.

[21] Compressing from Ar. *min al-naṣb fī.*

[22] In this sentence, al-Rijāl's source gives three synonyms for pearls, but the first and last words probably mean something else: *al-durr, al-law³law³,* and *al-ṣadaf.*

[23] This probably means "being in its fall" and "declining in the circle of the apogee," respectively.

decline in what is of that planet, from [its] share in the sign in which it is—what is of the water and the earth and air and fire.

10 And Abraham [ibn Ezra] the Jew [said]:[24] when Saturn is not in any of the stakes, it indicates cheapness; and [his] arrival in the stakes indicates expensiveness. **11** And if he was in any of the stakes, and he was in one of his shares,[25] it indicates excessiveness in that.

Chapter VIII.33.3: Filius the Roman[26]

37 And Filius the Roman said: If the Sun entered Aries, look at the planet which was in the Midheaven, or the planet to which the lord of the Midheaven is connecting: for that one indicates the price, by the permission of God. **38** If that planet in the Midheaven was a direct one [in] motion, then what is ascribed to that sign becomes elevated, and increases, and better and in a more persevering way if that sign were fixed. **39** And if it was turning back, or debased, or defective in light and number, it indicates lowness in what belongs to that sign in which that planet is.

40 And Dorotheus said: Look, in the expensiveness of prices and their cheapness, at the planet which was arising[27] in that year: it attacks[28] the things which belong to that planet, and they become expensive; and the planet which was descending[29] corrupts, and it cheapens what belongs to it, and it decreases. **41** And what is corrupting is if it was in its own descension or burned up or made unfortunate, or retrograde or separated[30] or in one of the reprehensible places, and the fortunes absent.[31] **42** And if it was good and bad, such as if it were retrograde in its own house, or burned up in its own exaltation, it peaks a little bit and is humble and sells poorly afterwards; God willing, it is raised [and] there is relief in the knowledge of increase and deficiency.

---

[24] This does not appear to be in either version of ibn Ezra's *Book of the World*.
[25] That is, some dignity.
[26] Omitting the Latin remark, "that is, a Christian." Since the Latin *filius* means "son" (just as Arabic *ibn/bin* means "son"), this could be read as "the son of the Roman."
[27] That is, "eastern" or rising out of the rays (Ar. *yashruq*).
[28] Reading *yughir* for *yafir* ("becomes plentiful"), because if they are scarce then the price should rise. But "Dorotheus" may be saying it will be more plentiful *and* expensive.
[29] Probably sinking under the rays.
[30] The Latin reads this as being cadent from the angles.
[31] That is, in aversion.

Section II.9: Ibn Labban on Prices

Comment by Dykes. In this Section I will summarize Kushyār ibn Labban's approach to prices, from Chapter II.8 of his *Introduction to Astrology*, where he largely borrows and streamlines material from other authors. One advantage of a summary like his, is its succinctness and clarity; a disadvantage is that he does not represent a single school of thought, but rather picks from here and there without explaining why. As with my summary of his weather material, bolded numbers represent numbered *paragraphs* in Yano's translation, not sentences.

𝒮ʘ   𝒮ʘ   ☊

General significators. Ibn Labban identifies four significators to watch when monitoring prices (**1**): [1] the Ascendant of the New/Full Moon preceding every quarterly ingress, [2] the lord of that same Ascendant, [3] the Moon,[1] and, in a secondary way, [4] the Ascendants of ongoing New/Full Moons. Thus ibn Labban does not want us to cast charts for the ingresses themselves, but only for the New/Full Moons, especially the ones most nearly preceding the Sun's seasonal ingresses.

Overall, ibn Labban seems to want us to look simply at the charts as a whole, and see whether various planets indicate high prices or not. But ibn Labban does provide a few special indications of high prices:

Indicators of high prices:
- The Moon applying to Saturn after the New/Full Moon, while Saturn is ascending in the circle of his apogee *or* in the apogee of his epicycle—especially if Mercury is somehow mixed with Saturn. But the high prices will only be relevant to thing indicated by Saturn's sign (**5**).
- The lord of the Ascendant of the year[2] being angular, increasing in motion (**6**). The precise angle it is in, indicates when the prices will

---

[1] This at least means the Moon in that chart itself, but as we will see, ibn Labban also tracks her ongoing transits.

[2] That is, at the Aries ingress (or rather, the New/Full Moon preceding it).

raise: for instance, if it is in the Ascendant, in the first quarter of the year; in the Midheaven, the second quarter; and so on.[3]

- Planets moving quickly, and in the angles (**6**).
- The Moon or the lord of the conjunction/opposition[4] being in the Ascendant, tenth, eleventh, or fifth, and being received, increasing in motion, exalted, or applying to such[5] a planet (**7**). But in the other two angles, or applying to one there, then if it is received it increases demand but not prices; if not received, not even demand increases. If the Moon is in the ninth or third and received, prices decrease but trade increases; without reception, prices increase[6] and trade decreases.
- Jupiter indicates cheapness, especially if his condition is weak; Saturn indicates expensiveness, especially if powerful (**8**). Angularity means a high price, while having dignities and reception indicate high trade (**8**). In this case, what ibn Labban seems to mean is that Jupiter normally indicates abundance (and thus a low price): therefore if his condition is weak, demand and trade are lowered, leading to even lower prices. Saturn normally indicates scarcity (and therefore high prices); but if in a good condition, he indicates high demand and trade, driving prices even higher.
- If the planets ruling the angles are strong (such as ascending in their apogees, being angular, being in dignities), the commodities they indicate will be expensive (**9**).

---

[3] Note the similarity to Jafar (Section II.12, sentences **206-07**). Jafar, though has the lord of the year increasing in calculation/computation, not motion.

[4] This probably means the lord of the Ascendant at that time.

[5] Yano's text simply says, "to a planet," but in context (and based on the next sentence) it must mean to a planet in one or more of these conditions.

[6] These statements by ibn Labban are puzzling to me, because he says that in general, reception leads to high demand but low prices, while a lack of reception leads to low demand and high prices (**7**). This is contrary to basic economic principles. But what seems to be happening is that *angularity* controls prices, while *reception* (or perhaps overall planetary condition) controls demand and trade. (But see Māshā'allāh's *On Prices*, which seems to be less systematic.) In that case, the planets being cadent would default to low prices, and reception would independently control the level of trade. In that case, ibn Labban's example of the Moon in the ninth or third should read that if she is not received, "prices *decrease* and trade decreases." See the next item in the list, where he says just this about Jupiter and Saturn: angularity means a high price, while good conditions and reception mean high trade.

- Planetary motion (9): fast planets bring something already expensive to an end;[7] if slow, the prices are steady; if decreasing,[8] the price goes down.

Finally, ibn Labban does make some comments about fertility which seem to derive from the same source as al-Rijāl VIII.31.2 (Section I.8, **11-14**). Jupiter being in the Ascendant of a New/Full Moon, indicates "dignities" (**4**).[9] It likewise indicates fertility if the lord of the Ascendant applies to benefics, the fourth (which indicates land) is free from the malefics, and the lord of the second is in a good relation to the lord of the Ascendant (**4**).

---

[7] This might mean that trade will go quickly, or that the high prices will come on fast but not last.

[8] This might mean, "retrograde." But it seems to me that a more natural division would be: faster than average speed, around average speed, slower than average speed.

[9] Or really, "claims" (*mazā'im*). This seems to be a misreading of al-Rijāl of his source, which wants Jupiter to be in the Ascendant, *especially* if he has dignity in the place of the lunation.

SECTION II.10: JIRJIS & "ARISTOTLE"

Comment by Dykes. These short selections from *Nine Judges* represent the summary views of the unidentified "Jirjis" and the equally unknown "Aristotle." As the reader of *Judges* may see, their views on horary questions are not incompatible with other, mainstream authors, but they often go their own way.[1] Here, they are primarily useful for associating the planets and signs with different commodities.

The first selection by Jirjis (§7.68) is notable for being very close to the last part of Abū Ma'shar's *Flowers*, Ch. III.1. But it has two unusual features in §7.68. First, he makes it seem as though the lord of the year in the annual Aries ingress *always* shows rising prices: this is probably a mistake, and what he means is that *if* the lord of the year shows rising prices, then the type of sign it is in, will indicate the type of commodities. Second, he associates the triplicities with different climes and cardinal directions. This is a normal thing to do in mundane revolutions, but here the scheme is incomplete and confusing, not to mention that it incorrectly associates the watery signs with the south, when they normally indicate the north.

℧   ℧   ♌

§7.68: On the price of things for sale—Jirjis

For having an understanding of this kind, the lord of the year should be noted. For, this [planet] traversing in a fiery[2] sign, makes gold, silver, and what comes to be through fire, more burdensome. In an earthy one, provisions[3] and germinating things. In a human one, living things and four-footed things. In a watery one, in fish and marine animals.

But[4] so that you may discern the place of this outcome, let the intention of your mind be drawn back to the sign of the Midheaven. Therefore, Aries in the Midheaven [indicates] it is in the middle of the second clime, toward

---

[1] But see Jirjis in §7.70: here, he is taking directly from Māshā'allāh's *Book of Prices*, sentences **L99-111**.

[2] Reading *igneo* for *aereo*.

[3] *Victualia*, here and below.

[4] In this paragraph, Jirjis is associating the signs on the Midheaven with the climes (areas of geographical latitude, from the equator to the north pole). The description here is incomplete and confusing. For different schemes of assigning signs and planets to climes, see Part IV of this book.

the east. Leo, the last parts of this clime, toward the east. Sagittarius, at the beginning of it, towards the east. Taurus too as the Midheaven, suggests the middle of the second clime, to the south. But Gemini [means] the last parts of the fourth clime, toward the west. But Libra, the beginning of the fourth and toward the west, and likewise Aquarius. But if Cancer, the last parts of the sixth toward the south.[5] But if Pisces, the beginnings of the seventh, to the south.

But these will only endure for a span of three months, up until the Sun undergoes the first degree of Cancer. With the east and the rest of the houses established, just as was done in the first point and degree of Aries, one will have to work thusly whenever he enters the rest of the turning [signs].

§7.69: On the same thing, through individual months—Jirjis[6]

But if you wish to distinguish what would happen through individual months, you will note the assembly of the Sun and Moon at that same point, and you will establish the east at that hour.[7] If therefore the lord of the east were adding in course, the price of provisions increases. But its average progression brings [the price of] provisions down.

Now, if it[8] would be lingering in the Midheaven, it makes the price most burdensome. It is not otherwise[9] if it[10] would apply to a star appearing in the Midheaven.

[Also, the pivots designate steadiness,[11] unless the Moon would apply to a star that is][12] in its own fall, or in the third or in the ninth: for thus provisions will be easier.

---

[5] This should be the north, as with Pisces in the next sentence.

[6] This section is a very abbreviated version of "Dorotheus" in §7.67 of *Nine Judges*, and is very similar to several sentences in Māshā'allāh's *Book of Prices*.

[7] That is, cast a chart for every New Moon throughout the year.

[8] "Dorotheus" reads this as being the Moon.

[9] That is, prices will go up.

[10] In "Dorotheus," this is now the lord of the Ascendant.

[11] In "Dorotheus," this seems to mean a steadiness of *increase*.

[12] Adding with "Dorotheus." Note the similarity with ibn Labban in Section II.9 above, his paragraph **7**.

§7.70: On the price of things for sale—Jirjis

Therefore, if the east of the annual cycle[13] were Aries, fish grow cheap but meat grows burdensome. With Taurus as the east, grain is dear, and meat will be cheaper. An east [comprised] of Gemini denotes that all things are burdensome, but wheat is cheap. But Cancer diminishes waters and dews, but multiplies conflagrations. But Leo as the east multiplies revenues and produce, [and] finally all provisions. Virgo makes olive oil very burdensome. Libra has few coins, whence silver is dear but gold grows cheap; finally, all provisions will be dear. Scorpio takes away from heavy rains, and makes moderate rivers, fertilizes trees, greatly increases proceeds,[14] and multiplies the waters of rivers. But Sagittarius stirs up battles, wars, and seditions, but the provisions will be many. Capricorn has the cheapest meats, but fruits or the dates of palm trees are dear; finally, vegetables[15] are cheap. But Aquarius as the east diminishes waters, [and] shows that provisions are more burdensome. An east of Pisces throws in mediocrity everywhere.

§7.71: On the price or status of things for sale—"Aristotle"

Whenever[16] it is asked about some thing, whether it is going to be dear in that month or year, the whole affair should be sought from the east and the rest of the pivots. For, any star traversing in a pivot will make the things of its own nature and proper quality dearer. But should it be staying after the pivots, it calls the things of its nature and proper quality back to a better status. And those in the remote [places] trample their own things with a cheap price.

But if he made the question about provisions, what is of a dearer price should be sought in the east and the tenth. In the second and eleventh the

---

[13] That is, the chart of the annual solar revolution. But I'm sure Jirjis also means this to pertain to the quarterly ingress charts as well (and perhaps the monthly ingresses). The previous section tracked prices based on the lord of the Ascendant, which must be why the sign on the Ascendant is addressed here.

[14] *Fructus*, which can also mean "fruit." I take it to mean "proceeds" here, since Hugo just contrasted it with *frux*, which has the more specific meaning of actual crops, produce, etc.

[15] *Olera*, a variant on *holera*.

[16] In this paragraph I believe "Aristotle" assumes the querent wants to *sell* something; but in the next paragraph, I believe he means that the querent wants to *buy* something (namely, essentials and provisions for life).

price is not wholly mediocre, because they look more to what is a burden.[17] In the third and ninth, the cheapness is greater.

Finally, let us see what things agree with which planets:

Therefore, Saturn has especially claimed lead and worse iron or Indian steel; of colors, the black; of clothing, woolens and what is of monastic (that is, poorly-made) quality,[18] and instruments of agriculture, but even hides.

But Jupiter has olive oil, and silk, raw silver, very white textiles, and white wine.

To Mars belong any arms, red wine and clothing of that color, moreover he has red gold and copper, more expensive or better steel and iron, mustard and pepper, euphorbia,[19] scammony,[20] and horses given to warlike uses.

But to the Solar power responds gold of a citrine color, and wine just like that, and saffron textiles, but even saffron-colored copper, and garnets[21] and *siricae*[22] clothing.

Venus has any fatness (lard, I say, and grease),[23] also sweet-smelling and any odiferous commodities, sweet water, and she has womanly ornaments.

But Mercury possess coins and millet (and middling or small grains), moreover filberts and what is of this kind.

Finally, the Moon has the beasts of common laborers and those that are put out for hire, olibanum, but she even claims milk and cheese.

---

[17] *Gravitatem.* I take this to mean that since they are moving towards the pivots (which indicate higher prices), they are somewhat middling in price, but more towards high or difficult prices.

[18] *Laneas et monachalis, id est, incompositi, ordinis.*

[19] A plant with a hot or stinging sap, used as a laxative.

[20] A plant used as a laxative.

[21] *Carbunculus*, lit. "live coals, embers."

[22] This word has a number of connotations, from red pigments (which might be considered solar) to various kinds of silk and finer textiles like velvet or damask.

[23] *Sepum (sebum)*. This can also include suet and tallow.

SECTION II.11: AL-QABĪSĪ (*ATTR.*)

Comment by Dykes. The following paragraphs were translated from a Latin text purporting to be by al-Qabīsī, *On the Conjunctions of the Planets in the Twelve Signs*, edited by Burnett in Appendix III of his edition of al-Qabīsī's *Introduction to Astrology* (2004). Burnett notes (p. 375) that it probably derives from a Western source, since references throughout the piece (but not here) make Arabs an enemy and point to other Western titles and phrases.

I have followed Burnett by numbering only the paragraphs, and I will probably translate the rest of the paragraphs for *AW2*. The method here is very simple: whatever planets are angular in the chart of the revolution, show that their commodities will be more expensive. The succeedent and cadent places are cheaper. Note also the similarity between ¶2 below, and "Aristotle" in Section II.10.

ಐ   ℘   ಜ

¶1 The treatise of the notable al-Qabīsī on the conjunctions of the planets in the twelve signs, and their prognostications in the revolutions of years, begins.

¶2 If you desire to know what things ought to be dear or cheap or middling in any year, see, when the Sun enters the first minute of Aries, what sign is arising and ascends at the horizon in which you are.[1] For the planet appearing in it then, will be called the lord of the year itself. Therefore, let there be a figure in which the twelve houses are put in order, thus,[2] and in which the twelve signs are put in order, and the seven planets are put in order in the individual houses just as they are then in the sky, with their true equation[3] having been made. And then look, and consider well the virtues of the signs and of the planets appearing in them, and judge with respect to the matters of that year as I will show [you], and as you could investigate it through the ingenuity of your mind.

¶3 If therefore Saturn were in the Ascendant, in the first house or sign, or in the tenth, then all things which are heavy and black will be very dear in that year, like lapis lazuli, iron, lead, and the like, and black woolen cloths (as

---

[1] That is to say, at your location.
[2] In Burnett's text appeared a blank, square-style chart. I omit it here.
[3] This refers to getting their exact position due to their movement on an epicycle, rather than their mean expected position.

are the vestments of monks and judges). Which if he were in the fourth or seventh house, they in particular will be dear, but not much. But if he were in the cadents, they will be neither cheap nor dear, but middling. And we say the same about the rest of the planets—the things which are signified by them (so as to speak briefly) being these: Jupiter signifies olive oil, cotton, honey, and silver; however, Mars signifies pepper, shields, and all arms; but the Sun signifies rough gold (that is, what is not worked); Venus signifies every fat, ointments, spices,[4] and white and nice-smelling wood, and pearls, and womanly ornaments; Mercury signifies tiny[5] grains and works of silk (both woven and not woven), and nuts, and what is like these; but the Moon signifies incense, milk, cheese, and the like.

---

[4] *Species.* This can also mean "medicines, drugs": think of medical ointments and creams.
[5] *Minuta.* Burnett also points out that this could refer to ingredients for fabrics.

SECTION II.12: JAFAR ON PRICES & MANSIONS

Comment by Dykes. This passage comes from the long Latin work attributed to "Jafar" or "Jafar Indus" (Jafar the Indian), which I partially translated for its weather material in Part I of this book. It concerns two methods of predicting prices using the lunar mansions.[1] It is intriguing and clearly comes from an alternate, perhaps Indian, tradition. Unfortunately, the first method is unclear at key points, and neither method really explains how to extract information on prices from a particular mansion: for instance, are rainy mansions better for prices? Should we look at the lucky and unlucky mansions listed in al-Bīrūnī's *Chronology* (p. 351)? Sentence **204** suggests the latter.

The first method (**197-204**) uses a Lot-like method to identify a key mansion. The instructions seem unclear at first, especially because 30° are immediately taken off the interval between 0° Aries and Saturn. The reason for this subtraction seems to be that what the author wants is the interval between the mansion of the Pleiades and Saturn:[2] since the Pleiades are near the beginning of the constellation of Taurus, it made sense to him subtract all of Aries, 30°. Of course, this would be an improper procedure even in a tropical zodiac, since the sums of various mansions do not fall into neat, 30° groups. And so, what the author really wants is the following: (1) cast the chart for the New/Full Moon; (2) measure the interval from the stars in the Pleiades, to Saturn; (3) project this distance from the Ascendant of the chart, and identify which sidereal mansion—i.e., based on the actual stars defining it—the counting stops in. Following this, Jafar recommends that we see what planets are in it, or are aspecting it, as well as combinations of Saturn, the Moon, or the benefics. Unfortunately, the method is so abbreviated that it is unclear how one would use it, especially if no planet is actually in that mansion.

The second method (**206-07**) is very simple and has a lot in common with other approaches: it looks at the lord of the east or its victor, and the lord of the year, and judges prices based on mansions and quarters.

In Section I.1 I have used al-Bīrūnī's designations of each of the mansions as being "lucky" or "unlucky" or "middling," as these might be seen to correlate with prices.

---

[1] That is, the 27-mansion system of the Indians.
[2] Probably because Saturn is a general indicator of agriculture.

ຽວ   ໊ວ   ໙

A treatment by the same man on the status of things for sale

197 Once a question about the status of things for sale is had, you will
note the established east of the assembly or opposition, [to see] which one of
the mansions of the Moon it holds onto; then, too, once the place of Saturn
is equally discovered, [then] collecting all of the degrees from the beginning
of Aries to the place of Saturn, once 30 from the whole sum have been
thrown away, divide what is left immediately by 13 1/3 (which is the size of a
mansion). **198** The parts of the division (however many there were), once the
beginning is taken up from the [mansion] which is the Pleiades, the method
urges [us] to distribute individual [parts] to individual mansions; and finally, it
being discovered which mansion from the east gets the end of the counting,
the diligent industry of the one observing [this] turns [to see] if any of the
stars were in it, while it would possess one knot[3] with any stars (or even
[with] Saturn), or at least should it be staying with the Moon. **199** If therefore
the star were corrupted by Saturn or it would be found in the same place or
in one knot with him, increasing in light and computation, and it was a mansion under the earth between the east and the fourth, it really introduces an
excessive burden [in price].[4] **200** For, it appearing between the fourth and the
seventh, there will be moderation everywhere; between the seventh and the
tenth, it chases after things for sale and demands them with the greatest desire; between the tenth and the east, it bears away the burdensomeness and
introduces cheapness—unless, I say, the regard of the fortunate ones would
help, or they would possess the same knot with [the star in question]. **201** For
thus they destroy the malice of Saturn and diminish his signification. **202**
Even the nature of the thing which becomes more burdensome may be diag-
nosed from the proper quality of the Saturnian mansion.[5] **203** Moreover, the
place of the Moon and her application with the fortunate ones, [and] likewise
her falling [away] from Saturn and his knot,[6] really means the quickest disso-
lution of easiness or burdensomeness [in price]. **204** A lucky mansion, or a

---

[3] In Section I.10 I suggested that a "knot" is a mansion.
[4] *Nimiam gravitatem.*
[5] This probably means that the mansion in which Saturn is, can reveal the kinds of things
which become expensive. Unfortunately, we do not have a list of what products correspond to the different mansions.
[6] Perhaps this means being in aversion to him (rather than separating from his aspect).

star traversing in it, remote from the regard of Saturn and that of the Moon, with the Moon being propitious, signifies cheapness.

Another chapter on the same thing

206 Therefore,[7] if the degrees from the east have not been taken up nor distributed, the minister-star[8] of the east and the lord of the year should principally be noted: for, they being found in an optimal place below the earth, adding in computation, while[9] they aspect the fortunate ones ([which are] adding in the same way) with an aspect of a certain configuration, as-cribed to the nature of their own place and [its] mansion, with the application being safe, above the earth, they denote burdensomeness; but if they were corrupted and bore themselves otherwise than what we said, it will be an indication of cheapness. **207** The leader[10] being in the east or the Midheaven indicates what is burdensome or cheap at the beginning of the year or por-tends it will be [so] in its first quarter; from the east to the pivot of the earth or in the fourth itself, it will convey it in the second quarter; from the fourth to the seventh, in the third quarter; from the seventh to the tenth, the out-comes of the signification will come forth in the last quarter of the year.

---

[7] For this paragraph, *cf.* ibn Labban's summaries in his paragraph 6 (Section II.9).

[8] *Stella…ministra.* This probably translates the Ar. *mustawlī* (which I elsewhere translate as "governor"), referring to a kind of victor: see for instance *Forty Chapters* Ch. 2.4.

[9] The middle of this sentence (from here up to "they denote burdensomeness") is com-plex and uncertain, and Hugo has done us no favors. It reads, *dum fortunatas eodem modo addentes configurationis cuiusdam aspectu naturae sui loci et mansioni relata applicatione salva super terram aspiciant….*

[10] That is, the governor-star.

SECTION II.13: AL-QABĪSĪ ON MUNDANE LOTS & PRICES

Comment by Dykes. This short excerpt from Book V of al-Qabīsī's *Introduction to Astrology*, is devoted to a rather rare subject in the literature: Lots for commodities. The translation is largely copied from my own *Introductions to Traditional Astrology (ITA)* §VI.5, but I have also consulted the Arabic text and made a few emendations to the Latin here and there. After describing a simple method for prices, al-Qabīsī gives the formulas for numerous Lots, all of which should presumably be projected from the Ascendant. Unfortunately, we currently have no way to know why these Lots were calculated with these planets, though in some cases the idea is clear (such as the Lot of poisons, which uses one of the Nodes and Saturn). Note the use of aspects and transits to the Lots.

The rules below may be summarized as follows. (1) For judging the supply of the commodity, a relationship of the Lot and its lord to benefics and/or the Moon indicates abundance; to the malefics, scarcity. (2) For price, the dignity, good condition, and angularity of the lord of the Lot will show a high price; in the contrary conditions, a low price.

ೞ   ೞ   ೞ

[V.19] Moreover, these are other Lots which we use in a revolution of the years of the world, and through them is known what would be more burdensome in [the price of] marketplace goods or what will be easier in price.[1]

And this is that you should look to see where the Lot fell—that is, into whose house or exaltation or bound or triplicity. Which if the planet were retrograde or burned up or in a malign place, that thing will become cheaper.[2] But if it were in a place of strength[3] or in an angle, and especially in the Midheaven, that thing will become more burdensome and will be of a greater

---

[1] Omitting a comment by John of Seville or a scribe: "and what is expensive or cheap, much or little."

[2] Omitting the comment: "and it will be of a small price."

[3] This could indicate some of the places of a planet's power as described in Book IV of *ITA*.

price.[4] And if the lord of that house arrived at the place of its own descension,[5] that thing will become more cheap.[6]

And look at the aspects of the fortunes and the bad planets to [the Lot], and also [to] the Moon and her lord.[7] If the fortunes and the Moon aspected the Lot, that thing will be multiplied; and if the bad ones aspected it, it will suffer detriment.[8]

The Lot of food:[9] from the Sun to Mars.
The Lot of water: from the Moon to Venus.
The Lot of barley: from the Moon to Jupiter.
The Lot of chickpeas: from Venus to the Sun.
The Lot of lentils: from Mars to Saturn.
The Lot of Egyptian beans: from Saturn to Mars.
The Lot of Indian peas: from Saturn to Mars.
The Lot of dates: from the Sun to Venus.
The Lot of honey: from the Moon to the Sun.
The Lot of rice:[10] from Jupiter to Saturn.
The Lot of olives: from Mercury to the Moon.
The Lot of grapes: from Saturn to Venus.
The Lot of cotton: from Mercury to Venus.
The Lot of sesame:[11] from Saturn to Jupiter or to Venus.
The Lot of watermelons:[12] from Mercury to Saturn.
The Lot of acidic foods: from Saturn to Mars.
The Lot of sweet foods: from the Sun to Venus.
The Lot of pungent[13] foods: from Mars to Saturn.
The Lot of bitter foods: from Mercury to Saturn.

---

[4] The Ar. explicitly says it will be rare, thus appealing to supply and demand: it will become more burdensome in price precisely because it is scarce.
[5] I.e., by transit. I assume that the transit could also be followed throughout the year and not only at the revolution.
[6] Omitting the comment: "and it will be of an easier price."
[7] Omitting the comment: "and see which one aspects the Lot itself, and how."
[8] This suggests that benefics will make it plentiful but also cheaper, while malefics will make it harmed and rare, albeit more expensive.
[9] The Latin and one Arabic manuscript read: "wheat."
[10] Omitting the comment: "which is a certain type of grain."
[11] Omitting the comment: "which is a certain kind of white seed like flaxseed, and medical doctors use it, and from it comes an ointment useful in medicine."
[12] Omitting the comment: "which are great and ripe orange melons."
[13] This Arabic word can also mean "spicy" (*harrīfah*). The Latin has "of the taste of celery [or parsley], or of herbs having a taste of this kind."

The Lot of purgative and sweet medicines: from the Sun to the Moon.
The Lot of purgative and acidic medicines: from Saturn to Jupiter.
The Lot of purgative and salty medicines: from Mars to the Moon.
The Lot of poisons: from the Node to Saturn.[14]

And all of these are projected from the Ascendant of the revolution.

[**V.20**] These are all of the Lots which have fallen to us. We have also introduced the latter Lots even though the description of them is weak, lest we omit something which could be an introduction to the mastery of the judgments of the stars by not mentioning it. With praise to God and for his support.

---

[14] Burnett notes here that other Arabic and Latin manuscripts contain additional Lots: see Bonatti's *Book of Astronomy* Tr. 8.2 for some of these.

PART III: ECLIPSES & COMETS

SECTION III.1: INTRODUCTION

In this Part we will look at eclipses and comets, both of which tended to be dreaded in the ancient and medieval world. As there is much more technical material on eclipses than on comets, most of my discussion will likewise be devoted to eclipses.

Eclipses

Modern, popularizing works in astronomy like to portray ancient and medieval people as idiots who were baffled by eclipses, as though they were so shocking that rich and poor alike fled for cover when they spotted one. As with so many other areas of ancient science and technology, the truth is rather different. For one thing, ancient people not only knew what eclipses were, but when they would occur. For instance, Aristotle himself uses the structure of eclipses to illustrate how logic shows that when we truly understand *what* something is, we also understand the explanation as to *why* it is (namely, that an eclipse of the Moon is the privation of the Sun's light from her, due to the earth's shadow).[1] Of course, knowledge about the types and regularity of eclipses was already possessed by the ancient Babylonians as well.

Let's begin by first explaining some terminology about eclipses and their types, and then I will discuss how our texts treat them astrologically—although the bulk of the method for eclipses may be seen in Section III.2, on Ptolemy.

First of all, an eclipse (of which there are several types) can only happen when the Moon is both (1) opposing or conjoined to the Sun and (2) close to one of the Nodes. She must be opposing the Sun for a lunar eclipse, and conjoined to him for a solar eclipse. But the relation to the Nodes is required because the Sun is by definition always on the ecliptic, and the Nodes are the very places where the Moon crosses the ecliptic. The farther away she is from the ecliptic when she is conjoined or opposed to him, the looser or

---

[1] *Post. An.* II.2, 90a14-17.

more partial the eclipse will be. We will be concerned with total eclipses, which I will distinguish from other types below.

Next, we should understand some terminology about the solar and lunar cycles, and how they relate to eclipses:[2]

Synodic month of Moon (29.531 days). This is the time between New Moons (Sun-Moon conjunctions). It is called "synodic" (Gr. *sunodos*, "meeting, assembly"), because at the New Moon she meets the Sun directly within the same sign. By definition then, the Moon has two chances to make an eclipse every 29.531 days: once at the conjunction or New Moon, and once at the opposition or Full Moon, provided that these places are also close to a Node.

Eclipse season/year. The luminaries and the Nodes each move, such that astronomers have defined periods in which they are coordinated together, called an eclipse *season* (173.31 days) and an eclipse *year* (two seasons, or 346.62 days). The eclipse year is shorter than our civil year (365.25 days) by 18.6 days.

Saros cycle. Since the Moon's synodic period, and solar eclipses, have to do with the Moon conjoining to the Sun, there is a mathematical relationship such that 223 *synodic months* (of 29.531 days apiece) is the same number of days as 19 *eclipse years* (of 346.62 days apiece): that is, 223 synodic months and 19 eclipse years are each about 6,585.5 days, or 18 years and 11.3 days in our civil calendar. This cycle is the *Saros* cycle, and simply means that those eclipses occurring 18 years and 11.3 days apart will have many of the same features, such as the type of eclipse and duration. For example, the solar eclipses of August 4, 1701, and August 15, 1719, were separated by exactly this amount of time, they were each total eclipses, and the Node was about 5° ahead of them in the zodiac. There are many overlapping series of Saros cycles in play at any time, although each ends after a long period of time due to various changes in celestial positions. Eclipses in odd-numbered Saros cycles occur at the North Node, and even-numbered ones at the South Node.

Each kind of eclipse is described in terms of how total it is, and its stages. For our purposes, we will only use the total eclipse:

Types of solar eclipse. Solar eclipses involve the Moon blocking out the light of the Sun. But because she does not always pass precisely in front of him,

---

[2] For some websites with much valuable information about eclipses see: (1) http://aa.usno.navy.mil/data/ and (2) http://sunearth.gsfc.nasa.gov/eclipse/eclipse.html.

and because she is sometimes closer to the earth than at other times, eclipses may only be partial, or the Moon might leave more light around her than in a normal total eclipse.

- Total: When the Moon fits virtually perfectly into the Sun, because she is visibly the same size as he is.
- Annular: When the Moon is a bit closer to the earth and so appears smaller than the Sun, creating a noticeable "ring" (Lat. *anulus*) of sunlight around her.
- Annular-total: A mixture of the first two.
- Partial: When the Moon does not really fit into the center but only passes by part of the Sun.

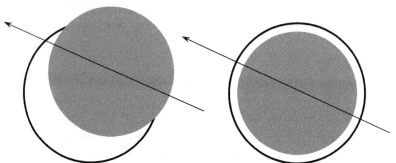

Figure 53: Partial (left) and annular (right) eclipses of the Sun (white) by the Moon (grey)

Stages of the total solar eclipse. The eclipse officially starts when the body of the Moon first appears to touch his body (P1), and ends when her body leaves his completely (P2). But when she is fully in the middle of his body, there are also two stages: first, when she is first completely within his body and their edges are still touching (U1), and when she reaches the other side of his body and touches it (U2). In the middle is the period of totality, which never lasts beyond about 7.75 minutes. These labels for the stages of solar eclipses are now standard in computer programs and astronomical tables.

- P1: When the edge of the Moon touches the edge of the Sun (eclipse begins).
- U1: When the Moon is fully "in" the Sun, but with the edges of each touching.

- Totality: When the Moon is considered to be in the center of the Sun.
- U2: When the Moon has passed totality, with the edges of each touching.
- P2: When the Moon's edge ceases to touch the Sun's (eclipse ends).

It is very important to find these values in programs or tables, because sometimes reports of eclipses are really only interested in the duration of the *totality*: thus a table may only list the duration as being (say) 7 minutes long, when in fact the entire eclipse lasted for several hours from start (P1) to finish (P2).

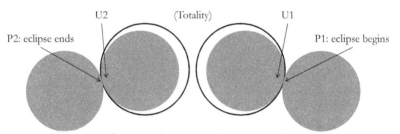

Figure 54: Stages of a total eclipse of the Sun (white) by the Moon (grey)

The visibility and timing of solar eclipses depends on when and where Moon's shadow touches the earth; and as the heavens turn, the place where the totality can be seen is called the path of the eclipse (therefore, totality will be seen at different times depending on where one is). Thus, the whole length of the eclipse is the time between the Moon's touching the Sun (P1) and her leaving him (P2), *for a particular location*. For example, at the total solar eclipse of June 21, 2001, some places in Angola were able to see the eclipse from start to finish (including totality) for 3 hours 11 minutes; but in Madagascar, for only 2 hours 20 minutes.

Figure 55: Path of totality of solar eclipse, June 21, 2001

The issue of the eclipse path is potentially important astrologically, because many contemporary astrologers (such as Robert Zoller) teach that the effects of the eclipse will be most strongly felt in countries along the eclipse path. But Ptolemy himself does not say this, as we will see below. For Ptolemy, places and things which pertain to the *sign* of the eclipse and to the Ascendant will be more strongly affected. But one might well imagine that the path of the totality should have something to do with the effects, even though this means that sometimes it will cross areas that do not seem to play a great role in world affairs: certain small islands, for example. Likewise, since much of the eclipse can be seen in places some distance from the path of the totality, we might ask whether it is enough to be able to see only part of it (even if not the totality itself) for that region to be affected.

Modern researchers on eclipses have added rules that are in harmony with certain Ptolemaic ideas. Recently I had the pleasure of hearing Bill Meridian give a talk about his work on eclipses,[3] which follows the research of Johndro, Jayne, and others. I do not know whether or not Johndro and Jayne were aware of Ptolemy's work, but it is worth saying a few words about how they and Meridian determine what regions and people are affected by eclipses—and I will deal only with solar eclipses here.

(1) Although a solar eclipse will primarily affect the people on and around the path of the center (since much politics is regional), there are two important ways to specify it further. First, see if the degree of the eclipse closely aspects the Ascendant, Midheaven or—especially—the Sun of the countries' *foundation charts* or its leaders' *nativities*. The eclipse will have a more intense effect on such people and places.

(2) People who are born on or about eclipses (and especially if the degree of the eclipse is on or closely aspecting important points) will often have an

---

[3] See Meridian 2011.

interest in, or interaction with, the ideas and peoples whose countries are crossed by the eclipse path. These interests will often be triggered the next time an eclipse in that Saros cycle occurs (every 18 years, 11 days).

(3) For the eclipses in a Saros cycle, the general path of the eclipse moves backwards by about 120° every time: thus every fourth eclipse (or 54 years, 33 days) will have a roughly similar path and so affect roughly the same region on earth. For example, the solar eclipse of October 2, 1959 (in Saros cycle 143) had a line connecting the United States and most of central Africa (at which time the Congo Crisis erupted). But the next two eclipses in the cycle (October 1977, October 1995) had lines in other areas. The line of the central-annular eclipse of November 2, 2013 (the next instance of Saros 143) will return to central Africa. This can be useful when looking at the path of any eclipse, because for the most part the same people and nations should have be affected.

(4) Solar eclipses occurring on one's natal Sun (or on the Sun of a country, etc.) can be forceful in a *supportive* way to the native, even if they bring change; but oppositions to one's Sun tend to be more destructive. Eclipses to any natal point can be important, but not so much as the Sun's position.

(5) Transits to the degree of a significant eclipse—whether before the eclipse or after—can have a triggering effect upon the events which are indicated by the eclipse itself. That is to say, an eclipse indicates a range of things, some of which will act as preludes to the main event, and others as after-effects.

As for lunar eclipses, they can pretty much be seen by anyone for whom it is night while the eclipse takes place, since by definition the eclipse is caused by the earth's shadow, which is on the nighttime side of the earth. The labels for the stages of a lunar eclipse are a little different from those of the solar eclipse, because shadows themselves have two "stages" or parts: you can see this by looking at the shadow of your own hand against a table. The darker, inner part of the shadow is the "umbra" (Lat. "shadow"), and the less dark region around it is the "penumbra" (Lat. "next to the shadow"). Proper total eclipses of the Moon take place in the Earth's umbra (U1-U4), even though the Moon must pass through the penumbra first to get there (P1, P2).

Types of lunar eclipse. As with solar eclipses, lunar ones come in several types, of which we will only look at the total ones.

- Total: When the whole Moon is covered in the Earth's umbra. Because of the size of the Earth's shadow, the period of totality might last up to 90 minutes.
- Partial: When only a portion of the Moon passes through the Earth's umbra.
- Penumbral: When the Moon only passes through the Earth's penumbra.

Stages of the total lunar eclipse. The stages at which the Moon passes through the penumbra are not astrologically important: what we care about is the umbric portion, from where the Moon's body first touches it, to where she finally leaves it completely.

- P1: When the Moon enters the penumbra. (This can sometimes be difficult to discern.)
- U1: When the Moon first touches the umbra (eclipse begins).
- U2: When the Moon is fully under the umbra.
- U3: When the Moon begins to leave the umbra.
- U4: When the Moon completely leaves the umbra (eclipse ends).
- P2: When the Moon fully leaves the penumbra.

Astrologically, the timing of the lunar eclipse begins at U1 and ends at U4; astronomical tables also give these values.

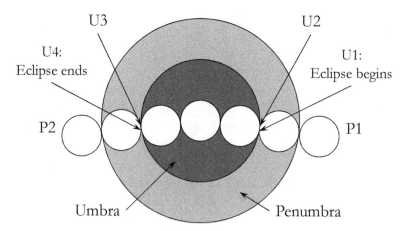

Figure 56: Stages of a total lunar eclipse

For example, at the total lunar eclipse of January 21, 2000, the Moon began to enter the umbra (U1) at 3:22 AM, and left the umbra completely (U4) at 6:26 AM, making the eclipse last 3 hours 4 minutes. During that time, she was totally covered for 1 hour 18 minutes, from 4:05 AM (U2) to 5:23 AM (U3). The total lunar eclipse of July 16, 2000, was longer: lasting 3 hours 56 minutes (U1-U4), with the Moon being totally covered for 1 hour 47 minutes (U2-U3).

We will look at Ptolemy's method for eclipses in detail in the next Section.

Comets

Comets receive a much less extensive treatment in the literature, perhaps because they are infrequent, less predictable, and were not obviously connected with the usual array of astrological concepts: planets, houses, *etc.* Still, enough information exists to begin to treat them in a formal astrological sense, and not just as general harbingers of drought and so on.

The word "comet" comes from the Gr. *komē* and *komētēs* ("hair," "long-haired"), describing the apparent mane of hair which attaches to the body of a comet (but which is really dust and other material emitted from it as it proceeds through our solar system). In Latin this was called a *cauda* ("tail"), so that comets are either "stars with hair" or "stars with tails." Arabic texts refer to tails as well.

Since comets are so small (and usually, far away), they are normally invisible to the naked eye until they suddenly appear with their bright tails. In antiquity this gave rise to several theories as to their origin and number. In his *Meteorology* I.6-7, Aristotle reviews three views of his predecessors before presenting his own, occasionally rambling or confusing objections, and then his own explanation. The first view is that of Anaxagoras and Democritus, who thought they were conjunctions of planets which are so close as to appear to be touching (and therefore, large and bright). Aristotle points out that all of the planets are near the ecliptic, but since comets are often seen far from the ecliptic, they cannot be composed of planets. Next, the Pythagoreans suggest that they are planets similar to Mercury: that is, that they revolve close by the Sun and so only appear briefly and occasionally. But this cannot be true, because (Aristotle says), comets do not fade away by going under the Sun's rays as planets do, but sometimes simply fade away where they are—unlike planets. This is also an argument against comets being bright conjunctions, because when they fade they do not leave just one planet behind, but nothing at all. (Nevertheless, the view that comets circulate close to the Sun most of the time, is echoed in later literature: see the opening sentences in Sections III.8, the second selection, and Section III.9.) Finally, there is the view of Hippocrates of Chios and his pupil Aeschylus, which is very close to that of modern astronomy: that the comet is something like a revolving planet, and its hair or tail is only an appearance caused by the Sun's light reflecting against moisture attracted by it. Comets appear so seldom, because they are only visible when appearing in certain parts of the heavens which can cause this reflection. But, Aristotle says, we do see comets in places where Hippocrates and Aeschylus say they shouldn't be seen, and anyway, why don't we ever see any of the usual seven planets with these tails (or a comet *without* a tail)?

Aristotle's last argument makes good sense if we assume (as he does) that celestial bodies are all made of the same material, because then we would expect even planets to have tails. Accordingly, his own explanation of comets and shooting stars is that they cannot be planetary or of the upper heavenly regions, but must belong to the region just below them. That is, the hot and dry (or fiery) region just below the Moon tends to ignite and burn any matter of the right consistency which enters it. If the matter provides a type of fuel so as to burn quickly, it appears as a shooting star; but if the matter is also rather fiery itself, then it will burn bright and long, forming a comet. The shape of the comet depends on the shape and type of fuel. Moreover, Aristotle seems to believe that if the influence creating the fuel comes from a fixed star or planet, then the planet or star itself will *seem* to be a comet; but if the influence comes from below the heavens, it will be a proper comet that is independent of any stellar or planetary motion.

The idea that an apparent comet could actually be a star or planet, may be one source for the later view that the color and style of the tail indicates a planetary *type* of comet: for example, that a red glow indicates that the comet will have Martial effects, or a blackish one Saturnian effects (see Ptolemy in Section III.2). Of course, interpreting comets in the context of horoscopic astrology virtually requires that they be associated with either planets or signs anyway. Otherwise, comets were thought generally to foreshadow drying winds and drought, precisely because of their physically fiery nature: that is, their heat would tend to move the air more violently and dry it out. Thus, however they may have been associated astrologically with particular planets later, according to Aristotle they were not really portents or omens, but simply the appearance of actually burning fuel which then directly caused changes in the natural world.

Not all later astrologers agreed with this view (although they did not necessarily present their opinions as a challenge to Aristotle). The 9ᵗʰ Century Christian astrologer ibn Hibintā claimed[4] that God shows us comets as *signs* when He allows some event (obviously one of some magnitude) to transpire somewhere. So this is a signification view, putting comets in the category of portents and omens. Abū Ma'shar (Section III.9 below) says that he himself saw a comet above the sphere of Venus, and others have reported them above the sphere of Saturn—thus they do not merely belong to the realm of elemental fire just below the Moon. Moreover, ibn Hibintā argued that comets circulate near the Sun (an echo of the Pythagorean view), despite the fact that they partake of the seven planetary natures.

As for the number of comets, Aristotle's view suggests that there are indefinitely many, since they would appear whenever there was enough fuel in the atmosphere to create one. And indeed Kennedy (1957) lists about a dozen named comets in Arabic, which suggests that some people identified them uniquely when they appeared, or else according to certain general shapes.

On the other hand, Ptolemy classifies comets by shape (such as "trumpets" or "casks"), but associates any individual comet with a planetary signification based on its coloring. Grosseteste (Section III.12 below) seems to follow Ptolemy. Other astrologers list a precise number of comets and associate them with the planets: for instance, while Hephaistio dutifully follows Ptolemy in mentioning trumpet and cask shapes, he describes seven comets (each belonging to one of the seven planets) and their effects. A pseudo-Ptolemy cited by Bonatti lists nine comets, seven of which are clearly those of Hephaistio. For these, see Section III.11.

According to Kennedy (1957), an apparently famous comet or other body is given in Arabic as *al-Kaid* ("the deception"),[5] which appears throughout many Arabic and Greek manuscripts, and is given a certain backwards zodiacal motion of about 2.5° per year. That would make it complete a revolution every 144 years, which to my mind makes its status as a comet suspect: for this is equivalent to moving one twelfth-part per year, and 144 being the square of 12 (the number of zodiacal signs) seems to be more than a coinci-

---

[4] Kennedy 1957, p. 44.
[5] But perhaps this should be *al-Qā'id*, "the leader"?

dence. Nevertheless, if it is a comet, Kennedy suggests[6] that it may have a period of 90 years between appearances. Ibn Hibinta[7] reports that it is bad if al-Kaid is in the signs of the pivotal degrees of some chart, and there are various interpretations for it when configured with various planets in various signs—so it was apparently tracked even when it did not actually appear. Neugebauer[8] notes that al-Kaid may actually be the Tail of the Dragon or South Node, called *Ketu* in Indian astrology: in a 14th Century Byzantine text, it is called *kait*, and explicitly associated with the Indians. And Kennedy[9] says that it might be what the Latin text of *Abū Ma'shar in Shadhān* describes as *kint*—which would make sense if it had originally been *Ketu*.

Before turning to a practical example of a comet, let us look at a famous "comet" from 1006, which was apparently really a supernova.[10] I have translated a first-hand account of it by ibn Ridwān from his (Latinized) commentary on the *Tetrabiblos*, but have used Goldstein 1965 to make certain corrections, as Goldstein published and translated the Arabic text. The Latin edition suggests that the "comet" of 1006 had a retrograde motion that lasted for about four months, which is what a comet might well do. According to Goldstein, this supernova influenced later astrological writing in Europe, and led to a flurry of scholarly activity which tried to figure out what comet it was. But Goldstein's publication of the Arabic shows that the object stayed still, while *the Sun* moved forward for four months—and when the Sun reached the sextile of the object, it disappeared. Nevertheless, it would be worth asking whether supernovas can also be interpreted in the manner of comets: following the ibn Ridwān text, I have translated several short Latin excerpts in which Latin-speaking contemporaries reported comet-like effects after seeing the supernova.

> [ibn Ridwān:] ...But I want to tell you about one omen which I saw when I was beginning to learn. For there appeared such an omen in the sign of Scorpio, in the opposition of the Sun: with the Sun in that hour appearing in 15° of Taurus; and that star itself[11] in 15° of Scorpio: and

---

[6] Kennedy 1957, p. 50.
[7] Kennedy 1957, p. 45.
[8] Neugebauer 1957, p. 211.
[9] Kennedy 1957, p. 46.
[10] This seems to have been the supernova SN 1006 (which Goldstein also identifies as NGC 5882), widely reported and seen all over the world.
[11] The Latin appears to give it a name, *Alanzadera*, but this is probably a mistaken transliteration (albeit a strange one) for the Ar. *al-nayzak* (originally from Persian), "meteor."

it had a great big round shape, and it could have been three times as great as Venus; and with respect to its brightness, the whole horizon light up, [and] the light could have been as much as one-fourth of the Moon's or a little bit more.[12] And always by moving it appeared in that sign with the motion of the firmament until [the Sun] put himself in its sextile from the sign of Virgo—and then it was destroyed. I saw the whole thing, as did many other sages. But the places of the planets of the appearance of this signal, were this: the Sun and Moon conjoined in 15° of Taurus; Saturn in Leo, 12° 11'; Jupiter in Cancer, 11° 21'; Mars in Scorpio, 21° 19'; Venus in Gemini, 12° 28'; Mercury in Taurus, 5° 11'; the Head of the Dragon in Sagittarius, 23° 28'; the star itself[13] which appeared, was ascending in 15° Scorpio. Likewise at Fustat, a city of Egypt, [the Ascendant of the conjunction at the time of the appearance of the meteor] was Leo 4° 02', [and the tenth house] Aries 26° 37', with [almost] all of Taurus. I say that it was in Scorpio, [and] that is the sign of the law of the Moors, and the sign of their conjunction.[14] Great battles took place among the Moors, strong wars, and killings. And on account of this, the great cities and regions of their lands were depopulated. And one great heretic left,[15] and rose up against the king of Mecca and Yathrib,[16] and great dryness happened, and a great dearth of provisions, and great mortality on account of the corruption of the air, and on account of pestilence and the sword, so that through famine, the sword, and infirmities, peoples without number perished, and military men and people. This evil and loss was continuous after the star appeared, for many years. We should speak of this when we put down examples of such things.

---

[12] Goldstein (p. 107) suggests that what ibn Ridwān means is this: (1) its diameter was 2.5—3 times as wide as Venus, and its brightness is that of the Moon when only one-fourth of the Moon is illuminated.

[13] Again, the Latin follows this with *Alazendera*.

[14] The Saturn-Jupiter conjunction of 571 AD (taken to herald Islam) was in Scorpio, so that Scorpio is an indicator for the Muslim community.

[15] Goldstein points out that this refers to the sect of the *Khawārij*, so ibn Ridwān is referring to a civil war during the time of the 'Umayyads.

[16] Another name for Medina.

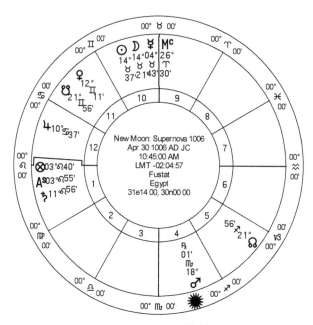

**Figure 57: Chart for the New Moon of the "comet"
(sc. supernova) of 1006 AD**

Other contemporary descriptions of the 1006 supernova and its effects[17]

[*Annales Laubiensis* 1841] There was the greatest famine with the appearance of a comet for a long time.

[*Johannes Chronicon Venetum* 1846, p. 36] The year 1006. And so, in that same time, there was a maned star (the human judgment of which always declares something scandalous),[18] appearing in the southern clime, which the greatest pestilence followed, throughout all the territories of Italy or Venice.

[*Hepidannus* 1826, p. 81][19] A new star of uncommon magnitude appeared, lighting up[20] in appearance and striking the eyes, not without

---

[17] I have used the Latin excerpts from Goldstein p. 108.
[18] *Flagicium*, which does not seem quite right. The writer might have meant something like *flagellationem*, "disaster."
[19] According to Goldstein, Hepidannus was a monk at St. Gall, who wrote records until the year 1044.

terror. In a surprising way it was sometimes more contracting, sometimes more spread out, [and] occasionally even extinguished. But it was seen for three months in the innermost territories of the south, beyond all of the signs which are seen in the heavens.

[*Annales Beneventani* 1844, p. 177] The year 1006….a most bright star shone forth, and there was great dryness for three months.

A recent comet

I thought it might be useful to apply some of the rules in our texts to the Hale-Bopp comet of 1996. The basic rules are these:

- Like eclipses, comets generally show great changes affecting politics in particular (usually due to some political death), but they also indicate economic changes due to agriculture.
- The sign in which a comet appears (or corresponds to), indicates the lands and beings affected. Since comets tend to move through multiple signs, longer-lasting comets will show far-reaching effects.
- The direction in which the hair or tail points, also indicates a terrestrial direction.
- The color of the comet can indicate the types of effects (e.g., red suggesting Martial effects)
- Eastern comets (rising before the Sun) shows that the effects happen sooner, western ones (setting after the Sun) show effects that happen later.
- The length of time for the effects is a bit murky, but Merrifield (1684, p. 33) suggests that we equate each zodiacal sign of the comet's travel, to a year.
- Merrifield (p. 32) also suggests that if the comet appears in the Ascendant of any city or nation, it will affect that nation as a whole; and likewise it will affect its honor or reputation if it appears in the Midheaven of the chart. Likewise, it will affect nations whose mundane ingress charts have that sign on their Ascendant.

---

[20] *Fulgurans*, the verb whence the Latin for "lightning" comes. Hepidannus wants to say that it was not only bright, but somehow reminded him of lightning.

Applying the rules to our example, the Hale-Bopp comet became visible between May-July 1996, and was eastern, in a position corresponding to the middle of Capricorn, and continued visible until October 1997, corresponding to late Leo. Since it was in 8 tropical signs, it indicated about 8 years of effects (about 1996-2005). Because it was eastern when it appeared, the effects should have begun early, say in the first half of the period (about 1996-2000). It had both a curved, reddish tail (signifying Mars), and a bluish tail (signifying Mercury), both of which signify death and war.

Because the comet appeared in so many signs, it should have affected much of the world. But what about Capricorn, where it first appeared? As for countries ruled by Capricorn, Ptolemy assigns it to regions in Asia which include parts of modern Afghanistan and Pakistan (Section IV.2 below); later Muslim sources such as Abū Ma'shar assign it to a region stretching from Ethiopia across the eastern and southeastern sides of the Arabian peninsula (Bahrain, Oman), through the portion of Asia which includes Afghanistan and Pakistan. As for ingress charts, I note that the annual Aries ingress chart for the United States in 1996 had 21° Capricorn rising. Thus when the comet was clearly visible, it was passing across the Ascendant of the ingress itself. This suggests that the people of the United States in particular would be affected by this comet.

The United States was the victim of numerous terrorist attacks between 1996 and 2000 or 2001. Some were relatively minor, such as the 1997 gun attack on visitors to the Empire State Building by an aged Palestinian, Ali Hassan Abū Kamal. Others were more spectacular, such as in Saudi Arabia (Khobar Towers, 1996), Yemen (U.S.S. Cole, 2000), and on its own soil (World Trade Center and Pentagon, 2001). On the other hand, the United States had already been bombing Iraq (most notably between 1998-2000), and officially went to war in Afghanistan in 2001 and Iraq in 2003. The bombing campaign in Afghanistan was concentrated on barren and mountainous places (Saturnian places).

A final note on eclipses, comets, and chorography

Four of our authors also pass on older lore on how an eclipse's or comet's location indicates the part of the earth affected; but the wording and meaning gets garbled from author to author, and changes from being instructions about eclipses (in Māshā'allāh) to instructions about comets in later authors. (Or perhaps, Māshā'allāh himself misunderstood the rules.)

In the background is a threefold way of dividing up the northern hemisphere according to the superior planets, mentioned both by Māshā'allāh in his Ch. 31 (see Section IV.9) and by al-Rijāl in his Ch. VIII.36 (Section IV.4). The northernmost latitudes of the hemisphere are ruled by Saturn and the Moon (whose domicile is opposite his), the middle latitudes by Jupiter and Mercury (ditto), and the hot southern latitudes by Mars and Venus (ditto). Based on where the eclipse or comet is located, it will indicate what region of the earth is affected. But what do we mean by its location, and is there a reason to prefer eclipses or comets as the proper object of the rule?

The first passage comes from Māshā'allāh,[21] says it is an *eclipse's* relation to the great circles of the *horizon and meridian* (i.e., the angles visible at an eclipse):

7 After this, look at the bad ones [at the time of an eclipse]: if they were in the Ascendant or closer to the Ascendant, there will be impediment in the middle part of the earth (which we said belongs to Jupiter and Mercury). **8** And if the bad ones were in the Midheaven, or closer to the Midheaven, it will be in the upper part of the orb (which we have said belongs to Saturn and the Moon). **9** But in the west, or closer to the west, it will be in the lower part of the earth (which belongs to Mars and Venus).

The problem with this view is that the relation of an eclipse to the horizon and meridian is location-sensitive. Since an eclipse will appear differently in different regions, it could indicate northern latitudes according to one view, but southern ones according to another. For example, if we cast charts for the maximum solar eclipse of August 11, 1999, for London, Munich, and Karachi, we see that the eclipse appears near the Midheaven of both London and Munich, but toward the Descendant in Karachi.

After Māshā'allāh, the rule seemed to be applied to comets instead. Sahl and Abū Ma'shar report virtually the same view but with ambiguous language about "elevated" paths or "lower" journeys. Only al-Rijāl's report is clear and makes sense: that the *ecliptical latitude* of the comet determines the position. That is, if it has extreme northern latitude so as to be far from the zodiacal belt, it indicates upper geographical regions; if in or around the signs, the middle regions; if outside the zodiac to the south, lower regions.

---

[21] Māshā'allāh's Ch. 40 (Section III.4).

[Sahl, Section III.7] **3** And look at the area in which [the comet] travels, [but] do not look for it as you look at the course of the planets and the eclipse and the aspects belonging to them. **4** If it was moving in the elevated path, that evil[22] was from the share of Saturn and the Moon. **5** And if it is in middle path, that was in the share of Jupiter and Mercury. **6** And if it was in the lowest path, it was in the share of Mars and Venus.

[Abū Ma'shar, Ch. 72, in Section III.9] **11** Look at the part [in] which [the comets] were: if they were in the lower journey, the evil will be in the part of Mars and Venus. **12** And if they were in the upper journey, the evil will be in the part of Saturn and the Moon and the Sun.

[Al-Rijāl, Ch. VIII.32.2, in Section III.8] **21** And if [the comet] was in the area of the sign, then indeed the evil is in the share of Jupiter and Mercury, in terms of countries and creatures. **22** And if it was in the belt of the highest (and that is what follows the north), that was in the share of Saturn and the Moon. **23** And if it was in the area of the lowest (and that is what follows the south), it was in the share of Venus [and Mars].

---

[22] Adding with Beatty.

SECTION III.2: PTOLEMY ON ECLIPSES & COMETS

Ptolemy's approach to mundane astrology revolves around two primary methods: the New/Full Moon preceding the seasonal ingresses (and later, throughout the season), and eclipses. In Section I.2 I described his method of interpreting lunation charts, which he uses mainly for weather prediction. Here I will describe his use of eclipses and then turn briefly to comets.

After describing his assignment of geographical regions to the signs (*Tet.* II.3),[1] Ptolemy turns to the method of eclipses itself (II.4-8). Here I will summarize the translation of Robbins, but use boldface numbers to indicate the sentences in Hübner's critical edition.

Tet. II.4: Preview. In II.4, Ptolemy says that we will look generally at features of eclipses themselves, as well as the behavior of the other planets at the time of them (**1**); in *Tet.* II.1, this had included both planets stationing and arising from the rays of the Sun.[2] In order to make the predictions more precise, in II.5 he identifies the regions and cities indicated by the eclipses or by the stations of the superior planets (**2**). Then in *Tet.* II.6, he discusses his timing mechanism, in II.7 the kinds of beings affected, and in II.8 what those effects will be (**3**).[3]

Tet. II.5: Identifying the terrestrial regions. At first (**1, 2**), Ptolemy makes it seem as though any eclipse may be judged, but "especially" those which may be observed more easily (in other words, the visible ones); but by the end of the chapter and in what follows, he seems to care only about those actually visible in a given location. I will follow Ptolemy and assume we are dealing with visible eclipses: this means total lunar eclipses visible to people in nighttime regions of the earth (so that the Moon appears above the horizon), and total solar eclipses visible especially along the path of the total eclipse (but perhaps also for people farther away, who can see it only in part). For those very far away, the Moon will not be seen to be totally covering the Sun.

In order to identify the region affected, we must note the following: [1] regions associated with the sign[4] of the zodiac in which the eclipse occurs, [2]

---

[1] For chorography and climes, see Part IV below.

[2] *Anatolē.* This probably does not mean just any planet already outside of the rays, but one which is actually emerging for the first time.

[3] *Tet.* II.8 also describes weather effects, which are used in his techniques for weather prediction.

[4] *Topon* ("place"), which I take to mean the sign itelf: namely the sign of the Sun in a solar eclipse, and the sign of the Moon in a lunar one.

regions associated with its triplicity, and [3] cities associated with it (**1**). The regions of [1] and [2] are part of Ptolemy's chorography (see Part IV), but the cities are identified in the following way (**1-2**): either the Ascendant of the city's founding,[5] and[6] the position of the luminaries at that time, or the Midheaven in the nativity of their leader at the time, must be "sympathetic" to the sign of the eclipse. What exactly counts as being "sympathetic" is a bit unclear to me, but it would definitely include the sign itself, and possibly in a trine to it (especially since Ptolemy is very interested in the triplicities). For example, if the eclipse took place in Gemini, then the eclipse will first of all affect [1] regions of the earth associated with Gemini (according to Ptolemy's chorography); then [2] regions associated with the airy triplicity, since Gemini is one of the airy signs. Finally, it will affect [3] cities whose foundational chart has Gemini rising (or perhaps any airy sign?), or perhaps has the luminaries in (or strongly aspecting?) Gemini, or else the Midheaven of the nativity of the city's founder ought to be Gemini (or perhaps any airy sign?).

In Section I.2 I mentioned that Ptolemy wants us to see if the planets ruling something like an eclipse have "familiarity" (Gr. *oikeiōsis, sunoikeioumenos, Tet.* II.8) with the regions and being affected. By "familiarity," he later clarifies (**22**) that he means being "lords of the countries." I believe what Ptolemy means is this. Suppose the sign of an eclipse were Libra: this means that the eclipse should especially affect Libran territories and the regions governed by the airy triplicity (Gemini, Libra, Aquarius).[7] We would then want to know whether Venus, who rules Libra, has rulership over some city or territory or beings in those areas—for instance, she may have special rulership in some but not others. If she does, then she has familiarity and this will affect such areas and beings in certain ways. So, (**21**), if the planets ruling the relevant sign are benefic, have familiarity with the things affected, and are not overcome by the malefic of the opposite sect, then they will be really beneficial in the relevant effects; if they are not familiar or are overcome, they will be less helpful. On the other hand (**22**), if the ruling planets were malefic, had familiarity and are overcome by benefics of the opposite sect, they will do less harm; but if they did not have familiarity and were not overcome by such

---

[5] In *Tet.* II.3 (equivalent to Huebner *Tet.* II.4, sentences **5-6**), Ptolemy also allows the other angles, but prefers the Ascendant.

[6] Or most likely, "or."

[7] See Ptolemy's chorography in Part IV.

benefics,[8] they will be more destructive. Finally (**23**), the general effects indicated by the planets will have special concern for people whose *nativities* have the sign of the eclipse or its opposite in chief places of the natal chart: such as if one of a native's luminaries or angles were on the sign and especially the degree of the eclipse or its opposite. For example, let the eclipse be at 9° Libra: then anyone whose (say) Ascendant, Moon, or Sun, were on Libra or Aries, and especially at 9° Libra or Aries, would be especially affected.

Tet. II.6: Timing. Ptolemy points out that because seasonal hours differ based on one's location, we must measure the length of the time of the eclipse using equinoctial or civil hours (**1**). And so, we should first cast a chart for the eclipse, and know how long it lasts. For a lunar eclipse, each hour of the eclipse equates to a month of effects, and each hour of a solar one equates to a year (**2**), although the effects will not be equally intense at all times (see below).

Now, both of these points (casting the chart, the different regional lengths of the eclipses) require comment. First, when Ptolemy speaks of seasonal hours, he is referring to what most of us think of as "planetary" hours:[9] that is, dividing the actual time of daylight in that location into 12 equal parts, to yield so many hours of daylight, and dividing the period of night into 12 equal parts in the same way. So for example, since winter has less daylight, the length of a day and of its 12 seasonal or planetary hours will be shorter in winter, and a night and its hours longer—these differences will be even more pronounced as one increases in latitude. However, Ptolemy says we must instead use "equinoctial" hours, which are nothing more than our normal civil hours of 60 minutes apiece.[10] This assertion is similar to his approach to weather prediction (II.10),[11] where he simply decides without argument that we ought to cast the New/Full Moon charts for all seasonal ingresses, even though he says there was a contemporary dispute about which seasons were the most important.

---

[8] Actually, here (**22**) Ptolemy says "planets that have familiarity," which would certainly be relevant. But the logic of his argument also suggests that benefics of the opposite sect would diminish the malefic qualities, too.

[9] See *ITA* V.13.

[10] They are called equinoctial, because at the equinox the length of daylight and nighttime are equal, so that each hour will by definition be 60 minutes long.

[11] In Hübner, this is *Tet.* II.11.

But why should we favor the equinoctial or civil hours? If an eclipse's effects are already relevant only to certain geographic regions, why couldn't we have longer effects for regions which see the eclipse as lasting a longer time, and shorter effects for regions which see it as lasting a shorter time? In fact, ibn Labban does something just like this (see below).

Ptolemy instructs us to cast the chart for the "hour" of the eclipse. This probably means the moment of the totality. Thus a lunar eclipse might last for 3 hours, but it only becomes total at a certain location when the Moon is in, say, the 9th house—the place of the totality matters for Ptolemy's timing technique, as we will see below. But other authors (like Sahl, but perhaps Ptolemy, see below) also want us to take note of the Ascendant of the eclipse. And since signs of different ascensional lengths arise faster or slower at different locations, and because the eclipse may last for quite a while, we run the risk of not knowing exactly what time to use if we are interested in the Ascendant and regions associated with it: should it be when the eclipse begins, or when it is total?[12] Perhaps we should cast charts for the beginning and end of the eclipse too, even if we do note where the totality takes place. For example, suppose the eclipse began while Aries was rising: in the northern hemisphere, Aries is a crooked sign which arises rather quickly; by the totality and end of the eclipse, Taurus might be on the horizon. If so, then perhaps the eclipse would have weaker effects for regions related to Aries, because the eclipse only began there; but it might have stronger effects for regions associated with Taurus, since Taurus was arising at the totality. But in either event, the sign in which the eclipse happened would still be important. Again, this is a matter which begs for research.[13]

Let's return to Ptolemy's method for determining the timing of the effects: their beginnings and intensifications are based on the eclipse's relationship to the axial degrees of the Ascendant-Descendant, and the Midheaven (2-3), as well as planetary events occurring during the relevant times (4).

Once we know the maximum length of the effects, the position of the eclipse gives us a starting point both for the effects in general, and for their intensification. That is, the effects will always begin within one year, and the

---

[12] In Ch. 28 (64, 75) of Hermann's summary of Sahl (Section III.5), he mentions that one ought to find the Ascendants for the beginning, middle, and end of the eclipse.

[13] An associated issue arises for lunar eclipses in particular: since so much of the earth at nighttime will be able to see a lunar eclipse, different regions will have different Ascendants at the moment of the totality.

position of the eclipse tells us both (a) when in that year they begin, and (b) when, during the *total* time of the effects, they will be most intense. If it takes place on the eastern horizon, the effects will *begin* within four months, with the *intensification* being in the first one-third of the total time; but if on the Midheaven, they begin between four and eight months, with the intensification being in the second third of the total time; and if on the Descendant, they begin between eight and twelve months later, with the intensification being in the last third of the total time (**2-3**). Let's take the following as a hypothetical example:

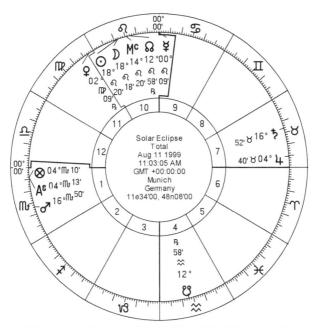

Figure 58: Solar eclipse of August 11, 1999 (Munich, Germany)

This chart is cast for the moment of totality during the solar eclipse of August 11, 1999. Munich was in the path of the totality, and in Munich the duration of the eclipse from P1-P2 was 2.75 hours. This means that the eclipse should have effects for 2.75 years. The eclipse is almost exactly on the Midheaven, but certainly in the middle one-third of the heavens.

According to Ptolemy's instructions, the effects must begin within 1 year. Because the eclipse is near the Midheaven or in the middle third of heaven, then the effects should *begin* within 4-8 months (the middle third of one year), and the *intensification* of them should likewise be within the middle third of the total time indicated (2.75 years). That is to say:

- The effects should *begin* between December 11, 1999 and April 11, 2000 (4-8 months after the eclipse).
- The effects should *last* for 2.75 years after that: until between September 11, 2002, and January 11, 2003.
- The intensification of the effects should begin in the middle third of 2.75 years. Since 1/3 of 2.75 is .916 (or 11 months), they will intensify for an 11-month period in the middle of the entire 2.75 years, depending on exactly when the effects began: so, between November 11, 2000 and March 11, 2001.

For a lunar eclipse, Ptolemy's rules are similar. Suppose this were the chart of a lunar eclipse, lasting 3 hours. The effects would last for 3 months, but would begin 4-8 months after the time of the eclipse, and the intensifications would be within the middle 1/3 of the 3-month duration of the eclipse.

Other authors, though, emphasize the actual position of the eclipse, which suggests another way of measuring the effects. If this solar eclipse lasts for 2.75 years, then let the entire upper hemisphere represent a span of 2.75 years. Let us suppose that the eclipse is in effect from the date of the eclipse itself. Since the eclipse is virtually 50% of the way across the heavens, then we might expect the intensifications to take place halfway through the 2.75-year period, namely after 1 year and 4.5 months, or at the end of December, 2000.

Then again, one might take Ptolemy's rules about when the effects begin, but use its precise position in the relevant third of the heavens, to identify a precise point within the relevant one-third of the intensification. For instance, again the eclipse here is almost exactly 50% through the heavens, which is in the center of the middle one-third of the heavens. This could indicate that the greatest intensification takes place in the middle of the 11-month period of the intensification I described above.

Finally, there is the seasonal hour method of ibn Labban, as described in Ch. II.9 of his *Introduction to Astrology* (and as clarified by Michio Yano). Ibn Labban says that the peak of the eclipse's effects will come according to the following ratio. The time to the peak effect equals:

(seasonal hours from ASC to eclipse * duration of eclipse) / 12

To put it arithmetically, ibn Labban first (a) finds the seasonal hours it takes for the degree of the eclipse to rise from the Ascendant to the place of the eclipse itself. Then, he (b) multiplies this by the duration of the eclipse (presumably as measured in equinoctial hours). Lastly, he (c) divides this product by 12. The result is the time from the eclipse to the peak effects.

Let's take the Munich chart as an example:[14]

(a) The time it takes for the degree of the eclipse (where the Sun is) to rise to the place at the totality, is nothing more than the time between sunrise and the time of the eclipse. In Munich, the Sun rose at 4:07 AM, and the totality was at 11:03 AM, a difference of 6:56 hours, or 416'. If we look at a program such as Janus, we see that on August 11 each seasonal or planetary hour during the day was 72' long—it is summer, so the seasonal hours will be longer than the usual civil length of 60'. If we divide 416' / 72', then we get 5.777 hours as the seasonal time between the Ascendant and the eclipse.

(b) The length of the eclipse in civil hours was 2.75 hours, as mentioned above. (Remember, for Ptolemy this is equivalent to 2.75 years.) Multiply 5.777 by 2.75 to yield 15.888.

(c) Divide by 12 to get 1.324. I take this to mean that the peak effects will take place after 1.324 years from the date of the eclipse, or about 1y 3m 26d. In this case, that gives us a date of December 7, 2000. Although this is not the place to delve into the terrorist attacks of September 11, 2001 in any detail, if we take this eclipse as indicating something about Germany, many of the future terrorists (including members of the Hamburg cell) were arriving in the United States in late 2000, getting certified as pilots, and 'Usama bin Laden picked his "muscle" men for the operation in December.

In the calculation above, I assumed that the measurement of the length of the eclipse was done in equinoctial hours (2.75). But what if ibn Labban wants us to use seasonal hours for it, as well? If so, then since the length of the eclipse was 165' long and the seasonal hours 72' apiece, that yields 2.29 hours or years. The result gives us a peak time of 1.102 years after the eclipse, or September 18, 2000.

Be that as it may, Ptolemy himself wanted to determine the more exact dates by certain planetary motions, to which we now turn. Above, Ptolemy

---

[14] For interesting commentary on this eclipse cast for Kabul, Afghanistan, see www.worldastrology.net/articles/equin.html.

also mentioned that planetary motions at relevant times will also show inten-sifications. This seems to mean the following (**4**): once we find out *when* the beginnings and intensifications are supposed to happen (see above), then observe the following: [1] conjunctions which take place in the relevant signs or in aspect to them, and [2] four phases of the planets which "effect the predicted event." As for [1], in other contexts Ptolemy seems to mean only the superior planets, and I imagine he is especially looking for their conjunc-tions in the sign of the eclipse or its Ascendant, but (knowing Ptolemy) probably also in their trine. When this happens, it shows either an intensifica-tion or abatement, but Ptolemy does not say how to tell the difference.[15]

As for [2], see when one of the planets which rules the eclipse or brings about its effects (see below) makes any of the following phases during the period in which the eclipse is effective, because it will also show intensifica-tions and abatements:

[2a] Arising [from the rays].[16] This produces an intensification.

[2b] Sinking [under the rays].[17] This produces an abatement.

[2c] Stationing: intensification.

[2d] Making an evening phase or advancing in the evening:[18] abate-ment.

This approach is in fact similar to the Persian method of combining profections and transits in annual predictions: the phases and transits of par-ticular planets will show changes throughout the year, but particularly if these things happen in the whole-sign angles of the sign of the annual profection.

Again, if we consider this eclipse in connection with the 2001 attacks, we might consider this. Mars and Saturn are each squaring the eclipse from the angles (in other texts, this is an indication of war). In December 2000 (when members of the Hamburg cell were entering the United States), Mars and

---

[15] These kinds of changes are what later authors like Māshā'allāh identify generally as "times" for observing changes in a phenomenon. See for example my introduction to *Choices & Inceptions*.

[16] *Anatolē.*

[17] *Duseis.*

[18] *Akronuktous phaseis* and *akronuktous...proēgēseis*, respectively. This is ambiguous to me. It might mean (for a superior planet) that it is opposing the Sun in such a way as to rise in the east at sunset (*akronuktous* literally means "at the tip of the night"), but it might also mean (for an inferior planet) that it is arising out of the rays on the western side of the Sun, moving in direct motion.

Saturn were again in these same signs: although Ptolemy does not mention this in the list above, it is something a later astrologer would have noticed, especially since Mars is the lord of the Ascendant of the eclipse. Jupiter, who is on the Descendant of the eclipse and also Ptolemy's mundane lord of the fiery triplicity (see Section IV.2) made an evening setting (setting on the horizon as the Sun rose). Shortly afterwards in January, Saturn and Jupiter both stationed.

Tet. II.7: The kind of beings affected. Having determined what regions will be affected, and for how long and just when, Ptolemy now turns to the kinds of events to expect. This will be shown by the natures and indications of the following (**1**):

[1] The sign of the eclipse itself.

[2] The nature[19] of the ruling planets over the sign of the eclipse and the pivot "before"[20] it.

[3] The sign of those ruling planets.

[4] The constellation of fixed stars ruling over the sign of the eclipse and its "preceding" angle.[21]

It is easy to understand the idea behind [1]: if the eclipse takes place in Gemini, then it will affect Gemini-type things within the regions associated with Gemini.[22] Ptolemy soon supplies a verbal table of such associations (**5-12**), which I insert here as a table:[23]

---

[19] Ptolemy does not bring this up explicitly until *Tet.* II.8 (in conjunction with weather), which is described in my summary of Ptolemy's weather material in Section I.2.

[20] *Pro tēs ekleipseōs.* But see below, where he seems to indicate the one "following" it.

[21] See below.

[22] But perhaps we might add any Gemini-type *places* or *things* anywhere in the world (see Abū Ma'shar's descriptions of landscapes in Section IV.5).

[23] Not every astrologer agreed on every member of these lists. I have followed Ptolemy where he has supplied the categories and their members, but have supplemented the list by people such as al-Qabīsī and Robbins's footnotes.

Type of sign/constellation	Kind of being affected
Human: ♊ ♍ ♎ ♒ ♐ (part); maybe Orion, etc.	Humans
Four-footed: ♈ ♉ ♌ ♐	Four-footed dumb animals
Creeping: ♏, maybe Draco	Creeping, snakes
Northern terrestrial:[24] ♈ ♉ ♊ ♌ ♍	Earthquakes
Southern terrestrial: ♎ ♏	Unexpected rains
Bestial:[25] ♈ ♉ ♌ ♑	Wild animals
Domesticated: ♈ ♉ ♑	Domestic/tamed/useful animals
Winged: ♍ ♐, Cygnus, Aquila	Winged animals, esp. used for food
Sea: ♋ ♑, Dolphin, Argo	Sea animals, fleets
Rivers: ♒ ♓, Argo	Rivers, springs, their animals
Solstitial, Equinoctial (all)	Weather, crop activities in that season
Solstitial	Weather, politics
Equinoctial	Sacred rites and worship
Fixed	Foundations and building
Common (double-bodied)	Humans, kings
Those close to the Ascendant	Crops, youth, foundations
Those near the MC	Rites, kings, middle age
Those near the Descendant	Changes of customs, old age, the dead

Figure 59: Effects of eclipse according to Ptolemy

The eclipse was in Leo, a fixed fiery sign: this indicates the fall of leaders and damage to buildings. In Ptolemy's chorography (Section IV.2), Leo and the fiery signs rule western Europe as well as the Near East, including portions of the Levant, Iraq, Iran, and Saudi Arabia.

As for [2] and [3], Ptolemy describes the determination of the lords in this way (**2-3**). First, we must take each of the following separately, and see which planet has the most relationships[26] to each:

---

[24] For these and the southern terrestrial ones below, I am relying on Robbins's translation of *Tet.* II.7, p. 173 n. 2.

[25] One might perhaps add the second (horse) half of Sagittarius.

[26] *Logous.* This seems to mean that we should treat each relationship equally, rather than assigning weighted points for different types of relationships, as in later medieval techniques of assigning victors. See below for the relationships themselves.

- The sign of the eclipse.
- The pivot or angle which is following upon it.[27]

Following are the types of relationships that matter: the nearest visible applications and separations,[28] those which have a configuration,[29] and the rulership by domicile, triplicity,[30] exaltation, and bound.

For the sign of the eclipse, let's suppose it was at 15° Gemini. I take Ptolemy to mean that we should see which planets are most closely aspecting it by degree (and which are in the upper hemisphere), aspecting by sign, and ruling it by the most of the four dignities just mentioned. The one which has the most of these relationships, will be the ruler over the sign of the eclipse.

The issue of the pivot or angle is less clear, since Ptolemy seems to contradict himself. For in describing the class of beings affected, he first mentioned the angle which was "before" the place of the eclipse (**1**): this suggests the angle to the right or more westward towards the Descendant, since that part of the sky will have arisen earlier and so precedes the place of the eclipse. But later, he spoke of the angle "following" it (**2**): this suggests the angle to the left, or more eastward towards the Ascendant, since that part will arise later and so follows the place of the eclipse. So for example, if the eclipse were in the eleventh house or sign, then the angle "before" the eclipse sounds like the Midheaven, while the angle "following" it sounds like the Ascendant. But if the eclipse were somewhere between the Midheaven and the Descendant, then the angle "before" it would be the Descendant and the one "following" would be the Midheaven. But Ptolemy's style is so brisk and free of examples, that it is hard to say which one he actually wanted.

At any rate, once we have found the ruler or victor over each category (the sign of the eclipse, and the angle), we are to see whether the same planet rules both, or different ones. If the same planet is the victor in each case, then it will obviously be the sole ruler (**3-4**). But if a different planet is a victor over each, use both of them but prefer the ruler over the eclipse (**4**). And if any of these places has more than one planet with the same number of relationships (such as if two planets each have three relationships to the same

---

[27] *Hepomenou.* Again, earlier he had said the one "before" it. See below.
[28] Perhaps this means applications and separations by degree to the *degree of the eclipse itself,* and to the *axial degree* in question.
[29] *Suschēmatismōn.*
[30] Ptolemy could mean the primary *mundane* triplicity rulers (Section IV.2): Jupiter (fire), Saturn (air), Venus (earth), Mars (water).

place), choose the one which is closest to an angle, or is more busy or advantageous,[31] or has a better sect-relationship (**4**). Once we have identified the ruling planet or planets, we must observe its conjunctions and phases as described above, in order to identify various intensifications in the effects of the eclipse.

As for [4] the fixed stars or constellations, we are to look at two possible fixed stars (**4**). The first is any fixed star (of those mentioned in *Tet.* I.9) which is on the "preceding" angle at the eclipse, if it is making one of the nine phases described in *Almagest* VIII.4.[32] The second is if a star of the "group visible at the time of the eclipse" is on the Ascendant or the Midheaven,[33] with the angle "following the place of the eclipse." He does not mention the planetary natures of the stars, but it stands to reason that if such an angular star were of the nature of Venus, then it would supply a Venusian meaning to the eclipse. But certainly, if the constellation were one of rivers or humans and such, it would also add that signification in accordance with the table above.

Tet. II.7: The portion of the beings affected. As for how many of these beings in that region will be affected, Ptolemy says that it will be based on how well eclipsed the luminary is, as well as the relative position of the ruling stars (**13**). The more complete the eclipse, the greater the number of beings. If the planets are in an evening position relative to solar eclipses or a morning one

---

[31] *Chrēmatistikōteron.* For different views on busy or advantageous places, see the Glossary and *ITA* III.4.

[32] This is a bit ambiguous, even though we know exactly what list of configurations Ptolemy means. Let me first explain the major phases, and then discuss how I think he means them. Ptolemy is specifically indicating the third group of configurations in *Alm.* VIII.4, of which there are nine types (and some subtypes). They have to do with stars being placed in such a way that *if* one of the planets (especially the Sun) is on an angle, the star will be on one, too. The nine main types are as follows. First, if the Sun is on the Ascendant, that the star is on the (1) Ascendant or (2) MC/IC or (3) Descendant. Next, if the Sun is on the MC/IC, that the star is on the (4) Ascendant or (5) MC/IC or (6) Descendant. Finally, if the Sun is on the Descendant, that the star is on the (7) Ascendant or (8) MC/IC or (9) Descendant. Now, since an eclipse's totality will rarely be exactly on an angle, Ptolemy must be saying that the *relationship* between the Sun and a star must be such that *if* he were on an angle at that latitude, the star would be too—even though neither of them is actually on an angle at the time of the eclipse. So for instance, one of the subvarieties of (1) is that the star is just emerging from the Sun's rays so as to be visible before dawn: so if it were dawn, they would both be rising somewhat together, but not exactly. In an eclipse chart, this must mean that *if* there were an important fixed star close to the Sun, so that *if* it were dawn it would be visible on the horizon just before sunrise, then that star would be relevant to the eclipse. In the chart of the 1999 eclipse above, such a star could be in early Leo, and probably would have to be in or close to the zodiac itself.

[33] I confess I am not sure what this means.

relative to lunar ones,[34] they affect fewer; if in opposition to the eclipse, one-half; if in a morning position to solar ones or an evening one relative to lunar ones, a majority. As Robbins points out (pp. 176-77), the more the planet's relationship to the eclipse matches the type of eclipse, the more it will affect matters on earth. So, when planets are evening stars in solar eclipses (setting after the Sun) or morning ones in lunar eclipses (rising before her), the positions and luminaries are mismatched, and so will affect fewer; but the contrary is true for the contrary positions.

Tet.II.8: The actual effects. Once we have discovered the region and class, we must examine the ruling planet(s), and its aspects. I have already summarized this in my introduction to Ptolemy's method of weather prediction in Section I.2.

Tet. II.9: [35] *The colors of comets*[36] *and eclipses.* Finally, I offer my own translation of Plato of Tivoli's 1138 Latin translation of the Arabic *Tetrabiblos*, but checked against the translations and editions of the Greek, as found in Robbins, Hübner, and Schmidt's translation of Hephaistio I.24. Again, the bolded sentence numbers refer to Hübner. (See also Sahl in Section III.5 below, Ch. 29, **1-8**).

Tet. II.9: On the colors of an eclipse, and on the tailed stars, and what is like that (*excerpt*)

1 Moreover, for future general matters, the colors appearing at the hour of an eclipse (that is, the colors of the luminaries themselves, and of those which are seen around them, such as those which are called "rods," "halos,"[37] and what is like these) should be observed by us.

When therefore they are black or as though green, they will signify those things which we have said imitate the nature of Saturn. And if

---

[34] I take this to mean that they set after solar eclipses, and rise before lunar ones (and the reverse later in the sentence). Note the relationship between this and positions of "body-guarding" or *doruphoria* in determining status and eminence in nativities (see *ITA* III.28).
[35] In the new critical edition of *Tet.* by Hübner (1998), this is Ch. II.10.
[36] Ptolemy's comments on comets are exceedingly short. Apart from a few comments in this chapter, he writes only a few more words. Following is my translation a short statement from Plato of Tivoli's translation (via Arabic), of *Tet.* II.13.10 (in Hübner, II.14.10): "In fact, tailed stars…always show winds and the dryness of the air; the strength of what happens from this will be according to the multitude of the things [in their heads], and the length of the distance [from head to tail]." That is, the greater and longer they are, the more intense the effects.
[37] Following Hübner's Greek, for Plato's *haleisi, halela.*

they were white, they are said to signify those things which are of the nature of Jupiter. Which if they inclined towards redness, they will designate those things which are of the nature of Mars. And if they appeared to be of the color of gold, they will indicate those things which follow the nature of Venus. But if they were of diverse colors, they will signify those things which are of the nature of Mercury. **2** If however the color will embrace the entire body of the luminary, or that of those which are around it, the future thing will happen in the majority of the regions; but if it occupied any one part of the luminary or of those which are around it, the future thing will come about only in that part which is in the direction of that part in which the color appeared.

3 Moreover, it is appropriate that we observe the tailed stars[38] which will have appeared at the hour of an eclipse (or [any] other time, and also the other general future things[39]): such as are those which are called "rods," "trumpets," or wine-casks,[40] and what is like these, whose natures are likened to the Martial and Mercurial natures which we stated before: which engage in battles, burnings, and qualities which make things be moved,[41] and accidents which happen on account of them.

We will even recognize the places in which future things will happen, from their places in the circle of signs,[42] and from the places which are in the direction of the tailed star.[43]

4 Also, we will discover the type of the signified future thing, and its essence [or] kind, from the form of the glowing [of their heads] which will then appear. But from the quantity of the time of the glowing which appears then, we will know the length [of time] of the future thing. At what hour the future thing will begin, will even be indicated from their affinity with the Sun: for when they will appear more in a morning position, their future thing will appear suddenly; when more in an evening position, their future thing will happen slowly.

---

[38] That is, comets. Some Latin writers viewed comets as having tails instead of hair.
[39] This phrase about general future things does not seem to appear in the Greek.
[40] Reading with the Greek for Plato's *haleisi, abbocat, halhaueni*, which are Arabic transliterations.
[41] Or rather, moved and changed around. The Greek suggests disturbances.
[42] That is, the sign it is in or corresponds to.
[43] That is, where the tail or mane points. But I am not sure if this refers to their cardinal direction, or perhaps a region ruled by another zodiacal sign to which it points.

SECTION III.3: DOROTHEUS ON ECLIPSES

Comment by Dykes. Following is my own translation of several sentences from 'Umar al-Tabarī's Arabic version of Dorotheus (*Carmen* I.1.4-6). One interesting thing about this passage (**4**) is in its use of the triplicities. For Ptolemy, the triplicity *signs* are especially important for indicating regions and things affected by the eclipse; but as reported here, the Arabic Dorotheus emphasizes the *lords* of the triplicity in which the eclipse takes place. For example, if the eclipse were in an earthy sign, then Ptolemy would focus on all of the earthy signs to identify the regions affected, even if the sign of the eclipse itself is most important of them. But Dorotheus would be interested in Venus, the Moon, and Mars, which are the triplicity *lords* of earthy signs, and they are different from the normal, domicile lords of the earthy signs. (The earthy signs are ruled by Venus, Mercury, and Saturn as domicile lords.) Unfortunately, there is no more information here about how to use them.

ℬ   ℘   ℛ

4 And I tell you that [for] every thing, he moreover demonstrates and indicates it as being from the lords of the triplicities;[1] and every thing of tribulation and calamity which strikes the people of the world and the whole of the people—the lords of the triplicities truly demonstrate that; and in an eclipse of the Sun and of the Moon, in [both of] which they[2] indicate the things which are, and until when they are, and in which class [of things] they are.

5 Indeed the Sun, if he is eclipsed and moreover his eclipse is for two hours, then every hour is a year;[3] [as for] what an eclipse of the Moon indicates, [if] her eclipse is for two hours, then every hour is a month.

6 And if the Sun was eclipsed in Aries, I have said that that calamity and tribulation is in the sheep; and if it was in Sagittarius, I have said it is in

---

[1] Pingree treats this part of the sentence as passive ("everything which is decided or indicated"); but since there is no relative pronoun, and 'Umar has put object pronouns on the verbs, I have rendered it as an indirect statement by 'Umar about Dorotheus.

[2] I have translated this passage rather literally. 'Umar is saying that the triplicity lords take a primary role in explaining the indications for both solar and lunar eclipses.

[3] 'Umar does not really mean that every hour is a year *only if* it lasts for two hours: the Ar. *'idhā* ("if") refers to situations which are likely or probable, so 'Umar is stating a likely situation.

workhorses and horses; although if it was in Leo, I have said it is in predatory beasts; and it is said likewise in every essential nature of the signs.

SECTION III.4: MĀSHĀ'ALLĀH ON ECLIPSES

Comment by Dykes. This Section contains material from the Latin versions of two of Māshā'allāh's mundane writings, of which the Arabic is lost.

First, I have included Chs. 5 and 7 (and two sentences from Ch. 8) of a famous short work often called the *Letter on Eclipses* (original Arabic title unknown, see Sezgin p. 106 #18). In my earlier translation of it for *Works of Sahl & Māshā'allāh*, I called it *On the Roots of Revolutions*, following the description in the manuscript BN 16204. I will include the complete text in either *AW2* or *AW3*.

Next I have appended Ch. 40 of *On the Revolution of the Years of the World* (*De Revolutione Annorum Mundi*), which was a Latin translation of the *Kitāb taḥāwīl sinī al-ʿālam.*[1]

℘   ℘   ℘

On the Roots of Revolutions Ch. 5:
On the eclipse of the Moon, and its signification

2 Māshā'allāh said: It behooves you to consider the eclipses of the year (both the lunar ones and the solar ones), and to know the Ascendant of the middle of the eclipse,[2] and the one who is in charge of that same Ascendant and its figure.[3] **3** Which if it were a bad one, it will signify impediment and destruction. **4** But if it were a fortune, it will signify fitness.

5 And know that the eclipse of the Moon, if it were in the cold signs, signifies the severity of the cold, and in watery ones the severity[4] of rains, if the season supported it (that is, if it were winter). **6** But if it were summer, it will signify the temperateness of the air. **7** Understand and test the rest thusly. **8** You should understand this: because if the fortunes aspected the Moon and received her, [the eclipse's] signification will be over those things which they signify concerning good and profit.[5]

---

[1] See Sezgin p. 105, #7.
[2] That is, the totality.
[3] Cf. Ptolemy's own guidelines for finding the victor in Section III.2.
[4] Hervagius 1533 reads, "excessiveness" (*nimietatem*).
[5] *Proficuum.* This should be taken broadly, to include whatever is beneficial or profitable (including good weather).

On the Roots of Revolutions Ch. 7:
On the eclipse of the Sun, and its signification

2 Māshā'allāh said:[6] Know that in the eclipse of the Sun, it cannot come to be but that some great accident[7] is signified, according to the quantity of the eclipse—that is, that it comes to be from the square of the Sun's body, and above that.[8] **3** But the knowledge of those things which happen from the eclipse of the Sun is that you should know the Ascendant of the middle of the eclipse, and the planets conquering over the figures of the eclipse. **4** Which if they were bad ones, they will signify evil and detriment, and the death of kings and the wealthy. **5** And if they were fortunes, they will signify fortune and the fitness of the condition of matters.

6 And you should know that the eclipse of the Sun, if it were in Aries, will signify the ruin[9] of kings and the wealthy, and dryness or the sterility of the earth, and famine; and so in the rest of the fiery signs. **7** But in the watery ones it will signify a multitude of rains, and detriment from them. **8** Understand also that if the fortunes aspected, they will subtract evil; but if the bad ones aspected, they will amplify [the evil] and will subtract fortune.

9 Know even that if the Sun or the Moon were someone's releaser or house-master,[10] and it was [the one] obscured, it will signify a great danger or

---

[6] This chapter and the next should be read along with Chs. 24, 35, and 40 of Māshā'allāh's *On the Revolution of the Years of the World*, which will be translated in *AW2*. I follow Hervagius 1533 through the rest of the paragraph. BN 16204 reads: "Know that in the eclipse of the Sun it cannot come to be but that something great is signified, happening according to the quantity of the eclipse and the planets conquering over the figure of the eclipse. Which if they were malefics, it will signify impediment and the corruption of kings and the wealthy; and if they were benefics, they will signify fortune and the fitness of the condition of matters."

[7] An "accident" is simply anything that befalls us.

[8] My sense is that this sentence and the next (which speaks of planets "conquering") are Māshā'allāh's version of ideas about victors and superior planets in Ptolemy (Section III.2). For at an eclipse, the superior planets in particular would be able to be in a square or trine to the Sun (by sign, if not by degree): thus they are either in a square or "more" or "above that" (i.e., a trine).

[9] *Interitum*, which can also mean "death," but I take it that the translator would have used *mortem* if he had meant death.

[10] *Hyleg vel alcochoden*, also known as the *hilāj* and *kadukhudāh*, two of the primary indicators of longevity in Perso-Arabic natal astrology.

serious infirmity for him whose releaser or house-master it was, unless the fortunes aspected.[11]

On the Roots of Revolutions Ch. 8 [part]:
On the conjunction of the planets and their effect

...8 And know that the conjunctions and the eclipse of the luminaries, if they were in fixed signs, will signify the lastingness of evil and its detriment; and if they were in movable signs, they will signify the smallness of the last-ingness of the evil and its detriment; but if they were in common signs, they will signify mediocre evil. 9 And say thus about the good.

ೞ   ೞ   ೞ

On the Revolution of the Years of the World Ch. 40:
On an eclipse, if there were one that same year

2 After this, look at the topic of an eclipse, if you knew that there would be an eclipse in that same year. 3 And so, look in that year at the lord of the sign in which the eclipse will be, what its condition is, and what kind of place it has with the lord of the Ascendant of the eclipse, and what kind of condition it has from the lord of the year and the significator of the king, and how the fortunes or bad ones aspect it. 4 Because if it were impeded by the aspect of the bad ones, what it signified will be irritated[12] and multiplied, and more strongly so if the lord of the eclipse were the significator of the king. 5 Be-cause if it was the significator of the king, and there were bad ones aspecting it, it will be feared concerning [the king] when the Sun arrives at the Mid-heaven of the eclipse; and if it was the lord of the year, it will be feared concerning the rustics when the Sun arrives at the Ascendant of the eclipse, according to the judgment[13] of the nature of the Ascendant: if it was ac-cording the image of a man, there will be impediment in men; and if it was according to the essence of animals, it will be in animals; and if it was under

---

11 Māshā'allāh probably means that at the moment of the eclipse, the benefics ought to aspect the eclipse position of the luminary. But perhaps their aspect to the *natal* position of the luminary would also be effective.

12 *Exasperabitur.* Or, "made angry."

13 *Rationem.*

the essence of water, it will be in waters, according to the essence of the ascending sign.

6 And know that, of the hours of the eclipse of the Moon, there is a dividing up of one month to every hour; and for the eclipse of the Sun, a year per every hour.

7 After this, look at the bad ones: if they were in the Ascendant or closer to the Ascendant, there will be impediment in the middle part of the earth (which we said belongs to Jupiter and Mercury). **8** And if the bad ones were in the Midheaven, or closer to the Midheaven, it will be in the upper part of the orb (which we have said belongs to Saturn and the Moon). **9** But in the west, or closer to the west, it will be in the lower part of the earth (which belongs to Mars and Venus).

SECTION III.5: SAHL ON ECLIPSES

Comment by Dykes. This Section was originally to be a translation of Chs. 26-29 of Hermann of Carinthia's Latin *Fatidica* ("Prophetic Sayings"), itself a paraphrase of Sahl's large mundane work, *Kitāb taḥāwīl sinā al-ʿālam*. But after comparing Hermann's cramped style to two Arabic manuscripts (Vatican 955, ff. 129-208; Beatty 5467, entire),[1] it was clear to me that his version as written was inappropriate. If his own style was not enough of a problem, Hermann's desire to compress complex material into a few sentences often leads him to skip long sections or omit key phrases, and sometimes he simply gets things wrong. Therefore, I have decided to provide a hybrid version of Hermann's text, which preserves his sentences to a great extent, but with a corrected text based on the Arabic. The number and order of sentences remains the same, and I have not included the Arabic material which Hermann skipped. But while the sentence numbers are still in boldface, I have put brackets around any sentence number for which I have made changes (i.e., the majority of them). In some cases I have only changed a word or two, but in others I have translated the entire sentence directly from Arabic. Where the Arabic is much more extensive, I have tried to balance accuracy against length, giving an accurate translation from Arabic but normally not going beyond what Hermann's Latin own summary covers. The result is something that is still roughly Hermann's summary, but more reliable. In the future I plan to translate this entire work of Sahl's, for a new Arabic series.

Sahl's material is rather straightforward, and the attentive reader will see that he is often reliant on Ptolemy's account of eclipses (which is not surprising), but also on Māshā'allāh. For instance, compare Hermann's Ch. 26, **13-14**, with Māshā'allāh's Ch. 7 of *On the Roots of Revolutions*, **3-5**; likewise Hermann's Ch. 26, **17-24**, with *On the Roots of Revolutions* Ch. 7, **6-7**; and Hermann's Ch. 26, **25-27**, with *On the Revolution of the Years of the World* Ch. 40, **2-5**.

ℬ   ℬ   ℭ

---

[1] Hermann's summary seems to come from the Arabic manuscript transmission represented by Beatty, as his readings are often closer to it. For example, Vatican's lists of significations for a planet are usually longer than Beatty's, and Hermann's summary tends to match the latter.

Chapter 26: Concerning an eclipse

[2] Know that the two eclipses have a powerful effect in the world, and I [will] explain to you what is needed for knowledge of it. 3 And so, one must know that an eclipse cannot happen except around the Head or the Tail. [4] The Tail is cold, its bond is with the two infortunes, and with Saturn especially; and the Head is hot, moist from the nature of the fortunes, and its bond is with the fortunes. 5 Therefore, with an assembly of the benevolents around the Head, there is no greater omen [of good]; with it conjoining the harmful ones, there is no greater misfortune than the Tail. [6] And if the Tail was with the fortunes, it breaks its evil; and the Head with the infortunes breaks their evil. [7] And the worst is [if] the eclipse is with the Head in a house of Mars, or with the Tail in a house of Saturn.

[8] And look at the sign in which the eclipse was: what belongs to it of the quarters of the earth, and of the division of the areas belonging to that triplicity, and what belongs to that sign in terms of cities and existence.[2] [9] And look at the viewpoint of the sign of the eclipse from the Ascendant and the quarters of the circle: for from that viewpoint in which the sign of the eclipse is, is the quarter from which the vice is: the east and the west and the north or the south. [10] And if the sign and the quarter disagreed, (such that one is eastern, the other western, and in this manner), one will have to mix the nature between each, and concede it to the one which was stronger.[3]

11 But an eclipse of the Sun must be feared for those parts of the lands whose sight it [actually] reaches. 12 For if it happens under the earth, it will harm nothing of the upper hemisphere.

[13] And look at the sign of the eclipse, and the place of the eclipse from the Ascendant of the middle of the eclipse, [14] and who is connecting at[4] the beginning of its eclipse, and its middle, and its end, and is it connecting with the infortunes or with the fortunes, [15] and with what colors it is being eclipsed, and what is the nature of the sign of the eclipse. 16 For, these things which are observed steer the certain path of the one judging.

---

[2] Ar. *al-kawn*.

[3] For example, if the eclipse were in a fiery sign (which indicates the east), but in the western quadrant, then one would have to see if there are any special indications for one or the other. William Lilly's approach to this may be found in *Christian Astrology* II, pp. 364-65, 391, and 393.

[4] Ar. *fī*, which can also mean "through, throughout."

[17] For Aries is in charge of all hairy things and four-footed things, but to Leo belong what has claws,[5] and to Sagittarius belongs what has hooves, and a share of the horse, and its liveliness.[6] **[18]** But in Taurus and its trigon, it is harmful to young boys and fruits and trees and vegetation and sheep, and it is like a scarcity of rain and planting. And cows belong to Taurus, **[19]** and to Virgo the plants and food, and it is without rain in it.[7] **[20]** And to Capricorn are goats and everything which is sown at high cost,[8] and vegetation. **[21]** But in Gemini and its triplicity, it is death and killing in men and birds, and the disaster of beasts, and the tyranny[9] of the winds; for Gemini belongs to kings and majesty, **[22]** and Libra belongs to the pious, and trade. **[23]** And Aquarius belongs to the lowest part of [society]. **[24]** But in Cancer and its trigon, it is dangerous enough for waters and aquatic things, for Cancer belongs to everything which descends from heaven, and Scorpio to every water which is flowing, and Pisces to every water which is stagnant.[10]

[25] Erect the Ascendant of the middle of the eclipse, and look at the lord of the sign of the eclipse: how is its place [from its own house][11] and what is its condition relative to the lord of the Ascendant of the eclipse, and what does it have from the lord of the Ascendant of the year and [from] the significator of kings, and how do the infortunes and fortunes look at it? **[26]** And if it looked at the eclipse in [the time of] the eclipse, and it was made unfortunate from an aspect to the infortunes, then what it indicated increases and intensifies. **[27]** And the strongest thing for that is if the lord of the house of the eclipse were the significator of kings: and if it was that, and the infortunes are aspecting it, [there is] injustice upon the king when the Sun reaches the Midheaven of the eclipse. And[12] if it were the lord of the year, there is injustice upon the citizens when the Sun reaches the Ascendant of the eclipse.

---

[5] In a later sentence, Sahl adds that an eclipse of the Sun in Leo has indications for kings.
[6] Ar. *wa-āsharhā*.
[7] Reading *yuqḥiṭu*.
[8] Reading *fī al-ghalāʾ*.
[9] Reading *ʿasf* for *ʿasūf* ("tyrant").
[10] Pisces and Scorpio should be reversed: Scorpio should rule stagnant water, and Pisces flowing water.
[11] Adding with Beatty.
[12] Adding this sentence from Vatican.

[28] And[13] if you wanted to know in which color the eclipse was, then if the eclipse was in Aquarius and its triplicity, or Saturn was in a stake of the [sign of the][14] eclipse, and Mercury in the square of Saturn,[15] then if the eclipse [was] in the bound of Mercury or in the bound of Saturn, then indeed the eclipse is made dusky [so as to be] black, and darkness. [29] And if the eclipse and Mars are in a stake[16] and in addition Mercury is in his[17] house, and he in a bound of Mars, and the Sun and Mercury connecting with Mars, and those two are in one of the bounds of Mars, and especially if the eclipse was in the houses of Mars, [then] indeed that eclipse was made dusky [so as to be] red. [30] And if Jupiter was in one of the stakes of the eclipse, and Venus is looking at him from a portion of the signs, and she was connecting with Jupiter, and Venus in one of their bounds, then indeed that eclipse is made dusky [so as to be] white.[18] [31 And an eclipse of the Head [inclines] toward the white.

[32] And if you wanted to know the greatness of the eclipse's harm (and its smallness), then know whether the eclipse did not emanate throughout the whole country for the number of hours of the eclipse. 33 Therefore, by how many equal hours were found in the whole space of time, [so many] years are counted for an eclipse of the Sun, but one observes [that] number of months for a lunar one. [34] And one appraises [it by counting] between the place of the eclipse up to the Ascendant of the middle of the eclipse, a month for every sign.[19]

[35] And look at the speed of the Moon, and her slowness: [36] for if she was going quickly, that evil is with quickness; and if she was slow, it is slow and lasts long. [37] Also, the superior stars are noted in an eclipse, because if they are found to be standing still, they add to the constancy of the evil, and it lasts long.

---

[13] This paragraph summarizes pp. 202a, ll. 19 – 202b, ll. 5. Beatty reads much differently for some of this, and indeed I do not understand what Sahl is doing. He seems to be saying that *if* certain planetary conditions exist, then the eclipse will be of such-and-such a color. But normally eclipses are observed by their color first, and the color gives an indication for their planetary meaning—regardless of what the planetary configurations happen to be. Sahl presents the usual method (derived from Ptolemy) below, in Ch. 29, **2-5**.
[14] Adding with Beatty.
[15] Beatty adds, "and Mercury with the Sun."
[16] Perhaps this means that Mars is in the stake of the eclipse, just as with Saturn.
[17] Probably Mars.
[18] Hermann now skips a few other color combinations.
[19] See below, Ch. 27, **2**.

[38] And beware in an eclipse of the Moon, three days before and three days after the eclipse, [to see] if these days are unfortunate; and in an eclipse of the Sun, seven days before it and seven days after it.

Chapter 27: On the time of the evil

2 Now, however, the arrival of the evils should be distinguished from their times. [3] For the astrologers portend [that] how many signs come in between, from the Ascendant of the middle of the eclipse up to the place of the eclipse, every sign is a month. [4] And if the Sun entered the sign of the eclipse or the Ascendant of the eclipse, it activates the matter and its animation. [5] However, what the Sun moves in the sign of the eclipse, the Moon will begin in the Ascendant of the eclipse; and conversely, if the Moon entered the sign of the eclipse, that matter emerges on that day.

[6] Moreover, if the sign of the eclipse were closer to the east, it prepares the outcomes of matters within the first four months of the year. [7] If it were closer to the Midheaven, in the following four months. 8 If however to the seventh, it defers the auspices of the matters to the last four. 9 For the emergence of the eclipse's signification by no means lasts [beyond] twelve full months.

[10] Then one must note with whom the Moon (when escaping the eclipse), is applying: a fortune or infortune, of the remaining stakes. [11] For if there were an infortune in the seventh with whom she would apply, or which she would approach [by body], one will have to see if it is in its bound at [their] meeting.[20] [12] For if it was in the seventh, then the country in which the infortune was,[21] is corrupted with a powerful corruption, along with the quarter in which the eclipse was; now if the infortune was in no bound of theirs, it is a little bit easier on the west.

13 Also, the place of the infortune from the Ascendant should be noted. [14] For if it were in a stake of the Ascendant, you know that the mishaps are quick, speedy, and it afflicts the countries which belong to the sign in which the infortune is, [and] what it afflicts more strongly is the quarter in which

---

20 I take this to mean that the malefic planet is in its own bound; see the next sentence.
21 This seems to mean the west, but certain bounds and degrees of the zodiac are also said to be associated with various countries. Sahl seems to be mixing up two different ideas here.

the eclipse was, except if the eclipse is in the Tail: for the Tail indicates people of the lower class in that quarter.

[15] But if that infortune which was in the seventh or in the stakes was Mars, he rejoices in much conflict and discord, he will even attack with hot diseases, and wield his every power with fury. **[16]** Which if it is Saturn, he will vex humankind with chronic sufferings, and introduce death and stomach pains to the people of the nation. **[17]** And if that sign is feminine, and the bound of the planet is feminine, more of it will be from[22] women.

[18] For Mars should be feared for [his effects upon] youths and middle-aged people, but Saturn for old men. **[19]** And if the Tail is with one of the two infortunes, the evil is greater [for] the nation, and the disease and death is from the lower types and the common people; and if the Head is with the infortunes it is in powerful people and their affairs, and the people of [great] houses and leaderships.

20 Then the lights should be considered. **[21]** Which if they apply with the fortunes, and they are in some of the pivots, look at the Ascendant or the lord of the Ascendant or the lord of its bound, and see the place of the Ascendant from that[23] fortune; and if you found the infortune falling away from[24] the place of the infortune, it takes away half of that evil from that quarter, and it does not afflict with any disease[25] the quarter which belongs to that stake in which the fortune was. **[22]** Which if [the luminaries] would apply first to [one kind of planet] and the depart and connect with [another kind], one will have to see with whom they do so first: for if it was first with a fortune, an unfavorable end will follow a prior good beginning, and likewise conversely.

[23] And look at the lord of the Ascendant of the eclipse, and at its Ascendant: does the Moon or the Sun have a claim of exaltation or good luck in it? And if you found one of them bearing witness, and the Ascendant made fortunate,[26] it will resist the evils; which if an infortune would regard the east from a pivot, it corrupts it equally with its parts.

---

[22] Or more likely, "in."

[23] Reading *dhalika* for *dat*.

[24] This must mean, "in aversion to."

[25] Reading *al-ʾāfah* for *al-ʾāfahi*.

[26] Reading the rest of this sentence with Hermann, who has greatly abbreviated the rest of the sentences in this section.

Chapter 28: On an eclipse through the twelve domiciles

2 Finally, one must pursue the diversity of the eclipse through all of the twelve houses or signs, the solution of which puts an end to the work. **3** And so, since one must fear the place of Mars more, he must be considered more powerfully through the whole circle. **[4]** Look at Mars from the sign of the eclipse, and what he has in it of the bound and power in the sign of the eclipse, and does he have a share in that bound, and is he aspecting it from a stake or by assembly, or from a square, or from friendship.

[5] If Mars alone is found to be the governor of that eclipse, [and it is] in Aries, it is agreeable to princes and the knightly order, but fatally unfavorable to the common people. **6** It threatens conflagrations and disputes and controversies to the lands of the sign of the eclipse. **[7]** Here however, if Jupiter regarded the Moon from a strong place, then the aspect to her or to him by the bound or eclipse,[27] [Jupiter] is more powerful than him based on the level of his strength and his share. **8** If even the Head would seem to be around the eclipse, it tempers the Martial violence. **[9]** But if an eclipse of the Sun was in [Aries], and he is aspecting Mars from the degree of his nobility, [and] the beginning of the eclipse is in the Ascendant, then the king of Babylon will [send] a man of the people of his own house upon him.

[10] If however the eclipse were in Taurus, but Mars [is] the governor, with Venus being corrupted by him or by Saturn, it signifies the corruption of the female sex, and an abundance of frequenting prostitutes; also it is dangerous for the kings and the people of the sign of the eclipse, [and] it even signifies the losses of cows and crops. **[11]** Now, if perhaps it happened in that same place around the Tail, it heralds the most severe mortality of boys, riding animals, and cows, and it is worse with Venus being scorched along with Saturn: for that is mortal to the female sex. **[12]** And if it was Mars, then all births [which] are born are annihilated, and it is [*unclear word*] and it corrupts every matter of Taurus based on its rulership.

[13] But if the eclipse were in Gemini, the place of Mercury must principally be noted. **[14]** If therefore Mars or Saturn were found to be the minister, and Mercury was corrupted by Mars, with the corruption of the Moon by one of the infortunes, it increases the killing by the people, and death, and the roads are corrupted by fear and the rain, and they spread death in the public. **[15]** Equally in that same year, whoever will be born in

---

27 Adding with Beatty.

that year will be occupied with death, and they will leave behind certain pains for their parents.

16 If however it were in Cancer, and the Moon was corrupted, and it was based on what I described to you in the matter of Mars or Saturn, and the Moon was corrupted by one of them, and Jupiter was falling,[28] it withdraws[29] the cold, and the snow increases, and rain decreases. **17** It even announces discord between the kings of Cancer, and at the same time diseases in men, corruption in aquatic things, even the eruption of cavities in the earth. **[18]** If Jupiter aspected the Moon from a strong place, it breaks the evil of Mars. **19** Therefore, wherever the eclipse was, one must always note which [stars] are either regarding the Sun or Moon, or are being joined with them. **[20]** And if the Moon is falling, and the infortunes are aspecting her, and Venus is aspecting the eclipse in that area, then the intentions and food and everything the people need for that daily, are corrupted, and at the same time the sprouts of that year; disputes will even be mixed in. **[21]** If Venus were conjoined to Mars in addition, or Mars was aspecting her, it even brings frequent anger into the nuptials of that year.

[22] But if the eclipse were in Leo, with the confusion[30] of the Moon by Mars, it signifies the disputes and discords of the knightly class and of the place belonging to that sign, earthquake, and the terror of the people. **[23]** If the infortunes regarded the Sun from a strong place, then say that one of the powerful kings of the east, the extent of his authority will be destroyed—and likewise in Aries.

[24] But if it were in Virgo, with the Moon being mixed with Mars [and] the benevolents being turned away from the view of the sign of the eclipse, they harm the regions of Virgo with the burden of famine, unless Mercury would be cleansed of the infortunes [and] is aspecting Jupiter: and if it were like that, there is a good condition after the corruption (and it corrupts the essence which belongs to Virgo).

[25] If however it were in Libra, with Saturn or Mars being the governor, and it would be corrupting Venus, some will be deceived by others, and corruption takes place in them, and powerful ones of the nobility of the Arabs will die, and it cuts off the kings, but it increases the rains in Babylon and its borders, and it increases disease.

---

[28] Certainly in aversion to Cancer, but perhaps even cadent from the angles as well.
[29] The mss. read اسلته or اسلّ, but Hermann reads that it will increase the cold (which makes more sense).
[30] Sahl seems to mean their "mixing" or "complexion," by body or aspect.

[26] Also, in Scorpio, with Mars or Saturn being the governor of it, it increases death and fear in the land of the Arabs.

[27] If however in Sagittarius, it harms the knightly order of the various regions, and it harms the assets of kings. **[28]** Here, if Jupiter were found in a pivot from the Moon, or he is aspecting one of the two infortunes from a strong place (Jupiter [having] a portion in it), it takes away from that evil depending on the strength of Jupiter, but there is a plague in horses and in whatever is of the nature of Sagittarius. **[29]** Which if Jupiter is equally turned away and corrupted, plague and disaster afflict science and the powerful and the noble, and the obliteration and harm and fear is great, depending on the place in which Jupiter is.

[30] Also, in Capricorn, with Mars being the governor, then there is corruption for what belongs to the noble and powerful in Capricorn, from the women and men of the common public; and the lower classes will rise up and be strong, and corrupt those of four-footed things, and what is planted, and the fruits [of that], and everything. **[31]** However, if Jupiter was aspecting it from a stake or would trine [it], Jupiter is strong and takes away from the evil of Mars and his corruption in that land.

[32] But if it were in Aquarius, look at the place of Saturn from it; and if Mars is the governor, and Jupiter is falling away from it, and Saturn is strong with the strength of Mars, that ruin belongs to the people of the west…and the Sudan and Ethiopia and Nubia.

[33] And if the eclipse was in the sign of Pisces, earthquakes appear and it confers fear upon the people from the waters and snow, and great collapses[31] in the lands. **[34]** And if Jupiter aspected it from a stake, it breaks the evil of Mars, just as his resources allow.[32]

[35] Finally, wherever the eclipse was, if it [were] around the Tail, it is worse for that sign; but if Saturn were found to be the governor over the place of the eclipse instead of Mars, he will arouse chronic illnesses. **[36]** If Jupiter was falling away,[33] it alters the matter of the Sultan and corrupts the waters and the lands, and vegetation which comes out of the earth. **[37]** Which if Jupiter or Venus would be in a stake, it breaks the evil of Saturn, indeed if they were in strong places belonging to them. **[38]** For the malignity of Saturn is most powerful in an eclipse if Jupiter was falling away from

---

[31] I.e., of things falling down.
[32] This last phrase was probably added by Hermann because Sahl's text goes on to explain other evils: thus Jupiter cannot wholly rescue the situation.
[33] That is, "in aversion."

him and the eclipse was in the houses of Mars, for the hostility of Saturn in these two signs. [39] But if it were in the houses of Venus, Mars however being weak, and the confusion of Venus with Saturn, it decreases cheer. [40] However, an eclipse of the Sun with Saturn is more intense than with Mars, [especially] if Saturn was the governor over the eclipse, and more intense is if his eclipse was in Aries and its triplicity; and if Jupiter was aspecting him from a stake, it diminishes the malignity of Saturn.

41 Then[34] the place of the eclipse from the Ascendant must be noted, and at the same time even the places of the infortunes must be noted, and one must judge, in the accidents of matter, in terms of the disposition and status of the star, and the dignity and nature of the place. [42] Even every scorched star is harmful to its portion [of places and things]. [43] After this, one must write down the Ascendant of the middle of the eclipse, [to see] in what sign or bound it is, even the place of the eclipse [to see] in whose bound it is, and which ones of the stars would be regarding [it] from whatever place.

[44] And so indeed if the eclipse was in the Ascendant, or the infortune was aspecting it from the Ascendant, the harm is to life; and if it was in the second from the Ascendant, in money, and thus through the order [of houses], according to the signification of each house and the nature of the sign. [45] And know that an eclipse of the Sun, if it was in the seventh from the Ascendant, and Saturn in the eighth, and Mars in the sixth or in the Ascendant in the degree of life, aspecting the Sun when he ascends and rises with the middle,[35] and that hour begins from the Sun at his setting [which] belongs to the place [Mars] is in and his strength,[36] then indeed the kings are afflicted, [and there is] starvation and death and epidemic and strong pain, based on the extent of the ascension of the sign at the height of the region.[37]

[46] If the eclipse were in an earthy sign, and the infortunes the governors, [there will be] earthquakes and the crashing and demolishing of large cities and great walls, and ruins and homes.

[47] If it was in the sign of Cancer and its triplicity, it corrupts the waters, and the harm is in the dew. [48] If the Moon and the lord of her house were increasing in computation, that corruption was from an abundance of dew; if

---

[34] This paragraph is redundant, and it suggests that Sahl is borrowing from some other source which contained it.

[35] Probably "the middle of the eclipse."

[36] I do not understand this long description of Mars's place.

[37] That is, based on the ascensional time of the sign: presumably, a short or crooked sign would have fewer problems or at least for a shorter amount of time.

decreasing, through the diminishment of moisture. **[49]** If the infortunes were aspecting the lights, they diminish waters and make the land parched. **[50]** And look, in an eclipse of the Moon in this triplicity, at the lord of the house of the eclipse, and at the lord of its bound, and at the Ascendant of the eclipse, and is it in an angle of the first (and that is the Ascendant), and the place of the Moon from the Ascendant. **[51]** For if the Moon was in the Ascendant or in a stake of the Ascendant, or the lord of the bound of the Moon was in the Ascendant, and it is one of the infortunes, the dew decreases and is held back, and especially if the eclipse was with the Tail (and it stimulates the blowing of winds). **[52]** But if it was with the Head, it does not start and there is no corruption. **[53]** But if the Sun suffers [eclipse] in this triplicity³⁸ around the Tail, and one of the infortunes is in that sign with the lights, and after the eclipse [the two lights] were moving towards the infortunes, it prevents that rain in all of that year. **[54]** If the two infortunes were in a square of the lights, or in the opposition, or it was in a trine, the damage is less. **[55]** Now, if they would be connected with the fortunes after the infortunes, they will give rains at the end [of the year], but without great advantage; and if their connection was with the infortunes after the fortunes, then the rain is at the beginning of the year.

[56] But if the eclipse were in a sign of feathers, such as Virgo and Sagittarius, or the image of fowl or the Flying Vulture³⁹ and what is like that, then the harm of the eclipse is in flying things and every feathered thing, and greater than that in whatever flying things are given to human use.

[57] And if the eclipse was in Pisces and Cancer and Capricorn and Aquarius, the harm is in animals of the sea, and ships; and animals of the river are Aquarius and Pisces, and they are the indicators over what happens in the river. **[58]** And if the eclipse was in a masculine one of the signs (a straight one),⁴⁰ then it is an indicator of the corruption of the atmosphere, and a corruption of the time which follows it, like Cancer belongs to the summer, and Libra the autumn.

---

³⁸ Omitting Vatican's parenthetical remark that this is the "earthy" or "dusty" one. Sahl still seems to be speaking of the watery triplicity.
³⁹ The constellation Aquila, called the Flying Vulture (*Vultur Volans*) by the Romans.
⁴⁰ Following Beatty and Hermann; Vatican lists both the crooked and the straight.

[59] And if it was in Aries it indicates the corruption of the trees and produce, and in Cancer[41] the harm is in vegetation and grasses, and in Libra the
harm is in plants and grasses and in Capricorn the harm is in legumes and in
birds, and fish. [60] And if it was in Aries and Libra (signs of equality),[42] the
harm is in mosques and the houses of those worshipping God. [61] Now, if
the eclipse was in the fixed signs, the harm is in foundations and structures;
and if it was in those of two bodies, the harm is in the people and kings.

[62] And if the place of the eclipse was towards the east, the harm is in
the youths of the people; and if it is in the Midheaven, the harm is in
mosques and kings and the middle-aged, and he of the people who is in the
middle;[43] and if the place of the eclipse is towards setting, the harm is in the
sheikhs and the elderly.[44]

[63] And[45] their harm is if the eclipse was on the longest day (that is, at
the beginning of Cancer), or it was an eclipse of the Moon at the longest
night (while the Sun enters Capricorn).

[64] Finally, one must especially observe where Saturn is from the Moon,
at an eclipse of the Moon: if he was aspecting from the Ascendant of the
beginning of the eclipse and its middle, and its completion. [65] No less
must one observe the place of the eclipse (perhaps the eclipse is beginning in
the Ascendant or in the Midheaven); and look at the lord of the completion,
and how are their places, and are they aspecting or not, and [by] how many
degrees their rays reach, towards the direction of the rays of the Sun and the
Moon. 66 Also, it will be good to consult the lord of the Moon, with the lord
of the bound of the eclipse, as to whether greater power in the eclipse would
be granted to them or to others.

[67-68] If the eclipse was not in a stake, and those planets are aspecting
from reverting[46] places or they were also withdrawing in the sixth and in the
twelfth, and the lord of the reception[47] was aspecting from the opposition in
a place of destruction, and in addition it is in the place of its setting, and
there was an eclipse of it in a defective sign, and the lord of its house was not

---

[41] Following Beatty and Hermann; Vatican gives a different list of significations, including
"plate armor," evidently due to the crab's hard shell. But this gives Cancer and Libra very
similar indications; only a critical edition will help distinguish these lists properly.
[42] Or, "the equator." Night and day are of equal length at the equinoxes.
[43] I take this to mean "the middle class."
[44] Hermann now skips the equivalent of 1.5 pages in the Vatican ms.
[45] This is actually a partial sentence, embedded in larger discussion about kings.
[46] That is, "cadent."
[47] I am not sure exactly how Sahl is using this word here.

aspecting it, and the infortunes are aspecting in addition, then say it is not good in that eclipse. **69** But[48] the regard of the benevolents or the harmful ones to the eclipse, must [also] be wholly observed.

[70] At any rate, once all things (in terms of the status and disposition of the stars) have been looked at by reason and intellect, the most certain things of the matters will come: so that if Mercury were the lord of the eclipse, it afflicts the youths of his type. **[71]** If he was with Mars, it is measles and smallpox and wounds and scabies; and if it was Saturn, the oppression is from spirits[49] and fear and a pain of the belly, and malicious diseases.

72 Thus if the eclipse were even in Aries, it is harmful more to the head and eyes, and especially if Aries is in the east. **[73]** And if there was Venus or Jupiter, it defends [against] some of this evil, if they were aspecting; and if Jupiter was the one with Saturn or Mars, aspecting him, it afflicts power and honor and the pious, namely[50] in terms of the admixed nature of the sign, in the way it was said about the four-footed or watery signs. **[74]** But the worst danger of an eclipse is whenever Mars regards by a tetragon, with the lord [of the eclipse] being scorched, opposing the Moon, and Jupiter in aversion.

[75] And look at Saturn and at the hour in which the eclipse begins, and: how is his strength and authority, and his place in terms of excellence, and [his] bearing towards the threefold Ascendant of the eclipse.[51] **[76]** And if he was in the Ascendant or aspecting it, it harms the world, and it is more intense for that if Mars was in the degree of the Midheaven. **77** Now, if both are in the east, they improve nothing.

Chapter 29: On colors

2 In the last place, the various significations [which are] interpreted by astronomical reason, and the power of the indicators enumerated, wholly attain the final end of the prophetic sayings.[52]

---

[48] This sentence is extremely generic and does not easily match either the previous sentences or the following ones in Vatican.
[49] So reads Beatty, but Hermann has "nocturnal terrors," and Vatican "friends of blackness," so this probably means nightmares.
[50] Hermann has now skipped a sentence, but his fundamental idea is correct.
[51] That is, at the beginning, middle, and end of the eclipse.
[52] Hermann wrote this prematurely, as Sahl then continues to discuss the rulership of the planets over the eclipse (see below).

[3] And so, if it is eclipsed by black, it harms the people and the earth which belongs to that sign, and its people, and prices increase, and diseases multiply, and a noble man perishes, a chief of the nature of Saturn. [4] And if it is eclipsed by red, it afflicts the nobility and the knights, and the majority of the nation, and the tribulation enters upon the people of the country which belongs to that sign, and it is of the nature of Mars. [5] And if it is eclipsed by white, and red mixes with it, it afflicts by prices, except that it is not like the first one in the people:[53] and this is of the nature of Jupiter. [6] And if it is eclipsed by black and red, it afflicts by means of the rain, and death spreads in the people, and the intensity enters upon the lower class of the people. [7] And if the wind blows from the side at the time of the eclipse,[54] it indicates tribulation which is in the area from which the wind blows.

8 Then[55] one must note in what quarter of the circle the eclipse happens, by night or day. 9 For if it were in the first [quarter], it is unfavorable to prominent people and the wise; but in the second one, it wounds princes and the knightly order; in the third, it harms the nobility and the powerful and the public; and if it was in the fourth quarter, it scatters the necessities of men.

10 Therefore, once the aspects to the eclipse have been considered, and the place of the eclipse itself, in whatever dignity it is, and once all of the planets have been placed throughout the circle, then finally the fixed [stars] will come into the judgment. 11 But not all of them: for, being unlimited, they exceed the ingenuity of a man. [12] So,[56] look at the light which was closer to the fixed star [in] the section of the sign of the eclipse, or the victor[57] which was in the stake of the tenth,[58] then see what was in the Ascendant in terms of these fixed stars, or in the Midheaven at the hour of the eclipse: and if you knew the fixed star, then it is the indicator over the matter of the eclipse, so know its manner and the manner of the sign in which the eclipse is, and the planetary manager from among the seven plan-

---

[53] Hermann reads this as though it means the harm to prices will be slight.
[54] But in Ptolemy (*Tet.* II.9.2), this has to do with how completely the color *surrounds* the eclipse. So if the color is only on the eastern side of the eclipse, then it will affect regions to the east; if fully surrounding the eclipse, then people everywhere; and so on.
[55] See a previous statement on this, in Ch. 28, **62**.
[56] Compare this with my discussion of *Tet.* II.7 above.
[57] This should probably read simply, "the fixed star." Perhaps Sahl means that a star on the Midheaven will be victorious over the other stars which may be in significant places.
[58] Vatican reads, "and the light which was in the tenth from it."

ets, and from that one knows in which type [of thing] that damage appears over the nature of that sign, based on what I am describing to you.

[13] And know that the lights are the two kings of the planets, and the managers of their matters, and overpowering belongs to them, and as they obtain the position of command in the effects of the stars, so does their suffering[59] [of eclipse] suggest the harms of the world to the senses. [14] And if the king of the stars is eclipsed, it harms the world and corrupts the essence of the signs and the images and bounds which are eclipsed in it, with the place of the eclipse from the Ascendant, and from the Ascendant of the conjunction[60] and the Ascendant of the year in which the eclipse was, unless perhaps the kings are weak and unlucky: they damage the people and it corrupts their kingdoms, and the tribulation enters upon the people because of the weakness of their kings, and likewise if these two kings are eclipsed they afflict the world.

[15] If Saturn was the ruler[61] of the management of the eclipse and of its bound, it produces the corruption of the cold and snow. [16] And if his indication was in people,[62] it makes prolonged pains appear in the people, and tuberculosis and moisture and the common cold, and quartan fever, and edema of the belly, and fear and death in the diseases of humans, and sheikhs and old people. [17] And if his indication was in animals which men use, it wears out their bodies and food. [18] And if his indication was in the air, it causes the most intense cold to manifest, and fog, and ice, and tribulation in it, [*unclear word*] and gloomy clouds, and abundant, corrupting rains which are unsuitable and not beneficial, and it increases the roughness of the earth, which harms the people. [19] And if his indication was in seas and rivers, it pollutes their waters and destroys ships, and reduces the fish and destroys them. [20] And if his indication was in produce and what comes from the earth, it corrupts and diminishes by means of worms and locusts and fire, and abundant rain and cold, until starvation and disaster reaches the people.

[21] And if Jupiter was the ruler of the management of the eclipse and its bound, it makes health and gentleness appear in people.[63] [22] And if his indication was in animals which belong to people, it increases [them], and it destroys and diminishes those which do not belong to people. [23] And if

---

[59] Reading *passiones* for *passionis*.
[60] Ar. *qirān*, normally referring to the Saturn-Jupiter conjunction.
[61] Ar. *wālī* (here and below), equivalent to a governor (*mustawlī*): basically, the victor.
[62] Here and throughout, Sahl seems to mean that the *planet* is in a *sign* of such a type.
[63] This must be provided that the *sign* is also a human one.

his indication was in air, the atmosphere is excellent,[64] suitable, windy, good, [and] normal for what is on the earth. **[24]** And if his indication was in rivers, it is healthy[65] and it makes ships safe on the seas. **[25]** And if his indication was in the fruits of the earth, then it is fertile.

[26] And if Mars was the ruler of the management of the eclipse and its bound, it perpetrates evil and corruption from dryness. **[27]** And if his indication was in people, it makes fighting manifest, and wars, and dryness, and servitude,[66] and the anger of the people, and death, and a disease from a fever of heat, and the effusion of blood. **[28]** And that is with juveniles and young men, and it causes difficult straits and yellowness[67] and fire, and killing, and thieving. **[29]** And if his indication was in air, it manifests intense heat, and a *simoom*[68] with its burning, and it causes the measles and smallpox, and lightning, and it reduces the rains and [there is] drought; and if his indication was in seas, it sinks ships by means of winds [and] lightning, and it burns them with lightning; and as for rivers, it reduces the waters in them and dries out springs and boils the rivers. **[30]** And if it was animals which belong to men, and trees and produce, then there manifests in it a great decrease and intense corruption from burning and the intensity of the wind.

[31] And if Venus was the ruler of the management of the eclipse and its bound, then she indicates the [kind of] value that Jupiter indicates, except that it is with pleasure and delight and rejoicing; and if her indication was in people, it makes weddings happen, and rejoicing, and thus and so on she answers to the teaching of Jupiter, through all things in which we offer congratulations.

[32] And if Mercury was the ruler of the management in an eclipse, it indicates approximately what is the nature of the planet which is mixed with him. **33** But if the leadership of the eclipse were committed to [Mercury],[69] he arranges travels, works at winds, quickly releases the business of commerce, [and] even is helpful for four-footed things and trees. **[34]** And if

---

[64] Reading as *mumtāz*.
[65] Reading as *yaʿdhā*, closer to Vatican.
[66] Reading with Beatty for an unclear word in Vatican.
[67] Reading as *al-ṣafār*. Perhaps this means jaundice, or else yellow bile (choler) and the angry attitudes which come with that.
[68] A kind of hot desert wind.
[69] Herman had read "the Sun." This apparently simple sentence summarizes about five lines of text in Vatican.

[Mercury's] indication was in the waters and rivers, then if he were western, it inundates[70] them; and if he was eastern, it expands them.

[35] And this is what the planets indicate if they were rulers of the management [of the eclipse] and of its bound. Which if the infortunes were mixed with them, they increase in evil, and if the fortunes were mixed with them, they subtract from the evil. [36] And if the infortunes were rulers of the management of the eclipse, and they were in agreeable places of it, and the fortunes were aspecting them, they subtract from their damage. 37 But[71] contrariwise, the benevolents being oppressed by the unfavorability of place and by the power of the harmful ones, become less effective.

---

[70] Reading as *yugharriq*. But Hermann reads this as though it depletes waters, which at least makes sense since he still increases them while eastern.
[71] I have left this sentence as it is, since it makes good astrological sense (although the Arabic does not quite read this way).

SECTION III.6: IBN EZRA ON ECLIPSES

Comment by Dykes. The following is my own summary of sections from the two versions (I, II) of Abraham ibn Ezra's *The Book of the World*, in the critical edition by Sela.

ೞ   ೞ   ೲ

(I.29-31, II.6-10). Solar eclipses have great power over mundane events,[1] provided they are total; if not, they will be minor. At any total solar eclipse, note the Ascendant at the time of the eclipse,[2] and the sign of the eclipse itself.

The effects will be indicated for the class of beings indicated by the sign of the eclipse: for example, humans if in human signs, or watery things if in watery signs.

Benefic planets aspecting the luminaries (or Mercury, provided he is also with benefics) will bring health and good effects, while malefics will bring misfortune. But beware of malefics and Mercury if they are closely conjoined with or aspecting the Sun at a solar eclipse, or the Moon at a lunar eclipse. Mercury is particularly malefic if he is with malefics in this condition. If any of the two malefics or Mercury are also in each other's houses, it is worse.[3] Under the rays, they cannot harm.

If there is harm, it will especially affect cities whose sign is the place of the eclipse, and the harm will come from cities whose sign is the place where the harmful malefic is,[4] and in accordance with the type of planet it is. But if any of the benefics or Mercury is in an angle, and also a malefic, then it is bad: if in the fourth and a malefic is there, it damages agriculture (and if it is Saturn

---

[1] *Book of the World* II.6.1. This implies that lunar eclipses are not as important.

[2] Ibn Ezra specifies the "true" conjunction of the luminaries (I.29.3), suggesting that for determining the effects, the Ascendant at the time of the totality is the desired one. See my introduction, where I suggest that one might also take the Ascendant at the *beginning* of the eclipse to indicate partial effects.

[3] *Book of the World* II.7.3. This must mean, "provided they are aspecting the Sun at a solar eclipse or the Moon at a lunar one."

[4] For example, if the eclipse happens in Cancer, and the luminaries are harmed by a malefic in Aries, then countries ruled by Cancer will be harmed by countries ruled by Aries.

in an earthy sign, by an earthquake); if the tenth, the government; if the seventh, wars and domestic unrest.[5]

The effects of solar eclipses will last for as many years as the equinoctial hours over which the eclipse takes place; those of lunar eclipses, for as many months as there are hours (but one should also factor in the fractions of hours).[6] Then see where above the horizon the eclipse takes place: if near the Ascendant, at the beginning of that period; if near the tenth, the middle; near the Descendant, the end. The most intense effects will happen at the moment corresponding to the proportional place of the total eclipse. But some people say that an eclipse in the southeastern quadrant will make things happen quickly, and in the southwestern one, later.[7]

For lunar eclipses, treat the whole region above the earth as being a maximum of one year. The position of the Moon at the total eclipse will show when, in that year, the intensification takes place. The effects will happen in cities whose sign is that of the eclipse or if that sign is one of the angles of the Ascendant of that city.

---

[5] This passage is worded confusingly and I am not sure that ibn Ezra is accurately reporting his source. Suppose that both benefics are in the fourth, with Saturn: why would they not overpower his malice?

[6] That is, if the eclipse is for 3.3 hours, then one should also include .3 of a year or month.

[7] This is not really different from Ptolemy's view, except that the view of these "others" is more general.

SECTION III.7: SAHL ON COMETS

Comment by Dykes. This Section contains a few sentences by Sahl on comets (here also called "meteors"), from the mundane work mentioned in Section III.5. Hermann's Latin summary of this material goes on to describe the indications of comets in the signs, but since I have not yet found these descriptions in the Arabic manuscripts, I have omitted them. (Hermann's summary may come from some later passages in Sahl's text.) As with the other passages from Sahl in Section III.5, I have primarily used Vatican 955 (p. 165b), but have also consulted Beatty 5467.

ಬ   ಬ   ಜ

Chapter: On the ascent of meteors, and the marks of the Sun[1]

2 Look, with respect to the appearance of stars which have tails, with the eclipse (or when[ever] they appear), for they bring about the nature of Mars and Mercury,[2] and it provokes fighting and war, and the generality of them indicate kings and scholars and the powerful.

3 And look at the area in which it travels, [but] do not look for it as you look at the course of the planets and the eclipse and the aspects belonging to them. **4** If it was moving in the elevated path, that evil[3] was from the share of Saturn and the Moon. **5** And if it is in middle path, that was in the share of Jupiter and Mercury. **6** And if it was in the lowest path, it was in the share of Mars and Venus.

7 And see in which sign it appears, and the condition of the lord of that sign in its own place, and how the infortunes and the fortunes are looking at it and at the patriarch [of it].[4] **8** And if it appeared in the signs of kings (and they are the ones of fire) and the lord of the sign is aspecting from a strong place, there goes out in that area one who contends in the dominion, of the people of the house of the king, and a notable person. **9** And if the lord of

---

[1] Sahl's material on the marks (or points, or signs) of the Sun is omitted here.
[2] This is very close to Hephaistio I.24, except that Hephaistio seems to say that only certain types of comets are Martial and Mercurial. Nevertheless, few of the indications for comets are at all positive, so perhaps Sahl is right to read things this way. See also comments by Ptolemy on this, in *Tet.* II.9 (see end of Section III.2).
[3] Adding with Beatty.
[4] Reading tentatively as *al-batrak*. Hermann seemed to read it this way, as he has "the lord."

the sign did not aspect it, he was one of the sons of the nobility, except that he is not suitable for a kingdom. **10** And likewise it decreases in all of the signs.[5]

11 And know that the houses of the Sun and of Jupiter and of Mars indicate the sons of kings, and likewise that of Saturn indicates those who are notable in the regions [and] their lineage in the world; and in Capricorn he perishes.[6] **12** And the house of the Moon is inferior to the house of the Sun, and the house of Mercury inferior to the house of Jupiter, and the house of Venus lower than the house of Mars.

13 And the harm is in the type of sign in which the tailed [star] appears, and in its manner; and the area in which the matter takes place, is known from the path of its tail; and the events are in the direction in which the planet [points][7] its tail (of the quarters of the circle). **14** And as for the time at which the evil begins, that is known from the easternness of it and its westernness.[8] **15** And indeed if it was eastern, what it indicated [begins] quickly [and] immediately. **16** And if it was western, there is a delay and slowing down in the appearance of the accidents. **17** And as for the length [of time] which it indicates, it is known from the time of its appearance and its concealment, and from the lodging-place[9] from the Sun.

---

[5] Reading *al-burūj* with Beatty and Hermann, for Vatican's *al-ḥurūb* ("wars").

[6] I take this to mean that if the comet is in Capricorn, the person *indicated by* Saturn will perish.

[7] Unclear word, in both Beatty and Vatican.

[8] That is, rising before the Sun (eastern) or after the Sun (western).

[9] *Manzil*, which normally means "mansion," but here may simply mean where it stands relative to the Sun.

SECTION III.8: THE ARABIC AL-RIJĀL ON COMETS

Comment by Dykes. The following three excerpts from al-Rijāl's *The Book of the Skilled* cover both comets and—it seems—shooting stars. All are a little unusual in their own way. I have translated them from the Arabic.

The first selection is a small portion of al-Rijāl's Ch. VIII.23, which describes the indications for comets which appear above the planets and the Nodes. The key question here is, what does it mean to be "elevated" or "raised up" (Ar. *'ashrāf*) over or above another planet? Normally, we can assume that this refers to "overcoming," a situation in which one planet is zodiacally "above" and aspecting another planet by being in an earlier sign, especially in the tenth sign from it.[1] An example would be a planet in Leo overcoming a planet in Scorpio—no matter which houses in the chart those signs actually occupy. And indeed, previous paragraphs speak of the planets being elevated over comets. But at the end of Ch. 23, al-Rijāl says: "And this judgment is said about the planet if any of them is elevated over any [other], and if any of them is conjoined to any, and if the lights of any of them are located on any [other]." So al-Rijāl's or his source does mean to speak more broadly about planetary configurations. In the case of comets below, I would like to suggest something else: that the comet is appearing spatially higher in the sky, right above one of the planets in the zodiac.

The next selection is the second half of Ch. VIII.32. The first half was from 'Umar's *Book of Questions* Ch. 138, which was already translated above in Section I.5. This second half is from an unknown author, but lacking 'Umar's complete text myself, it is possible that it continues the views of 'Umar. It is slightly unusual because it begins abruptly with comets after a discussion of general disasters shown by ingresses: the author seems to treat comets as though they are appearing during the ingress itself, but what about those appearing at other times?

The third selection is Ch. VIII.41, which in the Latin version is treated as though it deals with comets, but there is no indication of that here. Instead, the text speaks of stars that are shooting down or dropping down, which implies something like bright meteors. This is unusual, because large meteors (like shooting stars) are so transient, it seems highly unlikely that they should receive such a detailed treatment. Moreover, since they happen so quickly, how would anyone be sure exactly what constellation or sign they are appar-

---

[1] See Schmidt 2009.

ently dropping down from? I am tempted to say that the chapter is really about comets, but nothing prevented al-Rijāl from simply using the normal terminology for comets, and comets were always part of astrological lore, so why does he say that he used to doubt them? Perhaps if we can recover the texts of the two authors he mentions below, we will have the answer.

ℬ   𝔰𝔬   ℭℜ

The Book of the Skilled VIII.23 (part):
On the elevation of the planets, from The Book of Events

If[2] [a comet] is elevated above Venus, it indicates the decrease of the waters. And if it is elevated above Mercury, it indicates a scarcity of youths and their destruction. And if it is elevated above the Moon, it indicates the destruction of all assets. And if it is elevated above Saturn, it indicates intense illnesses. And if it is elevated above Jupiter, it indicates the killing of the nobles and people of distinction. And if it is elevated above Mars,[3] it indicates the union of weapons and intense fighting. And if it is elevated above the Head, it indicates the killing of the nobles and people of distinction. And if it is elevated above the Tail, it indicates the destruction of the fruit of the trees. And if it is elevated above Mercury, it provokes malice and evil.

The Book of the Skilled VIII.32 (second part):[4]
On knowing when conflicts, wars, burnings,
& submersions will happen

18 And know that that haired [star],[5] if it was arising[6] at the time of the transfer of a year or quarter in one of the signs, then indeed it appears in the place of Mercury in the year. **19** If he was eastern, then it is seen in the east; and if he was western, then it is in the west. **20** And it departs if Mercury is burned up.

---

[2] I have not added sentence numbers to this paragraph, as it comes at the end of a long chapter I have not translated.
[3] The Arabic suddenly uses the Persian term for Mars, Bahrām. This suggests a Persian background for the text.
[4] Original source for this part of the chapter unknown at this time.
[5] That is, a comet.
[6] That is, if it were appearing or making its presence known.

21 And if it was in the area of the sign, then indeed the evil is in the share of Jupiter and Mercury, in terms of countries and creatures. **22** And if it was in the belt of the highest (and that is what follows the north), that was in the share of Saturn and the Moon. **23** And if it was in the area of the lowest (and that is what follows the south), it was in the share of Venus [and Mars].

24 And see to which of the planets it belongs, and does it belong to a fortune or infortune, and how the fortunes look at it (or they are assembling with it), and judge that the evil is upon the people of the countries which that sign is in charge of. **25** And if it was of the signs of kings,[7] there appears a king from the side which the planet is on, fighting and capturing and burning and destroying. **26** And if it was of the signs of the powerful people,[8] the killing is among those [who are] below kings. **27** And the greatness of the evil and its smallness is based on the power of that hair or the fires[9] in its place, and the power of the aspect of the infortunes upon it.

The Book of the Skilled Chapter VIII.41:
On the shooting-down of the stars

2 I appended this section in my book when it [seemed] correct to me, with the experience of the death of ibn Alī al-Hussein and Sa'īd bin Hardūn,[10] since[11] before he died I did not hold nor believe that it had a signification nor any efficacy.

3 If a star shoots down from Aries, it splits the heavens and its activity remains; indeed the king dies, and in the land of the Romans and Babylon there is intense combat.

4 And if it dropped down from Taurus, then many cities among the Romans are destroyed, and the plague occurs in Babylon.

---

[7] Normally, these are the fiery signs.
[8] Probably the signs of the Sun, Jupiter, and Mars, as seen in Sahl (Section III.7, **11-12**) and Abū Ma'shar (Section III.9, Ch. 72, **17**).
[9] This could also be read as "lights," referring to the luminaries. But I think it makes more sense to treat this as the fiery light comprising the comet's tail.
[10] Nuruosmaniye reads this name as either Hazrūn or Hadhrūn. Both are unknown at this time.
[11] Reading the rest of the sentence with the Latin, as the Arabic does not quite make sense to me and may involve idiomatic expressions.

5 And if it dropped down from Gemini, then evil afflicts the land of the Romans and the king of Egypt dies in that year, and a good man will begin in his place, and there is plague and illness in the region of Persia.

6 And if it dropped down from Cancer, then there is evil in the Hijāz and the son of the king dies in battle, then a little later the king dies.

7 And if it dropped down from Leo, then the king dies and his enemy is made happy, and there goes out in the region of Babylon one who contends in the kingdom, and predatory beasts are aroused.

8 And if it dropped down from Virgo, then the king kills his enemy in the land of Egypt, and he sows discord in it.

9 And if it dropped down from Libra, the king encounters evil from [his] subjects in secret and [under] a veil.

10 And if it dropped down from Scorpio, it increases fires in countries and decreases the water of rivers.

11 And if it dropped down from Sagittarius, there is plague in the land of Babylon and Baghdad, and the king of them dies.

12 And if it dropped down from Capricorn, there is great evil in the Hijāz from wars, and other things besides that.

13 And if it dropped down from Aquarius, then a weak man goes out and takes the kingdom, and his survival in the kingdom is for a short time; then there is intense fighting after that.

14 And if it dropped down in Pisces, then the king acts justly with respect to [his] subjects, and there is security and an abundance of rains.

SECTION III.9: ABŪ MA'SHAR ON COMETS

Comment by Dykes. Following are two selections taken from Latin translations of Abū Ma'shar's works. The first selection is from the work *Scito horam
introitus*, which seems to be a translation of the Arabic *Book of the Revolutions of
the Years of the World* (Sezgin pp. 142-143). It must be based on Sahl or Sahl's
source. The translation here is based on Paris 16204, Erfurt 365, and London
Harley 1; the full translation will appear in *AW2*.

The second selection is a short excerpt from the end of the Latin *Flowers*,
which I have placed here for easy access; the rest of his statements on comets from the *Flowers* can be seen in Chapter VII.1 of that work, in *AW2*.

ༀ   ༀ   ༀ

Book of the Revolutions of the Years of the World
(Inc. *Scito horam introitus*)
Chapter 72 (excerpt): [Comets]

8 And[1] look at the flying stars which are specks of fire: because they always will appear in the place of Mercury. **9** And if Mercury were in the east,
they will be seen in the east; and if he were in the west, they will be seen in
the west. **10** And their receding will be the burning of Mercury.

11 Look at the part [in] which they were: if they were in the lower journey,
the evil will be in the part of Mars and Venus. **12** And if they were in the upper journey, the evil will be in the part of Saturn and the Moon and the Sun.

13 After this, see in what kind of sign they appear, and what is the being
of the lord of that same sign[2] in its place, and how the aspects of the bad
ones and the fortunes are, to the lord of the sign and of [its] mansion. **14**
Because if they were seen in a sign of wealthy people, and the lord of the sign
aspected from a strong place, it signifies that one will go out from that part,
who would contend in the kingdom, [and he will be] of the household members of the king, and he will be famous. **15** And if it were in a sign of wealthy

---

[1] This paragraph (itself based on Sahl) expresses the view that comets are closely related
to Mercury and circulate around the Sun. This is not Abū Ma'shar's own view, since he
apparently told his student Shadhān that some comets are as high as the sphere of Saturn
(see Section III.10).

[2] Reading with Harley and Erfurt; Paris has only the being or condition of the sign, not its
lord.

people in the way I said, and the lord of the sign did not aspect, he will be of the children of nobles, and he will be fit for a kingdom. **16** And judge likewise with all of the signs. **17** And know that the signs of the Sun and Jupiter and Mars signify the children of the wealthy, and the signs of Saturn famous people[3] among the old, and the house of the Moon[4] is below that of the Sun, and the house of Mercury below that of Jupiter, and the house of Venus below the house of Mars, and the house of Mars below the house of Jupiter, and the house of Jupiter below the house of Saturn, because their circles are below the circles of the ones which I said.

18 However, Saturn in Aquarius is a famous man, and associated with wisdom; but in Capricorn he is bad. **19** And the mansions, in their rising, do not signify [anything] except the condition of the common people, and [*unclear word*][5] of the wealthy and magnates generally.

The Flowers of Abū Ma'shar
[Chapter VII.1 (excerpt)]

52 However, if you wished to know the direction in which what the comet signifies will come, look at the [tip] of its tail, to see in what direction it is: and in that same direction will be what it signifies in terms of tribulation. **53** But for the remaining works [of the comet], the hour (which I told you in this book) in which everything which was said, will be, will be when [the Sun][6] has arrived at the sign which was of the substance of those things which I told you; or [at his arrival] at the planet whose nature is in [that] work, just like the nature of the event (which would appear to you) would be in that same year. **54** This is of the secrets of astronomy which is worth the trouble to be hidden.[7]

---

[3] Reading *nominatos* for *nominatus*.
[4] Reading the rest of the sentence with Harley; Paris omits most of it. By "below" (Lat. *infra*), the text is saying that certain planets indicate *types of people* which are *socially lower* than the others. So for instance, Mercury indicates people who are like Jupiterian people, but lower in the social order.
[5] Erfurt reads "likewise" (*similiter*), which does not make sense. I cannot read the word in Harley, and Paris omits it altogether.
[6] I have added this from Bonatti, who quotes this section virtually verbatim (*Book of Astronomy* Tr. 8 Part 1, Ch. 103). Indeed, without this phrase the predictive technique makes no sense.
[7] *Quod occultari opere precium est.*

SECTION III.10: SHADHĀN: EXCERPTS FROM THE *SECRETS OF ABŪ MA'SHAR*, ON COMETS

Comment by Dykes. The following short selection is taken from a Latin work called the *The Secrets of Abū Ma'shar*, which is itself an excerpt from a larger Arabic work by a pupil of Abū Ma'shar's, named Shadhān. I have used the new critical edition by Vescovini 1998 (p. 318), and in the future will translate the whole of this fascinating record of the conversations and practices (including numerous chart examples) of Abū Ma'shar.

ॐ   ॐ   ॐ

§24a: On Comets

1 Abū Ma'shar said, "The philosophers, and Aristotle himself, say that comets occur in the heavens, in the sphere of fire, and nothing of them comes to be in the heavens [themselves], and that the heavens do not take on [causal] influence.[1] **2** But they have all erred in such an opinion. **3** For I have seen a comet above Venus with my own eyes,[2] and I knew that the comet was above Venus because it did not alter its color. **4** And many people said to me that they saw a comet above Jupiter, and others saw a comet above Saturn. **5** However, you should know that appearing comets are always an evil portent, and they bring about great mishaps,[3] and the mishaps become analogous to their size. **6** For if the comet were large, it signifies great mishaps; but if small, very small."

---

[1] *Passionem.*

[2] Vescovini suggests that this was a supernova of 827 AD, but Goldstein suggests it might have been 844 AD. I would point out that 844 AD is a more likely date for Abū Ma'shar, since in 827 he would not only have been a young man but it would have been before his conversion to astrology—and so he might not have been able to make an appropriate judgment about the nature of comets at that time.

[3] *Symptomata.*

SECTION III.11: BONATTI ON COMETS

Comment by Dykes. This Section translates one chapter from Guido Bonatti's *Book of Astronomy* Tr. 8, which is based (sometimes verbatim) on a medieval Latin piece on comets attributed to Ptolemy.[1] This pseudo-Ptolemaic work is either directly or indirectly (via Arabic) based on a Greek source, as Hephaistio has a corresponding list of comets in his *Apotelesmatica* I.24.

Hephaistio I.24 (H)	Pseudo-Ptolemy (P)	Bonatti (B)
H1: Horseman (*hippeus*): ♀	P1: Soldier (*miles*): ♀	B4: Soldier (*miles*): ♀
H2: Swordfish (*xiphias*): ☿	P2: Lord of *aschona*: ☿	B5: Lord of *ascona*: ☿
H3: Torch (*lampadias*): ♂	P3: *Maculia* or golden (*aurea*): ♂	B6: Morning or dawn (*matutina, aurora*): ♂
H4: Haired (*kometēs*): ♃	P4: Silver (*argentum*): ♃	B7: Silver (*argentum*): ♃?
H5: Disk (*diskeus*): ♄	P5: Stick (*virga*): ♄	B9: Black (*nigra*): ♄; maybe B2: *coenaculum* (*tenaculum?*)
H6: Midwife (*eilēthuias*): ☽?	P6: Rose (*rosa*): ☽?	B8: Rosy (*rosea*): ☽?
H7: Typhon (*Tuphōn*): ☉?	P7: Javelin (*veru*): ☉?	B1: Javelin (*veru*): ☉?
	P8: Measuring rod (*pertica*): flexible	B3: Measuring rod (*partica* [sic]): flexible
	(P9: *Conaculum*— missing, see B2)	

Figure 60: Comets in Hephaistio, Pseudo-Ptolemy, and Bonatti

Clearly, then, Bonatti's list ultimately comes from a much earlier Greek source, which Hephaistio himself may have thought was authored by Ptolemy because so much of his own basic and natal astrological material is derived from Ptolemy. On the other hand, the list was augmented and changed a bit over time, and in my own opinion Bonatti has some better readings than the ones found in Baur's pseudo-Ptolemy. Bonatti also adds his own personal testimony and example of one of the comets.

In terms of the lists themselves, the Hephaistio list has 7 comets, of which the last two are unattributed but probably relate to the Moon and Sun. But the two Latin lists have 9 members, one of which is clearly a distinct comet (**P8/B3**), but the other may overlap with comet **H5** (**P9/B2**). The planetary attributions are pretty close between all of the lists, but the names are almost totally different apart from **H1/P1/B4**, which at least maintains a military theme despite being attributed to Venus.

---

[1] For an edited portion of pseudo-Ptolemy which corresponds to Bonatti, see the footnotes in Baur 1912, pp. 36-39.

In terms of Bonatti's readings, I believe his names make more sense for two of them, and he more properly has an adjective rather than a noun for another. That is, for **P3/B6**, pseudo-Ptolemy has the unknown *maculia* and the word for "golden" (*aurea*), but Bonatti has two synonyms which are close in spelling: *matutina* and *aurora* ("morning," "dawn"). Likewise for **P5/B9**, Bonatti reads the name as *nigra* ("black"), which makes sense because black is a color associated with Saturn. And although it is perhaps a minor point, **P6** is called a "rose," but Bonatti has the adjective "rosy." This suggests to me that Bonatti's text for pseudo-Ptolemy was better than Baur's.

There are however two names which do not quite make sense, and I have a suggestion for each. **P9/B2** is called a *conaculum* and *coenaculum*, respectively. *Coenaculum* (the only one of these which I can find) means a "dining room," and so is clearly inappropriate. It could possibly be *tenaculum*, which is a kind of hand-held instrument such as a tray (since the text speaks of a ray or smoke coming from underneath the head)—and I have tentatively suggested that below. But it might also be a diminutive of something like *comatus* or *conus*, which mean "long-haired" and "cone" respectively. Since comets are "haired" stars, and are sometimes given shapes such as disks or cones, these are also good contenders for the name.

The other name is "lord of *asconae/aschonae*" (**P2/B5**). Actually, the 1491 edition of Bonatti reads *astonae*, which suggests a misread for the Gr. *acontiae*, meteors or shooting stars with dartlike trains. But as with so many unusual words in medieval Latin astrological texts, we should consider an Arabic transliteration: in this case, something like the Ar. *al-sukhunah*, "lord of heat."

ಭ   ಭ   ಞ

Chapter 104: On haired stars

2 However, Ptolemy says there are nine haired stars, of which the first is called a javelin, the second a *coenaculum*,[2] the third a measuring-rod,[3] the fourth a soldier, the fifth the lord of *ascona*,[4] the sixth a morning or dawn

---

[2] See my introductory comments.
[3] Reading as *pertica* with pseudo-Ptolemy for Bonatti's *partica*. A *pertica* is a measuring rod used to measure grants of land (and it is said below to pertain to agricultural predictions); so perhaps it looks like two long rods.
[4] See my introductory comments.

one, the seventh silver, the eighth rosy, the ninth black. **3** And he said that the first four of these are likened to stars,[5] and they all signify wars and terrors and great events in the world. **4** And he said, "from their color will be known the evil that is to be, and from the nature of the sign in which they first appeared, and it will be known when that evil will be: for if it appeared in the east (or north, and went towards the south),[6] it will be quickly; and if in the west it will be delayed."

5 Indeed that which is called a javelin is horrible to look at, and it goes close to the Sun, and appears during the day; which, when it appears, it signifies the changing and diminution of the fruits of trees and of things born of the earth, and the mortality of kings and the wealthy and of those who are fit for a kingdom.

6 But that which is called a *coenaculum* is practically of the color of Mars, and has beneath it a ray in the manner of smoke under ashes: which, when it appears, signifies want (not however excessive [want])–but not famine. **7** And it signifies battles concerning which the religious interject themselves beyond the degree to which they are competent.

8 But that which is called a measuring-rod has a thick ray even though[7] it dragged a measuring-rod behind it, and is not very bright; which, when it appears, signifies dryness and a scarcity of waters, and the smallness of the grain supply. **9** Which if it were joined with one of the planets, it signifies other things according to the nature and disposition [of the one] to which it bodily joined: so that if it were joined with Saturn, there will be mortality, and much of it in old men and Jews and the religious and those who are dressed in Saturnian clothes. **10** If however it were joined with Jupiter, the things it signifies will appear in kings and magnates according to good and evil, in proportion to how he was disposed: made fortunate and strong, or made unfortunate and weak. **11** But if it were joined with Mars, it signifies even more battles, and mortalities by the sword and the shedding of blood, and the burning of fire. **12** With the Sun, however, it cannot appear. **13** But if it were joined with Venus, it signifies dryness and a great diminution of wa-

---

[5] Actually, the first five are explicitly related to planets or stars (see table above).

[6] I have put this remark in parentheses, because pseudo-Ptolemy does not include it (nor does Hephaistio), and it does not match the usual lore on comets. Normally, only easternness and westernness from the Sun is indicated. But Bonatti might also be suggesting that if a comet appears in a declination rather north of the Sun (so it is not exactly east or west), then it is like being eastern and so indicates quickness, while if it is far to the south it is like being western and so indicates delay.

[7] Reading *ac si* as *etsi*, but even so it should probably simply be read as "and it drags."

ters. **14** Indeed if with Mercury, it signifies the death of youths and the wise and scribes. **15** If with the Moon, it signifies mortality which is going to fall between the common people and other low-class persons.

16 That which is called a soldier is of the nature of Venus and is large, [inclining] toward the manner of the Moon; and it has a long ray and likewise hair, and extends [the ray or hair] behind itself; which if it appeared, it travels through the twelve signs. **17** And it signifies the harming of kings and of nobles and magnates, and that men will rise up in the world who wish to change the laws and ancient things, and lead new things [into being]; and its worse signification will appear from the direction toward which it extends its tail and hair.[8]

18 The lord of *ascona* is said to be of the condition of Mercury, and its color is blue, and it appears small in comparison with the other comets, and it has a long tail, and extends its rays to one side or another in the manner of a wing having heads underneath it, bringing it down to one place. **19** Which if it appeared, it signifies the death of kings or magnates and nobles who are fit for a realm, and especially toward the direction into which it extends its tail or rays; and it signifies battles. **20** And I saw it appear in the era of the Arabs, the 663rd year, in which Pope Alexander died; and not long afterwards King Manfred was killed by a certain brother of the king of France, by the name of Charles; and again, not long after that Conradin was killed by this same Charles in the kingdom of Apulia (and many dukes and many barons with him), and this was in the era of the Arabs, [year] 665. **21** And there were many battles and dissensions from the time of the appearance of this comet, and they lasted a long time.[9]

22 That which is called morning or dawn, is red, and it has a long tail (but less than that of the lord of *asconae*). **23** And it is of the nature of Mars, for it

---

[8] Hephaistio (I.24) says that the changes will happen in the countries "at which it is *deprived* of its hair" (emphasis mine).

[9] Pope Alexander IV died in May 1261, but Kronk (1999) does not give a comet for that year. Bonatti might be confusing Alexander's death with that Urban IV in late 1264, which was the Islamic year 663 and did coincide with a well-documented comet (C/1264 N1), which moved from Cancer to Taurus from July to October 1264 (Kronk, p. 218ff). This comet would have been especially associated with Urban's death, because it was discovered on July 17 and disappeared on October 9: Urban became ill on July 27 and died on October 2. Over the next few years, King Manfred of Sicily was killed in battle against Charles I of Anjou on February 26 or 27, 1266. Charles I of Anjou executed the teenage Conradin (then the popular King of Sicily and Jerusalem, and the last of the legitimate Hohenstaufens) in on October 29, 1268. In the East as well, there were many changes and upheavals in the Crusades.

has his significations: which if it appeared out of the direction of the east, having its head pressed down below it, [it signifies] battles and the burnings of fire, and pestilences and famine in the land of Babylon and in the lands of the Arabs and the Phorti;[10] and dryness in Egypt and a scarcity of waters, and this will be extended up to the western parts.

24 Indeed, that which is called silver, has a ray in the likeness of the purest silver, whose clarity exceeds the clarity of all nocturnal stars. **25** Which if it appeared while Jupiter is in Pisces or Cancer, it signifies an abundance of grain and produce in the directions in which it appeared. **26** But if Jupiter were in Scorpio, these things will happen, but somewhat less than this.

27 But that which is called rosy, is large and round, and the face of a man is observed in it, the color of which is between a golden and silver color. **28** Which if it appeared, it signifies the death of kings and magnates and the wealthy and nobles, and of those who are fit for a kingdom; and an event of great matters and of an appearance of [those things] themselves, and of the causes of ancient things, but they will change for the better.

29 But that which is called black is of the nature of Saturn, practically of a similar color to him: which if it appeared, it signifies mortality through natural death and death by the sword and beheading.

---

[10] *Phortorum.* Pseudo-Ptolemy seems to read this as the Phoenicians.

SECTION III.12: ROBERT GROSSETESTE, *ON COMETS*

Comment by Dykes. In this excerpt from Thomson 1933 (pp. 24-25), we see the medieval philosopher and scientist Robert Grosseteste's physical theory of comets, as well as some of the relationship between spirit and matter. For the most part the text is self-explanatory, except perhaps for his discussion of "complexioned" things. Grosseteste believes that spiritual bodily things (which here seem to be a form of fire) can be mixed or complected with terrestrial bodies. But when some of these fiery or spiritual bodies are released and rise up to their natural place in the heavens, they create what we call comets. Since what are left behind are less well-complexioned material things, the area of the earth which has released the fire or spirit, suffers changes. Thus, comets are the visible expressions of a process of corruption somewhere on earth, which is therefore subject to natural explanation.

ဢ ဢ ℭ

However, a star which has raised up a mane of hair is of the nature of one of the seven planets—because every star is of the nature of one of them, since it is even plain that the mane of hair is a lofty fire likened to the nature of one of the seven planets.

Now, in every complexioned thing of earth, there are spiritual bodily things [which are] likened to the heavenly natures; being embodied in those complexioned things, the spiritual things are separable from the things [though they have been] complexioned through the action of heavenly bodies. When this separation exists, the complexioned thing is left behind by the heavenly nature, and it is made infirm or corrupted. (However, the parts of this world are sensible, of an easier and quicker unraveling than are the parts of complexioned things, even though the entire sensible world is incorruptible, and every complexioned thing as a whole is corruptible.)[1]

---

[1] Grosseteste is making two points here. First, he is saying that a merely material object with no organizing spiritual nature mixed with it, will decompose more quickly than something which is still mixed with something spiritual: he must have in mind the difference between something like a corpse, and a living human body—each ultimately decomposes, but at different rates. Second, this fact only applies to *portions* of the earth, not to the earth as a whole (which he takes to be incorruptible). So, areas of the earth which have lost spiritual-fiery influences, will suffer problems, especially in those things ruled by the sign of the comet and its lord.

From these [facts], therefore, it appears that a comet, which is a sensible fire lifted up from a part of the world, is a sign of a preceding sublimation and separation of an uncorrupted spiritual nature [from] complexioned things and those likened to the earth, in a spiritual nature.[2] Wherefore, it is a sign of the weakening or corruption of those complected things which the planet (or another star of the nature of the planet) rules.

---

[2] I am a bit uncertain about the precise translation of this sentence, as there seems to be a word missing here and there. I am also not sure what function the last phrase plays here.

PART IV: CHOROGRAPHY
& CLIMES

SECTION IV.1: INTRODUCTION

In this Part of the book, we look at different ways of assigning astrological and other categories to the earth. As we have already seen, it is vital for Ptolemy to know such things as what places are ruled by the sign of an eclipse, since he makes predictions based on those attributions. The same is true of other authors. However, there are numerous ways of assigning planets and signs to the earth, not all of which are compatible. Here I provide a short guide to the approaches found in this book, and afterwards I will go into some detail about the rationale and mathematics behind the seven "climes." Please note that many authors have stray comments here and there about many different divisions of the earth: the guide below is not exhaustive.

In the last Section of this Part, I have compiled an exhaustive listing of all of the place names used, with (normally) the Arabic spellings and geographic coordinates where possible. In a few cases I have been unable to identify the names used.

Ascendants of cities. The first approach claims knowledge of the Ascendant of the founding of certain cities. Of course the most famous is that of the founding of Baghdad (through an election chart), which I reproduce below. Other sources here include al-Rijāl (Section IV.4, via a few references in his Ch. VIII.35), ibn Ezra (IV.7), and an unknown Greek source (IV.11). I have my doubts about the reliability of these, apart from the Baghdad chart below.

Individual assignments of signs and planets. Most of our authors also make individual assignments of signs and planets to various cities, apart from any claim that they reflect a foundation chart. A good example of these is the table in Section IV.5, from Abū Ma'shar. Sometimes these seem to be related to triplicity systems (see below), but in others it may derive from judgments about the qualities and activities of the peoples in that region.

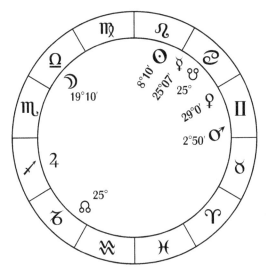

Figure 61: Foundation chart for Baghdad, from al-Bīrūnī[1]

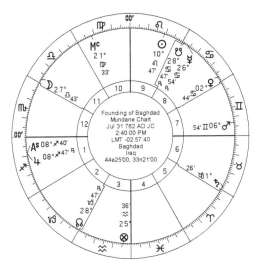

**Figure 62: Approximate chart for founding of Baghdad
(modern calculations)**

---

[1] The date in the Arabic calendar corresponds to July 31, 762 AD JC (see Holden 2003). Jupiter is in the Ascendant, though the exact rising degree is not known. According to al-Bīrūnī (*Chronology*, p. 262), Nawbakht the Persian was responsible for the timing of this chart. Other members of the team hired by Caliph al-Manṣūr for this purpose included Māshā'allāh and 'Umar al-Ṭabarī. Holden points out that the astrologers used "a fixed zodiac that differed by about 4 degrees from the tropical zodiac."

Peoples and religions. There are numerous authors (here and elsewhere) who relate the planets to certain ethnic peoples or religious groups—especially based on religious practices and political systems. For example, Arabs and/or Muslims are routinely assigned to Venus, perhaps due to the practice of daily ablution (since Venus governs cleanliness). Ibn Ezra (IV.7) lists four of these, and they can be found throughout the texts.

Landscapes. Abū Ma'shar (IV.5) has an interesting set of attributions for landscapes, which was influential even up to the time of William Lilly and beyond.

After these individualized attributions, our sources also have schemes of dividing up the whole world known to them:

Climes. The most important of these is the division by "clime" (Gr. *klima*),[2] normally seven lines or bands of latitude defined either by ascensional times or hours of longest daylight; many astrologers wanted to assign the traditional planets to these, in order to unify their understanding of the peoples, weather, and landscapes in these regions. Ptolemy (below) gave the most influential version of the climes in the *Almagest*, but defined the climes only as the lines of latitude themselves; al-Bīrūnī (Section IV.6) treats the climes as bands which are bordered by these lines. Al-Rijāl knows of Ptolemy's view, and lists certain cities and countries over which the climes pass (IV.4, in his Ch. VIII.36).

The three superiors. Māshā'allāh (IV.9) divides the region between the equator and the arctic circle into three, from Mars northward to Jupiter and thence to Saturn. Bonatti (IV.10) draws on Māshā'allāh, and this view is also mentioned by al-Rijāl in Section IV.4 (in his Ch. VIII.36).

Zodiacal climes. Bonatti (IV.10) attributes the zodiacal signs to the climes, and thus has planetary rulers over thin bands of climes. Al-Bīrūnī does likewise (IV.6).

Zodiacal bound longitudes. Since Ptolemy's geography was bounded in the west by the Canary Islands, and in the east by somewhere around the Ganges River,[3] one can imagine stretching each sign along its particular clime, and identifying terrestrial regions as corresponding to the bounds of the signs.

---

[2] In Arabic, the transliterated word for "clime" also simply means a "region," so it is sometimes hard to know whether al-Rijāl (the primary user of this term) and his sources mean a region of latitude, or simply a geographical region generally. I will tend to translate the Arabic as "region," to reflect this ambiguity.

[3] Berggren and Jones 2000, p. 21.

Bonatti (IV.10) does just such a thing, even going so far as saying how much territory is covered by each bound.

Triplicities. Both Ptolemy and ibn Labban employ a method of assigning the triplicities to regions of the known world, which Ptolemy then uses as a template to describe the characteristics of the people falling under them. Ptolemy's scheme is rather complicated and requires some explanation, while ibn Labban changes the attributions without explanation. Of course, such schemes could not account for most of the southern hemisphere, extreme east Asia, and the Americas.

Others. Finally, there are several other methods mentioned in our texts. The first is a way of counting the number of cities in each clime based on the number of minutes in the zodiacal circle: this is described briefly by al-Rijāl who quotes Hermes (Section IV.4, in his Ch. VIII.34), and by Māshā'allāh (IV.9). After that are a few schemes in al-Bīrūnī (IV.6) which I do not discuss, but the reader is invited to investigate them: various divisions into three parts justified by legends (attributed to a King Farīdūn or Afrīdūn, Noah, and the Greeks), the seven *kishwarāt* of the Persians (attributed to Hermes), and a nine-fold division attributed to the Indians.[4]

The seven climes[5]

A "clime" is a line of geographical latitude, but defined in terms of how many hours of daylight there are on the longest day of the year. Since daylight is a function of one's latitude, all positions in the same hemisphere with the same amount of daylight will share the same clime and latitude. The clime can be expressed as a ratio between the longest and shortest hours, as follows: suppose that a city has 14 hours of daylight on the summer solstice (the longest day). Since there are only 24 hours in a day, this means that there are 10 hours of night. And contrariwise, on the winters solstice (the shortest day), there will be 10 hours of daylight and 14 of night. So, the latitude of the city can be expressed as the ratio of longest to shortest, or 14:10 (by reduction, 7:5). Any place with this ratio will be on the same clime, provided it is in the same hemisphere: ancient astrologers knew only of the northern hemisphere, so they did not formally define the climes for the southern one, and certainly did not list any cities for it in their tables.

---

[4] For details, see al-Bīrūnī 1934, §240, and Kennedy (1973), pp. 73-74.
[5] In this section I am indebted to Neugebauer 1987, pp. 4-6.

Ancient astronomers were originally interested in casting charts using the climes of the most important cities of that time, namely Babylon and Alexandria, whose ratios of longest to shortest were taken to be 3:2 and 7:5, respectively. Of course, not all cities fall on one of these lines, nor even did Babylon and Alexandria, because the ratios of 3:2 and 7:5 are a little idealized. The longest daylight hours for Alexandria are really 14.179 hours, which means the shortest days are 9.821 hours, yielding a ratio that is not exactly 7:5 without some rounding up and down of the hours to 14 and 10. Nevertheless, calculating climes for regular intervals did allow for the creation of more accurate maps as well as the use of ascensional times tables for certain predictive methods in astrology (such as distributions through the bounds), not to mention other astronomical and astrological purposes.

The idea of climes and hours of longest daylight is closely related to the use of ascensional times for the signs of the zodiac, simply because the hours of daylight and the ascensional times are a function of one's latitude on the earth. As many readers know, the ascensional time of a sign is the amount of "time" (measured in degrees of right ascension) that it takes for a sign to ascend fully across the horizon in the east—which varies based on one's location.[6] Now, in the northern hemisphere the longest day is the summer solstice, when the Sun is at 0° Cancer.[7] If we measured the time between sunrise and sunset on that day (thus measuring the hours of longest daylight), then all of the signs between Cancer and Sagittarius—the so-called "straight" signs or signs of "long" ascension—would have completely arisen by the time the Sun set (see figure below).

Now, since there are 360° of right ascension, but 24 hours in a day, the relation between ascensions and hours of the day is 15: 360°/15 = 24.

Ascensions / 15 = hours of daylight

---

[6] My own website (www.bendykes.com/reviews/study.php) has a table of ascensional times for many latitudes, and the software for Delphic Oracle automatically calculates them for every chart.

[7] In the southern hemisphere, it is when the Sun is at 0° Capricorn.

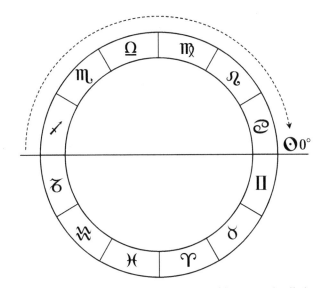

Figure 63: Signs arising on day of longest daylight (northern hemisphere)

Therefore, hours of longest daylight are nothing more than the number of ascensions of the longest or straightest signs at one's latitude, divided by 15. For example, the sum of ascensional times for Cancer through Sagittarius (from 0° Cancer to 0° Capricorn) at my location (Minneapolis, Minnesota, USA, 45° N) is 231.44 according to Delphic Oracle:

231.44 asc. times / 15 = 15.429 hours of longest daylight, or 15h 25m

Now, this number is mathematically correct, but slightly off in terms of actual daylight. If we use a program or newspaper to discover how long the period from sunrise to sunset was, we find it was about 15.36 hours, roughly 10 minutes longer than our calculation. Why was the actual period of daylight longer? Well, the reason is that the Sun is also moving forward through the zodiac, so that by the time we reach sunset, he will already have moved about 30' forward in the zodiac, taking longer to set than the actual degree of 0° Cancer. At any rate, the principle is this: the time of longest daylight, and the sum of the ascensional times of the longest signs, are directly correlated to the latitude of a place.

The Babylonians had two ways of calculating ascensional times, called System A and System B. These systems give the ascensional times for all of the signs at the latitude or clime of Babylon. Following are both systems,[8] along with the modern trigonometric values (for the latitude 32° 32' N):[9]

	System A	System B	Modern
♈/♓	20°	21°	20.47°
♉/♒	24°	24°	23.81°
♊/♑	28°	27°	29.66°
♋/♐	32°	33°	34.70°
♌/♏	36°	36°	36.01°
♍/♎	40°	39°	35.35°

Figure 64: Ascensional times for Babylon

Based on the descriptions above, we can figure out the longest hours of daylight for Babylon. Add together the ascensional times for the six signs Cancer through Sagittarius, and divide by 15:

System A and B: 216 / 15 = 14.40 hours
Modern: 212.12 / 15 = 14.14 hours

The modern calculations give Babylon slightly longer daylight hours, which means that it puts Babylon in a slightly higher latitude than Systems A and B do. Later astrologers decided to do the same thing for Alexandria:

	System A	System B	Modern
♈/♓	21° 40'	22° 30'	20.85
♉/♒	25°	25°	24.13
♊/♑	28° 20'	27° 30'	29.80
♋/♐	31° 40'	32° 30'	34.56
♌/♏	35°	35°	35.69
♍/♎	38° 20'	37° 30'	34.97

Figure 65: Ascensional times for Alexandria

---

[8] See Neugebauer and Van Hoesen 1987, pp. 3-4.
[9] Calculated using Delphic Oracle.

Again, add the ascensional times for the six signs Cancer through Sagittarius, and divide by 15:

Systems A and B: 210 / 15 = 14 hours
Modern: 210.44 / 15 = 14.03 hours

Now let us return to the climes. How many climes are there? The short answer is: as many as we want. Since a clime is defined by the hours of longest daylight at a given latitude, we could have as many as 66 climes (since the climes, like house systems, break down at the arctic circle). However, early astrologers decided upon seven climes, no doubt due to the number of the classical planets.[10] Using either System A or B, they calculated seven lines of latitude based on increments of 4 ascensional times. The table below uses the Alexandria model and my own table of ascensional times to discern which latitude corresponds to them:

Clime	Asc times	Latitude
(Equator)	180	0°
1	210	31°
2	214	34°
3	218	37°
4	222	40°
5	226	42°
6	230	45°
7	234	46° 30'

Figure 66: Early set of seven climes

In this table, the left column identifies the clime (the equator is not a clime in its own right). In the middle are the total ascensions of the longest signs (Cancer through Sagittarius), in increments of 4. By adding up these ascensions for each line of latitude on the table of ascensions, it is easy to see that each clime's sum corresponds to a particular degree of latitude, from 31° N to about 46° 30' N. Obviously, places such as London (51° 30' N) fall beyond the line of the 7th clime, while places such as Istanbul or Constanti-

---

[10] Neugebauer and Van Hoeson (*ibid.*, p. 4) point out that when an important city such as Constantinople fell in between the lines of the official seven climes, a special table was calculated especially for it so as not to interrupt the existing system of seven.

nople (41° 01' N) fall between two climes. Note that these latitudes are valid whether north or south of the equator, even though the ancient astrologers knew nothing of the latter.

In this older set of climes, the climes are derived from increments in ascensional times. But they could just as easily be derived from, or defined in terms of, hours of longest daylight. This is just what Ptolemy did in his *Almagest*, which did two things: (1) defined the climes in short increments[11] of longest daylight, and (2) identified a new set of seven climes. The smaller increments allowed Ptolemy to define more climes for greater accuracy in timekeeping and mapmaking, and his new seven climes were the basis of later discussions of the climes (such as in this book).

Following is a partial table of Ptolemy's version of the seven climes,[12] starting with the equator for reference and ending with the last clime:

Clime	Longest Daylight Hours	City Or Region	Ptolemy's Place Latitude	Correct Place Latitude	Correct Clime Latitude
(Equ.)	12		0°		0°
1	13	Meroë	16° 27'	16° 56'	16° 45'
2	13 ½	Syēnē	23° 51'	24° 05'	24° 15'
3	14	Lower Egypt	30° 22'	Varies[13]	31°
4	14 ½	Rhodes	36°	36° 10'	36° 30'
5	15	Hellespont	40° 56'	40° 13'	41° 30'
6	15 ½	Mid-Pontus	45° 01'[14]	45° 00'?	45° 35'
7	16	Borysthenes	48° 32'	46° 30'[15]	49° 10'

Figure 67: Ptolemy's seven climes, with modern values

Here we can see that the climes are defined by increments of 30 minutes in hours of longest daylight. Each is identified with a particular city or region,

---

[11] In most cases, in 15-minute increments.
[12] See *Almagest* II.13, pp. 124-30.
[13] The Nile Delta covers a large area, so Ptolemy's latitude is good enough.
[14] Pontus was a region of land on the southern edge of the Black Sea (the northern edge of modern Turkey), but Ptolemy's latitude corresponds more to the peninsula of land jutting out into the Black Sea, whose eastern edge encloses the Sea of Azov. Ptolemy probably means this, as the southern edge of the Black Sea (historical Pontus) is only at about 40°-41° N.
[15] Even if the shape and location of the delta has changed somewhat over time, Ptolemy's latitude is still far too high.

whose Ptolemaic latitude is given. Then, I have supplied the "correct" modern latitude[16] for the place, and have independently calculated the correct clime for the hours of longest daylight. Ptolemy's values are very close to the modern ones: in some cases he is identifying a river mouth or delta or similar region, which can only be approximated. We should also consider that since the earth is not a perfect sphere, actually measuring the hours of longest daylight in a place will give different values than the mathematically "correct" one.

The figure below is a map of the world, on which I have drawn Ptolemy's climes and included southern latitudes. Of course it includes more in the northern hemisphere than Ptolemy would have included, since the western edge of the world he knew ended at the Canary Islands.

As I will mention in the Section on al-Bīrūnī (IV.6), al-Bīrūnī treats climes not as single lines, but as bands which are defined by or bordered by these lines.

---

[16] Ascensional times are dependent not only on latitude, but also the obliquity of the ecliptic, which is not always constant; therefore my values will differ from Ptolemy's simply because of differences in the obliquity between his time and ours.

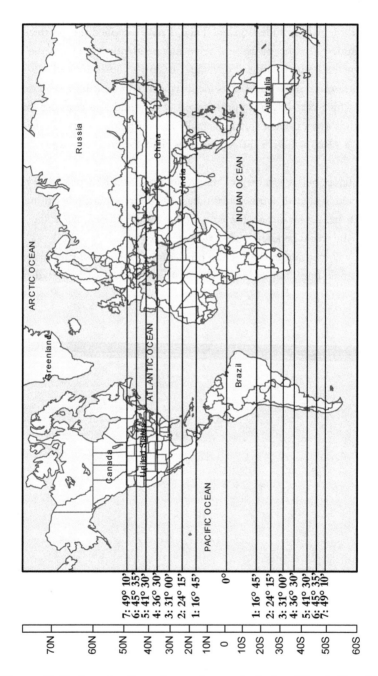

Figure 68: Ptolemaic climes by modern calculation (North/South)

SECTION IV.2: PTOLEMY'S TRIPLICITIES

According to Berggren and Jones,[1] Ptolemy's conception of the world and its size changed a bit between the *Almagest*, the *Tetrabiblos*, and the *Geography* (in that order). First of all, Ptolemy's world was much more limited than ours, and in his geographical discussions[2] he took the Canary Islands (about 28° N, 15° W) as being the western edge of the known world, and somewhere around the Ganges river and associated parts of China (perhaps near the end of the Silk Road) as the eastern edge. For the north, he identified 63° N and the seas containing the isle of Britain. The southern border was between 16°-17° S, at a latitude with about 13 hours of longest daylight, which he refers to generally as a land surrounding "Ethiopia," south of "Libya."

As for the size of this territory, Ptolemy had originally thought it fit into a 90° section of the northern hemisphere (as measured eastward from the Canary Islands), but by the time of the *Geography* he believed it encompassed 180° (although by then he thought the earth was somewhat larger than it is). To his credit, he was aware of the limits of contemporary geographical knowledge, and supposed that there were other land masses beyond these borders, including an uncertain land which formed the southern edge of what we now know as the Indian Ocean.[3]

The map in the figure below approximates his world—I say "approximates," because Ptolemy's proportions for land masses were not always correct—not to mention that he barely knew of India's geography, nor much of sub-Saharan Africa. And so, his *Geography* encompasses this territory by its *coordinates*, but not in all of its *details*.

---

[1] Berggren and Jones 2000, p. 21; I have relied broadly on their Introduction as well as their new translation of the theoretical chapters of Ptolemy's *Geography*.
[2] See Ptolemys' Book 7 of the *Geography*, in Berggren and Jones, pp. 108ff.
[3] Berggren and Jones, p. 108.

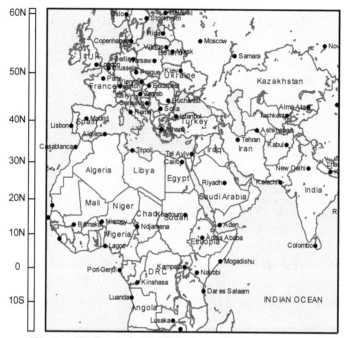

Figure 69: Geographical limits of Ptolemy's world

Later Persian and Arabic authors adopted his scheme of climes, as I mentioned in my Introduction above. But they also drew on another chorographical scheme described in the *Tetrabiblos*, which he devised[4] for astrological prediction: the assignment of the triplicities to territories on the earth.

In *Tet.* II.3, Ptolemy identifies two axes which divide the known world into four parts, and essentially define the center of the world. The horizontal axis goes from the Straits of Gibraltar through the Gulf of Issus, to the Taurus Mountains. The vertical axis goes from the Persian/Arabian gulf to the Black Sea and the Sea of Azov. Oddly, he also identifies the Aegean Sea as being on this line, but even in the old maps in Berggren and Jones, that is too far to the west even by Ptolemy's standards. At any rate, the map below illustrates the four regions, each of which Ptolemy assigned to certain triplicities and planets. He also used this scheme to help explain broad cultural differences between peoples of different regions.

---

[4] As with much of Ptolemy's astrology, it is hard to say how much he borrows straight from his predecessors, or streamlines or even invents himself.

In order to understand Ptolemy's triplicity scheme for geography, we must understand something about his concept of triplicities in general as well as his notion of winds, because both are necessary for dividing the earth as he does.

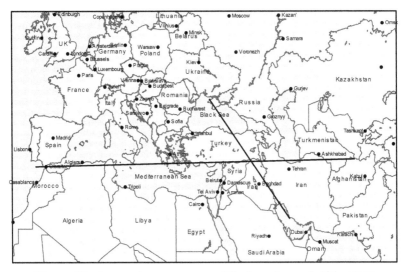

Figure 70: Approximate center of Ptolemy's earth (*Tet.* II.3)

Triplicities in general. A "triplicity" (Lat. *triplicitas*) is a group of three or something "threefold": in this case, a group of three signs. The Greek is a bit more straightforward, as a triplicity is simply a "triangle" (Gr. *trigon*), and one may easily see that the signs can be grouped into threes by overlaying triangles onto the zodiac.

Figure 71: Zodiacal triplicities or triangles

Most traditional astrologers in the Greek, Persian, and Arabic-speaking worlds used what are sometimes called the "Dorothean" triplicity lords, so-called because they were described by Dorotheus in his astrological poem; but Vettius Valens had described them as well. In this system, the signs joined by the points of each triangle are jointly ruled by a set of three planets: one in day charts, another in night charts, with a third, partnering planet assisting the others. However, these planets are *not* the same as the lords of these signs. For example, in the triplicity of Aries-Leo-Sagittarius, the three triplicity lords are the Sun (diurnal), Jupiter (nocturnal), Saturn (partner): but Saturn does not actually rule, nor is he even exalted in, any of these three signs.[5] These triplicity lords were used for a number of purposes, both interpretive (such as in judging eminence and life success) and predictive (assigning the lords to different periods of life).

Throughout the *Tetrabiblos*, Ptolemy tries to preserve many essential points of standard astrological doctrine, especially if he can explain them naturalistically by reducing them to processes such as heating and cooling: for example, that Mars causes heating and drying. On the other hand, sometimes he virtually rejects entire areas of astrological knowledge, such as the use of Lots (apart from his own version of the Lot of Fortune). When it comes to his

---

[5] Occasionally there has been speculation as to why these lords were assigned in the way they were, and in that order. I have some proposals to make which I will reserve for another time.

treatment of the triplicities (I.18), something very odd is happening, and his arguments often receive a strained reception. When all is said and done, Ptolemy has rejected the category of partnering planets, and only changes the lords of Cancer-Scorpio-Pisces. In the Dorothean system, the two main planets are Venus (diurnal) and Mars (nocturnal), but for Ptolemy they are Mars (diurnal *and* nocturnal), with the assistance of Venus (by day) and the Moon (by night).

	By Day/ Diurnal	By Night/ Nocturnal	Partnering
♈ ♌ ♐	☉	♃	♄
♊ ♎ ♒	♄	☿	♃
♋ ♏ ♓	♀	♂	☽
♉ ♍ ♑	♀	☽	♂

Figure 72: Dorothean triplicity lords

	By Day/ Diurnal	By Night/ Nocturnal
♈ ♌ ♐	☉	♃
♊ ♎ ♒	♄	☿
♋ ♏ ♓	♂ (♀)	♂ (☽)
♉ ♍ ♑	♀	☽

Figure 73: Ptolemy's version of standard triplicity lords

At first glance, this does not seem to be so great a change: after all, the partnering planets were always tertiary in importance, and Mars was always one of the two main triplicity lords of Cancer-Scorpio-Pisces anyway (and is still being assisted by Venus and the Moon). But when it comes to Ptolemy's actual arguments and explanations, *Tet.* I.18 makes little sense. First of all, Ptolemy seems to want to derive the triplicity lords from the lords of those signs, which does not always work (the Moon does not rule any earthy sign). The rules seem to change from triplicity to triplicity, with criteria for identifying one set of lords being dropped in favor of others in the next one. The discussion is permeated by talk about winds. Finally, while trying to derive roughly the same lords as the Dorothean model, Ptolemy suddenly introduces what will turn out to be alternative lords—for instance, wanting Jupiter and Mars for the Aries-Leo-Sagittarius triplicity, *even though* he also wants to keep the usual ones as well (the Sun and Jupiter). What is going on here?

The short answer is this. The reason *Tet.* I.18 is so strange, is because Ptolemy is trying to fulfill two projects which do not fit well together on this very topic. The immediate and subordinate project of the chapter is to reproduce and justify the traditional triplicity lords as much as possible. The dominant and broader project is to create a naturalistic astrology that includes effects over entire regions of the world, not just through individual nativities. Specifically, I.18 is a transition point between Ptolemy's earlier discussion of the planets, and the later treatment of chorography: we cannot understand them separately from his earlier discussions of natural processes, planets, and winds (see below).

Put differently, the odd jumble of winds, directions, and both regular and alternative lords in this chapter are not idiosyncratic and incidental: they are *essential for Ptolemy's larger astrological project.* The problem is that the Dorothean triplicity lords themselves were never derived from sign rulerships to begin with, nor from a consideration of winds—at least, not in the way that Ptolemy does it. Therefore, his arguments cannot really make sense in terms of mainstream astrological practice.

I hope to discuss all of these matters in greater detail in a later article. For now, let me focus more directly on Ptolemy's real interest, the alternative set of triplicity lords as they pertain to mundane astrology. I think the easiest way to understand his approach is to move backwards, as it were, and show the reader how to reach *Tet.* II.3 in a way that is faithful to Ptolemy's astrological essentials.

Ptolemy ultimately wants to show that the signs and planets can have special effects on a world which is divided into four primary parts by the axis of the four cardinal directions. We know from earlier chapters that he is interested in how the four primary winds have natural effects (*Tet.* I.10), and that certain planets are associated with them by having similar effects (I.4, I.10, I.18). We also know that the triplicities reduce the signs into four groups, which for him is convenient because the zodiac touches the circles which are responsible for the various seasonal effects when the Sun is in them (I.10, I.18). But there are seven planets, and so we must figure out a way to reduce them to four, each associated with only one of the four winds and directions.

The simple solution is simply this: remove the luminaries and Mercury from the equation. The effects of the luminaries is very general, and Ptolemy mostly leaves them out of his astrological discussions in natal interpretation. The Sun, for instance, defines the action of the winds themselves because of his creation of the seasons, so cannot be associated with any particular wind. Mercury is too indeterminate in his fundamental nature, in terms of both sect and in natural processes like drying and moistening (I.4, I.7). If we insert the domicile lords into the triplicity diagram and remove or grey out the luminaries and Mercury, we have the following:

Figure 74: Ptolemy's four mundane triplicity lords (black)

The four remaining planets are Saturn, Jupiter, Mars, and Venus. *These four are, precisely, the alternative and mundane triplicity lords which Ptolemy uses in his chorography.*

The next step is to identify which of the four planets go with each cardinal direction and wind. Ptolemy does this in I.18 and reaffirms it in II.3: Jupiter gets the north, Saturn the east, Venus the south, and Mars the southwest (but in practice, the west). The triplicities will now fit into the regions between the arms of this axis, and pairs of planets will rule over each. For instance, the eastern and northern planets (Saturn, Jupiter) will rule over the triplicity in the northeast region: E + S = SE.

What we don't know yet, is which triplicity fits into which region. They are not derived simply from the lords of the signs above, because while (for example) Jupiter and Mars are lords in the Aries-Leo-Sagittarius triplicity and do rule the NW in Ptolemy's chorography, the same is not true for what we call the watery and earthy triplicities:⁶ e.g., Jupiter and Saturn jointly rule the airy triplicity and the NE, but Jupiter himself does not rule any airy sign. We need a rule to decide where to put the triplicities. Ptolemy hints at just this rule in I.18, and it is this: the triplicity follows the lord of the same sect as those signs.

The whole procedure is consistent, and can be summarized as follows:

- Directions/Winds: Jupiter – North; Saturn – East; Venus – South; Mars – West
- Remove the luminaries and Mercury, as the luminaries are too general and Mercury is too ambiguous. This leaves four planets for the four directions.
- ♈ ♌ ♐ (Diurnal sect). After removing the Sun, Jupiter and Mars are left as lords. The triplicity follows Jupiter, because he is diurnal.
- ♊ ♎ ♒ (Diurnal sect). After removing Mercury, Saturn and Venus are left as lords. The triplicity follows Saturn, because he is diurnal.
- ♉ ♍ ♑ (Nocturnal sect). After removing Mercury, Venus and Saturn are left as lords. The triplicity follows Venus, because she is nocturnal.
- ♋ ♏ ♓ (Nocturnal sect). After removing the Moon, Mars and Jupiter are left as lords. The triplicity follows Mars, because he is nocturnal.

We are left with the following diagram, which Ptolemy will map onto the world as known to him:

---

⁶ Ptolemy does not use this terminology, but for the sake of convience I will begin to use it here.

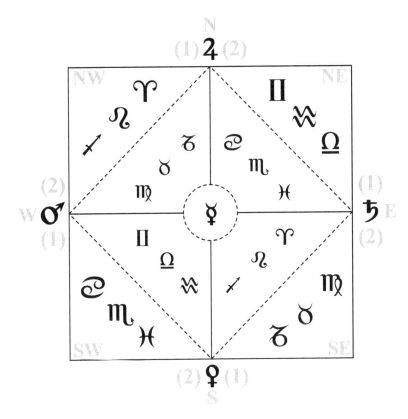

Figure 75: Ptolemy's complete astrological chorography

As we can see, the four mundane triplicity lords are in their appropriate cardinal directions. At the corners are triangles which contain the appropriate triplicities. The planets enclose the triplicities in pairs, with each triplicity being ruled primarily by the *domicile* lord within that triplicity which is of the sect of those signs. Each of these mundane triplicity lords has a (1) on the side of the triplicity which it rules primarily, and a (2) on the side which it rules secondarily: in each case, the primary planet is to the right, as though it is leading the triplicity as the heavens turn in clockwise order. Thus Jupiter and Mars are joint mundane rulers of the fiery triplicity, with Jupiter as the primary lord (on the right); Saturn and Jupiter jointly rule the airy triplicity, with Saturn as primary lord on the right. Likewise, Venus and Saturn for earth, with Venus to the right, and Mars and Venus for water, with Mars on the right.

The only feature of the diagram we must still discuss is the central portion. In the very center is Mercury, which Ptolemy says (II.3.) is because he is "mid-way between and common to the two sects," which I suggested above was a reason why he was excluded as a ruler of cardinal winds, like the luminaries.

But there is also another arrangement in the center, with the triplicities placed opposite their normal corners. According to Ptolemy (II.3.9-11), this is because just as the corners are triangular and point outwards, each of them near the center has, as it were, a triangle pointing inwards—so that each triangle pointing in the same direction will have the same triplicity, and the center portions will be attributed to the triplicity of the opposite side. This is because the geographical attributions are opposite the attributions of the winds "in the world." By this he is referring to what we normally think of as the quarters of a chart. Thus in the northern hemisphere, the southern part of the heavens near the MC is hotter, while the midnight position in the north is colder; but here, the planet in the north is Jupiter, a heating planet, while in the south is Venus, a cooling planet according to Ptolemy. So Ptolemy thinks that there is something oppositional between chart positions and terrestrial conditions.

Another way to look at it is as though the corner of the square may be folded inwards to create an inward-facing triangle, and this is important because Ptolemy specifically says that both inner and outer parts of the figure are triangular. For example, the fiery triplicity goes in the northwest, and the earthy triplicity is in the southeast—in the outer regions. But if we fold each corner inwards, we get two triangles that point in the opposite direction. So the *inner* portion of the northwest is a triangle pointing southeast, and so is also attributed to the earthy triplicity; likewise, the *inner* portion of the southeast is a triangle pointing northwest, and so is also attributed to the fiery triplicity. The same goes for the other two triplicities.

Following is the list of Ptolemy's country attributions based on this diagram when laid over the earth, both the outer portions and inner ones. As with all of the lists throughout this Part of the book, the place names are explained in Section IV.13 below:[7]

---

[7] This appears at the end of II.3 in Robbins, but the beginning of II.4 in Hübner. It may be significant that (as Robbins points out) there are 72 regions listed here. For there are also 72 bounds in the entire zodiac, and some texts say that the various bounds of the zodiac are associated with different regions. But I am not sure how to apply that concept here, since some signs have more than five countries attributed to them.

♈	*Outer (NW):* Britain, Galatia,[8] Germania, Bastarnia. *Inner (SE):* Koilē Syria,[9] Idumaia, Judaea.
♉	*Outer (SE):* Parthia, Mēdia, Persia. *Inner (NW):* the Kyklades Islands, Cyprus, the coast of Asia Minor.
♊	*Outer (NE):* Hyrcania, Armenia, Matianē. *Inner (SW):* Kyrenaikē, Marmarikē, Lower Egypt.
♋	*Outer (SW):* Numidia, Carthage, Africa. *Inner (NE):* Bithynia, Phrygia, Kolchis.
♌	*Outer (NW):* Italy, Gallia, Sicily, Apulia. *Inner (SE):* Phoenicia, Chaldaea, Orchenia.
♍	*Outer (SE):* Mesopotamia, Babylonia, Assyria. *Inner (NW):* Hellas, Achaia, Crete.
♎	*Outer (NE):* Bactriana, Kaspēria, Sērica. *Inner (SW):* Thebais, Oasis, Trōgodytikē.
♏	*Outer (SW):* Metagōnitis, Mauritania, Gaitoulia. *Inner (NE):* Syria, Kommagēnē, Cappadocia.
♐	*Outer (NW):* Tyrrēnia, Keltikē, Spain. *Inner (SE):* Arabia Felix.
♑	*Outer (SE):* India, Arianē, Gedrōsia. *Inner (NW):* Thrace, Macedonia, Illyria.
♒	*Outer (NE):* Sauromatikē, Oxiana, Sogdiana. *Inner (SW):* Arabia, Azania, Middle Ethiopia.
♓	*Outer (SW):* Phazania, Nasamōnitis, Garamantikē. *Inner (NE):* Lydia, Cilicia, Pamphylia.

Figure 76: Table of regions in Ptolemy's chorography

The following two maps show how the signs are actually distributed geographically. I have used dotted lines to show both the axes which divide the known world into four parts, and the subsections which contain the triplicity signs from the opposite side. Thus in the northwest, the fiery triplicity forms the outer regions of the quarter, while the inner regions are especially attributed to the earthy triplicity on the opposite side. Please notice that the north-south axis is particularly distorted and curved, because there is no way

---

[8] This is a region of ancient Gaul (Gallia) which Robbins reads as being Gaul north of the Alps.
[9] Hübner omits Palestine.

for Ptolemy to assign the signs in the way he does, while preserving a straight line from the Black Sea to the Arabian/Persian Gulf.

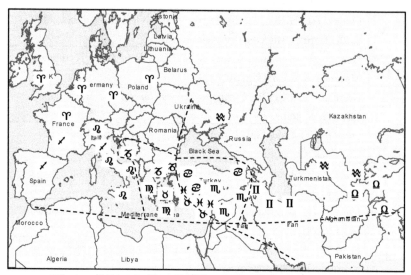

Figure 77: Northern regions of Ptolemy's chorography

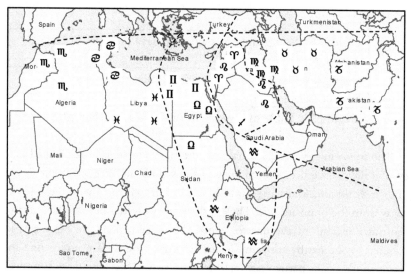

Figure 78: Southern regions of Ptolemy's chorography

One final note about the sign arrangements and maps has to do with the order of signs in each quarter and sub-quarter. Although it is sometimes hard tell (whether looking at Ptolemy's maps or these modern ones), it seems that in the outer regions the signs are meant to go counterclockwise in the following order: movable, fixed, common. Thus in the northwest, the movable sign Aries is near the top, then clockwise is a Leo region, then south of that a Sagittarian region. If I am correct, it has the interesting result that vertical pairs of signs on my "astrological chorography" diagram share the same ascensional times. That is, Aries in the northwest is directly above Pisces in the southwest, and both Aries and Pisces have the same ascensional or rising times. The same goes for Leo and Scorpio, Sagittarius and Cancer, and the rest of the signs on the eastern side. However, there does not seem to be a consistent pattern for the signs in the inner portion: on the eastern side the ascensional pattern still holds (Aries-Pisces, etc.), but not on the western one. Perhaps Ptolemy wanted it to be that way, but the placement of the regions on a map do not make that possible.

Ptolemy's astrological ethnology

Ptolemy uses his chorography to explain what he sees as the characteristics of the peoples in these regions. I have not listed everything he says about each region, but have tried to restrict it to the essentials. The delineations are interesting and could be used as the basis of understanding national characters even if we do not accept Ptolemy's own chorography. In all cases, Ptolemy understands these delineations to come primarily from the meanings of the mundane triplicity lords over the quarters, and the lords of the signs themselves.

NW Quarter	
♈ ♌ ♐ (Outer)	*All:* independent, loving freedom, warlike, leadership, great-souled; not given much to sex with women, manly, love of kin. *Aries:* add more fierceness and headstrong qualities. *Leo:* add more cooperativeness, sense of mastery, and benevolence. *Sagittarius:* add more independence, simplicity, cleanliness.

| ♉ ♍ ♑ (Inner) | *All:* still loving freedom and self-governance, and lawful, due to the nature of the whole quarter. *Taurus:* add more luxury and attention to the body. *Virgo:* add learning and focus on the soul rather than body. *Capricorn:* less social, less mild. |

NE Quarter	
♊ ♎ ♒ (Outer)	*All:* have or are interested in much wealth, clean, learned in religion, just, noble, hate evil, affectionate and loyal, sexually respectable, lavish. *Gemini:* add easily provoked and inclined to mischief. *Libra:* add following the Muses, more luxurious. *Aquarius:* add less gentle, more stern, bestial.
♋ ♏ ♓ (Inner)	*All:* interested in the mysteries, depraved, servile, slavers, destructive, women are obedient and full of labor. *Cancer:* add that the women are more warlike and masculine. *Scorpio:* add boldness and treachery and labor. *Pisces:* add wealthy and commercial, free, trustworthy.

SE Quarter	
♉ ♍ ♑ (Outer)	*All:* interested in predictive arts, sacred sexuality, the arts and adornment, indulgence, abhor same-sex practices, incest, effeminate in dress, noble, warlike. *Taurus:* add more luxury and cleanliness and finery. *Virgo:* add mathematics and astronomy. *Capricorn:* add ugliness, dirtiness, and beastliness.
♈ ♌ ♐ (Inner)	*All:* add more trade, unscrupulous, treacherous. *Aries:* bold, "godless,"[10] scheming. *Leo:* add simplicity, astrology, kindliness, and Sun worship. *Sagittarius:* add grace, a free spirit, a more mercantile attitude.

SW Quarter	
♋ ♏ ♓ (Outer)	*All:* incestuous rulers, bride-stealing, wives held in common, adornment, deception and recklessness, magic. *Cancer:* add more sociality, merchants. *Scorpio:* add more fierceness and war. *Pisces:* add more intelligence, work, cleanliness, and independence.

[10] Ancient people often thought that the rejection of familiar gods, gods of cities, etc., was akin to atheism, so Ptolemy may have Jews in mind (Robbins, p. 143 n. 2).

Ⅱ Ω ♒ (Inner)	*All:* worship planetary gods, lots of religious ceremony, superstitious, bury the dead, timid and suffering when ruled by courageous and great-souled when in power, polygamous and polyandrous, lecherous, fertile, eunuchs. *Gemini:* add intelligence and skill, especially in magic and religion and math. *Libra:* add liveliness and burning in the soul. *Aquarius:* eat much flesh and fish, nomads, a rough and bestial life.

Figure 79: Ptolemy's astrological ethnology

Fixed stars and Ascendants

Finally, at the end of II.3,[11] Ptolemy provides two rules which help attribute cities and regions to the signs. First, a given region will also be indicated by those fixed stars which co-rise or co-set with the sign already attributed to it. That is, suppose a region is already attributed to Scorpio: the fixed stars which co-rise or co-set with Scorpio at the latitude of that very region, will also be indicators for the region.[12]

Second, capital cities of a region will also be indicated and characterized by the signs in which the Sun, Moon, or axial degrees[13] were at the time of the city's founding. But if the chart of the founding is not known, one may use the sign on the natal Midheaven of the king or other rulers at the time of the founding.

---

[11] Hübner's II.4.

[12] At least, this is how I understand the rule: Ptolemy's sentence is rather complex.

[13] Probably the Ascendant and Midheaven. Ptolemy repeats this rule in his material on weather.

SECTION IV.3: DOROTHEUS ON
CHOROGRAPHY & CLIMES

Comment by Dykes. Following is a short list of country attributions by Dorotheus, as quoted in verse by Hephaistio (*Apotelesmatics* I.1). Dorotheus's use of "clime" (Gr. *klima*) does not seem to be strictly related to latitude, but is apparently a synonym for "region" (just like its transliterated form in Arabic, *'iqlīm*).

℥   Ω   ℧

♈	Ancient Babylon ("town of Tyrian Belos"), hindmost Arabia.
♉	Clime of Media, Arabia, "fine foot of fertile Egypt."[1]
♊	Clime of Cappadocia, Perrhaebia, Phoenicia.
♋	Clime of Thracia and Ethiopia.
♌	Hellas, Phrygia, mouth of the Pontus.
♍	The "virgin islands" of Rhodes and Kyklades, Ogygian trees, the stream of Oceanus, the Achaian clime of Laconia.
♎	Clime of Kyrēnē, Italy.
♏	Carthage, Libya, Sicily.
♐	Clime of the Gauls,[2] Crete.
♑	Cimmeria.
♒	Clime of Egypt, Mesopotamia
♓	Red Sea up to the flood of Oceanus

---

[1] Probably the fertile delta region.
[2] See *Gallia* in the list of regions in Section IV.13.

SECTION IV.4: THE ARABIC AL-RIJĀL ON CHOROGRAPHY & CLIMES

Comment by Dykes. All of the following excerpts have been translated from the Arabic version of al-Rijāl's *Book of the Skilled.* I have primarily used Br. Lib. 23399, but in some cases relied on Nuruosmaniye 2766. In some cases I have had to make choices about abridging the text or following Nuruosmaniye. For one thing, in these chapter of Book VIII Nuruosmaniye is often organized differently and even lists different countries and cities; but since the Latin often follows the Br. Lib. reading, I have usually followed the latter. But again, in some places Nuruosmaniye seems to have fewer misspellings and clearer readings, so I have followed it. Then, in Ch. VIII.37 al-Rijāl has listed Ptolemaic longitudes and latitudes for numerous cities (often, small towns) throughout Asia—but since many of these are spelled differently in the manuscripts, and especially since Ptolemy's longitudes (measured imprecisely from the Canary Islands moving eastwards) do not match ours, and do not contain astrological information anyway, I have omitted them.

There are two items of special interest in these selections. First, Chs. VIII.10 and VIII.34 below give some instructions as to how to begin interpreting ingress charts (which I have mainly reserved for *AW2*), showing how a planetary analysis can be applied mundanely to people and regions indicated by the planets. Second, in Ch. VIII.35 al-Rijāl begins to report an otherwise unknown book by an unknown Persian author, who according to Nuruosmaniye seems to have drawn on the Indian astrologer Kankah. Here, "Master Ibridaj" (if that is the correct spelling) first distinguishes all of Greater Iran (see below) from other regions to the west, and then subdivides Greater Iran into its own regions and cities. This is interesting because it suggests that Ibridaj was working entirely in the Sassanian Persian milieu and mindset, before the whole region was unified under the Islamic empires—and so was probably drawing on Persian material developed before the 8th Century.

൫ ൫ ൙

Chapter VIII.10: On knowing the places of the things which happen[1]

2 And if you wanted to know the places of the accidents, then look at the lord of the sign of the Ascendant: which one is it of the planets? **3** If Saturn was the king of the year[2] or the king of the quarter, then good strikes the land of Rome, and they will triumph over their enemy, and their king will die, and death will fall upon some of them. **4** And it will strike the land of Daylam well; and Jīlān and Tabaristān belong to the place of Saturn. **5** And if you found Jupiter or Venus clothed by Saturn, then take away from the evil we described about the land of Rome, and it elevates their king above death, [and] then they escape. **6** And what Saturn is, is worse if the Sun entered Aries and [Saturn] was in [the Sun's] opposition, going retrograde, or [the Sun] was connected with him and [Saturn] was in a foreign[3] sign: for it indicates evil and fighting between the people of the east and the west,[4] and wars in diverse places.

7 And if you found Jupiter to be the king of the year of the king of the quarter, then men will be fertile, and severity strikes the land of the Persians, and the wheat and barley increases, and a good condition increases in men. **8** And if Mars was clothed by Jupiter, and Mars had strength, then food becomes expensive at the end of that [quarter] and the end of the year, and depravity[5] will happen in the land in which you found Mars, according to his sign.

9 And if you found Mars to be[6] the king of the year or the king of the quarter, then look at the sign in which he was: for indeed he indicates an increase of rains in those countries, and the people of the lands which Mars falls around, will flourish. **10** And[7] an enemy will be located in the places of the land of Iraq. **11** And death will take place in the people, and more frequently in its occurrences, and especially in youths. **12** Mars, if he was standing [still] and moving the motion of Saturn,[8] it indicates disaster and the breaking of kinship, and slaves will not submit to their masters, nor will the young do so to adults. **13** And if you found Jupiter to be clothed with Mars,

---

[1] Title missing in the Ar.; I have used the Latin.
[2] This probably simply means "lord of the year," and not the significator of the king.
[3] That is, "peregrine."
[4] Or, "the Levant and the Maghrib."
[5] Nuruosmaniye reads, "earthquake."
[6] Omitting "Mars by the sign of it."
[7] Br. Lib. 23399 omits this sentence, which I have translated from Nuruosmaniye.
[8] That is, moving very slowly.

then take away from the evil based on the extent which you believe [there is] of the [good] condition of Jupiter.

14 And if you found the Sun to be the king of the year or of the quarter, then good will befall the land of Iraq, and some of the severity will strike the powerful ones of them, and death is increased in them. **15** And if Mars was clothed by the Sun, it indicates this.[9] **16** And if you found [it was] Saturn instead of Mars, it indicates an increase of diseases. **17** And if Jupiter and Venus were falling from[10] the Sun, then indeed [there will be] death in the land of Iraq, and [judge][11] the nobility and the kings based on the level of strength which you believed the Sun [had].

18 And if you found Venus to be the king of the year or of the quarter, then she indicates joy and delight, and fighting and plague strikes the people of Persia to the shore of the sea, toward India, or plague from the fighting [strikes] the youth. **19** And if you found Mars clothed by Venus, then famine and severity strikes the land of the Arabs,[12] and death increases in them. **20** And they will be changed from their own land to another land, [and] they will seek food from it, unless Jupiter and Venus are found to be aspecting, with power [being] from Jupiter: for then it takes away from that.

21 And if you found Mercury to be the king of the year or of the quarter, then good and joy strike the people of Isfahān, and severity and starvation and earthquake strike Azerbaijān, and good and benefit strike the people of Daylam and Hablān. **22** And if you found Mars clothed by Mercury, then fighting and forcefulness takes place in those countries whose sign Mars is in, from their nobility; and unrest will strike them, but their prices will decrease.

23 And if you found the Moon to be the king of the year or of the quarter, and she was clothed by Jupiter or Venus, then the rains and snow will increase in that year, and severity and earthquake will strike Rome, and tribulation will strike the people of India, and death in the nobility will strike the people of China up to the side of Sijistān.

---

[9] The Latin al-Rijāl has, "it signifies burning," which makes sense.
[10] This must mean, "in aversion to."
[11] Reading with the Latin for the uncertain فاعط.
[12] Reading al-ʿarab with the Latin for "the west" (al-gharb).

Chapter VIII.34: On what belongs to the signs & the planets, of the regions & the countries

2 Know that the world is divided into seven divisions; every division of them is a region, based on the number of the seven planets. **3** So, the first of them is Saturn, and the last of them is the Moon, based on the calculation of the succession of the planets in their circles.

4 The region of India belongs to Saturn, and the region of Babylon belongs to Jupiter, and the region of the Turks belongs to Mars, and the region of Rome[13] belongs to the Sun, and the region of the Hijāz belongs to Venus, and the region of Egypt belongs to Mercury, and the region of China belongs to the Moon.

5 And some of them[14] said that Aries and Jupiter belong to Babylon, and Capricorn and Mercury belong to India, and Leo and Mars belong to the Turks, and Libra and the Sun belong to Rome, and Scorpio and Venus belong to the Arabs.[15]

6 Look at each region according to its planet, if it entered its honor:[16] is it entering it and it is increasing in its course, and rising in its sector, appropriate in [its] condition, fortunate or in conflict? **7** And that is that you should know the news of the people of the clime from that, in the correctness of their issues and their disturbance. **8** And when there is a contrast[17] in the indication of Saturn[18] [and] the indication of Mars, and in the indication of Jupiter [and] the indication of Venus (and that is that one of them is the lord of the year, and the other the lord of the quarter), then what is good and what is evil in that year is stronger and greater. **9** And if the Sun was unfortunate in the year, one of the kings of the clime will die: and the knowledge of it is from the planet[19] which is bringing misfortune with the Sun, and the sign which it is in. **10** And so Jupiter and Aries, if they were both unfortunate, it destroys the king of Babylon; and Capricorn and Mercury [would destroy] the king of India, and Leo and Mars the king of the Turks, and Libra and the Sun the king of Rome, and Scorpio and Venus the king of the Arabs.

---

[13] Or rather, the Byzantine empire.
[14] Ibn Ezra credits an Enoch the Egyptian (probably a Hermes), in Section IV.7.
[15] Reading *ʿarab* for *gharb* ("West").
[16] That is, its exaltation (*sharaf*)
[17] Tentatively reading for what appears to be اعترضت.
[18] Omitting a repetition of "the indication of Saturn."
[19] Reading a singular for the plural, to match the verb here and below.

11 And the Indians and the Persians said that the first region belongs to Saturn, and the second one to Jupiter, and the third to Mars, and the fourth to the Sun, and the fifth to Venus, and the sixth to Mercury, and the seventh to the Moon. **12** Then they begin the allotment based on the signs:[20] so Aries and its triplicity belong to the east, and Taurus and its triplicity to the south, and Gemini and its triplicity to the west, and Cancer and its triplicity to the north.

13 And in every one of the regions of the planets are two powerful cities, by the reckoning of the houses of each planet. **14** In the region of the Sun there is one city, and likewise in the region of the Moon, because to each one of them belongs one house. **15** And in every one of them[21] there are (of the cities and forts) 21,600, a city and fort based on the amount of the minutes of the circle.[22]

16 And Hermes said that these minutes, if you [put it down as four],[23] it was the number of everyone who walks upon the earth: [and] if one of them died, another child is born.[24] **17** And [he said] that the first region which is at the ascending of the Sun[25] [has] 3,100 large cities and villages; and the second has, 2,713 large cities and villages; and the third has 3,970; and the fourth (and it is Babylon) has 2,974; and the fifth has 3,006 cities; and the sixth [has] 3,300 large cities and villages; [and the seventh has 2,537].[26] **18** Of all of them together, that is 400 cities in the Jazīrah.[27]

19 And if you gathered together the bounds of the planets from the course of the signs, what it conferred of the cities and villages with the amount of their degree and their minutes, [is] for every degree a city and for

---

[20] What follows is the usual assignment of the triplicities to the quarters based on Aries being in the east (in the northern hemisphere): Aries (and so fire) in the east, Capricorn (and so earth) in the south, Libra (and so air) in the west, Cancer (and so water) in the north. This arrangement is commonly found in horary questions about travel and lost objects.

[21] That is, in all of them *taken together:* see below.

[22] That is, every circle has 21,600 minutes (60' x 360° = 21,600').

[23] Reading uncertainly for جعلت روابع. Al-Rijāl seems to mean that the population of earth will be some multiple of 4.

[24] Omitting what seems to be a redundant *jaylān.*

[25] This could also be read as, "which is in/at the Ascendant of the Sun" (*fī ṭāliʿ al-shams*). But I am not sure what it means in any event.

[26] BL omits the seventh region, so I have added the number that would yield 21,600. The Latin al-Rijāl has 3,100 for the sixth, and 2,810 for the seventh, but that would be too many.

[27] Reading for *al-jazāʾir,* "Algeria."

every minute a village.[28] **20** And its bound from every sign is a place of its management of the countries. **21** And the planets especially have authority over the countries of that sign, such what belongs to Jupiter: he rules over the countries of Babylon, [and] the place of his bound in Cancer is the indicator of Iraq. **22** And like Venus, since she is the indicator of the Arabs: the place of her bound in Scorpio (which is the sign of the Arabs)[29] is the indicator of their desert. **23** And likewise, [the] indicator of the whole matter[30] is distinguished by its bound in the sign of their[31] countries. **24** And if you saw misfortune[32] in the entire sign, then I confirm it and I specify it in the bound of the planet of the king from that sign or the bound of the lord of its region.

Chapter VIII.35: On the knowledge of what cities belong to the signs[33]

Aries has, of countries:[34] Babylon, and Persia, and Azerbaijān, and Palestine, and Jazīrah, and Cyprus,[35] and the coast of the sea of Asia Minor, and the land of the Slavs, and Akhlāt, and Mūsul.

Taurus has, of countries: Sūwād,[36] and Māhīn, and Hamadān, and the country of the Kurds, and Isfahān up to the boundary of the island of Cyprus, and the coast of the sea of Asia Minor, and Lesser Armenia.

Gemini has, of countries: Armenia, and Jurjān, and Azerbaijān, and Egypt, and Mūqān, and Daylam, and Jīlān, and Tabaristān, and Burjān, and the sides of Isfahān, and Kirmān.

---

[28] I believe this means that since (for example) there are 76 degrees in Mercury's bounds, there are 76 Mercurial cities and 4,560 Mercurial villages.

[29] Removing the *qāf* (in "Scorpio") to yield "Arab."

[30] Reading *āmr* for *'ummahi.*

[31] Al-Rijāl seems to mean that the primary planet in the chart (or any planet) will affect the peoples ruled by its bound throughout all of the signs.

[32] A tentative translation for the seemingly ungrammatical منحه or ةمنحه. Still, what would al-Rijāl mean by the entire sign being unfortunate?

[33] For the first part of this chapter, I have decided to follow Nuruousmaniye. Br. Lib. 23399 (which the Latin seems to follow) has longer lists of attributions apparently from different sources, but contains many misspellings and unusual phrases (which might be due to misspellings). Since the list from Nuruosmaniye begins in the middle of a page as part of its Ch. VIII.34 (not VIII.35), I will simply translate it without sentence numbers, pending a future edition which will allow a comparison between both. I will resume with Br. Lib. starting with sentence **32**, which is identical in both sources.

[34] Reading for "cities," which is more properly part of the chapter title.

[35] But see below, where al-Rijāl has the "island of" Cyprus, not *"Jazīrah and"* Cyprus.

[36] Reading with Br. Lib. and Abū Ma'shar for اسوويدية, a kind of misspelling for Sweden.

Cancer has the land of Syria,[37] and Dūmah[38] and Halb, and Hamāh, and Hims, and Damascus, and Busrā and its territories.[39]

Leo has Antioch, and Tabaristān, and Nīshapūr, and Sicily, and the countries of the Yemen, and al-Kalwāniyyah.

Virgo [has] Babylon and the juncture of the two rivers[40] and their workings, and Eyvān, and Córdoba, and the Jazīrah of the Banī 'Umar.[41]

Libra has Khurāsān, and Bukhārā, and Tabaristān, and Kashmīr, and India, and Tibet, and some of the countries of Ethiopia, and Jurjān, and Tabaristān,[42] and the land of al-Sa'īd.[43]

Scorpio has the land of al-Sa'id, and the desolate earth,[44] and the land of Qayrawān and that ground, and the beginning of Tūnis and what follows it.[45]

Sagittarius has, of countries: Qūs, and the Taurus mountains, and the land of the Maghrib,[46] and the Island of Spain,[47] and al-Batr.[48]

Capricorn has the land of India, and the sphere[49] of Sijistān, and the upper regions,[50] and Macedonia, and Granada, and Sūs al-Aqsā.

Aquarius has from the sides of al-Madā'in, and Mīsān, and greater Alexandria.

Pisces has Tabaristān and the northern side of the land of Jurjān; and it has a partnership in Rome, and it has from Rome to the north, and it has the Jazīrah and lesser Alexandria, and the sea of Yemen, and it has Nanūniyyah and Sahūniyyah, and Lamūrīts, and Harmah, and the land of China, and the

---

37 Al-Shām.
38 This seems to be a city in NW Saudia Arabia, but perhaps should be identified with some place in Syria, given cities like Hamāh mentioned later.
39 Br. Lib. 23399 adds, "And it is the Ascendant of Babylon."
40 The Tigris and the Euphrates.
41 This seems to have been a tribe living in the Hijāz, somewhere between Mecca and Medīnah.
42 Note that Tabaristān has appeared twice here, another indication of how mixed-up some of these lists are—or that al-Rijāl is combining many sources together. Br. Lib. includes Tukhāristān, which might be a better reading for one of these.
43 Br. Lib. 23399 adds, "And it is the sign of Persia and the sign of Alexandria the Great, and and the Ascendant of Armenia, and the Ascendant of the Turks."
44 الارض المفقر, which may also refer to a particular desolate region.
45 Br. Lib. 23399 adds, "And it is the Ascendant of Persia."
46 Or perhaps, the "land of the west."
47 The Muslim lands in Spain, known as al-Andalus.
48 Br. Lib. 23399 adds, "And it is the Ascendant of Ahwāz, and the sign of Armenia, and the Ascendant of Babylonia, and the sign of Shāṭī al-Bahr."
49 كرة, which must be used metaphorically here because it normally means an actual spherical object.
50 راقية.

land of Ethiopia, and the Green Sea which is the sea of the west,[51] and Samarqand. **32** And it is the Ascendant of Rome.

33 And Master Ibridaj[52] the Persian mentioned that he had found [by means of Kankah],[53] in a book of the assignment of the lower world,[54] that the sign of the world is Aries, and its planet the Sun, and its Ascendant Cancer (and Jupiter in it).[55]

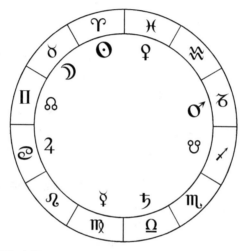

Figure 80: A Persian *Thema Mundi* (al-Rijāl Ch. VIII.35)

---

[51] Probably the Atlantic, but this term has also been used to describe the Arabian and Indian seas.

[52] This is my best guess at the name of this unknown Persian. In Br. Lib., his name is spelled twice without pointing and once with pointing (but without the letter that seems to be a *yaa*): see slides 318L line 1, 319R line 7, and 375R line 5. In Nuruosmaniye, his name is spelled once in a shortened form (278R lines 4-5), and twice in full (278L lines 20-21, 324L line 15). But the difference in pointing between all of these instances, makes it difficult to know the exact spelling.

[53] Adding *b-Kankah* (بكنكة) with Nuruosmaniye, suggesting that perhaps what follows is also reported in the works of Kankah the Indian.

[54] كناب عهد الدنيا. This could also be read as "a book of the age/epoch of the world," suggesting either an old book or one devoted to mundane epochs. Both readings are relevant here, since al-Rijāl proceeds to speak of a Persian *Thema Mundi* (chart of the beginning of the world), *and* the assignment of signs and planets to different countries.

[55] This is a very short version of a Persian *Thema Mundi*, in which Cancer is rising (as in the Greek *Thema Mundi*), but the planets are placed in the signs of their exaltations. The Persians (perhaps drawing on the Indians, who emphasize the lunar Nodes) also gave exaltations to the Nodes. For this use in mundane astrology, see Pingree 1968, pp. 62-63.

34 I distributed the regions among the seven planets and the twelve signs, and it came to be that Greater Irān[56] (which is Babylon) belongs to Jupiter and Aries; and Rome belongs to Libra and Saturn; and India and Sind and Makrān belong to Capricorn and Mercury, and the Hijāz and the land of the Arabs (all of it) belongs to Scorpio and Venus; and the Turks belong to Leo and Mars. **35** And as for what is beyond the Turks,[57] it belongs to the Moon and Virgo, and the land of Būdānjān[58] belongs to Aquarius and the Sun.

36 And I distributed Greater Irān[59] among the planets and the signs, and it came to be that Sūwād belongs to Aquarius and the Moon, and Māhīn and Māsdān and Fahrjān Burq and Hamadān belong to Taurus and Saturn, and the Alāns and Mūqān and Azerbaijān belong to Aries and Venus, and Persia[60] belongs to Virgo and Mercury, and Khūrasān belongs to Sagittarius and the Sun, and Rayy and 'Amad belong to Scorpio and the Moon, and Daylam belongs to Gemini and Mars, and Ahwāz belongs to Capricorn and Venus, and Jurjān and Tabaristān and Rayhān and al-Sa'ad and Samarqand and Sarakhs and Bust belong to Pisces and Mercury, and Marw al-Rūd and the Two Risings[61] and Murghāb[62] belong to Cancer and Saturn, and Sijistān and Kirmān belong to Libra and Mercury, and Ayward[63] and Nīshapūr and Tūs and Abrashahr[64]—they [belong to][65] Leo and Venus.

---

[56] Reading as ايران شهر (Irānshahr) for what seems to be Abranshahr or Abransahr (ايران شهر). For the first word, Br. Lib. has ايران ; Nuruosmaniye, ابرز or ابراز or ايران (below). Greater Iran refers to a large region of Iranian language speakers (and their culture), touching Syria, Irāq, and Azerbaijān in the west, to Pakistan and western China in the east, Uzbekhistān in the north, and to the Persian Gulf and Arabic Ocean in the south. Here, al-Rijāl's source (or perhaps al-Rijāl) identifies it broadly with Babylon, and distinguishes it from other cultures; then below, he divides it up and assigns signs and planets to various parts of it.

[57] Reading مرواء for ءموراء, from a Persian term that means "beyond." This term is also used in chorography to designate faraway places in Asia: see the entry for Marw al-Rūd in Section IV.13.

[58] Nuruosmaniye reads, "Azerbaijān.

[59] Again, *Abrān shahr* and its variants.

[60] Or more likely the province of Fars.

[61] الطالعان, unknown at this time. But Nuruosmaniye has الطالقان, al-Tālqān (unknown).

[62] Reading with Nuruosmaniye; Br. Lib has مرعات, Mara'āt.

[63] Reading with Br. Lib.; Nuruousmaniye has either *Anburd* or *Abnurd*.

[64] Reading with Br. Lib.; Nuruousmaniye has Aīn Shahr.

[65] Reading فهي with Nuruosmaniye for what seems to be بقي.

Chapter VIII.36: What regions & also villages belong to the planets

2 Saturn has the first region, and it is India[66] and China and the Zanj and the Sūdān and the higher[67] of the seas, and Ethiopia. **3** Jupiter has, in the statements of the Romans, the fourth region: and it is Babylon and the land of Persia and Khurāsān, and Iraq; in the statement of the Persians [he has] Aswān, and it is the region of Ethiopia and the Nubians. **4** Mars has, in the statement of the Romans, the seventh region, and the land of the Turks, and Syria,[68] and Rome; and in the statement of the Indians, the region of Alexandria and Syria.[69] **5** The Sun has, in the statement of the Romans, their own region and the second region, and the east,[70] and the land of China and what follows that, and Khurāsān; in the statement of the Persians,[71] Babylon. **6** Venus has, in [multiple] statements, the fifth region, and [it is] the Hijāz and the land of the Arabs, and Yemen. **7** And Mercury has, in the statement of the Romans, Alexandria and the land of the Greeks, and Syria;[72] and in the statement of the Persians, it is the sixth region and the third[73] region. **8** The Moon has, in the statement of the Romans, the sixth region and the land of the Maghrib[74] and the Franks, and Andalus and what follows it, up to the Turks and al-Jibāl; and in the statement of the Persians, it is the seventh region.

9 For[75] the cities of the signs which we said before, we named some cities of some of the signs, and the cities of other signs:[76] and this was in accordance with what we found in the statements of the scholars, and in the books—for example, the *Book of Regions and Countries*, and the book of Ptolemy, and the book of Abī Qimāsh and al-Muftī.[77]

---

[66] Nuruosmaniye has, "Sind."

[67] اعلى or اعلاء. This must refer to some region near the eastern coast of Africa.

[68] Al-Shām.

[69] Al-Shām.

[70] *Al-mushriq*, here probably meaning the Levant.

[71] Reading with Nuruosmaniye, for "al-Qūs."

[72] Al-Shām.

[73] Nuruosmaniye reads, "fifth."

[74] Or simply, the "west," especially when followed here by the Franks or Europeans.

[75] From the beginning of this sentence to the colon, I have translated from the Latin, as it is clearer.

[76] The Arabic also specifies that he has listed only those which were "worthy of mentioning," implying a much longer list at his disposal.

[77] Unknown at this time.

10 And Kasrī[78] [ibn Abū Sharwān][79] said, the[80] countries of the middle region [of the earth] are transferred,[81] and the countries in the extremes remain firm, for no one rules those regions except their own people. **11** And he said[82] that for the hot side, Mars manages it; and for cold one, Saturn manages it; and the middle one, Jupiter manages it: and [therefore the people living in the middle should be secure][83] based on that, and he is of the temperate [sort] of mind,[84] [but] the two on his sides are harmful.

12 And Abū 'Aun[85] related from his father Ibn Kisūn,[86] that he thought about this topic and he found the fixed stars to be spinning around the two [extreme] sides, the northern and the southern: and this was indicative of the constancy of the kingdom in them, and the moving, wavering planets spin around the area on the middle, and that was indicative of the movement in them.

[Remainder of chapter omitted.][87]

---

[78] Nuruosmaniye reads, "Kasbarī."

[79] Adding with Nuruosmaniye. Author unknown at this time.

[80] Omitting a phrase in Br. Lib. which begins with what might be an alternative name (البزر), and then says "he gathered together what is with the clans of the countries of the middle region…". Nuruosmaniye has, "the beginning of the middle region," perhaps a misspelling for "countries" (اول, دول).

[81] That is, there are many changes of government, empires, conquests, etc.

[82] The Latin says that other people *disagreed* with him, "and *they* said that…". But note that Māshā'allāh himself endorses this view in Ch. 31 of his *On the Revolutions of the Years of the World*: see Section IV.9.

[83] Reading with the Latin. The Ar. reads, "for he *[unknown word]* what he supplies." The Latin further goes on in more detail about the malefics, saying that the extremes in their qualities moves the nations under them to war.

[84] Reading *al-sarb wa-* with Nuruosmaniye, for *al-sharīq*.

[85] Nuruosmaniye spells this as A'aun (اعون).

[86] Nuruosmaniye reads, Kīsūn.

[87] The rest of this chapter attributes planets and signs to numerous cities, with the alleged authority of Ptolemy. But the lists in Br. Lib. and Nuruosmaniye differ wildly (including in their spelling, which affects the ability to locate them). Therefore I am omitting the remainder until I am better able to sort out and identify the cities.

Chapter VIII.37: On the longitudes of countries & their latitudes, based on what Habs[88] mentioned in his *Zij* (and they are from the extremity of the west), in addition to the position of every country[89]

2 It is mentioned by Ptolemy that the first clime begins from the east, from the extremity of the land of China, and it passes over it and over the coasts of the sea in the south of the land of India, then the country of Sind, then the mouth of the sea, over the island of al-Kūr[90] and cuts across the sea towards the Jazīrah of the Arabs and the land of Yemen, and cuts across the Red Sea, and passes through the country of Ethiopia, and cuts across the Nile of Egypt, and passes through the land of the Maghrib over the west of the land of the Berbers until it terminates at the [end of] the Maghrib. **3** And its greatest latitude is 16° 24', and the longest hour of its daylight 13 [hours] 29 [minutes], and its focus is on two cities, [and] they are behind the line of al-'Istiwayy, and they are affiliated with that. **4** The first of them is the city of al-Faqr: its longitude is 122°, and its latitude 3°. **5** And the other is the city of Barūnā: its longitude is 135°, and its latitude 3°. **6** And of its [other] cities, the city of: [*list omitted*].

7 The second clime begins from the east and passes over the country of China and India and Sind[91] and the juncture of the Green Sea and the Sea of Basrah,[92] and cuts across the Jazīrah of the Arabs in the land of Najd and Tihāmah, and cuts across the Red Sea and passes through Upper Egypt and cuts through the Nile and passes through the land of the Maghrib on the middle of the country of Ifrīqiyyah, then passes over the country of the Berbers and terminates until about the Maghrib. **8** And its greatest latitude is 29° 12', and the hours of its greatest daylight are [13 hours 49 minutes].[93] **9** And of its cities: [*list omitted*].

---

[88] حبس. Nuruosmaniye reads, "Khansh" (خنش). Unknown to me at this time.
[89] Throughout the rest of this chapter, al-Rijāl lists numerous cities (with their longitudes and latitudes) without interruption, in the form of a verbal table. Since these Ptolemy-based coordinates will not match modern geography and do not contain astrological information, I omit them here.
[90] Nuruosmaniye reads, "al-Tawl." Unknown at this time.
[91] Nuruosmaniye reads, "the north of the country of Sind."
[92] This probably refers to the Persian Gulf and Arabian Gulf, on either side of the United Arab Emirates and 'Omān.
[93] Reading with the Latin (which is correctly calculated). Missing in Br. Lib., and 14h 21m in Nuruosmaniye.

10 The third clime begins from the east and passes over the northern land of the country of China, then over the Indian country and the north of the country of Sind, then over the country of Kābul and Makrān up to the coasts of the Sea of Basrah and passes the *bakūr*[94] of Ahwāz, then passes over the country of Syria[95] and cuts across Lower Egypt and passes over the country of Ifrīqiyyah and terminates towards the sea of the west. **11** And its greatest latitude is 33° 40', and the hours of its greatest daylight 14 [hours], [15 minutes].[96] **12** And of [its] cities: [*list omitted*].

13 The fourth clime begins from the east and passes over the country of Tibet, then passes over Khūrasān and its cities, then over the north of Syria[97] and in its sea, and over the island of Cyprus and Rhodes, then it passes into the country of the Maghrib, over Tangiers toward the country of the west. **14** And its greatest latitude is 39°,[98] and the longest hours of its daylight 14 [hours], 49 [minutes]. **15** And in it are (of cities): [*list omitted*].

16 The fifth clime begins from the east, from the country of Yājūj and Mājūj, then passes over the north of Khurāsān and its cities, then it passes over Khersheh and passes over it from the country of Rome, then it passes by the coasts of the Syrian Sea from what follows after the north, then it passes over the country of al-Andalus toward the country of the Maghrib. **17** And its greatest latitude is 43°,[99] and the hours of its longest daylight [15 hours, 10 minutes].[100] **18** And in it are (of cities): [*list omitted*].

19 The sixth clime begins from the east and passes over the country of the Romans and Burjān, and passes over the sea of the west. **20** And its greatest latitude is 47° 02', and the longest of its hours of daylight 15 [hours], 41 [minutes].[101] **21** And in it are (of cities): [*list omitted*].

22 The seventh clime begins from the east, from the land of Yājūj, and it passes over the country of the Turks, then over the coasts of the sea of Jurjān, from what follows the north, and cuts across the sea of the Romans

---

[94] بكور. This word means "earliness," and has sunrise connotations. But I cannot understand it in this context.
[95] Al-Shām.
[96] Reading with the Latin (which is very closely calculated). Missing in Br. Lib., and listed as 12m in Nuruosmaniye.
[97] Al-Shām.
[98] Reading with Nuruosmaniye (and the Latin) for "40," as the former also gives the daylight hours.
[99] Nuruosmaniye reads either "42 [degrees] 33 [minutes]," or "42 [degrees] 38 [minutes]." The Latin has 43° 28'.
[100] Nuruosmaniye has 15° 12', the Latin 15° 15'.
[101] Reading the hours with Nuruosmaniye.

and passes over the country of Burjān and the Slavs, and terminates toward the sea of the west. **23** And its greatest latitude is 50° 30',[102] and the longest hours of its daylight [16 hours, 13 minutes].[103] **24** And in it are (of cities): [*list omitted*].

---

[102] Reading with the Latin, as it is missing in Br. Lib. and somewhat illegible in Nuru-osmaniye (but may be 53°).

[103] I have calculated this myself, but the Latin is very close (16° 16').

SECTION IV.5: ABŪ MA'SHAR ON CHOROGRAPHY

Comment by Dykes. This list from Abū Ma'shar's Arabic *Great Introduction* VI.9 includes significations for types of landscapes, which is useful in question ("horary") charts.

℧   ℩   ☋

♈	*Countries:* Babylon, Persia, Azerbaïjān, Palestine. *Landscapes and people:* Deserts, the pastures of sheep, small villages, places in which one works with fire, the shelters of thieves, houses covered with wood.

♉	*Countries:* Sūwād, Māhīr,[1] Hamadhān, the Kurds which are in the mountains.[2] *Landscapes and people:* Lands of little water in which one plants, every healthy cultivation, every place close to the mountains, gardens, forests,[3] trees, waters, the places of elephants and cows.

♊	*Countries:* Jurjān, Armenia, Azerbaïjān, Jīlān, Bazjān,[4] Mūqān, Egypt, the countries of Barqah, a partnership in Isfahān and Kirmān. *Landscapes and people:* The mountains, land which is cultivated, [flat broken ground],[5] hills, the places of fishermen, players of backgammon, the religious, singers.

---

[1] Probably Māhīn.
[2] Or specifically, al-Jibāl.
[3] Or, "jungles," reading with Lemay for الباغات.
[4] Probably a misspelling of Burjān, by pointing the ﺝ.
[5] This is the best I can make of دكادك, though related words include small hills.

Countries: Lesser Armenia, what is past Mūqān, Numidia (and it is part of Ifrīqīyyah), eastern Khurāsān, China,[6] Marw al-Rūd,[7] a participation in Balkh and Azerbaïjān.

Landscapes and people: Thickets, jungle, seashores, riverbanks, bluffs, the places of trees.

Countries: The Turks (to the end of the cultured region which follows it), Soghdiana, Arīn, the city of[8] Tūs.

Landscapes and people: Caverns,[9] the valleys of treacherous roads, those lands of gravel, every saturated land,[10] the mansions of kings, palaces, mountains, hills, elevated places of strongholds, impenetrable fortifications.

Countries: Jarāmaqa, Syria,[11] the Euphrates, the Jazīrah, and (of the countries of Persia) what follows Kirmān.

Landscapes and people: All land which is cultivated, the residences of women, jokers and singers, promenades.

Countries: The Romans and what is within their borders up to Ifrīqīyyah, and what is around them, Upper Egypt up to the borders of Ethiopia, Barqah, Kirmān, Sijistān , Kābul, Tu-khāristān, Balkh, Herāh.[12]

Landscapes and people: What is cultivated at the tops of mountains, every land with date palms on it, a place of hunting [with] falcons, every observatory[13] and road, a place of elevation [or] altitude, empty space, deserts.

---

[6] Probably the part close to Khurāsān.
[7] Reading a ﺪ for Abū Ma'shar's pointed ﺪ.
[8] *Shahr,* which is a Persian word for "city."
[9] Or, "depressions." Reading with alternate manuscripts for المغاوز or المفاوز.
[10] مشبعة: that is, saturated with enough herbage for sheep and goats.
[11] Al-Shām.
[12] Probably Herāt.
[13] This would probably include any kind of observation post.

♏	*Countries:* The land of the Hijāz, the desert of the Arabs and its sides up to Yemen, Tangiers, Qūmis,[14] al-Rāyy, a participation in Soghdiana. *Landscapes and people:* The places of grapevines and mulberries, and what resembles that in a garden, every place of stinking filth, prisons and the residences of anxiety and sadness, ruins, the hiding-places of scorpions.
♐	*Countries:* Jibāl, Rayy, Isfahān. *Landscapes and people:* Gardens, every place which is irrigated repeatedly, the places of the Herpads and the murmurers[15] and the places of the remaining religions, smooth deserts, the places of riding animals, oxen, and calves.
♑	*Countries:* Ethiopia, Makrān, Sind, the river of Kirmān and the shore of the sea which follows those areas, 'Omān, Bahrain up to India and its borders up to China, Ahwāz, the borders of the land of the eastern Romans.[16] *Landscapes and people:* The lands of castles and palaces[17] and gardens, every place irrigated by wadis and circling waters and rivers and irrigation canals, and ancient cisterns, every river edge with trees on it, a shore with a planting of vegetation as a cover on it, the places of dogs and foxes and beasts and lions, the residences of foreigners and the habitations of slaves,[18] the places in which fire has been kindled.

---

14 I have assumed an "and" should come between these, otherwise it would mean "the sea depth of Rayy."

15 Reading الزمزمة with Burnett in his edition of al-Qabīsī (I.33), for الزمزمه. The word refers to thunder and the roaring of lions, but the verb also means to murmur. Burnett has, "the murmuring songs of the fire-worshippers." So, the context suggests some sect that is known for chanting.

16 Probably Byzantine areas of modern Turkey.

17 Or, great halls.

18 Omitting an apparently redundant و.

Countries: Sūwād up to the side of the mountains, Kūfah and its sides, the back of the Hijāz, the land of the Copts in Egypt, the west of the land of Sind, a participation in the land of Persia.

Landscapes and people: The places of waters and flowing rivers, seas, canals and what is in them, every thing one digs with pick-axes, every place which water irrigates, the places in which water fowl are (and birds other than that), every place in which there are vineyards or alcohol is sold or whores reside, and every mountainous rural[19] land.

Countries: Tabaristān, the northern side of the land of Jurjān, a participation in the land of the Romans up to the land of Syr-ia,[20] the Jazīrah, Egypt, Alexandria and what is around Egypt, the Red Sea (I mean the sea of Yemen), the east of the land of India.

Landscapes and people: What is close to the seas and their shores, lakes, thickets, seacoasts, fish, the places of queens and the God-fearing, and a place of weeping and sadness.

---

[19] This can also refer to the steppes.
[20] Al-Shām.

SECTION IV.6: AL-BĪRŪNĪ ON CHOROGRAPHY

Comment by Dykes. In this Section I present two parts of al-Bīrūnī's cho-rography, from his *Book of Instruction*: his values for the seven climes, and place names along the climes. The values for the climes differ from Ptole-my's in that the climes are now treated as solid bands with borders: in the table below, I have given the beginning, middle, and end values for the long-est daylight hours and the associated latitudes. My computations were made using my table of ascensions (see Section IV.1 on the climes, and the citation there). The equator is not technically a clime, but like al-Bīrūnī I have includ-ed it.

Following is my own rendering of al-Bīrūnī's clime values from §236. As I mentioned above, the triple sets of values in the Longest Daylight and Lati-tudes columns represent the beginning, middle, and endpoints of the band for each clime.

Clime	Longest Daylight	Latitudes (Modern)
Equ.	(12h)	0°
1	12.75h - 13.00h - 13.25h	12° 45' - 16° 45' - 20° 36'
2	13.25h - 13.50h - 13.75h	20° 36' - 24° 15' - 27° 39'
3	13.75h - 14.00h - 14.25h	27° 39' - 30° 54' - 33° 48'
4	14.25h - 14.50h - 14.75h	33° 48' - 36° 36' - 39° 15'
5	14.75h - 15.00h - 15.25h	39° 15' - 41° 27' - 43° 36'
6	15.25h - 15.50h - 15.75h	43° 36' - 45° 34' - 47° 24'
7	15.75h - 16.00h - 16.25h	47° 24' - 49° 06' - 50° 36'

Figure 81: Climes of al-Bīrūnī

From §241 of the same work, the following table lists the countries along the path of each clime, from east to west. Al-Bīrūnī makes the interesting comment that the following account is only approximate, since "the latitudes of the cities in most of the books are far from correct," and he has not had the time to check every one. Note that although al-Bīrūnī would certainly have had access to Ptolemy's extensive coverage of Europe from the *Geogra-phy*, al-Bīrūnī (like other Islamic geographers and scholars) is almost wholly uninterested in anything outside the Islamic empires. This was a common feature of medieval Islamic scholarship, which routinely designated most Europeans indifferently as the *Franj*, the "Franks."

Clime	Cities and Countries, from East to West
Equ.	South Sea of China, Zanj/Zāvah Islands, Islands of Kalah and Sarīrah, south of Sri Lanka, Dībajāt/Dīva Islands, north of the Zanj and their islands, White Mountains, to Western Sea.
1	East of the Chinese empire, the Chinese Sea and its port cities such as Khānjū and Khānqū, Sri Lanka, Yemen south of Sanā' such as Zufār, Hadramaut, 'Aden; Dunqula (a city of Nubia), Ghānah of the west Sudān, to Western Sea.
2	Cities in China, India, the north of the Qāmrūn Mountains, Kīnaūj, Bārānāsī, 'Ujjain, some coastal cities, Thānah, Jīmur,[1] Sindān; of the countries of Sind: Mansūrah, Daybul; then 'Omān, the Arab areas of Hajar, Nejrān, Yamāmah, Mahrah, Sabā', Tabālah, al-Tā'if, Jiddah, Mecca, Medina, Kingdom of Ethiopia, land of the Bejah, Aswān, Qūs, al-Sa'īd al-A'lī, south of the cities of the Maghrib up to the Western Ocean.
3	East China and the capital of the empire, cities of the Indian Kingdom, Tanīshar, Qandahār; in Sind: Mūltān, Tahāma, Kūrūr,[2] the mountains of the Afghans, Zābulistān, Wālishtān, Sijistān, Kirmān, Persia, Isfahān, the Ahwāz, Basrah, Kūfah, Iraq, the country of the Jazīrah, Syria,[3] Palestine, the House of Reverence,[4] Qulzum, al-Tīh, Egypt, Alexandria, Barqah, Ifrīqīyah, the Berbers, Tāhart, Sūs, Tangier.
4	China, Tibet, the Qitāī and Khitan, Kashmir mountains, Bulūr, Wakhān, Bādakhshān towards Kābul and Ghūr, Herāt, Balkh, Tukharistān, Marw, Qūhistān, Nīshāpūr, Qūmis, Jurjān, Tabaristān, Rayy, Qumm, Hamadān, Mūsul, Azerbaījān, Manbij, Tarsūs, Harrān, Antioch, Cyprus, Rhodes, Sicily, the Straits of Gibraltar.
5	The eastern Turks, Yājūj and Mājūj, the wall (of China), the mountain Turks, Kāshgar, Balāsāghūn, Thāsht, Farghānah, Isbījāb, Shāsh, Ushrūshna, Samarqand, Bukhārā, Khwārizm, the Caspian Sea, Bāb al-Abwāb, Bard'ah, Mayyāfārqīn, Armenia, the paths of Rome and its countries, the country of Rome the Great,

---

[1] But the al-Bīrūnī manuscript looks like Jitmūr (جتمور).
[2] Reading with Wright, but the Arabic seems to read Kūzūz.
[3] Al-Shām.
[4] A title for Jerusalem.

	the land of Galicia and the cities of Spain.
6	The eastern Turks (the Qāy, Qūn, Kirghiz, Kimāk), the Toquz Oghuz toward the Türkmen and Fārāb, the city of the Khazars[5] and the north of their sea, the Alān between that sea and the Sea of Trabizond toward Constantinople, Burjān, France, northern Spain.
7	The Turks in northern forests and mountains, Bāshkhirt Mountains, the boundaries of Ghuzz and the Pechenegs, cities of Suwār and Bulghār, Russia, the Slavs, the Bulghars, the Magyars.

Figure 82: Countries in al-Bīrūnī's climes

Finally, I have included a map which represents al-Bīrūnī's coordinates in a rough form. Solid lines represent the *middle* of each clime, and numbers represent the primary cities and regions he describes. As one may see from the map, the equatorial regions fall widely off their line, those of the first clime are a bit better, and the rest fall pretty well into groupings along the other lines of the clime centers.

---

[5] That is, Atil (per Wright). "Their Sea" means the Caspian.

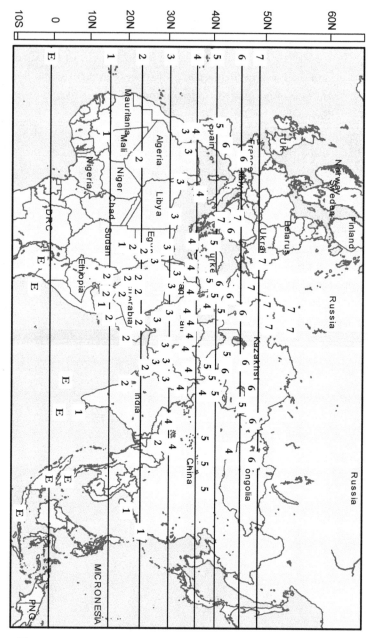

Figure 83: Al-Bīrūnī's chorography with middles of climes

SECTION IV.7: IBN EZRA ON CHOROGRAPHY

Comment by Dykes. In this Section, I summarize some chorographical statements by Abraham ibn Ezra, from the two versions of his *Book of the World* in the Sela critical edition. As with much of ibn Ezra's material in the *Book of the World*, his associations are usually taken from other authors with minimal commentary—normally, only the rules which he deems important. The statements are arranged by Sela's sections and boldface sentence numbers, and the two versions are distinguished by Roman numerals.

Two brief points about ibn Ezra's places: first, a couple of them (such as Edom, Canaan) were not directly relevant to the political reality in his times, but derive from Biblical references and metaphors. For example, Edom originally referred to a region of the Levant, but rabbinical literature had long since begun to refer to the Roman Empire as Edom—a double anachronism, since the Byzantine empire was no longer even the old western Roman Empire. Second, several of the names in his list of Ascendants (such as Egypt, Ifrīqīyyah) are not even cities. Perhaps ibn Ezra thought of these as referring to the founding or even conquest of large cities in them.

ༀ   ༀ   ༀ

Pairings of planets and signs (BW I.37, I.56, II.12-13). According to "Enoch the Egyptian" (I.37) or "Enoch the First" (I.56),[1] these pairs are associated with the following regions:

Source	Attribution	Variant
I.37, II.12	♃/♈: Iraq/Babylon, Persia	♃/♋: Iraq[2] (I.56)
I.37, I.56	♄/♎: Rome ("Edom")	
I.37, II.12	☿/♑: India	
I.37, I.56	♀/♏: Arabia (the Hijāz, Mecca)	
I.37	♂/♌: Barghān	
I.37	☉/♒: Canaan, Greece, Egypt	Israel, not Canaan (I.56)
I.37	☽/♍: Khurāsān	Add China (I.56)
II.12	♂/♉: Shur	
II.12	♀/♊: Egypt[3]	

---

[1] "Enoch" was one identity of Hermes Trismegistus, in Arabic and Hebrew texts. For this list, cf. the associations attributed to "some of them" by al-Rijāl in his Ch. VIII.34 (Section IV.4).

[2] Especially Jupiter's bound in Cancer.

II.12	♄/♌: Jerusalem[4]	
II.12	♂/♌: China[5]	
II.12	♂/♍: Spain	

In II.13, ibn Ezra credits Dorotheus with the following (cf. Section IV.3):

| ♄/♎: Edom (Rome?) | ♂/♐: Spain |
| ♀/♏: Qedar | ♎, ♏: See IV.3[6] |

In II.14, ibn Ezra changes course and makes some extra commentary. (**1**) Experience shows that Leo and the Sun rule "Edom" (by which he probably means the Romans or the Byzantines), since the Saturn-Jupiter conjunction took place in Leo before the birth of Jesus. (**2-5**) Although the Jewish sages say that Israel has no zodiacal sign, this is only when the Jews are properly following God's commandments: when they stray, they are ruled by Aquarius (see table above). (**6**) As with the Saturn-Jupiter conjunction before the birth of Jesus, the conjunction prior to the birth of Muhammad was in Scorpio, heralding Islam.[7] (**7**) According to one report, some astrologers associate Egypt with Capricorn.

The Ascendants of cities (I.38, II.15). Following is a list of the "signs" of some cities and regions. Only in II.15 does ibn Ezra clarify that these are the *Ascendants* of the cities. Note that the 8th Century foundation chart of Baghdad does not have Cancer rising, but Sagittarius.[8] Perhaps parts of this list come from much older sources.

---

[3] But see the Sun and Aquarius above.
[4] Ibn Ezra notes that "the ancients" erroneously attributed Cancer and Mars to Jerusalem.
[5] But see above, where China is associated by Enoch with the Moon and Virgo.
[6] Ibn Ezra simply says that Dorotheus was correct about Libra and Scorpio (Section IV.3). But ibn Ezra's list may not be the same as the one found in Hephaistio.
[7] In further volumes of the *Astrology of the World* series, I will explain conjunctional theory.
[8] See the chart in my *Choices & Inceptions*, in Ch. VII.2 of al-Rijāl's electional material. I also reproduce it in Section IV.1.

Almeria: 20° ♎	Ifrīqīyyah: 2° ♓	Pisa: 3° ♒[9]
Atābles/Alber: ♏[10]	Kirwān: 15° ♋	Rome: 15° ♌
Baghdad: 12° ♋	Lucca: ♋[11]	Saragossa: 6° ♈
Batelius: ♉	Lucena: 7° ♉	Seville: 7° ♓[12]
Béziers: ♓	Medīnah Sal'am: 6° ♑[13]	Toledo: ♍
Boujīah: 7° ♊[14]	Al-Mahdiyya: 3° ♌[15]	Tunis: 4° ♍
Córdoba, 22° ♊	Málaga: ♒	Valencia: 6° ♏
Egypt: 5° ♉	Mantua: ♎	Verona: ♉
Gabes: 2° ♓[16]	Marseilles: ♌	Washqā: 10° ♉
Granada: 10° ♋	Narbonne: ♒	Zawīlah: 15° ♍
Gūshqā: ♉	Palermo: 1° ♌	

Religions & peoples (I.66). The following planets are associated with various religions and peoples;[17] judge the status of these people according to how this planet is situated at the Aries ingress.

☉: Christians	♂: Arabs
♄: Philistines (Jews?)	♀: Muslims

Rules (I.56). Malefics on, squaring, or opposing a given degree (such as the bound of Jupiter in Cancer for Iraq) at the Aries ingress, will harm the relevant regions; a benefic will indicate the contrary. This is especially so for years in which there will be a Saturn-Jupiter conjunction.

---

[9] But in II.15, 6°. Ibn Ezra says that some have erroneously given Pisa to Pisces.

[10] Ibn Ezra says that Antares ("the heart of Scorpio") marks the Ascendant.

[11] Ibn Ezra notes that he has verified this by experience "several times," and that the Ascendant is in Jupiter's bound.

[12] In II.15, ibn Ezra says that in his opinion it is Aquarius. Since ibn Ezra spent time in Spain, he must have done some chart research to note the effects of these signs.

[13] But in II.15, Aquarius. Medīna al-Salām (or Salaam) is another name for Baghdad, which was already listed. Ibn Ezra may mean the Islamic holy city of Medīna/Medīnah, but its nickname is Medīna al-Nabī, "City of the Prophet."

[14] In II.15, ibn Ezra says that according to some it is 10° Gemini.

[15] In II.15, it is 6°.

[16] But in II.15, 10°.

[17] There are many versions of these attributions. See for example the planetary significations in *ITA* V.

SECTION IV.8: IBN LABBAN ON CHOROGRAPHY

Comment by Dykes. In Chapter II.9 of his *Introduction to Astrology*, al-Labban addresses chorography in the context of eclipses (drawing largely on Ptolemy). His list of signs and countries has many similarities with other medieval authors, but what stands out is his application of Ptolemy's triplicities to the Islamic world. For one thing, the orientation of his triplicities are totally different than Ptolemy's, circling clockwise in zodiacal order from the northeast. (Ptolemy's triplicities were placed according to planetary attributions to winds and the domicile lord of the triplicity which was of its sect.) Thus the airy triplicity was in the northeast in Ptolemy, but is here in the southwest.

Second, the association of individual countries with the signs does not seem to follow a pattern. That is, unlike in Ptolemy, ibn Labban does not seem to assign (for example) the fiery signs to the outer limits of one region, and the inner regions of its opposite. Perhaps ibn Labban and his sources are basing these attributions on social characteristics of the people in these regions, much as Ptolemy himself described people according to the lords of the signs (see Section IV.2).

ဢ   ဢ   ဢ

Triplicity	Quarter	Countries / Regions
Fire	NE	Turks, Shāsh, Farghāna, Khwārizm, river of Tabaristān, Bulgars, Khazars, Russia, Armenia.
Earth	SE	India, Islands,[1] Sind, Makrān, part of Khurāsān, Persia, Kirmān, land of Hajar, 'Oman, Arab desert, Yemen.
Air	SW	Sūdān, Hadham, shore of western sea,[2] Syrian sea, the Maghrib.
Water	NW	Spain, Jalāliqa, Burjān, Afrinja, greater Rumiyyz, the Slavs.

---

[1] Ibn Labban specifies that this is all manner of islands, but perhaps he means the islands in this quarter of the world.
[2] Probably the Atlantic Ocean.

Signs	Countries / Regions
♈	Babylon/Iraq, Azerbaïjān, Armenia, Persia, Palestine, Ramlah, Syria.
♉	Hamadān, Māhān, water of Kūfah, water of Basrah, Kurds, Sūwād to the mountains, the two sides of Tarsūs.
♊	Daylam, Jīlān, Egypt, Barqah, Jurjān, Mūqān, Qayrawān, Alexandria.
♋	Lesser Armenia, China to the east of Khurāsān, Marw, Marw al-Rūd, Ifrīqīyyah, Byzantium to behind the frontiers.
♌	Sogdiana, Tūs and its surroundings, Nīshāpūr, cities of the Turks to the end of the world, Antioch, inner Armenia, Bāb al-Abwāb.
♍	Algeria, Musūl, Jarāmaqah, the country by the harbors of Massīsa.
♎	Kirmān, Sijistān, Kābul, Tukharistān, Balkh, Herāt,[3] the Maghrib, Upper Egypt towards Ethiopia.
♏	The Hijāz, the Arabs' desert and toward Yemen, toward Tangiers, Qūmis, and Rayy.
♐	Baghdad, Isfahān, Saymara, Russia, al-Jibalīyya, Yemen.
♑	India, Ethiopia, Makrān, Sind toward Multān and 'Omān, the Ahwāz, Kābul, Ghūr.
♒	Kūfa, Sūwād and its surroundings, Copts, western Sind, back of the Hijāz toward Najd.
♓	Berber desert, cities of al-Hazar, al-Sarīr toward the sides of al-Hazar.

---

[3] Reading for "Heart."

SECTION IV.9: MĀSHĀ'ALLĀH ON
CLIMES & DIVISIONS

Comment by Dykes. Following are several excerpts from Māshā'allāh's *On the Revolutions of the Years of the World*, which only survives in Latin. I have re-edited it from the version in my *Works of Sahl & Māshā'allāh* (2008). Chapters 3 and 31 present two versions of climes, a seven-planet version and a superior planet version. Al-Rijāl's Ch. VIII.36 (in Section IV.4) has a little more on the division by superior planets. Chapters 32 and 34 assign zodiacal signs to regions of the world, and allot a certain number of cities to each region. These are obviously from the same source as parts of al-Rijāl's Ch. VIII.34, which is attributed by him to Hermes.

ℭ   ℭ   ℭ

Chapter 3: On the division of the earth

2 Know that the earth has two divisions: the east and the south is one, because they agree in heat; and the west and the north is the other, because they agree in cold. **3** After these, the earth is divided by the seven divisions of the seven planets in the climes, according to the order of the circles. **4** Therefore, the climes are known from the circle according to the order of the planets, just as with the lords of the hours. **5** For the first clime is Saturn's, the second Jupiter's, the third Mars's, the fourth the Sun's, the fifth Venus's, the sixth Mercury's, the seventh the Moon's.[1]

6 But the climes are according to the nature of the circle; after that is a known thing belonging to each sign, in terms of lands and cities;[2] and likewise for the bounds. **7** Because perhaps there will be a city belonging to some sign, and the bound of some planet of that sign conquers in [that city]. **8** Like Iraq, for example, which is said to belong to Cancer, and its planet is Jupiter, since the place of Iraq is in the place of the Jupiterian bound, from

---

[1] It is unclear to me whether Māshā'allāh is working numerically upwards, or geographically downwards. That is, if Saturn gets the first Ptolemaic clime, then Saturn's clime is closer to the equator and the Moon's is closer to the arctic circle. But if he is working geographically downwards, then Saturn really has the seventh clime higher in the north, and the Moon has the first clime closer to the equator.

[2] That is, the climes are derived astronomically from the order of planetary circles, while individual countries and cities are then associated with each zodiacal sign as a whole.

the nineteenth degree of Cancer up to its twenty-seventh, which is the bound of Jupiter.[3] **9** And the dismounting of the fortunes onto this place signifies fitness around Iraq in particular, and likewise the dismounting of the bad ones onto the same place signifies evil around Iraq. **10** Likewise you will know this from the dismounting of the fortunes and the bad ones in the rest of the bounds, as we have already expounded this to you. **11** Therefore, know them just as I have told you, because if you did this, it will not be concealed to you which sign or which bound a city belongs to.

Chapter 31: On the division of the world according to the three superior planets

2 Know that the world is divided into three divisions according to the natures of the three planets which are above the Sun: namely, according to their essences and complexions. **3** Therefore, the upper part of the world belongs to Saturn, and the middle part of the world belongs to Jupiter (and it is the temperate[4] part, like the substance of Jupiter); but the lower part belongs to Mars, which is the hot part, and it is according to the essence of Mars.

4 And the Moon participates with Saturn in his part, because her sign is opposite the sign of Saturn. **5** Therefore, from the quality of the intemperate years of this part of the citizens, there is a scarcity of wisdom and customs, and a cutting-off of piety, and forgetfulness; also, their colors are red and white, but the whiteness is like leadenness.[5] **6** The complexion of them and of their air is even of the darkness of the earth.

7 And Mercury participates with Jupiter, because his house is opposed to his house. **8** Also, the quality of the year of the citizens of this part effects wisdom, certitude, religion, variety and the conjoining of piety, and the unique shrewdness of [their] minds;[6] and their colors are of a diverse complexion, namely commingled of whiteness and blackness and redness, because their houses are commingled from the cold of the earth and the heat of the air. **9** Therefore the division of these is more worthy and more valua-

---

[3] The bound of Jupiter in Cancer runs from 19°—25° 59'.
[4] Remember that "temperateness" in traditional thought has to do with proper *mixtures*. So, Māshā'allāh is saying that the part of Jupiter is a harmonious mixture of the extreme qualities of Saturn and Mars, tempering their extremes.
[5] *Livido.* This word can also mean "black-and-blue."
[6] *Singularia ingeniorum acumina.*

ble than the rest of the divisions, and their land (the land of the philosophers and the wise) is better than the other lands.

10 And Venus participates with Mars, because her house is opposed to his house. **11** Also, just as we have said before in terms of the quality of the year of that same part of the citizens, there is the shamefulness and desire of Venus, and drinking parties and games, according to the places of its planets; and their colors are commingled from the heat of the earth and the air.

12 And the Sun participates with Jupiter and Mercury in their parts.

Chapter 32: On the division of the climes

2 Also, the climes are divided according to these ways, in worldly quality and colors of bodies, according to the order of the circle in the breadth[7] of its circle. **3** After this [the climes] are even divided over the twelve signs, which are the parts of the circle; and in these are 360 lesser segments divided by the degrees of the Sun, which make 21,600 minutes. **4** But the lesser minutes are not necessary, except in a revolution of the years of the world, and namely in a revolution of the year pertaining to the topic of the Sun,[8] so that the degree of the Ascendant and the quarters may not be concealed from you.

Chapter 34: On the number of cities in each clime

2 Also, they described that in the seven climes which is the world, there are cities and castles and villages according to the number of the twelve signs of heaven.

3 Likewise, the cities [are] just like the twelve signs, which are great cities, of which there are two in every clime: namely two of Saturn, two of Jupiter, two of Mars, two of Venus, one[9] of the Sun, one of the Moon, two of Mercury. **4** And I will reveal to you how many cities, villages and castles they said

---

[7] Or perhaps, "latitude" (*latitudine*).
[8] *In capitulis Solis.* I am uncertain what this means. It could refer to the direction of the Ascendant of a solar revolution (either of the world or a nativity) around the chart, as described by 'Umar al-Tabarī in *Persian Nativities II* or in my audio workshop on this same topic (www.bendykes.com/astrologylectures.php).
[9] Reading *una* for *duae*.

there were in the seven climes. **5** For[10] in the first clime they said there were 3,100; and in the second clime, 1,713; in the third, 1,077; in the fourth, 2,944; in the fifth, 3,006; in the sixth, 3,408; in the seventh, 3,300.

---

[10] These numbers do not add up to 21,600 as claimed. See the alternate values attributed to Hermes, described by al-Rijāl in his Ch. VIII.34, **16-18** (Section IV.4).

SECTION IV.10: BONATTI ON CLIMES & DIVISIONS

Comment by Dykes. This Section contains Chapter 8 from Tr. 8.1 of Guido Bonatti's *Book of Astronomy.* In the first part, Bonatti borrows—perhaps with the help of another source—from Māshā'allāh's material (see Section IV.9).

In the second part, on climes, Bonatti does something rather different. First, like al-Bīrūnī (IV.6), Bonatti assigns the zodiacal signs to the seven climes, and in the table below I have assumed that Bonatti is using the same hours of longest daylight as al-Bīrūnī does for the various climes and their subsections. Using these values, I have used my table of ascensions[1] to calculate what latitudes (whether north or south of the equator) the zodiacal climes belong to. Next, Bonatti imagines that these signs are stretched over the portions of the earth they are assigned to: so for example, all of Aries is stretched over the portion of the earth belonging to the first clime. Because each sign has five bounds, and since other authors have asserted that different countries are indicated by different zodiacal bounds,[2] Bonatti says that each bound of a sign is stretched over a certain portion of the earth along that clime, starting from east to west: this is a direct justification for the assigning certain bounds to certain countries, since a given region will have a certain bound stretched over it.

There are several points and cautions to make about Bonatti's account. First of all, the geography he is working with is still Ptolemy's: the most western point of the known world was the Canary Islands, and the most eastern point was somewhere in a line of longitude around the Ganges river. Thus, these bounds cannot be used directly to describe anything westward in the Americas or further east in Asia. Of course, this goes doubly for the southern hemisphere, although by Bonatti's time there were reliable reports and some geographical information about places below the equator.

Second, the bound system used by Bonatti here is Ptolemy's, not the Egyptian one we would expect from Perso-Arabic astrologers. This suggests that the scheme comes from someone with allegiance to Ptolemaic astrology and geography, and was not an independent notion by a Perso-Arabic astrol-

---

[1] See http://www.bendykes.com/reviews/study.php. Actually, I calculated directly with the equations used to construct the table. Remember that ascensional values will be slightly different depending on the method used; the program Delphic Oracle also computes ascensional times for each chart.

[2] For instance, the bound of Jupiter in Cancer (in the Egyptian bounds) indicates Iraq, and the bound of Venus in Scorpio the Arabs.

oger who happened also to know about Ptolemy's climes. Since Bonatti does not name his source, it is also possible that he is drawing on a medieval European; or perhaps Bonatti himself has invented this idea, since he himself uses the Ptolemaic bounds (or a version of them: see his *Book of Astronomy*, Tr. 2., Part 2).

Third, instead of saying that the bounds cover a region equal to a *proportion* of the length of the bound in the sign to the entire known world, Bonatti gives fixed values in a measurement of *miliaria* ("miles," exact value unknown). For example, suppose that the known world is 5000 "miles" across. In Ptolemy's bounds, Jupiter rules the first 6° of Aries. Since 6° is 1/5 of 30° (the whole of Aries), it should follow that the bound of Aries stretches over the first clime for a distance of 1,000 "miles" (.2 x 5000 = 1000)—and so on with the rest of the signs. But Bonatti makes the bound of Jupiter cover only 318 "miles" of territory; and when we reach the end of Aries after 1,590 "miles," we are supposed to start over with Jupiter if there is any remaining territory. To me it would make more sense to make each sign cover the entirety of its own clime, and assign the territories proportionate to the size of the bounds in the signs.

Related to this is the fact that all of Bonatti's distances are multiples of 53, a number which I cannot account for. That is, Jupiter's 318 *miliaria*, Venus's 424 *miliaria*, etc., are all multiples of 53: so if we divide each distance by 53 we get precisely the number of degrees in each planet's bound for that sign. So: why 53, and why fixed values instead of proportions? Bonatti does not say.

Finally, there is the question of the earth's curvature, which might explain why—given the use of fixed values—Bonatti speaks of starting over once one reaches the end of a sign. Based on the description below, it would appear that Bonatti or his source is looking at a flat map, and starting each sign in its own clime from the same beginning-point in the east. If so, then each sign will terminate in the same place on the western side of the map—and one might as well have used the proportional method I suggested above. On the other hand, if we started all of the climes at the same point of longitude in the east but wrapped them around a globe, then the distance around the earth will be greater for climes near the equator, and smaller for climes near the North Pole: thus, each sign will have to repeat its bounds, but the southern ones will have to repeat more often than the northern ones. Again, these problems disappear if we simply stretch each sign along the entirety of the clime around the earth (or along the entire map) and treat the position of each bound proportionally instead of using Bonatti's fixed values.

꙼   ꙼   ꙼

Chapter 8: How the earth is divided into seven other divisions

2 Again, these two and three divisions[3] are subdivided into another seven divisions according to the number of the seven planets—which are called climes, [and] which are fitted thusly to the seven planets. **3** For the first clime is fitted to Saturn, who is higher and superior and slower than the rest of the planets. **4** But the second clime is fitted to Jupiter, who immediately follows after Saturn in slowness, and succeeds [him] in the order of circles. **5** The third is fitted to Mars, who immediately follows after Jupiter and succeeds [him] both in slowness and in the order of circles. **6** The fourth is fitted to the Sun, who follows after Mars in the order of circles. **7** The fifth is fitted to Venus, who follows after the Sun in the order of circles. **8** The sixth is fitted to Mercury, who follows after Venus in the order of circles. **9** But the seventh and last one is fitted to the Moon, who follows after Mercury in the order of circles, wherefore she is lower than, and faster than, the rest of the planets.

10 Whence, every planet disposes more over the clime deputed to it than over the others, even though each of them has something to do over every clime—sometimes according to more, sometimes according to less. **11** And likewise the signs are in charge of regions, and imprint in them whatever is according to their nature. **12** Wherefore the fiery ones imprint more over the hot regions, the earthy ones over the dry ones, the airy ones over the moist ones, the watery ones over the cold ones.[4] **13** Because the signs do not signify over the parts of the world by places or through their position,[5] but through their [elemental] *nature*. **14** Whence, if the region over which a fiery sign was in charge, were hot, what is signified [by the sign] will happen more strongly than in a cold [region]: for it tempers the coldness in the cold one; and because [a wet sign] moistens in a wet [region], it tempers the dryness in a dry region, and *vice versa*.

---

[3] Bonatti is referring to his Ch. 7 (omitted here).
[4] The attributions here are not the standard Stoic or Aristotelian ones–they derive from a combination of wind and elemental considerations (see below).
[5] By this, Bonatti or his source might mean "not by their house position in a chart."

15 Just as Aries, Leo, and Sagittarius (which are the first triplicity), heat in the parts of the east, [so] in the parts of the north they temper the coldness—because they are fiery, and are eastern signs. **16** Whence if the Ascendant were one of those signs, it will strengthen what is signified, and will increase it; and the eastern wind is hot and dry.

17 And just as Taurus, Virgo, and Capricorn (which are the second triplicity) dry out in the parts of the south, [so] in the parts of the west they temper the moisture because they are earthy, and are southern signs. **18** Whence if the angle of the 10th were of those signs, it will strengthen what is signified, and will increase it; and the southern wind is hot and moist.

19 And just as Gemini, Libra, and Aquarius (which are the third triplicity) moisten in the parts of the west, [so] they temper the dryness in the southern ones because they are airy, and are western signs. **20** Whence if the angle of the 7th house were of those signs, it will strengthen what is signified, and will increase it; and the western wind is cold and moist.

21 And just as Cancer, Scorpio, and Pisces (which are the fourth triplicity) chill in the northern parts, [so] in the eastern ones they temper the hotness because they are watery, and are northern signs. **22** Whence if the angle of the 4th house were of those signs, it will strengthen what is signified, and will increase it; and the northern wind is cold and dry.

23 And even the planets help this: for if what is signified were in the north, and Saturn were in charge of what is signified, he will help it and will make it appear more, and more strongly so if Mercury helped him, and what was signified belonged to coldness. **24** And if it were in the west, and Jupiter were in charge of it, what is signified will be increased, and more strongly so if the Moon helped him, and what is signified belonged to moisture, and [Jupiter] will make it appear more. **25** And if it were in the southern parts, and Mars were in charge of it, it will be increased if what was signified belonged to dryness, and he will make it appear more. **26** And if it were in the eastern parts, and the Sun were in charge of it, and what was signified belonged to hotness, the Sun will help it, and will make it appear more, if however Venus were a participant, she will temper some of the heat.[6]

Another division of the earth

28 And after these two, and these three, and these seven divisions, again the earth is subdivided into another twelve divisions according to the number of the twelve signs, and according to the crossing of the degrees from the east to the west.

29 Now, Aries is fitted to the first clime: whence Mars, who is the lord[7] of Aries, is in charge of the things signified by that clime from the east to the west; but the lords of the bounds participate with him, and the virtue of the lord of the bound prevails over the virtue of the lord of the house in the particular significations of revolutions. **30** For Jupiter, who has the first bound of Aries, disposes over the significations of the revolution of the first clime, from the beginning of the inhabitable earth from the direction of the east toward the west, for 318 *miliaria*.[8] **31** And after him, Venus for 424 *miliaria*. **32** And after her, Mercury for 371 *miliaria*. **33** And after him, Mars for 265 *miliaria* (and his signification is stronger then, because he has the virtue of the bound and the virtue of the house—and so it happens with the others). **34** And after him, Saturn for 212 *miliaria*. **35** Then the disposition reverts to Jupiter and to the rest of the others until it reaches the end of the inhabitable region toward the west.

♈		♉		♊	
E	**B/P**	**E**	**B/P**	**E**	**B/P**
♃ 6	♃ 6	♀ 8	♀ 8	☿ 6	☿ 7
♀ 6	♀ 8	☿ 6	☿ 7	♃ 6	♃ 6
☿ 8	☿ 7	♃ 8	♃ 7	♀ 5	♀ 7
♂ 5	♂ 5	♄ 5	♄ 2	♂ 7	♂ 6
♄ 5	♄ 4	♂ 3	♂ 6	♄ 6	♄ 4

---

[6] Bonatti considers Venus to be primarily cold and moist, but with a certain "hidden heat" (Tr. 7, Part 1, Ch. 11).

[7] Reading *dominus* for *domus*.

[8] Bonatti is multiplying the number of degrees in each planet's bound by 53 *miliaria* (see above).

♋		♌		♍	
E	B/P	E	B/P⁹	E	B/P
♂ 7	♂ 6	♃ 6	♄ 6	☿ 7	☿ 7
♀ 6	♃ 7	♀ 5	☿ 7	♀ 10	♀ 6
☿ 6	☿ 7	♄ 7	♂ 5	♃ 4	♃ 5
♃ 7	♀ 7	☿ 6	♀ 6	♂ 7	♄ 6
♄ 4	♄ 3	♂ 6	♃ 6	♄ 2	♂ 6

♎		♏		♐	
E	B/P	E	B/P	E	B/P
♄ 6	♄ 6	♂ 7	♂ 6	♃ 12	♃ 8
☿ 8	♀ 5	♀ 4	♀ 7	♀ 5	♀ 6
♃ 7	☿ 5	☿ 8	♃ 8	☿ 4	☿ 5
♀ 7	♃ 8	♃ 5	☿ 6	♄ 5	♄ 6
♂ 2	♂ 6	♄ 6	♄ 3	♂ 4	♂ 5

♑		♒		♓	
E	B/P	E	B/P	E	B/P
☿ 7	♀ 6	☿ 7	♄ 6	♀ 12	♀ 8
♃ 7	☿ 6	♀ 6	☿ 6	♃ 4	♃ 6
♀ 8	♃ 7	♃ 7	♀ 8	☿ 3	☿ 6
♄ 4	♄ 6	♂ 5	♃ 5	♂ 9	♂ 5
♂ 4	♂ 5	♄ 5	♂ 5	♄ 2	♄ 5

Figure 84: Egyptian and Bonatti-Ptolemaic bounds

36 Taurus is fitted to the southern half of the second clime, and Venus (who is the lady of Taurus) is in charge of what it signifies, from the east to the west. **37** And Venus, who has the first bound of Taurus, is in charge of its significations and disposes over them from the beginning of the inhabitable earth from the east toward the west, for 424 *miliaria*. **38** And its significations will then be without the partnership of anyone, because she is the lady of the house and the lady of the bound, and therefore they appear more. **39** And after her, Mercury for 371 *miliaria*. **40** After him, Jupiter for 371 *miliaria*. **41** And after him, Saturn for 106 *miliaria*. **42** And after him, Mars

---

⁹ In this sign alone, Bonatti's list departs from the Ptolemaic bounds. Ptolemy has: *Jupiter 6*, Mercury 7, *Saturn 6*, Venus 6, *Mars 5*.

for 318 *miliaria*. **43** After him, the disposition reverts to Venus, and she is in charge of the significations for 424 *miliaria*, and so on for the rest of the lords of the bounds.

	Part	Clime	Daylight (Likely)	Latitudes (Likely)
♓	All	7	15.75h – 16.25h	47° 24' - 50° 36'
♒	N	6	15.50h – 15.75h	45° 34' - 47° 24'
♑	S		15.25h – 15.50h	43° 36' - 45° 34'
♐	N	5	15.00h – 15.25h	41° 27' - 43° 36'
♏	S		14.75h – 15.00h	39° 15' - 41° 27'
♎	N	4	14.50h – 14.75h	36° 36' - 39° 15'
♍	S		14.25h – 14.50h	33° 48' - 36° 36'
♌	N	3	14.00h – 14.25h	30° 54' - 33° 48'
♋	S		13.75h – 14.00h	27° 39' - 30° 54'
♊	N	2	13.50h – 13.75h	24° 15' - 27° 39'
♉	S		13.25h – 13.50h	20° 36' - 24° 15'
♈	All	1	12.75h – 13.25h	12° 45' - 20° 36'

Figure 85: Signs and climes (Bonatti)

44 But Gemini is fitted to the northern half of the second clime. **45** And Mercury, who is its lord, is in charge of the significations of that half from the east to the west, but [the lords of the bounds] participate with him in the bounds.[10] **46** Now Mercury himself is in charge of the first bound, and his signification will appear strong then (because he is the lord of the house and the lord of the bound) for 371 *miliaria*. **47** And after him, Jupiter for 318 *miliaria*. **48** And after him, Venus for 371 *miliaria*. **49** And after her, Mars for 318 *miliaria*. **50** After him, Saturn for 212 *miliaria*. **51** Then the disposition reverts to Mercury and thus for the rest, up to the end of the inhabitable earth to the west.

52 Cancer is fitted to the southern half of the third clime, from the east to the west: and its lady the Moon is in charge of the significations of the clime from the east to the west, and the lords of the bounds participate with her. **53** For Mars, who has the first bound of Cancer, is in charge of the significa-

---

[10] Reading *terminis* for *termino* (although the sentence is more truncated than its parallel ones in other paragraphs, and may have been garbled in transcription).

tions of the revolution, which ought to be from the beginning of the inhabit-able earth from the direction of the east to the west, for 318 *miliaria*. **54** And after him, Jupiter for 371 *miliaria*. **55** And after him, Mercury for 371 *miliaria*. **56** [And after him, Venus for 371 *miliaria*.][11] **57** And after her, Saturn for 159 *miliaria*. **58** Then the disposition reverts to Mars, and to the rest of the other planets, until the end of the inhabitable earth toward the west is reached.

59 Leo is fitted to the northern half of the third clime, from the east to the west: and the Sun, who is its lord, is in charge over the significations of that half generally, but the lord of the bounds [do so] with him particularly.[12] **60** For Saturn, who is the lord of the first bound of Leo, is in charge of the significations of the revolution from the beginning of the inhabitable earth from the direction of the east toward the west, for 318 *miliaria*. **61** And after him, Mercury for 371[13] *miliaria*. **62** After him, Mars for 265 *miliaria*. **63** After him, Venus for 318 *miliaria*. **64** After her, Jupiter for 318 *miliaria*. **65** Then the disposition reverts to Saturn and to the rest of the planets in succession, until the end of the inhabitable [earth] is reached.

66 Virgo is fitted to the southern half of the fourth clime, from the east to the west: and Mercury, who is the lord [of Virgo], is in charge of the signifi-cations of that half from the east to the west generally, but the lord of the bounds participate with him. **67** And he himself, who is the lord of the first bound of Virgo, is in charge of the significations of the revolution which ought to be from the beginning of the inhabitable earth toward the west, for 371 *miliaria*. **68** And after him, Venus for 318 *miliaria*. **69** And after her, Jupi-ter for 265 *miliaria*. **70** After him, Saturn for 318 *miliaria*. **71** After him, Mars for 318 *miliaria*. **72** Then the disposition reverts to Mercury, *etc.*, as was said about the others.

73 Libra is fitted to the northern half of the fourth clime from the east to the west: and Venus, who is its lady, is in charge of the significations of that half generally from the east to the west, but the lords of the bounds partici-pate with her. **74** Now Saturn, who is the lord of the first bound of Libra, is in charge of the significations of the revolution which ought to be from the beginning of the inhabitable earth from the direction of the east toward the west, for 318 *miliaria*. **75** And after him, Venus for 265 *miliaria*. **76** And after her, Mercury for 265 *miliaria*. **77** After him, Jupiter for 424 *miliaria*. **78** And

---

11 The text omits Venus, who fits here.
12 Remember, the luminaries do not rule any bounds.
13 Reading for "372."

after him, Mars for 318 *miliaria*. **79** Then the disposition reverts to Saturn, *etc.*, as was said about the others.

80 Scorpio is fitted to the southern half of the fifth clime: and Mars, who is its lord, is in charge of the significations of that half generally, from the east to the west, but the lords of the bounds participate with him. **81** For Mars himself, who is the lord of the first bound of Scorpio, is in charge of the significations of the revolution which ought to be from the beginning of the inhabitable earth from the direction of the east toward the west, for 318 *miliaria*. **82** And after him, Venus for 371 *miliaria*. **83** After her, Jupiter for 424 *miliaria*. **84** And after him, Mercury for 318 *miliaria*. **85** After him, Saturn for 159 *miliaria*. **86** Then the disposition reverts to Mars, *etc.*, as was said about the others.

87 Sagittarius is fitted to the northern half of the fifth clime, from the east to the west: and Jupiter, who is its lord, is in charge of the significations generally from the east to the west, but the lords of the bounds participate with him. **88** Now Jupiter,[14] who is the lord of the first bound of Sagittarius, is in charge of the significations of the revolution which ought to be from the beginning of the inhabitable earth from the beginning of the east toward the west, for 424 *miliaria*. **89** And after him, Venus for 318 *miliaria*. **90** After her, Mercury for 265[15] *miliaria*. **91** After him, Saturn for 318 *miliaria*. **92** After him, Mars for 265 *miliaria*. **93** Then the disposition reverts to Jupiter, *etc.*, as was said about the others.

94 Capricorn is fitted to the southern half of the sixth clime, from the east to the west: and Saturn, who is its lord, is in charge of the significations of that half generally from the east to the west, but the lords of the bounds participate with him. **95** For Venus, who is the lady of the first bound of Capricorn, is in charge of the significations of the revolution which ought to be from the beginning of the inhabitable earth from the direction of the east toward the west, for 318 *miliaria*. **96** And after her, Mercury for 318 *miliaria*. **97** After him, Jupiter for 371 *miliaria*. **98** After him, Saturn for 318 *miliaria*. **99** After him, Mars for 265 *miliaria*. **100** Then the disposition reverts to Venus, as was said about the others.

101 Aquarius is fitted to the northern half of the sixth clime, from the east to the west: and Saturn, who is its lord, is in charge of the significations of that half universally from the east to the west, but the lords of the bounds

---

[14] Reading *Juppiter* for *Saturnus*.
[15] Reading for "165."

participate with him. **102** Now this same Saturn, who is the lord of the first bound of Aquarius, is in charge of the significations of the revolution which ought to be from the beginning of the inhabitable earth from the direction of the east toward the west, for 318 *miliaria*. **103** And after him, Mercury for 318 *miliaria*. **104** And after him, Venus for 424 *miliaria*. **105** And after her, Jupiter for 265 *miliaria*. **106** After him, Mars for 265 *miliaria*. **107** Then the disposition reverts to Saturn, as was said about the others.

108 Pisces is fitted to the seventh clime, from the east to the west: and Jupiter, who is the lord, is in charge of the significations of that clime universally from the east to the west, but the lords of the bounds participate with him. **109** Now Venus, who is the lady of the first bound of Pisces, is in charge of the significations of the revolution which ought to be from the beginning of the inhabitable earth from the east toward the west, for 424 *miliaria*. **110** And after her, Jupiter for 318 *miliaria*. **111** After him, Mercury for 318 *miliaria*. **112** After him, Mars for 265 *miliaria*. **113** After him, Saturn for 265 *miliaria*. **114** Then the disposition reverts to Venus, as was said about the others.

115 If however the clime were not of such a length[16] that the things signified by the planets could be extended so much that the number of the *miliaria* could be completed, as was said, it does not refer [to anything]. **116** For with land missing, the signification of the bound of the planet expires.[17]

117 Whence, you ought to regard the disposition and being of the planets at the revolutions of years, both those of nativities, or questions, and of the world, and see if the being of the lord of the sign were good: because it signifies the good being of the clime generally, according to the part of which it is in charge. **118** And likewise look at the being of the planets in charge of the bounds: for if they agreed in one being, it will signify that what is signified by the revolution will appear more, both in what is good and what is evil. **119** So that if the being of the lord of the sign and the being of the lord of the bound were good, it signifies complete good in the region over which the lord of the bound is in charge. **120** If however the being of each were bad, it signifies that complete evil will appear in the region over which the lord of the bound is in charge. **121** If however they disagreed, what is signified by them will appear less, but what is signified by the lord of the sign will appear

---

16 That is, its length in longitude (*longitudinis*).
17 Bonatti seems to be referring to stretches of water: if the land ends in water with no land on the other side, then the indications for that clime cease.

less than what is signified by the lord of the bound, both in what is good and what is evil.

SECTION IV.11: FOUNDATION CHARTS

Comment by Dykes. In this Section I give the data from a "very old" Greek manuscript (Leid. B.P. Gr. 78) transcribed in the *CCAG* 9.2, pp. 177-79, which purports to give the planetary positions for the foundation charts of six famous cities. I have tried to find the appropriately-timed chart for each, and have translated some of the Latin comments by the editor, Stephan Weinstock.

Weinstock begins (p. 176) by saying, "The question arises as to why the author has selected these cities. We should hardly wonder why with respect to the first three, which in the age of the emperors were always 'imprinted cities.'[1] No one [else] would have related the last three, which seem to be Palestinian, except for an author stemming from that region. But there is nothing more which I may conjecture about him and his age." He also notes that the city of Cairo was said to have been founded medievally on July 9, 969 AD—that is, by the Fatimids.

In trying to date these charts, I found that only the Alexandria chart works for the known eras in which the cities were founded. But the data do work for these cities in *other* eras, all the way up to 833 AD. Could these "foundation" charts actually be the charts for coronations or battles on these dates?

ಬಿ   ಬಿ   ಬಿ

Constantinople: ☉: 12° 21' ♓ ☽: 15° 29' ♊ ♄: 19° 30' ♎ ♃: 16° 17' ♐ ♂: 9° 59' ♐ ♀: 21° 36' ♈ ☿: 5° 19' ♈ ASC: 17° 24' ♋ MC: 23° 09' ♓	*Weinstock*: The birth of Constantinople, which was first celebrated on the 11th day of May, 338 AD, is famous enough…but our chart does not square with these [other sources cited]: for the Sun was in Pisces in the months of February and March. *Dykes*: The superiors were in these signs (both tropically and by Fagan-Allen) in late 334-35 AD, but the closest chart up to 1000 AD is the figure below, from 833 AD. Note that Mercury and Venus are wholly wrong.

---

[1] Gr. *episēmoi.* This word can also mean "notable, remarkable." That is to say, these cities and their founding were commemorated on coins, often with astrological information. See below.

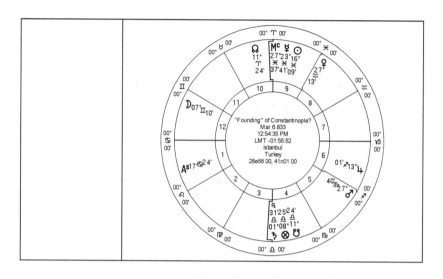

Antioch:

☉: 18° 09' ♊
☽: 7° 28' ♈
♄: 11° 04' ♌
♃: 14° 35' ♐
♂: 15° 38' ♓
♀: 19° 24' ♉
☿: 24° 07' ♊
ASC: 19° 27' ♈
MC: missing

Weinstock: Antioch was founded…on the 22nd day of the month of May, 300 BC…however, the coins of Antioch depict the Sun in Aries, which I do not observe.

Dykes: The chart matching this data is from 377 BC, much too early for Seleucus I. Currently I do not know what historical events this corresponds to.

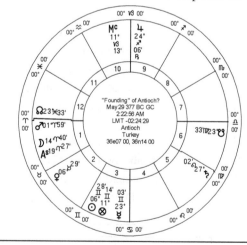

Alexandria:	*Weinstock*: Alexandria was founded in the year 330 BC...and our chart, as the very learned Otto Neugebauer has taught me well, rightly refers to the 16th day of April, with the exception of Jupiter, who ought to be in Sagittarius.
☉: 17° 03' ♈ ☽: 24° 09' ♎ ♄: 18° 07' ♓ ♃: 11° 09' ♉ ♂: 16° 24' ♒ ♀: 1° 03' ♉ ☿: 15° 07' ♈ ASC: 14° 11' ♌ MC: missing	

Dykes: Following is the chart suggested by Neugebauer, according to Weinstock.

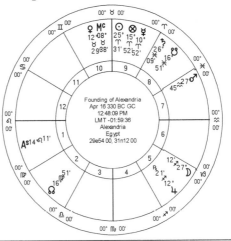

Gaza:	*Dykes*: Although Pompey the Great conquered Gaza during his Near East campaign, Gaza was more officially founded after rebuilding by his associate Aulus Gabinius, around 55-50 BC. Unfortunately, not even the superiors fit into these signs in that era. But in 196 AD all of the planets are in their proper signs except for Mars.
☉: 4° 11' ♈ ☽: 7° 35' ♉ ♄: 11° 03' ♒ ♃: 23° 15' ♓ ♂: 11° 04' ♈ ♀: 21° 06' ♉ ☿: 11° 54' ♓ ASC: 7° 19' ♉ MC: missing	

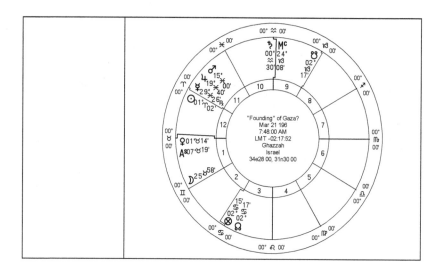

Caesarea:	*Weinstock*: Caesarea, if it is the city in Palestine, was
☉: 21° 31' ♓	founded around 22 BC.
☽: 7° 24' ♉	
♄: 17° 15' ♎	
♃: 7° 59' ♋	*Dykes*: Apart from Venus being in the wrong sign, this
♂: 15° 50' ♓	data can be matched to March 3, 70 AD.
♀: 13° 21' ♒	
☿: 14° 24' ♓	
ASC: 19° 21' ♉	
MC: 3° 16' ♒	

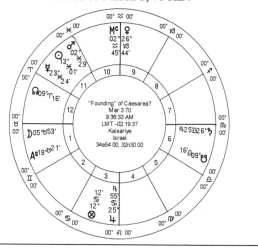

Neapolis:	*Weinstock*: Neapolis, if it is in Palestine, had its era start
☉: 26° 04' ♌	from the year 72 BC, according to coins.
☽: 14° 07' ♋	

♄: 17° 03' ♍
♃: 3° 43' ♍
♂: 7° 21' ♏
♀: 19° 27' ♎
☿: 28° 38' ♍
ASC: 46° 22' ♎
MC: missing

Dykes: The Palestinian Neapolis is now called Nablus. The numbers for the Ascendant are probably transposed, and should be 22° 46'. If so, then the most likely chart for this data is in 154 AD. I do not currently know what historical events this chart could be associated with.

SECTION IV.12: LILLY'S CHOROGRAPHY

Comment by Dykes. Following are astrological associations for countries throughout much of Europe and the Near East according to William Lilly (*Christian Astrology* I, pp. 93-99). They do not seem to be based on any scheme such as we find in Ptolemy or ibn Labban, so may be based on the charts of various treaties or other events. I have omitted Lilly's list of cities.

ཀྱ   ཀྱ   ཀྱ

Signs	Countries / Regions
♈	Germany, Sweden, Poland, Burgundy, France, England, Denmark, Upper Silesia, Judea, Syria.
♉	Greater Polonia, northern Sweden, Russia, Ireland, Switzerland, Lorraine, Campania, Persia, Cyprus, Parthia.
♊	Lombardy, Brabant, Flanders, W and SW England, Armenia.
♋	Scotland, Zeeland, Holland, Prussia, Tunisia, Algeria.
♌	Italy, Bohemia, the Alps, Turkey, Sicily, Apulia.
♍	Southern Greece, Croatia, Athenian territory, Mesopotamia, Africa, SW France.
♎	Upper Austria, duchy of Savoy, Alsatia, Livonia.
♏	Northern Bavaria, forests of Norway, Barbary, Kingdom of Fez.
♐	Spain, Hungary, Slavonia, Moravia, Dalmatia.
♑	Thrace, Turkish-ruled Macedonia, Albania, Bulgaria, SW Saxony, the West Indies, Styria, Orkney Islands, Hessia.
♒	Tartary, Croatia, Wallachia, Muscovia, German Westphalia, Piedmont in Savoy, W and S Bavaria, Media, Arabia.
♓	Calabria, Portugal, Normandy, northern Egypt.

SECTION IV.13: GUIDE TO PLACE NAMES

Comment by Dykes. This Section is a guide to the Arabic and Greek place names used in Part IV. I have been able to identify most of them, but some are still unknown, perhaps due to spelling errors in the texts. For most of the known places, I have provided modern longitudes and latitudes for the reader's reference, but not places whose location is obvious and well-known (for example, Italy). Please note that the *al-* (Ar. "the") is not part of the alphabetizing: thus al-Shām is listed under *S* rather than under *A*. Finally, some places have double entries if their ancient region (marked "Ancient") differed from their medieval or early modern one.

- Abādīyyah (أبادية). Possibly an ancient Egyptian city on the Nile, but also the city in western Turkey at 40° 10' N, 29° 44' E.
- Abrashahr (ابرشهر). An early name for the city (or perhaps region around) Nīshāpūr.
- Achaia (Ancient). The northern, mountainous portion of the Peloponnese Peninsula in Greece.
- Adanah (أدنة). A city in the province of the same name, in modern Turkey at 37° 00' N, 35° 19' E.
- 'Aden (عدن). A port city in Yemen, at 12° 48' N, 45° 02' E.
- Afrāqbah (أفراقية). Unknown at this time.
- Africa (Ancient). The area of northern Africa covering modern northern Tunisia and western Libya.
- Afrinjah / Afranj / Faranjah (فرنجة, افرنج, افرنجة), specifically the Franks or French, but often used in Arabic as a shorthand for all western Europeans.
- Ahwāz/Ahvāz (الأهواز). A city in western Iran, at 31° 19' N, 48° 40' E.
- 'Aīn al-Shams (عين الشمس). A village in modern Syria, at 34° 55' N, 36° 16' E.
- 'Aīn Dharīah (عين ذرية). Unknown at this time.
- Alān, the Alans (الان). A people speaking an Iranian language which later became Ossetian, living in and around the area just north of Georgia between the Black Sea and the Caspian Sea in the Caucasus (some of whom traveled with the Vandals westward to North Africa), variously under the control of the Turks or the Byzantines. Known to the Greeks as Αλανοι or Αλαννοι.
- Akhlāt / Ahlāt (اخلاط). A city in eastern Turkey, at 38° 45' N, 42° 29' E.

- Albania (Medieval/Modern). A small central southern European country just across the Adriatic Sea from the "heel" of the boot of Italy.
- Alber (אלבר). See Atābles.
- Alexandria (الإسكندرية). The city in northern Egypt on the Mediterranean, at 31° 12' N, 29° 55' E. Some Arabic texts distinguish between a greater Alexandria (العظى) and a lesser one (الصغري), but I am unsure of the difference at this time.
- Almeria. A city in eastern Spain, at 36° 50' N, 2° 28' W.
- Alsatia / Alsace (Medieval/Modern). A small region in NE France, bordering on Germany and Switzerland.
- 'Amad [sic?] (آمد). Unknown at this time.
- 'Amrān (عمران). An ancient city in modern Yemen, at 15° 40' N, 43° 57 E. But in al-Rijāl's Ch. VIII.35, this is associated with the land of the Turks and associated with Leo: thus it must refer to some other 'Amrān or 'Umrān closer to central Asia.
- Amul. See Amūya.
- Amūya. A city in Türkmenistan, anciently called Amul and nowadays Chardzou (Pers. چهارجوى) or Türkmenabat, at 39° 05' N, 63° 34' E.
- Al-Andalus (الاندلس). A medieval Arabic name for the conquests in modern Spain and Portugal (and surrounding areas such as Gibraltar).
- Antioch/Antākīah (أنطاكية). Probably "Syrian Antioch" or Antioch on the Orontes, nowadays in the city of Antakya in southern Turkey, at 36° 12' N, 36° 09' E.
- Apulia. The region of the Italian Peninsula the forms the "heel" and "ankle" of the boot.
- Arabia Deserta. The desert portion of the Arabian Peninsula.
- Arabia Felix. The greener, southwestern part of the Arabian Peninsula, part of what is now called the Hijāz.
- Arabia Petraia. The part of the Arabian Peninsula that adjoins Egypt (what we would call the Sinai Peninsula).
- Arabs, the Arabs (العرب). The Arab peoples and tribes generally in the Saudi Arabian deserts, but also as identified with Islam itself (which is highly identified with Arab culture).
- Arianē / Ariana (Ancient). A wide region between Central Asia and the Indus River, including modern Afghanistan, the east and SE of Iran, Tajikistan, and Turkmenistan.
- Arīn (أرين). Unknown at this time.

- Armenia (أرمينية), Greater and Lesser. Medievally, a people and region between and just south of the Caspian Sea and Black Sea. Lesser Armenia is a portion to the north and northwest of this region, bordering on the Black Sea. But in Ptolemy, Lesser Armenia is west of the Euphrates, and Greater is to the east.
- Arūqī Qāsīyah (اروقي قاسية). Unknown at this time.
- Al-As (الاس). See Alān.
- Asia Minor (آسية الصغرى). Also known as Anatolia, the region roughly equivalent to modern Turkey.
- 'Asqalān/Ascalon (عسقلان). A city in modern Israel and important center of Crusading, at 31° 40' N, 34° 34' E.
- Assyria (Ancient). In Ptolemy, an area around the upper Tigris in modern Iraq (according to Berggren and Jones); but according to MacBean, it was slightly east of this, with Armenia to the north and Media on the east.
- Aswān (أسوان) or Syēnē (Συηνη). A city in Egypt on the ancient frontier, at 24° 05' N, 32° 53 E.
- Atābles (אטאבלס). Unknown. According to ibn Ezra, it is also called Al-ber.
- Atil. The capital city of the Khazars along the Volga River delta at the NW corner of the Caspian Sea. Its ruins were recently claimed to be discovered SE of modern Astrokhan, at Samosdelka (46° 01' N, 47° 50' E).
- Atlas Mountains. A line of mountains in NW Africa, running SW to NE in what is now Morocco, Algeria, and Tunisia.
- Atrak River (اترك). A river in NE Iran, whose headwaters are at 37°10' N, 59° 00' E.
- Ayward [sic?] (ايورد). Unknown at this time.
- Azania. An inland region in east Africa between the cape of the Horn and the Tanzanian coast near Dar al-Salaam (around 6° N).
- Azerbāījān (أذربيجان). An ancient region (and modern nation) bordering the western coast of the Caspian Sea, on its southern half.
- Ba'albek (بعلبك). A city in Lebanon, at 34° 00' N, 36° 12' E.
- Bāb al-Abwāb (باب الابواب), lit. "Gate of Gates." Nowadays Derbent, a city on the Caspian Sea at 42° 04' N, 48° 17' E.
- Bābūniyyah (بابونية). Unknown at this time.
- Babylon (بابل). An ancient country centered around the city of Babylon, in central Iraq about 50 miles south of Baghdad.

- Babylonia (Ancient). The nation-state occupying what is now modern Iraq.
- Bactriana (Ancient). A region in modern northern Afghanistan.
- Bādakhshān (بدخشان). An area of NE Afghanistan and SE Tajikistan, containing the Wakhān Corridor.
- Baghdad (بغداد), also called the City of Peace, Medīnah al-Salaam (مدينة السلام), at 33° 19' N, 44° 25' E.
- Al-Bahrā' (البخراء). An Arab people who lived on the Euphrates and the plain of Hims (or Homs), initially loyal to the Byzantines.
- Bahraīn/al-Bahraīn (البحرين).
- Bahram (بهرم). Unknown at this time.
- Baīt al-Muqaddis / Beit al-Maqdis (بيت المقدس), lit. "House of Reverence/the Holy." A title for Jerusalem.
- Balāsāghūn (بلاساغون). An ancient city of Soghdiana, now in modern Kyrgyzstan, at 42° 44' N, 75° 15' E.
- Balkh (بلخ). A city in Afghanistan (36° 45' E, 66° 54' E), formerly an important city of Khurasān and now replaced by the nearby Mazar-i-Sharif.
- Balkhān (بلخان). A place allegedly near the headwaters of the Atrak River.
- Balqā' (البلقاء). A region (now in modern Jordan) east of the Jordan river.
- Bārānāsī [sic?] / Varanasi / Banaras (باراناسي ?), a city in India at 25° 17' N, 82° 57' E.
- Barāqiyyah (براقية). Possibly an early spelling or modern misspelling for the region of the Bariq (بارق) tribe and region, now in the 'Asir province of SW Saudi Arabia.
- Barbary (Medieval/Modern). A later European term for many of the coastlands of the Maghrib (but also further east to Libya), roughly corresponding to the Berbers.
- Bard'ah (بردعه), the modern Barda in Azerbaijan (at 40° 22' N, 47° 07' E).
- Barghān (برغان). See Firuzeh.
- Barqah (برقة). The eastern coastal area of Libya, anciently called Cyrenaica.
- Barūnā [برونا] (الفقر). Unknown city in the region of south Sudan (specifically, 'Istiwayy).
- Bāshkhirt, Bashkir (باشخرت). A Turkic people indigenous to the Ural mountains, on both sides.
- Al-Batr [sic?] (البتر). Unknown at this time.
- Basrah/al-Basrah (البصرة). A port city in SE Iraq on the Persian Gulf, at 30° 30' N, 47° 49' E.

- Bastarnia (Ancient). Roughly equivalent to modern Poland.
- Bavaria (Medieval/Modern). A large region in southern Germany.
- Bejah / Bejā (بجا / بجة). An African people primarily in Sudan and Upper Egypt.
- Belos / Belus. A river now in NW Israel, but identified by Dorotheus as being near Tyre (now in southern Lebanon).
- Berbers (البربر / البرابر). An ethnic people spread throughout northern Africa, nowadays more in Algeria and Morocco.
- Béziers. A city in southern France, at 43° 20' N, 3° 13' E.
- Bithynia (Ancient). A region of NW modern Turkey, on the southern coast of the Black Sea, connecting to the west with what is now the Asian side of the Istanbul/Constantinople area.
- Bohemia (Medieval/Modern). A European region in what is now the western Czech Republic, with its capital in Prague.
- Borysthenes River. Nowadays called the Dnieper River, passing south from Russia through to the Ukraine and into the Black Sea. The delta mouth is located at about 46° 30' N, 32° 20' E.
- Boujīah (Heb. בוגיאה / Ar. بوجية ?). A city, unknown at this time.
- Bozghān (بزغان). See Firuzeh.
- Brabant (Medieval/Modern). A duchy in what is now the modern Netherlands and Belgium.
- Britain/Brittania (برطانية).
- Būdānjān (بودانجان). An extinct city on the northern shore of Lake Bakhtegan in the Fars province of Iran, at about 29° 27' N, 54° 05' E.
- Bukhārā (بخارا). A city in the province of the same name, in modern Uzbekhistan at 39° 46' N, 64° 26' E.
- Bulgaria (Medieval/Modern). A SE European country on the western edge of the Black Sea.
- Bulgars, Bulghars. A semi-nomadic people living around the Sea of Azov and the Black Sea (and later on, on the Balkan peninsula north of Greece), with a mixture of Turkic and other ethnicities.
- Bulghār (بلغار). A Bulgar city on the Volga River, at 54° 59' N, 49° 03' E.
- Bulūr / Bolor (بلور). A region in the eastern Pamir Mountains of western China (near the conjunction of China, Tajikistan, Pakistan, Kyrgyzstan, and Afghanistan), around 72° E.
- Burgundy (Medieval/Modern). A region of central France, tending towards the NE quarter.

- Burjān (برجان). According to Kennedy (1973, p. 75), a name for the Bulgars living on the Danube just west of the Black Sea (800 AD at the latest). But there are several small towns in Pakistan and Iran with the same or a similar name.
- Burqān (برقان). A city in west-central Iran, at 34° 25' N, 49° 39' E.
- Busrā (بصرا / بصرى). A city in Syria, at 32° 31' N, 36° 29' E.
- Bust (بست). A city in Sijistān (in modern Afghanistan), on the Helmand River, coordinates unknown at this time.
- Byzantines/Romans (الروم رومية).
- Caesarea/Qaīsārīyyah (قيسارية). Any one of many Caesareas, of which the most famouse is Caesarea of Palestine (see below). But possibly also the Cappadocian Caesarea (modern Kayseri, at 38° 44' N, 35° 29' E) or the Cilician Caesarea (modern Anazarbus, at 37° 15' N, 35° 54' E), both in modern Turkey.
- Caesarea of Palestine/Qaīsārīyyah of Palestine (قيسارية فلسطين), also known as Caesarea Maritima, a city on the Mediterranean in modern Israel, at 32° 30' N, 34° 53' E.
- Calabria (Medieval/Modern). A region of Italy forming the toe and foot of the boot.
- Campania (Medieval/modern). A region of Italy on the western coast, forming the front of the "ankle" of the boot.
- Canaan, Canaanites. An ancient peoples or tribes of people living all along the Levant in what is now Lebanon, Israel, and parts of Syria.
- Cappadocia (Ancient). A region of modern east-central Turkey.
- Carthage. An ancient city in Africa, just north of modern Tunis.
- Chaldaea (Ancient).
- China/al-Sīn (الصين).
- Cilicia (Ancient). The most eastern region of the southern coast of modern Turkey.
- Cimmeria (Ancient). An ancient name for Crimea, a peninsula of the southern Ukraine jutting into the Black Sea, as well as some northern areas above it.
- Comoro Islands (قمر). A set of islands NW of Madagascar, at about 12° 08' N, 44° 15' E.
- Constantinople (القسطنطينية), the traditional name for modern Istanbul.
- Copts (قبط). The native Christians of Egypt.
- Córdoba (قرطبة). A city in southern Spain, at 37° 53' N, 4° 46' W.

- Crete (اقريطش / اقريطية).
- Croatia (Medieval/Modern). A southern European country and region on the eastern border of the Adriatic Sea.
- Cyprus/Qibrus (قبرس).
- Dabīl (دبيل). Unknown at this time.
- Dalmatia (Medieval/Modern). A portion of historic Croatia, on the eastern coast of the Adriatic Sea.
- Damascus/Damashq (دمشق).
- Dardanelles. See Hellespont.
- Dashti Maīsān (دشت ميسان). Unknown at this time, but Maīsān was a term for the region between Basrah and Wāsit (a town in eastern Iraq, at 32° 14' N, 46° 18' E).
- Dasmsār (دسمسار). Unknown at this time.
- Daybul / Debal (ديبل). An ancient port slightly SE of Karachi in Pakistan, at 24° 45' N, 67° 31' E.
- Daylam (الديلم). An ancient Persian region roughly corresponding to the modern Gīlān province in Iran, bordering the extreme southern point of the Caspian sea, about 37°N, 49.5°E.
- Dībajāt Islands (ديبجات). The Maldive islands in the Indian Ocean, whose modern capital is at 4° 10' N, 73° 30' E.
- Al-Diltā (الدلتا). See Lower Egypt.
- Dūmah (دومة). An ancient city in NW Saudi Arabia, at 29° 48' N, 39° 52' E.
- Dunqula (دنقلة). The city of Dongola in the modern Sudān, at 19° 10' N, 30° 28' E.
- Dūsh (دوش). Possibly the Iranian town at 34° 33' N, 46° 14' E.
- Edessa/al-Rahā' / Urfa (الرهاء). Now known as Sanliurfa and the capital of Sanliurfa province, in SE Turkey, at 37° 09' N, 38° 47' E.
- Edom. Originally a region of the southern Levant below the Dead Sea, but in later literature a catchphrase for Rome (esp. the Byzantines).
- Egypt/Misr/Egyptians (مصر).
- Ethiopia (Ancient). For Ptolemy, Africa south of Egypt and the ancient Libya Region: roughly, all of sub-Saharan Africa known to him.
- Ethiopia/al-Habshah (الحبشة).
- Eyvan / Aywān (ايوان). A city in western Iran, at 33° 49' N, 46° 18' E.
- Fahrjān Burq [sic?] (فهرجان برق). Unknown at this time.

- Al-Faqr [sic?] (الفقر). Unknown city in the region of south Sudan (specifically, 'Istiwayy).
- Fārāb, Pārāb (فاراب), modern Utrar or Otrar. A city on the Silk Road in modern Kazakhstan, at 42° 54' N, 68° 20' E.
- Farghānah, Farghāna (فرغانة). A city and capital of a province of the same name, in eastern Uzbekhistan, at 40° 23' N, 71° 47' E.
- Fas / Fez (فاس). A city and former kingdom in Morocco, at 34° 02' N, 5° 00' W.
- Fez. See Fas.
- Fīrūzeh (فيروزه). A city in NE Iran, at 36° 17' N, 58° 35' E.
- Flanders (Medieval/Modern). An area historically in NW Belgium, including portions of France and the Netherlands.
- France. See Franks.
- Franks / 'Ifranjah (إفرنجة). A generic Arabic term for any Europeans (about which most medieval Muslims knew little), but especially the French.
- Gabes. See Qābis.
- Gaitoulia / Gaetulia (Ancient). An ancient Berber people in the desert south of the Atlas mountains on the border of the Sahara.
- Galatia. See Gallia.
- Galicia. See Jalāliqah.
- Gallia (Ancient). A large region of ancient Europe, especially including modern France and the Benelux area, as well as some of Switzerland and northern Italy.
- Garamantikē (Ancient). A Saharan people, apparently south of the two Syrtis Gulfs in modern NE Libya.
- Gaza/Ghazzah (غزة).
- Gedrousia / Gedrosia (Ancient). An ancient name for modern Baluchistan, in SW Pakistan, SE Iran, and a bit of SW Afghanistan.
- German Westphalia (Medieval/Modern). A region of northern Germany.
- Germania (Ancient). An area of Europe east of the Rhine and north of the Danube.
- Germany/Jermānīyyah (جرمانية).
- Ghānah / Ghana (غانة). Medieval reference a bit uncertain, as the modern Ghana is south of the Ghana Empire, but both are in sub-Saharan Africa.
- Ghūr (غور). A province in modern Afghanistan, centered around 34° N, 65° E.

- Ghuzz. See Oghuz Turks.
- Granada (Ar. غرناطة). A city in Spain, at 37° 10' N, 3° 36' W.
- Greeks/al-Yūnān (اليونان).
- Gūshqā / Gūsqā (גושקא / Ar. جوسقا ?). A city, unknown at this time.
- Hablān (حبلان). Unknown at this time.
- Hadham (هذام?). Unknown at this time.
- Hadramaut (حضرموت). A region between Yemen and 'Omān on the Arabian Peninsula, centered around the city at 15° 58' N, 49° 01' E.
- Hajar. The mountains of NE 'Oman and the eastern United Arab Emirates, but Kennedy (1973) puts it closer to Bahraīn.
- Halb [sic?] (حلب). Unknown, but perhaps a misspelling for a city in Syria (al-Shām).
- Hamadān / Hamadhān (همدان / همذان). A city in the province of the same name in Iran, at 34° 48' N, 48° 31' E. Abū Ma'shar's use of "dh" is probably an error.
- Hamāh (حماة). A city in Syria, at 35° 08' N, 36° 45' E.
- Harmah (حرمة). A city in Saudi Arabia, at 25° 55' N, 45° 20' E.
- Harrān (حرّان). An ancient city important for astrological worship, now in modern Turkey at 36° 52' N, 39° 02' E.
- Al-Hazar. Probably an unpointed spelling for the Khazars.
- Hellas (Ancient). Greece, but especially the portion above the Peloponnese Peninsula.
- Hellespont. A narrow straight SW of Constantinople (Istanbul), connecting the Aegean Sea with the Sea of Marmara. It is located at about 40° 13' N, 26° 26' E.
- Herāt (هرات). Either the city in Afghanistan at 34° 20' N, 62° 12' E, or in Iran at 30° 03' N, 54° 22' E.
- Hessia / Hessen (Medieval/Modern). A region in central Germany, centered on Frankfurt-am-Main.
- Hijāz (الحجاز). A strip of western Saudi Arabia bordering on the Red Sea, which includes the cities of Mecca, Medina, and Jeddah.
- Hijr (هجر). Unknown at this time.
- Hims/Homs (حمص). A city in western Syria, at 34° 43' N, 36° 42' E.
- Hizāh or Hezāh (هزاه). Unknown, but possible a misspelling of Herāt (see above).
- Homs. See Hims.

- Al-Ḥūr (الحور). Unknown, but perhaps one of many villages in the Kirmān province of Iran.
- Hyrcania (Ancient). A region on the SE coast of the Caspian Sea, later called Jurjān.
- Hyrcania. See Jurjān.
- Idumaia (Ancient). A Greek word for Edom, a region of the southern Levant south of the Dead Sea and ancient Judea.
- Ifrīqīyyah (أفريقية). A largish area in northern Africa (derived from the Roman province of Africa), comprising Tunisia, western Libya, and eastern Algeria.
- Illyria (Ancient). The coastal region on the eastern side of the Tyrhennian Sea, such as modern Albania.
- India/al-Hind (الهند). Probably referring to the portion of NW India around the Indus River, rather than all of India; it is often paired with Sind (see below).
- Indikē / India. In Ptolemy, the northern portions of the Indian Peninsula.
- Iraq/al-ʿIrāq (العراق).
- Isbījāb (اسبيجاب / اسفيجاب), the modern city of Sayram in southern Kazakhstan, at 42° 18' N, 69° 46' E.
- Isfahān (إصبهان). A large city (and capital of the province of the same name) in central Iran, at 32° 38' N, 51° 39' E.
- Al-ʿIstiwayy (الاستوي / الاستوا). A region in modern south Sudan at around 5° N latitude.
- Italy/ʿItālīyyah (إيطالية).
- Jabal, Jibāl (جبل / جبال), lit. "mountain, the mountains." The mountainous central highland of Iran, esp. the western, Zagros mountains.
- Jalāliqah (حلالقة / جلالقة). Galicia, probably the Spanish Galicia at about 42° N, 8° W. (There was also a Galicia in what is now Poland and the Ukraine, NW of the Black Sea.)
- Jarāmaqah (جرامقة). Unknown at this time.
- Java / Zāvah (زاوة). The Indonesian island, at about 7° 29' S, 110° 00 E.
- Jazīrah (الجزيرة), lit. "the island." Sometimes this indicates a plain in NW Iraq and SE Syria (which may be called the Jazīra of Syria/Jazīra al-Shām [جزيرة الشام]), but otherwise it refers to the Arabian Peninsula, and may be designated the Jazīrah of the Arabs (جزيرة العرب).
- Jerusalem/Beït al-Qudds (بيت القدس).
- Jews/al-Hūd (الهود).

- Al-Jibalīyya (جبليا?). Possibly the town in the Gaza strip, at 31° 31' N, 34° 28' E. But the word itself means "the mountainous area," which is indeterminate.
- Jiddah / Jeddah (جدة). A city in Saudi Arabia, at 21° 32' N, 39° 10' E.
- Jīlān (جيلان). Possibly the same as the modern Gīlān province in Iran (see Daylam above).
- Jīmur (جيمور). Unknown at this time.
- Judaea (Ancient). In Ptolemy, also known as Palestine.
- Jurjān/Gurgān (جرجان). Derived from the ancient Hyrcania in the same area, a city in northern Iran near the extreme SE shore of the Caspian Sea, about 36° 50' N, 54° 26' E.
- Kābul (كابل). The capital of modern Afghanistan, at 34° 32' N, 69° 10' E.
- Kalah Island (كلة). The Malay peninsula, once thought to be an island, around 7° N, 100° E.
- Kalimah (كلمة). Unknown at this time.
- Kalwāniyyah (الكلوانية). Uncertain, but possibly the Indian city at 20° 34' N, 73° 49' E.
- Kāshgar (كاشغر). Probably the city in modern China, but on the border of Tajikistan and Kyrgyzstan, at 39° 28' N, 75° 59' E.
- Kashmīr (قشمير / كشمير). A northwestern region of India, specifically the valley between the Himalayas and the Pir Panjal mountains.
- Kaspēria (Ancient). A region in what is now modern Kashmir.
- Kāth (كاث). The capital of Khwārizm, at 41° 23' N, 60° 22' E.
- Kazan. A city on the Volga River, at 55° 47' N, 49° 08' E.
- Keltikē (Ancient). A portion of western Europe (probably throughout Gaul / Gallia) in which an uncertain people of this name lived. Based on Ptolemy's chorography, they would have lived closer to the Iberian peninsula and western France.
- Kerki (كركوه). See Zamm.
- Khānjū (خانجو). The modern Quanzhou in China, at 24° 55' N, 118° 35' E.
- Khānqū (خانقو). The modern Guangzhou in China, at 23° 08' N, 113° 16' E.
- Khazars/al-Khazar (الخزر). Probably referring to the Khazar Turkish people who had a powerful medieval state, centered on the northern part of the territory between the Caspian Sea and Black Sea, just north of Armenia.

- Khersheh (خرشه). Probably the village in SW Iran, at 31° 11' N, 48° 46' E.
- Khitan (ختن). Refers to a nomadic people originally from Mongolia and Manchuria, in NW modern China.
- Khurāsān (خراسان). A region in what is now NE Iran and northern Afghanistan, which includes cities such as Balkh, Merv, and Herat.
- Khūzistān (خوزستان). A province in SW Iran, whose capital is Ahwaz (see above).
- Khwārizm (خوارزم). An oasis region just south of the Aral Sea, overlapping Kazakhstan and Uzbekhistan).
- Kimāk, Kimek, al-Kāmiyyah (كماية). A Turkic tribe, one of the two tribes in the Kimek Khanate.
- Kimek Khanate. A Turkic state centered in the area around the Ob and Irtysh Rivers, northwards of the city of Balkhash (and its lake) at 46° 50' N, 74° 59' E.
- Kīnaūj / Kannauj (كنوج). An Indian city on the Ganges, at 27° 04', 79° 55' E.
- Kirghiz, Kyrgyz, Khirkhiyyah (خرخية). A Turkic tribe now living in Kyrgyzstan.
- Kirmān (كرمان). A city in SE Iran (in a province of the same name), at 30° 17' N, 57° 05' E.
- Kirwān. See Qayrawān.
- Koilē Syria (Ancient).
- Kolchis / Colchis (Ancient).[1] An ancient kingdom on the eastern shore of the Black Sea.
- Kommagēnē / Commagene (Ancient). An ancient kingdom between and just south of the Black Sea and Caspian Sea, including what is now Syria and parts of Iraq.
- Kūfah / Kūfa (الكوفة). An Iraqi city on the Euphrates, at 32° 02' N, 42° 24' E.
- Kūhistān (كوهستان?). See Jabal/Jibāl.
- Al-Kūr (الكور). Unknown, but according to al-Rijāl an island somewhere near the Horn of Africa.
- Kurds/al-Akrād (الأكراد). A set of peoples whose historical areas spread from eastern Turkey across Syria, northern Iraq, and northwestern Iran.
- Kūrūr / Kūzūz (كزوز / كرور). Unknown at this time.

---

[1] Is this Calchis?

- Kūsh (كوش). An ancient kingdom of great extent in Africa, but originating from the area around the Blue Nile, White Nile, and the River Atbara in modern Sudan.
- Kyklades Islands. An island group in the Aegean Sea, SE of Greece.
- Kyrēnaikē / Cyrenaica (Ancient). Roughly the eastern half of what is now modern Libya, especially the coastal regions; later called Barqah.
- Kyrēnē (Ancient). An ancient city in modern Libya (at 32° 49' N, 21° 51' E), whose name lent itself to the naming of the broader region, Kyrēnai-kē.
- Laconia (Ancient). The extreme southern region of Greece's Peloponnesian peninsula.
- Libya (Ancient). The broad Saharan region west of the Nile across to the Atlantic.
- Libya/Lūbīyyah (لوبية).
- Lamūrīts (الموريطس). Unknown at this time.
- Livonia (Medieval/Modern). A European region in the eastern Baltic which included the city of Riga (56° 56' N, 24° 06' E), but with variable borders over the centuries.
- Lombardy (Medieval/Modern). A region of Italy in the extreme north and center of the peninsula, bordering Switzerland to the north.
- Lorraine (Medieval/modern). A region of NE France.
- Lower Egypt. The Mediterranean delta in northern Egypt, at about
- Lucca. An Italian city in Tuscany, at 43° 51' N, 10° 30' E.
- Lucena. A city in southern Spain, at 37° 24' N, 4° 29' W.
- Lūniyyah (لونية). Unknown at this time, but it sounds very much like the *Lunia* which the medieval translator John of Spain (or John of Seville) claimed to be from.
- Lydia (Ancient). An ancient region of west-central Turkey, just west of Phrygia.
- Ma'rib (مأرب). See Sabā'.
- Macedonia (Ancient/medieval; Ar. مقدونية). A region in SE Europe, variously encompassing parts of modern Greece, Bulgaria, Albania, and Serbia.
- Al-Madā'in (المدائن), lit. "the cities," the combined cities of ancient Seleucia and Ctesiphon, near Baghdad at 33° 06' N, 44° 35' E.
- Madīnah al-Salām (مدينة السلام). A traditional name for Baghdad.

- Maghrib/Morocco (مغرب). Traditionally, the region including the Atlas mountains, Morocco, the northern plains of Algeria, and perhaps some portions of northern Tunisia.
- Magyars, Hungarians (مجار / مجع). The Hungarian people, earlier between the southern Ural Mountains and the Ural River, then in the Carpathian basin.
- Māhān (ماهان). A city in the district of the same name in the Kirmān province of Iran, at 30° 03' N, 57° 17' E.
- Al-Mahdiyya / Mahdia (المهدية). A city in Tunisia, at 35° 30' N, 11° 04' E.
- Māhīn (ماهين). Probably the modern village of Māhīn in northern Iran, at 36° 34' N, 49° 03' E.
- Mahrah (المهرة). The most eastern portion of Yemen, at about 16° 48' N, 51° 44' E.
- Mahrubān (مهروبان). An extinct port city near modern Behbehān in Iran (30° 35' N, 50° 14' E), on the edge of the Persian Gulf east of Basrah.
- Mājūj (ماجوج), also known as Magog (as in the Biblical Gog and Magog). An uncertain nomadic people or area in north-central Asia.
- Makrān (مكران). A coastal strip on the Indian Ocean in southern Sindh (see below) and overlapping with modern Balukhistan in Iran.
- Málaga. A city in southern Spain, at 36° 43' N, 4° 25' W.
- Malatia/Malatīyyah (ملطية). Probably the city (in the province of the same name) in eastern Turkey, at 38° 21' N, 38° 18' E.
- Manbij (منبج). The modern Membij in Syria, at 36° 32' N, 37° 57' E.
- Mansūrah (منصورة). According to Kennedy 1987, a city in modern Pakistan NE of Hyderabad, at 25° 53' N, 68° 47' E.
- Mantua. An Italian city in Lombardy, at 45° 10' N, 10° 48' E.
- Marāh (مراه). Unknown at this time.
- Marmarikē (Ancient). A coastal region on what is now the border region between modern Libya and Egypt.
- Marqān/Marq (مرقان / مرق). Unknown at this time.
- Marseilles. A city in southern France, at 43° 17' N, 5° 22' E.
- Marw al-Rūd (مرو الرود / مرورود, from Persian), later also called Marw al-Nahr, both of which mean "what is beyond the river," viz. the Oxus (nowadays, Amu) River in what was known as Transoxiana. The exact cite seems to be unknown, but Transoxiana was a broadish region beyond the river which is now occupied by the conjunction of Uzbekistan, Tajikistan, SW Kyrgyzstan, and southern Kazakhstan.

- Marw/Merv (مرو). An ancient city on the Silk road in modern Turkmenistan, at 37° 39' N, 62° 11' E.
- Māsdān (ماسدان). Unknown at this time.
- Mashriq (مشرق), qualified by al-Rijāl (Ch. VIII.35, **20**) with either al-Shām (viz. Syria) or Shams ("the Sun"). The Mashriq is a general area in the Near/Middle East, north of the Saudi Arabian peninsula and east of Egypt, as opposed to the Maghrib (the western lands in northern Africa).
- Massīsah (مصّيصة), also known as Mopsuestia and many other names (depending on its conquerers), a Cilician town in modern Turkey, at about 36° 57' N, 35° 37' E.
- Matianē (Ancient). An ancient kingdom in modern NW Iran.
- Mauritania, Mauritania Tingitana (Ancient). An ancient Roman province covering approximately modern Morocco and western Algeria.
- Maysān. See Mīsān.
- Mayyāfārqīn (ميافارقين), the modern city of Silvan in eastern Turkey, at 38° 08' N, 41° 00' E.
- Mazar-i-Sharif (مزار شريف), a city in modern Afghanistan, close to Balkh.
- Mecca/Makkah (مكّة). A city in the Hijāz of Saudi Arabia (and holy city of Islam), at 21° 25' N, 39° 49' E.
- Mēdia (Ancient). A region of ancient Persia, south and SW of the Caspian.
- Media. A region in NW Iran, formerly an empire, centered around the province of Hamadān.
- Medina/al-Madīnah (المدينة). A city in the Hijāz of Saudia Arabia (and holy city of Islam), at 24° 28' N, 39° 36' E.
- Mehrān river (نهر مهران). A river in southern Iran, flowing from the province of Fars (the original Persia) through the province of Hormozgan, to the Persian Gulf.
- Meroē (Gr. Μεροη, Ar. مرواه / مروى). An ancient city on the Nile (16° 56' N, 33° 45' E), and for a while the capital of the kingdom of Kūsh.
- Mesopotamia (Ancient).
- Metagōnitis (Ancient). A coastal region in ancient Mauretania, across from the city Cartagena (anciently, New Carthage) on the southern coast of Spain.
- Mid-Pontus. See Pontus.
- Mimsān (ممسان). Unknown at this time.
- Minah (منة). Unknown at this time.
- Mīsān (ميسان). A province in SE Iraq, bordered by the Tigris and Irān.

- Moravia (Medieval/Modern). A small central European region now in the east of the Czech Republic.
- Mosul. See Mūsul.
- Multān, Mūltān (ملتان / مولتان). A city in Pakistan, at 30° 11' N, 71° 28' E.
- Mūqān. An unknown region in central Asia, perhaps around the Black Sea or related to various Turkic peoples in the region.
- Murghāb (مرغاب). A city in Tajikistān, at 38° 10' N, 73° 57' E.
- Muscovia / Muscovy (Medieval/Modern). A Russian principality centered around Moscow.
- Mūsul/Mosul (الموصل). A city in northern Iraq, at 36° 20' N, 43° 07' E.
- Nahrawān (نهروان). A city (and canal with the same name) slightly east of Baghdād and the Tigris River, at 33° 22' N, 44° 42' E.
- Najd (نجد). The central highland region of the Arabian Peninsula.
- Najrān (نجران). A city in southern Saudi Arabia, at 17° 29' N, 44° 07' E.
- Nanūniyyah (نانونية). Unknown at this time; see the variant spelling, Babūniyyah.
- Narbonne. A city in southern France, at 43° 11' N, 3° 00' E.
- Nasamōnitis (Ancient). A people occupying a region that seems to have been inland and south of the NE coast of modern Libya (ancient geographers differ, and this people probably moved from place to place).
- Nīshāpūr (نيشابور). A city in NE Iran, at 36° 12' N, 58° 47' E.
- Normandy (Medieval/Modern). A region in northern France, on the English Channel.
- Nubia/al-Nubah (النوبة). A Nile region in southern Egypt and northern Sudan.
- Numidia (Ancient). A province of the African continent in what is now northern Algeria and some of western Tunisia.
- Numidia. Originally, a Libyan kingdom which covered what is now Algeria, eastern Morocco, and western Tunisia.
- Oasis (Ancient). Probably Ptolemy's Greater Oasis, a city on the Nile in Upper Egypt.
- Oceanus (Ancient). A personification of the bodies of salt water surrounding and in some ways permeating the known ancient world. Dorotheus refers to a "stream" and "flood" of Oceanus, which have Homeric and other pedigrees, but their geographical meaning is uncertain.

- Oghuz Turks (Ar. غُز), lit. "tribe of Turks." A medieval confederation of Turkish groups around the area of the Khazar state, whose descendants moved west and eventually became the Ottoman Turks.
- Ogygia (Ancient). A possibly legendary island mentioned by Homer (and apparently identified by some with Atlantis); some geographers place it in the Atlantic, others among the Greek islands. It was covered with many trees, hence Dorotheus's association of Virgo with "the Ogygian trees."
- Oman/'Omān (عمان).
- Orchēnia (Ancient). According to Ptolemy, a people in the desert of Arabia; but other ancient geographers put them closer to Chaldea and southern Iraq.
- Orkney / Orcades Islands (Medieval/Modern). A group of islands just north of Scotland.
- Otrar. See Fārāb.
- Oxiana (Ancient). A region around the Oxus River (now the Amu Darya), in northern Afghanistan and northwest in Turkmenistan and the Aral Sea.
- Palermo. A Sicilian city, at 38° 07' N, 13° 22' E.
- Palestine/Filastīn (فلسطين).
- Pamphylia (Ancient). The middle region of the southern coast of modern Turkey.
- Parthia (Ancient). A NE area of modern Iran, east of ancient Media and SE of the Caspian.
- Pechenegs, al-Bajākīah (البجاكية). A Turkic people from the central Asian Steppes, settling in about the 9th century into the steppes between the Ural and Volga Rivers.
- Perrhaebia (Ancient). A northern portion of Thessaly, in central Greece.
- Persia/Fārs (فارس). In its narrow sense, a province in southern Iran (the original homeland of the Persians).
- Phazania / Phasania (Ancient). A largely desert region in the SW of modern Libya
- Phoenicia (Ancient). A Mediterranean culture centered around what is now modern Lebanon.
- Phrygia (Ancient). A region in what is now west-central Turkey.
- Piedmont (Medieval/Modern). A region of NW Italy, closely associated with French Savoy just to its west.
- Pisa. An Italian city in Tuscany, at 43° 43' N, 10° 24' E.

- Polonia (Medieval/modern). An older (Latin) name for Poland; "Greater" Polonia is a region of west-central Poland, while "Lesser" Polonia is in the southern parts.
- Pontus, mid-Pontus. A region on the southern coast of the Black Sea, now in northern Turkey (about 40°-41° N, 33° 30' - 41° 30' E). It also refers to a river in this same region.
- Prussia (Medieval/Modern). A region of northern Germany on the Baltic Sea.
- Qabād (قبلد). Unknown at this time.
- Qābis (قابس). A city in Tunisia on the Mediterranean, at 33° 53' N, 10° 07' E.
- Qalī'iyyah (قليعية) or perhaps Qalīfiyyah (قليفية). Unknown at this time.
- Qāmrūn Mountains (قامرون). According to Kennedy (1987), probably the Kamrup Mountains in Bhutan.
- Qandahār (قندهار). A city in Afghanistan, at 31° 37' N, 65° 43' E.
- Qaramān (القرمان). A town in Azerbaïjän, at 40° 36' N, 47° 49' E.
- Qashā (قشا). Unknown at this time.
- Qāy (قاي). A Turkic tribe in eastern central Asia.
- Qayrawan, Kirwān (قيروان). A city in Tunisia, at 35° 40' N, 10° 06' E.
- Qedar, Kedar, Qedarites (قدار ?). An ancient group of northern Arab tribes living in the NW Arabian desert and perhaps as far north as modern Jordan. They seem to have ceased being independent after the first few centuries AD.
- Qinnasrīn (قنّسرين). An ancient Syrian city also known as Chalcis, at about 35° 59' N, 36° 59 E.
- Qitāī (قتاي). See Khitan.
- Qūhistān (قوهستان). A somewhat indeterminate area of medieval Persia, in Khurāsān.
- Qulzum (القلزم). A name for the Red Sea.
- Qūmis (قومس). Probably Shahr-e Qūmis, the site of the ancient Hecatompylos in Khurāsān, at 35° 57' N, 54° 02' E.
- Qumm (قمّ). A city in Iran, at 34° 38' N, 50° 52' E.
- Qūn (قون). A Turkic tribe in eastern central Asia.
- Qūs (قوص). A city in Egypt, at 25° 56' N, 32° 46' E.
- Ra's al-'Aīn (رأس العين), lit. "Head of the Spring." One of many cities with the same name throughout the Middle East, possibly near the ancient An-

tipatris, between Caesarea and Lydda in modern Israel. Or, the nearby Rosh ha-Ayn in Israel, at 32° 05' N, 34° 57' E.

- Ramlah (الرملة). A city in modern Israel, at 31° 56' N, 34° 52' E.
- Al-Raqqah (الرقّة). A northern Syrian city, at 35° 57' N, 39° 01' E.
- Rayhān (ريحان). A city in Iran, probably the one in the province of Kirmān, at 31° 05' N, 56° 44' E.
- Rayy/al-Rāyy (الريّ / الراي). An ancient city in Iran, today just SE of Tehran; destroyed by the Mongols in 1220.
- Rhodes (رودس). A Greek island, with a city of the same name at 36° 10' N, 28° 00' E.
- Rome. A city in Italy, at 41° 54' N, 12° 30' E. The name (in Ar. al-Rūm, الروم) was also used in medieval times by Latins and Arabic speakers alike to refer to the Byzantine Empire, including the region of Asia Minor (modern Turkey).
- Rūm. See Rome.
- Rumiyyz. Probably a misspelling for Rome or the Romans, the Byzantines.
- Russia, al-Rūs (الروس). More narrowly, Scandinavian traders living along the Russian rivers on the way to Constantinople.
- Sabā', Sheba (سبا), the nation of the Sabaeans. Its capital city of Ma'rib and nearby dam are in Yemen at about 15° 23' N, 45° 14' E.
- Sabab (سبب). Unknown at this time.
- Al-Sa'd (السعد). Unknown at this time, but possibly identical to Al-Sa'īd.
- Sahūniyyah (شحونية). Unknown at this time.
- Al-Sa'īd (الصعيد). Unknown at this time, but according to al-Bīrūnī it is in Africa west of Egypt.
- Al-Sa'īd al-A'lī (السعيد الاعلي), lit. "The Supreme Happiness." Unknown at this time, but probably al-Sa'īd.
- Samarkand. See Samarqand.
- Samarqand (سمرقند). An ancient city on the Silk Road, now in Uzbekhistan at 39° 39' N, 66° 57' E.
- Al-Samāwah (السماوة). An Iraqi city SE of Baghdad, at 31° 19' N, 45° 17' E.
- Samsat. A city in eastern Turkey, at 37° 34' N, 38° 28' E.
- Al-Saqāliba (صقالبة), the Slavs. This more narrowly includes Slavic people in Macedon and those Russians living along the river routes to Constantinople.

- Saragossa / Zaragoza / Saraqūstah (سرقسطة). A city in northern Spain, at 41° 39' N, 0° 53' W.
- Sarakhs (سرخس). A city in NE Iran (in a county of the same name), at 36° 32' N, 61° 09' E.
- Al-Sarīr (السرير ?). Probably Sarir, a medieval Christian state in what is now modern Dagestan, on the NW corner of the Caspian Sea, situated between the Khazars and the Georgians.
- Sarīrah Island (سريرة). The island of Sumatra, at about 0° N, 102° E.
- Al-Sās (الساس). Undoubtedly the unpointed spelling for al-Shāsh.
- Sauromatikē, Sarmatians (Ancient). A people living just north of the Black Sea, in what is now the Ukraine and southern Russia.
- Savoy (Medieval/Modern). A region of eastern France, bordering Italy and Switzerland.
- Saxony (Medieval/Modern). A region in eastern Germany, with its capital Dresden.
- Saymara. Perhaps an alternate spelling (or misspelling in ibn Labban) for Sāmarrā' (Samarra) in Iraq, at 34° 11' N, 43° 52' E.
- Sea of Trabizond. The SE portion of the Black Sea on which sits the city of Trabizond.
- Sea of Turkān/Jade Sea (بحر تركان). The fourth-largest salt-water lake in the world, overlapping Kenya and Ethiopia, at about 3° 35' N, 36° 07 E.
- Sērikē (Ancient). The country of the Sēres (inland China on the Silk Road), named after the production of silk. According to Ptolemy it was at about 40° N.
- Seville. A city in southern Spain, at 37° 22' N, 5° 59' W.
- Al-Shāsh (الشاش). The Arabic spelling for the old name of Tashkent (Chach), a city in modern Uzbekistan at 41° 16' N, 69° 13' E.
- Shātī al-Bahr (شاطي البحر). Unknown at this time.
- Shur (شور ?). Unknown, but many Iranian towns include this name. It is the Hebrew name for "Taurus/Bull."
- Al-Shūsh (الشوش). A city in western Iran, at 32° 11' N, 48° 14' E.
- Sicily/Siqillīyyah (صقلّية).
- Sīdon/Sīdā' (صيداء). A Lebanese city on the Mediterranean, at 33° 33' N, 35° 23' E.
- Sijistān/Sīstān (سجستان / سیستان). An ancient region in overlapping eastern Iran and southern Afghanistan, just south of Khurāsān.

- Silesia (Medieval/modern). A region in central Europe which includes parts of Poland, Germany, and Czechoslovakia.
- Sind / Sindh /al-Sind (السند). A region in the SE corner of modern Pakistan, along the Indus River.
- Sindān (سندان). Modern Sanjān, a city in India north of Mumbai at 20° 17' N, 72° 54' E.
- Sinjah (سنجة). Probably the city in Sūdān, at 13° 09' N, 33° 56' E.
- Slavonia (Medieval/Modern). A historic region now in eastern Croatia.
- Slavs. See al-Saqāliba.
- Soghdiana / Sogdiana (سغد). A region of central Asia centered around the conjunction of Uzbekistan, Kyrgyzstan, and Tajikistan, around 40° N, 70° E.
- Sri Lanka, Lank, Lankā (النكا / لنك).
- Styria (Medieval/Modern). A region in SE Austria.
- Al-Sūākhī (الصواخي). Probably an ethnic group, unknown at this time.
- Sūdān (سودان). Roughly, the area south of Egypt in eastern Africa, approximately the region of modern Sudan.
- Sūdāyyn (سودايين). Unknown at this time.
- Sūs al-Aqsa (سوس الاقصى, "remotest Sūs"). The westernmost part of Morocco, in the Sous/Sūs valley, nowadays identified with the city of Taroudant at 30° 28' N, 8° 52' W.
- Sūwād (سواد), lit. "blackness." A generic term for rich agricultural regions in Iraq, between and around the Tigris and Euphrates rivers.
- Suwār, Suar, Suvar (سوار). A Bulgar city on the Volga River, just south of Kazan.
- Syēnē. See Aswān.
- Syria/al-Shām (الشام). Generally, the land in the modern state of Syria. Al-Shām refers to something "on the left," just as someone facing east in the Arab Hijāz will find this land to their north or left. Our texts prefer this term for Syria.
- Syria/Sūrīyyah (سورية). This seems to have referred more particularly to Syrian Christians, rather than the region of Syria itself (al-Shām).
- Tabālah (تبالة). A village in eastern Yemen, at 14° 49' N, 49° 35' E.
- Tabaristān (طبرستان). An ancient territory embracing the southern coast of the Caspian Sea, in northern Iran.
- Tab'wādaltah (تبعوادلتة). Unknown at this time.

- Tahāma (تهامه ?). Unknown at this time. The manuscripts of al-Bīrūnī give variant readings, some with a completely different word.
- Tāhart (تاهرت). The modern Tiaret, a city in Algeria at 35° 22' N, 1° 19' E.
- Al-Tā'if (الطائف). A city in Saudi Arabia, at 21° 26' N, 40° 21' E.
- Tālibah (طالبة). An unknown city or region which al-Rijāl (Ch. VIII.35, **17**) says is close to Roman (Byzantine) territory.
- Tangier/Tanjah (طنجة). A city in northern Morocco on the coast near Gibraltar, at 36° 46' N, 5° 48' W.
- Tanīshar (تينشار / تانيشار). Unknown at this time.
- Tarsūs (طرسوس). A city in southern Turkey, at 36° 55' N, 34° 53' E.
- Tartary (Medieval/Modern). A western European name for the steppes of central Asia, inhabited by many Turkic, Tartar, and other tribes.
- Tashkent. See al-Shāsh.
- Thānah (ثانة). A city on the Indian coast, probably the Thānah in the district of the same name in Maharashtra, at 19° 10' N, 72° 57' E.
- Thāsht. Unknown, but Wright (citing Le Strange, p. 483) suggests Khāsht, an uncertain place in the hills of the land of Ilak (itself close to and sometimes confused with Shāsh), on the Syr Darya River (modern Kyrgystan).
- Thēbais (Ancient). A region of Upper Egypt on the Nile which contained the city of Thebes.
- Thrace (Ancient). A region east of Macedonia now on the European side of Turkey, NE Greece, and SW Bulgaria, and on the SE coast of the Black Sea.
- Tībet (تيبت / التبت).
- Al-Tīh (التيه). Unknown at this time.
- Tihāmah (تهامة). The narrow coastal plain (part of the Hijāz) on the western Arabian peninsula.
- Toledo. A city in central Spain, at 39° 51' N, 4° 01' W.
- Toquz Oghuz, Taghazghaz (البغزغز). A medieval alliance of Turkic tribes stretching across central Asia, from the Aral Sea eastwards through Mongolia.
- Trabizond (طرابزندة). A city now in modern Turkey, on the shore of the Black Sea at 41° 00' N, 39° 44' E.
- Tripoli/Tarāblus (طرابلس). The capital of Libya on the Mediterranean coast, at 32° 54' N, 13° 11' E.
- Trōgodytikē (Ancient, falsely called Trōglodytikē). Eastern sub-Saharan Africa, down to roughly the equator.

- Tuharistān/Tukharistān (طحرستان / طخرستان). A later name for Bactria, a region between the Hindu Kush mountain range and the Oxus river, which includes Surxondaryo Province (in SE Uzbekhistan), northern Afghanistan, and southern Tajikistan.
- Tunis (تونس). A city in and the capital of Tunisia, at 36° 48' N, 10° 11' E.
- Türkmen, Turcomen. See Oghuz Turks.
- Turks (الترك). Originally (and in our texts), Turkish nomadic peoples speaking numerous related languages, living across central Asia and especially in what is now western China. It is rarely clear which tribe or group is meant in our texts, but it probably includes those living in and closer to modern Turkey, such as the Seljuks.
- Tūs (طوس). An ancient city in modern Iran, at 36° 27' N, 59° 34' E.
- Tyre (صور). A city in modern Lebanon, at 33° 16' N, 35° 11' E.
- Tyrrēnia (Ancient). A region of northern central Italy.
- 'Ūjjaīn (اوجين). A city in India at 23° 11' N, 75° 46' E.
- Upper Austria (Medieval/Modern). A region of modern northern Austria, but earlier probably a region of larger extent in the Austro-Hungarian Empire.
- Ushrūsanah (اشروسنه). A region of Transoxiana, south of the Syr Darya River from about Samarqand to Khujand (40° 16' N, 69° 37' E), at the conjunction of Uzbekistan, Kyrgystan, and Tajikistan.
- Valencia. A city in eastern Spain, at 39° 28' N, 0° 23' W.
- Venice (بندقية).
- Verona. A city in northern Italy, at 45° 26' N, 10° 59' E.
- Wakhān (وخان / واخان). A rugged, mountainous part of Afghanistan near Tajikistan.
- Wālishtān (والشتان). The area around the city of Sibi or Sevi, in Pakistan at 29° 33' N, 67° 53' E.
- Wallachia (Medieval/Modern). A region in what is now southern Romania.
- Washqā (وشقة), the modern Huesca, a city in Spain at 42° 08' N, 0° 25' W.
- Wasīfīn (وصيفين). Unknown at this time.
- West Indies (Medieval/Modern). Islands in the Caribbean Sea; any group of these islands was also designated by the name of the European nation which ruled it (e.g., Dutch West Indies, French West Indies).

- White Mountains. The snowy peaks in Africa which include Kilimanjaro in Tanzania (3° 04' S, 37° 21' E) and the Rwenzori range in the Congo (around 0° 23' N, 29° 52' E).
- Yājūj (ياجوج), also known as Gog (as in the Biblical Gog and Magog), an uncertain nomadic people or area in north-central Asia.
- Al-Yamāmah (اليمامة). A region of central Saudi Arabia just east of the plateau of Najd.
- Yathrib (يثرب). The pre-Islamic name for Medina.
- Yemen (اليمن).
- Zābij (زابج). A name variously used for Java, southern Sumatra, or much of the Indonesian archipelago.
- Zābulistān (زابلستان). A region of Sijistān, the highlands NW of the Helmand River, now in southern Afghanistan.
- Zamm (زم؟). Nowadays Kerki or Atamurat, a town in Turkmenistan, at 37° 51' N, 65° 14' E.
- Zanj/al-Zanj (الزنج), the land of "the blacks," referring the southeastern part of Africa south of (and including part of) modern Somalia, encompassing Kenya, Tanzania, Mozambique, etc. Hence: "Zanzibar."
- Zaragoza. See Saragossa.
- Zāvah. See Java.
- Zawīlah (זוילה / زويلة), a western suburb of al-Mahdiyyah in Tunisia, at 35° 30' N, 11° 03' E. There is also a place of the same name in Libya, at 26° 11' N, 15° 06' E.
- Zeeland / Zealand (Medieval/Modern). A group of islands forming a western province of the Netherlands.
- Zufār (ظفار). A region of southern 'Omān bordering on Yemen, at about 18° N, 54° E.

GLOSSARY

This glossary is an expanded version of the one in my 2010 *Introductions to Traditional Astrology (ITA)*, with the addition of other terms from my translations since then. After most definitions is a reference to sections and Appendices of *ITA* (including my introduction to it) for further reading—for the most part, they do *not* refer to passages in this book (and if so, are labeled as such).

- **Accident** (Lat. *accidens*, Ar. *ḥādith*). An event which "befalls" or "happens" to someone, though not necessarily something bad.
- **Adding in course.** See **Course**.
- **Advancing.** When a planet is in an **angle** or succeedent. See III.3 and the Introduction §6.
- **Advantageous places.** One of two schemes of **houses** which indicate affairs/planets which are more busy or good in the context of the chart (III.4). The seven-place scheme according to Timaeus and reported in *Carmen* includes only certain signs which **aspect** the **Ascendant** by whole-sign, and suggests that these places are advantageous for the *native* because they aspect the Ascendant. The eight-place scheme according to Nechepso (III.4) lists all of the **angular** and **succeedent** places, suggesting places which are stimulating and advantageous for a planet *in itself*.
- **Ages of man.** Ptolemy's division of a typical human life span into periods ruled by planets as **time lords**. See VII.3.
- **Agreeing signs.** Groups of signs which share some kind of harmonious quality. See I.9.5-6.
- *Alcochoden.* Latin transliteration for *Kadukhudhāh*.
- **Alien** (Lat. *alienus*). See **Peregrine**.
- *Almuten.* A Latin transliteration for *mubtazz*: see **Victor**.
- **Angles, succeedents, cadents.** A division of houses into three groups which show how powerfully and directly a planet acts. The angles are the 1st, 10th, 7th and 4th houses; the succeedents are the 2nd, 11th, 8th and 5th; the cadents are the 12th, 9th, 6th and 3rd (but see **cadent** below). But the exact regions in question will depend upon whether and how one uses **whole-sign** and **quadrant houses**, especially since traditional texts refer to an angle or pivot (Gr. *kentron*, Ar. *watad*) as either (1) equivalent to the **whole-sign** angles from the **Ascendant**, or (2) the degrees of the **Ascendant-**

Midheaven axes themselves, or (3) **quadrant houses** (and their associated strengths) as measured from the degrees of the axes. See I.12-13 and III.3-4, and the Introduction §6.

- **Antiscia** (sing. *antiscion*), "throwing shadows." Refers to a degree mirrored across an axis drawn from 0° Capricorn to 0° Cancer. For example, 10° Cancer has 20° Gemini as its antiscion. See I.9.2.
- **Apogee.** Typically, the furthest point a planet can be from the earth on the circle of the **deferent**. See II.0-1.
- **Applying, application.** When a planet is in a state of **connection**, moving so as to make the connection exact. Planets **assembled** together or in **aspect** by sign and not yet connected by the relevant degrees, are only "wanting" to be connected.
- **Arisings.** See **Ascensions**.
- **Ascendant.** Usually the entire rising sign, but often specified as the exact rising degree. In **quadrant houses**, a space following the exact rising degree up to the cusp of the 2nd house.
- **Ascensions.** Degrees on the celestial equator, measured in terms of how many degrees pass the meridian as an entire sign or **bound** (or other spans of zodiacal degrees) passes across the horizon. They are often used in the predictive technique of ascensional times, as an approximation for **directions**. See Appendix E.
- **Aspect/regard.** One planet aspects or regards another if they are in signs which are configured to each other by a **sextile, square, trine,** or **opposition**. See III.6 and **Whole signs**. A connection by degrees or orbs is a much more intense of an aspect.
- **Assembly.** When two or more planets are in the same sign, and more intensely if within 15°. (It is occasionally used in Arabic to indicate the conjunction of the Sun and Moon at the New Moon, but the more common word for that is **meeting**). See III.5.
- **Aversion.** Being in the second, sixth, eighth, or twelfth sign from a place. For instance, a planet in Gemini is in the twelfth from, and therefore in aversion to, Cancer. Such places are in aversion because they cannot **aspect** it by the classical scheme of aspects. See III.6.1.
- *Azamene.* Equivalent to **Chronic illness.**
- **Bad ones.** See **Benefic/malefic.**
- **Barring.** See **Blocking.**

- **Bearing** (Lat. *habitude*). Hugo's term for any of the many possible planetary conditions and relationships. These may be found in III and IV.
- **Benefic/malefic**. A division of the planets into groups that cause or signify typically "good" things (Jupiter, Venus, usually the Sun and Moon) or "bad" things (Mars, Saturn). Mercury is considered variable. See V.9.
- **Benevolents**. See **Benefic/malefic**.
- **Besieging**. Equivalent to **Enclosure**.
- **Bicorporeal signs**. Equivalent to "common" signs. See **Quadruplicity**.
- **Blocking** (sometimes called "prohibition"). When a planet bars another planet from completing a **connection**, either through its own body or ray. See III.14.
- **Bodyguarding**. Planetary relationships in which some planet protects another, used in determining social eminence and prosperity. See III.28.
- **Bounds**. Unequal divisions of the zodiac in each sign, each bound being ruled by one of the five non-**luminaries**. Sometimes called "terms," they are one of the five classical **dignities**. See VII.4.
- **Bright, smoky, empty, dark degrees**. Certain degrees of the zodiac said to affect how conspicuous or obscure the significations of planets or the Ascendant are. See VII.7.
- **Burned up** (or "combust," Lat. *combustus*). Normally, when a planet is between about 1° and 7.5° away from the Sun. See II.9-10, and **In the heart**.
- **Burnt path** (Lat. *via combusta*). A span of degrees in Libra and Scorpio in which a planet (especially the Moon) is considered to be harmed or less able to effect its significations. Some astrologers identify it as between 15° Libra and 15° Scorpio; others between the exact degree of the **fall** of the Sun in 19° Libra and the exact degree of the fall of the Moon in 3° Scorpio. See IV.3.
- *Bust*. Certain hours measured from the New Moon, in which it is considered favorable or unfavorable to undertake an action or perform an **election**. See VIII.4.
- **Busy places**. Equivalent to the **Advantageous places**.
- **Cadent** (Lat. *cadens*, "falling"). This is used in two ways: a planet or place may be cadent from the **angles** (being in the 3rd, 6th, 9th, or 12th), or else cadent from the **Ascendant** (namely, in **aversion** to it, being in the 12th, 8th, 6th, or 2nd). See I.12, III.4, and III.6.1.
- **Cardinal**. Equivalent to "movable" signs. See **Quadruplicity**.
- **Cazimi**: see **In the heart**.

- **Celestial equator.** The projection of earth's equator out into the universe, forming one of the three principal celestial coordinate systems.
- **Centers of the Moon.** Also called the "posts" or "foundations" of the Moon. Angular distances between the Sun and Moon throughout the lunar month, indicating possible times of weather changes and rain. See *AW1*.
- **Choleric.** See **Humor.**
- **Chronic illness (degrees of).** Degrees which are especially said to indicate chronic illness, due to their association with certain fixed stars. See VII.10.
- **Cleansed.** Normally, when a planet is not in an **assembly** or **square** or **opposition** with a **malefic** planet, but possibly indicating being free of *any* **aspect** with a malefic.
- **Clothed.** Equivalent to one planet being in an **assembly** or **aspect/regard** with another, and therefore partaking in (being "clothed in") the other planet's characteristics.
- **Collection.** When two planets **aspecting** each other but not in an applying **connection**, each apply to a third planet. See III.12.
- **Combust.** See **Burned up.**
- **Commanding/obeying.** A division of the signs into those which command or obey each other (used sometimes in **synastry**). See I.9.
- **Common signs.** See **Quadruplicity.**
- **Complexion.** Primarily, a mixture of elements and their qualities so as to indicate or produce some effect. Secondarily it refers to planetary combinations, following the naturalistic theory that planets have elemental qualities with causal power, which can interact with each other.
- **Confer.** See **Pushing.**
- **Configured.** To be in a whole-sign **aspect**, though not necessarily by degree.
- **Conjunction (of planets).** See **Assembly** and **Connection.**
- **Conjunction/prevention.** The position of the New (conjunction) or Full (prevention) Moon most immediately prior to a **nativity** or other chart. For the prevention, some astrologers use the degree of the Moon, others the degree of the luminary which was above the earth at the time of the prevention. See VIII.1.2.
- **Connection.** When a planet applies to another planet (by body in the same sign, or by ray in **aspecting** signs), within a particular number of degrees up to exactness. See III.7.

- **Convertible**. Equivalent to the movable signs. See **Quadruplicity**. But sometimes planets (especially Mercury) are called convertible because their **gender** is affected by their placement in the chart.
- **Convey**. See **Pushing**.
- **Corruption**. Normally, the harming of a planet (see IV.3-4), such as being in a **square** with a **malefic** planet. But sometimes, equivalent to **Detriment**.
- **Counsel** (Lat. *consilium*). A term used by Hugo and other Latin translators of Arabic, for "management" (III.18). An **applying** planet **pushes** or gifts or grants its counsel or management to another planet, and that other planet **receives** or gathers it.
- **Course, increasing/decreasing in**. For practical purposes, this means a planet is quicker than average in motion. But in geometric astronomy, it refers to what **sector** of the **deferent** the center of a planet's **epicycle** is. (The planet's position within the four sectors of the epicycle itself will also affect its apparent speed.) In the two sectors that are closest to the planet's **perigee**, the planet will apparently be moving faster; in the two sectors closest to the **apogee**, it will apparently be moving slower. See II.0-1.
- **Crooked/straight**. A division of the signs into those which rise quickly and are more parallel to the horizon (crooked), and those which arise more slowly and closer to a right angle from the horizon (straight or direct). In the northern hemisphere, the signs from Capricorn to Gemini are crooked (but in the southern one, straight); those from Cancer to Sagittarius are straight (but in the southern one, crooked).
- **Crossing over**. When a planet begins to **separate** from an exact **connection**. See III.7-8.
- **Cutting of light**. Three ways in which a **connection** is prevented: either by **obstruction** from the following sign, **escape** within the same sign, or by **barring**. See III.23.
- *Darījān*. An alternative **face** system attributed to the Indians. See VII.6.
- **Decan**. Equivalent to **face**.
- **Declination**. The equivalent on the celestial **equator**, of geographical latitude. The signs of northern declination (Aries through Virgo) stretch northward of the **ecliptic**, while those of southern declination (Libra through Pisces) stretch southward.
- **Deferent**. The circle on which a planet's **epicycle** travels. See II.0-1.
- **Descension**. Equivalent to **fall**.

- **Detriment** (or Ar. "corruption," "unhealthiness," "harm."). More broadly (as "corruption"), it refers to any way in which a planet is harmed or its operation thwarted (such as by being **burned up**). But it also (as "harm") refers specifically to the sign opposite a planet's **domicile**. Libra is the detriment of Mars. See I.6 and I.8.
- **Dexter.** "Right": see **Right/left.**
- **Diameter.** Equivalent to **Opposition.**
- **Dignity** (Lat. "worthiness"; Ar. *ḥaẓẓ*, "good fortune, allotment"). Any of five ways of assigning rulership or responsibility to a planet (or sometimes, to a **Node**) over some portion of the zodiac. They are often listed in the following order: **domicile, exaltation, triplicity, bound, face/decan.** Each dignity has its own meaning and effect and use, and two of them have opposites: the opposite of domicile is **detriment,** the opposite of exaltation is **fall.** See I.3, I.4, I.6-7, VII.4 for the assignments; I.8 for some descriptive analogies; VIII.2.1 and VIII.2.2*f* for some predictive uses of domiciles and bounds.
- **Directions.** A predictive technique which is more precise than using **ascensions,** and defined by Ptolemy in terms of proportional semi-arcs. There is some confusion in how directing works, because of the difference between the astronomical method of directions and how astrologers look at charts. Astronomically, a point in the chart (the significator) is considered as stationary, and other planets and their **aspects** by degree (or even the **bounds**) are sent forth (promittors) as though the heavens keep turning by **primary motion,** until they come to the significator. The degrees between the significator and promittor are converted into years of life. But when looking at the chart, it seems as though the significator is being **released** counterclockwise in the order of signs, so that it **distributes** through the bounds or comes to the bodies or aspects of promittors. Direction by **ascensions** takes the latter perspective, though the result is the same. Some later astrologers allow the distance between a significator/releaser and the promittor to be measured in either direction, yielding "converse" directions in addition to the classical "direct" directions. See VIII.2.2, Appendix E, and Gansten.
- **Disregard.** Equivalent to **Separation.**
- **Distribution.** The **direction** of a **releaser** (often the degree of the **Ascendant**) through the **bounds.** The bound **lord** of the distribution is the

"distributor," and any body or ray which the **releaser** encounters is the
"**partner**." See VIII.2.2*f*, and *PN3*.

- **Distributor**. The **bound lord** of a **directed releaser**. See **Distribution**.
- **Diurnal**. See **Sect**.
- **Domain**. A **sect** and **gender**-based planetary condition. See III.2.
- **Domicile**. One of the five **dignities**. A sign of the zodiac, insofar as it is owned or managed by one of the planets. For example, Aries is the domicile of Mars, and so Mars is its domicile **lord**. See I.6.
- **Doryphory** (Gr. *doruphoria*). Equivalent to **Bodyguarding**.
- **Double-bodied**. Equivalent to the common signs. See **Quadruplicity**.
- **Dragon**: see **Node**.
- **Drawn back** (Lat. *reductus*). Equivalent to being **cadent** from an **angle**.
- **Dodecametorion**. Equivalent to **Twelfth-part**.
- *Duodecima*. Equivalent to **Twelfth-part**.
- *Dustūrīyyah*. Equivalent to **Bodyguarding**.
- **East** (Lat. *oriens*). The Ascendant: normally the rising sign, but sometimes the degree of the Ascendant itself.
- **Eastern/western (by quadrant)**. When a planet is in one any of the **quadrants** as defined by the axial degrees. The eastern quadrants are between the degrees of the **Ascendant** and **Midheaven**, and between those of the **Descendant** and *Imum Caeli*. The western quadrants are between the degrees of the Midheaven and Descendant, and between those of the *Imum Caeli* and the Ascendant.
- **Eastern/western (of the Sun)**. A position relative to the Sun, often called "oriental" or "occidental," respectively. These terms are used in two major ways: (1) when a planet is in a position to rise before the Sun by being in an early degree (eastern) or is in a position to set after the Sun by being in a later degree (western). But in ancient languages, these words also refer mean "arising" or "setting/sinking," on an analogy with the Sun rising and setting: so sometimes they refer to (2) a planet arising out of, or sinking under, the **Sun's rays**, no matter what side of the Sun it is on (in some of my translations I call this "pertaining to arising" and "pertaining to sinking"). Astrological authors do not always clarify what sense is meant, and different astronomers and astrologers have different definitions for exactly what positions count as being eastern or western. See II.10.
- **Ecliptic**. The path defined by the Sun's motion through the zodiac, defined as having 0° ecliptical latitude. In tropical astrology, the ecliptic (and

therefore the zodiacal signs) begins at the intersection of the ecliptic and the celestial equator.

- **Election** (lit. "choice"). The deliberate choosing of an appropriate time to undertake an action, or determining when to avoid an action; but astrologers normally refer to the chart of the time itself as an election.

- **Element**. One of the four basic qualities. fire, air, water, earth) describing how matter and energy operate, and used to describe the significations and operations of planets and signs. They are usually described by pairs of four other basic qualities (hot, cold, wet, dry). For example, Aries is a fiery sign, and hot and dry; Mercury is typically treated as cold and dry (earthy). See I.3, I.7, and Book V.

- **Emptiness of the course**. Medievally, when a planet does not complete a **connection** for as long as it is in its current sign. In Hellenistic astrology, when a planet does not complete a connection within the next 30°. See III.9.

- **Enclosure**. When a planet has the rays or bodies of the **malefics** (or alternatively, the **benefics**) on either side of it, by degree or sign. See IV.4.2.

- **Epicycle**. A circle on the **deferent**, on which a planet turns. See II.0-1.

- **Equant**. A circle used to measure the average position of a planet. See II.0-1.

- **Equator (celestial)**. The projection of the earth's equator into space, forming a great circle. Its equivalent of latitude is called **declination**, while its equivalent of longitude is called **right ascension** (and is measured from the beginning of Aries, from the intersection of it and the **ecliptic**).

- **Escape**. When a planet wants to **connect** with a second one, but the second one moves into the next sign before it is completed, and the first planet makes a **connection** with a different, unrelated one instead. See III.22.

- **Essence** (Lat. *substantia*). Deriving ultimately from Aristotelian philosophy, the fundamental nature or character of a planet or sign, which allows it to indicate or cause certain phenomena (such as the essence of Mars being responsible for indicating fire, iron, war, *etc.*). This word has often been translated as "substance," which is a less accurate term.

- **Essential/accidental**. A common way of distinguishing a planet's conditions, usually according to **dignity** (essential, I.2) and some other condition such as its **aspects** (accidental). See IV.1-5 for many accidental conditions.

- **Exaltation.** One of the five **dignities**. A sign in which a planet (or sometimes, a **Node**) signifies its matter in a particularly authoritative and refined way. The exaltation is sometimes identified with a particular degree in that sign. See I.6.
- **Face.** One of the five **dignities**. The zodiac is divided into 36 faces of 10° each, starting with the beginning of Aries. See I.5.
- **Facing.** A relationship between a planet and a **luminary**, if their respective signs are configured at the same distance as their **domiciles** are. For example, Leo (ruled by the Sun) is two signs to the **right** of Libra (ruled by Venus). When Venus is **western** and two signs away from wherever the Sun is, she will be in the facing of the Sun. See II.11.
- **Fall.** The sign opposite a planet's **exaltation**. See I.6.
- **Familiar** (Lat. *familiaris*). A hard-to-define term which suggests a sense of belonging and close relationship. (1) Sometimes it is contrasted with being **peregrine**, suggesting that a familiar planet is one which is a **lord** over a degree or **place** (that is, it has a **dignity** in it): for a dignity suggests belonging. (2) At other times, it refers to a familiar **aspect** (and probably the **sextile** or **trine** in particular): all of the family houses in a chart have a **whole-sign** aspect to the **Ascendant**.
- *Fardār.* See *Firdārīyyah*.
- **Feminine.** See **Gender**.
- **Feral.** Equivalent to **Wildness**.
- **Figure.** One of several polygons implied by an **aspect**. For example, a planet in Aries and one in Capricorn do not actually form a **square**, but they imply one because Aries and Capricorn, together with Libra and Cancer, form a square amongst themselves. See III.8.
- *Firdārīyyah* (pl. *firdārīyyāt*). A **time lord** method in which planets rule different periods of life, with each period broken down into sub-periods (there are also mundane versions). See VII.1.
- **Firm.** In terms of signs, the **fixed** signs: see **Quadruplicity**. For houses, equivalent to the **Angles**.
- **Fixed.** See **Quadruplicity**.
- **Foreign** (Lat. *extraneus*). Usually equivalent to **peregrine**.
- **Fortunate.** Normally, a planet whose condition is made better by one of the **bearings** described in IV.
- **Fortunes.** See **Benefic/malefic**.
- **Foundations of the Moon.** See **Centers of the Moon**.

- **Free.** Sometimes, being **cleansed** of the **malefics**; at other times, being out of the **Sun's rays**.
- **Gender.** The division of signs, degrees, planets and hours into masculine and feminine groups. See I.3, V.10, V.14, VII.8.
- **Generosity and benefits.** Favorable relationships between signs and planets, as defined in III.26.
- **Good ones.** See **Benefic/malefic**.
- **Good places.** Equivalent to **Advantageous places**.
- **Governor** (Ar. *mustawlī*). A planet which has preeminence or rulership over some topic or indication (such as the governor over an eclipse); normally, it is a kind of **victor**.
- **Greater, middle, lesser years.** See **Planetary years**.
- **Ḥalb.** Probably Pahlavi for "sect," but normally describes a rejoicing condition: see III.2.
- **Ḥayyiz.** Arabic for "domain," normally a gender-intensified condition of *ḥalb*. See III.2.
- **Hexagon.** Equivalent to **Sextile**.
- **Hīlāj** (From the Pahlavi for "releaser"). Equivalent to **Releaser**.
- **Hold onto.** Hugo's synonym for a planet being in or **transiting** a **sign**.
- **Horary astrology.** A late historical designation for **Questions**.
- **Hours (planetary).** The assigning of rulership over hours of the day and night to planets. The hours of daylight (and night, respectively) are divided by 12, and each period is ruled first by the planet ruling that day, then the rest in descending planetary order. For example, on Sunday the Sun rules the first planetary "hour" from daybreak, then Venus, then Mercury, the Moon, Saturn, and so on. See V.13.
- **House.** A twelve-fold spatial division of a chart, in which each house signifies one or more areas of life. Two basic schemes are (1) **whole-sign** houses, in which the **signs** are equivalent to the houses, and (2) **quadrant houses**. But in the context of dignities and rulerships, "house" is the equivalent of **domicile**.
- **House-master.** Often called the *alcochoden* in Latin, from **kadukhudhāh** (the Pahlavi for "house-master"). One of the lords of the longevity **releaser**, preferably the **bound lord**. See VIII.1.3. But the Greek equivalent of this word (*oikodespotēs*, "house-master") is used in various ways in Hellenistic Greek texts, sometimes indicating the **lord** of a **domicile**, at other

times the same longevity planet just mentioned, and at other times a kind of **victor** over the whole **nativity**.

- **Humor.** Any one of four fluids in the body (according to traditional medicine), the balance between which determines one's health and **temperament** (outlook and energy level). Choler or yellow bile is associated with fire and the choleric temperament; blood is associated with air and the sanguine temperament; phlegm is associated with water and the phlegmatic temperament; black bile is associated with earth and the melancholic temperament. See I.3.

- **IC.** See *Imum Caeli.*

- *Imum Caeli* (Lat., "lowest part of heaven"). The degree of the zodiac on which the lower half of the meridian circle falls; in **quadrant house** systems, it marks the beginning of the fourth **house.**

- **In the heart.** Often called *cazimi* in English texts, from the Ar. *kaṣmīmī.* A planet is in the heart of the Sun when it is either in the same degree as the Sun (according to Sahl ibn Bishr and Rhetorius), or within 16' of longitude from him. See II.9.

- **Indicator.** A degree which is supposed to indicate the approximate position of the degree of the natal **Ascendant,** in cases where the time of birth is uncertain. See VIII.1.2.

- **Inferior.** The planets lower than the Sun: Venus, Mercury, Moon.

- **Infortunes.** See **Benefic/malefic.**

- *ʾIttiṣāl.* Equivalent to **Connection.**

- **Joys.** Places in which the planets are said to "rejoice" in acting or signifying their natures. Joys by house are found in I.16; by sign in I.10.7.

- *Jārbakhtār* (From the Pahlavi for "distributor of time"). Equivalent to **Distributor;** see **Distribution.**

- *Kadukhudhāh* (From the Pahlavi for "house-master"), often called the *alcochoden* in Latin transliteration. See **House-master.**

- *Kardaja* (Ar. *kardajah,* from Sanskrit *kramajyā*). An interval used in the rows of astronomical tables such as in the *Almagest.* Each row begins with a value (called an "argument"), and one reads across to find the corresponding value used to correct such things as planetary positions. The increment or interval between each argument is a *kardaja.* A single table may use different increments based on theoretical considerations, levels of accuracy needed, *etc.* Some books of tables defined the *kardajas* in terms of sine functions. According to al-Hāshimī (1981, p. 143), the lower **sectors** of a planet's epicycle (closer to the earth, where it is retrograde) are the "fast" *kardajas*. But this probably also refers to the lower sectors of the eccentric or deferent circle, closer to a planet's **perigee**.

- **Kaṣmīmī**: see **In the heart**.
- **Kingdom**. Equivalent to **exaltation**.
- **Largesse and recompense**. A reciprocal relation in which one planet is rescued from being in its own **fall** or a **well**, and then returns the favor when the other planet is in its fall or well. See III.24.
- **Leader** (Lat. *dux*). Equivalent to a **significator** for some topic. The Arabic word for "significator" means to indicate something by pointing the way toward something: thus the significator for a topic or matter "leads" the astrologer to some answer. Used by some less popular Latin translators (such as Hugo of Santalla and Hermann of Carinthia).
- **Linger in** (Lat. *commoror*). Hugo's synonym for a planet being in or **transiting** through a **sign**.
- **Lodging-place** (Lat. *hospitium*). Hugo's synonym for a **house**, particularly the **sign** which occupies a house.
- **lord of the year**. The **domicile lord** of a **profection**. The Sun and Moon are not allowed to be primary lords of the year, according to Persian doctrine. See VIII.2.1 and VIII.3.2, and Appendix F.
- **Lord**. A designation for the planet which has a particular **dignity**, but when used alone it usually means the **domicile** lord. For example, Mars is the lord of Aries.
- **Lord of the question**. In questions, the lord of the **house** of the **quaesited** matter. But sometimes, it refers to the client or **querent** whose question it is.
- **Lord of the year**. In mundane ingress charts, the planet that is the **victor** over the chart, indicating the general meanings of the year.
- **Lot**. Sometimes called "Parts." A place (often treated as equivalent to an entire sign) expressing a ratio derived from the position of three other parts of a chart. Normally, the distance between two places is measured in zodiacal order from one to the other, and this distance is projected forward from some other place (usually the Ascendant): where the counting stops, is the Lot. Lots are used both interpretively and predictively. See Book VI.
- **Lucky/unlucky**. See **Benefic/malefic**.
- **Luminary**. The Sun or Moon.

- **Malefic.** See **Benefic/malefic.**
- **Malevolents.** See **Benefic/malefic.**
- **Masculine.** See **Gender.**
- **Meeting** (Ar. *ʾijtimāʿ*). The conjunction of the Sun and Moon at the New Moon, which makes it a **connection** by body.
- **Melancholic.** See **Humor.**
- **Midheaven.** Either the tenth sign from the **Ascendant**, or the zodiacal degree on which the celestial meridian falls.
- **Minister.** A synonym for **Governor.**
- **Movable signs.** See **Quadruplicity.**
- *Mubtazz.* See **Victor.**
- **Mutable signs.** Equivalent to "common" signs. See **Quadruplicity.**
- *Namūdār.* Equivalent to **Indicator.**
- **Native.** The person whose birth chart it is.
- **Nativity.** Technically, a birth itself, but used by astrologers to describe the chart cast for the moment of a birth.
- **Ninth-parts.** Divisions of each sign into 9 equal parts of 3° 20' apiece, each ruled by a planet. Used predictively by some astrologers as part of the suite of **revolution** techniques. See VII.5.
- **Nobility.** Equivalent to **exaltation.**
- **Nocturnal.** See **Sect.**
- **Node.** The point on the ecliptic where a planet passes into northward latitude (its North Node or Head of the Dragon) or into southern latitude (its South Node or Tail of the Dragon). Normally only the Moon's Nodes are considered. See II.5 and V.8.
- **Northern/southern.** Either planets in northern or southern latitude in the zodiac (relative to the ecliptic), or in northern or southern declination relative to the celestial equator. See I.10.1.
- **Not-reception.** When an **applying** planet is in the **fall** of the planet being applied to.
- **Oblique ascensions.** The **ascensions** used in making predictions by ascensional times or primary **directions.**
- **Obstruction.** When one planet is moving towards a second (wanting to be **connected** to it), but a third one in a later degrees goes **retrograde**, connects with the second one, and then with the first one. See III.21.
- **Occidental.** See **Eastern/western.**

- **Opening of the portals/doors.** Times of likely weather changes and rain, determined by certain **transits**. See VIII.3.4, and *AW1*.
- **Opposition.** An **aspect** either by **whole sign** or degree, in which the signs have a 180° relation to each other: for example, a planet in Aries is opposed to one in Libra.
- **Optimal place.** Also called "good" and "the best" places. These are probably a subset of the **advantageous places**, and probably only those houses which **aspect** the **Ascendant**. They definitely include the Ascendant, tenth, and eleventh houses, but may also include the ninth. They are probably also restricted only to houses above the horizon.
- **Orbs/bodies.** Called "orb" by the Latins, and "body" (*jirm*) by Arabic astrologers. A space of power or influence on each side of a planet's body or position, used to determine the intensity of interaction between different planets. See II.6.
- **Oriental.** See **Eastern/western**.
- **Overcoming.** When a planet is in the eleventh, tenth, or ninth sign from another planet (i.e., in a superior **sextile, square,** or **trine aspect**), though being in the tenth sign is considered a more dominant or even domineering position. See IV.4.1 and *PN3*'s Introduction, §15.
- **Own light.** This refers either to (1) a planet being a member of the **sect** of the chart (see V.9), or (2) a planet being out of the **Sun's rays** and not yet **connected** to another planet, so that it shines on its own without being **clothed** in another's influence (see II.9).
- **Part.** See **Lot**.
- **Partner.** The body or ray of any planet which a **directed releaser** encounters while being **distributed** through the **bounds**. But in some translations from Arabic, any of the **lords** of a place.
- **Peregrine.** When a planet is not in one of its five **dignities**. See I.9.
- **Perigee.** The position on a planet's **deferent** circle which is closest to the earth; it is opposite the **apogee**. See II.0-1.
- **Perverse** (Lat. *perversus*). Hugo's occasional term for (1) **malefic** planets, and (2) **places** in **aversion** to the **Ascendant** by **whole-sign**: definitely the twelfth and sixth, probably the eighth, and possibly the second.
- **Phlegmatic.** See **Humor**.
- **Pitted degrees.** Equivalent to **Welled degrees**.
- **Pivot.** Equivalent to **Angle**.

- **Place.** Equivalent to a **house**, and more often (and more anciently) a **whole-sign** house, namely a **sign**.
- **Planetary years.** Periods of years which the planets signify according to various conditions. See VII.2.
- **Possess.** Hugo's synonym for a planet being in or **transiting** a **sign**.
- **Posts of the Moon.** See **Centers of the Moon**.
- **Prevention.** See **Conjunction/prevention**.
- **Primary directions.** See **Directions**.
- **Primary motion.** The clockwise or east-to-west motion of the heavens.
- **Profection** (Lat. *profectio*, "advancement, setting out"). A predictive technique in which some part of a chart (usually the **Ascendant**) is advanced either by an entire sign or in 30° increments for each year of life. See VIII.2.1 and VIII.3.2, and the sources in Appendix F.
- **Prohibition.** Equivalent to **Blocking**.
- **Promittor** (lit., something "sent forward"). A point which is **directed** to a **significator**, or to which a significator is **released** or directed (depending on how one views the mechanics of directions).
- **Pushing.** What a planet making an **applying connection** does to the one **receiving** it. See III.15-18.
- *Qasim/qismah*: Arabic terms for **distributor** and **distribution**.
- **Quadrant.** A division of the heavens into four parts, defined by the circles of the horizon and meridian, also known as the axes of the **Ascendant-Descendant**, and **Midheaven-IC**.
- **Quadrant houses.** A division of the heavens into twelve spaces which overlap the **whole signs**, and are assigned to topics of life and ways of measuring strength (such as Porphyry, Alchabitius Semi-Arc, or Regiomontanus houses). For example, if the Midheaven fell into the eleventh sign, the space between the Midheaven and the Ascendant would be divided into sections that overlap and are not coincident with the signs. See I.12 and the Introduction §6.
- **Quadruplicity.** A "fourfold" group of signs indicating certain shared patterns of behavior. The movable (or cardinal or convertible) signs are those through which new states of being are quickly formed (including the seasons): Aries, Cancer, Libra, Capricorn. The fixed (sometimes "firm") signs are those through which matters are fixed and lasting in their character: Taurus, Leo, Scorpio, Aquarius. The common (or mutable or bicorporeal)

496 ASTROLOGY OF THE WORLD I: THE PTOLEMAIC INHERITANCE

signs are those which make a transition and partake both of quick change and fixed qualities: Gemini, Virgo, Sagittarius, Pisces. See I.10.5.

• **Quaesited/quesited.** In **horary** astrology, the matter asked about.

• **Querent.** In **horary** astrology, the person asking the question (or the person on behalf of whom one asks).

• **Questions.** The branch of astrology dealing with inquiries about individual matters, for which a chart is cast.

• **Reception.** What one planet does when another planet **pushes** or **applies** to it, and especially when they are related by **dignity** or by a **trine** or **sextile** from an **agreeing** sign of various types. For example, if the Moon applies to Mars, Mars will get or receive her application. See III.15-18 and III.25.

• **Reflection.** When two planets are in **aversion** to each other, but a third planet either **collects** or **transfers** their light. If it collects, it reflects the light elsewhere. See III.13.

• **Refrenation.** See **Revoking.**

• **Regard.** Equivalent to **Aspect.**

• **Releaser.** The point which is the focus of a **direction.** In determining longevity, it is the one among a standard set of possible points which has certain qualifications (see VIII.1.3). In annual predictions one either directs or **distributes** the longevity releaser, or any one of a number of points for particular topics, or else the degree of the **Ascendant** as a default releaser. Many astrologers direct the degree of the Ascendant of the **revolution** chart itself as a releaser.

• **Remote** (Lat. *remotus*, prob. a translation of Ar. *zāyīl*). Equivalent to **cadent**: see **Angle.** But see also *Judges* §7.73, where 'Umar (or Hugo) distinguishes being **cadent** from being **remote**, probably translating the Ar. *zāyīl* and *sāqiṭ* ("withdrawn/removed" and "fallen").

• **Render.** When a planet **pushes** to another planet or place.

• **Retreating.** When a planet is in a cadent place. See III.4 and the Introduction §6, and **Angle.**

• **Retrograde.** When a planet seems to move backwards or clockwise relative to the signs and fixed stars. See II.8 and II.10.

• **Return, Solar/Lunar.** Equivalent to **Revolution.**

• **Returning.** What a **burned up** or retrograde planet does when another planet **pushes** to it. See III.19.

- **Revoking.** When a planet making an applying **connection** stations and turns **retrograde**, not completing the connection. See III.20.
- **Revolution.** Sometimes called the "cycle" or "transfer" or "change-over" of a year. Technically, the **transiting** position of planets and the **Ascendant** at the moment the Sun returns to a particular place in the zodiac: in the case of nativities, when he returns to his exact natal position; in mundane astrology, usually when he makes his ingress into 0° Aries. But the revolution is also understood to involve an entire suite of predictive techniques, including **distribution, profections,** and *firdārīyyāt*. See *PN3.*
- **Right ascensions.** Degrees on the celestial **equator** (its equivalent of geographical longitude), particularly those which move across the meridian when calculating arcs for **ascensions** and **directions.**
- **Right/left.** Right (or "dexter") degrees and **aspects** are those earlier in the zodiac relative to a planet or sign, up to the **opposition;** left (or "sinister") degrees and aspects are those later in the zodiac. For example, if a planet is in Capricorn, its right aspects will be towards Scorpio, Libra, and Virgo; its left aspects will be towards Pisces, Aries, and Taurus. See III.6.
- **Root.** A chart used as a basis for another chart; a root particularly describes something considered to have concrete being of its own. For example, a **nativity** acts as a root for an **election,** so that when planning an election one must make it harmonize with the nativity.
- **Safe.** When a planet is not being harmed, particularly by an **assembly** or **square** or **opposition** with the **malefics.** See **Cleansed.**
- *Sālkhudhāy* (from Pahlavi, "lord of the year"). Equivalent to the **lord of the year.**
- **Sanguine.** See **Humor.**
- **Scorched.** See **Burned up.**
- **Secondary motion.** The counter-clockwise motion of planets forward in the zodiac.
- **Sect.** A division of charts, planets, and signs into "diurnal/day" and "nocturnal/night." Charts are diurnal if the Sun is above the horizon, else they are nocturnal. Planets are divided into sects as shown in V.11. Masculine signs (Aries, Gemini, *etc.*) are diurnal, the feminine signs (Taurus, Cancer, *etc.*) are nocturnal.
- **Sector** (Ar. *niṭāq*). A division of the **deferent** circle or **epicycle** into four parts, used to determine the position, speed, visibility, and other features of a planet. See II.0-1.

- **Seeing, hearing, listening signs.** A way of associating signs similar to **commanding/obeying.** See Paul of Alexandria's version in the two figures attached to I.9.6.
- **Separation.** When planets have completed a **connection** by **assembly** or **aspect**, and move away from one another. See III.8.
- **Sextile.** An **aspect** either by **whole sign** or degree, in which the signs have a 60° relation to each other: for example, Aries and Gemini.
- **Shift** (Ar. *nawbah*). Equivalent to **Sect**, and refers not only to the alternation between day and night, but also to the period of night or day itself. The Sun is the lord of the diurnal shift or sect, and the Moon is the lord of the nocturnal shift or sect.
- **Sign.** One of the twelve 30° divisions of the **ecliptic**, named after the constellations which they used to be roughly congruent to. In tropical astrology, the signs start from the intersection of the ecliptic with the celestial equator (the position of the Sun at the equinoxes). In sidereal astrology, the signs begin from some other point identified according to other principles.
- **Significator.** Either (1) a planet or point in a chart which indicates or signifies something for a topic (either through its own character, or house position, or rulerships, *etc.*), or (2) the point which is **released** in primary **directions.**
- **Significator of the king.** In mundane ingress charts, the **victor** planet which indicates the king or government.
- **Sinister.** "Left": see **Right/left.**
- **Slavery.** Equivalent to **fall.**
- **Sovereignty** (Lat. *regnum*). Equivalent to **Exaltation.**
- **Spearbearing.** Equivalent to **Bodyguarding.**
- **Square.** An **aspect** either by **whole sign** or degree, in which the signs have a 90° relation to each other: for example, Aries and Cancer.
- **Stake.** Equivalent to **Angle.**
- **Sublunar world.** The world of the four **elements** below the sphere of the Moon, in classical cosmology.
- **Substance** (Lat. *substantia*). Sometimes, indicating the real **essence** of a planet or sign. But often it refers to financial assets (perhaps because coins are physical objects indicating real value).
- **Succeedent.** See **Angle.**

- **Sun's rays** (or Sun's beams). In earlier astrology, equivalent to a regularized distance of 15° away from the Sun, so that a planet under the rays is not visible at dawn or dusk. But a later distinction was made between being **burned up** (about 1° - 7.5° away from the Sun) and merely being under the rays (about 7.5° - 15° away).
- **Superior.** The planets higher than the Sun: Saturn, Jupiter, Mars.
- **Supremacy** (Lat. *regnum*). Hugo's word for **Exaltation**, sometimes used in translations by Dykes instead of the slightly more accurate **Sovereignty**.
- **Synastry.** The comparison of two or more charts to determine compatibility, usually in romantic relationships or friendships. See *BA* Appendix C for a discussion and references for friendship, and *BA* III.7.11 and III.12.7.
- *Tasyīr* (Ar. "dispatching, sending out"). Equivalent to primary **directions**.
- **Temperament.** The particular mixture (sometimes, "complexion") of **elements** or **humors** which determines a person's or planet's typical behavior, outlook, and energy level.
- **Testimony.** From Arabic astrology onwards, a little-defined term which can mean (1) the planets which have **dignity** in a place or degree, or (2) the number of dignities a planet has in its own place (or as compared with other planets), or (3) a planet's **assembly** or **aspect** to a place of interest, or (4) generally *any* way in which planets may make themselves relevant to the inquiry at hand. For example, a planet which is the **exalted** lord of the **Ascendant** but also **aspects** it, maby be said to present two testimonies supporting its relevance to an inquiry about the Ascendant.
- **Tetragon.** Equivalent to **Square.**
- **Thought-interpretation.** The practice of identifying a theme or topic in a **querent's** mind, often using a **victor**, before answering the specific **question**. See *Search.*
- **Time lord.** A planet ruling over some period of time according to one of the classical predictive techniques. For example, the **lord of the year** is the time lord over a **profection.**
- **Transfer.** When one planet **separates** from one planet, and **connects** to another. See III.11.
- **Transit.** The passing of one planet across another planet or point (by body or **aspect** by exact degree), or through a particular sign (even in a **whole-sign** relation to some point of interest). In traditional astrology, not every transit is significant; for example, transits of **time lords** or of planets in the

whole-sign angles of a **profection** might be preferred to others. See VIII.2.4 and *PN3*.

- **Translation.** Equivalent to **Transfer.**
- **Traverse** (Lat. *discurro*). Hugo's synonym for a planet being in or **transiting** through a **sign.**
- **Trigon.** Equivalent to **Trine.**
- **Trine.** An **aspect** either by **whole sign** or degree, in which the signs have a 120° relation to each other: for example, Aries and Leo.
- **Turn** (Ar. *dawr*). A predictive technique in which responsibilities for being a **time lord** rotates between different planets. See VIII.2.3 for one use of the turn. But it can occasionally refer more generally to how the planets may equally play a certain *role* in a chart: for example, if the lord of the Ascendant is Saturn, it means X; but if Jupiter, Y; but if Mars, Z; and so on.
- **Turned away.** Equivalent to **Aversion.**
- **Turning signs.** For Hugo of Santalla, equivalent to the movable signs: see **Quadruplicity.** But *tropicus* more specifically refers to the tropical signs Cancer and Capricorn, in which the Sun turns back from its most extreme declinations.
- **Twelfth-parts.** Signs of the zodiac defined by 2.5° divisions of other signs. For example, the twelfth-part of 4° Gemini is Cancer. See IV.6.
- **Two-parted signs.** Equivalent to the double-bodied or common signs: see **Quadruplicity.**
- **Under rays.** When a planet is between approximately 7.5° and 15° from the Sun, and not visible either when rising before the Sun or setting after him. Some astrologers distinguish the distances for individual planets (which is more astronomically accurate). See II.10.
- **Unfortunate.** Normally, when a planet's condition is made more difficult through one of the **bearings** in IV.
- **Unlucky.** See **Benefic/malefic.**
- *Via combusta.* See **Burnt path.**
- **Victor** (Ar. *mubtazz*). A planet identified as being the most authoritative either for a particular topic or **house** (I.18), or for a chart as a whole (VIII.1.4). See also *Search.*
- **Void in course.** Equivalent to **Emptiness of the course.**
- **Well.** A degree in which a planet is said to be more obscure in its operation. See VII.9.
- **Western.** See **Eastern/western.**

- **Whole signs.** The oldest system of assigning house topics and **aspects.** The entire sign on the horizon (the **Ascendant**) is the first house, the entire second sign is the second house, and so on. Likewise, aspects are considered first of all according to signs: planets in Aries aspect or regard Gemini as a whole, even if aspects by exact degree are more intense. See I.12, III.6, and the Introduction §6.
- **Wildness.** When a planet is not **aspected** by any other planet, for as long as it is in its current sign. See III.10.
- **Withdrawal.** Equivalent to **separation**.

APPENDIX A:
THE *ESSENTIAL MEDIEVAL ASTROLOGY* SERIES

The *Essential Medieval Astrology* cycle is a series of books which is redefining the contours of traditional astrology. Comprised mainly of translations of works by Persian and Arabic-speaking medieval astrologers, it covers all major areas of astrology. Further series will include Hellenistic, Arabic, and later Medieval, Renaissance, and early Modern texts.

I. Introductions
- *Traditional Astrology for Today: An Introduction* (2011)
- *Introductions to Astrology: Abū Ma'shar & al-Qabīsī* (2010)

II. Nativities
- *Persian Nativities I*: Māshā'allāh's *The Book of Aristotle*, Abū 'Alī al-Khayyāt's *On the Judgments of Nativities* (2009)
- *Persian Nativities II*: 'Umar al-Tabarī's *Three Books on Nativities*, Abū Bakr's *On Nativities* (2010)
- *Persian Nativities III: On Solar Revolutions* (2010)

III. Questions (Horary)
- Hermann of Carinthia, *The Search of the Heart* (2011)
- Al-Kindī, *The Forty Chapters* (2011)
- Various, *The Book of the Nine Judges* (2011)

IV. Elections
- *Choices & Inceptions: Traditional Electional Astrology* (2012)

V. Mundane Astrology
- *Astrology of the World I: The Ptolemaic Inheritance* (2013)
- *Astrology of the World II: Conjunctions, Ingresses, & History* (2013)
- *Astrology of the World III: Abū Ma'shar's Book of Religions & Dynasties* (2014)

VI. Other Medieval Works
- Bonatti, Guido, *The Book of Astronomy* (2007)
- *Works of Sahl & Māshā'allāh* (2008)

BIBLIOGRAPHY:

Primary sources:

Al-Kindī, *De Mutatione Temporum* (*Letter on Air & Rains*, or *On the Change of Seasons*)
- Bos & Burnett 2000 (see below)

Al-Kindī, *The Forty Chapters* (all)
- Dykes 2011 (*The Forty Chapters of al-Kindī,* see below)
- Bos & Burnett 2000 (see below)

'Umar al-Tabarī & **the Tehran al-Kindī**
- Bos & Burnett 2000 (see below)
- Al-Rijāl 1485 (see below)
- Dykes 2011 (*The Book of the Nine Judges,* see below)

Māshā'allāh/Jirjis, *On the Rains in the Year*
- Dykes 2011 (*The Book of the Nine Judges,* see below)
- Della Vida 1934 (see below)

Māshā'allāh, *Letter on Rains* & *Winds*
- *CCAG* XII pp. 210-16 (see below)
- Paris BN lat. 7316a (69v-71v)

Al-Rijāl (all)
- Al-Rijāl 1485 (see below)
- Br. Lib. Ar. 23399
- Nuruosmaniye 2766

Ibn Labban (all)
- Ibn Labban 1997 (see below)

Jafar Indus (all)
- Burnett 2004 (see below)

The Sages of India
- Burnett 2004 (see below)

Hermann of Carinthia, *Liber Imbrium* (*Book of Heavy Rains*)
- Low-Beer 1979 (see below)
- Bernkastel-Kues, Cusanusstiftsbibl., 212, s. XV, f. 251r-253v.
- Cambridge, Trinity Coll., O.3.13 (1185), s. XVI, f. 116r-118r.
- Munich, BSB, Clm 11067, s. XV, f. 94ra-96vb.
- Oxford, BL, Auct. F.5.29, s. XIV, f. 29r-31r.

The Opening of the Doors
- Bos & Burnett 2000 (see below)

Saturn in Aries (Saturnus in Ariete)
- Munich, BSB, Clm 667, s. XV, f. 17v-20r.
- Bos & Burnett 2000 (see below)

John of Spain (attr.), *Epitome*
- Nuremburg, 1548

John of Spain, *Quadripartitum*
- Burnett 2004 (see below)

Robert Grosseteste, *On the Impressions of the Air*
- Baur 1912 (see below)

Dorotheus of Sidon (all)
- Dorotheus, *Carmen Astrologicum* (1976, see below)
- Hephaistio of Thebes, *Apostelesmaticorum Libri Tres* (1973, see below)
- Hephaistio of Thebes, *Apotelesmatics* Book III (2013, see below)

Māshā'allāh, *The Book of Prices*
- Berlin Lat. 246 (111vb-113ra)
- Munich Clm. 11067 (120ra-122ra)
- Oxford Hertford Coll. 4 (105r-107r)
- Erfurt Quarto 372 (56r-60r)
- Cambridge Emm. MS 70 (1.3.8; 147v-149r)
- Bodleian Marsh. 618 (225a-229b)

'Umar al-Tabarī on Prices
- Al-Rijāl 1485 (see below)
- Brit. Lib. Ar. 23399
- Dykes 2011 (*The Book of the Nine Judges*, see below)

Abū Ma'shar, *Flowers*
- *Flores Albumasaris* (Venice: Johannes Baptista Sessa 1488 or 1506)
- *Flores Albumasaris* (Augsburg: Erhard Ratdolt 1488)
- Paris BNF lat. 16208 (53vb-59ra)

Ibn Ezra (all)
- Ibn Ezra 2010 (see below)
- Ibn Ezra 1507 (see below)

Jirjis & "Aristotle"
- Dykes 2011 (*The Book of the Nine Judges*, see below)

Al-Qabīsī (attr. and authentic)
- Al-Qabīsī 2004 (see below)

Māshā'allāh on Eclipses
- Paris BNF lat. 16204
- Māshā'allāh 1549 (see below)
- Māshā'allāh 1533 (see below)

Sahl on Eclipses and Comets
- Hermann of Carinthia, *Fatidica* (Low-Beer 1979, see below)
- Vatican Ar. 955
- Beatty Ar. 5467

Abū Ma'shar (incl. Shadhān) on Comets
- Paris BNF lat. 16204
- Erfurt UFB, Amplon. Q. 365, 1r-27r.
- London BL Harley 1, 31r-40v.
- Abū Ma'shar's *Flowers* (see above)
- Vescovini 1998, p. 318 (see below)

Bonatti on Comets
- Bonatti 2007 (see below)
- Bonatti 1550 (see below)
- Hephaistio 1994 (see below)
- Baur 1912 (see below)

Robert Grosseteste on Comets
- Thomson 1933, pp. 24-25 (see below)

Dorotheus on Chorography
- Hephaistio 1994 (see below)

Abū Ma'shar on Chorography
- Abū Ma'shar 2000 (see below)
- Dykes 2010 (see below)

Al-Bīrūnī on Chorography
- Al-Bīrūnī 1934 (see below)

Māshā'allāh on Chorography
- Māshā'allāh, *On the Revolutions of the Years of the World* (in Dykes 2008, see below)
- Bonatti 2007 (see below)

CCAG Foundation Charts
- CCAG 9.2 (1953 pp. 176ff, see below)

Other Sources:

Abū Ma'shar al-Balhi (Richard Lemay ed.), *Liber Introductorii Maioris ad Scientiam Iudiciorum Astrorum* (Naples: Istituto Universitario Orientale, 1996)

Abū Ma'shar al-Balhi, *The Abbreviation of the Introduction to Astrology*, Charles Burnett ed. and trans. (Reston, VA: ARHAT Publications, 1997)

Abū Ma'shar, ed. and trans. Keiji Yamamoto and Charles Burnett, *On Historical Astrology: The Books of Religions and Dynasties (On the Great Conjunctions)* (Leiden: Brill, 2000)

Aristotle, *The Complete Works of Aristotle* vols. I-II, ed. Jonathan Barnes (Princeton, NJ: Princeton University Press, 1984)

Baur, Ludwig, *Die Philosophischen Werke von des Robert Grosseteste, Bischofs von Lincoln* (Münster i. W.: Aschendorffsche Verlagsbuchhandlung, 1912)

Berggren, J. Lennart and Alexander Jones, *Ptolemy's Geography: An Annotated Translation of the Theoretical Chapters* (Princeton and Oxford: Princeton University Press, 2000).

Al-Bīrūnī, Muhammad bin Ahmad, *The Book of Instruction in the Elements of the Art of Astrology*, trans. R. Ramsay Wright (London: Luzac & Co., 1934)

Al-Bīrūnī, Muhammad bin Ahmad, *The Chronology of Ancient Nations* (Lahore: Hijra International Publishers, 1983)

Bonatti, Guido, *De Astronomia Tractatus X* (Basel, 1550)

Bonatti, Guido, *The Book of Astronomy*, Benjamin Dykes trans. and ed. (Golden Valley, MN: The Cazimi Press, 2007)

Bos, Gerrit and Charles Burnett, *Scientific Weather Forecasting in the Middle Ages: The Writings of al-Kindī* (London and New York: Kegan Paul International, 2000)

Burnett, Charles, "Lunar Astrology: The Varieties of Texts using Lunar Mansions, with Emphasis on *Jafar Indus*," *Micrologus* XII (2004), pp. 43-133.

Catalogus Codicum Astrologorum Graecorum (CCAG), vol. 12, ed. Mstislav Šangin (Brussels: Mauritius Lamertin, 1936)

Catalogus Codicum Astrologorum Graecorum (CCAG), vol. 9.2, ed. Stephan Weinstock (Brussels: In Aedibus Academiae, 1953)

Della Vida, G. Levi, "Appunti e Quesiti di Storia Letteraria Araba," in *Rivista degli Studi Orientali* 14/1934, pp. 249-83.

Denningmann, Susanne, *Die Astrologische Lehre der Doryphorie: Eine soziomorphe Metapher in der antiken Planetenastrologie* (München and Leipzig: K.G. Saur, 2005)

Denningmann, Susanne, "The Ambiguous Terms ἑῴα and ἑσπερία ἀνατολή, and ἑῴα and ἑσπερία δύσις," *Culture & Cosmos*, vol. 11, nos. 1-2, 2007.

Dorotheus of Sidon, *Carmen Astrologicum*, trans. David Pingree (Abingdon, MD: The Astrology Center of America, 2005)

Dorotheus of Sidon, *Carmen Astrologicum*, ed. David Pingree (Leipzig: Teubner-Verlagsgesellschaft, 1976)

Dreyer, J. L. E., "The Comet of 1006," *The Observatory*, Vol. 30 (2007), p. 248-49.

Dykes, Benjamin trans. and ed., *Works of Sahl & Māshā'allāh* (Golden Valley, MN: The Cazimi Press, 2008)

Dykes, Benjamin trans. and ed., *Introductions to Traditional Astrology: Abū Ma'shar & al-Qabīsī* (Minneapolis, MN: The Cazimi Press, 2010)

Dykes, Benjamin trans. and ed., *The Forty Chapters of al-Kindī* (Minneapolis, MN: The Cazimi Press, 2011)

Dykes, Benjamin trans. and ed., *The Book of the Nine Judges* (Minneapolis, MN: The Cazimi Press, 2011)

Dykes, Benjamin trans. and ed., *Choices & Inceptions: Traditional Electional Astrology* (Minneapolis, MN: The Cazimi Press, 2012)

Evans, James, *The History and Practice of Ancient Astronomy* (Oxford: Oxford University Press, 1998)

ibn Ezra, Abraham, *In Re Iudicali Opera*, Peter of Abano trans. (Venice: Peter Leichtenstein, 1507)

ibn Ezra, Abraham, *The Beginning of Wisdom*, Meira Epstein trans., Robert Hand ed. (Arhat Publications, 1998)

ibn Ezra, Abraham, *The Book of the World*, Shlomo Sela trans. and ed. (Leiden and Boston: Brill, 2010)

Firmicus Maternus, James H. Holden trans., *Mathesis* (Tempe, AZ: American Federation of Astrologers, 2011)

Goldstein, Bernard R., "Evidence for a Supernova of A.D. 1006," *The Astronomical Journal*, Vol. 70 (February 1, 1965), pp. 105-114.

Goldstein, Bernard R., "The Arabic Version of Ptolemy's *Planetary Hypotheses*," *Transactions of the American Philosophical Society*, vol. 57/4 (1967), pp. 1-55.

Al-Hāshimī, 'Alī ibn Sulaymān, *The Book of the Reasons Behind Astronomical Tables*, trans. Fuad Haddad and E. S. Kennedy (Delmar, NY: Scholars' Facsimiles & Reprints, 1981)

Hephaistio of Thebes, *Apotelesmaticorum Libri Tres*, ed. David Pingree, vols. I-II (Leipzig: Teubner Verlagsgesellschaft, 1973)

Hephaistio of Thebes, *Apotelesmatics* Book I, trans. and ed. Robert H. Schmidt (Berkeley Springs, WV: The Golden Hind Press, 1994)

Hephaistio of Thebes, *Apotelesmatics* Book III, trans. Eduardo Gramaglia, ed. Benjamin Dykes (Minneapolis, MN: The Cazimi Press, 2013)

Holden, James H., "The Foundation Chart of Baghdad," *Today's Astrologer*, Vol. 65, No. 3 (March 2, 2003), pp. 9-10, 29.

Jenks, Stuart, "Astrometeorology in the Middle Ages," *Isis* Vol. 74 No. 2 (June 1983), pp. 185-210.

Kennedy, Edward S., "Comets in Islamic Astronomy and Astrology," *Journal of Near Eastern Studies*, Vol. 16, No. 1 (Jan. 1957), pp. 44-51.

Kennedy, Edward S., *The Astrological History of Māshā'allāh* (Cambridge, MA: Harvard University Press, 1971)

Kennedy, Edward S., *A Commentary Upon Bīrūnī's Kitāb Tahdīd al-Amākin* (Beirut: American University of Beirut, 1973)

Kennedy, Edward S. and M.-H., *Al-Kāshī's Geographical Table* (Philadelphia: The American Philosophical Society, 1987)

Al-Kindī, *The Forty Chapters (Iudicia Astrorum): The Two Latin Versions*, ed. Charles Burnett (London: The Warburg Institute, 1993)

Kronk, Gary, *Cometography: A Catalog of Comets Volume 1: Ancient-1799* (Cambridge: Cambridge University Press, 1999)

Kunitzsch, Paul, Tim Smart, *A Dictionary of Modern Star Names* (Cambridge, MA: Sky Publishing, 2006)

Kushyar ibn Labban, trans. and ed. Michio Yano, *Introduction to Astrology* (Tokyo: Institude for the Study of Languages and Cultures of Asia and Africa, 1997)

ibn Labban, Kušyar, *Introduction to Astrology* Part II, Michio Yano trans. and ed. (Tokyo: Institute for the Study of Languages and Cultures of Asia and Africa, 1997)

Le Strange, G., *The Lands of the Eastern Caliphate* (New York: Barnes & Noble, Inc., 1905)

Lilly, William, *Christian Astrology*, vols. I-II, ed. David R. Roell (Abingdon, MD: Astrology Center of America, 2004)

Linton, C. M., *From Eudoxus to Einstin: A History of Mathematical Astronomy* (Cambridge: Cambridge University Press, 2004)

Low-Beer, Sheila M., *Hermann of Carinthia: The "Liber Imbrium," the "Fatidica," and the "De Indagatione Cordis"* (New York: City University of New York, 1979)

MacBean, Alexander, and Samuel Johnson, *A Dictionary of Ancient Geography* (London: G. Robinson and T. Cadell, 1773).

Māshā'allāh, *Epistola in rebus eclipsis* (Basel: Iohannes Hervagius, 1533)

Māshā'allāh, *Messahalae Antiquissimi ac Laudatissimi Inter Arabes Astrologi, Libri Tres*, ed. Joachim Heller (Nuremberg: Joannes Montanus and Ulrich Neuber, 1549)

Meridian, Bill, *The Predictive Power of Eclipse Paths* (New York NY: Cycles Research, Ltd., 2011)

Merrifield, John, *Catastasis Mundi* (London: Rowland Reynolds, 1684), reprinted by *Renaissance Astrology Facsimile Editions*

Neugebauer, Otto, "The Rising Times in Babylonian Astronomy," *Journal of Cuneiform Studies*, Vol. 7, No. 3 (1953), pp. 100-02.

Neugebauer, Otto, "Notes on Al-Kaid," *Journal of the American Oriental Society*, Vol. 77, No. 3 (Jul.-Sep. 1957), pp. 211-215.

Neugebauer, Otto, and H. B. Van Hoesen, *Greek Horoscopes* (Philadelphia: The American Philosophical Society, 1987)

Al-Qabīsī, *The Introduction to Astrology*, eds. Charles Burnett, Keiji Yamamoto, Michio Yano (London and Turin: The Warburg Institute, 2004)

Pingree, David, *The Thousands of Abū Ma'shar* (London: The Warburg Institute, University of London, 1968)

Ptolemy, Claudius, *Tetrabiblos* (Venice: Bonatus Locatellus, 1493)

Ptolemy, Claudius, *Tetrabiblos* [*Cl. Ptolomaei Pheludiensis Alexandrini Quadriparti-tum*] (Basel: Johannes Hervagius, 1533)

Ptolemy, Claudius, *The Phases of the Fixed Stars*, trans. Robert Schmidt, ed. Robert Hand (Berkeley Springs, WV: The Golden Hind Press, 1993)

Ptolemy, Claudius, *Apotelesmatica*, ed. Wolfgang Hübner (Stuttgart and Leipzig: B. G. Teubner, 1998)

Ptolemy, Claudius, *Ptolemy's Almagest*, trans. and ed. G.J. Toomer (Princeton, NJ: Princeton University Press, 1998)

Al-Rijāl, 'Ali, *De Iudiciis Astrorum* (Venice: Erhard Ratdolt, 1485)

Al-Rijāl, 'Ali, *De Iudiciis Astrorum* (Basel: Henrichus Petrus, 1551)

Scofield, Bruce, "A History and Test of Planetary Weather Forecasting" (2010). *Open Access Dissertations*, Paper 221. Available at: scholar-works.umass.edu/open_access_dissertations/221

Thomson, S. Harrison, "The Text of Grosseteste's *De Cometis*," *Isis*, Vol. 19, No. 1 (Apr. 1933), pp. 19-25.

Thorndike, Lynn, *The Sphere of Sacrobosco and Its Commentators* (Chicago: The University of Chicago Press, 1949)

Travaglia, Pinella, *Magic, Causality, and Intentionality: the Doctrine of Rays in al-Kindi* (Sismel/Edizioni del Galluzzo, 1999)

Valens, Vettius, *The Anthology*, vols. I-VII, ed. Robert Hand, trans. Robert Schmidt (Berkeley Springs, WV: The Golden Hind Press, 1993-2001)

Vescovini, Graziella Federici, "La Versio Latina degli Excerpta de Secretis Albumasar di Sadan," *Archives d'Histoire Doctrinale et Littéraire du Moyen Âge*, Vol. 65 (1998), pp. 273-330.

Zoller, Robert, *Astrometeorology (Weather Prognostics)* (privately circulated, 2004)